CANADIAN HUMAN RESOURCE MANAGEMENT

A STRATEGIC APPROACH

TWELFTH EDITION

Dr. Hermann F. Schwind
Saint Mary's University

Dr. Krista Uggerslev
Northern Alberta Institute of Technology

Dr. Terry H. Wagar
Saint Mary's University

Dr. Neil Fassina
Athabasca University

ISBN-13: 978-1-25-965492-3
ISBN-10: 1-25-965492-3

4 5 6 7 8 9 M 23 22 21

Printed and bound in Canada.

Product Director, Canada: *Rhondda McNabb*
Product Manager: *Amy Clarke-Spencley*
Senior Marketing Manager: *Cathie Lefebvre*
Product Developers: *Lindsay MacDonald, Veronica Saroli*
Senior Product Team Associate: *Stephanie Giles*
Supervising Editors: *Janie Deneau, Jack Whelan*
Photo/Permissions Researcher: *Monika Schurmann*
Copy Editor: *Colleen Ste. Marie*
Plant Production Coordinator: *Michelle Saddler*
Manufacturing Production Coordinator: *Jason Stubner*
Interior Designer: *Michelle Losier*
Cover Design: *David Montle*
Cover Image: © *Panasonic*
Page Layout: *SPi Global*
Printer: *Marquis*

About the Authors

DR. HERMANN F. SCHWIND Dr. Schwind is Professor Emeritus (Human Resource Management) at Saint Mary's University in Halifax. He received his Ph.D. from the University of British Columbia, B.B.A. and M.B.A. degrees from the University of Washington, and mechanical and industrial engineering degrees from German institutions. He has 15 years of industrial experience and has taught as Visiting Professor at the University of Ottawa; at Sophia University in Tokyo; and at the Institute for International Studies and Training in Fujinomiya, a Japanese management training centre.

Dr. Schwind was a founding member and vice-president of the British Columbia Society for Training and Development, president of the Halifax and District Personnel Association (1984/86; now the Human Resource Association of Nova Scotia), and president of the Administrative Science Association of Canada. His research and publications focused on performance appraisal, training and development, motivation and compensation, and cross-cultural management. He also worked as a human resource consultant for 25 years.

DR. KRISTA UGGERSLEV Dr. Krista Uggerslev is the Applied Research Chair in Leadership and Talent at the Northern Alberta Institute of Technology. She holds Ph.D. and M.Sc. degrees in Industrial and Organizational Psychology from the University of Calgary, and was a tenured Associate Professor in the Asper School of Business at the University of Manitoba.

In her research, Dr. Uggerslev is a co-founder of metaBUS, creating Big Data tools for locating, curating, and synthesizing scientific research to propel the speed of science and disseminate information for evidence-based practice. Her research has appeared in the world's top academic journals in applied psychology and business and has been presented to national and international audiences, including NATO. In her consulting work, Dr. Uggerslev provides guest lectures on topics related to leadership, talent management, and demographic and economic changes in Canada and has developed and validated employee selection and performance appraisal systems for private, public, and non-profit organizations. She holds the Certified Human Resource Professional (CHRP) designation.

DR. TERRY H. WAGAR Terry H. Wagar is a Professor of Human Resource Management/ Industrial Relations at Saint Mary's University in Halifax. He has also taught at the University of South Australia, Wilfrid Laurier University, and the University of Western Australia. Dr. Wagar's degrees include an M.B.A. from the University of Toronto, a Master of Industrial Relations from Queen's University, an LL.B. from the University of Ottawa Law School, and a Ph.D. in labour relations, human resource management, and statistics/research methods from Virginia Tech.

Dr. Wagar has been a Visiting Scholar/Professor at several universities, including Flinders University of South Australia, University of Kentucky, University of Waikato, Queen's University, and the University of Western Australia. His research has been published in Canada, the United States, Europe, Asia, Australia, and New Zealand.

DR. NEIL FASSINA Dr. Neil Fassina is the president of Athabasca University. He received his Ph.D. in Management from the Rotman School of Business at the University of Toronto and his B.Sc. in Psychology from the University of Calgary. He is a Chartered Professional in Human Resources (CPHR) and a Designated Corporate Director (ICD.D) through the Institute of Corporate Directors.

In his research, Dr. Fassina addresses questions related to the areas of applied decision making—such as negotiations and strategic decision making—as well as social exchange relationships and talent management. As an educator, Dr. Fassina delivers seminars and workshops on effective negotiation strategies, strategic planning, conflict management, and communications, among other human resource–related topics, to clients at all levels of private, public, and not-for-profit organizations.

Letter to Students

Dear Student,

This book has a history of using orchestra themes as a cover picture. A high performance organization can be compared to a well-managed symphony orchestra, made up of dedicated individuals united in a common purpose and under the guidance and leadership of a conductor.

Creating that high-performance organization begins with effective human resource management. Like the conductor of the orchestra, the human resource professional takes responsibility for seeing the whole become larger than the sum of its parts. Through strategic planning, thorough recruitment, careful selection, ongoing training, effective motivation, helpful feedback, and progressive rewards, the human resource professional can help create an efficient organization and a positive work environment.

In this twelfth edition, an orchestra is again featured on the cover of the book. This time it is the only existing Philharmonic Turntable Orchestra of Japan, made up of 31 world-renowned DJs. Advances in technology and influences from around the world have enabled this orchestra to produce amazing music, which you can listen to on YouTube. These same advances impact the practice of human resource management, and you'll find current trends reflected in the content, examples, and "how to" steps used throughout this book.

Each chapter in this book includes many common elements, such as learning objectives, terms for review, research assignments and exercises, incidents, and discussion questions. Within all chapters, you will find a *Spotlight on HRM* box. These timely articles from journals and magazines in the field illustrate a manager's or consultant's point of view on HRM or offer a sharing of practical HRM experiences relevant to the chapter. Each chapter also contains a *Spotlight on Ethics*, where an ethics issue relevant to the chapter content is raised.

Photos of real job situations offer insights into work environments the book is discussing. Cartoons add some humour to the otherwise quite serious content. The *References* provide you with the sources for the information given in the chapter. They can also be used as a starting point for more detailed research.

There are two *Cases* associated with each chapter. The *WE Connections* case runs across all of the chapters. Each chapter also has an independent case focusing on individual and relevant contexts. Both the common and individual cases provide discussion questions for application and reflection of the chapter content within the case contexts.

If you have any feedback regarding the readability of the textbook or suggestions on how we could improve the next edition, please contact Krista Uggerslev via the e-mail address given below.

Good luck with your studies!

kristauggerslev@gmail.com

Brief Table of Contents

Table of Contents

Preface

We believe that human resource departments will play a critical role in determining the success of Canadian organizations in the twenty-first century.

—THE AUTHORS

Teachers and students ultimately determine the value of any university textbook. *Canadian Human Resource Management: A Strategic Approach* is no exception. Its eleventh edition passed the test of the marketplace by earning adoptions and re-adoptions in more than 70 colleges and universities in Canada and by becoming the best-selling human resource management text in this country. The book's thrust on presenting the key concepts, issues, and practices of this exciting field without being encyclopedic, its practical focus, and its emphasis on readability have endeared it to hundreds of instructors and thousands of students in Canada. Equally gratifying to the authors is that a large number of students retained this book for their professional libraries after course completion, suggesting that they found real value in the book.

Balanced Coverage

We attribute the book's popularity to its balanced coverage of both theory and practice, and of both traditional materials and emerging concerns. Regardless of their orientation, readers will sense our belief that people are the ultimate resource for any employer. How well an organization obtains, maintains, and retains its human resources determines its success or failure. And the success or failure of our organizations shapes the well-being of every individual on this planet. If the events of the last decade are any indication, the human race is entering a totally new phase in its evolution. The breakup of protectionist trade barriers and ideological walls that separate countries of the world may mean that the manager of the twenty-first century has to operate in a more complex and dynamic global setting that is also much more interdependent. Training in human resource management (HRM) will become even more critical in this new setting.

The twelfth edition of *Canadian Human Resource Management: A Strategic Approach* builds on the strengths of the eleventh edition. The book is divided into six parts.

- **Part 1: The Strategic Human Resource Management Model** introduces the strategic model that will be used as a guide through all chapters.
- **Part 2: Planning Human Resources** describes the two pre-hiring processes, analyzing the jobs in question and planning for future staff needs. New job options have to be integrated into the organization as part of the planning process.

- **Part 3: Attracting Human Resources** covers the legal aspects of any hiring decision and discusses recruitment and selection processes and the management of a diverse workforce.
- **Part 4: Placing, Developing, and Evaluating Human Resources** discusses the importance of preparing employees for new challenges through training and development and providing timely performance feedback.
- **Part 5: Motivating and Rewarding Human Resources** reviews the many ways a human resource department can contribute to a more effective organization through a fair and equitable compensation system and proficient benefits administration. Creating a motivating environment is another responsibility of the HR manager.
- **Part 6: Maintaining High Performance** brings up the issues related to workplace safety, which is of concern to every manager. This concern has to be conveyed to all employees through an effective communication system. Good interpersonal relations require appropriate and fair discipline procedures. This part also discusses in detail the union–management framework, union organizing, collective bargaining, and collective agreement administration.

Updated in the Twelfth Edition

The chapters in the new edition have been streamlined and organized for easier reading and retention of material by students. The focus of the text continues to be the strategic contribution of HR function in organizations; but an explicit recognition of the relationship between HR strategies, tactics, and systems has been incorporated into the model and throughout the text material. Within this format, both present and emerging concerns of a significant nature are highlighted. Key terms are bolded and an extensive glossary of HR terms is included at the end of the text.

This edition has a thorough coverage of Canadian human rights legislation and many recent legal precedents. A number of trends and potentially promising HRM strategies have been incorporated into appropriate chapters of the new edition. HRM has recently played a more important role in the overall strategy of companies. This trend is strongly reflected in the new edition. All chapters now include a discussion of how the topic dealt with in the chapter should be mirrored in the HRM strategy and how this strategy fits into the overall strategy of the organization.

All chapters have been updated. Information on legislative changes, especially in the area of employment equity (women, sexual orientation, disabled people, and Indigenous people), statistics, and demographics, is the latest available. New work options provide organizations not only with opportunities to be more effective but also offer employees more flexible work opportunities, better suited to their needs. Growing internationalization of companies and international trade are reflected in the contexts and examples throughout the text. In this edition, we have integrated global and international content into each chapter. The text provides over 100 examples and anecdotes of Canadian and global firms—private and public, local and national, and large and small.

In this edition, a new running case is introduced spanning all of the chapters. In addition, new individual chapter cases touching upon recent and important issues within the topic in varied contexts and circumstances have been included for each chapter.

Chapter-by-Chapter Changes

- **Chapter 1:** Includes new running and individual chapter cases and updates to all figures to be current with the latest Canadian workplace trends.

- **Chapter 2:** All generic examples were replaced with real-world samples and how-to checklists.

- **Chapter 3:** Two new cases and a new incident provide students with current and relevant scenarios faced by HR practitioners, highlighting the balancing act of HR supply and demand.

- **Chapter 4:** This chapter provides a thoughtful advance in how the focus on inclusion may be advantageous to the previous focus on diversity management. Updates to statutes and recent case examples are present throughout the chapter.

- **Chapter 5:** Canadian companies from across the country as well as global companies (e.g., Facebook, Google) appear prominently. Recent digital advances in recruiting and commentary on their potential implications are provided.

- **Chapter 6:** New Canadian and global examples with varied contexts bring the chapter material to life.

- **Chapter 7:** The career planning content was revised with more detail and application. The onboarding content is updated to keep current with best practices, and new images reflect developments in virtual and augmented reality in training.

- **Chapter 8:** Includes greater focus on talent management, linking employee potential along with

employee performance to organizational and employee objectives. Steps to improve employee performance from an HR standpoint are discussed in significant detail.

- **Chapter 9:** This chapter has undergone a significant revision in this edition, including updates to compensation philosophies, methods for determining direct compensation and pricing jobs, and matching employees to pay.

- **Chapter 10:** Boutique-style benefits options and benefit provider options now available to Canadian employers are highlighted. New cases, exercises, and figures show how benefit practices are used by employers.

- **Chapter 11:** New examples expand on the Canadian context and bring the employee relations concepts in the chapter alive.

- **Chapter 12:** A new health and safety case builds on the WE Connections case from the previous 11 chapters. A new individual chapter case highlights how judgment in a critical moment can lead to safety risks.

- **Chapter 13:** New cases give students the opportunity to examine a union drive in a workplace and reactions of HR and management to the union drive. A new individual chapter case provides students with the opportunity to examine grievances in a hotel chain.

Key Features

In addition to new features, important key features from previous editions have been retained.

WE Connections and Org Chart

WE CONNECTIONS: PERFORMANCE MANAGEMENT

Performance Appraisal Meeting

Project Manager Oliver Caine skimmed his notes as he waited for Ben Robins to come to the meeting room. He hoped Ben would arrive soon, as he wanted to get the conversation finished quickly. He had a lot of other people to get through. It was performance appraisal season, and Oliver had to sit down with each of his seven software engineers, just as he had done the year before. Oliver had promised the HR people that he would hand in the forms by Friday, which had seemed like a good idea three weeks ago when he had agreed to it. Unfortunately, there had been some unexpected issues with his project in the meantime so now he had to squeeze all of the performance management activities into a couple of days.

Ben walked into the conference room, and smiled as he said, "Hi, Oliver. I hope I didn't keep you waiting."

Oliver replied, "No, I was a little early. Come on in and sit down. Let's get this performance appraisal done."

Smiling good-naturedly, Ben shrugged and chuckled as he said, "Sounds good to me. Just tell me how great I am and I'll get out of your hair."

need improving, however. Let me tell you what you need to work on. First, I've noticed you coming in late a couple of times. That's never a good idea, especially for a junior person. Please do what you can to cut that out."

Leaning forward in his chair, Ben looked startled as he said, "Well, okay. I guess it's true I was late on two mornings, but that's because I've been having some car trouble this month. You know that I work late most nights, sometimes till 11:00 p.m. And I've never taken a sick day. I can't believe that being 10 minutes late twice is at the top of your list. That really doesn't seem to be significant in my mind."

Looking uncomfortable, Oliver replied, "You don't need to get so upset, Ben. I'm trying to help you here. And actually, this reminds me of another area that needs improvement. You seem to get upset too easily. Come to think of it, I've seen you react strongly to things that people say in our project meetings. I wish you would make more of an effort to stay calm and reasonable."

Shaking his head, Ben said, "Excuse me? I honestly don't know what you are talking about. I have never gotten upset in a project meeting! I may have defended an idea,

A partial organizational chart to accompany the WE Connections case study is available for reference below.

TABLE 1

WEC Performance Appraisal Form

WEC Performance Appraisal Form

Employee Name _____
Employee Role _____
Supervisor Name _____
Appraisal Period _____ to _____

Performance Contributions:
Please indicate three areas where the employee performed well:
1. _____
2. _____
3. _____

Cases—This is the only Canadian HR text to have a running case anchored to material in every single chapter and a second individual chapter case for each chapter. The *WE Connections* cases feature a tech start-up that is struggling with human resources management challenges as the company continues to grow. The additional individual chapter cases highlight unique HR contexts and the strategic role of HR in today's organizations. Both of the cases that appear at the end of each chapter allow the student to further learn about how HR can make a significant contribution to organizational success and growth through the application of chapter content.

CASE STUDY

Starbright Casino

Using Job Analysis for Job Rotation and Redesign

The casino was all set for another busy and profitable Friday night. The tribute band would be starting in another hour and the restaurants and bar stools were nearly full with preshow diners. Many of the show seekers would return to try their hand at tables or slots before the evening was out. As Shea looked around the casino floor, she could feel the energy just starting to ramp up as the night's hopeful gamers were trickling in, replacing the coffee-drinking day crowd now cashing in their remaining chits and chips.

Shea scanned the day shift employees, knowing they would be counting down the time until they could rest their tired backs and feet with their shift behind them. As shift manager, she couldn't help but keep a casual lookout for the table-game dealers, slot-machine attendants, and casino cashiers who would be taking over as the evening crew during the shift change in 15 minutes.

Just then, Shea spotted Bin walking quickly in her direc-

Her mind switched to solving the problem at ha The two cages each needed two cashiers for that nig shift. With one now away, she would have to pull on the table-game dealers or slot-machine attendants. No would be happy to forego their scheduled work for a shi the cage. Shea aimed to schedule cage shifts evenly ac all of the table-game dealers and slot-machine attend for each night they normally worked to be as fair as sible in giving each staff member time on the floor. V *except for the crap table dealers*, Shea thought. They di have to take a turn in the cage, and Shea knew this w point of contention for the other staff. Four-person te managed each crap table, and the quick math and comp ity of the game, owing to the number of gamblers and to keep track of, meant that fewer staff could handle game. Other employees coveted the crap table, in par they could avoid the cage.

Shea looked to the remaining table game dealers

Spotlights—All chapters provide a *Spotlight on HRM*, focusing on an emerging practice, issue, or HR opportunity. Some Spotlights from previous editions have been retained at the request of reviewers; the new ones reflect current trends and practices.

Spotlight on HRM

Human Capital: A Key to Canada's Competitiveness

What makes an economy accelerate or stagnate? In answering this question, many will point to key economic indicators such as Real GDP, consumer price index (CPI), or consumer confidence. Others may point to effective policy or the flow of goods and services among the numerous individuals and companies in an economy. Regardless of the micro- or macro-economic drivers, the shape of an economy is highly influenced by people. It is people who set policy and regulations. It is people who lead the many micro, small, medium, and large organizations that make up our economy. It is people who purchase or use the goods and services within an economy.

With people at the core of an economy, the importance of human resources or human capital cannot be overstated. Part of the human capital equation is productivity, that is, how much output an individual can create in relation to

an increased focus is being placed on the role of human capital in creating long-term and sustainable productivity improvements.

The role of human talent in creating long-term sustainable economic and social benefits to organizations and communities through productivity necessitates a collaborative and long-term approach among organizations, governments, communities, and numerous other support structures.

Among the key elements to creating innovation and, in turn, productivity is education.[95] Because knowledge is a necessary precursor to realizing the full potential of human capital in creating productivity improvements, governments, communities, and education systems must come together in developing and enhancing citizens' overall knowledge base. Canadian communities must also understand the importance of life-long

Ethics Box—A significant feature is the *Spotlight on Ethics,* in which an ethics issue relevant to the chapter content is discussed.

Spotlight on ETHICS

What Is a "Right" Behaviour?

Ethics are moral principles that guide human behaviours and are often based on a society's cultural values, norms, customs, and beliefs, which means that different cultures and even individuals within the same society have widely varying standards of behaviour. How are we to differentiate "right" from "wrong" or "good" from "bad"? There are no simple answers. Many adopt one of the following postures in dealing with such ambiguous situations:

1. *Universalist approach:* Persons who embrace this view assert that some moral standards are universally applicable. In other words, regardless of society or place, a wrong act (such as killing, stealing, or lying) is wrong. There are no exceptions to moral "rights" and "wrongs."

2. *Situational approach:* What is right or wrong

Another useful model to understand and guide ethical behaviour is offered by Lawrence Kohlberg. Kohlberg, an American psychologist, posits six stages that form an invariant and universal sequence in individual development; thus, everyone is supposed to go through the same stages in the same sequence. It is, however, possible for a person to be "stuck" at one of the following stages and not proceed to the next level. The six stages of moral development identified by Kohlberg[77] are as follows:

Stage 1: Obedience and Punishment Stage: The only reason for a person to perform the "right" act at this stage is obedience to others who have the power to punish.

Stage 2: Reciprocity Stage: Here, the individual enters into reciprocal agreements with others so that he or she receives the greatest good

Research—To assist students in making optimal use of Internet resources for more information on HR topics, HR-related websites are provided throughout the text and hotlinked in the ebook. To facilitate class discussion, research questions have been added at the end of every chapter. We have also included a handy reference list of important homepages related to human resource management on *Connect.*

Global Knowledge, a leader in business and IT training, in conjunction with Deloitte, a leading professional services firm, was awarded gold honours by the Canadian Society for Training and Development (CSTD) for their Managers 1 and 2 programs. These programs are designed to prepare the new managers to increase their confidence and capability. The program offers originality, instructional design, virtual class elearning, self-paced elearning, live labs, and a knowledge centre that includes webinars, blogs,

In-Text Glossary—Important terms and concepts are highlighted with boldface type in the text. Allowing students to find critical definitions at a glance, all terms appearing in boldface are also defined in the text in the margins and referenced in the *Terms for Review* section at the end of each chapter. They can also be found in the *Subject Index*, highlighted in a secondary colour. Finally, a full list of glossary terms is also provided in the end matter of the text.

Figures—Charts and diagrams are included to illustrate relevant ideas and concepts.

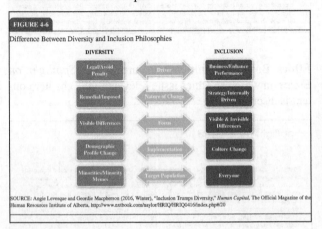

FIGURE 4-6

Difference Between Diversity and Inclusion Philosophies

SOURCE: Angie Levesque and Geordie Macpherson (2016, Winter), "Inclusion Trumps Diversity," *Human Capital*, The Official Magazine of the Human Resources Institute of Alberta, http://www.nxtbook.com/naylor/HRIQ/HRIQ0416/index.php#/20

Terms for Review—All important terms and buzzwords are included. This is an excellent tool for self-testing.

Learning Objectives—This useful tool enables students to gauge their progress and understanding while working through each chapter.

End-of-Chapter Summaries—The authors provide an abbreviated version of the main ideas, theories, and strategies of each chapter.

SUMMARY

Human resource planning is a proactive approach to ensuring that the organization has the right people at the right place with the right skills at the right time and in the right environment. The human resource planning process signals the beginning of an organization's ability to "manage its talent." The planning process directs the organization to decide what talent it needs and suggests several ways in which to source that talent. It is an attempt by companies to estimate their future needs and supplies of human resources as well as the business processes to effectively enable that talent.

Through an understanding of the factors that influence the demand for workers, workforce planners can forecast specific short- and long-term needs. Given some anticipated level of demand, planners try to estimate the availability of present workers, both internal and external to the organization, to meet that demand. Such estimates begin with an audit of present employees. Possible replacements are then identified. Internal shortages are resolved by seeking new employees in the external labour markets. Surpluses are reduced by normal attrition, leaves of absence, layoffs, or terminations. Both external and internal staffing strategies can be used to meet human resource needs.

Planners use various tools to gather information and can provide meaningful information to their stakeholders. Effective use of technology has afforded HR the opportunity to demonstrate enhanced service delivery and offer greater strategic services to its stakeholder.

The HR plan can be considered as a *road map* for HR professionals, as it directs the recruitment, selection, and training and development processes. Once HR professionals understand an organization's human resource needs and available supply, they then will be able to decide how best to recruit that resource and establish the framework for the selection criteria. Once onboard, employees' capabilities will need to be understood and their talents and skills optimized so they can perform effectively. Future value-added contributions will depend on how the organization develops its employees and successfully aligns its needs with its employees' developmental paths. Talent management is an important HR activity to ensure organizational sustainability. Later, in Chapter 5, Chapter 6, and Chapter 7, we will discuss those HR functions that support effective talent management processes.

Before that, it is important to study the impact of governmental policies on a firm's human resource policies and practices. This will be attempted in the next chapter.

Review and Discussion Questions—These questions test students' understanding of the chapter material and suggest topics for class or group discussions.

REVIEW AND DISCUSSION QUESTIONS

1. What are the key steps in workforce planning in organizations? Which of your actions, if any, would be different if you were planning human resources for a smaller firm (that employs fewer than 50 persons in all) instead of a larger firm (which has 500 employees)?
2. What are staffing tables and replacement charts? Of what use are they to a human resource manager?
3. Discuss any three techniques for estimating the demand for human resources. Provide examples where relevant.
4. What are some popular approaches to match the supply and demand of human resources? Briefly discuss two approaches (each) for situations when demand exceeds and is less than supply of human resources, highlighting their advantages and limitations.
5. "Alternate work arrangements are useful approaches for both the employer and the employee." Discuss.
6. What are some of the security considerations organizations must understand when implementing a human resource information system? Provide an example of one way that security profiles are set up.

Critical Thinking Questions—These questions challenge students to expand on what they have just learned, discussing broader relationships and interactions of the concepts in the chapter.

CRITICAL THINKING QUESTIONS

1. Suppose a workforce planner estimated that due to several technological innovations your firm will need 25 percent fewer employees in three years. What actions would you take today?
2. Suppose you managed a restaurant in a winter resort area. During the summer it was profitable to keep the business open, but you needed only half of the cooks, table servers, and bartenders that you employed during the winter. What actions would you take in April when the peak tourist season ended?
3. If your company locates its research and development offices in downtown Windsor, Ontario, the city is willing to forgo city property taxes on the building for 10 years. The city is willing to make this concession to help reduce its high unemployment rate. Edmonton, Alberta, your company's other choice, has a low unemployment rate and is not offering any tax breaks. Based on just these considerations, which city would you recommend and why?
4. Assume you are the human resource manager in a Canadian university employing approximately 300 faculty members. Since these faculty members constitute a "valuable" resource of your organization, you decide to install an accounting procedure for changes in the value of this asset. How will you go about it? What problems do you anticipate in the process?
5. For a high-tech organization where the job specifications and customer needs continually change, which of the forecasting techniques discussed in the text are likely to be relevant? Why?
6. Some fire departments and hospital staff are using the 3-day, 36-hour schedule. Do you see any negative aspects to this schedule?
7. Assume you work for a firm that employs 30 managerial and 70 clerical/sales employees. As a cost-cutting strategy, your firm is forced to terminate the services of 10 percent of your managers and 5 percent of your clerical staff. What specific actions will you take to help the departing employees?

Incidents—These short cases test students' understanding of concepts and their impact on the organization.

INCIDENT 3-1

Case Incident: Temporary Foreign Workers

Canada's Temporary Foreign Worker (TFW) program was designed to bring workers to Canada from other countries to fill urgent, short-term job vacancies when domestic workers can not be found. Recent data suggests that about 35 percent of foreign workers stay five years or longer, and an overwhelming majority of those eventually become permanent residents. Recent data also suggests that there is a weak correlation between the presence and length of stay of temporary workers and unemployment levels in various parts of Canada. Thus, it may be that TFWs are not just acting as a "last resource" for employers who can not find domestic workers.

At present, there are inconsistencies in how the TFW program is enacted across Canada. Regional inconsistencies mean that the same worker might be able to stay in one part of the country but must return to his or her home country after a year when in another part of the country. Meanwhile, Canada has targets of the number of immigrants it hopes to attract into the country.

It seems there is a direction decision for Canada to permanent residents, then paths for temporary workers to become permanent residents should be made across all TFW categories.

For more information, see https://globalnews.ca/news/3993108/temporary-foreign-workers-canada-unemployment/

DISCUSSION QUESTIONS

1. If temporary workers are allowed to apply for permanent residency after one year of work, how will this impact other new immigrants who may have less experience in Canadian workplaces?
2. If temporary workers are restricted to one-year terms but employers seek an ongoing supply of trained and readily available foreigners, should employers be forced to provide training to domestic workers who are not in post-secondary education?

Exercises—These offer students the opportunity to apply strategies to specific situations and arrive at their own conclusions or discuss with the instructor and fellow students.

EXERCISE 2-1

Strengths and Weaknesses of Job Descriptions*

Step 1. Students should bring several job descriptions to class. Pick job descriptions from O*NET OnLine if needed.

Step 2. Create teams of three. Discuss the job descriptions. Do they adequately reflect the responsibilities and KSAOs

that the employee will need to perform? Compare the job descriptions to the information in your text. What are the weaknesses and strengths of the job descriptions? What specific changes would make the job descriptions more measurable?

* Exercise suggestion: C. Fitzgerald, Okanagan College, Kelowna, BC.

Subject Index—All chapter topics are indexed by subject. Glossary terms and page references are included in a secondary colour.

Reference Notes—Specific cases and other source references are gathered at the end of the text for more detailed research purposes.

References

CHAPTER 1

1. Leif Edvinsson, accessed September 22, 2018, from https://www.12manage.com/quotes_hr.html

2. Canadian Business, Canada's 15 top companies by market cap: Investor 500 2016, 2016, accessed September 18, 2018, from http://www.canadianbusiness.com/lists-and-rankings/best-stocks/2016-biggest-companies-by-market-cap/

3. How stuff works, downloaded September 18, 2018, from http://www.howstuffworks.com/innovation/inventions/top-5-nasa-inventions.htm#page=1

4. National Aeronautical and Space Administration, downloaded September 18, 2018, from http://mars.jpl.nasa.gov/mars2020/

5. Ulrich, D., Yonger, J., Brockbank, W., and Ulrich, M. (2012), HR talent and the new HR competencies, *Strategic Human Resource Review*, downloaded September 18, 2018, from http://www.researchgate.net/publication/235295245

6. Bloomberg BMA (2015), HR department benchmarks and analysis 2015–2016,

11. Purpose and Values, Target, downloaded September 22, 2018, from https://corporate.target.com/about/purpose-values

12. Verma, S. (2012), The relentless pursuit of perfection: The Lexus brand strategy, *Business 2 Community*, accessed January 6, 2018, from https://www.business2community.com/branding/the-relentless-pursuit-of-perfection-the-lexus-brand-strategy-0307457

13. van der Hoop, J. (2016), *10 examples of innovative HR practices and policies that amplify success*, accessed September 18, 2018, from https://www.talentsorter.com/10-examples-innovative-hr-practices-policies/

14. SHRM (2016), *2016 human capital benchmarking report*, accessed September 18, 2018, from https://www.shrm.org/hr-today/trends-and-forecasting/research-and-surveys/Documents/2016-Human-Capital-Report.pdf

15. *State of the American workplace: Employee engagement insights for US business leaders* (2013), accessed September 18, 2018, from http://www.gallup.com/file/services/176708/

23. Conference Board of Canada (2017), *Canadian outlook long-term economic forecast: Mid-year update—2017*. Ottawa: The Conference Board of Canada.

24. The World Bank (2016), *Exports of goods and services (% of GDP) 2016*, accessed September 22, 2018, from https://data.worldbank.org/indicator/NE.EXP.GNFS.ZS

25. Schwab, K. (2017), World Economic Forum, *The global competitiveness report: 2017-2018*.

26. Immigration, Refugees and Citizenship Canada (2017), *2017 annual report to Parliament on immigration*, accessed September 22, 2018, from https://www.canada.ca/en/immigration-refugees-citizenship/corporate/publications-manuals/annual-report-parliament-immigration-2017.html

27. Gerszak, R. (2017), Canada aims for immigration boost to buttress economy as population ages, *Global and Mail*, accessed September 22, 2018, from https://www.theglobeandmail.com/news/politics/canada-to-admit-40000-more-immigrants-a-year-by-2020-

Glossary—The most comprehensive glossary in the HR field—over 300 items—completes the book, allowing students to find definitions of most HR terms and concepts.

Glossary

360-degree performance appraisal: Combination of self, peer, supervisor, and subordinate performance evaluation.

ability tests: Tests that assess an applicant's capacity or aptitude to function in a certain way.

ads: Advertisements in a newspaper, magazine, and so on, that solicit job applicants for a position.

alternate work arrangements: Nontraditional work arrangements (e.g., flextime, telecommuting) that provide more flexibility to employees while meeting organizational goals.

alumni associations: Associations of alumni of schools, colleges, or other training facilities.

applicant tracking system (ATS): A database of potential candidates that enables a good match between job requirements and applicant characteristics and also enlarges the recruitment pool.

apprenticeships: A form of on-the-job training in which junior employees learn a trade from an experienced person.

arbitration: The settling of a dispute between labour and management by a third party.

assumption of risk: Meaning the worker

benefit audit: A system to control the efficiency of a benefit program.

biographical information blank (BIB): A type of application blank that uses a multiple-choice format to measure a job candidate's education, experiences, opinions, attitudes, and interests.

blind ads: Job ads that do not identify the employer.

blogs: Web logs—online journals, diaries, or serials published by a person or group of people.

bona fide occupational requirement (BFOR): A justified business reason for discriminating against a member of a protected class; also known as bona fide occupational qualification (BFOQ).

burnout: A condition of mental, emotional, and sometimes physical exhaustion that results from substantial and prolonged stress.

business unionism: A type of unionism whose mission is to protect workers, increase their pay, improve their working conditions, and help workers in general; it recognizes that a union can survive only if it delivers a needed service to its members in a businesslike manner.

in terms of a career, and engages in a lifelong series of activities in pursuit of that career.

careless worker model: The early approach to safety in the workplace, which assumed that most accidents were due to workers' failure to be careful or to protect themselves.

Chartered Professional in Human Resources (CPHR): Human resource practitioner, formally accredited to practice, who reflects a threshold professional level of practice.

collective agreement: A labour contract that addresses a variety of issues, such as wages and benefits, hours of work, working conditions, grievance procedures, safety standards, probationary periods, and work assignments; usually negotiated between the local union's bargaining committee and the human resource or industrial relations department.

communication standards: Formal protocols for internal communications within an organization to eliminate sex/gender, racial, age, or other biases in communications.

compa-ratio: An index that indicates how an individual's or a group's salary relates to the midpoint of their relevant pay grades.

comparative evaluation methods: A col-

Market Leading Technology

connect®

Learn without Limits

McGraw-Hill Connect® is an award-winning digital teaching and learning platform that gives students the means to better connect with their coursework, with their instructors, and with the important concepts that they will need to know for success now and in the future. With *Connect,* instructors can take advantage of McGraw-Hill's trusted content to seamlessly deliver assignments, quizzes, and tests online. McGraw-Hill *Connect* is a learning platform that continually adapts to each student, delivering precisely what students need, when they need it, so class time is more engaging and effective. *Connect* makes teaching and learning personal, easy, and proven.

Connect Key Features:

SmartBook®

As the first and only adaptive reading experience, *SmartBook* is changing the way students read and learn. *SmartBook* creates a personalized reading experience by highlighting the most important concepts a student needs to learn at that moment in time. As a student engages with *SmartBook,* the reading experience continuously adapts by highlighting content based on what each student knows and doesn't know. This ensures that he or she is focused on the content needed to close specific knowledge gaps, while it simultaneously promotes long-term learning.

Connect Insight®

Connect Insight is *Connect's* one-of-a-kind visual analytics dashboard—now available for instructors—that provides at-a-glance information regarding student performance, which is immediately actionable. By presenting assignment, assessment, and topical performance results together with a time metric that is easily visible for aggregate or individual results, *Connect Insight* gives instructors the ability to take a just-in-time approach to teaching and learning, which was never before available. *Connect Insight* presents data that helps instructors improve class performance in a way that is efficient and effective.

Simple Assignment Management

With *Connect,* creating assignments is easier than ever, so instructors can spend more time teaching and less time managing. With *Connect,* instructors can do the following:

- Assign *SmartBook* learning modules.
- Edit existing questions and create their own questions.
- Draw from a variety of text-specific questions, resources, and test bank material to assign online.
- Streamline lesson planning, student progress reporting, and assignment grading to make classroom management more efficient than ever.

Smart Grading

When it comes to studying, time is precious. *Connect* helps students learn more efficiently by providing feedback and practice material when they need it, where they need it. *Connect* does the following:

- Automatically scores assignments, giving students immediate feedback on their work and comparisons with correct answers
- Accesses and reviews each response; manually changes grades or leaves comments for students to review
- Tracks individual student performance—by question, assignment, or in relation to the class overall—with detailed grade reports
- Reinforces classroom concepts with practice tests and instant quizzes
- Integrates grade reports easily with Learning Management Systems, including Blackboard, D2L, and Moodle

Mobile Access

Connect makes it easy for students to read and learn using their smartphones and tablets. With the mobile app, students can study on the go—including reading and listening using the audio functionality—without constant need for Internet access.

Instructor Library

The *Connect Instructor Library* is a repository for additional resources to improve student engagement in and out of the class. It provides all the critical resources instructors need to build their course. The previous edition's Maple Leaf Shoes Case Study will be available as an instructor resource. The Library allows instructors to do the following:

- Access instructor resources.
- View assignments and resources created for past sections.
- Post their own resources for students to use.

INSTRUCTOR RESOURCES

- Instructor's Manual
- Computerized Test Bank

- Microsoft® PowerPoint® Presentation Slides
- Videos
- Manager's HotSeat Videos
- Application-Based Activities

Manager's HotSeat Videos

The *Manager's HotSeat* is a resource that allows students to watch real managers apply their years of experience to confronting certain management and organizational behaviour issues. Students assume the role of the manager as they watch the video and answer multiple choice questions that pop up during the segment, forcing them to make decisions on the spot. Students learn from the managers' unscripted mistakes and successes, and then do a report critiquing the managers' approach by defending their reasoning. The *Manager's HotSeat* is ideal for group or classroom discussions.

Application-Based Activities

The *Connect Application-Based Activities* are highly interactive and automatically graded, application- and analysis-based exercises wherein students immerse themselves in a business environment, analyze the situation, and apply their knowledge of managerial strategies to real-world situations. Students progress from understanding basic concepts to using their own knowledge to analyze complex scenarios and solve problems.

The *Connect Application-Based Activities* provide students with valuable practice using problem-solving skills to apply their knowledge to realistic real-world situations. Students progress from understanding basic concepts to using their knowledge to analyze complex scenarios and solve problems.

SUPERIOR LEARNING SOLUTIONS AND SUPPORT

The McGraw-Hill Education team is ready to help instructors assess and integrate any of our products, technology, and services into your course for optimal teaching and learning performance. Whether it's helping your students improve their grades or putting your entire course online, the McGraw-Hill Education team is here to help you do it. Contact your Learning Solutions Consultant today to learn how to maximize all of McGraw-Hill Education's resources.

For more information, please visit us online:

http://www.mheducation.ca/he/solutions

Acknowledgements

Writing a textbook requires the co-operation and support of many people. *Canadian Human Resource Management* is no exception. We are thankful to the many students, instructors, researchers, and practitioners who have used and commented on our last edition. Ultimately, it is the users of a book who can tell us about what we did right in the past and what we should do in the future. We hope the readers will find this twelfth edition even more useful in teaching and learning about human resource management.

A very special thank you goes to Amy Clarke-Spencley, Veronica Saroli, Jack Whelan, Colleen Ste. Marie, Monika Schurmann, Michelle Saddler, and Michelle Losier who, with their special expertise, guided us toward a better product.

And, finally, we would like to express our deeply felt thanks to those who assisted us in many tangible and intangible ways: Hermann, Ruth, Neil, Leslie, and Krista.

Hermann F. Schwind
Krista L. Uggerslev
Terry H. Wagar
Neil E. Fassina

The Strategic Human Resource Management Model

As a strategic business partner, human resource management helps organizations and their employees attain their goals. This section explores some of the pressures and opportunities faced by organizations and outlines how strategic human resource management provides a framework from which success can be built and sets the frame for the rest of this book.

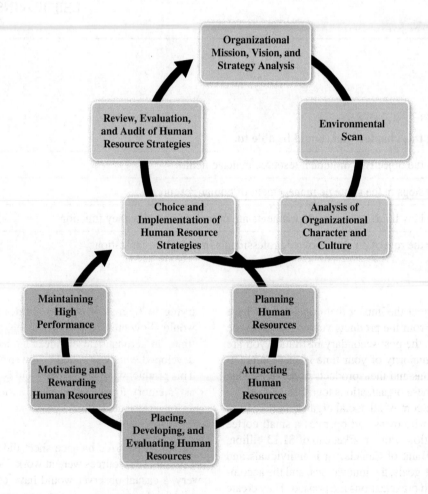

Strategic Human Resource Management

The only vital value an enterprise has is the experience, skills, innovativeness, and insights of its people.

LEIF EDVINSSON[1]

LEARNING OBJECTIVES

After studying this chapter, you should be able to:

LO1 Discuss the objectives of human resource management.

LO2 Identify steps in the strategic management of human resources.

LO3 Explain how human resource departments are organized and how they function.

LO4 Discuss the role of human resource professionals in today's organization.

Consider for a moment the impact that organizations have on your daily life. From the products you consume, to the services you use, to the post-secondary institution you are attending, the vast majority of your time is spent interacting with organizations and their products or services. One element ties all of these organizations together: people.

People are at the core of all social organizations—from the sole proprietor who owns and operates a small coffee shop to an organization with a market cap of $1.13 billion, such as the Royal Bank of Canada.[2] It is individuals and teams that create the goals, the innovations, and the accomplishments for which organizations are praised. They create the work environments that win awards, such as Deloitte's award for "Canada's Best Managed Companies." From the organization's perspective, people are resources. They are not inanimate resources, such as land and capital; instead, they are *human* resources. Without them, organizations would not exist.

At the beginning of the 1960s, the National Aeronautics and Space Administration (NASA) was trying to figure out how to build a spacecraft that would allow humans to return safely to earth.[3] At the time, an aeronautical engineer named Charles Yost developed what was called "slow spring back foam." This product was later adapted and is now referred to as "memory foam" and is found in football helmets, airline seats, and pillows.

Although NASA's balance sheet did not list its human "assets," these resources were at work. Before the foam discovery, a casual observer would have considered NASA's tangible infrastructure as the company's most important asset. With each discovery and innovation necessary to enable space travel, NASA's assets continued to grow. A keen observer would note that neither the tangible assets nor the innovation would be of great value without capable people to manage them. Amazingly, today NASA faces similar challenges; however, rather than returning from the moon safely, a major innovation challenge is how to return humans safely from Mars.[4]

Organizational success depends upon careful attention to human resources. An organization's strategies are dependent on the people brought together to create them. In turn, the success of an organization relative to these strategies is dependent upon the practices used to organize and lead human resources. Some of the best managed and most successful Canadian organizations are those that effectively make employees meet societal challenges creatively.

LO1 What Is Human Resource Management?

To understand what human resource management is, we need to first consider why people come together to form organizations. In short, organizations bring people together in a coordinated manner to accomplish goals or objectives that could not be accomplished by a single individual. The goals that organizations set may be as varied as the organizations themselves. Many **organizational goals**, however, may be categorized into economic (e.g., profit, shareholder value), social (e.g., ethical practices), and environmental (e.g., reduction of carbon footprint) goals. For an organization to achieve its goals, employees must engage in actions and behaviours that move the organization toward accomplishing them. If employees do not contribute to an organization's goals—or worse, engage in behaviours or actions that move the organization away from its goals—the organization will stagnate and potentially fail. This principle applies to all forms of organizations—including for-profit, not-for-profit, nongovernmental, social, and governmental, to name a few.

> **organizational goals** An organization's short- and long-term outcomes that human resource management aims to support and enable.

At its core, **human resource management** is the leadership and management of people within an organization using systems, methods, processes, and procedures that identify, select, motivate, and enable employees to achieve outcomes individually and collectively that enhance their positive contribution to the organization's goals. Thus, human resource management is not an end in itself; it is a means of structuring the organization to facilitate and enable the organization to achieve its objectives. The role of human resource management is therefore critical to the success—indeed, even the very survival—of the organization.

> **human resource management** The leadership and management of people within an organization using systems, methods, processes, and procedures that enable employees to optimize their performance and in turn their contribution to the organization and its goals.

The Difference between Human Resource Management and a Human Resource Department

Before moving on, it is important to differentiate between the field of human resource management and a human resource department. Although human resource management is central to all organizations, not all organizations will have a dedicated human resource department. The field of human resource management thus focuses on what leaders and managers should do regarding organizing human resource systems, policies, and procedures. These systems, in turn, create value by facilitating and enabling employees to achieve individual goals that in turn contribute to corporate or organization goals.[5]

A human resource department, on the other hand, is a specialized group with the primary focus of ensuring the most effective use of human resource systems across an organization to enhance employee performance and accomplish organizational goals. The contribution of a human resource department should be kept at a level appropriate to the organization's needs and resources. In a new venture or micro-business, for example, human resource management may be performed by the entrepreneur or one individual who has numerous other duties within the organization. As the organization grows, the organization may decide to hire a professional human resource manager. Within large-scale organizations, it is not uncommon to have numerous people dedicated to organizing human resource practices. However, resources are wasted when the human resource department is more or less sophisticated than the organization demands. A 2015 study conducted by Bloomberg BMA found that HR teams tend to comprise approximately 1.6 human resource staff for every 100 employees in organizations smaller than 250 employees. That number changes to about 0.6 human resource staff per 100 employees in organizations over 2,500 employees.[6]

Regardless of the size of an organization and whether or not the organization has a human resource department, the responsibility for the day-to-day management of human resources most often rests with individual managers throughout the organization. As a result, all leaders and managers must be familiar with the fundamentals of human resources.

Human resource management as a specialist function evolved from very small beginnings. (See Appendix A at the end of this chapter for the growth of human resource functions over time.) Inseparable from key organizational goals, product-market plans, technology and innovation, and an organization's strategy, the field of human resource management comprises numerous activities—many of them discussed in depth throughout this textbook. Although each topic within human resources is addressed individually, it is important to recognize that the activities within human resource management are all interconnected. Figure 1-1 highlights some of this interconnectedness. When a change

FIGURE 1-1

The Interconnectivity of Human Resource Management Activities

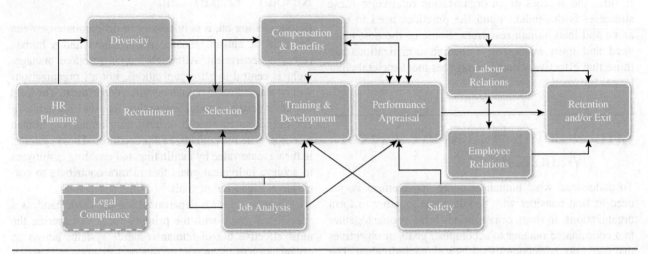

is made to one activity or system, it often has an impact on another activity. For example, if an organization acts to engage long-term employees in order to prevent them from leaving, it may spend fewer dollars recruiting and hiring new employees.[7] In order for human resource management systems, practices, and activities to be effective, leaders must consider how changes may affect the system overall.

LO2 Making Human Resource Management Strategic

Human resource management must operate within the framework of an organization. Like other activities, human resource management activities must contribute to the organization's goals and performance.[8] In response to a growing call for accountability, recent decades have witnessed an increased attention to *strategic* human resource management. Strategic human resource management seeks to recognize that the choice of human resource tools will depend on what the organization is trying to achieve. As a strategic business tool, the human resource management activities must anticipate, align with, and contribute to the organization's strategies. Similar to any other investment made by an organization, financial, technological, and infrastructure investments made in human resource systems, processes, and tools need to create a return on that investment that exceeds the investment itself.

An organization's strategy is similar to a game plan: It involves large-scale, future-oriented, integrated ideas and initiatives to achieve organizational goals and respond to uncertain and competitive environments facing the organization. In part, a strategy identifies how the organization will change and create long-term sustainable value given the environment the organization is in.[9] Strategies can vary significantly, even within the same market.

> Walmart uses the slogan "Save money. Live Better."[10] As a result, Walmart tends to follow a low-cost strategy. Target's slogan, on the other hand, is "Expect more. Pay less."[11] As a result, Target tends to follow a value-based strategy.

In some cases, strategies may even differ within a company.

> For instance, Toyota uses the slogan "Let's go places," which is focused on innovation. Lexus, Toyota's luxury vehicle division, focuses on quality, as indicated by its slogan, "The relentless pursuit of perfection."[12]

Strategic human resource management is the process of integrating the strategic needs of an organization into the organization's choice of human resource management systems and practices to support the organization's overall mission, strategies, and performance. Strategic human resource management is a value-driven, proactive focus on how best to deploy human resource practices and activities to enable an organization of any size to achieve its goals. This is done while also recognizing that the people who make up an organization's human resources department will have needs and goals of their own. We start with a discussion of strategic human

> **strategic human resource management** Integrating the strategic needs of an organization into the organization's choice of human resource management systems and practices to support the organization's overall mission, strategies, and performance.

resource management because it lays a foundation from which the topics discussed throughout this textbook can be integrated into a human resource system.

At the core, human resource strategies and tactics must be mutually consistent and must reflect the larger organizational mission and strategy. Even the best-laid strategies may fail if they are not accompanied by sound human resource programs or procedures.

> Costco Wholesalers has a strategy based partly on high volume and value-based sales. To support this strategy, it has few people on the retail floor to help shoppers and instead employs a large number of cashiers to process orders more quickly. This could be compared to Holt Renfrew, which has a strategy based partly on high quality and high-value products. As such, Holt Renfrew employs proportionately more sales associates, to assist shoppers in product choice, and fewer cashiers.

By integrating corporate strategies with the choice of human resource practices, managers of human resources can remain proactive and anticipate challenges or problems both inside and outside the organization and make adjustments before they impact the organization or its people.

The challenge facing human resource leaders is that often the human resource strategy needs to be put in place before the corporate strategy can be successful. That is, the human resource strategy needs to be implemented so that the right people are in the right place at the right time to even initiate the corporate strategy.

> Marriot Hotel uses gamification to recruit potential Millennial employees. Alternatively, Zappos offers successful job candidates $3,000 to leave the recruitment process. Their aim is to invite candidates who are not going to stay long term to exit the company early. Those who do not take the exit offer (which is 97 percent of candidates) have a better understanding of the corporate culture.[13]

The strategy of attracting talent through **gamification** is an example of how proactive strategies can meet the needs of organizations. Understanding the forces that may impact organizations and their strategies is critical in strategic human resource management and will be discussed later in this chapter.

> **gamification** The use of rules, competition, and teamwork to encourage engagement by mimicking games.

Just as each member of an organization is expected to generate positive contributions to accomplishing an organization's goals, so too is every human resource system. That is, each and every human resource system, practice, process, or tactic should generate value for the organization. The challenge for managers of human resources is to understand that within a system of people, a decision to change one thing will often have an impact on other human resource practices or activities. Moreover, these decisions are often influenced by the organization and its environment. To this end, managers of human resources need to be able to integrate and synthesize information about an organization, its environment, its culture, and its strategies to make the most effective human resource decisions for the organization:

> A number of organizations are installing workout facilities within their physical space. At first glance, this may appear to be simply a cost centre for an organization with respect to the installation and ongoing maintenance and operation of the facility. A closer consideration, however, may reveal increased employee morale, decreased expenses associated with sick days and health benefits, and a time savings for employees, who no longer need to leave the office early to drive to a gym.

Although HR managers must be consistently strategic in their mindset, human resource issues are also dominating corporate strategic priorities. Consider first that employee salaries may account for more than 50 percent of the operating expenses in some organizations.[14] Complicating matters are findings such as those in a 2013 study in the United States that suggests that actively disengaged employees cost the U.S. economy between $450–$550 billion dollars a year.[15] As a result, the expectations for human resource departments are regularly on the rise:

> A survey of 200 CEOs and other top executives in the United States, United Kingdom, France, Spain, Germany, and Australia indicates that four of the five top strategic priorities most commonly identified by business executives are HR related (ranks in parentheses): attracting and retaining skilled staff (1); improving workforce performance (3); changing leadership and management behaviours (4); and changing organizational culture and employee attitudes (5). The other priority, rated second overall, was increasing customer service—while a marketing priority, customer service is still closely linked to HR activities such as training, compensation, and performance management. Only 13 percent of the respondents, however, reported satisfaction with the way their HR departments achieved these priorities, thus underscoring the major strides HR has yet to make to fulfill organizational expectations.[16]

To meet these demands, HR teams and senior leaders in HR need to be strategic business partners who are able to make evidence-informed recommendations and decisions that enable individuals and teams to create more value for the organization. The gradual shift to strategic HR is evidenced by the 62 percent of senior HR leaders now reporting to the CEO or president of the organization.[17]

Understanding the Strategic Human Resource Management Process

To be effective, a human resource management strategy and system should be formulated after careful consideration of an organization's environment, mission and objectives, strategies, and internal strengths and weaknesses, including its culture. For purposes of discussion, we will break the human resource strategy formulation and implementation process into five major steps, as outlined in Figure 1-2. Alternative sources may provide different stages and descriptions. Regardless, the logic remains consistent: Know what you are aligning to, understand your external and internal environment, make decisions, and evaluate decisions.

Step 1: Organizational Mission, Goals, and Strategy Analysis

The way in which an organization defines its mission often significantly influences human resource strategies. A **mission statement** specifies what activities the

organization intends to pursue and what course is charted for the future. It is a concise statement of "who we are, and what we do" and gives an organization its own special identity, culture, and path of development.

Two similar pork producers may have varying missions. One may define the mission as "to be a sustainable pork producer," whereas the other may define it as "to be a leading pork producer." The associated strategies are likely to show significant differences. Apart from finding efficient ways to raise hogs, the former may also seek ways to improve the effectiveness and safety of manure recycling or seek strategies to raise antibiotic-free hogs while the focus of the second producer may be expansion and profitability.

Even organizations with similar goals may show remarkable differences in

mission statement A statement outlining the purpose and long-term objectives of the organization.

FIGURE 1-2

A Model of Strategic Human Resource Management

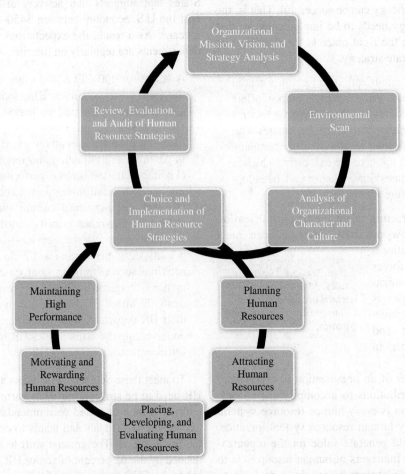

their strategies to achieve those goals. There are three generic business strategies: cost leadership, differentiation, or focus.[18]

Firms that pursue a **cost leadership strategy** aim to gain a competitive advantage through lower costs. They aggressively seek efficiencies in production and use tight controls (especially in managing costs) to gain an advantage over their competitors.

> **cost leadership strategy** Strategy to gain competitive advantage through lower costs of operations and lower prices for products.

The BIC pen company is a good example of a firm that attempts to compete successfully by producing pens as cheaply as possible. Similar cost leadership strategy is demonstrated by Walmart and Acer Inc.

Product **differentiation strategy** focuses on creating a distinctive or even unique product that is unsurpassed in quality, innovative design, or other features. This may be accomplished through product design, through unique technology, or even through carefully planned advertising and promotion. Firms that use this strategy may even be able to charge higher than average prices for their products.

> **differentiation strategy** Strategy to gain competitive advantage by creating a distinct product or offering a unique service.

Apple, Samsung, and Stella Artois are firms that use a differentiation strategy.

Under the **focus strategy**, a firm concentrates on a segment of the market and attempts to satisfy it with a low-priced or a highly distinctive product. Within this specific market or target customer group, a focused firm may compete on the basis of either differentiation or cost leadership. The target market in this instance is usually set apart either by geography or by specialized needs.

> **focus strategy** Strategy to gain a competitive advantage by focusing on the needs of a specific segment of the total market.

An automobile manufacturer sells its sport utility vehicles primarily in North America because of the local demand. The same firm sells its smaller and fuel-efficient economy car in less-developed countries because consumers there have lower disposable income or require smaller vehicles.

Regardless of an organization's strategic direction, human resources are required to formulate and fulfill the organization's strategies. In all cases, the human resource strategies should be chosen for their ability to enable successful completion of the organization's strategies. In some cases, a single human resource strategy may be used to accomplish different corporate strategies.

Many organizations are also now including specific strategies that directly consider their employees. For example, many organizations have set as a strategy to become one of Canada's "Best Managed Companies."[19] The setting of corporate strategies directly related to human resources is a growing trend as HR professionals continue to demonstrate their strategic value.

Consistent with the setting of corporate strategies, managers of human resources must consider how the external environment will influence their decisions. This is the focus of the second step.

Step 2: Environmental Scan

Through careful and continuous monitoring of economic, social, and labour market trends and by noting changes in governmental policies, legislation, and public policy statements, effective human resource management will be able to identify environmental threats and opportunities that in turn serve as a foundation for new action guidelines. Some of these environmental forces facing Canadian organizations today are listed in Figure 1-3. For discussion purposes, the forces facing a Canadian organization (especially those affecting human resource management) can be grouped under five headings: *economic* (e.g., recession), *technological* (e.g., automation), *demographic* (e.g., workforce composition), *cultural* (e.g., ethnic diversity), and *legal* (e.g., changing laws). The first four forces will be discussed in this chapter. The critical importance of legal compliance for the human resource function warrants a more elaborate

FIGURE 1-3

Major Forces Facing Canadian Business

review of the subject matter. Hence, this topic is discussed in detail in Chapter 4.

Economic Forces

Economic Force: Economic Cycles The first of four critical **economic forces** is *economic cycles*.

Economies go through boom and bust business cycles. The Canadian economy is no exception to this. In today's globally connected world, strengths and misfortunes originating in one economy are soon passed on to others. Human resource professionals must consider economic cycles in designing practices, policies, and the broader system. For instance, human resource managers face special challenges during a recessionary period, as they often have to carry out the unpleasant task of planning, communicating, and implementing employee layoffs or terminations. Often, wage concessions have to be sought from labour for the sheer survival of the firm. Workforce morale, by and large, is low during a recessionary period; supplementary employee counselling may become necessary. At times, the entire organization may assume a crisis management posture, which creates new challenges for the human resource manager with respect to policy formulation, communication, and implementation.

> **economic forces** Economic factors facing Canadian business today, including global trade forces and the force to increase one's own competitiveness and productivity levels.

The challenges are equally daunting coming out of a recession, as human resource managers consider how best to grow the organization's talent base. During growth cycles, organizations may be faced with the opportunity of recruiting employees with a different skill set than those that may have been let go during the recessionary cycle.

> By the middle of 2017 Canada's economy was growing at an unprecedented pace. According to the ministry of finance, the economy is growing at over 3.5 percent, a far cry from the 0.9 percent in 2015 and 1.5 percent in 2016.[20] This pace of growth puts Canada at the head of the G7 countries.[21] The Conference Board of Canada, however, suggests that growth will fall to 2.0 percent in 2018 because the economy is approaching full capacity.[22] Moreover, economic growth will slow to 1.7 percent until 2023[23] because of our aging population, discussed below.

Note that boom and bust cycles may not be the same across the country. For instance, the manufacturing sector in Southern Ontario often cycles based on the value of the Canadian dollar against the American dollar. The oil and gas sector in Alberta, on the other hand, tends to vary based on the price of crude oil on the world market. This results in localized challenges for finding or shedding talent. Thus, managers of human resources need to consider economic forces at the local, national, and international level—which are discussed next.

Economic Force: Global Trade International trade has always been critical to Canada's prosperity and growth. Canada ranks high among exporting nations: on a per capita basis, we export much more than either the United States or Japan.[24] The combination of a relatively small population and a large natural resource base gives Canada an international trade advantage.

Although our ability to compete in the international marketplace has been generally strong, Canada's competitiveness has fallen. In 2011, Canada was the twelfth most competitive nation in the world; in 2015, we had fallen to fifteenth and, as of 2017, we are fourteenth (Figure 1-4).[25]

The ever-growing shift toward the global marketplace forces organizations to consider how they manage their employees. The emergence of open borders has presented newer opportunities to Canadian firms and professionals—resulting in both an increase in Canadians working abroad and an increase in economic immigration to Canada. Canada currently accepts approximately 300,000 immigrants per year; of these, approximately 156,000 join the workforce.[26] Progressive human resource practices and new government policies may be critical to meet these growing realities. Indeed, the Canadian government is looking to increase immigration to Canada in an attempt to boost the economy as our population ages, with a focus on economic immigration as compared to family- or refugee-based immigration.[27]

Economic Force: Productivity and Innovation Improvement **Productivity** refers to the ratio of an organization's outputs (e.g., goods and services) to its inputs (e.g., people, capital, materials, and energy). Productivity increases as an organization finds new ways to use fewer resources to produce its output. For example:

> **productivity** The ratio of a firm's outputs (goods and services) divided by its inputs (people, capital, materials, energy).

> A restaurant may seek to improve productivity by using fewer ingredients in recipes (reduction in raw materials) or by asking a server to also clear, clean, and reset tables (increase in responsibility and associated reduction in the need for additional staff). Alternatively, the restaurant may seek to increase the number of outputs by having more people come to the restaurant. The latter, however, may require increased marketing efforts, which would result in an increase in inputs.

In a business environment, productivity optimization is essential for long-run success. Individuals can even gain

FIGURE 1-4

How Competitive Is Canada Compared to Other Nations?

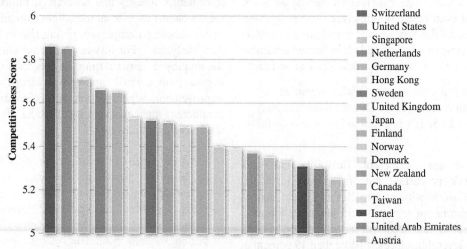

Legend:
- Switzerland
- United States
- Singapore
- Netherlands
- Germany
- Hong Kong
- Sweden
- United Kingdom
- Japan
- Finland
- Norway
- Denmark
- New Zealand
- Canada
- Taiwan
- Israel
- United Arab Emirates
- Austria

SOURCE: Based on data from *The Global Competitiveness Report 2017–2018*, Klaus Schwab, World Economic Forum.

accreditation in optimization processes through organizations such as the International Association for Six Sigma Certification. Through gains in productivity, managers can reduce costs, save scarce resources, and enhance profits. In turn, improved profits allow an organization to provide better pay, benefits, and working conditions. The result can be a higher quality of work life for employees, who are more likely to be motivated toward further improvements in productivity. Human resource professionals contribute to improved productivity directly by finding better, more efficient ways to meet their objectives and, indirectly, by improving the quality of work life for employees.

Unfortunately, optimizing productivity is not simply a matter of increasing outputs or decreasing inputs. In either case, the employees must adapt how work is done. As a result, a major challenge facing Canadian managers is optimizing productivity while maintaining a high quality of engaged work life for the employees. Moreover, strategic human resource management seeks to address more than just financial productivity.[28] Some of the strategies to address productivity will be discussed in Chapter 3.

What is worrisome today is the gap between the productivity levels of Canada and its biggest trade partner, the United States.[29] For over a decade, U.S. productivity has been consistently outpacing that of this country. Canada is steadily losing its ability to innovate and create wealth compared with other countries. According to the Conference Board of Canada, Canada is ranked ninth of sixteen peer countries of the Organisation for Economic Co-operation and Development.[30] Even more troubling is that without enhanced management skills, something enabled through HR, the future is not likely to shift.

If Canada is to improve—even maintain—its competitiveness, innovation on two fronts, namely people management and technology, are a must.

> Among peer nations, Canada receives a poor rating for the number of patents filed per capita. Indeed, we are 15 of 16. Japan and Switzerland are ranked number 1 and 2.[31]

Without innovation, productivity differences tend to increase. As such, without innovation, Canadian employers and their human resource professionals will be faced with the challenge of creating additional productivity improvements. As a progressive human resource strategy, numerous organizations are starting to recruit or develop innovative staff to create a culture of innovation within the organization.

Technological Forces

Technological Force: Flexible Work Design Technology influences organizations and the way people work. Often it can affect an entire industry, as the following example illustrates:

> With a history dating back to 1880, Kodak was among the major producers of photographic film. The advent of digital photography and technology is among the factors that contributed to Kodak's filing for bankruptcy in 2012. Of note, Kodak had invented the digital photography technology but (clearly, in retrospect, unwisely) chose not to commercialize it.[32]

Canada has witnessed the rapid growth of technology and access to high-speed information transmission systems affecting almost all walks of life. In December 2016, the Canadian Radio-television and Telecommunications Commission declared that access to high-speed Internet should be a base service for all Canadians.[33] An unprecedented degree of technology has changed the way we work, play, study, and even entertain ourselves. Access to information has affected the way several organizations conduct their business. Nevertheless, Canada lags behind a number of developed nations in technology development and use.

> Canada ranks fourth in the OECD countries, up from eleventh place in 2012. Of note, approximately 90 percent of Canada's population has access to the Internet.[34]

Technology brings considerable flexibility into when and where work is carried out. In several instances, employees can work without ever leaving their homes. Such *telecommuting* (or remote work) has been found to cut greenhouse gases and boost worker perceptions of communications in several instances.[35] More than 19 percent of Canada's working population works from a nontraditional workplace, such as their home.[36]

> TELUS has arranged for half of its 30,000 employees to be able to work from home if they choose. In its teleworking pilot test, TELUS found that having 170 employees working from home saved 114 tonnes of greenhouse gases and 14,000 hours of traffic time. In the same pilot, TELUS found that morale as well as productivity increased as a result of telecommuting.[37]

Telecommuting, however, is not without its human resource challenges. For instance, a challenge related to telecommuting is how an organization can best ensure that the employee's home workstation is safe.

Not all jobs lend themselves to less traditional workspaces; but with the advances in technology, virtually any job—or any part of a job—that involves work that is independent of other people and special equipment could be performed away from the workplace. Careful planning, training, and piloting may be required before telecommuting is rolled out in an organization, as managing from a distance is simply different from managing in person.[38]

More recently, a greater focus has been placed on cyber security.[39] With employees working distally, the probability of data breaches is also likely to climb. From a strategic human resource perspective, many organizations have taken to hiring cyber security experts to not only protect their sensitive data but also make attempts to breach their security systems in an effort to better protect their data.

Technological Force: Connectivity Connectivity and technology have disrupted the way organizations operate, often reducing costs or capitalizing on new opportunities.

More effective *knowledge management*—the process of capturing organizational knowledge and making it available for sharing and building new knowledge—has been

another outcome of digital information systems. It has given rise to potentially boundless information.[40] Intranets and integrated information systems help store and access information quickly and accurately. Information management systems capture an incredible amount of digital information about an employee, giving rise to human resource data analytics.[41] For instance, such systems can store what the employee learns during various training programs (or over a time period) and give evidence of performance improvement. When the annual performance interview is conducted, managers can identify the on-the-job competencies of an employee.

> Even the field of human resources is being shaped by big data trends. For instance, metaBUS is a technology-based research hub that is seeking to bring together and synthesize every correlation within the field of human resources over a 25-year period to enable human resource practitioners to make better data-informed decisions about their practices and systems.[42]

As a platform for communication and interaction, the Internet has had a profound impact on human resource management activities. Social networking sites, video-sharing sites, wikis, blogs, and other interactive opportunities allow users to own and control data as well as add value to the applications they use. This has resulted in rapid use of the technology for a variety of human resource purposes. It has also resulted in organizations needing to create human resource policies about the limitations of social networking within organizations.

Technological Force: Automation **Automation** continues to be a technological force and opportunity that has affected Canadian organizations and their human resource management practices.

Organizations tend to mechanize for speed, reliability, or flexibility. Competition from other countries has made it imperative that we

> **automation** The shift toward converting work that was traditionally done by hand to being completed by mechanical or electronic devices.

improve the speed of our manufacturing practices if we want to stay competitive. This trend has led to the development of mechatronics programs at some post-secondary institutions.

By moving to a mechanized process, better service may be provided to the customer through *increased predictability and reliability* in operations and *higher standards* of quality in production. Machines do not go on strike, nor do they ask for raises.

Mechanization allows for *flexibility* in operations. In several automated production facilities, even small production batches become economically viable since the time, cost, and effort involved in changing setups are minimal. The ability to produce small batches in turn enables a firm to focus on the needs of different customers and market segments and speed up delivery schedules.

> Shapeways is an organization that specializes in rapid prototyping and small-batch production through three-dimensional printing in materials such as plastic and metal. These products can be created in minutes.

Mechanization and automation is not without human resource challenges. Negative union attitudes toward mechanization are a barrier to the introduction of technology in the workplace. Automation may result in a smaller workforce together with fewer opportunities for socialization on the job. To use expensive technology effectively (during an automation), more and more manufacturing facilities may find it necessary to schedule two or three shifts a day. In addition, the technologies used in industries such as additive manufacturing may require highly skilled designers, operators, and technicians.

> Improvements in technology and automation have helped the British Columbia lumber industry. Interestingly, while automation has led to job losses in some roles, British Columbia's forest industry is facing a talent shortage due to retirements and technology advances. Thus, automation has created an environment in which there are too many employees and too few employees simultaneously, just for different segments of the industry.[43]

In some cases, however, mechanization is seen as a solution to labour shortages. The farming industry in the United States, as an example, is experiencing a labour shortage. As a result, companies are turning to mechanization as a solution.[44]

Courtesy of neuroArm, University of Calgary.
Robots are increasingly being used in places not yet seen before. The neuroArm developed at the University of Calgary is a surgical robotic system that is controlled by a surgeon working at a computer and guided by continuous magnetic resonance images.

In summary, the technology employed by different firms shows considerable variation. In organizations such as a large steel factory or lumber mill, the production processes are fairly routine. In several such organizations, improving predictability of operations assumes great importance. This often requires human resource managers to focus more on predictability of employee performance (e.g., by providing explicit job descriptions and job-specific training, and by focusing on performance monitoring). In contrast, in firms with nonroutine production processes (such as advertising firms and software developers), flexible human resource practices that foster creativity, innovation, and entrepreneurship may add more value.

Demographic Forces

Demographic Force: Gender Balance in the Workforce
The demographics of the labour force describe the composition of the workforce: the education levels, the age levels, the percentage of the population participating in the workforce, and other population characteristics. While **demographic changes** occur slowly and can be predicted in most instances, they still exert considerable influence on organizational decisions. Each demographic change will have a different impact on the choice of human resource practices and activities, but may also have an additive effect. As a result, managers of human resources must consider demographic shifts both in isolation and as an integrated system.

> **demographic changes**
> Changes in the demographics of the labour force (e.g., education levels, age levels, participation rates) that occur slowly and are usually known in advance.

While the figures that follow refer to gender, one must recognize from an inclusiveness lens the importance of differentiating biological gender from gender identity. An understanding of demographic forces in both gender and gender identity will serve human resource professionals in their pursuit to create inclusive workplaces. For example, a recent job fair in Toronto focused on the transgender community.[45]

> As of 2017, Canada's labour force consisted of almost 19.6 million people aged 15 years or older, up from 14.2 million in 1990.[46] Just over 47 percent of the workforce in 2015 were women.[47] Moreover, the participation rate of women in health care and professional, scientific, and technical services also continues to grow (see Figure 1-5). More women than men tend to work part-time (see Figure 1-6).

Demographic Force: Shift Toward Knowledge Workers
Recently, there has been a shift from employment in primary and extractive industries (such as mining and fishing) to service, technical, and professional jobs. The relative contribution to Canada's employment in various

---

FIGURE 1-5

Distribution of Gender in the Workforce by Industry

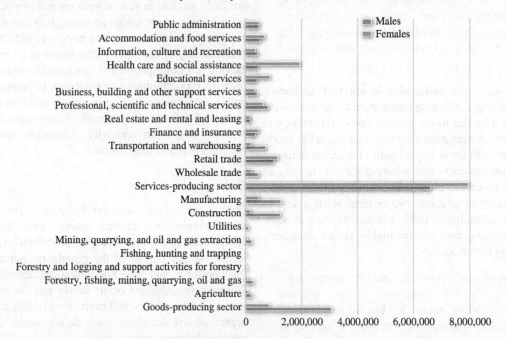

SOURCE: Adapted from Statistics Canada, "Labour force characteristics by industry, annual," 2017. Table: 14-10-0023-0.

FIGURE 1-6

Labour Force Employed Full-Time and Part-Time by Gender

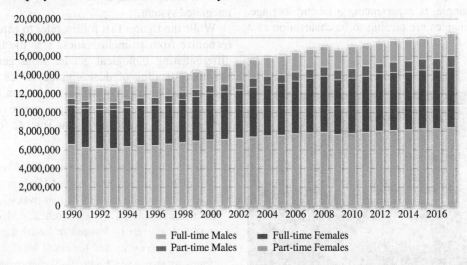

SOURCE: Adapted from Statistics Canada, "Labour force characteristics by sex and detailed age group, annual," Table 14-10-0018-01.

---

industries is shown in Figure 1-7. Service industries such as education, health care, tourism, trade, and public administration make significant contributions to our national wealth today.

The move away from extractive industries increases the need for innovation. In part, it creates an environment that requires not only knowledge workers, but individuals who bring innovative thinking to their organization.

FIGURE 1-7

Employment by Industry in Canada

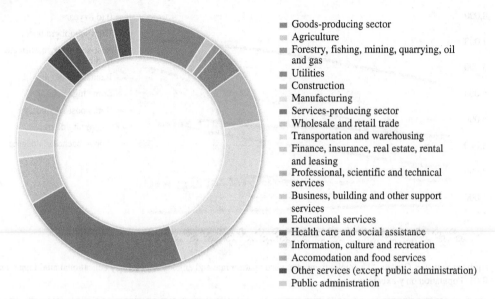

- Goods-producing sector
- Agriculture
- Forestry, fishing, mining, quarrying, oil and gas
- Utilities
- Construction
- Manufacturing
- Services-producing sector
- Wholesale and retail trade
- Transportation and warehousing
- Finance, insurance, real estate, rental and leasing
- Professional, scientific and technical services
- Business, building and other support services
- Educational services
- Health care and social assistance
- Information, culture and recreation
- Accomodation and food services
- Other services (except public administration)
- Public administration

SOURCE: Adapted from Statistics Canada, "Labour force characteristics by industry, annual," 2018, Table 14-10-0023-01.

Knowledge workers form the basis of a knowledge-based economy grounded in the production, distribution, and use of knowledge and information. Indeed, modern economies are becoming dependent on knowledge, information, and highly skilled individuals.[48] It is estimated that by 2021, there will be a shortage of over 40,000 knowledge workers in the province of Alberta alone.[49]

The ability of organizations to find, keep, and continually retrain these workers might spell success in the coming years. This is not only a trend in North America. China has taken great strides toward moving away from a production-based to a knowledge-based economy.[50] Moreover, some have even signalled that the term *knowledge workers* needs to be changed to *learning workers*.[51] With an increased reliance on knowledge workers, organizations also start to face challenges associated with employees hiding and withholding knowledge.[52] A further challenge facing human resource professionals in a growing knowledge-based economy is that educational attainment is not keeping pace.

Demographic Force: Educational Attainment of Workers
A look at the **educational attainment** of Canadian workers presents an intriguing picture. The educational attainment of Canadians has increased dramatically over the past several years and is expected to maintain its upward trend (see Figure 1-8).

knowledge workers
Members of occupations generating, processing, analyzing, or synthesizing ideas and information (such as scientists and management consultants).

In 2016, 54 percent of Canadians aged 25 to 44 years were post-secondary graduates.[53] Over 28 percent of Canadians aged 25 or above hold a university degree or better (the corresponding figure in 2002 was less than 10 percent).[54]

Primary and secondary education systems play a key role in generating the new supply of skills needed by our post-industrial society. By and large, Canadian schools appear to be ready for this task.

In one study, approximately 30,000 students from more than 1000 Canadian schools were compared on their mathematical and scientific literacy with students in 31 other countries. Canadian students performed well compared to others, ranking second in reading, seventh in science, and eighth in mathematics. In a majority of provinces, students' performance in reading, science, and mathematics placed these provinces among the top-ranked countries.[55]

The disturbing news, however, is that 48 percent of Canadians aged 16 or over fall below adequate levels of literacy.[56] Not only do such low literacy rates reduce the overall productivity levels in our industries, they may also be a major contributor to safety violations and accidents. Moreover, as the nature of work shifts to that of knowledge-based industries, the demand for

educational attainment
The highest educational level attained by an individual worker, employee group, or population.

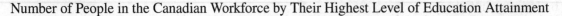

FIGURE 1-8

Number of People in the Canadian Workforce by Their Highest Level of Education Attainment

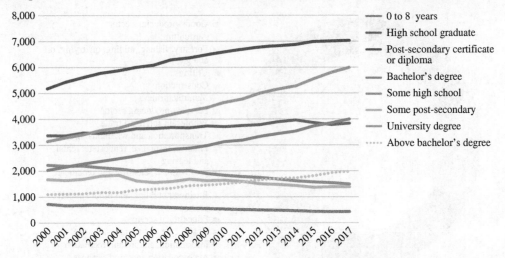

SOURCE: Adapted from Statistics Canada, "Unemployment rate, participation rate and employment rate by educational attainment, annual," Table 14-10-0020-01. Population on y-axis in *thousands*.

individuals with post-secondary education will outpace the rate at which people attain a post-secondary education.

> About 17 percent of women and 19 percent of men drop out of school before they graduate high school.[57] It is estimated that currently more than 5.2 million Canadians lack a basic school certificate or diploma.[58]

Some of the more progressive employers have recognized workplace literacy as a serious issue and have taken proactive action to minimize its adverse consequences. For instance, human resources professionals are encouraged to use accessible and plain language in communications.[59]

Faced with this disheartening prospect, the Corporate Council on Education identified a set of "employability skills" consisting of basic academic skills (e.g., communication, thinking, learning), personal management skills (e.g., positive attitudes and behaviours, ability to accept responsibility, adaptability to new challenges), and teamwork skills (e.g., ability to work with others, ability to lead a team). These skills were considered to be the foundation skills for employability in the future.[60]

Demographic Force: Aging Population One of the issues for human resource managers is what *Maclean's* termed our old age crisis.[61] In 1996, about 28 percent of the population (or almost 7.6 million Canadians) were more than 50 years old. The proportion of the population in the age group 65 and over is now expanding rapidly, reinforced by a low birth rate and longer life expectancy. In 2016, people aged 65 and over formed 16.5 percent of the population. By 2060, this proportion will increase to 25.4 percent. Conversely, the age category between 15 and 30 years

old will decrease from 19.3 percent to 16.9 percent of the population over the same time frame.[62] In short, human resource professionals will face an ever-increasing trend of more people leaving the workforce than entering it. This is because the average age of the Canadian population has been steadily increasing (see Figure 1-9). Like economic cycles, the impact of population aging is different depending on your location.

> In 2016, the provinces with the highest proportion of the labour force aged 65 and over were Quebec, New Brunswick, Nova Scotia, and Prince Edward Island, all at 19 percent compared to 16.5 percent for Canada as a whole.[63] At the other end of the scale, Nunavut had only 7 percent of its population over the age of 65 in 2016. By 2038, Prince Edward Island will pull in front with 32 percent of its population over the age of 65, whereas Nunavut will continue to have the lowest percentage, at 15 percent.

The exact consequences of this trend for the human resource management function are hard to predict. An increasingly hectic scramble for jobs (especially in the traditional sectors) may be one consequence. This is because the fear of post-retirement poverty (fuelled by uncertainty about government-sponsored pension plans and the recent volatility in the stock market, which eroded the savings of many Canadians) may motivate employees to hold on to their current jobs. This may create unprecedented bottlenecks in professional and unionized industries. That said, older workers may face ageism in technology jobs.[64]

> According to Statistics Canada, the age of retirement has been on the rise since the 1990s. The average age

FIGURE 1-9

Projected Population of Canada by Age Category

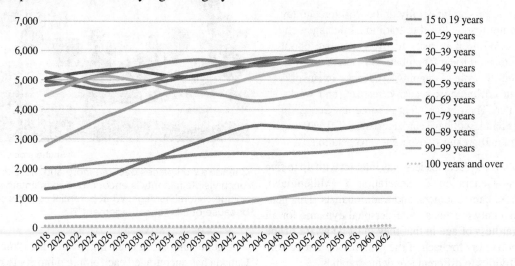

SOURCE: Adapted from Statistics Canada, "Projected population, by projection scenario, age and sex, as of July 1," 2018, Table 17-10-0057-01. Population on y-axis in *thousands*.

for retirement in 2000 was 61.6, whereas the same number in 2014 was 63.[65]

Pressures for expanded retirement benefits, variable work schedules, coordination of government benefits (e.g., Canada/Quebec Pension Plan benefits) with company benefits, and retraining programs are just a few of the challenges that await human resource specialists in the future. This effect is compounded by recent changes to old age security. Specifically, workers now have to wait until they are 67 to claim old age security.

One major challenge facing Canadian organizations is retaining older, more experienced, and skilled employees whose expertise is in demand in the labour market. The past view of people as expendable cogs who are responsible for managing their own careers has encouraged employees to leave their employers as soon as a better opportunity emerges elsewhere. To retain older workers, employers have to show respect and appreciation, facilitate career growth within the organization, offer flexible work and opportunities to telecommute, and recognize their skills and experience.[66]

The abolition of mandatory retirement has also brought in new challenges as well as opportunities. An aging population affects many human resource functions, especially recruitment and selection, job design, training, appraisal, and compensation and benefits administration.

The availability of retirees provides an opportunity to employers who are looking for experienced, part-time employees. The reduction in the supply of young workers (a staple source of recruits by many fast-food restaurants and grocery chains) may be compensated by the availability of older workers willing to work part-time. Experienced and highly motivated retirees may be a welcome source of recruits for employers and nonprofit/voluntary agencies searching for persons who can accept supervisory responsibilities.

The age crisis is not limited to older generations. A declining youth population—those under age 25—entering the workforce has implications for Canada on a global scale. While Canada's youth population is falling in relation to the population overall, developing economies, such as India, are experiencing an increase in the youth population relative to the population overall.

Demographic Force: Generational Shift Generation X employees, who are born between 1966 and 1980, are considered to be different from the baby boomers (the previous generation). While Generation Xers are not averse to hard work, they place a premium on work–life balance and like to be active participants in decision making.[67] They are likely to show disdain for a "command and control" culture and are likely to have more loyalty to their profession and competency building than to their employers.

Some writers claim that Gen Xers think of work as a job while boomers view it as a career. Xers are unfazed by power and authority; boomers are impressed and attracted by it. Xers mistrust most business practices; boomers instituted many of them. Xers are self-reliant; boomers are team-oriented.[68]

The newest generations in the labour market are Generation Y and Generation Next (or Gen Z), and they are qualitatively different from either of the above groups:

> Generation Yers are now fully in the workforce today and may not respond well to traditional management practices. While it is risky to overgeneralize about any group, significant numbers of Gen Yers seek continuous learning, ongoing feedback, teamwork, up-to-date technology, security, respect, and work–life balance. Their biggest fear is boredom. Gen Z, on the other hand, will have characteristics of fiscal conservatism and greater transparency expectations.[69]

In today's workplace, leaders may interact with up to five generations—Generation Z, Generation Y (Millennials), Generation X, baby boomers, and traditionalists. This generational diversity creates an interpersonal dynamic for all leaders regardless of age in that they must be aware of the different motivators for each of the generations and be able to tailor activities to different age demographics.

Generational shifts in North America are also having complex implications for human resource managers that are somewhat outside their control. For example, certain industries will be facing an impending skilled trades shortage in part because of the increasing average age of the skilled trade worker and in part because of challenges attracting young people to the skilled trades in post-secondary education.

Cultural Forces

Cultural Force: Diversity As cultural values change, human resource departments discover new challenges. While several **cultural forces** face Canadian managers, we will only discuss diversity and ethics briefly here as an important consideration in the formulation of HR strategy.

In 1971, Canada became the first country to declare multiculturalism as a state policy.[70] By 2016, the Canadian population was made up of over 250 ethnic origins.[71] The coexistence of numerous national, racial, and ethnic groups, each with its unique cultural and social background, makes Canadian society a **cultural mosaic**.[72] Economic immigrants have often acted as engines of economic growth in this country, while shifts in the country of origin of immigrants have added to this country's cultural diversity and richness.

> **cultural forces** Challenges facing a firm's decision makers because of cultural differences among employees or changes in core cultural or social values occurring at the larger societal level.

> **cultural mosaic** The Canadian ideal of encouraging each ethnic, racial, and social group to maintain its own cultural heritage, forming a national mosaic of different cultures.

© Shutterstock/Rawpixel.com

Canada's workplaces become more and more diverse as each visible minority is encouraged to maintain his or her unique cultural heritage. What potential conflicts can develop because of this "encouragement"?

Unlike the American notion of the "melting pot," Canada has encouraged each ethnic minority to maintain its unique cultural heritage to form part of the Canadian cultural mosaic. Canada is no longer a two-language nation; millions of Canadians have neither English nor French as their mother tongue.

> Today, over 3.6 million Canadians are referred to as *allophones*, which literally means "other speaking." For example, today, more Canadians speak Chinese than Italian, and it is the most common nonofficial language.[73]

For the practising manager, this cultural diversity simultaneously brings additional opportunities and challenges. Often, it is the human resource department's responsibility to maximize the beneficial outcomes and minimize the challenges posed by a diverse workforce. A large focus of current HR practices is to create inclusive work environments in which differences are embraced and leveraged for the betterment of the organization.

Cultural Force: Ethics There is a great demand today for more ethical conduct of business. The unethical practices of several large companies, including Bre-X, Enron, and WorldCom, underscored the social costs of unethical and fraudulent business practices. Businesses, especially big corporations, have been accused of acting totally out of self-interest and furthering the interest of a few members of top management. In recent years, a variety of unethical practices have been reported, including creative accounting, insider trading, securities fraud, excessive payments made to top management not reflective of their contributions, and bribery and kickbacks. Indeed, greed and short-term orientation accompanied by creative accounting played no small role in the stock market meltdown and the acceleration of personal bankruptcies in 2008.

> A global survey indicated that nearly 75 percent of respondents had felt pressure to compromise

their standards at work.[74] The most important ethical issues confronting Canadian firms today would seem to relate to sexual harassment, cyber espionage, avoiding conflicts of interest and maintaining honest governance, employee and client privacy, environmental protection, and security of information.[75]

This has resulted in many Canadian firms instituting a code of ethics or code of conduct for their employees. Over 70 percent of the responding firms in a survey[76] had also instituted a program to promote ethical values and practices. Needless to say, the human resource department will be a key player in this important activity.

Spotlight *on* ETHICS

What Is a "Right" Behaviour?

Ethics are moral principles that guide human behaviours and are often based on a society's cultural values, norms, customs, and beliefs, which means that different cultures and even individuals within the same society have widely varying standards of behaviour. How are we to differentiate "right" from "wrong" or "good" from "bad"? There are no simple answers. Many adopt one of the following postures in dealing with such ambiguous situations:

1. *Universalist approach:* Persons who embrace this view assert that some moral standards are universally applicable. In other words, regardless of society or place, a wrong act (such as killing, stealing, or lying) is wrong. There are no exceptions to moral "rights" and "wrongs."

2. *Situational approach:* What is right or wrong depends essentially on the situation or culture surrounding the actor. While telling the truth is desirable, there may be situations in which lying is acceptable or even necessary, or other cultures may not value truth to the same extent. Similarly, while killing is bad, there may be situations in which this act is justified. It all depends on the situation. While high morals are to be followed, an individual may have to make exceptions when the context justifies them.

3. *Subjectivist approach:* In this approach, the individual decision maker facing a situation determines what is right and wrong after considering all aspects of the situation. Moral decisions are based on personal values and preferences. Needless to say, the standards imposed by individuals are vastly different depending on their upbringing, current circumstances, values, and beliefs.

Another useful model to understand and guide ethical behaviour is offered by Lawrence Kohlberg. Kohlberg, an American psychologist, posits six stages that form an invariant and universal sequence in individual development; thus, everyone is supposed to go through the same stages in the same sequence. It is, however, possible for a person to be "stuck" at one of the following stages and not proceed to the next level. The six stages of moral development identified by Kohlberg[77] are as follows:

Stage 1: Obedience and Punishment Stage: The only reason for a person to perform the "right" act at this stage is obedience to others who have the power to punish.

Stage 2: Reciprocity Stage: Here, the individual enters into reciprocal agreements with others so that he or she receives the greatest good or reward. The focus is on achieving one's own objectives and on self-interest; for this, the individual concerned is willing to take actions that others want him or her to take.

Stage 3: Interpersonal Conformity Stage: What is "right" is determined by expectations of others who are close to the individual. Close relatives, friends, and other "reference groups" help the individual identify the "right" action in any setting.

Stage 4: Law and Order Stage: Doing one's duty and obeying society's rules is considered the "right" behaviour at this stage.

Stage 5: The Social Contract Stage: Here, the individual goes beyond the minimal standards established by laws and rules. "The greatest good of the greatest number" in the society is the maxim that guides the individual's behaviour at this stage.

(Continued)

Stage 6: Universal Ethical Principles Stage: At this stage, the individual is guided by high moral principles. People are to be treated as ends in themselves, not just as means to one's ends or even to the ends of a whole group or society. People are considered as inherently valuable and to be treated in the "right" way. Very few individuals reach this level.

The field of human resource management is full of situations that involve hard choices between good and bad, right and wrong, desirable and undesirable.

The Spotlight on Ethics feature in this book will introduce you to one or more ethical challenges associated with the topic discussed in each chapter. Once you have identified your responses, compare your answer to those of your friends or family members. Find out why each person chose differently. Try to categorize the responses under the three categories and six stages of moral development listed above. Which approach seems to be used by most of your friends and acquaintances? At what stage of moral development are you and your friends?

Why? What are the implications for you and for your employer? What prevents you and your friends from moving to the next stage?

Instructions: Consider the following situation. Make a note of your answer and compare it with those of your friends and acquaintances.

Challenge with the Organization's Pension Fund
Your organization currently offers a pension plan that provides employees with a defined benefit of 2 percent of an employee's salary at retirement per year of service. Your pension fund manager has just informed you that the pension fund cannot sustain the current defined benefit because of the combination of an extraordinary number of predicted retirements in the next 10 years, the cumulative years of service provided by retiring employees, and a general increase in life expectancy. The pension fund manager has suggested that the fund be amended such that the defined benefit would be reduced to 1.8 percent of an employee's salary per year of service. What would you do?

Step 3: Analysis of Organizational Character and Culture

In addition to external scans, human resource strategies should be formed only after a careful consideration of the internal environment and elements such as character and culture. Similarities between organizations can be found among their parts, but each whole organization has a unique character. A key element of organizational character is its structure. **Organization structure** is the product of all of an organization's features and how they are arranged: its employees, its objectives, its technology, its size, and its policies, to name a few.[78] Organization structure reflects the past and shapes the future. Human resource specialists should be familiar with and adjust to the organization's structure. For example, sometimes objectives can be achieved in several acceptable ways. This idea, often overlooked, is called *equifinality,* which means there are usually many paths to any given objective. The key to success is choosing the path that best fits the organization's character.

Take, for example, how several key managerial decisions are made and their impact on HR practices. In some

> **organization structure**
> The product of all of an organization's features and how they are arranged—people, objectives, technology, size, age, and policies.

organizations, an autocratic decision-making style is used along with a strong organizational hierarchy. In contrast, other organizations consciously make an effort to create an egalitarian, participative, and entrepreneurial work climate. HR practices such as seniority- and rank-based pay and top-down communication channels are likely to work best in the former situation while results-oriented (and competency-based) pay and organic communication channels are likely to work best in the latter.

The managerial philosophy also influences the type of organization structure and the HR department's role within the firm. For instance, in a highly formal bureaucracy that is structured along functional lines (e.g., marketing, finance, production, etc.), HR's role is often to preserve the existing division of work by providing clear job descriptions, hiring specialists for each division, and introducing training systems that foster functional expertise. In contrast, in organizations that have flexible structures, the socialization of employees to create an organization-wide perspective and the creation of broad job classes may assume greater importance. Finally, an **organizational culture**, the core beliefs and assumptions that are widely shared by all organizational members, shapes work-related

> **organizational culture**
> The core beliefs and assumptions that are widely shared by all organizational members.

and other attitudes and significantly influences overall job commitment and performance. Clearly, human resource management has a role in shaping this; however, even here, the culture has to be consistent with the overall mission and strategy of the organization concerned.

Step 4: Choice and Implementation of Human Resource Strategies

Giving consideration to both the internal and external environments provides the opportunity for the human resource professional to begin evaluating potential human resource practices and activities and whether each is viable. Unsuitable strategic options must be dropped from consideration. The ones that appear viable should be scrutinized in detail for their advantages and weaknesses before being accepted for implementation.

Strategic choice and implementation involves identifying, securing, organizing, and directing the use of resources both within and outside the organization. Ultimately, there should be a clear line of sight between the human resource strategy and the corporate goals (see Figure 1-10). Similarly, the strategic human resource plan needs to integrate with other plans in the organization.

As the above example shows, the human resource strategy must reflect every change in the organizational strategy and support it. Simply stating that "we are strategic in our focus" does not, in fact, result in a contribution to organizational strategy.

A survey of 700 HR professionals found that 66 percent of the respondents felt that many human resource professionals who think they are strategic are simply not so in their actions. Only 4 percent of the respondents felt that human resource professionals are, on the whole, strategic and recognized for their strategic thinking by relevant others. However, 73 percent of the respondents believe that the word *strategic* is overused in human resources.[79]

Identifying an organization's HR strategy is often a complex task. Because of the dynamic nature of both the internal and external environments, it is not uncommon to see a difference between an organization's stated HR strategy and its "emergent" HR strategy.[80] Although in any given organization, there tends to be a *dominant* HR strategy, multiple bundles of HR practices are likely to develop to cater to the unique needs of organizations in a subgroup or industry.[81] Mere use of the term *strategic* without clear actions that support it simply reduces the credibility of the HR profession and its members. In formulating strategies, the human resource department must continuously focus on the following five major groups of activities:

1. Planning Human Resources

Human resource planning enables the determination of demand and supply of various types of human resources within the firm. It is also a systematic review of the current state of human resource practices in an organization and the identification of needed human resource processes, tools, and activities. The results of human resource planning shape the overall human resource strategies in the short run and identify any gaps in people or processes that need to be fulfilled.

A second element of the planning process is the eventual choice of appropriate human resource practices that

FIGURE 1-10

Line of Sight in Human Resource Strategy

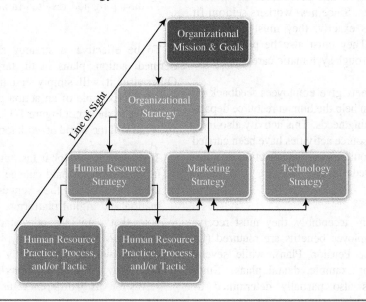

will fill the gaps identified in the first stage of planning. While details of this choice will be discussed in the chapters that follow, here are some of the initial questions human resource professionals are able to ask themselves and others:

- Are their assumptions realistic?
- Does the organization have the skills and resources to make its strategy viable?
- Does the organizational strategy hang together with the organization's structure, or will the strategy be at risk due to the structure?
- What are the risks of the strategy, and can we afford them?
- What do we need to do to make the strategy viable?

2. Attracting Human Resources

Following the planning of human resources, managers must begin to take action in filling apparent gaps in either people or practices. For instance, in recruiting and selecting workers, a human resource manager should meet all legal requirements (e.g., equal employment opportunity laws). Recruitment is the process of finding and attracting capable individuals to apply for employment and to accept a job offer if/when one is made to them. The selection process is a series of specific steps used to decide which recruits should be hired and aims to match job requirements with an applicant's capabilities.

3. Placing, Developing, and Evaluating Human Resources

With the right talent in the right place, attention must turn to optimizing both the employee's time as well as the activities and processes that guide human resources in a company. Once hired, new employees need to be oriented to the organization's policies and procedures and placed in their new job positions. Since new workers seldom fit the organization's needs exactly, they must be trained to perform effectively. They must also be prepared for future responsibilities through systematic career planning and development.

Performance assessments give employees feedback on their performance and can help the human resource department identify future training needs. This activity also indicates how well human resource activities have been carried out: Poor performance could mean that selection or training activities need to be redesigned.

4. Motivating Employees

When employees perform acceptably, they must receive compensation. Some employee benefits are required (for example, Canada/Quebec Pension Plan), while several others are voluntary (for example, dental plans). Since employee motivation is also partially determined by

internal work procedures, climate, and schedules, these must be continually modified to maximize performance.

It has often been observed that people leave their bosses, not their organizations. Many times, an employee may quit because the boss does not inspire, make good decisions, possess relevant knowledge, or treat employees fairly and with respect. Recognizing this fact, many progressive HR departments have initiated actions to identify problems before they cause an employee to leave the firm. One tool used is the employee opinion survey with its specific questions on managers. The other is the employee call centre, which allows employees to convey their problems anonymously.

5. Maintaining High Performance

The human resource strategy should ensure that the productive contribution from every member is at the maximum possible level. Most effective organizations have well-established employee relations practices, including good communication between managers and employees, standardized disciplinary procedures, and counselling systems. In today's work setting, internal work procedures and organizational policies must be continuously monitored to ensure that they meet the needs of a diverse workforce and ensure safety to every individual. In many organizations, employees may decide to join together and form unions. When this occurs, management is confronted with a new situation: union–management relations. To respond to the collective demands by employees, human resource specialists may have to negotiate a collective agreement and administer it.

Canada's record in work stoppages is by no means flattering. Between 2014 and 2017, Canada experienced 771 work stoppages that were an average of 77 days long and resulted in nearly 5.4 million days lost.[82]

To be effective, a strategy should also have clearly defined action plans with target achievement dates. Otherwise, it will simply end up being an exercise on paper. An example of an action plan with specific targets and dates is shown in Figure 1-11.

What will the world of work look like in the next decade?

The McKinsey Global Institute outlined a series of influences that would change the nature of work in the future. Among the strongest influences are automation and digital platforms. The McKinsey group notes that many jobs today stand the chance of being automated.[83] Needless to say, HR's role in the future of work will be significantly different. This means that today's HR departments should prepare themselves for vastly different future roles.

FIGURE 1-11

Metro Hospital's Strategic Approach to Human Resource Management Background Information

Background Information

Metro Hospital, a large hospital in a major Canadian city, currently faces an 18 percent turnover among its nursing staff. In fact, the turnover among nurses has been on the increase in the last two years. Kim Cameron, the hospital's newly appointed human resource manager, would like to reverse this trend and bring down the turnover rate to under 5 percent in the near future. As a first step, she looks through all available company records to find out more about the background of nurses who left the organization. She interviews 14 nurses who left the hospital recently and another 10 nurses who are currently employed in the hospital. Here are some of Cameron's findings:

- Forty percent of the nurses who left the hospital commented that their supervisors did not "treat them well"; only about 25 percent of the nurses who are currently with the hospital made the same comment.

- Six of the nurses who left and five of the present staff complained that the heating and air conditioning systems in the hospital do not work well so that it is very hot inside the hospital in the summer months and too cold in the winter.

- Fifty-five percent of those she talked to said that the benefits in the hospital were not as good as elsewhere, while the salary level was found to be similar to that available elsewhere.

- Research of hospital records indicated that only about 10 percent of the nursing supervisors had undergone any type of supervisory leadership skills training in the past.

Kim Cameron's Objective

After her initial research, Kim Cameron identifies the following as one of her major objectives for the immediate future: "To reduce the turnover among nursing staff from the present 18 percent to 4 percent by July 1, 2020, by incurring costs not exceeding $——(at current dollars)."

Kim Cameron's Overall Strategy

To achieve the above goal, Kim Cameron realizes that it is critical that the overall job satisfaction of nurses (especially their satisfaction with supervisors, working conditions, and rewards) be monitored and improved (if necessary). She sets out the following action plans for the immediate future for herself and others in her department.

Kim Cameron's Action Plans

Action Number	Action Description	Person Responsible for Action	Date by Which Action to Be Completed	Budget Allocated
1.	Conduct an attitude survey among all nurses; collect information on their attitudes toward their job, supervisor, pay, benefits, working conditions, and colleagues.	Asst. HRM	31-3-2019	$5,000
2.	Identify steps for improving morale among nurses.	Self (in consultation with others)	30-5-2019	——
3.	Ask physical plant to check condition of A/C and heating systems.	Self	25-1-2019	——
4.	Complete training program for 50 percent of nursing supervisors.	Training manager	15-2-2020	$9,000
5.	(Depending on the survey findings, other actions that have to be initiated will be listed here.)			

Without a future orientation, the human resource department becomes reactive, not proactive. And reactive approaches allow minor problems to become major ones.

Step 5: Review, Evaluation, and Audit of Human Resource Strategies

Human resource strategies, however effective they prove to be, must be examined regularly. An organization's contextual factors, such as technology, environments, government policies, and so on, change continuously; so too do several of its internal factors, such as membership characteristics, role definitions, and internal procedures. All these changes necessitate regular strategy evaluation to ensure their continued appropriateness.

> For example, a study by Statistics Canada reported that attempts at innovative human resources have actually increased labour turnover in Canadian manufacturing operations. The study examined how six specific alternative work practices—problem-solving teams, self-managed teams, flexible job design, profit sharing, merit pay, and formal training on team work—affect turnover. Although human resource professionals have always argued that innovative practices cause lower turnover, this particular study did not support that claim.[84]
>
> Hewlett-Packard has carried out formal research to identify links between employee experience and the firm's operational performance. The company grouped employees based on their function, recognizing that certain functions have more direct impact on operational outcomes. Results from the study indicate that "effective collaboration" combined with "empowerment to make decisions" tend to be related to customer attitudes.[85]

Results of program evaluation such as the above produce valuable *feedback,* which is information to help evaluate success or failure. Such information, in turn, helps the firm to fine-tune its practices or even abandon some actions that do not seem to have performance potential. Alternatively, additional resources can be allocated to successful projects to reap full benefits.

A holistic review of the human resource strategies in an organization with the intention of identifying and correcting deficiencies is referred to as a **human resource audit**. The audit may include one division or an entire company.

human resource audit
An examination of the human resource policies, practices, and systems of a firm (or division) to eliminate deficiencies and improve ways to achieve goals.

The benefits of a human resource audit are many and include the following:

- The audit helps align the human resource department's goals with larger organizational strategies.

- It almost invariably uncovers better ways for the department to contribute to societal, organizational, and employee objectives. This, in turn, clarifies the human resource department's duties and responsibilities.

- It ensures timely compliance with legal requirements.

- It discloses how well managers are meeting their human resource duties.

- It uncovers critical human resource problems and possible solutions.

- It reduces human resource costs through more effective procedures.

- It provides specific, verifiable data on the human resource department's contributions.

- It stimulates uniformity of human resource policies and practices.

- It helps review and improve the human resource department's information system.

- It enhances the professional image of the department among various stakeholders.

Human resource research grows more important with each passing year, for several reasons. First, human resource work carries with it many legal implications for the employer. Failure to comply with equal employment or safety laws, for example, subjects the organization to potential lawsuits. Second, "people costs" are significant. Pay and benefits often are a major operating expense for most employers. Improper compensation plans can be costly, even fatal, to the company's survival. Third, the department's activities help shape an organization's productivity and its employees' quality of work life. Fourth, the critical resource in many organizations today is not capital but, rather, information and knowledge. This means that an audit of the calibre of a critical resource—namely, human resources—is necessary for the success of the organization. Human resource audits provide the information needed by human resource managers to validate the alignment (or misalignment) of human resource strategies with those of the organization as well as the organization's key performance indicators.

Finally, the growing complexity of human resource work makes research necessary. Today, more than ever before, human resource activities aimed at productivity improvement, succession planning, and cultural change are critical to competitive survival. More and more executives expect the department to make strategic contributions and place the function at a higher level in the organizational hierarchy.

> Over 50 percent of organizations surveyed in one study were found to have human resources departments report to the CEO or the president/owner of the organization.[86]

Moreover, HR departments are being reviewed for their effectiveness. One study, conducted by Aon, found that 68 percent of HR's time continues to be spent on administrative functions. The same study found that 35 percent of typical HR functions could be automated.[87]

Today, organizations are participating in human resource metric benchmarking. Through this process, organizations contribute information about human resource practices and associated metrics. In return, the participating organizations have access to aggregated data about other organizations so that they may benchmark their own practices and performance.[88]

The metrics established through an audit also result in the initiation of new programs, such as literacy training, and better responses to employees with disabilities, which can significantly improve employee productivity and morale. The steps involved in a human resource audit are outlined in Figure 1-12, and the major areas covered in such an audit are described in Figure 1-13.

FIGURE 1-12

Steps in a Human Resource Audit

FIGURE 1-13

Major Areas Covered in a Human Resource Audit

Human Resource Management Information	
Human rights legislation and employment legislation • Information on compliance	**Human resource plans** • Supply and demand estimates • Skills inventories • Replacement charts and summaries
Job analysis information • Job standards • Job descriptions • Job specifications	**Compensation administration** • Wage and salary levels • Benefit package • Employee value proposition

Staffing and Development	
Recruiting • Source of recruits • Availability of recruits • Employment applications	**Selection** • Selection ratios • Selection procedures • Human rights legislation compliance
Training and orientation • Orientation program • Training objectives and procedures • Learning rate	**Career development** • Internal placement success • Career planning program • Human resource development effort
Performance appraisals • Standards and measures of performance • Performance appraisal techniques • Evaluation interviews	**Labour–management relations** • Legal compliance • Management rights • Dispute resolution problems
Human resource controls • Employee communications • Discipline procedures • Change and development procedures	**Human resource audits** • Human resource function • Operating managers • Employee feedback on human resource department

Preparing for the Future

Evaluations and audits are necessary, but they are backward-looking. They uncover only the results of past decisions. Although past performance should be evaluated, human resource departments also should look to the future to be proactive. A proactive approach requires human resource managers and their staff to develop a future orientation. They must constantly scan their professional and social environment for clues about the future. New developments may mean new challenges.

LO3 The Organization of Human Resource Management

The responsibility for human resource management activities rests with each manager. If a manager does not accept this responsibility, then human resource activities may be done only partially or not at all. This is not to suggest that every manager needs to be a human resources professional, but even when an HR team is created, the manager continues to have a key role in enabling, following, and administering HR practices.

As noted earlier, a separate HR department usually emerges only when human resource activities need to be coordinated in a manner that cannot be done organically or when the expected benefits of a human resource usually exceed its costs. Until then, managers handle human resource activities themselves or may delegate them to subordinates. When a human resource department emerges, it is typically small and reports to a middle-level manager. Figure 1-14 illustrates a common placement of

a human resource department at the time it is first formed. The activities of such a department are usually limited to maintaining employee records and helping managers find new recruits. Whether the department performs other activities depends upon the needs of other managers in the firm.

As demands on the department grow, it increases in importance and complexity. Figure 1-15 demonstrates the increased importance by showing the head of human resources reporting directly to the chief operating officer, who is the company president in this figure. The greater importance of the head of human resources may be signified by a change in title to vice-president. In practice, increased complexity also results as the organization grows and new demands are placed on the department or as jobs in the department become more specialized. As the department expands and specializes, it may become organized into highly specialized subdepartments.

The Service Role of the Human Resource Department

Although they are organizational strategic partners, human resource departments continue to be a service and support department. They exist to assist employees, managers, and the organization. Their managers do not have the authority to order other managers in other departments to accept their ideas. Instead, the department has only **staff authority**, which is the authority to advise, not direct, managers in other departments.

> **staff authority** Authority to advise, but not to direct, others.

FIGURE 1-14

The Human Resource Department in a Small Organization

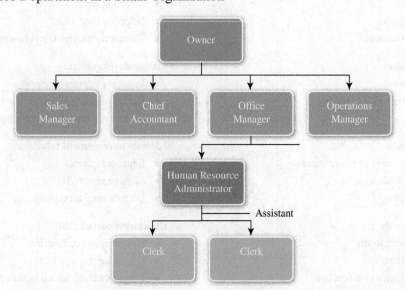

FIGURE 1-15

A Large Human Resource Department

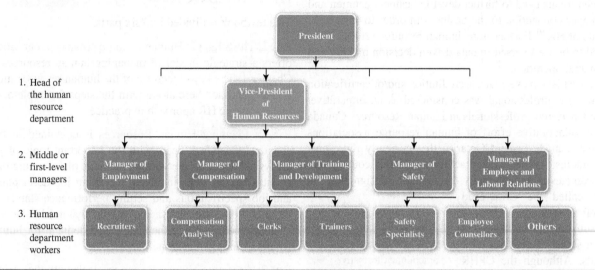

In contrast to staff authority, **line authority**, possessed by managers of operating departments, allows these managers to make decisions

> **line authority** Authority to make decisions about production, performance, and people.

about production, performance, and people. It is the operating managers who normally are responsible for promotions, job assignments, and other people-related decisions. Human resource specialists advise line managers, who alone are ultimately responsible for employee performance.

For something like recruitment and retention, the line manager may provide details of performance standards and job success, interview job candidates, and utilize the information provided by human resources to make a final decision. The human resource professional, on the other hand, will ensure compliance with human rights laws and organizational policies regarding equity in addition to planning and organizing all of the activities related to recruiting, interviewing, hiring, and communicating about a new employee. In the case of employee and labour relations, the line manager is likely to communicate with employees, implement motivational structures, coach employees, provide conflict resolution, and promote teamwork. The human resource professional is then left to focus on establishing grievance handling procedures, negotiating with the bargaining unit, and planning and initiating change initiatives. In short, human resource departments tend to provide the technical expertise while line managers use this expertise to effectively manage their subordinates.

In highly technical or extremely routine situations, the human resource department may be given functional authority. **Functional authority** gives the department the right to make decisions usually made by line managers or top management. For example, decisions about fringe benefits are technically complex, so the top manager may give the human resource department the functional authority to decide the type of benefits offered to employees. If each department man-

> **functional authority** Authority that allows staff experts to make decisions and take actions normally reserved for line managers.

ager were to make separate decisions about benefits, there might be excessive costs and inequities. To provide control, uniformity, and the use of expertise, functional authority allows human resource specialists to make crucial decisions effectively.

LO4 Today's Human Resource Management Professional

In the last 40 years, there has been a surge in the number of human resource managers. In 1971, there were only 4,055 human resource managers in this country.[89] In 2018, the corresponding number is more than 50,000.[90] However, historically, the status of human resource professionals within organizations has not been high.

Despite its enormous growth, human resource management was slow to evolve into a full-fledged profession. Since the actual capability of practising human resource experts varied widely, however, it became increasingly evident that professionalism of the human resource management field was needed.

In a recent study, a majority of CEOs reported that HR professionals need to further develop business acumen and a deeper connection to the business in order to enrich the value of HR.[91] Furthermore, human resource professionals need to be well versed in data-driven decision making and financial operations.[92]

To achieve these goals, accreditation and/or certification of the HR professional was considered as an imperative. The Chartered Professionals in Human Resources Canada is a collaborative effort of human resource associations across Canada (except Ontario) that currently represents the interests of most HR practitioners in this country and coordinates the nationally recognized designation in HR called the **Chartered Professional in Human Resources (CPHR)**, based on a series of national standards. Although the CPHR is granted by each provincial HR association, it is recognized and transferable across Canada—except in Ontario.

Chartered Professional in Human Resources (CPHR) Human resource practitioner, formally accredited to practice, who reflects a threshold professional level of practice.

Based on extensive national and regional consultations with employers, human resource professionals, and researchers, CPHR Canada has identified a set of competencies referred to as the "Chartered Professional in Human Resources Competency Framework" in key HR areas, such as strategy; engagement; labour and employee relations; learning and development; human resource metrics, reporting, and financial management; professional practice, workforce planning and talent management; health, wellness, and safe workplaces; and total rewards. These standards are regularly being reviewed and updated. For a summary of the requirements for the CPHR designation, see CPHR Canada (https://cphr.ca/).

Ontario Human Resource Professionals are accredited through the Human Resource Professional Association (HRPA). In Ontario, a series of HR designations are available, including the Certified Human Resources Professional (CHRP), Certified Human Resources Leader (CHRL), and Certified Human Resources Executive (CHRE). Similar to the CPHR, the designations available through the HRPA are based on a set of competencies.

A third credentialing body for human resource professionals is the International Personnel Management Association.

Certification or designation alone does not make human resource management a profession or improve its status in the eyes of organizations. One approach to improving the human resource manager's status within the organization may be to strengthen the position's contribution to the enhancement of organizational performance and effectiveness. This is already beginning to take place. The higher status given to human resource experts in job ads and organizational charts indicates that the importance of human resource management activity is being recognized.

The Framework Used in This Book

This textbook is divided into six parts.

Part 1: The Strategic Human Resource Management Model offers a strategic model of managing human resources in Chapter 1. The key objectives of the human resource function are outlined here along with the steps for implementing a strategic HR approach in practice.

Part 2: Planning Human Resources is contained in two chapters. Chapter 2 deals with the important topic of job analysis—detailing the various methods of collecting data about jobs, the steps involved in writing job descriptions and job specifications and setting performance standards. Chapter 3 discusses the various factors that need to be considered when planning the supply and demand for human resources in organizations.

Part 3: Attracting Human Resources deals with the various steps in acquiring human resources. Chapter 4 details key provisions of human rights legislation and the Canadian Constitution along with their implications for hiring employees. It also discusses the issue of diversity. Chapter 5 (Recruitment) and Chapter 6 (Selection) deal with the various tools, options, and strategies open to the human resource manager in attracting and selecting qualified applicants for the job.

Part 4: Placing, Developing, and Evaluating Human Resources deals with all key activities involved in orienting, training, developing, and evaluating employees. Chapter 7 outlines the key steps involved in the orientation and training of employees; it also focuses on the development of employees to take on greater responsibilities in the future, including career counselling to staff. Chapter 8 deals with various appraisal techniques that help an organization to monitor and improve employee performance.

Part 5: Motivating and Rewarding Human Resources discusses the critical tasks of motivating and rewarding employees. Chapter 9 deals with direct compensation, including methods of evaluating the worth of each job and the incentive schemes currently available. Chapter 10 discusses how careful planning enables an organization to make the most out of its benefits package. It also deals with various work options and other arrangements that have implications for employee motivation.

Part 6: Maintaining High Performance focuses on the various human resource actions to ensure high performance. Chapter 11 details the methods of improving communication and enforcing discipline when employees violate organizational policies. Chapter 12 discusses two types of security offered by modern human resource departments: financial and physical. Chapter 13 discusses strategies for dealing with unions and outlines the human resource manager's role during negotiations with unions.

Spotlight *on* HRM

Human Capital: A Key to Canada's Competitiveness

What makes an economy accelerate or stagnate? In answering this question, many will point to key economic indicators such as Real GDP, consumer price index (CPI), or consumer confidence. Others may point to effective policy or the flow of goods and services among the numerous individuals and companies in an economy. Regardless of the micro- or macro-economic drivers, the shape of an economy is highly influenced by people. It is people who set policy and regulations. It is people who lead the many micro, small, medium, and large organizations that make up our economy. It is people who purchase or use the goods and services within an economy.

With people at the core of an economy, the importance of human resources or human capital cannot be overstated. Part of the human capital equation is productivity, that is, how much output an individual can create in relation to the inputs. According to the Conference Board of Canada, Canada scores a B for productivity and growth.[93]

At points in history, organizations have turned to technology as the basis for improving productivity. Today, however, this approach is insufficient for Canada to keep pace or to catch up with the productivity improvements in other developed countries. The Conference Board of Canada has pointed to the importance of innovation in strengthening Canada's productivity.[94]

Similar to productivity, human ideas and ambitions rest at the core of innovation. As a result, an increased focus is being placed on the role of human capital in creating long-term and sustainable productivity improvements.

The role of human talent in creating long-term sustainable economic and social benefits to organizations and communities through productivity necessitates a collaborative and long-term approach among organizations, governments, communities, and numerous other support structures.

Among the key elements to creating innovation and, in turn, productivity is education.[95] Because knowledge is a necessary precursor to realizing the full potential of human capital in creating productivity improvements, governments, communities, and education systems must come together in developing and enhancing citizens' overall knowledge base. Canadian communities must also understand the importance of life-long learning. Because of the time required for learners to progress through education systems, a long-term approach to planning in relation to the development of human talent must be taken.

More recently, we have seen growing examples of how productivity enhancements are often found through new innovations. Similar to developing a learning city, significant lead time and planning is needed to create a community in which innovation thrives. Examples abound of communities that have come together to create ecosystems in which innovation and entrepreneurism are strong (e.g., Silicon Valley).

SUMMARY

The central challenge for organizations today is to survive and prosper in a highly complex and continuously changing world. To do this, most organizations find it necessary to maintain high productivity and effectiveness levels and to have a global focus. Strategic management of organizations is one approach to adapting to a continually changing global context. Human resource management *aims to optimize the contribution of employees to the organization's goals.* The field of human resource management thus

focuses on what managers—especially human resource specialists—do and what they *should* do.

This chapter pointed out that human resource management is the responsibility of every manager. The human resource department provides a service to other departments in the organization. In the final analysis, however, the performance and well-being of each worker is the dual responsibility of that worker's immediate supervisor and the human resource department.

Strategic human resource management is systematically linked to the strategic needs of an organization and aims to provide the organization with an effective workforce while meeting the needs of its members and other stakeholders. It is important that human resource strategies and tactics are mutually consistent and provide direct support to the organization's mission, goals, and strategies. Even the best-laid strategies may fail if they are not accompanied by sound programs or procedures and aligned with organizational strategies.

Strategic human resource management necessitates an exhaustive evaluation of an organization's internal and external environments. This chapter discussed factors that should be reviewed before formulating human resource strategies. These include economic, technological, demographic, and cultural challenges. As well, the chapter pointed out that continuous evaluation of strategy and proactive management are critical to ensure the successful management of human resources.

This section of the text has emphasized a strategic approach to human resource management. This is because,

increasingly, human resource managers are expected to contribute to the organization's strategic thinking and be strategic business partners to other executives in organizations. Marketing, production, and financial strategies depend upon the abilities of the firm's human resources to execute these plans. The status of the human resource function within an organization is likely to be determined by its contribution to the organization's overall success. Strategic management of human resources may be one key to this success. To assist with the "people side" of implementation, human resource directors will be forced to uncover, through audits and research, the causes of and solutions to people-related problems. Their diagnostic abilities to assess present and potential human resource issues will be needed as they and their staff increasingly serve as internal consultants to others who are facing human resource–related challenges. They then will be called on to facilitate changes in the organization that maximize the human contribution. In short, the traditional administrative skills associated with human resource management must grow to accommodate diagnostic, assessment, consulting, and facilitation skills.

TERMS FOR REVIEW

automation 10
Chartered Professional in Human Resources
(CPHR) 26
cost leadership strategy 7
cultural forces 16
cultural mosaic 16
demographic changes 11
differentiation strategy 7
economic forces 8
educational attainment 13
focus strategy 7
functional authority 25

gamification 5
human resource audit 22
human resource management 3
knowledge workers 13
line authority 25
mission statement 6
organization structure 18
organizational culture 18
organizational goals 3
productivity 8
staff authority 24
strategic human resource management 4

SELF-ASSESSMENT EXERCISE

How Knowledgeable Are You about Human Resource Management?

A successful human resource manager should possess knowledge in a number of areas, including job design, human resource planning, recruitment, selection and

training of employees, and employee relations. The following self-test helps you assess your present knowledge level in some of these areas. Read each statement and indicate whether the statement is true or false.

1.	A human resource manager should take corrective actions only after a problem has been crystallized and well understood.	T	F
2.	When assigning jobs to employees, I should ensure that there is no significant variation in job challenges from one employee to the next.	T	F
3.	Two experienced workers and three trainees can complete a project in 10 days; three experienced workers and two trainees can do the same project in 8 days. If I hire two experienced workers and one trainee, they should be able to complete the project in 11½ days.	T	F
4.	When designing a job application form, I should make sure to ask for the applicant's social insurance number in order to complete the employee file.	T	F
5.	When I visit campuses to recruit graduates, I should focus on the quality of education they received in the school rather than on whether they meet specific job requirements.	T	F
6.	When hiring an administrative assistant, the best way to assess the candidate's skills is by requiring the person to undergo a word processing or other performance test.	T	F
7.	The best way to teach a person a new accounting program is to give a short lecture on the subject matter.	T	F
8.	Measuring the students' learning before they begin this course and again at the end of the course may be a better indicator of this course's effectiveness than asking the students about their satisfaction level about what they learned in this course.	T	F
9.	Today, in Canada, women and men get paid equally in all occupations.	T	F
10.	If a person has to choose between two jobs that are alike in all respects, except that one job pays $45,000 in straight salary and the second one pays $35,000 in salary and $10,000 in benefits, the individual is better off accepting the second job.	T	F

SCORING

For statements 1, 2, 3, 4, 5, 7, and 9, if you answered false, you get one point each. For questions 6, 8, and 10, if you answered true, you get one point each. Add up your scores.

Scores of 8–10: Wow! You already know several important HR concepts. You can build on these by carefully studying the text chapters and actively participating in class discussions. You will also be a valuable source of information to others. So, participate actively in and outside the classroom!

Scores of Less Than 8: As you read the various chapters in this text, you will find the rationale behind the above statements. (The question numbers correspond to the chapter in this book in which this material is discussed.) Human resource management is an exciting profession—it also means that several assumptions that are popularly considered to be true are not. Keep reading!

REVIEW AND DISCUSSION QUESTIONS

1. What are the goals of a human resource department? Choose an organization that you are familiar with and indicate which of these goals will be more important in this organization and discuss why.

2. Draw a diagram of a human resource department in a firm that employs over 5,000 persons and name the likely components of such a department. Which of these functions are likely to be eliminated in a small firm employing 50 persons?

3. Identify and briefly describe three major external challenges (choosing one each from economic, technological, and demographic categories) facing human resource managers in Canada, and their implications.

4. Outline the three major strategies pursued by Canadian businesses. What implications do they have for the human resource function within the firms? Illustrate your answer with suitable examples.

5. What are four trends (or attributes) in the Canadian labour market that have implications for a human resource manager? Explain your answer, citing which of the human resource functions will be affected and how.

CRITICAL THINKING QUESTIONS

1. Suppose your employer is planning a chain of high-quality restaurants to sell food products that it already produces. Outline considerations that may be made by a strategic human resource professional prior to a roll-out of the planned restaurants.

2. If a bank is planning to open a new branch in a distant city, with what inputs will the human resource department be concerned? What activities will the department need to undertake in the transition to a fully staffed and operating branch? What type of feedback do you think the department should seek after the branch has been operating for six months?

3. Find two recent news stories and explain how the developments outlined in the stories might impact a human resource professional in a related organization.

4. If the birth rate during the early 2020s were to double from the low rates of earlier decades, what would be the implications in the years 2040 and 2050 for (a) grocery stores, (b) fast-food restaurants, (c) the Canadian Armed Forces, (d) large metropolitan universities?

5. Assume you were hired as the human resource manager in a firm that historically has given low importance to the function. Most of the human resource management systems and procedures in the firm are outdated and administrative. Historically, this function was given a low-status, "record-keeping" role within the firm. Armed with sophisticated HR training, you recently entered the firm and want to upgrade the department's HR systems and status. In other words, you want to make the management recognize the true importance of sound HR practices for strategic success. What actions will you take in the short and long term to achieve your goal? Be specific in your action plans, and illustrate your steps where relevant.

ETHICS QUESTION

After graduation, you are hired as a management trainee in the human resource department of a large organization with widely held stock. Your boss, the human resource manager, is away on holidays and asked you to make all decisions in her absence, including the hiring of an assistant in your department. A senior manager in the company recently indicated to you how much he would like the position to be given to Bob, his nephew, who had applied for the position. When you look through the records, you find that while Bob meets the basic requirements, there are at least two other better candidates—one male and one female. (Your firm recently indicated a commitment to employment equity initiatives.) You realize that the senior manager has considerable influence in the company and may even be able to influence your career progress within the firm. Consider how you would address this situation.

RESEARCH EXERCISE

Select three jobs: one knowledge-based, one manufacturing, and one in the service sector. Based on your search of websites of Employment and Social Development Canada, Statistics Canada, and other relevant online sources, what patterns in employment and job vacancies do you see? What are the implications for large human resource departments in these industries?

INCIDENT 1-1

Human Resource Decision Making at Canada Importers Ltd.

Canada Importers Ltd. (CIL) is a large importer of linens, china, and crystal from a number of Asian, European, and South American countries. While nearly 55 percent of linens are imported from China, nearly 70 percent of crystals and diamond items originate in India. Most of the china comes from European and South American countries.

Several other handicrafts and household products are imported from other East European countries and Japan. Different geographical offices of CIL specialize in different products; for example, the Toronto and Vancouver offices primarily deal with suppliers in India (specializing in different industry groups), while the Calgary office conducts all negotiations with South America. CIL's offices in Montreal and Halifax primarily deal with their European counterparts. Over time, management practices, including HR activities, in various CIL offices have begun to show considerable differences, posing problems for the senior managers. Recently, the following conversation took place between Rob Whittier, the vice-president of human resources, and Henri DeLahn, the vice-president of distribution.

Rob Whittier: You may not agree with me, but if we are going to have consistency in our human resource policies, then key decisions about those policies must be centralized in the human resource department. Otherwise, branch managers will continue to make their own decisions, focusing on different aspects. Besides, the department has the experts. If you needed financial advice, you would not ask your doctor; you would go to a banker or other financial expert. When it comes to deciding compensation

packages or hiring new employees, those decisions should be left to experts in salary administration or selection. To ask a branch manager or supervisor to make those decisions deprives our firm of all of the expertise we have in the department.

Henri DeLahn: I have never questioned your department's expertise. Sure, the people in human resources are more knowledgeable than the line managers. But if we want those managers to be responsible for the performance of their branches, then we must not deprive them of their authority to make human resource decisions. Those operating managers must be able to decide whom to hire and whom to reward with raises. If they cannot make those decisions, then their effectiveness as managers will suffer.

DISCUSSION QUESTIONS

1. If you were the president of Canada Importers Ltd. and were asked to resolve this dispute, whose argument would you agree with? Why?

2. Can you suggest a compromise that would allow line managers to make these decisions consistently?

INCIDENT 1-2

Canadian Bio-Medical Instruments Ltd.

Canadian Bio-Medical Instruments Ltd., founded 10 years ago, manufactures a variety of biomedical instruments used by physicians and surgeons, in both clinics and hospitals. The high quality of the company's products led to quick market success, especially for products such as artificial heart valves, operating-room pumps, and respiratory modules. The company, which had sales of less than $900,000 in the first year, today enjoys an annual revenue of $150 million. However, the industry is competitive and the research development and promotional budgets of some of the key players in the industry are several times that of the firm.

Given the successful track record for its existing products and the competitiveness of the North American market, the management of the firm believed that gaining new market shares in Europe would be easier than expanding against well-entrenched domestic producers. Preliminary market studies supported management's thinking.

A decision was made to open a small sales office in Europe, probably in Frankfurt, Germany, given the

nonstop flight facilities that currently exist from Toronto, where the firm's head office is located. Three employees were sent to Germany to identify possible office sites and to learn about European testing procedures and what documentation would be legally required to prove the safety and effectiveness of the company's medical instruments. All three employees were fluent in German. If the reports on Germany are favourable, the firm expects to have about 20 employees working in Europe within the next year.

DISCUSSION QUESTIONS

1. Assume you are the vice-president in charge of human resources. What additional information would you want these three employees to find out?

2. What human resource issues or policies are you likely to confront in the foreseeable future?

WE CONNECTIONS: GETTING STRATEGIC ABOUT HR

Jake's Resignation*

Alex Wong, president of WE Connections (WEC), could not believe his ears. He shook his head as if to clear it, and stammered, "What did you just say, Jake?"

The employee sitting across from him looked uncomfortable and fidgeted in the visitor's chair in Alex's office. Quietly, he said, "I'm really sorry, Alex. I know I am leaving you in a bind. But I don't think I have a choice. This is my two weeks' notice that I'm leaving the company."

Running his hand through his already messy black hair, Alex leaned forward and pressed for an explanation. "But why? Why are you leaving us? I thought you were happy here."

Jake Morisson shrugged, and replied, "This is a good place to work. But I'll be honest with you. I haven't had a raise in the last 15 months, and that's a pretty clear indication that I'm not valued. I heard Julie Moore got a raise last month, and I think I work a lot harder than her. Actually, hearing about her raise is what got me looking around for another job. I want to work somewhere that treats me right."

Alex's mouth dropped open as he listened, then he smiled, and said, "It's about money? Why didn't you say something? You have to come and ask if you want a raise. That's what Julie did. Anyway, we can match what you're getting at this new job you found. In fact, I'll go higher!"

Jake shook his head sadly. "I'm sorry, Alex. I have already signed the offer letter, and I don't want to let them down. And it sounds like it's a really good fit for me. But please know that I'll do whatever I can to make the transition as easy as possible for you."

He stood then and held out his hand, a signal that the conversation was over. Resigned, Alex accepted it before walking him out of his office.

After he left, Alex sat down at his desk with a sigh. He reached into his desk drawer for yet another antacid. This was a problem. Jake was the project manager of a key project, one that was due to launch in less than six weeks. Alex was not sure who was going to be able to step into Jake's shoes. Beyond that question, Alex experienced a more general feeling of anxiety. This was the second key person to leave WEC within a few months. In addition, there was some indication that the employees in the company were not working together as effectively as they used to. In the early days when they were a small start-up, every new client or technical breakthrough had been celebrated by everyone as a shared success. Growth had led to the development of departments and physical expansion of their office space. But now it seemed that the departments

had some communication problems and even some rivalries. Alex had the uneasy feeling that what had made WEC successful in its start-up years would not make the company thrive through its expansion.

WEC Background

It hadn't been like that in the beginning. When Alex had started the company with his co-founder, Selina Everett, things were tough but relatively simple. They spent most of their time working on the technology that they loved. Alex and Selina were techies who had met at the University of Waterloo, where they had completed their undergrad degrees in software engineering. With an eye toward opening his own company, Alex had broadened his skills by enrolling in the double degree program with the nearby business school at Wilfrid Laurier University. The two founded WEC the year after Alex graduated, which was seven years ago.

WEC was a B2B (business-to-business) software company offering organizations a way to increase efficiency and effectiveness by connecting information located in different systems. Rather than simply tracking data, WEC specialized in bridging unaligned systems to achieve company-wide collaboration. About 40 percent of WEC's business involved customizing software to track the parts being used on a client organization's production line/process, so that the system could automatically order refills from designated suppliers when stock got low. With its software, clients could check delivery status with real-time data from the delivery truck itself, dramatically lowering the chances that they would unexpectedly run out of parts. Another 40 percent of WEC's business stemmed from building custom software applications designed to increase organizational efficiency by sharing information across departments. For instance, WEC had connected production schedules to the HR, quality, and safety departments in order to align resources with needs in real time for one client. For other clients, WEC had built software to enable clients to collect data from their customers and to translate that information into responsive actions at lightning speed. Over time, WEC found that companies did not just want software help, they wanted WEC expertise in designing better data flow and even enterprise-wide systems. WEC's growing consulting department focused on helping clients think through their broader communication strategies, forming the final 20 percent of the company's revenue.

The ability to connect different systems, and even different platforms, was a huge value-add to organizations, and WEC quickly began to fill a niche overlooked by the large software providers. Alex and Selina had added 178 employees over the seven years they had been in business and remained in the Kitchener/Waterloo area. Most of their recruiting focused on hiring innovative software engineers who could solve tough technical problems, but they had also added other staff, including administrative, marketing, and quality departments as these functions got too big for Alex and Selina to handle directly.

A few years in, Alex had realized that the people issues were taking up a lot of time, and so they had hired a human resources specialist, the very sharp Charlotte Huang, and eventually she had hired an assistant. However, Alex had to admit that while they had a strong mission and set goals that directed the company's overall business strategy, there was no clear direction when it came to managing the people of WEC. He knew how to build software. He even had a pretty clear idea of how the business should fit into the market. But he had no clear vision on how to ensure that all of the HR decisions were aligning with his overall business strategy. He simply dealt with the people issues in isolation as they arose, and moved on, hoping for the best. On some level, he had thought that if he focused on the technology, everything else would follow. But he was starting to see evidence that his piecemeal approach to people management was not working.

Alex had a hunch that he had to put some serious thought and effort into this core driver of the business. Neglecting it just wasn't an option any longer if he wanted to continue to deliver to his customers with a high-functioning, cohesive team that could solve almost any information-sharing problem. He had to be able to deliver inspired solutions in a timely way, and he needed all of his people and systems aligned with that objective.

Moving Forward

Alex clicked on the laptop keyboard on his desk to open his calendar. He was going to have to carve out some time to work on this key problem. He stifled an urge to berate himself for letting this go for so long. Sure, it would have been preferable to deal with this before he lost Jake, but he knew that all he could do was move forward. While it might be true that he wasn't an expert at dealing with the organization's talent, he was pretty confident that he could learn. As he began blocking time slots in his calendar, he wondered where he should start.

DISCUSSION QUESTIONS

1. Is Alex's approach of blocking time in his calendar to become strategic about HR consistent with the process of strategic human resource management? Is this approach common for start-up organizations? Why?

2. Imagine that Alex has asked you to advise him as he is about to develop the strategic human resource management process for WEC. Describe for him how economic, demographic, technological, and cultural forces are likely to affect WEC.

3. Alex asks you to conduct a human resource audit; how would you go about doing that? What things would the audit cover?

4. Who else might Alex want to involve in the development of a strategic HR framework for WEC?

In the next installment of the WE Connections story (at the end of Chapter 2), job design elements are seen to influence the motivation level of employees.

---

* This WE Connections case was prepared by Steve Risavy and Karen MacMillan.

CASE STUDY

DigiTech

Connecting Organizational Strategy to Human Resource Strategy

Gail's phone buzzed as she stepped into the DigiTech office first thing Monday morning. Having been the director of human resources for three years, Gail was accustomed to her phone buzzing as soon as the day began, but this time was different. Stephanie, the company's chief operating officer (COO) had sent a text requesting an urgent meeting with Gail.

DigiTech was an educational gaming provider specializing in peer-to-peer games for kids between the ages of 12 and 15 that provided the foundations for software coding. DigiTech had been in business for 12 years and employed

about 125 people in various functions from user experience, to graphic design, through to technology support. It was an exciting time at DigiTech, as the company had recently created a new strategic plan and digital transformation plan that would take DigiTech into the next generation of computing power and gain back the market share it had recently lost.

Late last year, the business analyst at DigiTech had discovered that the company was losing clients because its connectivity was not fast enough and the quality of its games was falling behind the market. While DigiTech had no problem improving the quality of its games, the company discovered that when its games had become more detailed, its connectivity speed had dropped, leaving clients frustrated. As part of its digital transformation plan, DigiTech made the decision to move everything to the cloud to improve connectivity speed and give the company access to the computing power required by the higher quality games.

Stephanie was frustrated. She expressed to Gail that the operations team at DigiTech was not successfully implementing the projects that would take its software into the cloud. This put the implementation plan that was supposed to take five months nearly two months behind. This was a problem for Stephanie and the company's CEO because they had both promised the owners that everything would be up and running by June—a mere three months away. Stephanie's immediate reaction was that the operations team simply needed to work harder and learn whatever they needed to in order to get it done. To that end, Stephanie wanted Gail's help so that HR could make it happen.

Gail asked Stephanie what she meant by the operations team's needing to "learn whatever they needed to in order to get it done." Stephanie indicated that the operations team was having difficulty getting things "set up right" in the cloud because things needed to be configured differently than before and that they had seen an increase in security breaches since starting the project. Probing further, Gail asked what the operations team needed to learn, specifically, to which Stephanie replied, "I'm not sure, I just know that they need some training, and fast."

DISCUSSION QUESTIONS

1. What do you believe has led to the emergency meeting between Stephanie and Gail from (1) an organizational perspective and (2) a strategic HR perspective?
2. What internal and external forces were influencing DigiTech?
3. In hindsight, what should Gail have done before this eventful Monday morning?
4. What should Gail do now?

APPENDIX A

Origins of Human Resource Management

The origins of human resource management are unknown. Probably the first cave dwellers struggled with problems of utilizing human resources. During the thousands of years between cave dwellers and the Industrial Revolution, there were few large organizations. Except for religious orders (the Roman Catholic Church, for example) or governments (particularly the military), small groups did most of the work. Whether on the farm, in small shops, or in the home, the primary work unit was the family. There was little need for formal study of human resource management.

The Industrial Revolution changed the nature of work. Mechanical power and economies of scale required large numbers of people to work together. Large textile mills, foundries, and mines sprang up in England and then in North America. Collectively, people were still an important resource, but the Industrial Revolution meant greater mechanization and unpleasant working conditions for many workers.

By the late 1800s, a few employers reacted to the human problems caused by industrialization and created the post of welfare secretary. Welfare secretaries existed to meet worker needs and to prevent workers from forming unions. Social secretaries, as they were sometimes called, helped employees with personal problems, such as education, housing, and medical needs. These early forerunners

of human resource specialists sought to improve working conditions for workers. The emergence of welfare secretaries prior to 1900 demonstrates that the personnel activities in large organizations had already become more extensive than some top operating managers alone could handle. Thus, social secretaries marked the birth of specialized human resource management, as distinct from the day-to-day supervision of personnel by operating managers.

Scientific Management and Human Needs

The next noteworthy development was scientific management. The scientific management proponents showed the world that the systematic, scientific study of work could lead to improved efficiency. Their arguments for specialization and improved training furthered the need for HR management. The first decades of the twentieth century saw primitive "personnel departments" replace welfare secretaries. These new departments contributed to organizational effectiveness by maintaining wages at proper levels, screening job applicants, and handling grievances. They also assumed the welfare secretary's role of improving working conditions, dealing with unions, and meeting other employee needs.

By the First World War, personnel departments were becoming common among very large industrial employers. But these early departments were not important parts of the organizations they served. They were record depositories with advisory authority only. At that time, production, finance, and marketing problems overshadowed the role of personnel management. The importance of personnel departments grew slowly as their contribution and responsibilities increased.

From the end of the First World War until the Great Depression of the 1930s, personnel departments assumed growing roles in handling compensation, testing, unions, and employee needs. Greater attention was paid to employee needs. The importance of individual needs became even more pronounced as a result of the research studies in the United States at Western Electric's Hawthorne plant during this period. These studies showed that the efficiency goals of scientific management had to be balanced by considerations of human needs. These observations eventually had a profound impact on personnel management. But the Depression and the Second World War diverted attention to more urgent matters of organizational and national survival.

Modern Influences

The Depression of the 1930s led citizens to lose faith in the ability of business to meet society's needs. They turned to government. Government intervened to give workers minimum wages and the right to join labour unions. In 1940, Canada started an unemployment insurance program to help alleviate financial problems during the transition from one job to another. In general, the government's emphasis was on improving employee security and working conditions.

This drafting of legislation during the 1930s helped to shape the present role of personnel departments by adding legal obligations. Organizations now had to consider societal objectives and the need for legal compliance, which elevated the importance of personnel departments. In practice, personnel departments were made responsible for discouraging unionization among employees. But with newfound legal protection, unions grew dramatically. These organizing successes startled many organizations into rethinking their "management knows best" approach to employee welfare. Personnel departments began replacing this paternalistic approach with more proactive approaches that considered employee desires. When workers did organize, responsibility for dealing with unions also fell to the personnel department, sometimes renamed the industrial relations department to reflect these new duties.

Personnel departments continued to increase in importance during the 1940s and 1950s. The recruiting and training demands of the Second World War added to the credibility of the personnel departments that successfully met these challenges. After the war, personnel departments grew in importance as they contended with unions and an expanding need for professionals, such as engineers and accountants. The increasing attention given to behavioural findings led to concern for improved human relations. These findings helped underscore the importance of sound personnel management practices.

In the 1960s and 1970s, the central influence on personnel was again legislation. Several laws were passed that affected the working conditions, wage levels, safety, and health and other benefits of employees. These acts began to provide personnel department managers with a still larger voice—a voice that began to equal that of production, finance, and marketing executives in major corporations.

While the human resource function has now been around for several decades, it is only more recently that human resource specialists have started to exert great influence on organizational strategy or have been chosen as chief executives. Today, in many organizations, there is a genuine recognition that human resources spell the difference between strategic success and organizational decline. The emphasis placed on strategic human resource management and the formal certification of HR specialists are evidence of this growing role of human resource management.

PART 2

Planning Human Resources

This part introduces you to the important task of planning for human resources. Chapter 2 discusses the various approaches to conducting a job analysis. Steps to create valid job descriptions, specifications, and performance standards are outlined in this chapter. Chapter 3 discusses the various factors that need to be considered

when forecasting the demand for and supply of human resources. It also outlines several popular techniques for making such forecasts. Together, these two chapters help you to identify the type, number, and degree of sophistication of human resources needed by your firm.

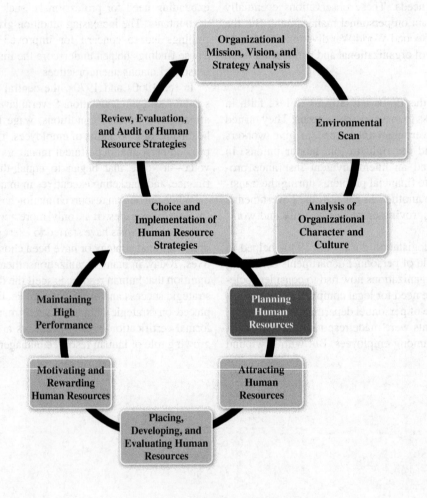

CHAPTER 2

Job Analysis and Design*

Job analysis is considered by many HR practice leaders to be a pivotal aspect of effective human resources administration. It has the potential to impact every major core competency area of HR.

SAGAR JIVANI[1]

LEARNING OBJECTIVES

After studying this chapter, you should be able to:

LO1	Describe the uses of job analysis information for human resource managers.
LO2	Discuss the various steps in conducting job analysis and methods of job data collection.
LO3	Describe the contents of a job description and a job specification.
LO4	Discuss the various approaches to setting performance standards.
LO5	Define what competencies are and describe competency models.
LO6	Outline the key considerations in job design.

In this part of the book, we will explain how knowledge about jobs and their requirements must be collected through **job analysis** (see HR-Guide.com) before any other HR functions can begin. From making the right hiring decision, to developing training programs, to dismissing employees who are not performing to expectations, and more, decision-makers need accurate information about a variety of aspects of the job in question.

job analysis Systematic study of a job to discover its specifications, skill requirements, and so on, for wage-setting, recruitment, training, or job-design purposes.

Job analysis and design knowledge is vital to the effective functioning of an organization, as shown in the following example:

At Purolator, which employs 11,600 Canadians, including 3,000 couriers, 300 line-haul truck drivers, and 500 call centre operators, the Workers' Compensation Board bill came in at $13 million. Purolator traced 90 percent of the workers' compensation claims to employees in two occupations: couriers and sorters. These two jobs require constant lifting, hauling, pushing, and pulling, leading to soft tissue,

---

* It has been suggested that we reverse the sequence of Chapters 2 and 3—that is, that we discuss human resource planning before job analysis. However, we feel that job analyses come first. Without them, no human resource planning is possible.

orthopaedic, and joint injuries—and the majority of the WCB claims. By conducting job analyses for the 25 jobs where most of the injuries were occurring, Purolator was able to identify suitable modified or transitional duties for injured workers. Through its early and safe back-to-work initiative, Purolator was able to reduce its lost day severity, total number of lost days, and number of modified or accommodated days, and keep workers engaged within their workgroups.[2]

Jobs are at the core of every organization's productivity. If they are not well designed and done right, productivity suffers, profits fall, and the organization is less able to meet the demands of society, customers, employees, and other stakeholders.

For a human resource department to be effective, its members must have a clear understanding of the jobs found throughout the organization. A **job** consists of a group of related activities and duties. A job may be held by a single employee or several persons. The collection of tasks and responsibilities performed by an individual employee is called a **position**.

> **job** A group of related activities and duties.
>
> **position** A collection of tasks and responsibilities performed by an individual.

In a department with one supervisor, three animators, and twelve programmers, there are sixteen positions, but only three jobs.

With hundreds—or even thousands—of positions, it is nearly impossible for the human resource professionals in large companies to know the details of every one. It is, however, unnecessary to collect information on identical positions separately. Consider this example:

One transmedia storytelling company has 20 game developers. Each position is the same. Rather than study each position separately, the job analyst can collect data from a random sample of the positions to generate an accurate understanding of the game developer job.

LO1   Uses of Job Analysis Information

Figure 2-1 lists major human resource actions that rely on job analysis information. For example, without job analysis information, human resource specialists would find it difficult to evaluate how environmental challenges or specific job requirements affect employees' quality of work life. To match job applicants to openings, human resource specialists must understand what each job requires and know what information to place in job advertisements. Similarly, compensation analysts cannot determine a fair salary without

---

FIGURE 2-1

Major Human Resource Activities That Rely on Job Analysis Information

1. Careful study of jobs to improve employee productivity levels

2. Elimination of unnecessary job requirements that can cause discrimination in employment

3. Creation of job advertisements used to generate a pool of qualified applicants

4. Matching of job applicants to job requirements

5. Planning of future human resource requirements

6. Determination of employee onboarding and training needs

7. Fair and equitable compensation of employees

8. Identification of realistic and challenging performance standards

9. Redesign of jobs to improve performance, employee morale, and/or quality of work life

10. Fair and accurate appraisal of employee performance

---

detailed knowledge of each job. Human resource departments formalize the collection, evaluation, and organization of this information.

This chapter describes the information sought by job analysts and the techniques to collect it. The chapter also describes how such data are converted into a useful *human resource information system (HRIS)*. A sophisticated HRIS permits easy retrieval of relevant job details; it also provides a variety of information about the job, jobholders, and past performance standards. Further details about designing an HRIS are in the next chapter.

LO2   Steps in the Job Analysis Process

Job analysis has three phases: preparation, collection of job information, and use of job information for improving organizational effectiveness (see Figure 2-2). Each phase consists of several actions, discussed below.

FIGURE 2-2

The Job Analysis Process

Phase 1			Phase 2			Phase 3
Preparation for Job Analysis			**Collection of Job Analysis Information**			**Use of Job Analysis Information**
Step 1	**Step 2**	**Step 3**	**Step 4**	**Step 5**	**Step 6**	• Job description
Become familiar with the organization and the jobs	Determine uses of job analysis	Identify jobs to be analyzed	Determine sources of job data	Identify the data required	Choose method for data collection	• Job specification • Job performance standards • Job redesign • Designing HRIS • Changing HR systems (e.g., compensation) • Organization change (e.g., redesigning workflow in plant)

Phase 1: Preparation for Job Analysis

Three key activities are performed in this phase:

Step 1: Become Familiar with the Organization and Its Jobs

Before studying jobs, it is important to have an awareness of an organization's objectives, strategies, structure, inputs (people, materials, and procedures), and desired outcomes. Job analysis procedures are influenced by the organization character, discussed in Chapter 1. In unionized organizations, job analysis steps also have to meet the various provisions of the collective agreement between the management and the union (more details about this relationship are discussed in Chapter 13). Job analysts may also study industry and government reports about the jobs to be analyzed. In all instances, the intent is to collect relevant and accurate information about jobs and factors determining job success.

Step 2: Determine Uses of Job Analysis Information

As shown in Figure 2-1, job analysis plays a critical role in many HR functions. The most common uses of job analysis information are in the recruitment process, the design of performance appraisal, compensation systems, and training.[3] Job analysis may also be done to ensure fair treatment across all employee groups[4] or to assist in job redesign, as shown in the following example:

Jobs in traditional print journalism have declined dramatically. The emergence of digital media in the newspaper industry beginning in the early 2000s transformed the skills required by journalists. Although writing, print design, and editing copy were the top three skills required 30 years ago and are still required today, multimedia skills including multimedia production, video shooting, and social media skills are now fundamental to many journalism jobs.[5]

The details collected during a job analysis are influenced by the objectives of the study; hence, it is critical to define the objectives early on.

Step 3: Identify Jobs to Be Analyzed

Although almost all jobs might benefit from an in-depth analysis, resource and time constraints often preclude organizations from conducting job analyses. Likely targets of job analysis are jobs that are critical to the success of an organization; jobs that are difficult to learn or perform (to determine the extent of training); jobs in which the firm continuously hires new employees (identification of clear job requirements assumes great importance); or jobs that exclude members of the protected classes described in Chapter 4. Jobs should also be analyzed if new technology or altered work environments affect how the job is performed (see HR Guide.com).

If inappropriate job requirements are used, the organization may even be in violation of laws, as the following example illustrates:

In the past, the Vancouver Fire and Rescue Services required that all successful job applicants be at least 175 centimetres (five feet, nine inches) tall. After one of the applicants complained, the Human Rights Board looked into the department's selection practices and could not find any correlation between the height of a firefighter and injuries or employee productivity. The department was found to be in violation of the Human Rights Act.[6]

In general, senior management and all key supervisors of the firm should be consulted before selecting jobs for in-depth analysis, as the jobs selected for analysis can affect the firm's strategic success and overall human resource

© Tyler Stableford/Stone/Getty Images

Discriminatory practices for firefighters are prohibited as long as a person is able to do the job. Women usually are able to carry less weight than men. Should that be taken into account during hiring?

policies (e.g., hiring, training). The type, number, and geographical dispersion of the jobs selected for analysis also influence the choice of data collection method.

Phase 2: Collection of Job Analysis Information

This phase contains three interrelated activities: determining the source of job data, identifying the data required, and choosing the method of collection.

Step 4: Determine Sources of Job Data

Although the most direct source of information about a job is the jobholder, various other sources— both human and nonhuman—may be used for this purpose. Figure 2-3 lists alternative sources of job information.

Occasionally, materials published in professional journals and magazines provide information about how jobs are performed in other organizations and settings. This information can be valuable when establishing performance standards and benchmarks for quality. The *National Occupational Classification (NOC)* in Canada (discussed in greater detail later in this chapter), and the U.S. Department of Labor Employment and Training Administration's electronic database, the *Occupational Information Network (O*NET),* provide information on various jobs. As well, the websites of several professional associations and private consulting firms offer a wealth of material relevant to job analysis and job descriptions.

The jobholders, along with their supervisors and colleagues, provide the most valid information about the way jobs are performed. However, other parties can also provide important information about jobs:

In the case of a salesperson, contacting past customers provides additional insights about job behaviours.

FIGURE 2-3

Sources of Job Data

Nonhuman Sources	Human Sources
Existing job descriptions and specifications	Job incumbents
Equipment design blueprints	Supervisors
Equipment maintenance manuals and records	Job experts
Training and safety manuals	Work colleagues
Organization charts and other company records	Subordinates
National Occupational Classification	Customers
Videos supplied by appliance/ machine manufacturers	
Professional journals/magazines/ publications	
Internet sources	

In the case of college or university faculty, students may be able to provide important information on in-class behaviours related to effective job performance.

Step 5: Identify the Data Requirements

To study jobs, analysts must establish the data about the job that must be known for the uses identified in Step 2. Figure 2-4 shows an outline of types of information the job analyst may seek, which can be modified to suit the needs of specific situations.

Data requirements typically fall into the following six categories:

- **IDENTIFICATION** The information in this section includes job title, division, and title of supervisor(s), and sometimes a job identification number, such as an NOC code. Without these entries, users of job analysis data may rely on outdated information or apply the information retrieved to the wrong job. Because most jobs change over time, outdated information may misdirect other human resource activities:

  At IC&RC, the world leader in addiction-related credentialling, a new job analysis for alcohol

FIGURE 2-4

Information Sought in the Job Analysis

A. Job Analysis Identification:

1. Job analysis date:
2. Job title:
3. Department:
4. Reports to:
5. NOC code:
6. Job analysis process: (Describe the collection of job analysis information)
7. Verification signatures:

B. Duties:

1. Job summary: (Briefly describe the purpose of the job, its scope, and how the job is done)
2. List duties and the proportion of time each involves:

    a. _____%
    b. _____%
    c. _____%

3. What constitutes the successful performance of each of these duties?

C. Responsibilities: (What are the responsibilities involved in this job and how great are these responsibilities?)

a. Decision-making authority: (Indicate level of discretion or authority allowed under company policies, procedures, and practices)
b. Supervisory responsibility: (Extent to which position controls, directs, or is accountable for work of others)
c. Equipment operation: (Use of tools and materials, protection of equipment, tools, and materials.)
d. Safety: (Personal safety and safety of others)
e. Travel: (Percentage of travel time expected for the position, where the travel occurs such as local or in specific countries, and whether the travel is overnight)
f. Other: (Please specify)

D. Human Characteristics:

a. What are the physical attributes or skills necessary to perform the job and how important are they (unnecessary, helpful, essential)?

    i. Vision (near acuity, far acuity, depth perception, accommodation, colour vision, field of vision)
    ii. Hearing
    iii. Tasting or smelling
    iv. Talking
    v. Walking
    vi. Standing
    vii. Lifting
    viii. Climbing
    ix. Kneeling, stooping, or crawling
    x. Pulling or reaching
    xi. Hand-eye coordination
    xii. Height
    xiii. Attention
    xiv. Reading
    xv. Arithmetic
    xvi. Writing
    xvii. Mental functions (such as comparing, copying, computing, compiling, analyzing, coordinating, synthesizing)
    xviii. Money skill
    xix. Other (Describe)

b. Describe the education or training requirements for the job: (Indicate levels of training, formal education, and required credentials)

(Continued)

c. Outline the experience required for the job:

    i. Amount of experience required in years

    ii. Type of expertise (academic, technical, or commercial)

    iii. Prerequisite job experience (list previous job titles)

    iv. Specific expertise requirements (such as languages, office or other equipment, required licenses)

d. Describe the equipment used:

    i. Office equipment (e.g., computer, specific software capabilities)

    ii. Hand tools (e.g., hammer, shovel, screwdriver)

    iii. Power tools (e.g., radial saw, reciprocating saw, drill, pneumatic hammer)

    iv. Vehicles (e.g., automobile, tractor, lift, crane)

E. Working Conditions:

a. Describe the working conditions of the job including environmental conditions and physical surroundings encountered on the job:

    i. Exposure to weather (hot, cold, wet, humid, or windy conditions caused by the weather)

    ii. Extreme cold or heat (exposure to nonweather-related cold or heat temperatures)

    iii. Wet and/or humid (contact with water or other liquids or exposure to nonweather-related humid conditions)

    iv. Noise (exposure to constant or intermittent sounds or a pitch or level sufficient to cause marked distraction or possible hearing loss)

    v. Vibration (exposure to a shaking object or surface)

    vi. Atmospheric conditions (exposure to conditions such as fumes, noxious odours, dust, mists, gases, and poor ventilation that affect the respiratory system, eyes, or skin)

    vii. Confined/restricted working environment (work is performed in a closed or locked facility providing safety and security for clients, inmates, or fellow workers)

b. Describe safety and health features:

    i. Is there exposure to any hazards (such as high heights, electrical shock, toxic or caustic chemicals)?

    ii. Safety training requirements:

    iii. Safety equipment requirements:

F. Performance Standards:

a. Describe how performance in the job is measured:

b. Describe identifiable factors that contribute to successful performance on the job:

---

and drug counsellors was released in February 2015. All new candidates seeking the Alcohol and Drug Counsellor designation have to complete a test based on the four domains revealed in the job analysis to be essential for practice and knowledge in that field: screening, assessment, and engagement; treatment planning, collaboration, and referral; counselling; and professional and ethical responsibilities. The job analysis for alcohol and drug counsellors is updated every five to seven years to stay relevant to current trends and practices for counselling people with alcohol and drug addictions.[7]

- **DUTIES** A job analysis explains the purpose of the job, what the job accomplishes, and how the job is performed. Often both a summary and specific duties are listed to give detailed insight into the position.

- **RESPONSIBILITIES** Questions on responsibility are expanded significantly when the checklist is applied to management jobs. Additional questions map areas of responsibility for decision making, controlling, organizing, planning, and other management functions.

- **HUMAN CHARACTERISTICS** Besides information about the job, analysts need to uncover the particular skills, abilities, training, education, experience, and other characteristics that jobholders need. This information is invaluable when filling job openings or advising workers about new job assignments.

- **WORKING CONDITIONS** Information about the job environment improves understanding of the job. Working conditions may explain the need for particular skills, training, knowledge, or even a particular job design. Likewise, jobs must be free from recognizable health and safety hazards. Knowledge of hazards allows the human resource department to redesign the job or protect workers through training and safety equipment.

- **PERFORMANCE STANDARDS** The job analysis questionnaire also seeks information about standards, which are used to evaluate performance. Performance standards describe to what level an employee needs to be doing the job to be a good performer versus an average or a poor performer. This information is collected on jobs with objective standards of performance. When standards are not readily apparent, job analysts may ask supervisors or industrial engineers to develop reasonable standards of performance.

Various standardized forms designed to collect information on these six categories are currently available for job analysis. Although many forms are available online, three of the more popular ones are O*NET, Position Analysis Questionnaire, and Critical Incident Method:

- **OCCUPATIONAL INFORMATION NETWORK (O*NET)** The O*NET website (https://www.onetcenter.org/) contains generic questionnaires for specific domains of information (e.g., abilities, generalized work activities, work context) that can be easily customized to particular organizational needs and branded with the company logo.

- **POSITION ANALYSIS QUESTIONNAIRE (PAQ)** Designed to apply to all types of jobs, the PAQ[8] is a survey designed to determine the degree to which 194 different task elements in six divisions (information input; mental processes; work output, including physical activities and tools; relationships with others; job context, including the physical and social environment; and other job characteristics, such as pace and structure) are involved in performing a particular job. The PAQ allows grouping of job elements in a logical and quantitative manner and enables easy comparisons between jobs. Past research, however, has indicated the PAQ to be more useful for lower level jobs.[9] Job analysts must purchase the PAQ for each job they analyze.

- **CRITICAL INCIDENT METHOD (CIM)** The CIM involves identifying and describing specific events (or incidents) when an employee performed really well and when that employee performed very poorly (such as inducing an accident). From these incidents, the job analyst identifies critical components of the job relating to the situation leading up to the event, the employee's actions, the results of the employee's actions, and the effectiveness of the employee's behaviour. The goal of the CIM is to create a behaviourally focused description of work and related performance standards, in particular, those that differentiate excellent from average or poor performance.

When asked to provide critical incidents, train engineers from CP Rail may recall a train derailment near Golden, British Columbia, on December 27, 2011.[10] The job analyst will ask the train engineers about the behaviours and circumstances that led up to the event as well as the duties and tasks that are necessary to prevent this type of incident.

The job analyst will translate descriptions of critical incidents into specific job responsibilities, such as these for the position of train engineer found on O*NET:

- Observe tracks to detect obstructions.
- Interpret train orders, signals, or railroad rules and regulations that govern the operation of locomotives.
- Confer with conductors or traffic control centre personnel via radiophones to issue or receive information concerning stops, delays, or oncoming trains.[11]

For job analysis purposes, about 10 statements will suffice.

Step 6: Choose Method for Data Collection

There is no one best way to collect job analysis information. Analysts must evaluate the trade-offs between time, cost, and accuracy associated with each method. Once they decide which trade-offs are most important, they use questionnaires, interviews, focus groups, employee logs, observations, or some combination of these techniques.

Questionnaires

A fast and cost effective option is to survey sources using **job analysis questionnaires**. These questionnaires are used to collect job information uniformly. They uncover the duties, responsibilities, human characteristics, working conditions, and performance standards of the jobs investigated. Analysts want differences in job information to reflect differences in the jobs, not differences in the questions asked. Therefore, it is important to use the same questionnaire on similar jobs.

> **job analysis questionnaires** Checklists used to collect information about jobs, working conditions, and other performance-related information in a uniform manner.

Questionnaires are particularly important when collecting information from human sources. However, depending on the sources surveyed, there can be issues associated with misunderstood questions, incomplete responses, and low response rates. Using multiple sources can help to verify employee responses.

Interviews

An **interview** is an effective way to collect job information. The analyst has the job analysis questionnaire as a guide but can add other questions as needed. Although the process is slow

> **interview** An approach to collecting job- and performance-related information by a face-to-face meeting with a jobholder, typically using a standardized checklist of questions.

and expensive, it allows the interviewer to explain unclear questions and probe into uncertain answers. Typically, both jobholders and supervisors are interviewed. The analyst usually speaks with a limited number of workers first and then interviews supervisors to verify the information. This pattern ensures a high level of accuracy. The validity of the information received depends on the representativeness of the sample of the respondents and on the types of questions used. For all of the interviews, a structured list of questions similar to those that appear in Figure 2-4 should be used.

Focus Groups

In a **focus group**, typically five to seven jobholders or others who are knowledgeable about the job are brought together by a facilitator to interactively discuss the job's duties and responsibilities. Focus groups are useful to allow ideas from participants to build off one another and to gain consensus on job duties and responsibilities. One uncertainty, however, is whether jobholders will be willing to share their opinions if a supervisor is included in the focus group as well.

> **focus group** A face-to-face meeting with five to seven knowledgeable experts on a job and a facilitator to collect job- and performance-related information.

Employee Log

In an **employee log**, workers periodically summarize their tasks and activities. If entries are made over the entire job cycle, the diary can prove quite accurate. However, logs are not a popular technique because they are time-consuming for jobholders and human resource specialists, which makes them costly. Managers and workers often see them as a nuisance and resist their introduction. Moreover, after the novelty wears off, accuracy tends to decline as entries become less frequent. Infrequently performed tasks may be challenging to capture if they are not performed during the span of keeping the employee log.

> **employee log** An approach to collecting job- and performance-related information by asking the jobholder to summarize tasks, activities, and challenges in a diary format.

Observation

Another approach is direct **observation**. Accuracy of observations may be low because the analysts may miss irregularly occurring activities, and workers may perform differently when they know they are being watched. But observation is the preferred method in some situations. When analysts question data from other techniques, observation may confirm or remove doubts. The existence of language barriers with foreign-language-speaking workers may also necessitate the observation approach.

> **observation** An approach to collecting job- and performance-related information by direct observation of jobholders by a specialist.

FIGURE 2-5

Job Analysis Methods in Common Use

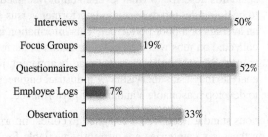

SOURCE: Based on SHRM Survey Findings: Job Analysis Activities, December 11, 2014, http://www.shrm.org/research/surveyfindings/articles/pages/2014-Job-Analysis-Activities.aspx

In the famous Hawthorne studies, while trying to examine the effects of lighting on productivity, observers found that employee performance went up under conditions of bright light and light as dim as moonlight. The conclusion? Employee performance went up because they knew they were being watched and interest was taken in their performance, not because of lighting conditions.[12]

Combinations

Since each method has its shortcomings, analysts often use a combination of two or more techniques concurrently, especially if locations are geographically dispersed.

A survey of 459 HR professionals revealed the most common job analysis methods used in their organizations, as shown in Figure 2-5.[13] Key considerations in the choice of job analysis method should include method–purpose fit, practical feasibility, cost, and reliability of the data collected for making valid decisions.

Phase 3: Use of Job Analysis Information

The information collected about various jobs is put into such usable forms as job descriptions, job specifications, and job standards, and, more recently, competency models. Together, these applications of job analysis information provide the minimum human resource information system and data necessary to formulate various HR strategies. The remainder of this chapter discusses using job analysis to assist with job design.

Job Description

A **job description** is a written statement that explains the duties, working conditions, and other aspects of a specified job.

> **job description** A recognized list of functions, tasks, accountabilities, working conditions, and competencies for a particular occupation or job.

LO3 Contents of a Typical Job Description

Within a firm, all the job descriptions follow the same style; between organizations, however, form and content may vary. One approach is to write a narrative description that covers the job in a few paragraphs. Another typical style breaks the description down into several subparts, as shown in Figure 2-6. This figure shows a job description that parallels the job analysis checklist that originally generated the data (see Figure 2-4).

The key parts of a job description are as follows: job identity, job summary, job duties, and working conditions. Most job descriptions also identify the author, the work supervisor, and the date on which it was prepared.

Job Identity

The section on **job identity** typically includes job title, job location, job code, job grade, and whether or not it is exempt from overtime laws. A **job code** uses numbers, letters, or both to provide a

> **job identity** The key part of a job description, including job title, location, and status.
>
> **job code** A code that uses numbers, letters, or both to provide a quick summary of the job and its content.

quick summary of the job and to provide comparisons between jobs. Figure 2-7 explains the coding used in the **National Occupational Classification** (NOC). The two major attributes of jobs

> **National Occupational Classification (NOC)** An occupational classification created by the federal government, using skill level and skill types of jobs.

that were used as classification criteria in developing the NOC were *skill level* (amount and type of education and training) and *skill type* (type of work performed). Four skill level categories describe the educational and training requirements of occupations. Skill type is defined generally as the type of work performed and is divided into 10 broad occupational categories (0 to 9) in the NOC. Figure 2-8 gives some sample NOC codes. Other factors, such as industry and occupational mobility, were also taken into consideration.[14]

Job Summary and Duties

Following the job identification (in Figure 2-6), the next part of the description is the job summary. It summarizes the job in a few sentences, telling what the job is, how it is done, and why.

Then, in a simple, action-oriented style, the job description lists the job's responsibilities or duties. In essence, this

---

FIGURE 2-6

Sample Job Description

Job Title: Retail Sales Associate

Job analysis date: January 16, 2019

Reports to: Sales Manager

NOC Code: 6421

Department: Consumer electronics

Signatures:

Job Summary: Sells a range of electronics products (e.g., TVs, computers) directly to customers. Interacts with customers, promptly responding to all inquiries with detailed and comparative product knowledge in a courteous and efficient manner. Encourages the sale of company products.

Duties and Responsibilities:

- Greet customers and ascertain what each customer wants or needs.
- Describe merchandise and explain use, operation, and care of merchandise to customers.
- Recommend, select, and help locate or obtain merchandise based on customer needs and desires.
- Display and stock merchandise on shelves.
- Compute sales prices, total purchases, and receive and process cash or credit payment; balance accounts at the end of each shift.
- Answer questions regarding the store and its merchandise, product warranties, and delivery terms.
- Interact with the store's gift registry database, Lightspeed POS point of sale system, and respond to customer email inquiries using Microsoft Outlook.
- Watch for and recognize security risks and thefts and know how to prevent or handles these situations.

Working Conditions:

- Works in a well-ventilated retail store environment. Must be able to work shifts.

A comprehensive job description for a retail sales associate can be found on O*NET OnLine (https://www.onetonline.org/link/summary/41-2031.00).

NOC Skill Type and Skill Level Categories

When the First Digit Is . . .	the Skill Type Category Is . . .
1	Business, Finance, and Administrative Occupations
2	Natural and Applied Sciences and Related Occupations
3	Health Occupations
4	Occupations in Education, Law and Social, Community, and Government Services
5	Occupations in Art, Culture, Recreation, and Sport
6	Sales and Service Occupations
7	Trades, Transport and Equipment Operators, and Related Occupations
8	Natural Resources, Agriculture, and Related Production Occupations
9	Occupations in Manufacturing, and Utilities

When the Second Digit Is . . .	the Skill Level Category Is . . .	and the Education Level Is . . .
1	Skill Level A	University education (Professional Occupations)
2 or 3	Skill Level B	College education (Technical, Paraprofessional, and Skilled Occupations)
4 or 5	Skill Level C	High school (Intermediate Occupations)
6	Skill Level D	On-the-job training (Labouring and Elemental Occupations)

SOURCE: Based on Employment and Social Development Canada, National Occupation Classification. Reproduced with permission of the Minister of Public Works and Government Services Canada, 2011.

Examples of NOC Unit Groups and Codes

NOC Coding System. A two-digit code is assigned at the major group level. A third digit is added at the minor group level, and a fourth digit is added at the unit group level. For example:

- Major Group 31—Professional Occupations in Health
- Minor Group 314—Professional Occupations in Therapy and Assessment
- Unit Group 3142—Physiotherapists

Using the above coding system, some sample occupations with codes include:

0211	Engineering Managers
0212	Architecture and Science Managers
2231	Civil Engineering Technologists and Technicians
4163	Marketing Consultant–Market Research
6531	Tour and Travel Guides
4012	Tutor–Post-Secondary Teaching Assistant
5241	Graphic Designers and Illustrators
1226	Conference and Event Planners
1123	Professional Occupations in Advertising, Marketing, and Public Relations

SOURCE: Based on Employment and Social Development Canada, National Occupation Classification. Reproduced with permission of the Minister of Public Works and Government Services Canada, 2011.

section explains what the job requires. The effectiveness of other human resource actions depends upon this understanding because each major duty is described in terms of the actions expected.

Working Conditions

A job description also explains **working conditions**, which may go beyond descriptions of the physical environment. Hours of work, safety and health hazards, travel requirements, and other features of the job expand the meaning of this section.

> **working conditions**
> Facts about the situation in which the worker acts; includes physical environment, hours, hazards, travel requirements, and so on, associated with a job.

Approvals

Because job descriptions affect most human resource decisions, their accuracy should be reviewed by selected jobholders and their supervisors. Then, supervisors are asked to approve the description. This approval serves as a further test of the job description and a further check on the collection of job analysis information.

There are many form-fillable templates available online to assist in creating job descriptions. One useful template can be found at hrcouncil.ca. Employment and Social Development Canada (ESDC) has a downloadable handbook to guide generating job descriptions on the NOC website (http://noc.esdc.gc.ca/English/home.aspx).

Job Specifications

Whereas the job description focuses on the job tasks and duties, the **job specification** indicates the human knowledge, skills, abilities, and other characteristics (KSAOs) necessary to do a job. These requirements include experience, training, education, and physical and mental demands. Whether part of a job description or a separate document, job specifications include the information illustrated in Figure 2-9. The data to compile specifications also come from the job analysis checklist.

> **job specification** A written statement that explains what a job demands of jobholders and the human skills and factors required.

A job specification should include specific tools, actions, experiences, education, and training (i.e., the individual requirements of the job).[15] For example, it should describe "physical effort" in terms of the special actions demanded by the job. "Lifts 40-kilogram bags" is better and more specific than "Lifts heavy weights." Clear behaviour statements give a better picture than vague generalities. Specifications of mental effort help human resource experts to determine the intellectual abilities needed to perform the job. Figure 2-9 contains several examples of the kind of information about physical and mental efforts needed by customer service representatives working for a department store.

© CP/Fred Chartrand

The job specifications for these hydro workers should clearly state that working outdoors under extreme conditions is a regular part of the job. What consequences could there be if that information was not provided?

Do the working conditions make any unusual demands on jobholders? The working conditions found in job descriptions may be translated by job specifications into demands faced by workers. Figure 2-10 provides examples for the job of hospital orderly and helps to show how tasks and duties from a job description can produce human requirements for a job specification. It shows that a simple statement of working conditions found in the job description can have significant implications for jobholders. For example, compare points 2 and 3 under the job description column with points 2 and 3 under job specifications.

LO4 Job Performance Standards

Job analysis has a third application: **job performance standards**. These standards serve two functions. First, they become objectives or targets for employee efforts.

> **job performance standards** The work performance expected from an employee on a particular job.

The challenge or pride of meeting objectives may serve to motivate employees. Once standards are met, workers may feel accomplishment and achievement. Second, standards are criteria against which job success is measured. They are indispensable to managers or human resource specialists who attempt to promote good work performance. Without standards, there is no yardstick for good versus average or poor job performance.

Job performance standards are developed from job analysis information, and then actual employee performance is measured. When measured performance strays from the job standard, corrective action is taken. The corrective action, in turn, may result in changes in either the standards (if they were inappropriate) or feedback to improve actual job performance.

Sample Job Specification

Job Specification—Retail Sales Associate

Job Title: Retail Sales Associate

Job analysis date: January 16, 2019

Reports to: Sales Manager

Education: High school diploma or equivalent

NOC Code: 6421

Department: Consumer electronics

Signatures:

Experience: Prior selling experience of 1 year in a consumer goods industry is desirable

Knowledge:

- Customer and Personal Service—Knowledge of principles and processes for providing customer and personal services (including assessing customer needs, meeting quality standards for services, and evaluating customer satisfaction)
- Sales and Marketing—Knowledge of principles and methods for showing, promoting, and selling products or services (including marketing strategy and tactics, product demonstration, sales techniques, and sales control systems)
- English language—Knowledge of the structure and content of the English language, including the meaning and spelling of words, rules of composition, and grammar
- Mathematics—Knowledge of arithmetic, statistics, and their applications

Technology Skills:

- Database user interface and query software: Gift registry software
- Email software: Microsoft Outlook
- Point of sale (POS) software: Lightspeed POS

Skills:

- Active Listening—Giving full attention to what other people are saying, taking time to understand the points being made, asking questions as appropriate, and not interrupting at inappropriate times
- Persuasion—Persuading others to change their mind or behaviour
- Speaking—Talking to others to convey information effectively
- Service Orientation—Actively looking for ways to help people
- Negotiation—Bundling product offerings together and achieving optimal sales

A comprehensive job description for a retail sales associate can be found on O*NET OnLine (https://www.onetonline.org/link/summary/41-2031.00).

Translation of Working Conditions for Job Description to Job Specification

Hospital Orderly	
Job Description: Statement of Working Conditions	**Job Specification: Interpretation of Working Conditions**
1. Works in physically comfortable surroundings	1. (Omitted. This item on the job description makes no demands on jobholders.)
2. Deals with physically ill and diseased patients	2. Exposed to unpleasant situations and communicable diseases
3. Deals with mentally ill patients	3. May be exposed to verbal and physical abuse

Spotlight *on* **HRM**

Job Descriptions Can Help Meet New Hires' Expectations of the Job

Sixty-one percent of employees participating in a survey by Glassdoor said aspects of their new job differed from expectations set during the hiring process. Employee morale was most commonly cited to be different from what new hires expected, followed by job responsibilities, work hours, and the supervisor's personality.[17]

Job postings and information conveyed by recruiters during hiring should both accurately reflect the duties, responsibilities, and working conditions of the job. However, some aspects of the job can be difficult to convey, such as company culture and characteristics of the work group and supervisor. How can you create a comprehensive job description to minimize unmet new hire expectations? Beyond the job description, how else can you ensure that new hire expectations are met on their first day?

TD Bank was in the news after anonymous salespeople suggested that they were pressured to make sales "by not acting in their customers' best interest, behaving unethically, and sometimes breaking the law."[16] Performance standards were reviewed to determine whether they needed to be lowered to serve customers' best interests, or whether employees required additional training to meet customer interests along with sales targets.

When the standards are wrong, they alert managers and human resource specialists to problems that need correction. The example also underscores the need for keeping job analysis information current.

Job performance standards are obtained either from job analysis information or from alternative sources. For example, industry standards may be used as benchmarks for performance in certain jobs (especially service functions such as human resource management).[18] Job analysis information is usually sufficient for jobs that have the following features:

- Performance is quantified.
- Performance is easily measurable.
- Performance standards are understood by workers and supervisors.
- Performance requires little interpretation.

Jobs with short work cycles often exhibit these features. An example is an assembly-line job. For these jobs, questions on the job analysis checklist may generate specific, quantitative answers. When confirmed by supervisors, this information becomes the job performance standard. In the case of some service jobs, quantifiable "outputs" may not be readily available; but even here, performance can be appraised by looking at the behaviours of the jobholders. More details of behaviourally oriented performance appraisals will be discussed in Chapter 8.

LO5 Competency Models

More recently, competency-based job descriptions and specifications have become increasingly popular. A **competency** is a knowledge, skill, ability, or behaviour required to be successful on the job.[19] Competencies are broader in scope than the KSAOs

> **competency** A knowledge, skill, ability, or behaviour associated with successful job performance.
>
> **competency model (competency framework)** A list of competencies required in a particular job.

discussed earlier in this chapter; examples are interacting and presenting, leading and deciding, and creating and conceptualizing.[20] A **competency model (competency framework)** describes a group of competencies required in a particular job, with typical jobs defined with between 10 and 15 competencies. Competency models can be developed for individuals, specific jobs, teams, work units, or the total organization.

There are three key differences between competency-based job analyses and other forms of job analyses. First, whereas duties or tasks might apply only to a single job within an organization, competencies might be job spanning, meaning that they contribute to success on multiple jobs (or even all jobs) within the organization. All jobs within the organization may require a particular competency, albeit how the competency should be enacted for strong performance will vary across jobs.

A product knowledge competency may span multiple jobs, including sales associates and product maintenance staff. However, product knowledge may be demonstrated differently in the varying roles. Whereas sales associates might demonstrate their product knowledge by answering customer inquiries on product features, prices, services, and delivery terms, product knowledge for maintenance staff might include troubleshooting when a product is not functioning properly.

A second difference is that job-spanning competencies may vary in importance across job roles. A **competency matrix** lists different levels of skill for a combination of competencies and indicates to what level multiple jobs across the firm should have mastery of each competency. Figure 2-11 shows an example of a competency matrix in an engineering firm. Each of the six competencies is measured at seven levels (Level 1 being the lowest; Level 7, the highest). Employees may be expected to possess all competencies, albeit to varying degrees. An engineer may be required to possess high technical expertise and medium problem-solving abilities, whereas a manager may have to possess more sophisticated higher problem-solving skills and lower levels of technical expertise; both are expected to have adequate communication abilities. Use of a competency matrix shifts the focus from performing specific duties to developing broader skills. It also empowers employees to assume new responsibilities. Such a system must be supported by an effective training and development strategy and a competency-based compensation system. These will be discussed in later chapters.

A third distinct feature of competency-based job analyses is that competencies contribute not only to job performance but also to the success of the organization.

competency matrix A list of the level of each competency required for each of a number of jobs.

Competencies explicitly support the firm's vision, strategic direction, and values.

At the YMCA of Greater Toronto, seven association-wide competencies and seven leadership competencies support the organization's vision, values, and strategic plan, and they are the foundation for all jobs. The 14-competency framework helps employees to understand what is expected of them, how to be successful, and how they will be rewarded. These competencies are used in job descriptions, training and development, recruitment and selection, performance evaluation, and succession planning. They are also a critical component used in the Y's employment branding.[21]

Some organizations have used competencies as the foundation for job design, new performance management systems, selection and career paths, compensation, training and development, and, in a few cases, a highly integrated human resource management system called *competency-based management*. Competencies are identified after a careful analysis of the work of high performers and a thorough examination of the organization's strategic direction. This may be done through observation, listings of critical incidents at work, interviews, focus groups, employee logs, or otherwise, and by examining the organization's mission, vision, and values.[22] In generating job-specific competencies, the process of data collection and sources discussed earlier in the chapter for job analysis will be useful. Consistent with job analysis, the process for generating the competency model should be well documented.[23]

FIGURE 2-11

An Example of a Competency Matrix in an Engineering Firm

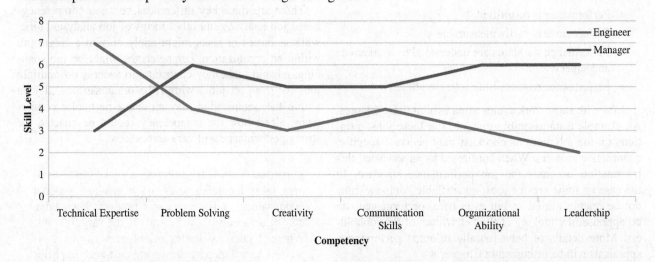

Spotlight *on* **ETHICS**

Job Design: Happy Workers or Higher Profits?

A small manufacturer of snowboards and skateboards faces a dilemma. His 15 employees work in loose production teams on cutting, layering, edging, pressing, drilling, painting, drying, mounting, and printing the boards. Job satisfaction is high and there is almost no turnover. But because of competition, the company had only small profits for the last two years, and the manufacturer wants to change that. His choice is to ask his employees to accept a significant pay cut, switch to an assembly-line system, or, the most profitable solution, install an automated machine that would require only 3 workers, making the remaining 12 redundant. All of his employees are married and have children and have been with him for 15 and more years. He feels a strong obligation toward them but is convinced that a workflow change is necessary.

Of what nature are his obligations toward his employees? What is the optimal solution for (a) his employees? (b) his company? (c) himself?

However, it is important to offer one cautionary note: When competencies become increasingly job-spanning and are no longer supported by specific duties and tasks, the legal defensibility of decisions based on these competencies is unknown. As competency models are tested within the legal system in Canada over the coming years, HR professionals will have a better indication of how broad or narrow competencies can be to support their staffing practices and decisions and to avoid unintentional discrimination.

LO6 Job Design

Worldwide competition, complex technology, and increasing worker expectations have necessitated the redesign of many jobs. Technological advances have brought about a revolution that has changed millions of jobs. While some jobs have grown more challenging, others are increasingly being automated or eliminated altogether. And yet, despite this vast increase in automation and computerization, human resources have become more, not less, important in today's organizations. For example, the cost of human error in a nuclear plant or in flying a supersonic jet can be enormous. Whether it is the high-speed computer or the traditional auto assembly plant now run by robotics, the contribution of human beings continues to be critical. Indeed, new technologies may be dangerous or unforgiving when operated by uncommitted or poorly skilled persons.

A good example of human error is the meltdown in the reactor of the Chernobyl nuclear power station in April 1986 in Ukraine, caused by a faulty test execution. The explosion released 100 times more radiation than the atomic bomb explosions in Hiroshima and Nagasaki. The long-term impact to the health of over seven million people is still unfolding. The contamination stretched to Norway and Germany.

How well people perform is shaped, at least in part, by the characteristics designed into their jobs. Not only is productivity affected, but quality of work life is also tied to **job design**.[24] Jobs are the central link between employees and the organization. Poorly designed jobs not only lead to low productivity, but they can cause employee turnover, absenteeism, complaints, sabotage, unionization, resignations, and other problems. One high-end purse and bag maker's experience of redesigning jobs is noteworthy in this context:

> **job design** Identification of job duties, characteristics, competencies, and sequences, taking into consideration technology, workforce, organization character, and environment.

At Louis Vuitton, each worker had narrowly defined responsibilities, such as cutting leather or canvas, attaching zippers or buckles, and stitching seams. Each worker performed a specific function and sent the product to the next person in the line of 20 or 30 workers. The result was that no one was responsible for completion of a single product. Vuitton moved to a team-based design where workers were trained to complete multiple tasks and could shift production quickly according to consumer demands. Workers learned new skills, job satisfaction went up, and the time to produce the same bag dropped from eight days to one day.[25]

In this case, the company had to consider the various environmental, organizational, and employee-related factors before redesigning the jobs. Typically, job redesign results in some trade-offs. Under the new structure at

FIGURE 2-12

Key Considerations in Job Design

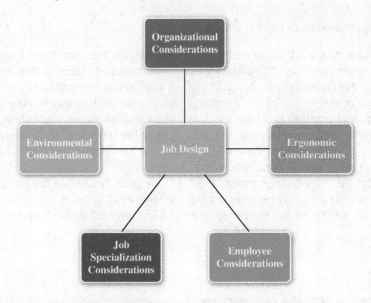

Vuitton, each worker needed to have knowledge of several activities. Therefore, more training for these workers was necessary. And, as the workers became more qualified, the company needed to pay them higher salaries.

Figure 2-12 illustrates five critical elements that deserve consideration when designing jobs: organizational, ergonomic, employee, job specialization, and environmental. Each is discussed below.

Organizational Considerations

Simply put, each job should contribute to the overall organizational objectives effectively and efficiently. The overall organizational mission is accomplished through a series of interrelated tasks or activities. If the organization is to remain successful and grow, these tasks and activities should be performed in a timely, effective, and efficient manner. This involves focus on two interrelated concepts: efficiency and work flow.

Efficiency

High task **efficiency** is concerned with achieving maximum output with minimum expenditure of time, effort, or other resources. As discussed earlier, time standards are established by recording the time needed to complete each element in a work cycle. Industrial engineers study work cycles to determine which, if any, job elements can be combined, modified, or eliminated to reduce the overall time needed to perform

> **efficiency** Achieving maximal output with minimal input.

the task. *Task specialization* was suggested as a key strategy to improve efficiency. According to these engineers, when workers are limited to a few repetitive tasks, output is usually higher because specialized jobs lead to *short job cycles*. The automotive industry is a good example of such industrial engineering practices:[26]

> For example, an assembly-line worker may pick up a headlight, plug it in, twist the adjustment screws, and pick up the next headlight within 30 seconds. Completing these tasks in 30 seconds means this worker's job cycle takes half a minute. The job cycle begins when the next headlight is picked up.

Headlight installation is a specialized job, so specialized that training takes only a few minutes. The short job cycle means that the assembler gains much experience in a short time. Said another way, short job cycles require small investments in training and allow the worker to learn the job quickly. Training costs remain low because the worker needs to master only one job.

The above approach stresses efficiency in effort, time, labour costs, training, and employee learning time. Today, this technique is still widely used in assembly operations. But the efficient design of jobs also considers such organizational elements as work flow, ergonomics, and work practices.

Work Flow

The **work flow** in an organization is strongly influenced by the nature of the product or service. The product

> **work flow** The sequence of and balance between jobs in an organization needed to produce the firm's goods or services.

or service usually suggests the sequence of, and balance between, jobs if the work is to be done efficiently. For example, the frame of a car must be built before the fenders and doors can be added. Once the sequence of jobs is determined, the balance between jobs is established:

> Suppose it takes one person 30 seconds to install each headlight. In two minutes, an assembler can put on four headlights. If, however, it takes four minutes to install the necessary headlight receptacles, the job designer must balance these two interrelated jobs by assigning two people to install the receptacles. Otherwise, a production bottleneck results. Therefore, the work flow demands two receptacle installers for each headlight installer.

Ergonomic Considerations

Optimal productivity requires that the physical relationship between the worker and the work be considered in designing jobs. Derived from the Greek words *ergo* meaning "work" and *nomos* meaning "laws," **ergonomics** in a general sense means the "laws of work" and focuses on how human beings physically interface with their work.[27] The study of ergonomics is multidisciplinary, using principles drawn from biology (especially anatomy and physiology), the behavioural sciences (psychology and sociology), and physics and engineering. Although the nature of job tasks may not vary when ergonomic factors are considered, the locations of tools, switches, and the work product itself are evaluated and placed in a position for ease of use. In other words, ergonomics focuses on fitting the task to the worker in many instances rather than simply forcing employees to adapt to the task.[28]

ergonomics The study of relationships between physical attributes of workers and their work environment to reduce physical and mental strain and increase productivity and quality of work life.

> On an automobile assembly line, for example, a car frame may actually be elevated at a work station so that the worker does not become fatigued from stooping. Similarly, the location of dashboard instruments in a car is ergonomically engineered to make driving easier.

Attention to details of work settings can lead to significant improvements in efficiency and productivity:

> As seen in the video clip at https://www.youtube.com/watch?v=0lsZvPInD6w&=&feature=relmfu, Ford uses state-of-the art manufacturing and job design techniques—including industrial engineering, ergonomics, and behavioural considerations. Cars pass through the assembly line on hydraulic lifts that allow employees to raise or lower the cars to suit their own height. Employees are allowed to ride the platform to minimize their steps walking to and from cars, thereby conserving energy. Industrial engineers

© Adam Gault/age fotostock

If an employee has to remain in a seated position for many hours, an ergonomically correct seat and a suitably placed monitor are essential. What are other benefits of ergonomic considerations?

videotape employee actions and simplify operations to minimize motion.

Ergonomic considerations are also important to maintain safety in the workplace. Ignoring a proper fit between work station and worker can be catastrophic.

> In Canada in 2013, 640,000 workplace accidents were reported to the provincial Workers' Compensation Boards. These claims came at a cost to Canadian firms of $11.7 billion.[29] A significant percentage of these accidents stemmed from poor workplace or task design.

Ergonomics will become more important in the future as the Canadian workforce ages:

> On July 1, 2014, 15.7 percent of Canada's population (nearly one in six Canadians) was aged 65 and older, up from only 10 percent 30 years prior. In 2016, the number of seniors in Canada surpassed the number of children aged 15 and under. The number of people aged 15 to 24 in Canada (the age when people typically enter the workforce) is now smaller than the number of people aged 55 to 64 (the age when people typically exit the workforce). Thirty years ago, there were two people aged 15 to 24 for every person aged 55 to 64.[30] Because aging results in a decrease in several hand functions (e.g., grip strength, precision), lowered muscular strength, and reduced vision and hearing, the need for ergonomics-based work improvements to reduce physical demands will be higher than ever before. Items such as mechanical assists for lifting (e.g., tilters, vacuum lifts) and for assembly (e.g., screw guns, adjustable tables) will be essential. Such improvements will also be needed for lighting arrangements and size of character displays in terminals to respond to older workers' diminished visual capabilities.[31]

Employee Considerations

Jobs cannot be designed by using only those elements that aid efficiency. To do so overlooks the human needs of the people who are to perform the work. Instead, job designers draw heavily on behavioural research to provide a work environment that helps satisfy individual needs. In general, jobs have to be designed not only to maximize productivity but also to help employees achieve better work–life balance.

> Research studies indicate that employee productivity can be up to 20 percent higher in organizations that implement work–life balance programs.[32]

This section briefly describes the job characteristics model, shown in Figure 2-13, which discusses the importance of high autonomy, variety, task identity, feedback, and task significance in a job design context.[33] According to this model, these five characteristics result in three psychological states: meaningfulness, responsibility, and knowledge of outcomes. Employees who find themselves in jobs that provide these experiences tend to have higher motivation, job satisfaction, and productivity.

Autonomy

Autonomy refers to the concept of assuming responsibility for what one does. It is the freedom to control one's response to the environment. Jobs that give workers the authority to make decisions tend to increase employees' sense of recognition, self-esteem, job satisfaction, and performance. The absence of autonomy, on the other hand, can cause employee apathy or poor performance:

> **autonomy** In a job context, independence—having control over one's work and one's response to the work environment.

> A common problem in many production operations is that employees develop an indifferent attitude because they believe they have no control over their jobs. On the bottling line of a small brewery, however, teams of workers were allowed to speed up or slow down the rate of the bottling line as long as they met daily production goals. Although total output per shift did not change, there were fewer cases of capping machines jamming or breaking down for other reasons. When asked about this unexpected development, the supervisor concluded, "Employees pride themselves on meeting the shift quota. So they are more careful to check for defective bottle caps before they load the machine."

Variety

A lack of **variety** may cause boredom. Boredom in turn leads to fatigue, and fatigue causes errors. By injecting variety into jobs, human resource specialists can reduce fatigue-caused errors.

> **variety** An attribute of jobs wherein the worker has the opportunity to use different skills and abilities, or perform different activities.

> Being able to control the speed of the bottling line in the brewery example added variety to the pace of work and probably reduced both boredom and fatigue.

Past research studies have found that variety in work may be related to effective performance and can be a major contributor to employee satisfaction.

Task Identity

One problem with some jobs is that they lack any **task identity**. Workers contribute to one part of the piece of work but do not get to point to a complete piece of work.

> **task identity** The feeling of responsibility or pride that results from doing an entire piece of work, not just a small part of it.

FIGURE 2-13

The Job Characteristics Model

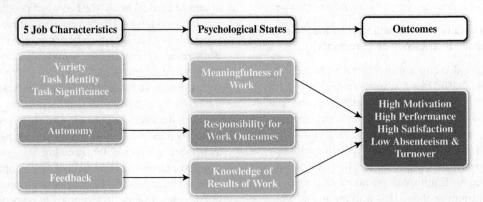

They have little sense of responsibility, may lack pride in the results, and have little sense of accomplishment. When tasks are grouped so that employees feel they are making an identifiable contribution—to see the job through to completion—job satisfaction may be increased significantly.

> In the earlier Louis Vuitton example, we saw that productivity and satisfaction increased when employees became responsible for an identifiable and sensible group of tasks.

Feedback

When jobs do not give the workers any **feedback** on how well they are doing, there is little guidance or motivation to perform better.

> **feedback** Information that helps evaluate the success or failure of an action or system.

> For example, by letting employees know how they are doing relative to the daily production quota, the brewery gives workers feedback that allows them to adjust their efforts. Providing feedback leads to improved motivation.

Task Significance

Closely related to the above dimensions is **task significance**. Doing an identifiable piece of work makes the job more satisfying for employees. Task significance, knowing that the work is important to others within the organization or outside it, makes the job even more meaningful for incumbents. Their personal sense of self-importance is enhanced because they know that others depend on what they do. Pride, commitment, motivation, satisfaction, and better performance are likely to result.

> **task significance** Knowing that the work one does is important to others in the organization or to outsiders.

> A good example was the Porsche car company. Mechanics, who assembled complete engines, punched their names into the engine block, a cause of extreme pride but also useful for feedback purposes. Rationalization eliminated this procedure, resulting in lower satisfaction, lower quality, and higher turnover.

Job Specialization

As workers become more educated and affluent, routine jobs that are very specialized, such as assembly-line positions, hold less and less appeal for many people. These jobs seldom offer opportunities for accomplishment, recognition, psychological growth, or other sources of satisfaction. To increase the quality of work life for those who hold such jobs, human resource departments often use a combination of *job rotation, job enlargement, job enrichment,* and *employee involvement and work teams.*

Job Rotation

Job rotation moves employees from job to job. Jobs are not actually changed; only the workers are rotated. Rotation breaks the monotony of highly specialized work by calling on different skills and abilities. The organization benefits because workers become competent in several jobs rather than one. Knowing a variety of jobs improves self-image, provides personal growth, and makes the worker more valuable to the organization.

> **job rotation** Moving employees from one job to another to allow them more variety and to learn new skills.

> Job rotation was introduced by the Volvo car company back in the 1970s to reduce the monotony of the assembly line. Work teams exchanged jobs during the day. Job satisfaction increased and turnover decreased.

A caution about the use of job rotation: it does not improve the jobs, as the relationships between tasks, activities, and objectives remain unchanged. It may even delay the use of more effective techniques while adding to training costs. Implementation should occur only after other techniques have been considered.

Job Enlargement

Job enlargement expands the number of related tasks in the job. It adds similar duties to provide greater variety although the duties are not more complex. Enlargement reduces monotony by expanding the job cycle and drawing on a wider range of employee skills.

> **job enlargement** Adding more tasks to a job to increase the job cycle and draw on a wider range of employee skills.

> When looking to prevent musculoskeletal injuries in poultry processing, the U.S. Occupational Safety and Health Administration found that risk factors were reduced when employees were cross-trained so that sufficient support was available for peak production, to cover breaks, and when job enlargement programs were instituted.[34]

Job Enrichment

Job enrichment adds new sources of needs satisfaction to jobs. It increases responsibility, autonomy, and control. Adding these elements to jobs is sometimes called *vertical loading.* Enrichment views jobs as consisting of three elements: *plan, do,* and *control.* Whereas job enlargement (or horizontal loading)

> **job enrichment** Adding more responsibilities and autonomy to a job, giving the worker greater powers to plan, do, and evaluate job performance.

adds more related tasks, enrichment (vertical loading) attempts to add more *planning* and *control* responsibilities. This, coupled with rethinking the job itself, often leads to increased motivation and other improvements:

> Every year since 1999, Statistics Canada has sampled information from over 6,000 Canadian workplaces about workforce characteristics and job organization, with specific questions regarding decision making, quality circles, teams, suggestion programs, feedback, and self-directed work. Two researchers used the data to determine whether enriched jobs result in higher motivation and job satisfaction. The study included feedback from 43,917 employees. The results strongly support the hypothesis that enriched jobs increase motivation and satisfaction.[35]

Job enrichment, however, is not a cure-all. Job enrichment techniques are merely tools, and they are not applicable universally. When the diagnosis indicates that jobs are unchallenging and limit employee motivation and satisfaction, human resource departments may find job enrichment to be the most appropriate strategy.

Employee Involvement and Work Teams

To increase employee involvement at the workplace, work teams are often used. Work itself is increasingly being organized around teams and processes rather than activities or functions. Over 40 percent of the respondents in a national survey by the Conference Board of Canada reported use of teams in their workplaces.[36] Self-managed and autonomous work teams have become a normal part of many Canadian organizations, including CIBC, Xerox Canada, and Vancity. These and other employee involvement approaches are discussed in detail in Chapter 11. The intent of all such approaches, however, is to provide more autonomy, feedback, and task significance to workers, and they may also lead to increased innovation:

> Multinational giant IBM uses innovation portals in the form of specially designated chat rooms, where employees with new ideas or projects can recruit team members, secure resources, or tap into location or domain expertise across the entire firm within hours. More than 90,000 IBM employees have worked on these global teams, decreasing project launch times from six months to 30 days.[37]

As in the case of job enrichment, employee involvement and teams may not be appropriate for all organizations or all situations. The complexity of the task involved, the prevalence of the shift system, and the skill levels of employees involved may moderate the applicability of such systems in a particular situation.[38] The introduction of team management, if not accompanied by changes in other systems (e.g., performance appraisal, compensation), may cause frustration. To be successful, top management has to be truly committed to the notion of employee empowerment—that is, granting employees the power to initiate change and take charge of what they do.

Use of Job Families in HR Decisions

Often, in the context of job design, the human resource manager looks at **job families** rather than single jobs. Job families are groups of jobs that are closely related by similar duties, responsibilities, skills, or job elements. The jobs of barber, hairstylist, hairdresser, and cosmetologist constitute a job family, for example.

> **job families** Groups of different jobs that are closely related by similar duties, responsibilities, skills, or job elements.

Job families can be constructed in several ways. One way is by careful study of existing job analysis information. Matching the data in job descriptions can identify jobs with similar requirements. A second method is to use the codes in the National Occupational Classification discussed earlier in this chapter. Similarities in the job codes indicate similarities in the jobs. A third approach is to use the PAQ, also discussed earlier in this chapter, and statistically analyze information on tasks and worker traits to identify clusters of similar jobs.

Job families allow human resource managers to plan job rotation programs and make employee transfer decisions. The compensation levels of jobs that form a family should also be comparable; this means that equitable compensation strategies cannot be formed without considering the entire job family. In some instances, it may also be economical to use similar recruitment methods and sources to hire individuals who belong to the same job family.

Environmental Considerations

The environments within which the firm and job exist also need to be considered when redesigning jobs. As with most human resource activities, job designers cannot ignore **environmental considerations**—the influence of the external environment, which affects workforce availability, values, and practices.

> **environmental considerations** The influence of the external environment on job design; includes employee ability, availability, and social expectations.

Workforce Availability

Efficiency considerations must be balanced against the abilities and availability of the people who will actually do the work. An extreme example underlines this point:

Governments of less developed countries often think they can "buy" progress. To be "up to date," they seek the most advanced equipment they can find. Leaders of one country ordered a digital oil refinery, necessitating a level of technology that exceeded the abilities of the country's available workforce. As a result, these government leaders hired expatriate Europeans to operate the refinery.

In less developed nations, the major risk is jobs that are too complex. But in industrialized nations with highly educated workers, jobs that are too simple can produce equally disturbing problems.

For example, even when unemployment rates are high, many simple and overly specialized jobs are sometimes hard to fill, as longstanding ads for janitors attest.

Social Expectations

The acceptability of a job's design is also influenced by **social expectations**. For example, working conditions that would have been acceptable to some early Canadian immigrants are no longer acceptable to our present generation.

> **social expectations** The larger society's expectations about job challenge, working conditions, and quality of work life.

When rail lines were being laid across Canada, many persons were willing to work long hours of hard labour. They had fled countries where jobs were unavailable, which made a job—any job—acceptable to them. Today, industrial workers are much better educated and have higher expectations about the quality of work life.

Even where work flow might suggest a particular job design, the job must meet the expectations of workers. Failure to consider these expectations can create dissatisfaction, poor motivation, and low quality of work life.

Work Practices

Work practices are set ways of performing work. These methods may arise from tradition or from the collective wishes of employees. The human resource department's flexibility to design jobs may be constrained, especially when such practices are part of a

> **work practices** The set ways of performing work in an organization.

union–management relationship. Failure to consider work practices can have undesired outcomes:

> General Motors decided to increase productivity at one of its American plants by eliminating some jobs and adding new tasks to others. These design changes caused workers to stage a strike for several weeks because traditional practices at the plant had required a slower rate of production and less work by the employees. The additional demands on their jobs by management were seen as an attempt by the company to disregard past work practices.

Job Analysis in Tomorrow's "Jobless" World

Global competition, fast technological obsolescence, changing worker profiles, and rapid increases in knowledge requirements for various jobs have made accurate and timely job descriptions difficult. Today's global village has resulted in "boundary-less" and "de-jobbed" organizations, in which traditional boundaries between a firm and its suppliers, customers, and even competitors have disappeared. Many employees are no longer responsible for producing specific outcomes; rather, they are members of teams entrusted with many responsibilities.

How do organizations that operate in such fast-changing environments conduct valid job analyses? How can the task and person requirements identified today be relevant for an unknown tomorrow?

Of course, there are no simple solutions. A few attempts have been made to meet the newfound challenges. One strategy has been to adopt a future-oriented style when describing job activities and specifications. Rather than asking what the current jobholder does, the focus is on what the jobholder must do to effectively carry out and further organizational strategies and the new competencies required of the jobholder. Thus, present and future requirements, rather than past actions, guide job descriptions and the hiring and training of employees.

Regardless, job analysis will continue to be relevant for legal compliance and defensibility in the event of a court action.[39] Traditional sources of information (such as jobholders, supervisors) may, however, need to be supplemented by data emerging from customers, peers, and technical experts to incorporate the ever-changing job demands.

SUMMARY

Job analysis information provides the foundations of an organization's human resource information system. Analysts seek to collect specific data about jobs, jobholder characteristics, and job performance standards. Job analysis information can be collected through interviews, focus groups, questionnaires, employee logs, direct observation, or some combination of these techniques. Once collected, the data are compiled into job descriptions, job specifications, and job standards. Competencies have emerged as another approach to collecting job information. Job analysis information is then used when these specialists undertake

other human resource management activities, such as job design, recruiting, and selection.

Job analysis information is used for job design. Essential elements of job design include organizational considerations (such as efficiency and work flow), ergonomic considerations, employee considerations (such as autonomy, feedback, variety, task identity, and task significance), job specialization (and increasing quality of work life through job rotation, job enlargement, job enrichment, and work teams), along with environmental considerations (such as workforce availability, social expectations, and work practices).

TERMS FOR REVIEW

autonomy 54
competency 49
competency matrix 50
competency model (competency framework) 49
efficiency 52
employee log 44
environmental considerations 56
ergonomics 53
feedback 55
focus group 44
interview 43
job 38
job analysis 37
job analysis questionnaires 43
job code 45
job description 44
job design 51

job enlargement 55
job enrichment 55
job families 56
job identity 45
job performance standards 47
job rotation 55
job specification 47
National Occupational Classification (NOC) 45
observation 44
position 38
social expectations 57
task identity 54
task significance 55
variety 54
work flow 52
work practices 57
working conditions 47

SELF-ASSESSMENT EXERCISE

How Enjoyable Was That Work or Project?

Consider a job that you held in the past. If you have no work experience, consider a course project or other effort where you had to work for a reward. Please respond frankly to the questions on the following page.

SCORING

For the odd-numbered statements, assign a score of 1, 2, 3, or 4 for Strongly Disagree, Disagree, Agree, and Strongly Agree, respectively. For the even-numbered statements, reverse the scoring—that is, Strongly Disagree gets a score of 4 and Strongly Agree gets a score of 1. Add up your scores for all 10 statements.

Your score should lie somewhere between 10 and 40. If you received a score of 32 or higher, you had an enjoyable experience with your past work or assignment—at least most of the time. If you scored less than 20, it is unlikely that you had much fun doing the job or project.

Although this is not a validated instrument, statements 1 and 2 above indicate the overall autonomy you had in doing the project; 3 and 4 measure the dimension of variety; 5 and 6 reflect task identity; 7 and 8 measure feedback; and 9 and 10 measure task significance. On each dimension, your scores can range anywhere from 2 to 8. It is possible for you to get a high score on one dimension and a low score on another, although an "enriched" project would have had high scores on all dimensions.

Statement about Your Work/Project	Strongly Disagree	Disagree	Agree	Strongly Agree
1. I felt that I had control over the quality and performance of my job.				
2. I was not allowed to plan the optimal pace at which I could work.				
3. The work/project involved various activities.				
4. It was the same routine every day; I did the same things day after day.				
5. At the end of a day, I could see a finished job or part of the project.				
6. There were many days when I had little sense of accomplishment.				
7. My boss/supervisor always told me whether I did the work well or poorly.				
8. I got little feedback from anyone about how well I performed during the course of the project.				
9. The work I did (or the project I completed) was an important one.				
10. Often I felt that it made little difference how I did on this job/project.				

REVIEW AND DISCUSSION QUESTIONS

1. Suppose you work for an organization that does not conduct job analysis. What arguments will you make to introduce it? What method(s) of collecting job analysis information will you recommend and why?

2. Define *job descriptions* and *job specifications,* illustrating how the two are related yet different.

3. Why are clear job specifications important? What are the costs of imprecise specifications?

4. How can performance standards be set for production jobs when job analysis information is insufficient? How would you set performance standards for a research scientist if you were chief scientist?

5. What factors need to be considered when redesigning jobs? Of these, which is (are) most important?

CRITICAL THINKING QUESTIONS

1. Suppose you were assigned to write the job descriptions for a shirt factory in British Columbia employing mostly Filipino immigrants who speak little English. What methods would you use to collect job analysis data?

2. You work in the human resource department of a large brewery in Atlantic Canada. You are in the process of writing job descriptions for all managerial and supervisory staff. One manager who is in the production division of the brewery refuses to complete a job analysis questionnaire.

   a. What reasons would you use to persuade that individual to complete the questionnaire?

   b. If, after your best efforts at persuasion failed, you still wanted job analysis information on the manager's job, how would you get it?

3. Suppose that you have been assigned to design the job of ticket clerk for a regional airline in Ontario. How would you handle the following trade-offs?

   a. Would you recommend highly specialized job designs to minimize training or very broad job designs with all clerks cross-trained to handle multiple tasks? Why?

   b. Would you change your answer if you knew that employees tended to quit the job of ticket clerk within the first six months? Why or why not?

4. Assume that you are told to evaluate a group of jobs in a boat-building business. After studying each job for a considerable amount of time, you identify the following activities associated with each job. What job redesign techniques would you recommend for these jobs, if any?

   a. *Sailmaker:* Cuts and sews materials with very little variety in the type of work from day to day. Job is highly skilled and takes years to learn.

   b. *Sander:* Sands rough wood and fibreglass edges almost continuously. Little skill is required in this job.

   c. *Sales representative:* Talks to customers, answers phone inquiries, suggests customized additions to special-order boats.

   d. *Boat preparer:* Cleans up completed boats, waxes fittings, and generally makes the boat ready for customer delivery. Few skills are required for this job.

5. What are the key performance dimensions of the instructor who is teaching this course? How would the instructor go about setting performance standards for the individual? Establish performance standards and associated time-bound, specific objectives in any two areas of your choice.

ETHICS QUESTION

Your firm, an importer of a large number of consumer goods, including garments, sent you to a developing country to negotiate a deal with a local exporter. Under the proposed contract, your firm will invest 25 percent of the capital necessary to open a new garment tailoring plant, with the exporter investing the balance. During your week-long stay in the country, you realize that child labour is fairly common in this country, although a number of local employers categorically refuse to employ anyone under 18 years of age in their plants. During discussions with the local plant manager, you understand that he plans to use 12- to 15-year-old children in the factory, and the children will have performance standards at levels equal to or higher than a typical adult Canadian worker in the same industry. You know that a couple of other foreign firms are currently interested in reaching a deal with this exporter because he has a reputation for reliability and quality. This is your first visit to this country.

What action, if any, will you take?

RESEARCH EXERCISE

Make a list of three jobs you have held or are held by members of your family. Go to the O*NET OnLine webpage (https://www.onetonline.org/).

1. Enter the first job into the occupation search bar. Is the occupation you are looking for one of the first five options? Click on the category that best describes the first job. How well does the information provided about the tasks, activities, skills, and so forth, match your impression of the first job?

2. Next, consider the second job that you held or that was held by a member of your family. Using the Find Occupations search bar, select Bright Outlook. Is the second job listed as one that is expected to grow significantly in the next few years? Look down the list of jobs with bright futures. Are there any that you are surprised to find on this list? Are there any jobs that appeal to you on this list?

3. Finally, consider the tools or technology that are required in the third job that you held or that was held by a member of your family. Use the Advanced Search bar to explore Tools and Technology. Are you able to find the third job you have in mind from the tools or technology used on the job? How might the O*NET resource be useful to you as you explore career options over the course of your working life?

INCIDENT 2-1

Hillary Home Appliances Corporation

Hillary Home Appliances and Furnishings Corporation (HHAC) is a medium-sized manufacturer of home appliances. Historically, the firm has followed a low-cost strategy to successfully operate in a highly competitive industry. Recently, increasing global competition has made it necessary for the firm to revise its strategy in favour of improved customer service. The organization had paid virtually no attention to the human resource function; its human resource department focused primarily on compensation administration and staffing. Now, however, the firm's top management is convinced of the need for strategic use of its human resources. An indication of this new thrust is the hiring of Leslie Wong, who has a reputation as a results-oriented HR manager. However, progressive HR practices have been slow to find acceptance at lower levels. In a recent meeting with two work supervisors, Jeff Gidoe and Mike Tarson, Leslie Wong, the newly hired human resource manager, faced these arguments:

Jeff Gidoe: I agree that good employee relations are important. But I simply cannot afford to let the HR staff interrupt our daily work with job analysis. Already, with the arrival of two new competitors, we have lost most of our cost advantage. Spending time on activities such as this further reduces our production and increases our costs.

Mike Tarson: Your plan to invite ideas from employees for product improvement is good; however, I should warn you that many of the workers in my section are high school dropouts. They simply cannot accept responsibility.

They care only for the wages they get and are constantly looking at the clock for quitting time.

Jeff Gidoe: At least a few of my employees will object to the time spent on job analysis. As you know, we have a production bonus plan in this plant. Every minute they spend on activities such as this costs them money. Already, several of them feel that the production standards are too high.

Mike Tarson: Your new idea of employee involvement teams is also likely to create problems. Already, they waste a fair bit of time each day jesting and horseplaying. If you put them into groups, things will only get worse, not better.

Leslie Wong: I value your comments. As supervisors, you know your employees best. I recognize that you are experts in your production areas. However, I can tell you this: The facts you have provided have simply reconfirmed the need for job analysis. Even more, they tell me that HR has a key role to play in this firm. I'll tell you why.

DISCUSSION QUESTIONS

1. What prompted the HR manager to make the above statement?

2. If you were the HR manager, what arguments would you provide to convince the two supervisors of the desirability of job analysis and employee involvement teams?

EXERCISE 2-1

Strengths and Weaknesses of Job Descriptions*

Step 1. Students should bring several job descriptions to class. Pick job descriptions from O*NET OnLine (https://www.onetonline.org/) if needed.

Step 2. Create teams of three. Discuss the job descriptions. Do they adequately reflect the responsibilities and KSAOs

that the employee will need to perform? Compare the job descriptions to the information in your text. What are the weaknesses and strengths of the job descriptions? What specific changes would make the job descriptions more measurable?

---

* Exercise suggestion: C. Fitzgerald, Okanagan College, Kelowna, BC.

WE CONNECTIONS: MOTIVATION THROUGH JOB DESIGN

No Use Crying over Spilled Coffee . . .

Coffee sloshed over the rim when Charlotte placed her cup heavily on the desk. She shook her head, cursing at her sloppiness. She thought, "Come on, woman. Get it together already." She reached into a drawer for a napkin to mop up the mess as she unloaded the pile of files she was carrying onto an already disordered desktop.

Coffee stains on these documents were the last thing she wanted. These were the notes she had compiled on the different projects Alex had her working on. She had thought that her role as an HR specialist was busy before, but Alex, the founder of WEC, had recently been loading her up with even more tasks than usual, and she didn't know how she was going to get them all done. She had just left an update meeting with him and was feeling frustrated. She now had several new tasks and didn't get closure on any of the outstanding tasks she was leading.

Fast and Furious

Part of the problem was that Alex had a very fast-moving mind. He would get an idea and instruct Charlotte to look into it, but by the time she made any progress, he was already thinking about something else. She would have to drop the first project to work on the latest. Eventually, he would remember the first one, and she would feel negligent that she hadn't done more on it. Sometimes she felt as though she was chasing wisps of smoke.

As an example, the week before Alex had asked her to do an exit interview with Jake, the project manager who had resigned. The conversation with Jake had been enlightening. He had indeed left because he had found out that someone else had gotten a raise ahead of him, as he had told Alex. But it turned out that he had been frustrated for quite some time, and that event had simply been the last straw. He told Charlotte that since he had started at the company, he was always given projects that bridged two particular platforms; that was his specialty, so it had made sense, but he had been craving new challenges. Even though he asked to get involved in something different, the company kept putting him off by saying "not until things slowed down," but that never seemed to happen. Another problem was that he was always asked to launch new projects, but once they were running, he rarely heard about them again. Any issues that arose were handled by a service department. In one case, he had found out that his solution had been abandoned six months after implementation, but he never found out why. He worried that maybe he had done something wrong or could have made some modifications based on the client's feedback to fix the issue, but he couldn't be sure. Charlotte had hoped to report her findings from Jake's exit interview to Alex in the meeting, but she hadn't been given the chance. In an effort to be more systematic in her review of employee opinions, Charlotte had also wanted to talk to Alex about implementing an employee engagement survey across all WEC staff. She wanted to collect data about the areas of employee satisfaction as well as discontent in the workplace to guide and prioritize future HR efforts.

Anna Comaro, Charlotte's assistant, walked into her office and sat down on one of the visitor's chairs. She asked, "What did Alex say about the plan for the new wellness initiatives? Which ones did he like the most?"

Charlotte sighed, and replied, "We didn't even get to that. He was too excited about a training program he had heard about. He wants me to look into maybe bringing it here."

Anna slapped her hand on the desk, and said, "Really? But you did so much work researching everything. And there were a lot of things on that list that I think we really need!"

Charlotte smiled, and nodded. She said, "I know, Anna. But it's not up to me. He's the boss."

Anna leaned forward with a furrowed brow, and said, "I admire your patience. I think I would lose it if it were me. I hope he knows how hard you work."

Charlotte shrugged, and said, "I don't know what he thinks about me or the things I do. You know, when I was working toward my Chartered Professional in Human Resources (CPHR) designation, it was so exciting. Being an HR professional seemed like a perfect job to me. I could help businesses make the most of their people, and I could help potentially hundreds or even thousands of people have a better work life. But, wow, it's hard to have a clear impact when you're moving in 10 directions at once."

The phone rang, and Anna jumped out of her chair. "Speaking of moving, I had better get back to work, or *my* boss is not going to be happy with me."

Charlotte laughed as she reached to pick up the phone, "You're right, Anna. No more goofing off. Maybe if I work fast enough, I can get something done before my to-do list changes again!"

DISCUSSION QUESTIONS

1. What consequences are arising from job design in this case?

2. Imagine that you are a consultant hired by WEC. Use the job characteristics model to analyze (a) Jake's job and (b) Charlotte's job. Based on your analysis, what changes would you recommend for (a) Jake's job and (b) Charlotte's job?

3. Recognizing that HR is not Alex's area of expertise, what recommendations would you have for Charlotte in conducting a job analysis of her own job? (a) Using Figure 2-4, for guidance, what duties and responsibilities should Charlotte include in the analysis of her own job? (b) How should she prioritize them?

4. How might Charlotte be able to design a job description for her own job to be more proactive as opposed to reactive when issues arise and when Alex makes requests of her time?

In the next installment of the WE Connections story (at the end of Chapter 3), a senior leader struggles to balance staffing levels as she copes with having too many of some employees and not enough of others.

CASE STUDY

Starbright Casino

Using Job Analysis for Job Rotation and Redesign

The casino was all set for another busy and profitable Friday night. The tribute band would be starting in another hour and the restaurants and bar stools were nearly full with preshow diners. Many of the show seekers would return to try their hand at tables or slots before the evening was out. As Shea looked around the casino floor, she could feel the energy just starting to ramp up as the night's hopeful gamers were trickling in, replacing the coffee-drinking day crowd now cashing in their remaining chits and chips.

Shea scanned the day shift employees, knowing they would be counting down the time until they could rest their tired backs and feet with their shift behind them. As shift manager, she couldn't help but keep a casual lookout for the table-game dealers, slot-machine attendants, and casino cashiers who would be taking over as the evening crew during the shift change in 15 minutes.

Just then, Shea spotted Bin walking quickly in her direction, a grim look on his face. "Angelo was supposed to be working in the cage tonight, and he just called in sick."

Shea could tell from the tone of Bin's voice that he was questioning whether Angelo was actually sick or just avoiding taking his turn exchanging bills for chips and turning chips into cash as a cashier in the cage. Shea silently acknowledged that the absence rates when staff members were scheduled to work cage shifts were significantly higher than when they were scheduled to work the tables or slots. She knew that being closer to the gambling action was more exciting than being in the cage and made the shift pass by more quickly. As well, there was always the possibility that lucky gamblers would share a chip or two with their dealers.

Her mind switched to solving the problem at hand. The two cages each needed two cashiers for that night's shift. With one now away, she would have to pull one of the table-game dealers or slot-machine attendants. No one would be happy to forego their scheduled work for a shift in the cage. Shea aimed to schedule cage shifts evenly across all of the table-game dealers and slot-machine attendants for each night they normally worked to be as fair as possible in giving each staff member time on the floor. *Well, except for the crap table dealers,* Shea thought. They didn't have to take a turn in the cage, and Shea knew this was a point of contention for the other staff. Four-person teams managed each crap table, and the quick math and complexity of the game, owing to the number of gamblers and bets to keep track of, meant that fewer staff could handle the game. Other employees coveted the crap table, in part so they could avoid the cage.

Shea looked to the remaining table-game dealers and slot attendants. They would have to offer one fewer table game tonight, which meant the casino would likely leave some gamblers with a little more money in their pockets at the end of the night than Starbright would have hoped. She glanced at the evening shift staff now entering the floor, mentally eliminating the four who had worked the cage last Friday. Shea could move one of the slot attendants into the cage, and then one of the table-game dealers to the slots, but then realized she would be disappointing two staff instead of only one. She saw Marcel heading toward the Texas Hold 'Em tables, but she dismissed the idea of moving him to the cage. He had covered for another last-minute absence in the cage last Saturday. Her gaze rested on Cecilia. Shea knew Cecilia handled disappointment better than some of the others, but that meant she was called upon all too frequently to cover these absences. Just then, Shea saw Gabe walking in and recalled he was set to deal blackjack. She went to tell him the news that he would be working in the cage that night.

DISCUSSION QUESTIONS

1. What recommendations would you make for Shea to improve her implementation of job rotation? How could she make the system fair to all employees (including Angelo following his absence)?

2. What are some other strategies that Shea could use to enrich the cashier job?

3. How would you go about conducting a job analysis for the cage attendant job? Referring back to Figure 2-2, make an action plan for each of the six steps.

4. The table games have a clear hierarchy in terms of staff desire to work at them, with the crap table the most desired, followed by other table games, then the slots, then working as a cashier. How is job analysis useful in determining hiring, training, and compensation requirements across these four jobs in this job family?

CHAPTER 3

Human Resource Planning

> Human resource planning is . . . designed to translate strategic objectives into targeted quantitative and qualitative skill requirements, identify the human resource strategies and objectives necessary to fulfill those requirements . . . and . . . assess progress.
>
> ABDUL RAHMAN BIN IDRIS AND DEREK ELDRIDGE[1]

LEARNING OBJECTIVES

After studying this chapter, you should be able to:

LO1 Explain the importance of human resource plans for strategic success.

LO2 Describe the human resource planning process.

LO3 Discuss methods for estimating an organization's demand for human resources.

LO4 Explain the various methods of estimating a firm's supply of human resources.

LO5 Identify solutions to shortages or surpluses of human resources.

LO6 Discuss the major contents of a human resource information system (HRIS).

LO7 Explain how HRIS has contributed to enhancing HR service delivery.

In Chapter 1, we addressed how different organizational strategies and tactical plans require different human resource practices, strategies, and tactics in order to be successful. In this chapter, we elaborate on this concept by addressing human resource planning—a fundamental step in strategic human resource management. Recall that strategic human resource management enables leaders and human resource professionals alike to align the human resource systems, policies, and practices to the organizational strategy. Human resource planning, in turn, enables organizations to ensure that the right people are in the right place at the right time to support the completion of organizational strategies. It is also the opportunity to consider whether there is a gap in the current HR practices and procedures to enable success

in the organization's strategic plan. Perhaps, more than any other human resource activity, planning allows the human resource department to be proactive and strategic. Planning is a critical HR process—particularly over the long term, since without planning, an organization may find itself with an office without the employees or the business processes to run it effectively. HR plans themselves range from simple frameworks based on past trends to highly sophisticated modelling based in live-time data analytics. However, it is important that some form of planning exists.

In 1924, International Business Machines was created. Better known today as IBM, the company has made major shifts in business strategy over the last 95 years. With origins in creating and manufacturing hardware (including clocks), IBM has undertaken a strategy of "making markets by transforming industries and professions with data."[2] To undertake a strategy focused on big data and data analytics, an appropriate shift in human resources would have needed to take place to ensure that the right individuals with the right skill sets were in place well in advance of executing this strategy. Without an appropriate human resource plan, the leaders at IBM would likely be addressing the age old phenomena. That is, they would be rushing to hire people in a reactive way rather than in a proactive way.

LO1 Relationship of Human Resource Planning to Strategic Planning

Human resource planning (HRP) is a strategic and proactive process used to determine future human resource requirements and the business processes that will be needed to support and enable those resources by anticipating future business demands, analyzing the impacts of these demands on the organization, determining the current availability of human resources and the applicable business processes, and making decisions on how to effectively adapt and utilize firms' human resources. HRP helps identify what human resources are needed to ensure that the organization can respond to change and provides plans to help the organization respond effectively.[3] Although the term *human resource planning* has been used interchangeably with other terms, such as *employment planning, human capital planning,* and *human capital management,* the process of human resource planning has expanded well beyond simply predicting the number of employees an organization will need. Because of the interdependence of organizational strategy and human resources, HR planning is often referred to as *strategic human resource planning* (SHRP).

One major objective of human resource planning is to ensure that the organization has the *right people with the right skills at the right time* in order for the organization to fulfill organizational objectives.[4] Simply putting the right people in the right place at the right time, however, does not ensure success. Having the appropriate human resource practices in place to create the *right environment* and enable and

> **human resource planning** A process used to determine future human resource requirements and the business processes that will be needed to support and enable those resources by anticipating future business demands, analyzing the impacts of these demands on the organization, determining the current availability of human resources and the applicable business processes, and making decisions on how to effectively adapt and utilize firms' human resources.

motivate people to do *the right things* is equally important. Complementing the "people resource" element, planning also involves planning for the appropriate human resource practices and activities. For example, consider an organization that is planning a major expansion into a new market when employees are resistant to change, lack trust in leadership, and have generally low morale. In a case like this, human resources will need to figure out how to attract, hire, and retain more employees while simultaneously developing and implementing strategies to improve the organization's culture.

By anticipating the number and types of employees and the activities that will be needed, the human resource leader helps improve the utilization of its human resources, attempts to achieve economies of scale by securing the right type of resources, and aligns its activities with the organization's overall strategic direction.

However, getting the right people in the right place at the right time does not ensure organizational success. For discussion purposes, this chapter focuses on creating a workforce plan and introduces concepts and tools that will be more fully developed throughout Part 2 of the text. Enabling and motivating "people" resources to do the right things is the focus of Part 3 of this text.

Linking Strategy to Planning

In Chapter 1, we outlined a number of forces—both internal and external—that would impact an organization's ability to successfully achieve its goals. Adopting a strategic focus on human resources enables managers to proactively anticipate the long-term "people" and "process" needs of an organization and to create a human resources strategy that brings those elements together. It is important to recognize, however, that a firm's long-range strategic plan is accomplished by the thoughtful execution of a series of short-range, tactical (or operational) plans that focus on current needs and operations. Purchasing a new information management system to improve efficiency, recalling a defective product, and managing inventory more effectively are some examples of tactical activities. Whatever the plan, it is made and carried out by people, which necessitates the proper staffing of an organization. As such, each tactic also requires managers and leaders to consider the short-range human resource needs.

Consider the interaction between performance consulting and digital learning. Performance consulting is a systems approach to enabling people in their jobs by focusing on the knowledge, skills, and abilities they need to be successful. In many cases, organizations are turning to asynchronous, online, modular, and on-demand learning to enable these skills.[5] Organizations that operate using traditional classroom-based learning and performance management systems would need to pivot their short-term human resource needs to adapt to current technology and approaches to enable long-term HR goals.

When Nordstrom, an upscale U.S. retailer, announced that it would open a flagship store in Toronto, the underlying HR system would have gone to work. To be ready to execute this major initiative, Nordstrom must have had the proper staff available with specific skills. For example, to staff its stores, Nordstrom needed retail clerks, managers, merchandizers, and cashiers. In addition, it required regional managers, a country manager, and an executive to oversee this expansion.[6]

Figure 3-1 shows the relationship between an organization's strategic plans and its human resource plans. As illustrated, the overall organizational strategy defines the human resource objectives that are accomplished through the implementation of appropriate human resource plans. Successful organizations—both large and small, and public as well as private—recognize the importance of *intellectual* or *human capital*. An effective human resource plan is a critical tool to take advantage of this valuable asset.

HR Planning Can Vary from Capturing Basic Information to a More Sophisticated Approach

Organizations are unique; they use different approaches for planning the allocation of human resources. It is typical to expect that, as organizations grow, they develop more robust planning practices, largely due to the significant impact on labour costs. Large Canadian employers, such as ONEX (161,000 employees), George Weston (200,000 employees), Magna International (159,000 employees), and RBC Royal Bank (78,000 employees), pay considerable attention to employment planning since even a 1 percent increase or decrease in the total workforce can result in significantly different labour costs. In some cases, organizations have hired "chief human resources officers," asserting that organizations need to bring together strategy, research, data, planning, and employee engagement

and well-being to create high performance organizations.[7] However, this type of planning is exceptional. Some organizations think very short term, their planning is informal, and their resource plan is static. One author has described these differences in terms of levels of planning sophistication.[8] From this perspective, organizations may be categorized into one of five levels of planning (see Figure 3-2).

LEVEL ONE companies can be described as not engaging in any form of planning, whether it is business- or human resource–related. Recruitment and training are considered an afterthought. An example would be family-owned small organizations where the leadership style is paternalistic in nature.

LEVEL TWO companies do engage in some long-term business planning, but minimal human resource planning. Resource planning is solely focused on how many people will be needed in the future. However, the planning is static in nature and receives minimal weight in terms of importance within the organization.

LEVEL THREE companies engage in moderate planning activities, creating longer term forecasts, projecting their needs three to five years ahead. However, these organizations still do not integrate their people planning efforts into the long-term business plan.

LEVELS FOUR AND FIVE companies are considered advanced in terms of their planning sophistication, engaging in long-range human resource planning, spanning three to six years. Human resource planning now becomes a core process and is considered a key priority. Managers are enthusiastic about planning, and there is a growing recognition that anticipating resource requirements for the future is imperative to ensure organizational sustainability. The plan is formal, flexible, and dynamic. It adjusts to change as circumstances dictate. The human resource components are fully integrated with the business plan. Recruitment and training are anticipated and succession planning is considered a critical activity to ensure sustainability. The key difference between levels 4 and 5 is that level 5 organizations utilize *robust* evaluation tools and

FIGURE 3-1

Relationship between Strategic and Human Resource Plans

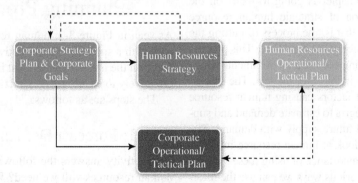

FIGURE 3-2

The Five Levels of Planning Activities

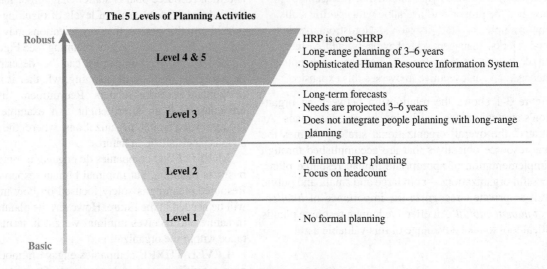

The 5 Levels of Planning Activities

Robust

Level 4 & 5
· HRP is core-SHRP
· Long-range planning of 3–6 years
· Sophisticated Human Resource Information System

Level 3
· Long-term forecasts
· Needs are projected 3–6 years
· Does not integrate people planning with long-range planning

Level 2
· Minimum HRP planning
· Focus on headcount

Level 1
· No formal planning

Basic

highly sophisticated technology to create long-range plans to improve returns on investment.

This is not to suggest that all organizations eventually progress through the levels. In some cases, an organization may not make it past level 1. This may be due to a lack of knowledge or simply a lack of time.

The behaviours described in level five require a great deal of resources and time. For some organizations, this investment is not only important, it is essential, to the point that they are turning to companies like SAP to create software solutions to predict certain events, such as employee turnover.[9] This has created a new challenge for human resource professionals—namely, how to use data analytics without creating concern from employees.[10]

According to the Chartered Institute for Personnel Development, HR analytics is using people-centric data in analytic procedures to solve business problems.[11] In creating evidence-informed decisions, the field of HR is still coming into its own. Some authors argue that the primary challenge for HR is to use data at all simply because the appropriate type of data doesn't exist in most companies today.[12]

The remainder of the chapter is going to focus on the workforce planning portion of strategic human resource planning (see Figure 3-3), that is, the process of putting the right people in the right place at the right time. This process is complemented by creating the right environment, which will be developed robustly in Part 3 of the text. The discussion begins with a look at factors causing human resource demand, followed by strategies to estimate demand and supply and match current and future supply with demand. The chapter ends with a brief look at human resource information systems (HRIS), the importance of using these systems to manage talent, and the various ways we can use the information to effectively utilize our human resource capabilities.

FIGURE 3-3

The Workforce Planning Process

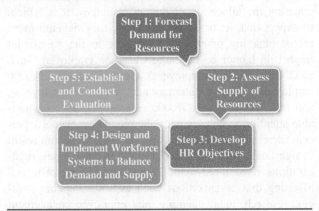

Step 1: Forecast Demand for Resources

Step 2: Assess Supply of Resources

Step 3: Develop HR Objectives

Step 4: Design and Implement Workforce Systems to Balance Demand and Supply

Step 5: Establish and Conduct Evaluation

LO2   The Human Resource Planning Process

As seen in Figure 3-3, human resource planning is a process with a specific order of activities helping managers to focus on the issues that are most important so they can plan effectively to ensure that organizational objectives are met.

The steps are as follows:

Step 1: Forecast Demand for Resources

This activity answers the following questions: *How many* human resources will we need? *When* will we need them? *Where* will we need them? It forecasts demand by looking at the many factors that cause a labour need to exist and uses various forms of forecasting techniques.

Step 2: Assess Internal and External Supply of Resources

This phase assesses the internal and external supply of labour. It answers these questions: *What resources* do we have available both inside the organization and in the external environment? *What skills and competencies* do these resources possess?

Step 3: Develop HR Objectives

This step identifies what the planners expect to accomplish as a result of their actions. Planners carry out an analysis to determine the differences between demand and supply, and write HR objectives that will determine the choice of programs.

Step 4: Design and Implement HRM Programs

Here the planners decide what type of human resource programs will be developed to achieve their objectives. These programs attempt to balance demand and supply. For example, if the organization is projecting a shortage, it may choose to outsource or use overtime, or, if a surplus is expected, it may decide to allow employees to job share as opposed to downsize.

Step 5: Establish Program Evaluation

With any process it is important to evaluate its effectiveness, using some form of quantitative or qualitative measurement. Evaluation of the process answers this question: Is there a tangible link between investments in human resource programs and organizational sustainability, and, if so, to what degree?[13]

Forecasting Labour Demand

A challenge facing organizations is that "people" resources are rarely in a state of being perfectly balanced. Because organizations and their environments are continually changing, organizations quite likely will find themselves either in a position of having too many employees or not enough. This underscores the importance of effective human resource planning. While it may not completely eliminate it, a good human resource plan reduces the risk of being out of balance. To have an effective human resource plan, organizations need to have a clear understanding of what they need in terms of employees, what they have, and what the difference is between the two. Moreover, a good human resource plan will identify and anticipate shifts in either an organization's demand or supply of human resources.

The best place to begin is to forecast the need for resources. To this end, we need to consider the factors that cause a demand to exist.

Forecasting: Identifying the Causes that Will Drive Demand

To understand how to forecast demand, we need to consider what would cause an organization's need for employees or specific skill sets to change in one direction or another. Note that the examples provided are not exhaustive but, rather, provide some illustration of what may impact human resources demand. As well, some forces may create either an undersupply or oversupply, depending on other factors. For example, sales projections may create an oversupply if sales projections are falling or an undersupply if sales projections are increasing. Some of these causes are within the organization's control, and others are not. Human resource **forecasts** are attempts to predict an organization's future demand for employees.

forecasts Estimates of future resource needs and changes.

Strategic Plan

As discussed earlier in the text, the organization's strategic plan commits the firm to long-range objectives, such as growth rates, new products, markets, or services. These objectives determine the numbers and types of employees needed in the future. Obviously, a fast-growing firm has more beginning-level vacancies. The number of higher-level openings also depends on how well the human resource department assists employees to develop their capabilities. If workers are not encouraged to expand their capabilities, they may not be ready to fill future vacancies.

Demographic Impacts

In Chapter 1, a series of demographic impacts were identified, including age and gender. Like national, regional, or even local demographics, each organization will have a demographic profile of its own. This profile helps inform human resource leaders regarding impending changes in their workforce. For instance, human resource leaders may capture the average age of employees against the average retirement ages to gain insight into future retirements. Consider the impact of the shrinking population of Newfoundland on employability and on the cost of healthcare.[14]

Turnover

Turnover is the departure of employees from an organization. In some cases, such as resignations, the decision to leave the organization is made by the employee. In other cases, the employer makes the decision, such as in terminations. In yet other cases, the turnover may be temporary (e.g., leaves of absence). As will be discussed later in the text, turnover may be functional (i.e., good) or dysfunctional (i.e., bad). Regardless of the cause, effective human resource planning needs to be prepared to understand and predict employee departures as well as possible. For example, as of February 2018, the number of employees voluntarily leaving their jobs in the U.S. is at the highest point in 17 years. This is due to individuals' confidence that they will find another job because of a strong U.S. economy.[15]

Legal Changes

Changes occurring in social, political, and legal spheres are easier to predict, but their implications are seldom clear. As demographics change, so do employee attitudes toward work and their employers. The impact of the *Canadian Human Rights Act* on human resource planning, passed more than 40 years ago, is still somewhat unclear. Major judicial verdicts, changes in employment laws (such as minimum wages),[16] and federal and provincial government regulations all have great implications for the human resource planner. Although many large firms have established employment equity programs, the results of a change from the notion of equal pay for equal work to that of equal pay for work of equal value (see Chapter 4) will have profound implications.

Technological Changes

Technological changes, which are normally difficult to predict, can affect both demand for, and supply of, human resources and appropriate human resource practices and tools.[17] As an example, many thought the computer would mean mass unemployment. While it is true that digitization and automation have eliminated certain types of jobs, the high-tech and electronics industry today employs hundreds of thousands of people and is a high-growth business. In some cases, it is the high-tech jobs that are in the highest demand. An example is the artificial intelligence sector.[18] Very often, technological changes tend to reduce employment in one department while increasing it in another, making planning tricky. The rapid automation, digitization, and technology of many work activities may necessitate new skills on the part of employees.

> A study by McKinsey notes that automation may affect 50 percent of the world economy or 1.2 billion employees and 14.6 trillion wages.[19]

Competitors

Competitors affect an organization's demand for human resources, though not in any uniform manner. Employment in some of the traditional sectors (such as the steel industry) barely grows because of foreign competition and a push for productivity improvement. But in the high-tech and electronics industries, competition causes lower prices, larger markets, and additional employment. In yet other cases, the arrival of a competitor may create demand because employees leave to work for the competitor or an organization fails to compete.

Budgets and Revenue Forecasts

Budget increases or cuts are the most significant short-run influence on human resource needs. Related to budgets are revenue forecasts. While less exact than budgets, revenue forecasts may provide even quicker notice of short-run changes in human resource demand.

> If a sharp decline in sales were to occur, retailers might quickly discard the short-run human resource plan and impose an employment freeze. Consider Bombardier's needing to potentially lay off hundreds of workers because the company was not successful on a bid to build new trains for the city of Montreal.[20]

Historical sales and production forecasts can be used as the operational index to which HR planning forecasts its future human resource demands.

New Ventures

New ventures mean new human resource demands. When initiated internally to the organization, the lead time may allow planners to develop short-run and long-run employment plans. But new ventures begun by acquisitions and mergers cause an immediate revision of human resource demands. A reorganization, especially after a merger or an acquisition, can radically alter human resource needs. Several positions or jobs may have to be eliminated to avoid duplication, while new integrating roles may have to be created for smooth operating of merged units.

> For example, consider the takeover of Whole Foods by Amazon in 2017. Following the takeover, employees begin to fear the deployment of drones, which would lead to layoffs.[21]

Organizational and Job Design

Changes in the organization structure have major implications for human resource needs. In some cases, new roles may be created. In others, roles may be eliminated.

> Prior to 2014, Nokia, a Finnish company, was heavily invested in the cellphone market. Recognizing that it could no longer be profitable in the device market, Nokia sold its interests in cellphones to Microsoft. In doing so, Nokia swung more heavily into the networking equipment industry. After buying out a partnership with Siemens, Nokia shifted its strategy, corporate structure, business plan, and management team—all resulting in a need for the HR team at Nokia to pivot and adapt.[22]

FIGURE 3-4

Techniques for Estimating Future Human Resource Needs

Expert	Trend	Other
• Informal and instant decisions	• Extrapolation	• Budget and planning analysis
• Formal expert survey	• Indexation	• New-venture analysis
• Delphi technique	• Statistical analysis	• Simulation models

LO3 Forecasting Techniques for Estimating Human Resource Demand

As Figure 3-4 shows, forecasting techniques range from the informal to the sophisticated. Even the most sophisticated methods are not perfectly accurate; instead, they are best viewed as approximations. Most firms make only casual estimates about the immediate future. As they gain experience with forecasting human resource needs, they may use more sophisticated techniques (especially if they can afford specialized staff).

Each of the forecasting methods in Figure 3-4 is explained below.

Expert Forecasts

Expert forecasts rely on those who are knowledgeable to estimate future human resource needs. At the first level of complexity, the manager may simply be convinced that the workload justifies another employee. The idea that workload justifies a recruit illustrates an informal and instant and often inaccurate forecast. The primary risk in doing so is that it is not part of a systematic planning effort. A better method is for planners to survey managers, who are the experts, about their department's future employment needs, identify differences in perspectives, and place the data in context. The centralization of this information permits formal plans that identify the organization's future demand.

The survey may be an informal poll, a written questionnaire, or a focused discussion using the **nominal group technique** (NGT).[23] The NGT presents a group of managers with a problem statement, such as, "What will cause our staffing needs to change over the next year?" Then each of the participants writes down as

nominal group technique A focused group discussion where members meet face-to-face or digitally, write down their ideas, and share them. All new thoughts on a topic are recorded and ranked for importance.

many answers as he or she can imagine. These ideas are then shared in round-table fashion until all written ideas and any new ones they stimulated have been recorded. The group's ideas are then discussed and ranked by having each member of the group vote for the three to five most important ones.[24]

If the experts cannot be brought together, sophistication can be added to the survey approach with the **Delphi technique**.[25] This technique solicits estimates from a group of experts, usually managers. Then human resource department planners act as intermediaries, summarizing the various responses and reporting the findings to the experts. The experts are surveyed again after they get this feedback. Summaries and surveys are repeated until the experts' opinions begin to agree on future developments. For example, the human resource department may survey all production supervisors and managers until an agreement is reached on the number of replacements needed during the next year. The main difference between the two techniques is that in the NGT they meet face-to-face, whereas in the Delphi technique they utilize a lead coordinator to collect, summarize, and disseminate the information to and from the experts.

Delphi technique The soliciting of predictions about specified future events from a panel of experts, using repeated surveys until convergence in opinions occurs.

Trend Projection Forecasts

Perhaps the quickest forecasting technique is to project past trends. The two simplest methods are extrapolation and indexation. **Extrapolation** involves extending past rates of change into the future. For example, if an average of 20 production workers were hired each month for the past two years, extrapolation indicates that 240 production workers will probably be added during the upcoming year.

extrapolation Extending past rates of change into the future.

© Ingram Publishing

By analyzing the staffing needs of existing oil rigs, planners of a new rig can forecast their human resource needs until changes in technology occur. How can planners react to shortages of skilled staff?

Indexation is a method of estimating future employment needs by matching employment growth with a selected index. A common example is the ratio of production employees to sales. For example, planners may

> **indexation** A method of estimating future employment needs by matching employment growth with a selected index, such as the ratio of production employees to sales.

discover that for each million-dollar increase in sales, the production department requires 10 new assemblers. The relevant business factor here is sales figures in dollars. That is, an overall productivity index for all relevant sales personnel is computed. This ratio, with appropriate modifications, enables the firm to estimate its demand for personnel for the next period. However, the growth or decline rate in the labour force may be different during growth and downsizing periods (typically, the growth of the management tier happens at a somewhat faster pace than its compression). When using indexation, this factor must be recognized.

Extrapolation and indexation are crude, short-run approximations because they assume that the causes of demand—external, organizational, and workforce factors—remain constant, which is seldom the case. They are inaccurate for long-range human resource projections. More sophisticated statistical analyses make allowances for changes in the underlying causes of demand.

Other Forecasting Methods

There are several other ways planners can estimate the future demand for human resources with more accuracy.

Budget and Planning Analysis

Organizations that need human resource planning generally have detailed long-range plans, short-term operational plans, and budgets to support those plans.

A study of department long-range planning may show planned growth or contraction. Analysis of these plans plus extrapolations of workforce changes (resignations, terminations, and the like) can provide short-run estimates of human resource needs. Short-term operational plans along with budgets can then be used to validate these projections.

New-Venture Analysis

When new ventures complicate employment planning, planners can use *new-venture analysis,* which requires planners to estimate human resource needs by comparison with firms that already perform similar operations.

For example, an integrated steel company that owns steel plants and iron ore mines decides to explore iron ore at a new site. The management can estimate its employment needs in the new mine by looking at employment levels of other iron ore mines and making necessary adjustments for productivity improvements.

Simulation and Predictive Models

As we discussed earlier, the most sophisticated organizations used robust technology to forecast effectively. *Data analytic models* are a series of mathematical formulas and algorithms that simultaneously use extrapolation, indexation, survey results, and estimates of workforce changes to compute future human resource needs. They simulate and forecast changes in demand for human resources caused by various internal and external factors.

Converting a Forecast into Human Resource Requirements

Forecasts translate the causes of demand into short-range and long-range statements of need. The resulting long-range plans are, of necessity, general statements of probable needs. Specific numbers are either omitted or estimated. To summarize forecasts, organizations often turn to creating staffing tables.

A **staffing table** may be a specific number or an approximate range of needs, depending on the accuracy of the underlying forecast. Staffing tables are neither complete nor wholly accurate; they are only approximations. But these estimates allow human resource specialists to match short-run demand and supply. They assist HR departments in writing HR objectives, they help operating departments run more smoothly, and they can enhance the image of the human resource department with specific estimates of future human resource needs, allowing human resource specialists to become more proactive and systematic.

> **staffing table** A list of anticipated employment openings for each type of job.

FIGURE 3-5

A Partial Staffing Table for a City Government

Metropolis City Government Staffing Table
Date Compiled:

Budget Code Number	Job Title (as found on job description)	Using Department(s)	Anticipated Openings by Month of the Year												
			Total	1	2	3	4	5	6	7	8	9	10	11	12
100-32	Police Recruit	Police	128	32			32			32			32		
100-33	Police Dispatcher	Police	3	2					1						
100-84	Meter Reader	Police	24	2	2	2	2	2	2	2	2	2	2	2	2
100-85	Traffic Supervisor	Police	5	2			1			1			1		
100-86	Team Supervisor— Police (Sergeant)	Police	5	2			1			1			1		
100-97	Duty Supervisor— Police (Staff Sergeant)	Police	2	1					1						
100-99	Shift Officer— Police (Inspector)	Police	1	1											
200-01	Car Washer	Motor Pool	4	1			1			1			1		
200-12	Mechanic's Assistant	Motor Pool	3				1			1			1		
200-13	Mechanic III	Motor Pool	2	1									1		
200-14	Mechanic II	Motor Pool	1						1						
200-15	Mechanic I (Working Supervisor)	Motor Pool	1	1											
300-01	Clerk IV	Administration	27	10			5			6			6		

For example, a review of Figure 3-5 shows that the city's human resource department must hire 32 police academy recruits every three months. This knowledge allows recruiters in the human resource department to plan their recruiting campaign so that it peaks about six weeks before the beginning of the next police academy class. The advanced planning allows the department to screen applicants and notify them at least three weeks before the class begins. For those still in school or otherwise unable to be ready that quickly, recruiters can inform them when the following class begins. If the human resource department waited for the police department to notify them, notification might come too late to allow a systematic recruiting and screening process. Staffing tables enable recruiters to be proactive and to better plan their activities.

LO4 The Supply of Human Resources

Once the human resource department makes projections about future human resource demands, the next major concern is filling projected openings. There are two sources of supply: internal and external. The internal supply consists of present employees who can be promoted, transferred, or demoted to meet anticipated needs.

Internal Supply Estimates

Estimating the internal supply involves more than merely counting the number of employees in an organization. Planners audit the present workforce to learn about the capabilities of present workers. This information allows planners to tentatively estimate which openings can be filled by present employees. These tentative assignments usually are recorded on a replacement chart. Considering present employees for future job openings is important if workers are to have careers with their employer and feel engaged. The patterns of employee transitions among jobs must be carefully assessed and taken into consideration. Audits, replacement charts, and employee transition matrices (more popularly called Markov analysis and discussed in detail below) also are important additions to the human resource department's information base. With greater knowledge of employees, the department can more effectively plan recruiting, training, and career-planning activities. A human resource department can also help meet its employment equity goals by identifying internal minority candidates for job openings.

An economic force that is making internal supply estimates more difficult is the increase of voluntary temporary work, or the gig economy. This is because transitions in and out of roles in an organization are happening faster, leading to greater complexity in prediction. Temporary work will be discussed more fully later in the chapter.

Human Resource Audits

Human resource audits summarize the employee's knowledge, skills, and abilities, and they generate skills and management and leadership inventories that, in turn, facilitate the preparation of a replacement chart and replacement summaries. Following is a brief discussion of skills inventories in the context of human resource planning.

Skills Inventories

An inventory catalogues the capabilities found in the organization's workforce. **Skills inventories** may be applied to both managerial and non-managerial roles.

A skills inventory will bring together data about specific employees. This may include, but is not limited to,

skills inventories Summaries of each worker's knowledge, skills, abilities, experiences, and other attributes.

an employee's educational history, work history, extra-work experiences, core skills, knowledge, abilities, and key project accomplishments. From these profiles, planners learn about the mix of employee knowledge, skills, and abilities and whether the current staff will be able to meet the organization's goals.[26] One may note the similarities between a skills inventory and a typical applicant résumé. In many ways, a résumé that covers these key areas enables HR professionals to determine if an applicant can fill a gap in the organization's skills, knowledge, and abilities.

Skill inventories may also summarize an employee's potential by describing the employee's performance history and readiness for promotion, as well as any deficiencies in the employee's profile.

To be useful, inventories of human resources must be updated regularly. A robust review and update every two years is often sufficient for most organizations if employees are encouraged to report major changes to the human resource department when they occur. Major changes include new skills, degree completions, changed job duties, and the like. Failure to update skills inventories can lead to present employees being overlooked for job openings within the organization and may create an inaccurate profile of the organization's available skills. As the average length of term that employees have with a company decreases, managers may need to reconsider the length of time between refreshing information. To make the process easier and more efficient, inventories are more often being conducted electronically. For example, Cognology has developed a digital skills audit platform.[27]

Some organizations are complementing skills audits with competency audits. As the nature of work continues to change, having a robust understanding of employees' competencies allows human resource managers to mitigate the risks associated with an under- or oversupply of human resources.

Management and Leadership Inventories

An audit of management talent is called **management or leadership inventory**. As in the case of skills inventories, these are comprehensive reports of available management and leadership capabilities in the organization. Like skills inventories, management inventories should be updated periodically since they also are used for key human resource–related decisions. In fact, some employers use the same form for managers and nonmanagers. When the forms differ, the management inventory requests information about management activities. Common topics include the following:

management or leadership inventory Comprehensive reports of available management capabilities in the organization.

- Number of employees supervised
- Types of employees supervised
- Total budget managed

- Management training received
- Duties of subordinates
- Previous management duties

Skill inventories and leadership inventories are not mutually exclusive. The 9-box grid (discussed in Chapter 8) is an example of an individual evaluation tool that integrates an employee's current contribution to the organization (i.e., skills inventory) with that employee's potential level of contributions to the organization (i.e., leadership inventory).[28]

Recently, a great deal of attention has been paid to the domain of talent management. Understanding who in an organization may be transferred into a management or leadership role is a fundamental component of talent management. In some organizations, leaders at all levels are issued leadership profiles, such as the Leadership Practices Inventory (LPI).[29] By accumulating information on employees' leadership behaviours, organizations are able to more accurately identify who from within the organization may be suitable to put in a leadership role.

Replacement Charts

Replacement charts are a visual representation of who will replace whom in the event of a job opening. The information for constructing the chart comes from the human resource audit.

> **replacement charts**
> Visual representations of who will replace whom when a job opening occurs.

Figure 3-6 illustrates a typical replacement chart. It shows the replacement status of only a few jobs in the administration of a large city.

With mandatory retirement abolished, it becomes increasingly unnecessary to include age in replacement charts. It may, however, be desirable to gather retirement intentions to facilitate long-term planning. Alternatively, organizations may compare someone's age with the average age of retirement from the organization to predict when someone may retire.

Although different firms may seek to summarize different information in their replacement charts, the figure indicates the minimum information usually included or needed.

FIGURE 3-6

A Partial Replacement Chart for a Municipal Government

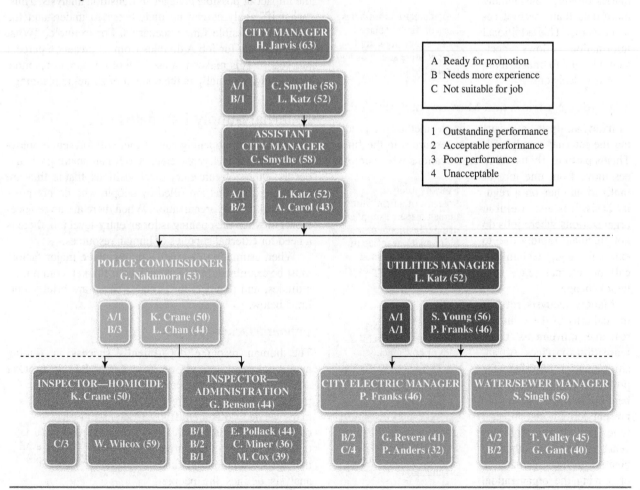

The chart, which is much like an organization chart, depicts the various jobs in the organization and shows the status of likely candidates. Replacement status consists of two variables: present performance and promotability or potential. Present performance is determined largely from supervisory evaluations. Opinions of other managers, peers, and subordinates may contribute to the appraisal of present performance. Future promotability is based primarily on present performance and the estimates by immediate superiors of future success in a new job. The human resource department may contribute to these estimates through the use of psychological tests, interviews, and other methods of assessment. This information is also captured in the 9-box example mentioned earlier.

Human resource and management decision makers find that these charts provide a quick reference. Their shortcoming is that they are built on the assumption that the organizational structure is quite static. They also contain little information.[30] To address the lack of information, replacement summaries may be prepared, as discussed next.

To supplement the chart—and, increasingly, to supplant it—human resource specialists develop **replacement summaries**. Replacement summaries list likely replacements and their relative strengths and weaknesses for each job. As Figure 3-7 shows, the summaries provide considerably more data than the replacement charts. This additional information allows decision makers to make more informed decisions.

> **replacement summaries**
> Lists of likely replacements for each job and their relative strengths and weaknesses.

Transition Matrices and Markov Analysis

Markov analysis is a fairly simple method of predicting the internal supply of human resources in the future. This is particularly useful in organizations where employees move from one job (or rank) to another on a regular basis. It is also useful in organizations where jobs do not fluctuate rapidly due to external (e.g., technological) or internal (e.g., strategic) change.

Markov analysis reflects the patterns in these human resource movements using **transition matrices**. A transition matrix describes the probabilities of an incumbent's staying in his or her present job for the forecast time period (usually one year), moving to another job position in the organization, or leaving the organization.

> **Markov analysis**
> Forecast of a firm's future human resource supplies, using transitional probability matrices reflecting historical or expected movements of employees across jobs.

> **transition matrices**
> Describe the probabilities of how quickly a job position turns over and what an incumbent employee may do over a forecast period of time, such as stay in the current position, move to another position within the firm, or accept a job in another organization.

When this matrix is multiplied by the number of employees in each job at the beginning of a year, the forecaster is easily able to identify the number of persons who will remain in the job at the end of the year.

Figure 3-8 shows a sample transition matrix. It indicates that 80 percent (or 0.80) of the incumbents in Job A remain in their present position at the end of the year, 10 percent (or 0.10) move to Job B, 5 percent (or 0.05) move to Job C, none of them move to Job D, and 5 percent (or 0.05) leave the organization (through resignations or otherwise). When these probabilities are multiplied by the number of persons in Job A at the beginning of the year (namely, 200), we see that 160 of them remain in their present position, 20 of them move to Job B, 10 of them move to Job C, and the remaining 10 leave the organization. When similar calculations are performed for all the jobs (in the case of this firm, for Jobs A, B, C, and D), we are able to predict the approximate number of employees who will remain in each job position.

Markov analysis is popular because of the ease of its use. However, it is only as good as the transition probabilities used. The probabilities are not very reliable if there are only a few incumbents in each job. This makes it appropriate only for medium-sized and large organizations.

Markov analysis can also be used speculatively to assess the impact of possible changes in transition analysis. Thus, "what if" analyses can be undertaken to understand the impact of possible future scenarios. For example, "What if the quit rate for Job A doubles from its present 6 percent per year?" This makes it a useful tool for human resource forecasting, especially in the context of strategic planning.

External Supply Estimates

Not every future opening can be met with present employees. Some jobs lack replacements to fill an opening when it occurs. Other jobs are entry-level positions; that is, they are beginning jobs that are filled by people who do not presently work for the organization. When there are no replacements or when the opening is for an entry-level job, there is a need for external supplies of human resources.

When estimating external supplies, three major factors must be examined: trends in the labour market, community attitudes, and demographic trends. These are briefly outlined below.

Labour Market Analysis

The human resource department's success in finding new employees depends on an accurate **labour market analysis**. Even when unemployment rates are high, many needed skills are difficult to find. This is a key distinction for human resource managers. A labour market analysis defines the people

> **labour market analysis**
> The study of a firm's labour market to evaluate the present or future availability of different types of workers.

FIGURE 3-7

A Replacement Summary for the Position of City Manager

Replacement Summary for the Position of City Manager			
Present Office Holder	Harold Jarvis	**Age**	63
Probable Opening	In two years	**Reason**	Retirement
Salary Grade	99 ($86,000)	**Experience**	8 years
Candidate 1	Clyde Smythe		
Current Position	Assistant City Manager		
Current Performance	Outstanding	**Explanation** Clyde's performance evaluations by the City Manager are always the highest possible.	
Promotability	Ready now for promotion	**Explanation** During an extended illness of the City Manager, Clyde assumed all duties successfully, including major policy decisions and negotiations with city unions.	
Training Needs	None		
Age	58		
Experience	4 years		
Candidate 2	Larry Katz		
Current Position	Utilities Manager		
Current Performance	Outstanding	**Explanation** Larry's performance has kept costs of utilities to citizens 10 to 15 percent below that of comparable city utilities through careful planning.	
Promotability	Needs more experience	**Explanation** Larry's experience is limited to utilities management. Although successful, he needs more broad administrative experience in other areas. (He is ready for promotion to Assistant City Manager at this time.)	
Training Needs	Training in budget preparation and public relations would be desirable before promotion to City Manager.		
Age	52		
Experience	5 years		

An Example of Markov Analysis

(a) Transition Probability Matrix

Year Beginning	Year End				
	Job A	Job B	Job C	Job D	Exit
Job A	0.80	0.10	0.05	0.00	0.05
Job B	0.10	0.70	0.00	0.10	0.10
Job C	0.00	0.00	0.90	0.05	0.05
Job D	0.00	0.00	0.00	0.90	0.10

(b) Expected Movements of Employees

	Initial Staffing Level	Job A	Job B	Job C	Job D	Exit
Job A	200	160	20	10	0	10
Job B	70	7	49	0	7	7
Job C	60	0	0	54	3	3
Job D	100	0	0	0	90	10
Predicted End-of-the-Year Staffing Level		167	69	64	100	30

potentially available for work. A skills market, however, narrows the available people to those who have the appropriate skill set.

In the short run, the national unemployment rate serves as an approximate measure of how difficult it is to acquire new employees. Human resource specialists realize that this rate varies for different groups, as well as from province to province and city to city.

A significant challenge with using employment rates as a measure of potential employee recruitment opportunities is that it represents only a moment in time. That is, it provides a measure of how many people are unemployed during a certain historical period. It does not identify what the future looks like. To address this shortcoming, some jurisdictions have undertaken an analysis to determine what the future supply and demand is for specific occupations.

The province of Alberta conducts analyses on both a short-term and long-term basis. Alberta's short-term employment forecast analysis predicts surplus or undersupply of potential employees in Alberta over a three-year period for a series of job types.[31] The same province conducts a longer term analysis that predicts labour markets in Alberta through to 2023.[32]

Regardless of the unemployment rate or regional demand outlook, external needs may be met by attracting employees who work for others or in other regions. In some professions—such as teaching and engineering—labour mobility between provinces is quite high.[33] In other industries, such as the infrastructure trades, there is less mobility relative to university graduates.[34]

In the long run, local developments and demographic trends have the most significant impact on labour markets. Local developments include community growth rates and attitudes.

For example, labour shortages in Canada's agriculture industry have doubled over the last 10 years and are expected to double again before 2025. This labour gap is forcing agricultural companies and farms to turn to temporary foreign workers to fill the gap.[35]

The lack of jobs results in still more people leaving the local labour market. This is particularly so in the case of minorities and other under-represented groups of society.

During a recessionary period, the job prospects of minorities and new immigrants are more adversely affected. As an example, during the global economic downturn in late 2000, a study out of Ireland demonstrated that immigrants were losing jobs at a rate of 20 percent, whereas domestic Irish persons were losing jobs at a rate of 7 percent. [36]

While people move across labour markets, language and cultural barriers may often act as deterrents. Sometimes, migrants from other areas may receive a hostile welcome in the local labour market:

In 2014, the Temporary Foreign Worker Program came under great scrutiny when the program was linked to joblessness.[37]

This experience is troubling in that a strong source for external workers for Canadian employers is the Canadian Temporary Foreign Worker Program.[38] This program was overhauled in 2014 to ensure that employers were putting Canadian workers first in their hiring decisions.[39] As of 2018, Canada is seeing an increase in temporary foreign workers gaining permanent residency.[40] This has not slowed the back and forth opinions on the program. As recently as March 2018, the program continues to be contested because of the policies associated with it.[41]

Community Attitudes

Community attitudes also affect the nature of the labour market. Anti-business or nongrowth attitudes may cause present employers to move elsewhere. An example of this is activist investing.

In 2013, an activist investor group tried to break apart Agrium—a Calgary-based fertilizer company—into its wholesale and retail businesses. This action would have divided Agrium into two companies and would likely have had a dramatic effect on the employee pool.[42] Agrium was later merged with PotashCorp to form Nutrien.[43]

Demographic Trends

Chapter 1 provided a detailed account of a number of demographic influences on an organization. Demographic trends are another long-term development that affects the availability of external supply. Fortunately for planners, these trends are known years in advance of their impact. Two examples serve to illustrate such trends:

Consider the 2011 research study released by the Information and Communication Technology Council. It found that a major technology labour crunch is looming in Canada. The study predicted that there will be 106,000 openings in the five years that followed in the Information and Technology sector, and the study highlighted the specific skills sets needed.[44] Driven by baby boomer retirements, the lack of hiring during the prior recession, and the significant changes in technology requirements, a major shortage exists for these types of skills.

Another example relates to the shipping industry. A shortage of truck drivers in the United States is forecast to reach 900,000 as fewer people enter this industry. A career in driving is not one that all people aspire to and, as a result, this industry is experiencing a staffing shortage. Finding ways to attract people to trucking careers is difficult. Taken in combination with the observation that 70 percent of goods sold in the United States are transported by truck, some companies are needing to stop nonessential shipments.[45]

There are several sources of information available to planners. For example, major sources of data include Statistics Canada and Employment and Social Development Canada (ESDC). Another source of information is the Conference Board of Canada, which generates excellent research reports on many other HR-related topics.

Statistics Canada publishes reports on labour force conditions on a monthly, quarterly, annual, and occasional basis. Information available on total labour force projections includes geographic, demographic, and occupational variables, and labour income, census data, and population projections by sex and province over various years.

The **Canadian Occupational Projection System (COPS)** was designed by Employment and Social Development Canada. The COPS provides a highly detailed projection of the Canadian economy up to 10 years in the future.[46]

Job Bank (https://www.jobbank.gc.ca/home) is a group of products available from ESDC that identifies

> **Canadian Occupational Projection System (COPS)** Provides up to 10-year projection of Canadian economy and human resource needs.

trends in the world of work. It outlines job outlooks by occupation as well as by field of study and estimates the prospect of finding jobs in a specific occupation or field in a specific location. Job Bank provides Canadians with the latest information available about work—information that is important for anyone in the process of making decisions or advising others in the area of career planning.

For example, Job Bank forecasts that the chance of finding work as a registered nurse in Edmonton, Alberta, and Thunder Bay, Ontario, is very strong. Of note, however, it also identifies that the average wage in Edmonton is $42.00/hour whereas the rate in Kenora is $37.00/hour.

FIGURE 3-9

FIGURE 3-9

Summary of HR Tools Used to Estimate Internal and External Supply of Labour

Internal Supply Indicators	External Supply Indicators

• Human Resource Audits
   • Skill inventories
   • Management inventories
   • Replacement charts/summaries
• Transition matrices and Markov analysis
	• Labour market analysis
	• Community attitudes
	• Demographic trends

Figure 3-9 provides a summary of the HR tools used to estimate internal and external supply of labour.

HR Objectives

The identification of supply and demand forecasts and summaries only provides the human resource professional with context and information. It does not address the process by which any gaps can be addressed. As such, the next step in the process identifies what the organization expects to accomplish as a result of its actions. It directs the planning process of the organization, identifies what the planner will do to achieve its goals, and sets a baseline to determine whether the organization has achieved its goals. For example, if the organization's strategy were to grow its market share by 20 percent, the HR objective would be to add a certain number of "head count" with a certain set of skills by a predetermined date. However, if the organization's objective is to reduce labour costs by 20 percent, then the objective might be to reduce the workforce in each department by 5 percent by a certain date, carefully taking into account the preservation of individuals with critical skills sets and significant ongoing potential. Once these objectives are identified, then the planner can decide what specific HR programs and strategies will be appropriate.

LO5 HRM Strategies to Achieve Objectives in Supply and Demand

Typically, human resource planners face two decision situations: They find that the available supply of human resources is either less or greater than their future needs. It is only the rare, fortunate planner who finds that the supply and demand are equal. Each of the above two situations requires somewhat different corrective actions, which are discussed next.

Strategies to Manage an Oversupply of Human Resources

When the internal supply of workers exceeds the firm's demand, a human resource surplus exists. There are various strategies that HR can consider. It can group each of these strategies under three main headings: head-count reduction, attrition, and work arrangements.

Head-Count Reduction

Here are four main ways to ensure a head-count reduction: layoffs, leaves without pay, incentives for voluntary separation, and termination.

Layoffs Layoffs, the temporary withdrawal of employment to workers, are used in cases of a short-run surplus. Layoffs are the separation of employees from the organization for economic or business reasons. The separation may last only a few weeks if its purpose is to adjust inventory levels or to allow the factory to retool for a new product. When caused by a business cycle, the layoffs may last many months or even years. However, if the layoff is the result of restructuring or rescaling of an industry, the "temporary" layoffs may be permanent.

As unpleasant as layoffs are for both workers and management, they may be required when attrition (see below) is insufficient to reduce employment to acceptable levels. In some organizations, each employee who is laid off may receive a supplemental employment benefit over and above government EI benefits. However, during severe economic downturns, the employer's ability to provide these benefits may be seriously jeopardized.

While the terms of a collective agreement dictate layoff procedures in unionized settings, nonunion employers may have to consider other factors or be exposed to constructive dismissal claims.

For example, in Ontario, the province's *Employment Standards Act* permits a temporary layoff of an employee without pay for up to 13 weeks in a consecutive 20-week period. If the unpaid layoff exceeds that period, it will no longer be deemed "temporary" and the employer will become liable for reasonable notice and severance pay, if applicable.[47]

When the layoffs are expected to be of a short duration—as when an automobile plant temporarily closes to change its tooling for a new model—layoffs may not follow the normal pattern of forcing the most recently hired employees to accept unemployment. Rather than following seniority, some contracts have "juniority" clauses. Juniority provisions require that layoffs be offered first to senior workers. If the senior worker wants to accept the layoff, that person collects employment insurance and the other organizational benefits, and the juniors keep their jobs. Senior workers are likely to accept layoffs of short duration because they receive almost the same take-home pay without working. When the layoff is of an unknown duration, the seniors usually decline to exercise their juniority rights and fewer senior employees are put on layoff.

Leaves Without Pay One way to temporarily reduce the number of employees on the payroll is to give them an opportunity to take a leave of absence without pay, either to attend college or university or to pursue other personal interests. Employees who are offered this leave are usually those who are financially able to leave the organization for a little while and whose jobs may be eliminated in the future. Thus, this strategy might help some employees to prepare for oncoming changes.

Incentives For Voluntary Separation Sometimes organizations decide to offer employees some form of an "enticement" to leave the organization early. This practice is referred to as a "buyout." At one large telecom during the recession, employees were offered a buyout. It was called Voluntary Severance Package (VSP) and contained a cash bonus, bridging for one's pension, and outplacement services.

Termination *Termination* is a broad term that encompasses the permanent separation from the organization for any reason. Usually this term implies that the employee was fired as a form of discipline. When employees are discharged for business or economic reasons, it is commonly, although not always, called a layoff. Sometimes, however, the employer needs to separate some employees for business reasons and has no plans to rehire them. Rather than being laid off, those workers are simply terminated.

The blow of discharge may be softened through formal **outplacement** procedures, which help present employees find new jobs with other firms. External consultancy firms are typically used to provide services such as résumé writing, job search, and interview preparation. Not only do such efforts help the former employee, but they also give evidence to the remaining employees of management's commitment to their welfare.[48]

A recent study highlighted that only about 30 percent of firms in the United States focused on outplacement

> **outplacement** Assisting employees to find jobs with other employers.

services. That said, the same study highlighted that $1.5 billion was spent on outplacement services in 2001 in the United States.[49]

Attrition Strategies

Attrition is the normal separation of employees from an organization as a result of *resignation, retirement,* or *death.* It is initiated by the individual worker and not by the company. In most organizations, the key component of attrition is resignation, which is a voluntary separation. Although attrition is a slow way to reduce the employment base in an organization, it presents the fewest problems. Voluntary departures simply create a vacancy that is not filled, and the staffing level declines without anyone being forced out of a job. Two common attrition strategies are hiring freeze and early and phased retirement offers.

> **attrition** Loss of employees due to their voluntary departures from the firm through resignation, retirement, or death.

Hiring Freeze Most employers initially respond to a surplus with a hiring freeze. This freeze stops the human resource department from filling openings with external applicants. Instead, present employees are reassigned.

> Faced with a drop in heavy oil commodity prices in early 2015, Suncor cut 1,000 jobs and announced a hiring freeze.[50]

Early and Phased Retirement Offers A special form of attrition is *early retirement.* It is one form of separation that the human resource department can actively control. It is used to reduce staffing levels and to create internal job openings. Early retirement plans are designed to encourage long-service workers to retire before the normal retirement age in the organization (say, 65 years). Since employees who retire before age 65 will draw benefits longer, their monthly retirement benefits may be reduced proportionately.

Some companies are allowing older employees to reduce their work activity and gradually *phase into* retirement without loss or reduction of pension benefits. The most typical pattern in **phased retirement** is to allow gradually shortened workweeks, a preferred schedule among older workers according to some surveys.[51] Most companies in the survey required that an employee first work a minimum of five years in the firm and be at least 55 years old in order to participate in a phased retirement program, and over half allowed employees to later change their minds.

> **phased retirement** Gradual phase in to retirement with loss or reduction of pension benefits.

An example of phased retirement is provided by the University of Toronto:

> The University of Toronto offers its faculty members a pre-retirement package that allows them to scale down their workload over three years provided they are between 57 and 68.[52]

Alternative Work Arrangements

If the head count of employees is not to change, other options are to adjust the work term, either by reducing the number of work hours by using part-time workers, job sharing, transferring employees where resources are needed, or loaning employees to other organizations.

Job Sharing Reducing the number of total work hours through **job sharing** is the first of the above options to adjust the work term. Job sharing, also called *job splitting*, involves dividing duties of a single position between two or more employees. From the employer's perspective, this eliminates the need to lay off one employee completely. But the employees also benefit by having more free time at their disposal and maintaining employment.

> **job sharing** A plan whereby available work is spread among all workers in a group to reduce the extent of layoffs when production requirements cause a substantial decline in available work.

> A more recent twist on the concept of job sharing is whether jobs can be shared with artificial intelligence. In a 2018 blog, author Ceilidh Higgins described how technologies such as building information management systems enable her as an architect to focus on design rather than on repetitive tasks as an architect.[53]

Work sharing programs are also used to avoid layoffs. A major initiative is the federal work sharing program administered by ESDC. It allows employees to voluntarily reduce their hours to spread available work around.[54]

The major advantage claimed for job sharing is increased productivity from workers who are not fatigued. Problems arise from the increased paperwork and administrative burden associated with two employees doing the job of one. Another problem is that of benefits. Human resource specialists are forced to decide whether job sharers should be given benefits equal with other employees or benefits that are scaled down in proportion to the employee's hours. Employers may also need to pay for a crossover day.[55]

Using Part-Time Employees Eliminating full-time positions and replacing them with part-time positions, thus reducing the total work hours and labour costs, is another strategy used in several settings.

Very often, **part-time employees** are paid no benefits. The significant decrease in total benefit costs, especially health care and pensions, provides a great incentive for employers to make more use of regular *part-time work*. Employers that do pay benefits tend to be in the public sector, such as health care facilities and municipal governments. Another advantage of part-time work is that it increases flexibility so that employers can match the workforce with peak demands. Part-time employment is also popular for a few other reasons, such as the following:

> **part-time employees** Persons working fewer than the required hours for categorization as full-time workers and who are ineligible for many supplementary benefits offered by employers.

- The higher demand in the service industries, which employ more than 40 percent of all part-timers[56]
- The need for cost-cutting

Part-time work has public costs. Part-time employees have limited entitlement to government-run employment insurance and disability benefits, resulting in potentially serious financial problems should they be unable to work. Without disability benefits they have no income and may end up on the welfare rolls. In some settings, converting full-time to part-time work may be fraught with legal challenges as well.

Strategies to Manage Shortages of Employees

A **labour shortage** occurs when there is not enough qualified talent to fill the demand for labour and organizations cannot fill their open positions. A skill shortage refers to specific skills that the organization requires. It occurs when the demand for workers with specific skills exceeds the available supply of workers with these specialized skills.

> **labour shortage** Insufficient supply of qualified talent to fill the demand for labour.

Organizations that are effective at HR planning utilize a variety of staffing strategies to ensure that they have the right people with the right skills at the right place and at the right time to do the right things. There are several staffing options available to choose from, depending on the sense of urgency, economic conditions, and productivity gains. The staffing options to consider are as follows: hire employees, contract out the work to another firm, develop existing employees, and leverage existing work arrangements. A summary of these options is shown in Figure 3-10.

Hire Employees

One way to address a labour shortage is simply to hire an employee to fill the open position. However, whether to hire a full-time or part-time employee or an internal or an external candidate is an important decision that managers make. A more fulsome discussion of the hiring process is found later in the text.

FIGURE 3-10

Alternative Staffing Strategies

Hire Employees	Source Service Providers	Develop Employees Internally	Existing Work Arrangements
• Full-time	• Independent contractor	• Replacement charts	• Overtime
• Part-time	• Third party	• Succession planning	• Flexible schedules
• Temporary	• Outsource	• Career development	• Flexible time and location
	• Crowdsource	• Float and transfer	• Flex policies

Full-Time Employees For several positions, hiring **full-time employees** is the only alternative. This may be the case for key roles such as the CEO. Many organizations are averse to this strategy since it incurs additional fixed costs. Hiring full-time staff also requires a more detailed look at their competencies in terms of the organization's long-term strategies. Full-time work in Canada is defined as more than 30 hours per week.[57]

> **full-time employees**
> Employees who work 37.5 to 40 hours in a workweek.

Some organizations have sought to mitigate some of the risk of hiring full-time employees by bringing them on first as probationary employees. These employees are hired on a full-time basis but can be released from the organization at any time during their probationary period for any reason. This enables organizations to more effectively assess the skill set of full-time employees before committing indefinitely to them.[58] For instance, a probation period of 90 days is outlined in legislation in Alberta.[59]

Part-Time Employees An increasingly popular strategy for meeting human resource needs is to use part-time employees. Part-time employees are an attractive option to the employer since using them adds flexibility in scheduling. Traditionally, part-timers have been employed by service businesses, such as restaurants and retail stores, that experience considerable fluctuation in demand during peak and off-peak times. However, more recently, many firms, after a downsizing or restructuring, employ part-timers to provide services that had previously been offered by full-timers.

> For example, in the past, United Parcel Service created 25-hour-per-week part-time jobs for shipping clerks and supervisors who sort packages at its distribution centres.[60]

Employment of part-timers reduces overall payroll costs since part-timers are, typically, not eligible for several of the expensive benefits offered to the full-time workforce. However, there are variations across provinces, and the human resource manager should carefully check the legal requirements before introducing new policies. For example, Saskatchewan has extended a number of benefits to part-time workers under specific conditions:

> In Saskatchewan, a full-time employee is anyone who works 30 hours or more per week. All businesses with 10 or more full-time equivalent employees must provide benefits to eligible part-time employees. To qualify, part-time employees must have been employed for 26 consecutive weeks and have worked 390 hours in those 26 weeks. To maintain eligibility, the employee should work for at least 780 hours in a calendar year. Eligible benefits include dental plans, group life, accidental death or dismemberment plans, and prescription drug plans.[61]

Contract Out the Work

The next alternative that organizations may consider to manage a labour shortage is to enter into a service agreement with a **contract (or contingent) worker**. A contract worker is a freelancer who is not part of the regular workforce and who provides goods or services to another entity under the terms of a specific contract. Contractors are not employees of an organization. They are governed under contract law, not employment legislation. The contractor typically invoices the organization, and the organization pays for these services via the accounting function. The contractor's "contract" ends when the services that he or she had agreed to provide are complete and the services have been delivered. On occasion, organizations will choose to engage a "consultant." **Consultants**, by definition, are professionals who provide expert advice and counsel in a particular area.

Contractors determine their own work hours, typically have their own offices, and can work on multiple

> **contract (or contingent) worker** A freelancer (self-employed, temporary, or leased employee) who is not part of the regular workforce who provides goods or services to another entity under the terms of a specific contract.

> **consultants** Professionals who provide expert advice and counsel in a particular area.

FIGURE 3-11

Key Tests to Determine Contractor/Employee Status

Control	• Is the person under the direction and control of another with respect to the time the person works, where the person works, and the way in which the work is done? • The greater the control, the more likely the person is an employee. The contractor determines the result. As an employee, the employer has the right to determine the way the task is carried out.
Ownership of Tools	• Does the person use the tools, space, supplies, and/or equipment owned by someone else? If so, this may be an indicator. • Contractors supply their own tools.
Profit	• Does the person make a profit? • If the person profits, then he could be a contractor. If the person's income is the difference between the cost of providing the service and the price charged, then the person is deemed an independent contractor.
Risk of Loss	• An employee has no risk of loss. • If the person risks losing money if the cost of doing the job is more than the price charged, then he or she she can be considered to have contractor status.
Sub-Contracting	• Does the individual need to complete the work herself? • If the person does not need to complete the work herself and can hire someone else to do it, she is considered to be a contractor.

---

contracts at the same time. They can hire other persons to perform the work, they are not eligible for benefits, and they provide their own equipment and supplies. Revenue Canada has provided a number of tests that can be used to determine whether someone is a contractor. They are strict and assess companies' practices to ensure that the relationship is at arm's length. The tests are related to control, ownership of tools, chance of profit, and risk of loss and payment (see Figure 3-11).

Outsourcing The term *outsourcing* has been used extensively in the past decade. **Outsourcing** work refers to a formal agreement an organization makes with a third party to perform a service rather than using internal resources. Outsourcing or "contracting out" work is typically associated with work that is *noncore* to that organization and one where the outsourcing firm has special skills, technology, and expertise to manage this work. Outsourcing is a business decision made by executives and human resource leaders. It allows the organization to save money, improve quality, or free company resources for other activities so that the organization can focus on those activities that it does best. *Offshoring,* a subset of *outsourcing,* also implies transferring jobs to another

> **outsourcing** Contracting tasks to outside agencies or persons.

country, either by hiring local subcontractors or building a facility in an area where labour is cheap.

> Outsourcing can often be a source of disruption in organizations as evidenced by the backlash toward CIBC when it announced it was outsourcing some Canadian operations to India.[62]

Human resource management plays a significant role when HR is outsourced. It must focus on service delivery and ensure that the transition is seamless. Ultimately, human resource management has direct responsibility for service quality and results, and it must manage the vendor to ensure that the service is value added and that business objectives are met.

Crowdsourcing—A Novel Way To "Source Talent" **Crowdsourcing** is a term that describes how companies meet their resource requirements by taking a function once performed by employees and outsourcing it to an undefined (and generally large) network of people in the form of an open call.

> **crowdsourcing** The act of a company or institution taking a function once performed by employees and outsourcing it to an undefined (and generally large) network of people in the form of an open call.

In this model, the organization has a need for human resources. It then communicates this need to the public via the Internet. It is an *open call* to interested parties on the web who decide, based on their own interests and their own time, whether they want to help the organization with its problem, provide a service, or fill the need in some way. A large network of potential labour exists. These individuals use their time to help the company solve their problems. The work is done outside the traditional company walls. If the organization feels that the contribution is valuable, the organization will pay the contributors for their efforts in some way.

In outsourcing, the organization typically sends out a formal *Request for Proposal (RFP),* and it reviews potential vendors before deciding on the best one. Typically, lower paid professionals do the work itself. In crowdsourcing, the problem is communicated through the net or social networks for those individuals who are interested to respond.

The main advantage of crowdsourcing is that innovative ideas can be explored at relatively low cost. Furthermore, it also helps reduce costs and makes use of the *crowd* to communicate its requirements.

> In 2014, McDonald's crowd-sourced new ideas for burgers that the public would like to see in store.[63]

Co-Sourcing A recent trend in technology and audit services is co-sourcing. Co-sourcing is a form of contracting that brings together an external team to support and work with an organization's internal team to achieve the goals of the organization. A co-sourcing model represents more of a collaboration than a contracting out of business goals.

Develop Employees Internally

Another option to be considered, which can address a shortage in human capital, looks at leveraging the current supply of existing employees within an organization. This option considers the strength of an organization's internal workforce with respect to the skills and knowledge employees possess and the future skills and knowledge employees will need for the organization to meet its human capital requirements. Organizations use various mechanisms, such as promotions and replacement charts and succession and career plans, to ascertain employees' interests, the types of training and development required, and when employees will be ready to fill a future labour requirement. Organizations utilize their internal HR-related processes to facilitate these activities, optimizing their human resources' talent pool. Chapter 7 will discuss this option in more detail.

Create Flexible Work Arrangements

The last staffing option focuses on the various types of work arrangements. A **work arrangement** refers to a firm's use of work hours, schedules, and location to ensure that the goals of the organization and the needs of employees are optimally met. We will be discussing three types

of arrangements: overtime, flexible retirement, and float and transfer.

These types of arrangements are all based on *choices:* The organization can make a choice to offer these options to the employees, and the employees make a choice whether to accept. In this reciprocal relationship, both the employer and employees typically receive a benefit as a result. For example, if employees agree to overtime, then they will receive money or time off in lieu, and the organization will be able to meets its staffing shortage.

> **work arrangement** A firm's use of work hours, schedules, and location to ensure that the goals of the organization and the needs of employees are optimally met.

Overtime A popular strategy is to ask existing employees to work beyond the normal hours. Indeed, even during a nonshortage situation, regular overtime has become a fact of life in many firms that do not want to incur additional fixed expenses of hiring permanent employees.

> In many organizations, employees—especially, supervisory and managerial staff—are expected to work overtime, most of it unpaid. The culture of the organization requires the employee to put in the extra effort without expecting any reward. This is particularly so in nonunionized settings. This, however, can have detrimental effects on employee morale.

Higher employee fatigue, stress levels, accident and wastage rates, and so on, are some of the unwanted consequences of using overtime on a recurring basis. Recognizing this fact, some progressive employers have gone against the mainstream—namely reducing the number of work hours—and ended up improving their productivity levels and competitiveness in the labour market. One U.S. manufacturer's experience is noteworthy:

> Metro Plastics Technologies Inc. in Columbus, Indiana, could not fill eight vacancies in its plant as the unemployment rate in the area hovered between one and three percent. To get a recruiting advantage, it adopted an innovative "30-hour work week for 40-hour pay" strategy under which an employee had to put in only 30 hours a week instead of the traditional 40 hours. A single newspaper ad brought hundreds of qualified applicants to the firm and the firm was able to fill the vacancies immediately. The benefits did not stop there. Within two years, customer returns had fallen by 72 percent and many internal costs had dropped dramatically. The same results have been reported in a number of other plants, in a variety of industries.[64]

Flexible Retirement Another opportunity for firms to manage shortages is to target those employees who are close to retirement with a view to extending their contributions. The challenge has been how to balance the needs of these employees with the needs of the organization. A relatively new approach to managing retirement is called **flexible retirement**. This term has been used to describe an approach to optimizing the talent of these recent retirees, thus extending their contributions and continuing their engagement in organizational activities. Called "retiree-return" programs, these programs provide retirees with the opportunity to work after they have retired and provide them with significant flexibility in terms of how they work, what they work on, when they work, and where. These programs are flexible in the sense that they take into account the retirees' needs and tailor the work accordingly. These programs typically begin prior to retirement and continue after the employee has *officially* retired. One can say that these retirees take on an *active* retiree status, whereby they continue their involvement in the organizations long after they have *officially* retired.

flexible retirement
Programs that provide retirees with the opportunity to work after they have retired and provide them with significant flexibility in terms of how they work, what they work on, when they work, and where.

The benefits are substantial as the organization will be able to retain its intellectual capital long after employees have *left* the organization. The firm will be able to retain its talent to fill unexpected gaps; institutional knowledge and transfer of this knowledge will not be lost; and the organization will be able to control its labour costs, as *retirees* do not receive any additional benefits. It is projected that phased retirement programs will double over the next several years, from 26 to 55 percent. However, employers have a duty to accommodate workers who suffer from age-related health issues as age is a protected ground from discrimination.[65]

Float And Transfer Another flexible arrangement that organizations use to manage shifts in work is to use a flexible policy that enables its full-time resources to be transferred when needed; or, if the need is for a very short time, they *float* the worker. These organizations rely on their training programs to ensure that their employees are cross-trained and that they can secure these resources when they need them and for the length of time necessary. Another term that we can use to describe this arrangement is *job rotation*. For example, Fidelity Investments Canada uses this arrangement to cover leaves and develop a talent pipeline.[66] That said, job rotation is not without its challenges.

Spotlight *on* ETHICS

Cutting Costs

Like other human resource management activities, HR planners often face ethical challenges. Consider the following two situations and respond to them. Once you have written down your answers, compare them with those of your team or classmates. Are there differences in your approaches? What facts and arguments seem to justify one action over the other?

Facing fierce price-based competition, your firm, which employs over 470 persons, has been trying to reduce costs in a variety of ways.

1. One action currently being considered is to move Production Unit 1 from its present location in an interior Canadian town to a developing country. Your manufacturing unit is the sole employer in that town and currently employs 128 persons. Most of the employees are semi-skilled and would find it hard to find employment elsewhere. You know that in the case of many employees, they are the sole breadwinner for their families. Your firm located in this town because of a variety of tax advantages and subsidies the province offered to you for the first two years of your operations. Under those terms, your firm was expected to operate for a minimum period of four years. This is your sixth year in the province.

2. Your firm is also considering converting a number of your full-time employees in the head office and Production Unit 2 to a part-time workforce. (You may assume that this is legal in the province where you are employed.) Approximately 200 persons will be affected by this plan. This can generate significant savings for your firm, since a number of benefits currently offered to full-time employees need not be offered any more to the part-timers. You realize that a number of your employees depend on the company benefits to take care of their children and the elderly in the family.

Arrangements such as the above not only enhance organizational flexibility and efficiency and help reduce costs, but also enable human resource departments to better respond to employee needs. To ensure that HR is actually achieving these goals, evaluation and measurement must be an integral part of the HRP process.

Program Measurement and Evaluation

A major goal of human resource measurement is to enhance decisions about human capital and to connect human resources to strategy. The final step in the process is to evaluate the workforce planning activities. In many ways, workforce planning assessment serves as a starting point. As noted earlier, goals must be established for workforce planning to occur. Inherent in these goals is defining what success looks like for workforce planning and how it will be measured.[67] For instance, a goal of workforce planning may be to reduce vacancy times for key roles in an organization. Alternatively, a measure of effectiveness might be the percent of internal versus external candidates who are hired within a given year. To measure human capital effectively, the planner is responsible for evaluating its processes and continuously improving on the technical and strategic aspects of this process.

> Even with the best planning, however, context may impact plans and outcomes significantly. Take Target Canada, for instance. In 2015, after posting billion dollar losses and filing for creditor protection, Target Canada moved to close all 133 Canadian locations. These closures would result in the loss of 17,600 full- and part-time jobs across the country. This represents one of the largest mass layoffs in Canadian history.[68]

Improvement must be evident from year to year based on human resource planning. To ensure continuous improvement, all processes must be measured, a baseline developed, and initiatives put in place. It is imperative that the human resource professional use key business metrics and develop a thorough understanding of how human resource planning can contribute to the bottom line. Evaluation is dependent on the criteria the organization uses to discern whether the human resource planning function is effective. Typically, processes are measured in terms of time and cost associated with their deployment. For example, a measure might be the time it took to find an appropriate resource to fill a particular position and include the cost of recruiting and time to interview.

There are a variety of mechanisms or tools that can be used to ascertain this value, and the ability to do this in a comprehensive way largely depends on the organization's level of technological sophistication and the robust nature of the tools chosen.

A 2015 *Harvard Business Review* article cited talent-related concerns as the primary issues facing CEOs.[69] It is no surprise, therefore, that human resource planning is a key function of human resource professionals. Technology influences have added further complexity to the planning environment. At the same time, technology is enabling human resource professionals to be more effective in contributing to organizational strategy and success. One such technology arena is data analytics and evidence-informed decision making. What began out of a need to support payroll in the 1940s,[70] modern day human resource information systems (HRIS) provide human resource professionals with live-time data and business intelligence to make effective decisions.

LO6 Human Resource Information Systems

A **human resource information system (HRIS)** is used to collect, record, store, analyze, and retrieve data concerning an organization's human resources. This is most often done at the enterprise level (i.e., organization wide). These systems are comprised of different software applications that work with various relational databases. All good human resource decisions require timely and accurate information. A good HRIS enables the HR department to be responsive to its customers' needs and is critical for the effective functioning of the HR department and the larger organization. The major stakeholders who use the information from an HRIS are HR professionals, managers, and employees. Each of these "customers" expects a responsive HR department that can provide accurate and timely information. The larger the organization and the more dynamic an organization's environments, the greater the need for a sophisticated HRIS.

> **human resource information system (HRIS)** A system that gathers, analyzes, summarizes, and reports important data for formulating and implementing strategies by HR specialists and line managers.

HRIS Functions—Breadth and Size

Not all HRISs are the same. In fact, there are many different systems to choose from, depending on the organizational requirements. Key considerations that organizations take into account when deciding on an appropriate HRIS to match their needs, include the following:

- The size of the organization
- What information needs to be captured
- The volume of information transmitted
- The firm's objectives
- Managerial decision needs
- The importance of reporting capability
- Technical capabilities
- Available resources

Typically, a small firm may begin with a simple HRIS as its information needs are very basic and used solely for the purposes of HR administration. The type of employee information captured may include the employee name, address, emergency contact, employment status, position held, how much the employee is paid, benefit coverage, birth date, and gender. The technology is also low tech as these firms typically use generic software applications like Excel, and their entire database is maintained on one computer or a few networked computers and in one database. The application itself is "nonrelational," meaning that information on employee name, home address, job title, pay rate, and so on, will have to be separately entered into the payroll file, the benefits file, performance appraisal records, and several other places. Any change in employee information will have to be updated separately in each file. The probability of an error in inputting information is very high in nonrelational systems. Probability of delays and inconsistencies in information updating is also higher.

As organizations grow and their information needs become more complex, they typically require a more sophisticated HRIS. These systems can vary considerably in price depending on their degree of functionality and system integration capabilities. Given the recent increase in people analytics, even large organizations find it difficult to integrate systems that cover the entire organization, including finding the talent to run them.[71]

Firms may choose an HRIS that is self-contained and relational, meaning that each HR module relates to one another. In this type of system, information about an employee only needs to be entered once. In addition, these systems have the capabilities to prevent errors and catch inconsistencies. This feature, called *referential integrity,* ensures that an organization's policies are operationalized or implemented consistently throughout the organization. Referential integrity is a very important function as it enables HR to build into the HRIS its policies and set up parameters. An example illustrates this function:

> Take sick leave. A company's policy might require a doctor's note after four days, and, in terms of pay, an employee may be entitled to 100 percent pay for four weeks and then 60 percent of pay for the balance of leave. The system will flag this parameter and a report will be generated indicating the action required. An example of a relational system with referential integrity is Sage HRMS Software.[72]

Firms may also choose what is called a "gold standard" system. These systems not only have significant relational abilities within the HR environment, but they are also part of an enterprise-wide IT infrastructure. These systems are typically found in very large organizations. They are called **enterprise-wide systems** and link an organization's entire software application environment into a single enterprise solution. This means a seamless integration of data from the various functions, such as sales, operations, distribution, and HR. This integration offers a single and shared view. Therefore, the information is not only entered once, but it is accessible within other system applications and can be viewed in real time.

enterprise-wide systems Systems that link an organization's entire software application environment into a single enterprise solution.

> For instance, an organization has decided on an annual salary increase for all employees. The information will appear instantly on the employee file and also in the general ledger within the financial module. The transaction is seamless and updated in "real time" only once. This information will appear in all appropriate tables (viewed on all permissible computer screens and resonant in the appropriate files). The system behind the HRIS will know how to use this new information for all relevant decisions affecting this employee—for example, compensation, skills listing, performance competencies, benefits, and so on.

These systems often possess several technological features. They have the ability to offer web-based and mobile applications, linking to the employer's **intranet** and databases. A common feature of a web-based system is to offer intranet applications, such as **employee self-service (ESS)** and **manager self-service (MSS)** functions. ESS allows employees to access and view their own records and make changes where applicable. An example would be updating address or banking information. MSS refers to managers being able to access their employees' records and view and add relevant information, such as a performance appraisal rating, or review their employees' performance records. In addition to these web-based applications, these systems also possess exceptional reporting capabilities and seamlessly link to payroll and benefit providers. Examples of these systems are Oracle, and its affiliated application PeopleSoft, and SAP.

intranet An organization-specific internal computer network.

employee self-service (ESS) A feature of an HRIS that allows employees to access and view their own records and make changes where applicable.

manager self-service (MSS) A feature of an HRIS that allows managers to view and access their employees' records and add relevant information.

Enterprise information management is a growing industry. In many respects, it has emerged out of the risks identified by companies in relation to the data they create, collect, and store. HRIS is a key element of enterprise information and may become a cornerstone in predictive data analytics and knowledge transfer.

Components of an HR System and Common Data Fields

The most common components of an HRIS are recruitment and applicant tracking, time and attendance, training and development, performance management, career planning, compensation, benefits and pension administration, employment equity information, performance evaluation, health and safety, and labour relations (see Figure 3-12). However, the number of data fields, where information can be stored, will largely depend on the functionality of the system. For example, within the training component some common data fields available would be the type of training an employee took, the cost of the training, the vendor who delivered the training, and the method of training delivery. Within the performance module, the data fields might be the performance appraisal rating of the employees, the actual appraisal details, and various productivity data for a particular role. Some systems allow the organization to identify which data fields are important to them while other systems have the data fields predetermined and hard coded. Having a robust data set enables HR to generate more meaningful reports. Next we will discuss the types of reporting capabilities and why this information is so important for organizational effectiveness. Examples of the types of information contained within an HRIS and common reporting capabilities of the system are shown in Figure 3-13.

Type of Outputs—Reporting Capabilities

All HRISs produce some regular reports, such as employee records, salary and benefit details, retirement benefits, and so on. However, as a firm's HRIS increases in sophistication, it goes beyond these regular reports and is able to produce special reports, answer questions interactively, and play an important role in supporting organizational decision makers.

For example, suppose an organization is considering a new dental benefit program. A sophisticated HRIS will be able to generate predictions of not only how many employees are likely to qualify for and probably accept the new program, but also how much it will cost the firm over a specific period of time and how it will affect recruitment success, employee turnover, and other relevant data.

Today, even moderately sophisticated HRISs have a number of modules that perform specific functions, such as applicant tracking, recruitment source evaluation and costing, performance appraisal recording, compensation and payroll, training records maintenance, and human resource forecasts.

For example, one Canadian university's HRIS enables the institution to pay employees and scholarship recipients; enroll and unenroll employees in benefit plans; and record all hires, terminations, leaves, and salary increases, applying all the appropriate rules that pertain. It will provide timely reports and will automatically calculate service, statutory holiday pay, sick time, vacation entitlements, and much more.[73]

Access to HRIS Information—Privacy and Security Considerations

Who should have access to the information contained in an HRIS? Obviously, HR staff and key managers should have access to all information that enables them to make informed decisions; however, this should be weighed against the need for confidentiality and the need to respect employees' privacy. Most HRISs collect and retain only the employee information needed for business or legal reasons and establish controls for internal use and external release

---

FIGURE 3-12

Components of a Human Resource Information System with Relational Features

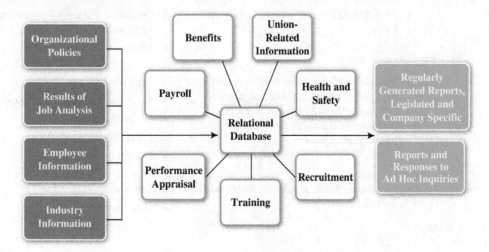

FIGURE 3-13

HRIS Database Information and Reporting Outcomes

HR Function	Typical Information Contained within an HRIS	HRIS Reporting Outcomes
HR Administration	• Employee information/demographics (all relevant data for tax and pension plan purposes, staff profiles, etc.) • Organizational data (structure, levels, reporting pattern) • HR policies	• Time and attendance data; absenteeism data • Division, department, and job categories • Employee records and employment histories • Employee positions and progressions
Compensation/ Payroll	• Pay structure • Wage/salary histories of employees • Raises received by employees • Types of benefits and choices available	• Salary budget information • Pension and retirement plan information • Benefits utilization categorized by benefit type or employee group • Cost summaries and projections of benefits programs • Job evaluation information
Recruitment & Selection	• Job postings • Job descriptions/specifications • Selection decision criteria	• Applicant tracking • Recruitment costs • Number of job postings filled • Number of external hires vs. internal promotions • Employment equity reports • Diversity statistics
Training & Development	• Types, dates offered, training records of employees, training needs of personnel, training costs	• Training data on courses and vendors • Career paths • Training ROI
Health & Safety	• Accidents, costs, tolerance limits for various dangerous substances	• Health and safety records and trends • Short- and long-term disability records
Performance Management	• Performance records, appraisals, productivity data	• Performance records—performance appraisal data • Employee rating percentages
Strategic HR Planning	• Succession plans (skills, specialties, work experience, performance record, promotion capabilities of employees), career planning—job families (jobs, number, training needs, salary)	• Turnover indices • Employee movements/redeployments • Skills inventories • Succession plans • Human resource plans
Labour Relations	• Grievances (types, frequency, decisions by adjudicator)	• Union contract details • Grievance statistics • Costing models

of this information. Sensitive information—such as security and medical reports, investigative and grievance files, insurance and benefit records, information related to performance and disciplinary actions, and so on—should be tightly protected and offered to persons only on a *need-to-know* basis. The decision about who should have the right to change input data is also critical. On the one hand, restricting data entry to a few persons can improve consistency and prevent errors; on the other hand, it can also result in delays and a complete lack of flexibility.

A key feature of any HRIS is how effective it is at providing the tools with which to manage these security issues. The more robust systems enable the organization to set up "security profiles." These profiles are based on "role" and whether the holder of the role can *view* the information or *change* it and what *data fields* are accessible. For example, what information can an HR consultant, payroll staff, or manager view? Should these roles have the ability to view or change information? Consider social insurance numbers. The only role that can view this number is the employee and the payroll department. What about banking information? The only role that can view and change this information would be the payroll department, once the employee provides the appropriate documentation. An employee will be able to view it, but only payroll can change it. Consider emergency contact information. Should a manager, HR, and payroll have access to this information? Security profiles take a lot of time to create and to set up, but they are critical to ensure that proper security measures are in place.

LO7 HRIS—An Important Tool for Strategic HRM

As previously noted, the major stakeholders who use the information from HRISs are HR professionals, managers in each functional area, and the employees. With the increasing need for HR professionals to meet the needs of all its stakeholders, HR professionals recognize the importance of leveraging the system capabilities to deliver greater value-added services. By leveraging the automation and system capabilities, HR professionals can spend more time working at the strategic level rather than at the transactional level. As a result, the HR role has evolved in several ways to enhance its service delivery to the organization. There are several ways that illustrate HR's transformation.

Increased Efficiency—Enhanced Service Delivery

Advances in technology have enabled HR to decrease its involvement in administrative transactions and compliance requirements. HR has successfully automated the day-to-day activities and, where possible, downloaded the data entry at the source. It has established applicable security

profiles and assigned relevant roles, identified key reporting criteria, developed meaningful reporting practices, and purchased applications that implemented self-service options using web-based technology. Not only is the information more readily available, but it is more accurate, timely, and accessible. As a result, HR is better equipped to provide *just-in-time* service delivery to all its stakeholders on an as-needed basis. Consider this example:

> When employees need to change their address or their emergency contact information in a system that has a self-service option, these employees no longer have to contact anyone, fill in any paperwork, or get approvals. They simply log on to the system into their employee file, enter the new information, and save it. The payroll department will automatically have an updated address so that the pay stub can be sent to the correct address and the HR department will automatically have the correct emergency contact in case a need arises.

Increased Effectiveness—Helping Stakeholders Make Better Decisions

Fewer transactions means that the HR department can focus more on strategic issues. Now HR has the time to focus on understanding which HR metrics are important to help the organization achieve its business goals and objectives. Choosing the appropriate data and analyzing them has become an integral part of how HR helps managers make better decisions. Using predictive analysis, HR helps managers to detect trends. **Predictive analysis** is the process of selecting, exploring, analyzing, and modelling data to create better business outcomes. From this system, HR can collect applicable information, analyze it, and use it to *predict* how best to address future events, develop future strategies, or manage human resource–related issues. Consider how HR data can be used to help managers make better decisions.

> **predictive analysis** The process of selecting, exploring, analyzing, and modelling data to create better business outcomes.

> Organizations such as DBS Bank in Singapore utilize HRIS data to increase productivity, reduce turnover, and recruit more effectively.[74] Similarly, HR technology companies are creating HRIS to increase retention and performance through machine learning solutions.[75]

Increased Contribution to Organizational Sustainability—Talent Management

Throughout the text we refer to how important it is for organizations to value their human resources and to effectively manage their talent, optimizing the skills and competencies resonant within the firm. The term *talent management* was coined by McKinsey and Company in 1997 and appeared in its report on the "War on Talent." This report took into account a number of HR processes critical for organizational sustainability. **Talent management** refers to "a systemic attraction, identification, development, engagement/retention and deployment of those individuals with high potential who are of particular value to the organization."[76]

> **talent management** "A systemic attraction, identification, development, engagement/retention, and deployment of those individuals with high potential who are of particular value to the organization."

The information that is generated from the HRIS helps managers and HR leverage these employees' capabilities and skills and design opportunities for development. A robust HRIS, such as SAP and PeopleSoft, will possess several development modules, such as Career Planning, Succession Planning, and Training & Development. On the infrastructure side, HR can populate these modules with career paths and the corresponding skills and competencies needed. They can create replacement charts and succession models and then generate a list of employees who have the skills and are ready to move into the next role, or they can generate what type of development would be appropriate for these individuals to pursue. The opportunity to use this information to ensure that the organization can deploy its high-potential workforce when needed is invaluable to organizational sustainability, especially as organizations manage unforeseen challenges. We will discuss talent management in more detail in Chapter 7.

Increased Visibility—Enhanced HR Competencies

Not only has technology enabled HR to provide greater value-added services, but it has also afforded the HR professional the opportunity to interact at a more sophisticated level with client groups regarding their business informational needs. Clients expect HR to possess knowledge of their financial and strategic business challenges and to explore the various technological solutions that will meet their needs. This expectation has enabled HR to demonstrate a greater degree of professionalism and has raised the credibility of human resource professionals' knowledge within the organization.[77] In addition, HR has had to work with IT departments to integrate and maintain these systems. This has resulted in HR becoming more technologically savvy, gaining greater credibility with IT departments, and working with IT as a strategic business partner instead of using it as a service department.

Human Resource Accounting

More recently, some organizations have considered examining the impact of human resource capital development in organizations using a financial model. This approach considers "human resources" as an asset and an investment and measures from a financial perspective the return of those investments.[78] This value is quantified using a process method called **human resource accounting (HRA)**. HRA is the process of identifying, measuring, accounting, and forecasting the value of human resources in order to facilitate effective management of an organization.[79] HRA attempts to put a dollar figure on the human assets of an organization using a cost or a value model. The cost model is based on some kind of cost calculation—acquisition, replacement, or opportunity costs—while the value-based models strive to evaluate human resources on the basis of their economic value to the organization.

> **human resource accounting (HRA)** A process to measure the present cost and value of human resources as well as their future worth to the organization.

HRA is a managerial tool that can help managers make better decisions. It can be a blessing to salary administrators, trainers, human resource planners, and union–management negotiators if it provides them with the kind of objective and reliable information they have long needed to plan these functions.

Spotlight on HRM

Dedicated to Diversity

By Sarah Dobson

We talked to five CEOs to get their take on diversity at work.

Bill McFarland CEO and senior partner of PwC

The professional services firm has 6,000 employees in Canada

Bill McFarland, CEO and senior partner of PricewaterhouseCoopers (PwC), grew up with three older, "way smarter" sisters, he says, so he learned early in life about the talent available. That may be part of the reason why he has made diversity and inclusion priorities at the 6,000-employee professional services firm based in Toronto.

"It really means creating an environment at PwC where people feel safe to voice their opinion, they're inspired and empowered to bring their best and, I'll call it, real selves to work every day, and use the rich and different experiences and perspectives that they have to team together on client projects. So really it's about the firm and all of our people having the opportunity to meet their full potential," he says. "Our goal at PwC would be to acknowledge, respect and thrive off each other's differences, whether that's gender, religion, sexual identity or race."

Diversity is also good for business, he says.

"If you bring together different people with different experiences and you team them together, you're going to come up with better ideas which will help us provide more value to our clients, which will ultimately lead to better people and a better bottom line."

Even customers will point out the need for diversity, as one client did years ago, saying: "Well Bill, if you have three white males on the cover of a proposal, you shouldn't really expect to win that work," says McFarland. "We strongly believe we need to mirror within PwC the communities in which we work."

McFarland also made a point to change the management structure when he came on board by having a broader group.

"It allows me to have more diversity, be more inclusive and have very different perspectives, and I can tell you we have very different conversations today than we had historically at the executive team level."

And PwC has focused on educating partners and employees about diversity and inclusion, he says, "both from a fairness perspective to our people, and from a business case perspective."

That's meant training around unconscious bias.

"We all have biases, we may not be aware of them, and we need to become aware of them so that we treat people fairly. So that was a key part, and that is still continuing today," says McFarland.

PwC is also a founding impact champion for the United Nations' HeForShe initiative.

"It empowers both men and women to take an online pledge that confirms their support for gender diversity, and we have close to 2,000 of our men at PwC Canada who have taken that pledge, so I'm really proud of that fact; that tells you it also resonates with a broad group within our staff and our people—but it also says we've got more work to do."

Members of the extended leadership team each sponsor two women to make sure they're having the right experiences and opportunities at the firm.

"In our succession planning process, we look at whether we have diverse candidates for each senior position, and we also have worked hard at taking the unconscious bias out of promotion and compensation decisions," he says.

PwC Canada also set a goal of 50-50 gender parity for new partner admits by 2020, says McFarland.

"That promotes a different level of dialogue, is the way I'd put it, and actively managing our partner pipeline and our talent mix. And I think that's been extremely well-received by our people, and the business community and it ties back to (the fact) we hire slightly over 50 per cent females, and so, therefore, we should be reflecting that in ultimately who ends up as partners in the firm."

As for any backlash or resentments, it's more about making sure diversity stays a priority.

"We have lots of priorities in big businesses; therefore, people are always wondering, 'Is this the flavour of the day or how do I know this is actually important?' and they're watching very closely," he says.

"The leadership commitment is one of the most important things—that tone from the top."

It's also about having the backbone to call out bad behaviour, such as bias in hiring decisions, says McFarland.

"These are all tests of leadership, and our staff and our partners take the cues on how we respond to those over a period of time, so it isn't about one day, it's about having a consistent approach over the longer term."

(Continued)

Sue Tomney CEO of YWCA Calgary
The women's organization has about 350 employees

As an organization that began with a focus on women, diversity should come naturally to the YWCA Calgary. But diversity is more of an evolving culture piece, according to Sue Tomney, CEO.

"It's so expansive. It's around gender, age, religion, mental health, economic viability, so really for us, it even goes past culture, it's more of a mindset of how we approach our work, and it's really about continuing to change. And it has always had to be something that's been responsive in terms of how it relates to our community, not only our employees but our clients, so it is just forever evolving."

A focus on diversity has always been there, but it hasn't been overt, says Tomney.

"We're an organization that serves such a diverse spectrum of clients, it can be easy for us to become the shoemaker's children, so it's more we look at diversity around our clients and how best we're serving them and then tend not to look inward in terms of how we're evolving as an organization, as a group of employees. So I think that this is something just in the last six to 12 months that we said, 'Boy, we'd better be paying attention to this as much internally as we are externally,'" she says.

"Without being intentional, it's very easy for us to take our eye off the ball."

As a social services agency, the YWCA can be so focused on the client that it doesn't pause and understand what it's doing itself, says Tomney.

"We are constantly trying to help them and we forget we have to do work here. That's a real mind shift, and I think it's exacerbated by having a large female staff . . . women put themselves last a lot of time, so there has to be discipline in making sure we pay attention to how we operate as a team."

Diversity has to start at the top, and that means the board, particularly in the not-for-profit sector, she says.

"They really set the tone and so it needs to be something that's clearly understood and something that is practised there. There's more opportunity for rigour that way because boards have terms that expire, and new board members that come in, so it's a more ongoing process, whereas employees may be here for 20 years."

Leadership buy-in has to be there, and sometimes that means recognizing you're not making progress or there are still some obstacles, says Tomney. "Everybody needs to be accountable to someone."

It's about using a diversity lens in informing all of the organization's work, she says.

"Then, we're actually able to achieve the culture of inclusion, which is what we talk about: 'Inclusion for our clients, are we doing that here?'"

That means looking at recruitment and onboarding, and striving to continually improve, says Tomney. Diversity is also a strength because it ensures the YWCA will continue to be relevant and serve the needs of the community.

"We're an old broad, we're 106 years old, and we feel like we're still young but that's because we continue to reflect the needs of the community, so the way to do that is ensuring we are diverse."

Some of the more tangible initiatives around diversity include a culture statement created in 2014, done with input from employees, along with a practice framework created in 2015 that talks about the importance of issues such as language, ethnicity and economic and mental health status, she says.

It's also about ensuring policies and benefits reflect the diversity of the workforce, as people are in different stages of their life or have different family circumstances, says Tomney.

"It's less about 'Oh, what's the cost of the dental plan?' and it's more around 'How do our benefits, how do our vacation and time off reflect who we are, and ensure that . . . there are choices for our employees because of our diversity?'"

Age is another area of diversity that's starting to become more of an issue, says Tomney, with many people working longer.

"You have now arguably four different generations in any workplace, so the needs are different there on how people view things . . . and I think it makes us a richer organization as a result. We have to realize there are different needs and wants when you're in a different age bracket, and different motivators."

When it comes to measuring diversity, the YWCA is working on benchmarking and tracking but, anecdotally, it can be striking to see the diversity at meetings, she says.

"It's really exciting, it says we are paying attention to our hiring practices."

When it comes to challenges around diversity, there's the danger of getting caught in a perception of fairness, and it's about understanding that it's equity versus equality, she says.

"Equity means having the same opportunities for a fair outcome, so that's where it can be challenging."

Generally, feedback on diversity is positive, but where it gets challenging is the fact that diversity means different things to different people, says Tomney.

"You could come in here and say we're not as diverse as we need to be strictly from gender, and a lot of that is because of the type of agency we are."

As a 106-year-old organization with a solid reputation, there's farther to fall, she says.

"It doesn't take much to take that down . . . that's why we know we have to continually look at this because there's a lot to lose."

Mike Mallen Acting CEO of the Museum of Vancouver
The non-profit organization has about 35 employees

Mike Mallen, acting CEO of the Museum of Vancouver, has worked at much larger organizations, with tens of thousands of employees but, in a way, focusing on diversity at a smaller workplace like the museum can be more challenging, he says.

"You interact with everyone on a daily basis, and they challenge you because if you say you're going to do something and it's not done . . . they hold me to task . . . I expect the same from them as from me . . . they don't let me off the hook," says Mallen. "They see you every day, and they see you live those values or you don't. So, in some ways, it's more difficult."

A lot of what the Museum of Vancouver does is project-based, and to tell a story properly, it's important to hire the right people for the work, he says.

"It's important to go back and say, 'We need people from the community to tell the stories, and not just the people here.'"

But since the museum can't always have someone full-time, it's about making a point to hire appropriately. For example, the museum is looking to do an exhibition on the Chinese-Canadian experience, primarily around immigration, so it's looking to hire a Chinese-Canadian curator "to help us understand what's important to the community," he says.

But taking that approach can be hard.

"We're trying to hire for a finite amount of time, so trying to find the right person at the right time can be a challenge," says Mallen.

Much of the museum's renewed focus on community comes from the board. About two years ago, one of the museum's mandates was to reshape the board, which led to a "very interesting and very strong mix that we hadn't seen in a long time," says Mallen.

And the board chair, Jill Tipping, has made a point to look at finding people not just from the museum community but different businesses and areas, he says.

"When you start looking at our board, it's diverse through gender, we have First Nations, we have people from the academic side of things, people from the business community, we have lawyers—it's such a different group of people . . . who are able to offer different perspectives and guidance when it comes to how we hire externally and how we hire for projects."

This year, the Museum of Vancouver also hired a permanent First Nations associate curator.

"It's been so uplifting for staff to see it's not a one-time (hire), it's something that's resonating throughout the organization—from education, public programming, hiring, even the gift shop, ethically. It's really brought a realness to it. (If it's) project-based, it can really fall apart if you don't live it every day, and it's always interesting to hear someone's perspective who's there and can understand it and connect the dots."

Gentil Mateus CEO of CSSEA
The Community Social Services Employers Association of BC has 23 employees

Born in Portugal, Gentil Mateus has many employees who are also first-generation immigrants. As CEO of CSSEA (the Community Social Services Employers Association of BC), he thinks it's important that the makeup of the organization reflects the larger society in which it operates and, to a certain extent, its client base.

"For me, that's what diversity means, is that people can identify with the people who are

(Continued)

working in the organization . . . and you're more likely to be sensitive to the needs and aspirations and the challenges of the community you serve," says Mateus, in Vancouver.

Diversity also enhances an organization in providing different viewpoints and perspectives when tackling an issue or developing a strategy.

"I've seen organizations where leaders surround themselves with people who think like they think and they have the same cultural background and I always try to do the opposite of that—I actually want people that think differently than I do, bring different perspectives to the table—and together it usually makes for better outcomes," he says.

But there will be times when people's suggestions are not accepted or adopted. Then, it's a matter of leadership circling back to thank the people and say their opinions are still valued, says Mateus.

"It requires more thoughtfulness in how you interact with staff."

However, by and large, diversity has been "quite a bit of a passive exercise," he says, in the sense of being aware of the makeup of his workforce, but "not necessarily prescriptive."

"I always surround myself with the best people—regardless of race, gender, religion, colour—because I feel comfortable with that, and it makes for better outcomes, so it's never really been an issue," says Mateus, citing as an example his recent decision to hire a lawyer who held quite different viewpoints than him.

"For me it's more 'Be alive, be connected to the people you serve and the community you work in, and does your organization by and large reflect that?'"

Employers will be more successful with diversity if they truly believe in it, instead of being forced to adopt it and put in place a policy, he says.

"If you do value diversity, you will inevitably surround yourself with people of diverse backgrounds, so if you honestly truly believe that, then you more often than not are going to be fostering a culture of diversity . . . it almost happens organically."

Leadership needs to articulate the values they want to promote and foster within the organization, and be clear and transparent.

"Where organizations fall short is that their words and actions do not match, or they're often incongruent, and when managers and others see the incongruency in the words and actions of leadership, it's almost permission for them to do whatever they want," he says.

"It starts first and foremost with valuing diversity, and then recruitment is just the means by which you ensure those values manifest themselves in the organization."

And that doesn't mean hiring "tokens," says Mateus.

"First of all, you started from the wrong premise, as far as I'm concerned, and there's an inherently prejudicial bias that goes into the decision-making," he says.

"I know you can legislate or create policies about certain stuff, but it's so much better if you actually believe what you're doing instead of it being forced upon you or the organization."

And the inclusion part of the equation is important. That means flexibility, for example, when people make requests around accommodation, as organizations are often more rigid than they need to be, he says.

But it's also about communication to avoid any potential backlash, says Mateus.

"The piece that you need to circle back is make sure folks in the organization, to the extent possible . . . are aware everybody is being treated equally—and that doesn't mean the same because some may have different needs than others, and that's OK—but people need to feel if they have a similar concern, they would be given the same consideration."

Leigh-Anne Palter CEO of Chestermere Utilities

The utility is based in Chestermere, Alta., and has 30 employees

As a woman who's only ever worked in roles considered non-traditional for her gender, Leigh-Anne Palter knows well the value of diversity.

"Diversity is everything," says the CEO of Chestermere Utilities.

Back when Palter started working in the 1990s at a large natural gas utility, diversity was about creating respectful workplaces for women—such as taking down pin-up calendars in the receiving docks.

But at its core, diversity is recognizing the importance of having differences, and being very deliberate about it, she says.

"There's a human nature in all of us that we like to spend time with the people who are most like us, and that can be great for cocktail hours or after-hours type activities, but I don't believe it brings the best results to organizations. And if you're mindful about that, and challenge yourself to think outside of your comfort zone when you're looking at adding team members, (it's about being) very deliberate about making sure that you're really checking all the boxes in terms of the organization's needs."

Along with gender, diversity can be about experience or socioeconomic or educational differences, she says. Palter, for example, spent time in executive recruitment and has done a lot of board work.

"It's fascinating to watch the dynamic," she says as, more often than not, diversity meant hiring more women and visible minorities. But once that was achieved, the companies found the decision-making hadn't really improved and they weren't attracting more representative groups.

"You sit down and say to them 'All you've done is brought on more people exactly like you—you haven't really dug down deep and done the hard work around diversity, and so a whole bunch of middle-class people, irrespective of their gender or skin colour, isn't really diversity because you all share a degree at a post-secondary and you all enjoy the same means of life, and struggle with the same things.'"

But diversity can make for tough dynamics at the leadership table.

"You think about (for example) how to be inclusive of First Nations peoples—they have very different interaction styles, and for your traditional board or your traditional leadership team of a utility, (it's about being) committed to understanding what does that mean and how do you have to adapt, how do you make your organization welcoming to the kind of diversity you want?" says Palter.

And since she joined the utility two years ago, things have changed.

"We've completely turned things over. We have first-generation Canadians, we have young people, we have some folks who are returning for third careers, so they're bringing lots of experience, we have (LGBTQ) folks as part of our team, and people who speak different languages," she says. "We look more like the community that we serve."

But there can be backlash, as Palter has seen at much larger organizations. When there was a women's leadership lunch, for example, people would ask if there would be a similar event for men.

"Sadly, that's to be expected—people start feeling threatened when there's deliberate action," she says.

Leadership is everything because people will model the behaviours that are expected of them, says Palter.

"There's nothing worse than having a leadership team where maybe the CEO and typically the senior vice-president of HR say, 'This is important, this is what we're going to do,' and yet other leadership team members say, 'Ah, this'll die soon' or they're not being held accountable."

It's important to hire leaders with qualities that say, "This is part of who we are," says Palter. It's also about challenging each other and in the hiring process, making sure people are involved from different areas.

"You're forcing diversity into the conversation just by the fact of not having people of the same background making hiring decisions."

And maintaining that drive requires focus every single day.

"Once you get a critical mass in organizations, it can become self-sustaining, it becomes the way that you do things," she says.

But one of the challenges is the inclusion side, says Palter. It might be great, for example, to hire a woman who speaks two different languages, but if people can't understand her on the phone, then the employer has to figure out a way to make that work.

"It's a constant—I wouldn't say it's a struggle—but it has to be a constant point of focus. If (for example) you say you want young, professional women in the workplace, you have to acknowledge they're also the ones having babies, so how do you create a workplace where they feel like they can have both? It's about creating flexible work schedules and understanding kids get sick and they need to call from home for meetings. Lots of people say it but then they don't adapt the expectations of the workplace."

SOURCE: Sarah Dobson, "Dedicated to diversity: We talked to five CEOs to get their take on diversity at work," *Canadian HR Reporter,* October 30, 2017. Reprinted by permission of Canadian HR Reporter. © Copyright Thomson Reuters Canada Ltd. (2017), Toronto, Ontario, 1-800-387-5164. Web: http://Human.hrreporter.com

SUMMARY

Human resource planning is a proactive approach to ensuring that the organization has the right people at the right place with the right skills at the right time and in the right environment. The human resource planning process signals the beginning of an organization's ability to "manage its talent." The planning process directs the organization to decide what talent it needs and suggests several ways in which to source that talent. It is an attempt by companies to estimate their future needs and supplies of human resources as well as the business processes to effectively enable that talent.

Through an understanding of the factors that influence the demand for workers, workforce planners can forecast specific short- and long-term needs. Given some anticipated level of demand, planners try to estimate the availability of present workers, both internal and external to the organization, to meet that demand. Such estimates begin with an audit of present employees. Possible replacements are then identified. Internal shortages are resolved by seeking new employees in the external labour markets. Surpluses are reduced by normal attrition, leaves of absence, layoffs, or terminations. Both external and internal staffing strategies can be used to meet human resource needs.

Planners use various tools to gather information and analyze the data, such as HRIS and HRA, so that they can provide meaningful information to their stakeholders. Effective use of technology has afforded HR the opportunity to demonstrate enhanced service delivery and offer greater strategic services to its stakeholder.

The HR plan can be considered as a *road map* for HR professionals, as it directs the recruitment, selection, and training and development processes. Once HR professionals understand an organization's human resource needs and available supply, then they will be able to decide how best to recruit that resource and establish the framework for the selection criteria. Once onboard, employees' capabilities will need to be understood and their talents and skills optimized so they can perform effectively. Future value-added contributions will depend on how the organization develops its employees and successfully aligns its needs with its employees' developmental paths. Talent management is an important HR activity to ensure organizational sustainability. Later, in Chapter 5, Chapter 6, and Chapter 7, we will discuss those HR functions that support effective talent management processes.

Before that, it is important to study the impact of governmental policies on a firm's human resource policies and practices. This will be attempted in the next chapter.

TERMS FOR REVIEW

attrition 81
Canadian Occupational Projection System (COPS) 79
consultants 83
contract (or contingent) worker 83
crowdsourcing 84
Delphi technique 71
employee self-service (ESS) 88
enterprise-wide systems 88
extrapolation 71
flexible retirement 86
forecasts 69
full-time employees 83
human resource accounting (HRA) 92
human resource information system (HRIS) 87
human resource planning 66
indexation 72
intranet 88
job sharing 82

labour market analysis 76
labour shortage 82
management or leadership inventory 74
manager self-service (MSS) 88
Markov analysis 76
nominal group technique 71
outplacement 81
outsourcing 84
part-time employees 82
phased retirement 81
predictive analysis 91
replacement charts 75
replacement summaries 76
skills inventories 74
staffing table 72
talent management 92
transition matrices 76
work arrangement 85

SELF-ASSESSMENT EXERCISE

How Do External Supplies Affect Your Chosen Career?

Consider the job you plan to search for after graduation. (If you are already working and do not plan to leave your present job, you can look at the job rank [or grade] you want to have in five years after graduation.) This self-test involves looking at the external labour market and forming conclusions about how it affects your career. If you are not familiar with the labour market conditions, you may have to conduct an Internet search to identify answers to the following questions. You can start with Statistics Canada and Employment and Social Development Canada websites but need not restrict your search to these. Once you have done this, please respond to the following statements.

Statement	Strongly Agree	Agree	Undecided	Disagree	Strongly Disagree
1. The way the job is done is significantly affected by technological changes.					
2. The growth rate in the number of jobs in this profession/job category is more than rate of employment growth rate.					
3. The career/job position I aspire to is likely to be found attractive by persons in all age and social groups.					
4. Because of demographic changes, there are fewer persons like me likely to be applying for a job/career such as the one I am aspiring to.					
5. The job position I have in mind is a glamorous or high-paying one.					
6. Most persons in my age or socioeconomic group are unlikely to apply for the job position that I have in mind.					
7. The job I have in mind is likely to be found attractive by even individuals who live thousands of kilometres away.					
8. The location or the nature of the job may make it unattractive to persons who live in other provinces.					
9. Currently the unemployment rate in this job category is over 6 percent.					
10. There is hardly any unemployment in this job category, especially if a person is prepared to relocate.					

SCORING

For statements 1, 3, 5, 7, and 9, assign a score of 5, 4, 3, 2, and 1 for Strongly Agree, Agree, Undecided, Disagree, and Strongly Disagree, respectively. For statements 2, 4, 6, 8, and 10, assign a score of 1, 2, 3, 4, and 5 for Strongly Agree, Agree, Undecided, Disagree, and Strongly Disagree. Add up the scores for all 10 statements.

INTERPRETATION

The total score may lie anywhere between 10 and 50. If the score is 33 or higher, you are aspiring for a job position that is very much in demand and likely to be found attractive by a large number of persons. This means that you have to equip yourself with additional competencies or unique skills to be attractive to employers. Even if the total score is lower, changes in economy or technology may change the picture considerably any time in the future!

REVIEW AND DISCUSSION QUESTIONS

1. What are the key steps in workforce planning in organizations? Which of your actions, if any, would be different if you were planning human resources for a smaller firm (that employs fewer than 50 persons in all) instead of a larger firm (which has 500 employees)?

2. What are staffing tables and replacement charts? Of what use are they to a human resource manager?

3. Discuss any three techniques for estimating the demand for human resources. Provide examples where relevant.

4. What are some popular approaches to match the supply and demand of human resources? Briefly discuss two approaches (each) for situations when demand exceeds and is less than supply of human resources, highlighting their advantages and limitations.

5. "Alternate work arrangements are useful approaches for both the employer and the employee." Discuss.

6. What are some of the security considerations organizations must understand when implementing a human resource information system? Provide an example of one way that security profiles are set up.

CRITICAL THINKING QUESTIONS

1. Suppose a workforce planner estimated that due to several technological innovations your firm will need 25 percent fewer employees in three years. What actions would you take today?

2. Suppose you managed a restaurant in a winter resort area. During the summer it was profitable to keep the business open, but you needed only half of the cooks, table servers, and bartenders that you employed during the winter. What actions would you take in April when the peak tourist season ended?

3. If your company locates its research and development offices in downtown Windsor, Ontario, the city is willing to forgo city property taxes on the building for 10 years. The city is willing to make this concession to help reduce its high unemployment rate. Edmonton, Alberta, your company's other choice, has a low unemployment rate and is not offering any tax breaks. Based on just these considerations, which city would you recommend and why?

4. Assume you are the human resource manager in a Canadian university employing approximately 300 faculty members. Since these faculty members constitute a "valuable" resource of your organization, you decide to install an accounting procedure for changes in the value of this asset. How will you go about it? What problems do you anticipate in the process?

5. For a high-tech organization where the job specifications and customer needs continually change, which of the forecasting techniques discussed in the text are likely to be relevant? Why?

6. Some fire departments and hospital staff are using the 3-day, 36-hour schedule. Do you see any negative aspects to this schedule?

7. Assume you work for a firm that employs 30 managerial and 70 clerical/sales employees. As a cost-cutting strategy, your firm is forced to terminate the services of 10 percent of your managers and 5 percent of your clerical staff. What specific actions will you take to help the departing employees?

ETHICS QUESTION

Two months ago, you joined Canada Construction and Design Incorporated, an engineering firm that designs and builds large residential and office complexes, as its human resource manager. Of the 320 employees in the firm, 84 are engineers with various specializations. You find that engineers work routinely for 60–70 hours a week, often taking their work home or coming to the office even on the weekends or in the late evenings. Under the firm's job classification, the engineers are considered to be managerial or supervisory and hence not eligible for any overtime benefits. You also recognize that the culture of the organization expects people, especially managerial and supervisory staff, to put in extra effort. While there is no formal rule requiring overtime, it is clear that "nonperforming" engineers do not receive promotions or even merit increases. You are concerned about the impact of the current setup on the long-term mental health and family welfare of the engineers, yet don't know whether you should "make waves" so soon after your arrival in the firm. However, you feel that it is morally wrong to make an individual work without giving any rewards.

What actions, if any, will you take? Why?

RESEARCH EXERCISE

Visit the websites of agencies such as Statistics Canada and ESDC and identify trends in employment and occupational demand patterns for the following positions in one Western and one Atlantic province: electricians, fishers, nurses, and blue-collar workers in the pulp and paper industry.

What patterns do you see? What are the implications for students about to graduate from high school this year? For employers? Compare your findings and present your summary findings to the class.

INCIDENT 3-1

Case Incident: Temporary Foreign Workers

Canada's Temporary Foreign Worker (TFW) program was designed to bring workers to Canada from other countries to fill urgent, short-term job vacancies when domestic workers can not be found. Recent data suggests that about 35 percent of foreign workers stay five years or longer, and an overwhelming majority of those eventually become permanent residents. Recent data also suggests that there is a weak correlation between the presence and length of stay of temporary workers and unemployment levels in various parts of Canada. Thus, it may be that TFWs are not just acting as a "last resource" for employers who can not find domestic workers.

At present, there are inconsistencies in how the TFW program is enacted across Canada. Regional inconsistencies mean that the same worker might be able to stay in one part of the country but must return to his or her home country after a year when in another part of the country. Meanwhile, Canada has targets of the number of immigrants it hopes to attract into the country.

It seems there is a direction decision for Canada to make. One one hand, if temporary workers are only meant to fill extreme short-term shortages, then one year maximums could be imposed across the country. On the other hand, if temporary workers are another source of

permanent residents, then paths for temporary workers to become permanent residents should be made across all TFW categories.

For more information, see https://globalnews.ca/news/3993108/temporary-foreign-workers-canada-unemployment/

DISCUSSION QUESTIONS

1. If temporary workers are allowed to apply for permanent residency after one year of work, how will this impact other new immigrants who may have less experience in Canadian workplaces?

2. If temporary workers are restricted to one-year terms but employers seek an ongoing supply of trained and readily available foreigners, should employers be forced to provide training to domestic workers who are not in post-secondary education?

3. What is the impact of the TFW program on underemployed and unemployed domestic youth? What is the impact of permanent economic immigrants on those same youths?

WE CONNECTIONS: BALANCING EMPLOYEE SUPPLY AND DEMAND

A Run to Clear Her Head

The sun was just coming up as Selina, co-founder of WEC, stepped onto the trail and inserted her ear buds. She took a quick glance at her watch in order to track her time.

The loop she was going to follow was about eight kilometers, and she was hoping she could finish it in about 45 minutes, which would be a stretch. As with most things in her life, she liked to challenge herself. As she started her run, she felt grateful for the relative quiet. All she could hear was her music and the sound of her feet hitting the ground in a steady fashion, one in front of the other: bam, bam, bam. Occasionally, sounds from the city would break in—a horn or a siren—but these were few and far between, and Selina had trained herself to filter them out. Outside, moving, wrestling with big problems in her mind—this was her happy place.

For the first several minutes, Selina tried not to think about anything except running the trail. She focused on her pace and her breath to get herself into a good rhythm. As she got further into her run, she allowed thoughts from the back of her mind to come forward to claim her attention. As the vice-president of operations at WEC, there were always thorny issues to wrestle with. Her partnership with Alex was, like many other founding duos, complementary. He was the "idea person," he thought big picture, while she excelled at implementing their plans. But making things happen was not always easy. Thinking through tough problems as she ran was a strategy that she had developed years before. She found that being alone with dilemmas and giving herself time to mull them over was a great way to find innovative solutions.

When she eventually opened up her mind to work issues, the problem that jumped forward first was a persistent one. It had been resurfacing over the past couple of weeks, and Selina felt that she needed to do something, but she had not been able to figure out what. The problem was connected to their employee base. WEC had grown quickly, and she had to admit that the company didn't always look long term when adding positions.

Oversupply

A year earlier there had been several projects that required heavy administrative support. Although the majority of contracts relied mostly on programmers, several projects had come in that needed a large amount of data entry. Instead of using highly paid programmers to complete these tasks, Selina and the team had calculated data entry speeds divided into the total quantity of data entry along with the timeline requirements and had determined that the workload could be handled by six administrative personnel. She had tasked Charlotte with hiring the additional six administrative positions, and it had worked out very well. These staff members had made a substantial contribution. Each was considered a strong worker and well-liked. However, those projects were almost completed, and the new projects that had come in since their hiring did not require a lot of data entry. Selina was well aware that within the next month or two, there would only be enough work for about two of these employees. WEC was always getting new projects, so it was possible that greater need would arise over the coming year. It was just difficult to know for sure. Selina didn't know what she should do.

Undersupply

In a related issue, Selina knew that there would be a need for the addition of new technical talent in the coming months for a couple of upcoming projects that required expertise the company currently did not have in-house. By her calculations, WEC would need three new developers with experience in blockchain technology. It would probably require this talent for eight months on a full-time basis. Normally, Selina would simply approve the hires and assume that she could find work for the employees afterwards, but after struggling with the administrative overstaffing, she didn't want to make the same mistake twice.

The Long and Winding Road

Options for dealing with these two problems swirled around her in mind. Selina grimaced when she saw that she was almost back to her starting point on the trail. She didn't feel any closer to knowing what to do. She knew that as soon as she got to the office, email messages, texts, and meetings would pull at her attention. Selina sighed as she began to slow down her pace, dejected that she had not found the answers she wanted. Suddenly it occurred to her that perhaps this wasn't a puzzle that she could work out on her own. She realized that it might help to bounce ideas around with WEC's HR specialist. Charlotte had been trained in dealing with people. That is why they had hired her, after all. Although, if she was being honest, sometimes Selina worried that maybe they should have hired a more experienced HR person. Charlotte was bright, but sometimes she struggled with knowing how to handle the complicated people issues. Nevertheless, Selina felt that a good starting point would be to connect with Charlotte about this. With her mind turning back to her run, Selina smiled as she glanced at her watch and then sprinted the last hundred yards with a feeling of satisfaction. She hadn't landed on the answer she was hoping for, but the run had helped her figure out what to do next. Sometimes that was enough.

DISCUSSION QUESTIONS

1. Imagine that you are Charlotte and that Selina asks for your help with (1) the administrative staff oversupply issue, and (2) the developer undersupply issue. Outline potential strategies that could be used to deal with each of these issues.

2. From the potential strategies outlined in your response to the first discussion question, offer your recommendations regarding the best solution(s) for Selina to pursue.

In the next installment of the WE Connections story (at the end of Chapter 4), the HR staff manage a diversity issue as they react to allegations of sexual harassment and discrimination in the company.

CASE STUDY

InfoServe

Planning for Human Resource Needs

Steve is the Western Canada regional manager for InfoServe. InfoServe has been contracted by a national car dealership company to provide multi-media information and support services for its vehicle maintenance and repair clients. The team at InfoServe responds to questions and inquiries about vehicle problems and troubleshooting for clients across the country via phone, Twitter, Facebook, Snapchat, and various other social media interfaces.

InfoServe's front-line team tends to be younger adults just out of school looking to make an income. They are often interested in cars and trucks, but not always. To this end, InfoServe has a significant training program and a large searchable database of frequently asked questions to help them troubleshoot with clients.

InfoServe has always prided itself on "promoting from within." In an industry marked by high turnover rates, the management at InfoServe believes that by providing opportunities for advancement, it can keep people interested in working for InfoServe longer and reduce the company's turnover rates. For every ten people hired by InfoServe to work on the front line, three resign or are terminated within three months. On average, InfoServe loses another two during the first year, leaving five out of every ten hires at the one-year mark. Of these five, one is typically promoted to "team lead" within a year as well because of exceptional performance on the front line.

Steve has found it increasingly difficult to find new staff for InfoServe. Five years ago, he used to receive about 15 résumés for every job opening he posted. He has found that this number has dropped to only six résumés for every job posting in recent months.

In addition to the reduced number of applications, Steve has also noticed something else. When a front-line staff member is promoted to team lead, the team often loses an additional staff member. In some cases, exit interviews have found that these resigning employees felt that they should have been given the job as team lead or could not work for someone they used to consider a friend. In some cases, however, the resigning employees comment that the recently promoted "team lead" is a terrible manager.

DISCUSSION QUESTIONS

1. What tools could Steve use to better understand the high turnover rate at InfoServe?

2. What factors might be leading to the reduced number of applications at InfoServe?

3. How might technology solutions support Steve in his role at InfoServe?

4. Steve has recently begun to question whether InfoServe should promote from within or hire team leads from outside the organization. What are the pros and cons of each approach? Which approach would you recommend, and why?

PART 3

Attracting Human Resources

A company hires employees to meet its objectives. First, it has to identify potential employees and find the ways and means to get the necessary information to them, taking into account the requirements of human rights legislation. Then it has to select those candidates who best meet its needs.

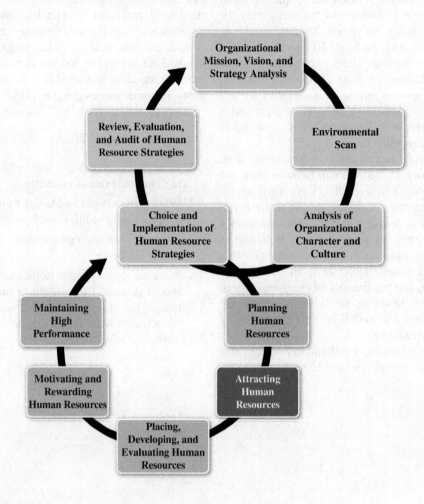

CHAPTER 4

Legal Requirements and Managing Diversity

All human beings are born free and equal in dignity and rights.

ARTICLE 1, UNIVERSAL DECLARATION OF HUMAN RIGHTS, DECEMBER 1948, UNITED NATIONS

All individuals should have an equal opportunity to make for themselves the lives that they are able and wish to have, consistent with their duties and obligations as members of society, without being hindered in or prevented from doing so by discriminatory practices based on race, national or ethnic origin, colour, religion, age, sex, sexual orientation, marital status, family status, disability or conviction for an offence for which a pardon has been granted.

SECTION 2, *CANADIAN HUMAN RIGHTS ACT*

LEARNING OBJECTIVES

After studying this chapter, you should be able to:

LO1 Explain the impact of government on human resource management.

LO2 List the major provisions of the *Canadian Human Rights Act*.

LO3 Define *harassment* and explain what is meant by the term *sexual harassment*.

LO4 Outline an employment equity program.

LO5 Explain the effect of human rights legislation on the role of human resource specialists.

LO6 Describe the strategic importance of diversity for Canadian workplaces.

LO7 Discuss a diversity perspective versus an inclusion perspective.

LO1 Government Impact

Few challenges encountered by human resource departments are as overwhelming as those presented by government. Government, through the enforcement of laws, has a direct and immediate impact on the human resource function. The federal and provincial laws that regulate the employee–employer relationship challenge the methods human resource departments use. The impact of these laws has helped elevate the importance of human resource decisions.

Many aspects of human resource management are affected by human rights legislation. This chapter will focus on compliance with government legislation and the organizational implications for managing a diverse workforce.

At appropriate points throughout this book, employee-related laws are explained to illustrate the challenges modern human resource departments encounter and the actions they must take.

To avoid flooding the courts with complaints and the prosecution of relatively minor infractions, federal and provincial governments often create special regulatory bodies, such as commissions, tribunals, and boards, to enforce compliance with the law and to aid in its interpretation. Examples are the various human rights commissions and labour relations boards, which evaluate complaints and develop legally binding rules, called **regulations**. Human resource specialists become involved because legislation and regulations affect the employment relationship. The involvement creates three important responsibilities. First, human resource experts must stay abreast of the laws and the interpretation of the laws by regulatory bodies and court rulings. Second, they must develop and administer programs that ensure company compliance. Failure to do so may lead to the loss of government contracts, to poor public relations, and to lawsuits by regulatory bodies or affected individuals. Third, they must pursue their traditional roles of obtaining, maintaining, and retaining an optimal workforce.

> **regulations** Legally enforceable rules developed by governmental agencies to ensure compliance with laws that the agency administers.

The Charter of Rights and Freedoms

An example of government legislation that has profound implications for employers is the *Constitution Act* of 1982, which contains the **Canadian Charter of Rights and Freedoms**.[1] The Charter provides some fundamental rights to every Canadian. These are as follows:

> **Canadian Charter of Rights and Freedoms** Federal law enacted in 1982, guaranteeing individuals equal rights before the law.

- Freedom of conscience and religion
- Freedom of thought, belief, opinion, and expression, including freedom of the press and other media of communication
- Freedom of peaceful assembly
- Freedom of association

The Charter provides protection to every Canadian in the following specific areas:[2]

- Fundamental freedoms
- Democratic rights

- The right to live and seek employment anywhere in Canada
- Legal rights: the right to life, liberty, and personal security
- Equality rights for all individuals
- Officially recognized languages of Canada
- Minority language education rights
- Canada's multicultural heritage
- Aboriginal (or Indigenous) peoples' rights

The Canadian Charter of Rights and Freedoms is probably the most far-reaching legal challenge for human resource managers. A review of the application of the Charter to human resource and industrial relations issues reveals that its impact has been important but limited at times. One reason is that it takes considerable time for cases to reach the Supreme Court, the ultimate interpreter of the Charter.

Section 1 of the Charter guarantees rights and freedoms "subject only to such reasonable limits prescribed by law as can be demonstrably justified in a free and democratic society." Of course, such adjectives as "reasonable" and "demonstrably justified" will lead to different interpretations by different judges. This is one of the reasons why many cases are winding their way through the judicial system up to the Supreme Court, just to get a final opinion. Every time a court invokes one of the rights or freedoms, it must determine if the infringement is justified.

Section 2 of the Charter guarantees freedom of association, a very important aspect in industrial relations, especially for unions. A key question in this context is whether the freedom to associate carries with it the right to bargain collectively and the right to strike, the main reasons for the existence of unions. As will be shown, these rights cannot be taken for granted anymore.

Section 15—the equality rights part—came into effect on April 17, 1985, having been delayed to allow the federal government and the provinces to create or change laws to ensure compliance with the Charter. It states in its first paragraph:

> Every individual is equal before the law and under the law and has the right to the equal protection and benefit of the law without discrimination and, in particular, without discrimination based on race, national or ethnic origin, colour, religion, sex, age, or mental or physical disability.

This section of the Charter was expected to—and has—caused a flood of litigation that will take many years to resolve.

The Charter of Rights and Freedoms applies only to individuals dealing with federal and provincial governments and agencies under their jurisdiction, but its impact is far-reaching, since potentially every law can be challenged.

Courts have the delicate task of balancing individual and collective rights. Consider this arbitration case:

> Quebec arbitrator Jean-Pierre Lussier ruled that a collective agreement provision providing for 24-hour shifts at the McGill University Health Centre violated both the Canadian Charter of Rights and Freedoms and the Quebec Charter of Human Rights and Freedoms. Grievor Alain Bestawros and other residents claimed that the long shifts affected their health and safety, reduced the ability to concentrate, resulted in fatigue when driving home, and led to difficulty in remembering common knowledge. According to Arbitrator Lussier, "A condition of employment exposing a doctor to greater risk of physical or mental injury for himself, higher risk of errors, incorrect diagnoses and even causing injury to individuals when his mission is to take care of them is an unfair, unreasonable condition of employment."[3]

Human Rights Legislation

While the Charter of Rights and Freedoms guarantees equality before the law for every Canadian, human rights legislation seeks to provide equal employment opportunities and prohibits discrimination on all prohibited grounds. In short, human rights legislation has a major impact on human resource management.[4]

Scope

Usually, employment-related laws and regulations are limited in scope; their impact on the human resource management process is confined to a single human resource activity. For example, minimum-wage laws specify the lowest amount an employer can pay for each hour worked; in spite of their importance, these laws affect only the compensation management function. Other human resource activities—selection, training, and labour relations—are largely unaffected.

Human rights legislation, however, is an exception. Its role is not limited to a single human resource activity.

Instead, human rights legislation affects nearly every human resource function: human resource planning, recruiting, selection, training, compensation, and labour relations.

Overview

Human rights legislation is a family of federal and provincial acts that have as a common objective the provision of equal employment opportunity for members of protected groups. Figure 4-1 summarizes these two layers of employment laws. Discrimination between workers on the basis of their effort, performance, or other work-related criteria remains both permissible and advisable.

Human rights legislation permits employers to reward outstanding performers and penalize insufficient productivity. Its only requirement is that the basis for rewards and punishments be work-related, not based on a person's race, sex, age, or other prohibited criteria.

The following discussion focuses on federal human rights legislation because **provincial human rights laws** tend to differ only slightly, mainly in terminology (e.g., some provinces use "national origin," others use "ethnic origin"). The examples used in the discussion of federal legislation are also typically representative of provincial situations.

> **provincial human rights laws** All provinces have their own human rights laws with discrimination criteria, regulations, and procedures.

LO2 The *Canadian Human Rights Act*

The **Canadian Human Rights Act** was passed by Parliament on July 14, 1977, and took effect in March 1978. The Act proclaims the following:

> **Canadian Human Rights Act** A federal law prohibiting discrimination.

> The purpose of this Act is to extend the laws in Canada to give effect, within the purview of matters

FIGURE 4-1

Types, Sources, Objectives, and Jurisdiction of Canadian Human Rights Legislation

Type	Source	Objectives and Jurisdiction
Federal Law	Passed by Parliament and enforced by federal Human Rights Commission/Tribunal	To ensure equal employment opportunities with employers under federal jurisdiction
Provincial Law	Enacted by provincial governments and enforced by provincial human rights commissions/tribunals	To ensure equal employment opportunities with employers under provincial jurisdiction

coming within the legislative authority of Parliament, to the principle that all individuals should have an opportunity equal with other individuals to make for themselves the lives that they are able and wish to have and to have their needs accommodated, consistent with their duties and obligations as members of society, without being hindered in or prevented from doing so by discriminatory practices based on race, national or ethnic origin, colour, religion, age, sex, sexual orientation, marital status, family status, disability or conviction for an offence for which a pardon has been granted.[5]

The Act applies to all federal government departments and agencies, Crown corporations, and business and industry under federal jurisdiction, such as banks, airlines, railways, and interprovincial communication (radio and TV) companies—in their dealings with the public and in their employment policies. In areas not under federal jurisdiction, protection is given by provincial human rights laws. Each of Canada's provinces and territories—with the exception of Nunavut, which is still under federal jurisdiction—has its own antidiscrimination law, which is broadly similar to the federal law. Figure 4-2 compares federal and individual provincial human rights legislation as to different grounds of discrimination prohibited in employment. While discrimination in the provision of services is also prohibited, the grounds are often very similar to employment and are not provided in the table.

Discrimination Defined

Collins English Dictionary defines *discrimination* as "the practice of treating one person or group of people less fairly or less well than other people or groups."

© CP PHOTO/Toronto Star/Bernard Weil

Former Iraq hostage James Loney says that a Catholic youth camp, where he was on staff, was ordered to close down because he is gay. Should sexual orientation play a role in staffing decisions in religious organizations?

Discrimination is neither defined in the Charter of Rights and Freedoms nor in any federal or provincial human rights legislation with the exception of Quebec. Section 10 of the Quebec Charter states the following:

> Every person has a right to full and equal recognition and exercise of his human rights and freedoms without distinction, exclusion, or preference based on race, colour, sex, gender identity or expression, pregnancy, sexual orientation, civil status, age except as provided by law, religion, political convictions, language, ethnic or national origin, social condition, a handicap or the use of any means to palliate a handicap. Discrimination exists where such a distinction, exclusion, or preference has the effect of nullifying or impairing such right.

What grounds of discrimination occur most frequently? When examining the annual reports of the various human rights commissions/tribunals, the ground alleged most frequently is discrimination on the basis of disability (alleged in about 45 to 60 percent of claims). For example, in the federal jurisdiction for 2016, about 60 percent of the claims involved disability (with about 48 percent of these claims related to mental health), 15 percent were based on sex, 16 percent on national or ethnic origin, and 17 percent on race. In New Brunswick, 46 percent of the complaints involved disability (25 percent were physical and 21 percent were mental disability). Note that a complainant may allege more than one ground of discrimination.[6]

One area that is particularly challenging for employers involves "competing rights" cases. For example, what if a male employee refuses to work on a team with female workers? According to lawyer Katherine Ford, the employer has a duty to accommodate but none of the rights is absolute and there is no hierarchy of rights. It is important to determine whether the request is a right or preference and to recognize that each case will be decided on its merits.[7]

Direct Versus Indirect (Systemic) Discrimination

Normally, intentional direct discrimination on grounds specified in the human rights legislation is illegal. However, under certain circumstances intentional direct discrimination is acceptable. A fashion store catering to women will be allowed to advertise for female models, and schools controlled by religious groups are permitted to limit their hiring to members of the specific faith. This legal discrimination is called a **bona fide occupational requirement (BFOR)**.

bona fide occupational requirement (BFOR)
A justified business reason for discriminating against a member of a protected class; also known as bona fide occupational qualification (BFOQ).

FIGURE 4-2

Prohibited Grounds of Discrimination in Canada (Employment)*

Prohibited Ground	Jurisdiction	Comments
Race or Colour	All jurisdictions	In addition, Saskatchewan prohibits discrimination on the basis of "perceived race."
Religion	All jurisdictions	Manitoba's Code and Yukon's Act read "religion or creed, or religious belief, religious association or religious activity." In addition, Saskatchewan prohibits discrimination on the basis of "religious creed." Ontario uses the term "creed." Nunavut's Act says "creed [and] religion."
Physical or Mental Disability	All jurisdictions	Quebec uses the phrase "handicap or use of any means to palliate a handicap." Ontario has prohibition on the basis of "both current and previous disabilities as well as the perception that one may have or have had a disability." Nunavut uses the word "disability."
Dependence on Alcohol or Drugs	All except Yukon and Northwest Territories	Policy to accept complaints in British Columbia, Alberta, Saskatchewan, Manitoba, Ontario, New Brunswick, Northwest Territories, and Prince Edward Island. Included in "handicap" ground in Quebec. Previous dependence only in New Brunswick and Nova Scotia. Included in "disability" ground in the Yukon, Alberta, and Nunavut.
Age	All jurisdictions	British Columbia: 19+; Alberta: 18+; Saskatchewan: 18+; Ontario: 18+; Newfoundland: 19+; Quebec: except as provided for by law; Nunavut: applies with no age restrictions in the Act.
Sex (includes pregnancy and childbirth)	All jurisdictions	Alberta uses the term "gender"; Manitoba includes gender-determined characteristics; British Columbia and Ontario include breastfeeding; Ontario recognizes the protection of transgender persons and accepts complaints related to "gender identity"; Ontario accepts complaints related to female genital mutilation; in Quebec, pregnancy as such is considered a ground of discrimination; in the Northwest Territories, gender identity as such is considered a ground of discrimination; Nunavut Act says "sex, sexual orientation, marital status, family status, pregnancy."
Marital Status	All jurisdictions	Quebec uses the term "civil status."
Family Status	All except New Brunswick and Newfoundland and Labrador	Saskatchewan defines family as being in a parent–child relationship; Quebec uses the term "civil status"; Northwest Territories have prohibition on the grounds of "family status" as well as "family affiliation."
Sexual Orientation	All jurisdictions	The Supreme Court of Canada read sexual orientation into the *Alberta Human Rights, Citizenship and Multiculturalism Act* in 1998.

(Continued)

Prohibited Ground	Jurisdiction	Comments
National or Ethnic Origin (including linguistic background)	All except British Columbia	Saskatchewan and Northwest Territories use the term "nationality"; Manitoba Code uses "nationality" or "national origin"; Manitoba Code uses "ethnic background or origin"; Ontario's Code includes both "ethnic origin" and "citizenship"; Alberta uses the term "place of origin."
Ancestry or Place of Origin	Yukon, British Columbia, Alberta, Saskatchewan, Manitoba, Northwest Territories, Ontario, Nunavut, and New Brunswick	
Language	Ontario, Quebec, New Brunswick, Northwest Territories, and Yukon	Ontario accepts complaints on the grounds of ancestry, ethnic origin, place of origin, and race; New Brunswick and the Northwest Territories will accept language-related complaints filed on the basis of ancestry, although it is not an enumerated ground; included under "linguistic background" in Yukon; Nunavut: no specific mention in the Act.
Social Condition or Origin	Quebec, Northwest Territories, New Brunswick, and Newfoundland and Labrador	
Source of Income	Alberta, Saskatchewan, Manitoba, Quebec, Yukon, Prince Edward Island, and Nova Scotia	Defined as "receipt of public assistance" in Saskatchewan; included under social condition in Quebec and New Brunswick; Nunavut says "lawful source of income."
Assignment, Attachment, or Seizure of Pay	Newfoundland and Labrador and Quebec	Included under "social condition" in Quebec.
Based on Association	Yukon, Manitoba, Ontario, New Brunswick, Nova Scotia, Northwest Territories, Nunavut, and Prince Edward Island	Northwest Territories has prohibition on basis of "political association."
Political Belief	Yukon, Newfoundland and Labrador, British Columbia, Manitoba, Quebec, Nova Scotia, Prince Edward Island, New Brunswick, and Northwest Territories	Newfoundland and Labrador has prohibition on basis of "political opinion"; Manitoba Code includes political activity and political association.
Record of Criminal Conviction	Yukon, Manitoba, British Columbia, Quebec, Ontario, and Prince Edward Island	Manitoba and Yukon's Act read "criminal charges or criminal record"; Ontario has prohibition on basis of "record of offences."
Pardoned Conviction	Federal, Yukon, Ontario, Nunavut, and Northwest Territories	Ontario has prohibition on basis of "record of offences."

* This document provides comparative information on the grounds of discrimination covered by federal, provincial, and territorial human rights legislation in Canada. In some instances, prohibited grounds for employment differ from those for the provision of services.

SOURCE: Based on data from Canadian Centre for Diversity and Inclusion (2018, January), *Overview of Human Rights Codes by Province and Territory in Canada,* https://ccdi.ca/media/1414/20171102-publications-overview-of-hr-codes-by-province-final-en.pdf

Indirect, unintentional, or **systemic discrimination** takes place if there is no intention to discriminate, but the system, arrangements, or policies allow it to happen. Such employment practices may appear to be neutral and may be implemented impartially, but they exclude specific groups of people for reasons that are neither job-related nor required for safe or efficient business operations.

systemic discrimination Any company policy, practice, or action that is not openly or intentionally discriminatory but has an indirect discriminatory impact or effect.

Examples include the following:

- Minimum height and weight requirements for employment with police forces, which make it more difficult for women and Canadians of Asian origin to be hired
- Minimum scores on employment tests, which discriminate against distinct groups (e.g., the use of culturally biased intelligence tests, which tend to screen out a disproportionate number of minorities)
- Internal hiring policies, word-of-mouth hiring, or the requirement to submit a photograph with the application form
- Limited accessibility of buildings and facilities, which often makes it impossible for persons with disabilities to be employed with organizations using such places
- Psychological inability of people to deal with persons with disabilities
- Unavailability of alternative formats or forms of tools (e.g., publications in Braille for the blind or telephone devices for the deaf)
- Job evaluation systems that tend to undervalue jobs traditionally held by women (e.g., give more points to compensable factors that favour men, such as physical strength, and fewer points to such factors as dexterity)
- Promotion criteria that favour factors such as seniority and experience in traditionally male-dominated organizations in which women have not had the chance to acquire either
- An organizational culture in which minority groups feel unwelcome and uneasy, resulting in a disproportionate turnover rate for such groups
- Lack of explicit anti-harassment guidelines, which allows an atmosphere of abuse to develop in the workplace

Indirect or systemic discrimination is more difficult to detect and to fight because often it is hidden and requires a special effort to deal with effectively. The **Canadian Human Rights Commission (CHRC)** has

Canadian Human Rights Commission (CHRC) Supervises the implementation and adjudication of the *Canadian Human Rights Act.*

taken specific steps to define and detect the causes and sources of indirect or systemic discrimination.

When looking globally, some airlines have a height requirement for flight attendants, such as being at least five feet tall. Others may have a minimum vertical reach requirement to ensure that flight attendants can reach high enough to secure overhead bins.[8]

There is a growing acknowledgement of the importance of "unconscious or implicit bias," which is a bias that may affect our decisions but which we are unaware of. Factors such as a person's background, personal experiences, societal stereotypes, and cultural context can impact our decisions. For instance, a recruiter may unknowingly select (or not select) a job candidate based on the person's name on the résumé. This issue can be addressed by removing all names before examining résumés:[9]

The federal government implemented a pilot project to examine whether hiring outcomes varied based on "name-blind recruitment" (where information such as a candidate's name, email, and country of origin will be omitted) or traditional evaluation procedures. The project follows one that was implemented in the United Kingdom in 2015. According to one expert, "If you go down a résumé, there are roughly 18 to 20 different signals that are all triggers for implicit bias."[10]

Starbucks recently announced that it was going to provide implicit bias training for all of its U.S. employees:

Two black men went into a Starbucks coffee shop in Philadelphia to meet an acquaintance. They asked to use the washroom but were told that only patrons buying something could get the access code. The men refused to leave the café so a Starbucks employee called police and reported that the men were trespassing. The men were arrested but eventually released for lack of evidence that a crime was being committed. Videos of the incident were posted online, and this was followed by protests at the coffee shop and a strong backlash on social media.

Starbucks CEO Kevin Johnson met with the men and apologized. He also announced that on the afternoon of May 29, 2018, Starbucks stores and corporate offices would be closed so that the 175,000 U.S. employees could go through training to address "implicit bias, promote conscious inclusion, prevent discrimination and ensure that everyone inside a Starbucks store feels safe and welcome."[11]

Race and Colour

It is sometimes difficult to see which of these two characteristics is the actual basis of discrimination; often both are involved. The discrimination can be intentional or unintentional, subtle or very open:

> The Armour Group, a property management firm in Halifax, decided to change cleaning contract companies, resulting in the layoff of seven black janitors at historic Founders Square. The new contractor has decided to hire only one employee from the former contractor—a white janitor. The Armour Group is alleging that the decision to change contractors was based on a dissatisfaction with the quality of cleaning services being provided and said that more than 200 complaints had been received in 2017. The seven janitors believe that they are the victims of racial discrimination and plan to lodge a human rights complaint.[12]

It is important that employers respond appropriately if a human rights violation is alleged:

> Priti Shah, a Winnipeg lawyer born in Canada, was told to "go back to my own country" by another patron at the Fort Garry Hotel after she spoke to a server about a problem with her meal. The employer took more than half an hour to intervene and failed to conduct a thorough investigation or ask the perpetrator to move to another table. Under Manitoba human rights law, the employer has a duty to not harass people and also an obligation to ensure that no one else knowingly harasses people at the employer's place of business.[13]

A *Canadian HR Reporter* survey found that almost 75 percent of the 235 participants agreed that First Nations people are underutilized in the workforce. Less than one-third of respondents indicated that their organization had a clear mission to recruit First Nations candidates. The most important factors limiting the recruitment of First Nations people included lack of candidates (67 percent), lack of academic qualifications (55 percent), lack of appropriate experience (47 percent), and location of candidates (35 percent).[14]

National or Ethnic Origins

It is also illegal for human resource decisions to be influenced by the national or ethnic origins of applicants or of their forebears. Although discrimination on the basis of national or ethnic origins may be indirect, on some occasions there is clear, documented evidence:

> Ottawa Valley Cleaning and Restoration was ordered to pay $8,000 to a foreign-born job applicant after a human rights tribunal found multiple violations of discrimination based on the applicant's race, colour, and place of origin. Among the text messages sent to the applicant, who during an initial phone call indicated that he was not from Canada, were "Try learning English you will have better luck I don't hire foreners [sic] I keep the white man working," and "Go file a

complaint he will probably be a white man and he will probably laugh at you and tell you to go away."[15]

Does your name affect the likelihood of your getting a callback after applying for a job? A study from Metropolis British Columbia probed the impact of name discrimination. The study authors sent out about 8,000 résumés to online job postings in three Canadian cities (Toronto, Montreal, and Vancouver). Some résumés had common Anglophone names while others contained common Chinese, Greek, or Indian names. The results revealed that applicants with Anglophone names were 47 percent more likely to get a callback compared with individuals with Chinese or Indian names in Toronto, 39 percent more likely in Montreal, and 20 percent more likely in Vancouver. The authors suggest that subconscious or implicit discrimination may help to explain why applicants with non-Anglophone names were less likely to receive a callback.[16]

Another study revealed that about 40 percent of minority job applicants may engage in résumé "whitening" (such as anglicizing their name or excluding work experience related to an ethnic group). However, résumé whitening was considerably less likely when job candidates were applying to organizations that promoted diversity. The study involved sending out 1,600 résumés (half of which were "whitened") to an equal number of pro-diversity employers and organizations that did not mention diversity in their job advertisement. The results showed that the "whitened" résumés were two to two-and-a-half times more likely to get a callback, regardless of whether the employer indicated that he or she was pro-diversity. In other words, it appeared that minority résumés were being discriminated against, even by employers that indicated they favoured diversity.[17]

Religion

A person's religious beliefs and practices should not affect employment decisions. An employer has a **duty to accommodate** an employee's religious practices, unless those practices present undue hardship to the employer:

> **duty to accommodate**
> Requirement that an employer must accommodate the employee to the point of "undue hardship."

> A Muslim employee of a communications company lost his job over the question of having time off each week to attend prayers at his mosque. After conciliation, a settlement was reached that did not impose undue hardships on the employer and by which the employee was allowed to take one-and-a-half hours per week of leave without pay. He was reinstated with retroactive pay and benefits.

If an employer does not make a reasonable attempt to accommodate workers' religious practices, he or she can be found guilty of violating the *Human Rights Act*.

The terms "undue hardship" and "duty to accommodate" were examined in an important decision by the Supreme Court of Canada in a ruling against Central Alberta Dairy Pool (1990). The complainant worked at a milk-processing plant. After becoming a member of the Worldwide Church of God, he requested unpaid leave for a particular Monday in order to observe a holy day of his church. The request was refused because Mondays were especially busy days at the plant. When the employee did not report for work, he was fired.

The court ruled that Dairy Pool had discriminated on the basis of religion. Although the company had not done so directly, it had an adverse effect on the complainant due to his religion. The court stated that the employer must meet the "duty to accommodate" up to the point of "undue hardship."

The court did not define "undue hardship." However, it stated that relevant considerations would include financial cost, health and safety, disruption of a collective agreement, interference with other workers' rights, the size of the operation, problems of morale of other employees, and interchangeability of workforce and facilities. It found that Dairy Pool could cope with employee absences on Mondays because of illnesses. Therefore, it could also accommodate a single instance for absence due to religious reasons, particularly if the employee had tried to accommodate the employer.[18]

Age

The use of age as an employment criterion has also received considerable attention in the past. Many employers consider that establishing a minimum or maximum age for certain jobs is justified, although evidence is rarely available that age is an accurate indication of one's ability to perform a given type of work: In recent years, we have seen

© Paul Henry—Material republished with the express permission of Sun Media, a division of Postmedia Network Inc.

A Supreme Court judgment forced the RCMP to accommodate its Sikh officers' religious requirement to wear a turban at all times. What other uniform accommodations might need to be made to accommodate a diverse workforce?

the abolishment of mandatory retirement in jurisdictions across the country. Still, older workers may be the victims of indirect or subtle discrimination.

Home Depot is very active in recruiting older workers and has partnered with CARP (using career fairs, newsletters, and advertising campaigns) to make older workers aware of job opportunities. About 31 percent of Home Depot's employees are age 50 and older, and 6 percent are 65 or older. However, a survey of small- and medium-sized employers revealed that more than 70 percent of respondents said it is unlikely that job openings now or in the future will be filled by a person who is at least 65 years of age. The main reason given by employers is that they want to hire people who might stay with the organization for a long period of time.[19]

Do Canadians want to retire? The 2015 *Sunlife Retirement Index* revealed that for 2014, 32 percent of Canadians expected to be working full-time at age 66 (compared with only 16 percent in 2009). About 59 percent reported that they would be working because they needed to (compared to 41 percent who wanted to continue working), and a recent HSBC survey revealed that about 17 percent of Canadians reported that they will never have sufficient funds to retire.[20] Some employers have developed programs to assist in the transition to retirement. For instance, Jane McVeigh, vice-president of HR at C4 Systems International, found that the use of a phased-in retirement program (where employees reduce their time at work over a year or two) has been very successful in her company.[21]

More and more Canadians are working past age 65. Results from the 2016 Census revealed that about 20 percent of Canadians over 65 are doing some kind of work and the number of workers staying on past 65 has doubled since 1995. Two important factors in the decision to remain in the workforce are the increased health of older workers and the decline in pension coverage.[22]

As mentioned earlier, the law may make an exception for certain occupations when it comes to retirement age. It is not considered a discriminatory practice if a person's employment is terminated because that person has reached the normal age of retirement for employees working in similar positions. The last few years have seen a growth in age discrimination lawsuits. It is important that employers are aware of ageism discrimination and are able to provide clear evidence that employment-related decisions relating to older workers are based on legitimate business reasons.

In one case, a 60-year-old was not selected for an interview because the organization was looking for applicants who were "more junior in their experience and salary expectations." Putting pressure on an older worker to retire or trying to "push an older worker out the door" could lead to a human rights complaint. Rather, it is advisable to rely on the performance management system to distinguish between good and poor performers.[23]

Sex

The *Canadian Human Rights Act* also prevents discrimination on the basis of an individual's sex (often erroneously referred to as *gender;* the Act specifically uses the term *sex*). Consider the following case where the employer tried to force a pregnant employee to quit her job:

> The new owner of a Vancouver sports bar reduced the number of shifts of a server who was six months pregnant from four shifts to about one per week in an effort to get the employee to quit. The tribunal held that the server was in an inhospitable, discriminatory work environment and the bar was unable to show that not being pregnant was a bona fide occupational requirement. Consequently, the server was awarded $2,000 in lost wages and $7,500 for injury to dignity and self-respect.[24]

It should be noted that the Ontario Human Rights Commission updated its policy on discrimination on the basis of pregnancy to include protection for women trying to become pregnant.[25] As well, the Supreme Court of Canada, in *Dionne v. Commission scolaire des Patriots,* made it clear that an employer may not discriminate against a pregnant employee who refuses to work because of a risk to the person's health and safety. In that case, Dionne refused to work because her doctor had advised her that she was susceptible to several harmful viruses and that her work environment constituted a health risk because children are frequent carriers of a number of viruses.[26]

Not only is it illegal to recruit, hire, and promote employees because of their sex, it is unlawful to have separate policies for men and women. For example, it is discriminatory to reserve some jobs for men only or women only. It is even illegal to apply similar standards to men and women when such standards arbitrarily discriminate against one sex more than the other. When standards (such as a height or physical test requirement) discriminate against one sex (or race, national or ethnic origin, religion, age, or marital status), the burden is on the employer to prove that the standards are necessary.

> A recent Ontario Human Rights Commission report entitled *Not on the Menu: Inquiry Report on Sexual and Gender-based Dress Codes in Ontario Restaurants* is aimed at the issue of some restaurant dress requirements. In one case, a visibly pregnant server working at a sports bar indicated that she was uncomfortable wearing the new form-fitting uniform. In response, the bar reduced her shifts. The Ontario Human Rights Tribunal awarded the woman close to $3,000 in lost wages and $17,000 for injury to her dignity.[27]

One study showed that the words used in job ads had little effect on men, but for women, words stereotypically associated with men (such as *independent, aggressive,* or *analytical*) made the ad less appealing and decreased the likelihood that a woman would apply for the position. The research suggests that subtle cues may affect how an ad is perceived.[28] Another study revealed that about 46 percent of women working in the technology sector perceived that they were treated differently because of their sex, 57 percent in senior management positions believed that they had been passed over for a promotion in favour of male colleagues, and around two-thirds stated that benefit packages in the industry are not adapted to women. One-third of women indicated that they lacked the confidence to ask for a pay raise, a quarter did not feel comfortable speaking up at business meetings, and 36 percent felt that their opinion was not valued.[29]

A far-reaching Supreme Court decision relating to sex discrimination concerns the earlier mentioned bona fide

Spotlight *on* ETHICS

The Hiring Dilemma

The manager of an accounting department has to hire the replacement for a retiring accountant. Over 20 applicants have applied, and 3 were put onto the short list. One of the shortlisted candidates is a 60-year-old CPA, more experienced than the other two, who also have a CPA designation. The manager knows that the department will change accounting practices in the near future (no date has been set yet) and introduce new accounting software, which will require extensive retraining of current staff. If the more experienced candidate is hired, the manager will be faced with the question of whether investing a considerable amount in retraining a person who may retire soon after is justified. But if one of the younger candidates is hired, the company might face an age discrimination charge. What should the manager do?

occupational requirement. The case involved a woman who had been employed by the Province of British Columbia in an elite firefighting unit for more than two years.

> In 1994, Ms. Meiorin failed one of several new fitness tests, a 2.5-kilometre run to be completed in 11 minutes, and lost her employment. A subsequent grievance launched by her union was appealed to the Supreme Court. The court decided in favour of Ms. Meiorin, agreeing with an earlier arbitrator's ruling that the government had failed to justify the test as a BFOR by providing credible evidence that her inability to meet the standard created a safety risk.[30]

The court established three new criteria to assess the appropriateness of a BFOR:

1. Is the standard rationally connected to the performance of the job?
2. Was the standard established in an honest belief that it was necessary to accomplish the purpose identified in stage one?
3. Is the standard reasonably necessary to accomplish its purpose?

The stricter rules may make it more difficult for human resource managers to establish and defend BFORs. However, one report suggests that the promise of Meiorin—that human rights legislation would take adverse effects discrimination seriously—is under attack, with intensified efforts to prevent complainants from going beyond the prima facie stage of discrimination. According to the report, "For many people with disabilities, the duty to accommodate as it is being applied today, simply does not go far enough to ensure their equality and inclusion in the world they live in."[31]

Sexual Orientation

Consider this recent case:

> Robert Ranger, a gay correctional officer, alleged harassment and discrimination based on his sexual orientation. While the main antagonist was a fellow union member, the employer knew the environment was poisoned and did nothing to accommodate Ranger when he was able to return to work. Ranger suffered from "profoundly humiliating homophobic harassment" and eventually went on long-term disability. He still suffers from anxiety attacks and depression. Ranger was awarded $53,000 in compensatory damages for the employer's failure to accommodate, $244,000 for lost wages, and $45,000 in compensatory damages for discrimination, harassment, and a poisoned workplace. In the words of vice-chair Deborah Leighton, "There is no case before me where the complainant has suffered such extensive harm."[32]

As stated in the 1999 Canadian Human Rights Commission's annual report, that year may come to be regarded as a watershed year for gay and lesbian Canadians. The issue of discrimination against same-sex relationships was effectively addressed by the Supreme Court of Canada when it decided that same-sex couples must be treated the same way as heterosexual couples.

In 1996, a human rights tribunal ordered the federal government to extend medical and dental benefits to the same-sex partners of its employees. The same year, the government amended the *Human Rights Act* to add sexual orientation as a prohibited ground of discrimination. Since then, several Supreme Court decisions have forced provinces to amend their benefit and tax laws to include same-sex couples in their considerations. In 2000, Parliament passed legislation treating same-sex partners the same as legally married and common-law couples for all purposes of federal law, but left the traditional definition of marriage as between a man and a woman. Finally, in June 2005, Parliament also changed the definition of marriage to include same-sex couples.[33]

In a recent case, a supervising engineer working on a road construction project was subject to repeated negative comments and emails relating to his race, religion, and sexual orientation by a foreman also working on the project but for a different company. The engineer argued that he was a victim of employment discrimination but the foreman's company asserted that the relevant human rights legislation did not apply because the engineer and foreman were not in a direct employment relationship. In late 2017, the Supreme Court of Canada held that "the code is not limited to protecting employees solely from discriminatory harassment by their supervisors in the workplace . . . This may include discrimination by their co-workers, even when those co-workers have a different employer."[34]

Still, not all workplaces are safe for LGBTQ employees:

> About one-third of Canadians do not believe that their workplace is safe and inclusive for gay and lesbian employees (and 45 percent do not feel the workplace is safe and inclusive for transgender employees). In addition, more than 85 percent of LGBTQ employees would be more likely to consider working for an organization that is LGBTQ-friendly.[35]

Gender Identity

All Canadian provinces and territories have legislation protecting "gender identity" or "gender identity and expression." In June 2017, the Senate passed Bill C-16, which prohibits discrimination on the basis of gender identity or expression. However, while some countries are introducing legislation to advance LGBTQ rights, there has been a backlash in other parts of the world (including the United States). Shortly before Bill C-16 was passed, an 18-year-old Malaysian youth was beaten, burned with cigarettes, and sodomized because he was considered effeminate. He was brain dead by the time medical personnel arrived.[36]

A number of employers may not have policies relating to transgender employees. Brian Kreissl, managing editor at Consult Carswell, makes the following suggestions: (1) meet with the employee beforehand to determine how and what should be communicated, (2) hold information sessions with other employees before the transgender employee commences work, (3) have a respectful workplace policy, (4) inform employees to call the employee by his or her chosen name and pronoun, (5) allow the employee to dress in accordance with the dress code matching his or her gender identity, and (6) permit the employee to use washroom facilities consistent with the person's gender identity.[37]

A Toronto job fair for transgender employees involved about 15 employers, including Parks Canada, the Armed Forces, and Indigo:

> According to Greg Bryant, HR manager in Peterborough for Parks Canada, "In some communities, people don't think of us as an employer. So we do outreach like this; this is a great example of a diverse community that maybe we're not meeting. We've had an LGBTQ working group for about 20 years now, and it's pretty darn active."[38]

Service Canada recently issued a directive asking managers and team leaders to use gender-neutral or gender-inclusive language, and to use a client's full name or ask how the person would prefer to be addressed. Helen Kennedy, executive director of Egale Canada (a national LGBTQ human rights organization), supported the initiative and indicated that "it needs to be accompanied by more awareness training and education around non-binary and gender-neutral language." However, some opposition members of Parliament were highly critical of the directive.[39]

Marital Status

The idea of what constitutes a family has undergone considerable change in Canadian society over the course of its history. Single-parent families, or nontraditional families, such as those resulting from common-law marriages, are now far more numerous than in the past. But some still hold a strong feeling that the traditional family is a unique institution deserving special consideration.

The *Canadian Human Rights Act* spells out quite clearly that any discrimination based on marital status is illegal:

> A woman was denied a job with the CBC because her husband was already employed by the corporation at the same station. After a complaint and hearing, the CBC changed its employment practices, which formerly discriminated on the basis of marital status, and placed the woman in a position in the same station in which her husband was employed.

Family Status

In a widely cited case regarding family status, the CHRC initiated action against the Canada Employment Insurance Commission (CEIC).

> Ms. Ina Lang alleged that the CEIC denied her application for funding under the Challenge 86 program because she wished to hire her daughter to help in her family child-care business. A tribunal held that the CEIC had discriminated against Ms. Lang on the basis of her family status when it denied her the funding she sought, and awarded her $1,000 for hurt feelings. The CEIC appealed the decision to the Federal Court of Appeal, but the court upheld the decision.

Some recent human rights decisions relating to family status suggest that employers may have a duty to accommodate employees with child-care obligations unless such accommodation results in undue hardship. A number of the cases have dealt with work schedule issues and whether the employer would adjust the timing of shifts:

> In the case of *Miraka v. ACD Wholesale Meats,* a delivery truck driver informed his manager that he would need to be off work the next day because his wife was ill and unable to care for their two young children. The manager gave him permission to be absent for the day. His wife's condition did not improve so he stayed home the day after to care for the children. However, he did not contact his manager until later that day because he assumed his manager knew he was home caring for his children and no one from work contacted him regarding his absence. Upon returning to work, Mr. Miraka suffered a workplace injury and asked to leave early. His employer responded by terminating his employment, arguing that Mr. Miraka had not made sufficient efforts to find an alternative solution, such as finding a babysitter. The Human Rights Tribunal found in favour of Mr. Miraka and awarded him $10,000 for injury to his dignity, feelings, and self-respect. The Tribunal distinguished between long-term accommodation needs and short-term accommodation such as the need to care for an unexpected illness of a child.[40]

However, it appears that voluntary family activities (such as vacations or extracurricular sporting events) would not fall under the duty to accommodate.[41]

Disability

No person should be denied employment or terminated from a job because of a disability. However, in the 2017 *Elk Valley Coal* decision (discussed in Chapter 11), the Supreme Court of Canada confirmed the principle that terminating an employee with a disability is not always a violation of human rights law.[42]

The principle of **reasonable accommodation** has been established. It means that an employer can be expected to take reasonable measures to make available a suitable job to a person with a disability if it does not impose undue hardships on the organization:

> **reasonable accommodation**
> Voluntary adjustments to work or workplace that allow employees with special needs to perform their job effectively.

> Coffee giant Starbucks was sued by a barista in El Paso, Texas. The woman, who is a little person, was hired on a trial basis and she requested that she be able to use a stool or step ladder to help her perform her job. The company decided that using a stool was not reasonable accommodation considering the work environment and argued that the woman could represent a danger to customers and co-workers. The case was ultimately settled with Starbucks agreeing to pay the woman $75,000 and to provide training on disability issues to all managers and supervisory staff in its El Paso locations.[43]

The labour force participation rate is about 54 percent for people with disabilities, and almost 800,000 Canadians are not working even though their disability does not prevent them from doing so (with about half of these people having post-secondary education).[44]

> Mackenzie Whitney has a math degree from the University of Alberta but was working marginal jobs owing to his autism. Eventually, he started working at Meticulon Consulting in Calgary as a junior tester monitoring quality assurance. Company co-founder Garth Johnson stated that he looks for people with autism because they offer unique skills, such as precision, diligence, attention to detail, and an ability to sustain focus.[45]

Many organizations have established rigid physical standards for certain jobs without being able to show that these standards are truly relevant to the requirements of the job. Some complainants have been refused jobs when their disability might be a problem in a speculative situation; for example, a firm might argue that a deaf person would be unable to hear a fire alarm. Other complainants have been disqualified for jobs not because they are physically disabled now but because they may become so in the future.

Being alcohol or drug-dependent can also be interpreted as a disability. Employees with a dependency on drugs or alcohol must be reasonably accommodated to the point of undue hardship on the employer. Typical requirements include providing an employee assistance program or giving an employee time off to attend such a program. However, an employer is not obligated to accept long-term absences unrelated to rehabilitation.[46]

Recent Ontario legislation addresses workplace issues relevant to employees with disabilities. The *Accessibility for Ontarians with Disabilities Act* (AODA) requires employers to make workplaces accessible to members of the public with disabilities. It is estimated that one in seven people in Ontario has a disability, and that number is projected to increase. The Integrated Accessibility Standards Regulation requires that emergency procedures and plans be available in accessible formats if requested and that employers develop an individualized workplace emergency response plan for employees with a disability.[47] However, complying with the legislation can be challenging for employers:

> A partially deaf transit user is alleging that the Toronto Transit Commission (TTC) is failing to communicate with all passengers because it is not providing hearing-impaired riders with the same information as other customers. Although the TTC provides written information on screens, it frequently relies on audio messages to make passengers aware of service disruptions or route changes. TTC's accessibility policy provides that it will "communicate with persons with disabilities in a manner that takes into account their disability" and "ensure information is available in accessible formats to persons of all abilities, across all modes of transit."[48]

It appears that the federal Liberal government will introduce legislation in 2018 aimed at increasing accessibility in federally regulated sectors (such as banking, interprovincial transportation, and federal government services such as Canada Post). The legislation may follow the lead of Ontario and focus on broad areas, such as customer service and employment. Currently, only Ontario, Manitoba, and Nova Scotia have accessibility legislation while other countries, including the United States, Australia, and the United Kingdom, have had laws to meet the needs of people with disabilities for years.[49]

Scotiabank changed its funding relating to accommodation to include services:

> According to Deanna Matzanke, director, Global Employment Strategies (Diversity & Inclusion; HR Policy & Compliance) at the bank, "A lot of episodic disabilities (such as multiple sclerosis and chronic fatigue syndrome) don't actually need assistive technology or an electronic door. What they need more often are types of services like a job coach to help organize the workplace." About one-third of employers indicated that their knowledge of how to support people with episodic disabilities was low. Accommodations for people with episodic disabilities may include such things as providing flextime, working from home, adjusting work duties, and providing a private space at the workplace where employees can rest or take medications.[50]

Also consider the experience of a Tim Hortons' franchisor:

> Over the years, Mark Wafer's Tim Hortons' franchises have employed more than 125 employees with disabilities. Currently, 46 of his 250 employees have a disability (ranging from intellectual challenges to mental health issues to multiple sclerosis). While more than 15 percent of Canadians have a disability, there are about 450,000 school graduates with a disability (270,000 of whom have post-secondary education) who have never worked a day over the past five years. Wafer notes that the absenteeism rate for his 46 employees with disabilities is 85 percent lower than for the 200 employees without disabilities, and employee turnover is under 40 percent (compared to the 100 percent norm in the quick-service sector). Morever, Wafer has never filled out a workplace safety form for an employee with a disability.[51]

A *Canadian HR Reporter* survey revealed that about 50 percent of employers have a policy encouraging the hiring of people with disabilities, and 70 percent have hired an individual who self-identified as having a disability. In terms of performance, 9 percent of respondents indicated that employees with disabilities performed better than other employees, almost 80 percent said there was no difference, and only 6 percent perceived that employees with disabilities performed worse than other workers. The three types of assistance that would be most beneficial include workplace support for employees with disabilities (such as a short-term job coach), disability awareness training for staff, and financial assistance with training and workplace modifications.[52]

In an effort to replace older workers who are retiring, the energy sector is looking at increasing the hiring of people with disabilities. A 2017 survey indicated that only about half of Canadians with a disability have a full- or part-time job. Electricity Human Resources Canada has developed an on-line portal with strategies to assist people with disabilities to find employment in the sector. There is also information outlining how hiring people with disabilities makes good business sense and leads to many positive outcomes, including higher productivity and morale as well as employee retention.[53]

Pardoned Convicts

The *Canadian Human Rights Act* prohibits discrimination against a convicted person if a pardon has been issued for the offence. Pardon may be granted by a parole board after five years following release, parole, or the completion of a sentence:

> A person convicted and paroled on a drug offence applied for a job with a government agency dealing with drug abuse. He was denied employment because of his conviction. Subsequently, the National

Parole Board granted his request for a full pardon. The government agency maintained, however, that pardoned or not, he remained a security risk and that being without a criminal record was a BFOR of a correctional service's staff. He appealed to the Canadian Human Rights Commission, and after the Commission's investigation, the government agency decided that a criminal record would not, in fact, inhibit the applicant's ability to meet the requirements of the job, and, satisfied that he was suitable, offered him the position.[54]

The CHRC has also been approached by persons who claim to have been refused employment on the basis of their arrest record, even when the arrest did not lead to a conviction. These persons are without legal protection because the *Canadian Human Rights Act* does not address this type of discrimination. For the human resource manager, this does not mean that all applicants can be asked for their arrest record. It must still be shown that doing so is relevant to the job. For this reason, the Commission has advised employers under federal jurisdiction that applicants should not be asked, "Have you ever been convicted of an offence?" It is recommended—if such information is legitimately needed for employment purposes—that the question be phrased as "Have you ever been convicted of an offence for which you have not received a pardon?"

LO3 Harassment

The *Canadian Human Rights Act* contains the following prohibition against harassment:

> It is a discriminatory practice,
>
> a) in the provision of goods, services, facilities or accommodation customarily available to the general public,
>
> b) in the provision of commercial premises or residential accommodation, or
>
> c) in matters related to employment,
>
> to harass an individual on a prohibited ground of discrimination.

Such behaviour may be verbal, physical, deliberate, unsolicited, or unwelcome; it may be one incident or a series of incidents. Protection against harassment extends to incidents occurring at or away from the workplace, during or outside normal working hours, provided such incidents are employment-related.[55] Consider a class action lawsuit against the RCMP:

> A former member of the RCMP initiated a class action lawsuit against the RCMP with the goal of purging the toxic attitude against women. Janet Merlo, who spent 19 years in the RCMP, alleges that

she was subject to ongoing sexist comments, sexual pranks, derogatory remarks, and double standards. According to Merlo's lawyer David Klein, "Part of the problem is that the complaints women made were not taken seriously by the force. They need a new structure and it's something that has to come from the top down."[56]

Following the 2016 settlement of two class action lawsuits, Merlo says that the RCMP is "failing in its responsibility to make female employees safe and to end the toxic work environment that's plagued the RCMP for more than 40 years." More than 4,000 women have come forward alleging sexual harassment or discrimination following the 2016 settlements (which involved the government's setting aside $100 million for payment of claims ranging from $10,000 to $220,000 based on the severity of the claim).[57]

Although somewhat controversial, a website in the United States, Ebosswatch, allows employees to provide anonymous ratings of their supervisors. While the founder of the website argues that this information will allow people to evaluate potential bosses, managerial candidates, and employers, there is the risk of false allegations or defamation complaints.[58]

harassment Occurs when a member of an organization treats an employee in a disparate manner because of that person's sex, race, religion, age, or other protective classification.

What is harassment? **Harassment** may include the following:

- Verbal abuse or threats
- Unwelcome remarks, jokes, innuendo, or taunting about a person's body, attire, age, marital status, ethnic or national origin, religion, and so on
- Displaying of pornographic, racist, or other offensive or derogatory pictures
- Practical jokes that cause awkwardness or embarrassment
- Unwelcome invitations or requests, whether indirect or explicit, or intimidation
- Leering or other gestures
- Condescension or paternalism that undermines self-respect
- Unnecessary physical contact, such as touching, patting, pinching, or punching
- Physical assault

It will be assumed that harassing behaviour has taken place if a "reasonable person ought to have known that such behaviour was unwelcome."[59]

A City of Woodstock parks department employee with 20 years of service and no previous disciplinary problems was demoted for sexually harassing a female employee and her co-workers during their summer employment. In addition to making sexually inappropriate comments, the employee asked two female summer students (and one of the complainants' 16-year-old sister) to come to his hot tub, sent texts asking if all girls liked to be choked, and stated that he would like to marry the complainant. The employee's work computer also revealed he had pictures of the complainant taken away from the worksite and inappropriate pictures of her at work. The city decided to dismiss the employee, who, through his union, grieved the dismissal (arguing that he was unaware that his behaviour was unwanted and that there was no policy prohibiting fraternization between supervisors and other workers). The arbitrator noted that the grievor had no previous disciplinary offences on his record and the harassment did not go beyond verbal and texted comments. As a result, the arbitrator gave the grievor a two-month suspension and an indefinite demotion to a nonsupervisory position.[60]

Although most organizations have strong policies on harassment, an issue that is frequently overlooked is workplace ostracism. Ostracism is a form of bullying and can be overt or subtle but it is often omitted from harassment policies. It is important to make managers aware of the problem, provide training to employees, and emphasize that ostracism will not be tolerated.[61]

There is also growing concern about cyberbullying. An AVG Technologies study of employees in 10 countries revealed that about one-quarter of companies do not have a cyberbullying policy and only 37 percent of employees are aware of a comprehensive policy. Almost 10 percent of employees have had a manager use information against them that was obtained from a social media site, 53 percent believe that workplace privacy has been eroded due to social media, and 11 percent have had embarrassing photos or videos taken at a work event and then uploaded onto social media. Common forms of cyberbullying include sending unpleasant or defamatory remarks to or about a colleague and posting negative comments on a social media site about a colleague's appearance.[62]

From a policy perspective aimed at addressing cyberbullying, employers need to (1) revise harassment and bullying policies to include cyberbullying; (2) create a procedure for investigating and reporting cyberbullying; (3) provide training on cyberbullying; (4) provide EAP support to employees who are victims of bullying; (5) have a zero tolerance policy; (6) respond to allegations in a timely manner; (7) raise awareness of cyberbullying; (8) make sure that a respectful workplace policy is in place; (9) regularly monitor emails, social media, and text messages for incidents of cyberbullying; and (10) require employees to sign an antibullying agreement.[63]

Sexual harassment is an important topic in human resource management, evidenced by the increased number of complaints lodged. A Canadian Human Rights Tribunal identified three characteristics of sexual harassment:

> **sexual harassment**
> Unsolicited or unwelcome sex- or gender-based conduct that has adverse employment consequences for the complainant.

1. The encounters must be unsolicited by the complainant, unwelcome to the complainant, and expressly or implicitly known by the respondent to be unwelcome.
2. The conduct must either continue despite the complainant's protests or, if the conduct stops, the complainant's protests must have led to negative employment consequences.
3. The complainant's co-operation must be due to employment-related threats or promises.

How common is sexual harassment? A recent Angus Reid survey revealed that 52 percent of Canadian women report being subject to sexual harassment at work during their lifetime, and 28 percent indicate that they have been subject to nonconsensual sexual touching. More than 60 percent of respondents have been closely following news reports on this topic, and a similar percent believe that the #MeToo campaign has had an effect on their attitudes toward workplace gender relations. About 91 percent of men and 94 percent of women agree that "men need to take more responsibility for the way they behave toward women" while 74 percent of men and 81 percent of women agree that "there is no forgiveness for sexual harassment." In addition, more than 80 percent of women indicate that they take some type of action to prevent or avoid sexual harassment.[64]

A survey by Employment and Social Development Canada revealed that 60 percent of respondents reported experiencing workplace harassment over the previous two years, while 30 percent stated that they had been sexually harassed, 21 percent had experienced violence, and 3 percent had experienced sexual violence. Ninety-four percent of respondents experiencing sexual harassment were women. About half of respondents reporting harassing or violent behaviour said that the perpetrator was an individual with authority over them while 44 percent said that the behaviour was by a co-worker. Although about three-quarters of people experiencing harassment or violence took action, 41 percent stated that no attempt was made to resolve the issue. Employees experiencing harassment or violence were most likely to discuss the matter with a co-worker (64 percent) or supervisor (58 percent), with only 22 percent talking to a human resources professional.[65]

Further information on sexual harassment was revealed in a December 2017 study by the NRG Research Group. About 82 percent of participants believed that stalking or cyber stalking were examples of sexual harassment or sexual violence. Other examples included asking someone on a date more than once after being told no (47 percent) and greeting someone and telling them they look nice today (5 percent). About 51 percent of respondents indicated that recent sexual harassment allegations of high-profile individuals (such as Harvey Weinstein and Kevin Spacey) have had a very large or somewhat large impact on reducing the occurrence of sexual harassment at work. In addition, 50 percent of participants were very or somewhat aware of the #MeToo campaign, and 84 percent of those aware of #MeToo felt that the campaign was very or somewhat effective in raising awareness of sexual harassment and sexual violence.[66]

A landmark case involving sexual harassment was *Robichaud v. Department of National Defence (DND),* which went to the Supreme Court. The court ruled that the employer shared the responsibility for the actions of one of its supervisors, who had sexually harassed Ms. Robichaud. It added that "only an employer can remedy undesirable effects [of discrimination]; only an employer can provide the most important remedy—a healthy work environment." The DND was ordered to pay Ms. Robichaud $5,000 for pain and suffering, to issue a written apology, and to post the written apology in all DND facilities.

Women are not the only employees who may be subjected to sexual harassment. Evidence from the United States Equal Employment Opportunity Commission indicates that about 16 percent of all sexual harassment claims are by men and the percentage has doubled over the past 20 years. Most of the charges of sexual harassment filed by men involve men harassing other men.

Employer Retaliation

It is a criminal act to retaliate in any way against those who exercise their rights according to the *Canadian Human Rights Act.* Those who file charges, testify, or otherwise participate in any human rights action are protected by law. If a supervisor tries to get even with an employee who filed charges, he or she violates the Act.

Enforcement

The responsibility for the administration of the *Canadian Human Rights Act* lies in the hands of the Canadian Human Rights Commission (CHRC). The Commission consists of up to eight members, including the chief commissioner, who is a full-time member appointed for a term of not more than seven years. Other full-time members are also appointed for a term not to exceed seven years, and part-time members are appointed for a term of not more than three years.

The role of the CHRC is to investigate and try to resolve allegations of discrimination in employment and the provision of services within the federal jurisdiction. The CHRC also administers the *Employment Equity Act.* The Commission is also mandated to develop and conduct

FIGURE 4-3

Remedies for Violations

The Canadian Human Rights Tribunal has several remedies at its disposal. For example, it can order a violator to do the following:

- Stop the discriminatory practice.
- Restore the rights, opportunities, and privileges denied the victim.
- Compensate the victim for wages lost and any expenses incurred as a result of the discriminatory practice.
- Compensate the victim for pain and suffering.
- Develop and implement employment equity programs to equalize opportunity for certain groups that have suffered from discriminatory practices in the past.

information and prevention programs, to conduct and sponsor research, and to report annually to Parliament. The Commission is not a tribunal and does not rule on cases. If a complaint cannot be resolved, the Commission may recommend mediation or ultimately ask the Canadian Human Rights Tribunal to hear the case. Figure 4-3 describes some of the remedies available to the tribunal in settling a complaint. Should the tribunal find that the discriminatory practice was maintained purposely or recklessly, or that the victim's feelings or self-respect have suffered as a result of the practice, it may order the person or organization responsible to compensate the victim appropriately.

A person who obstructs an investigation or a tribunal, or fails to comply with the terms of a settlement, or reduces wages in order to eliminate a discriminatory practice can be found guilty of an offence punishable by a fine or jail sentence or both. On summary conviction, such a person can be liable to a fine not exceeding $50,000.[67]

Spotlight *on* HRM

How to Handle an Employee Sexual Harassment Complaint

When an employee complains that he or she is experiencing sexual harassment of any type, the employer has a legal, ethical, and employee relations obligation to investigate the charges thoroughly. The employer can't decide whether to believe the employee but must take him or her at their word.

If an employer hears rumors that sexual harassment is occurring, the employer must investigate the potential harassment.

- It can include hearing gossip from other employees.

- It can involve instances in which noninvolved employees or friends of the targeted employee bring up the subject with Human Resources to help their coworker or friend who is embarrassed to go to HR.

- It can also include any instance in which an employee tells HR about questionable behavior that they have witnessed.

These are examples of how seriously employers must take sexual and any other form of employee harassment that is or may be occurring in their workplace.

As an HR staff person, one of the most common requests that will occur when you are approached by an employee to talk is that they want to tell you something, but you must first promise to keep it confidential. Confidentiality in HR is not well understood by employees.

You must be prepared to answer that request by responding that if you can, you will keep the matter confidential. Some issues you are required by law to pursue whether the employee wants you to pursue the allegations or not. Sexual harassment is one of them.

How to Handle Sexual Harassment in the Workplace

1. Before a complaint is filed, make sure you have posted and informed all employees of your organization's policy relative to sexual

(Continued)

harassment. It won't be tolerated; it will be investigated.

2. Provide several different ways in which an employee can make a formal charge or complaint. You will not want to make complaints to the manager or supervisor the employee's only option as this may be the individual about whom the employee needs to complain. Human Resources offices are an excellent option. So is the CEO, president, or company owner unless they are the harasser. A manager is also a good option if he or she is not involved.

3. Assign a staff member to own the complaint. This individual should be knowledgeable about the organization, the people in the organization, and the history of the organization.

4. Map out a plan that covers the important people and situations to investigate from the initial complaint. Plan the investigation, based on current knowledge.

5. Talk with the employee who is complaining. Guarantee that he or she is safe from retaliation and took appropriate action in reporting the incident or general situation no matter what the results of the investigation found.

6. Inform the employee that you need to know immediately about any retaliation, purported retaliation, or ongoing harassment the employee experiences.

7. Ask the employee to tell you the whole story in his or her own words. Listen with care; take notes to document the conversation thoroughly. Write down relevant facts such as dates, times, situations, witnesses, and anything else that seems relevant.

8. Tell the person accused that a complaint has been filed and that no acts of retaliation or unethical actions will be tolerated. Ask the person to be patient while you conduct a thorough investigation.

9. Assure the person accused that a fair and just investigation will be conducted on their behalf as well as that of the accuser.

10. Interview any potential witnesses in the same manner. Ask open-ended questions and seek facts that support or disprove the employee's allegations.

11. Interview the person who is accused of sexual harassment. Apply the same listening and respectful approach you accorded the person who filed the complaint and the other witnesses.

12. Take all the information you received and attempt to reach a decision. Make the best decision that you can with the information you have. Consult with other HR colleagues to do the right thing.

13. Consult with an attorney to ensure that you are looking at the whole situation fairly based on the evidence you have. Make sure the attorney supports the direction you are taking.

14. Based on all of the documentation and advice from colleagues and your attorney, make decisions about whether sexual harassment occurred. Provide the appropriate discipline to the appropriate people, based on your findings. Make work or assignment setting adjustments, or change a reporting assignment if necessary.

15. Recognize that you are not perfect, no situation can be perfectly investigated. Even when harassment may have occurred, and you believe it may have occurred, you may have no facts or witnesses that corroborate a complainant's statement.

16. Assure that no further incidents occur by following up, and documenting your follow-up with the employee who made the original harassment claim. Keep documentation separate from the personnel file.

17. Afford the employee, who may have been wrongly accused, the same courtesy of follow-up and documentation. Adjust working situations fairly where necessary for the comfort and productivity of all.

Tips to Consider

1. Legally, the employer will want to avoid any possibility or appearance that the employee's complaint was disregarded. Respond immediately.

2. Ethically, the employer will not want to allow such behavior to exist in their workplace.

3. The trust, morale, and fair treatment of employees are at stake. An employer's actions send powerful signals about what another employee can expect in similar circumstances.

4. You may want to consider reposting and reiterating your sexual harassment policies across your whole workplace. Let the circumstances guide your judgment.

5. In all cases, make sure that you write and keep complete and accurate documentation.

Employees who are unhappy with the results of your investigation may take additional legal action.

Disclaimer: Please note that the information provided, while authoritative, is not guaranteed for accuracy and legality. The site is read by a worldwide audience, and employment laws and regulations vary from state to state and country to country. Please seek legal assistance, or assistance from State, Federal, or International governmental resources, to make certain your legal interpretation and decisions are correct for your location. This information is for guidance, ideas, and assistance.

SOURCE: "How to Handle an Employee Sexual Harassment Complaint" by Susan M. Heathfield. © 2018 Reprinted with permission of Dotdash.

As mentioned previously, provinces have their own rules regarding human rights violations. Some employer lawyers are expressing concerns about the increasing awards associated with human rights cases. There appears to be a trend toward greater damages for injury to dignity and punitive damages.[68]

Provincial Human Rights Laws and Human Rights Commissions

Most provinces and two territories (Northwest Territories and Yukon) have their own human rights laws and commissions with similar discrimination criteria, regulations, and procedures. British Columbia abolished its commission in 2003, but retained its Human Rights Tribunal. Nunavut has a human rights act and a tribunal, and Ontario has both a commission and tribunal.

If a person feels discriminated against, he or she will contact a provincial human rights officer, who will investigate the complaint and attempt to reach a settlement that will satisfy all parties. Experience has shown that the majority of cases are settled at this stage. Should there be no agreement, the case will be presented to the provincial human rights commission. The members of that commission study the evidence and then submit a report to the minister in charge of administration of the relevant human rights legislation. Depending on the jurisdiction, a case may be sent to the relevant human rights tribunal or board of inquiry (which has powers similar to those of a tribunal). Noncompliance with the course of action prescribed by the board/tribunal may result in prosecution in a provincial court of law. Depending on the jurisdiction, individuals can be fined between $500 and $25,000. If an issue at hand

has nationwide implications, a decision may ultimately be appealed to the Supreme Court of Canada.

There has been a trend recently to try and improve the dispute resolution programs administered by human rights commissions. For example, since 2012, the Nova Scotia Human Rights Commission began using a "resolution conference" in an effort to deal with complaints better, faster, and in a manner helping to restore or repair relationships. The objective is to have the parties create their own solution to the complaint. If a resolution conference fails to resolve a complaint, information from it will be used to make a recommendation to commissioners, who can dismiss the complaint or send it to a board of inquiry.[69]

A 2017 survey by the Ontario Human Rights Commission provides information on people's opinions on human rights:

Fewer than half of the respondents reported having positive feelings toward transgender people (46 percent), Muslim (45 percent) or Arab (44 percent) people, or people receiving social assistance (39 percent). Only 55 percent of respondents indicate some familiarity with the *Ontario Human Rights Code,* and views toward the most common reasons for discrimination include race or colour (63 percent), sexual orientation (34 percent), and disability (25 percent). Just under half of respondents indicated that they had experienced discrimination in the past five years, with the most common grounds being age (21 percent), gender (16 percent), or race (15 percent). Only 14 percent of people stating that they had been discriminated against had complained to someone in the organization where the discrimination occurred.[70]

LO4 Employment Equity

The Abella Commission on Equality in Employment (chaired by Judge Rosalie Abella) was appointed in 1983 to inquire into the most effective, efficient, and equitable methods of promoting employment opportunities for four designated groups: women, persons with a disability, Indigenous people (many of whom, but not all, prefer the term *Indigenous* to *Aboriginal* although *Aboriginal* appears in the legislation), and members of a visible minority. The Commission recommended that all organizations set mandatory equality programs and urged the provincial and federal governments to pass equity legislation—a recommendation that has since been implemented by the federal and all provincial governments. The Commission also recommended using the term *employment equity* in Canada to distinguish it from the U.S. term *affirmative action* because, in the opinion of the Commission, the latter carried too many negative associations.*

As a result of the Abella Commission's report, the federal government proclaimed the **Employment Equity Act** in August 1987. Its intent is to remove employment barriers and promote equality of the four designated group members. The Act requires employers with 100 and more employees under federal jurisdiction to develop annual plans setting out goals and timetables and to maintain these plans for three years. The Act requires further that each employer submit annual reports describing the progress in attaining the goals set out in the above-mentioned plans. The Canada Employment and Immigration Commission forwards employer reports to the Human Rights Commission. Employers who do not comply may be investigated by the Human Rights Commission and, if necessary, prosecuted under the *Canadian Human Rights Act.*

> **Employment Equity Act**
> Federal law to remove employment barriers and to promote equality.

The *Employment Equity Act* was amended in 1996. It now contains two specific provisions regarding "reasonable accommodation." Section 5 provides that:

"Every employer shall implement employment equity" by, among other measures, "making such reasonable accommodations as will ensure that persons in a designated group" achieve a degree of representation commensurate with their representation in the Canadian workforce and their availability to meet reasonable occupational requirements.

As noted above, the four designated groups are women, Indigenous people, persons with a disability, and members of a visible minority. (This is in contrast to human rights legislation, which requires equal treatment of *all* groups.)

Section 10 of the Act specifies that an employer shall prepare an "employment equity plan" that provides for "reasonable accommodation . . . to correct . . . under-representation." Some examples of reasonable accommodation are as follows:

- Providing a sign-language interpreter for a job interview with an applicant who is deaf
- Providing telephone or computer equipment to accommodate persons who are hard of hearing or seeing
- Constructing a barrier-free worksite for wheelchair-bound employees
- Allowing religious minorities to alter their work schedules to accommodate religious obligations
- Altering dress or grooming codes to allow Indigenous people to wear braids

The amended Act also established the CHRC as the monitoring agency that would carry out compliance audits for federally regulated public- and private-sector employers.

Functional Impact

Virtually every human resource function is affected by employment equity plans:

- *Human resource plans* must reflect the organization's employment equity goals.
- *Job descriptions* must not contain unneeded requirements that exclude members of protected classes.
- *Recruiting* must ensure that all types of applicants are sought without discriminating.
- *Selection* of applicants must use screening devices that are job-relevant and nondiscriminatory.
- *Training and developmental* opportunities must be made available for all workers, without discrimination.
- *Performance appraisal* must be free of biases that discriminate.
- *Compensation programs* must be based on skills, performance, and/or seniority and cannot discriminate against jobholders in other respects.

Even when human resource specialists know that their intent is not to discriminate, they must carefully review the results of these human resource functions to ensure that the results are not discriminatory. Otherwise, lawsuits may arise and the current employment equity plan may need to be revised or scrapped.

U.S.-based Uber recently announced plans to increase the pay of thousands of employees and to require pay equity between men and women and diverse groups.

---

* The major difference between Canadian employment equity and U.S. affirmative action programs is that the former are based on the principle of equitable access in all employment systems, while the latter are based on the principle of righting past wrongs.

There are several challenges facing the company. These include issues relating to occupational choices, experience and performance differentiation, the elimination of bias by managers, getting rid of subjectivity, and dealing with self-promotion.[71]

Employment Equity Programs

The *Employment Equity Act* gives the CHRC great latitude in pursuing the enforcement of the Act. One way for the Commission to comply with the intent of the Act to improve equal employment opportunities for special groups is for it to encourage **employment equity programs**.

> **employment equity programs** Developed by employers to undo past employment discrimination or to ensure equal employment opportunity in the future. Called affirmative action programs in the United States.

Section 16(1) of the *Canadian Human Rights Act* specifies special programs as a legitimate mechanism for improving the opportunities of a group through the elimination, reduction, or prevention of discrimination:

> It is not a discriminatory practice for a person to adopt or carry out a special program, plan, or arrangement designed to prevent disadvantages that are likely to be suffered by, or to eliminate or reduce disadvantages that are suffered by, any group of individuals when those disadvantages would be based on or related to the prohibited grounds of discrimination, by improving opportunities respecting goods, services, facilities, accommodation, or employment in relation to that group.

Such programs are developed by employers to remedy past discrimination or to prevent discrimination in the future. For the organization, such a program usually involves a self-evaluation of its hiring, promotion, and compensation policies. If discrepancies are found, it would be good human resource practice to check the criteria used for different decisions, adjust them if necessary, and make sure that they are consistently applied.

Employment equity programs exist for several reasons. From a practical standpoint, employers seldom benefit by excluding people who belong to a particular group. To exclude an entire class of workers, such as women or visible minorities, limits the labour pool available to the human resource department. Open discrimination can also lead to negative public relations, boycotts by consumers, and government intervention. To ensure that such discrimination does not occur, employers often develop equity programs voluntarily.

It should be noted that mandated equity programs take place mainly at the federal level—that is, in organizations and industries under federal jurisdiction. At the provincial level, such programs are implemented almost exclusively

---

FIGURE 4-4

Major Steps in Employment Equity Programs

1. Exhibit strong employer commitment.
2. Appoint a high-ranking director.
3. Publicize commitment internally and externally.
4. Survey the workforce for underutilization and concentration.
5. Develop goals and timetables.
6. Design remedial, active, and preventive programs.
7. Establish control systems and reporting procedures.

---

on a voluntary basis. Regardless of the reasons or goals of such programs, human resource departments should adhere to the guidelines discussed below and summarized in Figure 4-4.

- *Exhibit commitment.* No matter how favourably the human resource department is viewed by others in the organization, the CEO/president of the company should support the program in writing. Anything less than total support from top officials raises questions about the sincerity of the organization's commitment in the eyes of government agencies, courts, and employees. To exhibit this commitment forcefully, company officials may make raises, bonuses, and promotions dependent upon each manager's compliance.

- *Appoint a director.* Some member of the organization should be responsible for equity issues. Commonly, the vice-president of human resources is appointed director, although day-to-day implementation may be delegated to a compliance specialist in the human resource department.

- *Publicize commitment.* An employment equity program is ineffective unless publicized externally and internally. Outside the company, sources of potential recruits must be made aware of the new policy. School guidance counsellors, employment agencies, and officers of Canada Employment Centres are likely candidates for notification. Organizations should include the phrase "An equal opportunity employer" on company stationery and in employment ads to further publicize its policy. Internally, the practice should be conveyed, in strong enough terms, to everyone involved in the hiring process. Otherwise, top management may pursue one policy; and lower levels, another.

- *Survey the workforce.* The human resource department needs to know how the composition of the employer's workforce compares with the composition of the workforce in the labour market.

For example, if the employer's mix of male and female employees differs significantly from the labour market from which the employer attracts workers, it is possible that discrimination has occurred. When a survey of the employer's workforce indicates such differences, the employer may find examples of underutilization or concentration. **Underutilization** exists when a company or department has a smaller proportion of protected class members than is found in the labour market. **Concentration** is just the opposite, occurring when protected class members are concentrated in a few departments, out of proportion with their presence in the labour market.

underutilization A condition that exists when a department or employer has a lesser proportion of members of a protected class than are found in the employer's labour market.

concentration A condition that exists when a department or employer has a greater proportion of members of a protected class than are found in the employer's labour market.

- *Develop goals and timetables.* When, through surveys, underutilization and concentration are found (possibly as consequences of past discrimination), human resource specialists should set up goals and timetables to eliminate them.

- *Design specific programs.* To reach goals, human resource specialists must design remedial, active, and preventive programs. *Remedial programs* correct problems that already exist. *Active programs* imply that management goes beyond instructing supervisors about new hiring policies and waiting for things to happen. It means going to high schools in areas dominated by minorities, approaching community leaders in such areas for assistance, inviting residents to attend information sessions, and advertising in newspapers or other media outlets accessible to minorities and special target groups:

In 1985, the law school at Dalhousie University (now the Schulich School of Law) in Halifax developed an Indigenous Blacks and Mi'kmaq Initiative to train more black and Mi'kmaq lawyers. The program director visits high schools and universities and holds information sessions at reserves and community centres. An advisory board made up of law school representatives, community leaders, and the two student groups assists in identifying ways to reach the target groups. To date, the program has more than 150 graduates.[72]

Preventive programs are more proactive. They involve an assessment of human resource management policies and practices. Policies that discriminate (such as height rules) or practices that continue past discrimination (such as hiring exclusively from employee referrals) must be eliminated.

- *Establish controls.* An employment equity program is likely to fail unless controls are established. Human resource specialists and line managers must perceive their rewards as depending upon the success of the program. To evaluate that success, monthly, quarterly, and yearly benchmarks should be reported directly to the director of the program and to the CEO/president or another senior official.

Contract Compliance Policy

In addition to companies or agencies under federal jurisdiction, the federal government requires compliance with the *Employment Equity Act* from any company doing business with the federal government. Companies with 100 or more employees bidding on contracts for goods and services of $1,000,000 or more are subject to the employment equity criteria listed in the Act. Under this policy, companies are required to certify in writing at the tendering stage of a contract their commitment to implement employment equity. Employers will be subject to random reviews to ensure their compliance with the Act.

Pay Equity

Women aged 25–54 earn about 87 percent as much per hour as male employees, and the gap has shrunk by about 10 cents since 1981.[73] There are many reasons for this pay gap, including differences in work experience, education, major field of study, occupation and industry of employment, as well as reasons that are still not understood. Pay equity legislation attempts to remedy these inequities. At the federal level, the *Canadian Human Rights Act* prohibits discrimination based on sex; it is therefore illegal to pay women less than men if their jobs are of equal value, a principle known as "equal pay for work of equal value," which is discussed in more detail in Chapter 9. Pay equity policy frameworks exist in British Columbia and Saskatchewan, and pay equity negotiations with public sector unions exist in Newfoundland and Labrador. Legislation in Nova Scotia, Manitoba, New Brunswick, and PEI applies to public service employees but only Quebec and Ontario have laws covering the public and private sector. At the federal level, the Public Sector Equitable Compensation Act regulates remuneration for public servants.[74]

That the "equal pay for work of equal value" concept can be very costly was shown in the case of 390 federal library science employees—mostly women—who earned less than historical researchers—mostly men—though the library science work was claimed to be of equal value. The settlement, requiring individual salary increases of up to $2,500 a year, cost the federal government $2.4 million.

On October 19, 1999, the longest and largest pay equity case was resolved when Justice John Evans upheld a Human Rights Tribunal's ruling that the federal government owed about 230,000 (mostly female) workers 13 years of back pay. The final settlement cost the Treasury Board over $3.5 billion. The federal government decided not to appeal this decision.

In November 2011, the Supreme Court of Canada decided in favour of female Canada Post workers in a pay equity case that was brought 28 years ago. Originally, about 2,300 employees worked in the affected classification (office workers), but about 6,000 employees (including some men) have been in the classification at some point in time. It is estimated that workers employed in the classification between 1983 and 2002 will share about $250 million. The main issue was whether it was appropriate for the Human Rights Commission to compare the office group with a male-dominated group that had some female members.[75]

The implication for human resource people is that they must make very sure the wage and salary system does not subtly discriminate on the basis of sex.

Reverse Discrimination

The use of employment equity programs can lead to charges of reverse discrimination against employers. The charges usually arise when an employer seeks to hire or promote a member of a protected group over an equally (or better) qualified candidate who is not a member of a protected group. For example, if an employer has an employment equity program that gives preference to women over men when promotions occur, a qualified male may sue the employer and claim that he was discriminated against because of his sex.

Charges of reverse discrimination may put human resource departments in a difficult position. On the one hand, the human resource manager is responsible for eliminating concentration and underutilization. On the other hand, to give preference to members of a protected class (such as women) raises questions about whether the human resource department is being fair. Although preferential treatment will always raise questions of fairness, the *Canadian Human Rights Act* declares employment equity programs nondiscriminatory if they fulfill the spirit of the law.

The Principle of Natural Justice

Many people in an organization have the power of making decisions that can greatly affect the life or career of organization members. To ensure that a decision-making process is fair, the principle of **natural justice** has been accepted internationally— for example, as nonlegal

natural justice Minimum standards of fair decision making imposed on persons or bodies acting in a judicial capacity.

guidelines for arbitrators or mediators, but also by courts in their legal judgment process. The rules of natural justice are minimum standards of fairness and are implied obligations for decision makers. Some of the rules are as follows:

- The right to a fair hearing
- The right to a bias-free proceeding (e.g., a person adjudicating a dispute should have no personal interest in the outcome of the proceedings)
- The right to present the opposing argument
- The right of legal representation
- The right of timely notice of a hearing
- The right to a timely process (according to the principle, "Justice delayed is justice denied")

Court decisions have decreed that natural justice rules supersede organizational policies and regulations. This means that human resource managers have to make sure that organizational procedures follow the above rules.

Other Legal Challenges

This chapter has dealt mainly with legal discrimination and harassment issues. Of course, there are many other potential legal challenges, not all of which can be detailed here. The following are some of these relevant issues, most of which will be discussed in later chapters:

- *The Canada Labour Code.* The *Industrial Disputes Investigation Act* of 1907 was modified and re-enacted in 1971 as the *Canada Labour Code.* It regulates union certification, the right to organize, union prosecution, and mediation and arbitration procedures, all of which are discussed in more detail in Chapter 13. Provincial equivalents to the code are the *Employment* (or *Labour*) *Standards Acts.*
- *Dismissal.* According to common law, every employee has a contract with his or her employer, even if there is nothing in writing. An employee or employer can terminate an employment relationship by giving reasonable notice. An immediate dismissal is possible if an employee is compensated through appropriate severance pay (see Chapter 11).
- *Hours of work and overtime regulations.* The *Canada Labour Code* sets the standard workday at eight hours and the standard workweek at 40 hours, and overtime pay at one-and-a-half times the regular pay.
- *Minimum wages.* These are set by provincial and federal boards and discussed in Chapter 9.
- *Occupational health and safety.* The *Canada Labour Code* also regulates occupational health and safety issues, discussed in Chapter 12.

- *Weekly rest day.* The *Canada Labour Code* specifies that employees must be given at least one full day of rest during the week, preferably on Sunday.
- *Workplace Hazardous Material Information System (WHMIS).* WHMIS regulates the handling of dangerous material, discussed in Chapter 12.

These are some of the federal laws that have an impact on human resource managers. Most of them have their provincial equivalent. It is ultimately the human resource manager who is responsible for knowing and enforcing the law.

LO5 Strategic Implications of Legal Challenges

If there is one basic rule in human resource management, it is "Obey the law." The human resource manager must make sure all policies and rules take legal aspects into account (e.g., hiring and termination procedures, pay equity regulations, health and safety rules, and the handling of dangerous products). Given the current priority accorded employment equity, human resource managers also have to ensure that all long-range strategic plans that have an impact on staff and staffing follow employment equity requirements. Not doing so can be costly, as some of the examples given in this chapter have shown.

It is also desirable for a corporation to be perceived by the public as being a "good corporate citizen." One of the objectives of an organization is to project equity, which determines its attractiveness as perceived by job applicants (discussed in Chapter 5, Chapter 6, and Chapter 9).

Following legal requirements also has implications for training:

> A Sears employee in Winnipeg asked a customer to have his children get off the lawn tractors on display. The employee also said, "Let me guess, you just came off the boat?" The two parties got into an argument and a part of the incident was captured on video. The employee was ultimately fired. The incident shows how quickly an issue can become viral and also points to the need for detailed customer service training. Sears has a code of conduct, a code of ethics, and a respect-in-the-workplace policy and every employee has to complete online training with exams every year. However, as business coach Janice Martin put it, "When you are faced with a ticked-off customer, you are not thinking of the role-playing you did months ago in training."[76]

Managers and supervisors have to be familiar with the laws as they apply to human resource management. Sexual harassment is an issue that has cost business and government organizations large amounts of money in fines, court costs, and compensation to the victims. Unjust dismissal is another prominent issue. More and more employees dismissed for unsatisfactory performance or other reasons have challenged their dismissal, and management has had to prove that the decision was valid.

Diversity in Canadian Workplaces

Dimensions of Diversity

Given the myriad differences among humans, it is very difficult to arrive at a broad and universally acceptable definition of diversity that is inclusive yet does not overwhelm us in the process. Broadly, **workplace diversity** may be defined to include important human characteristics that influence an employee's values, perceptions of self and others, behaviours, and interpretation of events around him or her. Diversity, at a minimum, includes age, ethnicity and culture, sex/gender, race, religion, sexual orientation, and mental and physical capabilities (see Figure 4-5). Several writers consider seven areas to be the **core dimensions of diversity** because they exert

> **workplace diversity** Includes important human characteristics that influence employee values, their perceptions of self and others, behaviours, and interpretations of events.
>
> **core dimensions of diversity** Age, ethnicity and culture, sex/gender, race, religion, sexual orientation, and capabilities.

FIGURE 4-5

Core and Secondary Dimensions of Diversity

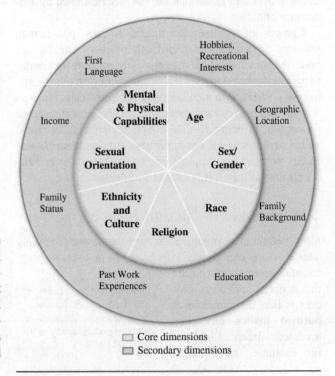

☐ Core dimensions
☐ Secondary dimensions

considerable impact on our early socialization and a powerful, sustained impact throughout our lives.

For example, regardless of whether a particular employee is currently 20, 40, or 60 years old, his or her age has a bearing on how that person is perceived by others as well as on the individual's ability to learn, perform (several tasks), and relate to the environment. Age, thus, is a core dimension that affects an individual's workplace perceptions and behaviours.

Several other **secondary dimensions of diversity** such as education, family status, language, and even income levels play important roles in shaping our values, expectations, behaviours, and experiences. Hence, their impact on employee behaviours at the workplace should not be underestimated. They are, however, less visible, more mutable, and more variable in their impact on individual behaviours.

> **secondary dimensions of diversity** Education, status, language, and income levels.

Can sports bring people of diverse backgrounds together? The Canadian Football League (CFL) recently introduced its Diversity Is Strength campaign. T-shirts with the Diversity Is Strength logo also include names of players from diverse backgrounds. Critics of the initiative argue that the CFL is trying to promote diversity and multiculturalism as a way to increase business and attract more fans.[77]

Consider some of these statistics on Canadian diversity:

- According to the 2016 census, Canada has a total of 72,880 same-sex common-law couples representing 0.9 percent of all couples in the country.[78] The number of same-sex couples increased by 60.7 percent between 2006 and 2016.

- With the legalization of same-sex marriage in July 2005, Canada became the third country in the world to legalize same-sex marriage after the Netherlands (2000) and Belgium (2003).

- 21.9 percent of Canadians were born outside the country, and this is expected to increase to between 25 and 30 percent by 2036.

- Nearly 7.7 million Canadians, or 22.3 percent of the total population (based on 2016 data), were visible minorities. About 70 percent of visible minorities live in Toronto, Montreal, or Vancouver.

- About 3.8 million Canadians (13.7 percent) reported having a disability. Women (14.9 percent) were more likely to report a disability than men (12.5 percent).[79]

Most of us tend to group people using dimensions such as race, sex/gender, and age. However, the same person may belong to multiple categorical groups:

The same individual's identity can be composed of various facets: One can be an African-Canadian (race) woman (sex) who is older (age), married (marital status), and from a low-income family (income status).

This raises an important question: On which one or more of these identities should a human resource manager focus? Grouping people often results in **stereotyping**; yet, a grouping that gives added insights into the person's unique background, capabilities, and individuality is likely to generate better workplace outcomes. Further, the differences between groups need not be intrinsic or innate; they can be differences attributed to history or prevailing culture and subject to change.

> **stereotyping** The process of using a few observable characteristics to assign someone to a preconceived social category.

In 1993, about 46 of federal government employees were women and 2 percent were Indigenous people. Women now make up 54.4 percent of the federal public service and 4 percent are Indigenous. Visible minorities now make up almost 9 percent of the federal workforce, compared to just under 4 percent in 1993. However, there are major differences when comparing across government departments. Some observers are attributing the changes to an employment equity program that depends on public disclosure rather than a mandatory quota system.[80]

Such attributed differences play a key role in human interaction. Cultural conventions and values set "rules" when interacting with others and reduce uncertainty for individuals in a society. These largely unwritten rules themselves have been changing. For some people, many of these "rule changes" are welcome since they reduce inequity and injustice. For others, the pattern and pace of change heightens anxiety and discomfort because longstanding ideals are being eroded.

Challenges for Diverse Workers

Historically and even currently, members of diverse groups experience specific challenges in Canadian workplaces owing to their diversity. Several of these challenges are described next.

Many women are hindered by lack of access to the **old boys' network**, the set of informal relationships that develop among male managers and executives.[81] This results in exclusive fraternizing of men with men that reinforces a "culture" of men without women's perspective and condones behaviour that devalues women. The friendships and contacts built through the network become the basis for assignments and promotions, and the network becomes the informal communication link

> **old boys' network** Set of informal relationships among male managers providing increased career advancement opportunities for men and reinforcing a male culture.

that provides vital information about business from which women are excluded. This means that many women never reach positions of power.

Even in judicial settings, women find themselves subject to harassment:

> Errol Massiah, an Oshawa Justice of the Peace, was found guilty of judicial misconduct for sexually harassing female court staff. Six complainants stated that Massiah made comments about their physical attributes during the period 2008 to 2010. A review by a panel of the Justices of the Peace Review Council considered Massiah's efforts to address his misconduct, including writing letters of apology to the six complainants and attending sensitivity and remedial human rights training. However, Massiah was not terminated but rather given a 10-day suspension without pay but with benefits.[82]

A global study by Oliver Wyman revealed that 25 percent of executives at financial services firms in Canada are female, placing Canada third in the world behind Norway (33 percent) and Sweden (32 percent) and ahead of the United States (20 percent). Japan ranked last of 19 countries, with 2 percent of women holding executive roles at major financial institutions. The Back to Bay Street program, which assists women returning to the financial sector after taking time off to have children, was cited as part of a web of support.[83]

The Canadian Board Diversity Council's Fifth Annual Report Card (2016) revealed that women held about 22 percent of board seats in FP500 companies (up from 13.7 percent in 2009). Women were more likely to be on the board of firms in retail and trade (29.4 percent), utilities (29.0 percent), and finance and insurance sectors (27.4 percent). About 23 percent of board seats in manufacturing and 9.7 percent in mining, oil, and gas were held by women.[84]

Although it is projected that visible minorities will make up about one-third of the country's population in 15 years, representation on the boards of public institutions and agencies tends to not be reflective of the community. An initiative called DiverseCity onBoard is aimed at addressing the issue by developing networks and providing boards with real-life candidates in front of them.[85]

About 95 percent of board directors agreed that board diversity is very or somewhat important to them (up from 85 percent in 2010). However, 74 percent of female directors indicated that board diversity is very important to them, compared with 45 percent for male directors. Just under 40 percent of boards have a target for the percentage of directors that are women. When considering diversity of board directors, about 4.5 percent are visible minorities, 3 percent report having a disability, less than 1 percent are Indigenous peoples, and 2 percent are LGBTQ.[86]

The existing values, norms, and patterns of interactions among managers may also act as a **glass ceiling** that stunts the career growth of women and minority persons beyond a certain level. Promotional opportunities are visible, but invisible obstructions seem to block the way. The perception of the existence of a glass ceiling results in frustration, reduced job and career satisfaction, alienation from the workplace, and ultimately higher employee turnover. However, some organizations are making major strides in advancing promotional opportunities for female and visible minority employees.

> **glass ceiling** Invisible but real obstructions to career advancement of women and people of visible minorities, resulting in frustration, career dissatisfaction, and increased turnover.

> Michael Bach founded the Canadian Institute for Diversity and Inclusion in 2012 with the objective of supporting employers in their diversity and inclusion journey. In 2011, Catalyst Canada recognized Bach, then director of Diversity, Equity, and Inclusion at KPMG, for his activities in supporting the advancement of women in Canadian business.[87]

Despite the transformation of Canadian cities and towns into multicultural mosaics, prejudices against visible minorities continue to exist in the workplace. In addition, the stereotypes faced by women belonging to specific religious groups prevent them from gaining even lower-level jobs:

> Discriminatory hiring practices and workplace racism toward Muslim women are common in Toronto, according to a study by Women Working with Immigrant Women, a nonprofit organization that works with immigrants. Of the 32 Muslim women surveyed, 29 said that employers had commented on their hijab and 13 women reported that an employer told them they would have to take the hijab off if they wanted a job. The study also included a field experiment where three teams of applicants—matched in every way except that one wore the hijab and one didn't—visited 16 job sites to apply for a job. At more than half of the sites, the applicant without the hijab was asked to fill out an application or leave a résumé while the applicant with a hijab was not. At two job sites, the woman without the hijab was told there was a job available while the woman with the hijab was told there weren't any jobs.[88]

Every year employers are honoured for their contribution to diversity. Some of the 2018 winners of Canada's Best Diversity Employers include Air Canada, City of Saskatoon, Home Depot, the Nova Scotia Government, and the Toronto Transit Commission. For each of the winners, one can read about the diversity initiatives in place at the organization as well as statistical data, such as percentage of employees who are women, percentage of employees who are visible minorities, and average age.

LO6 Strategic Importance of Diversity

A diverse workforce requires managers with new leadership styles who understand their varying needs and creatively respond by offering flexible management policies and practices. **Managing diversity** recognizes that an organization is a mosaic where employees with varying beliefs, cultures, values, and behaviour patterns come together to create a whole organization and where these differences are acknowledged and accepted. Managing diversity has three major dimensions.[89] First, it assumes that effective management of diversity and differences among employees can add value to an organization; second, diversity includes all types of differences and not simply obvious ones such as sex/gender, race, and so on; and third, organization culture and working environments are key items to focus on in managing diversity.

> **managing diversity**
> Ability to manage individual employees with different cultural values and lead teams made up of diverse employees.

Managing diversity requires an organization to treat its employees as individuals rather than as numbers or categories. Several factors make diversity management strategically important.

Changing Workforce

As detailed in Chapter 1 and Chapter 3, the Canadian labour market is undergoing rapid and continuous transformation. Years ago, the average member of the workforce was male, white, approximately 30 years old, and usually held a high school diploma or lower. These men also worked within the region of their birth, were married, and had children. In contrast, today's workforce is considerably more diverse. Given this change, diversity management is

© Darryl Estrine/Getty Images RF

Canada's cultural mosaic raises several challenges for the manager who must successfully manage a diverse workforce. What advantages and disadvantages would a team made up of members from different cultures have?

not merely desirable but mandatory if an organization is to effectively attract, utilize, and develop human resources.

Importance of Human Capital

Changes in production technology have dramatically increased the importance of human capital. In today's world of "intellectual capitalism" and knowledge-intensive firms, it is not clear who owns the company, its tools, and its products. The knowledge worker may be the key to the success or failure of the firm. Often the departure of even a few key workers can spell disaster for the firm. The most valuable parts of the firm's operation may be reflected in human tasks of sensing, judging, and making decisions. In today's information age (and the growing advancement of artificial intelligence, machine learning, and digitization; see Chapter 11), the importance of human capital is critical.

> The vast majority of employers believe that they have programs aimed at the successful integration of foreign-trained employees into their workplaces. However, a study of 560 professionals who earned their degrees outside of Canada, but have been in the country for between 6 and 15 years, found that only 49 percent of participants felt that the places they worked had policies to integrate non-Canadian employees. There was a perception that employer orientation programs should include more information on the culture at Canadian workplaces. Less than half of employers reported having a way to assess whether foreign credentials are adequate.[90]

Diversity as a Competitive Advantage

Proactive organizations recognize that competitive strength often lies in focusing on their employees and their clients. Globalization and changing domestic markets (because of demographic changes, immigration, etc.) mean that a firm's customers are no longer a homogeneous group of persons. For Canada, this is particularly important since our biggest trading partner, the United States, itself is undergoing rapid transformation in its population, resulting in greater workforce diversity.

Further, many of the growing export markets for Canadian firms are located in Asia, Latin America, and Africa. It is imperative that we understand the needs of a diverse population and respond effectively and in a timely fashion to maintain our competitive advantage.

Although the great majority of organizations report that diversity, inclusion, human rights, and equity are strategic initiatives at their workplaces, a study by the Canadian Institute of Diversity and Inclusion revealed that only about 19 percent of employers are measuring the impact, efficiency, or return on investment (ROI) of their diversity initiatives. In addition, very few employers measure the diversity impact over an employee's life cycle.[91]

Increasing Role of Work Teams

Teams play a dominant role in modern organization. While teams always reflected some degree of diversity, today the differences among members are even greater. The differences must be considered as "value added" rather than as "problematic" and the team leader today must have the skills to facilitate and inspire (rather than coach and control as in the past). Valuing differences can result in improved creativity and innovative problem solving.

Does diversity matter? Based on a review of research on workplace diversity and firm performance published in nine leading journals from 2000–2009, McMahon found that the relationship was curvilinear—the effects are stronger in more stable environments and more dramatic in service industries compared to manufacturing. Diversity alone cannot explain firm performance—resources, capabilities, and core competencies are stronger predictors of performance. However, diversity that enhances these variables is associated with better performance.[92] Similarly, Herring, using data from a sample of for-profit firms in the United States, found that racial diversity was related to greater sales revenue and market share, higher relative profits, and more customers. In addition, gender diversity was associated with all of the above outcomes except for greater market share.[93]

Diversity is more than a human resource management issue and affects all strategies and processes of the organization. Diversity management is tied to the strategic plan, and every employee from senior executive to the lowest-level employee contributes to fostering a diverse workforce.

LO7 Diversity and Inclusion

While diversity may be defined as "all the ways in which we differ," inclusion involves establishing and maintaining work practices and a work environment where everyone can be fully themselves and make contributions. Many organizations are now moving from only a diversity management approach toward leveraging inclusion. One primary reason behind this shift is that "managing diversity" requires first a label or classification of a person along a dimension of diversity (for instance, older, female, gay, Lebanese, transgender). Inclusion leapfrogs this labelling and moves right into creating practices and conditions where *all* employees are able to contribute effectively *regardless* of their differences. Figure 4-6 describes the differences between diversity and inclusion philosophies.

For organizations seeking to move toward an inclusive environment, one of the first steps is to articulate the ideal future state the organization would achieve through inclusion. Creating an inclusive culture is not accomplished merely by stating it within the organization's vision and

---

FIGURE 4-6

Difference Between Diversity and Inclusion Philosophies

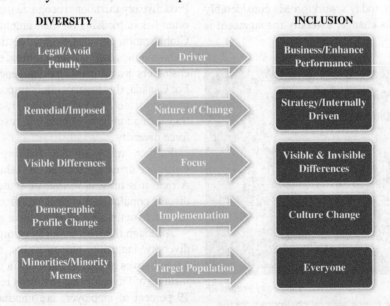

SOURCE: Angie Levesque and Geordie Macpherson (2016, Winter), "Inclusion Trumps Diversity," *Human Capital,* The Official Magazine of the Human Resources Institute of Alberta, http://www.nxtbook.com/naylor/HRIQ/HRIQ0416/index.php#/20

values, but these statements provide guideposts for the organization to develop practices and conditions toward living inclusion.

Another step is to examine how the present systems are operating through examining "people analytics." A good and honest survey of employees will indicate how well the organization is currently doing in terms of supporting inclusion.

> Part of RBC's strategy of diversity is asking employees to examine their blind spots and banish their mind bugs. RBC's unconscious bias campaign is part of the company's commitment to progress in all areas of diversity, including women, visible minorities, people with disabilities, LGBTQ, and Indigenous communities. According to senior VP Rod Bolger, diversity has evolved from an initiative seen as "the right thing to do" to a business strategy conferring competitive advantage to today's drive for inclusiveness.[94]

Current policies, systems, practices, rules, and procedures have to be examined for their appropriateness for an inclusive culture. Included here are work assignments, recruitment and hiring, onboarding, training, compensation, employee communication, human resource development, and performance appraisal. As one example, recruitment practices may need to be revised, as seen in this example:

> Shopify, a recipient of the 2018 Employer Excellence Award from Hire Immigrants Ottawa, launched an Android Bootcamp in 2017. This program involves reaching out to software developers who are recent immigrants to Canada, selecting candidates for a two-and-a-half day Android Bootcamp, and considering Bootcamp participants for employment. According to Meghan Herman, "Diversity and inclusion are integral tenants of Shopify's culture."[95]

Senior management commitment to inclusion is one of the most important elements of ensuring the success of inclusion efforts; so is whole-hearted support from the unions. Inclusion efforts will fail unless all managers and employees see them as an integral part of the firm's business philosophy. This means that particular attention should be paid to communication, hiring, and reward structures to promote inclusion. A number of managers do not know what their specific role is when it comes to managing inclusion. According to Siu, "A lot of managers are saying 'I know how great diversity is but exactly what can I accomplish to prove that and align what I am doing with the senior management agenda?'"[96]

In the past, several organizations have confused diversity with hiring women, members of visible minorities, and people with disabilities. However, simply hiring more women or other minorities in the absence of a genuine commitment to diversity and inclusion is not sufficient.

© Robert Kneschke/Shutterstock

Today's workforce includes more women participating in careers that were typically exclusive to men. Still, the glass ceiling remains. How can it be cracked?

Indeed, some recent research studies indicate that women often leave organizations and start their own companies to avoid "glass ceilings" at work.

At times, human resource practices represent major impediments to inclusion and may discourage people from applying for a job. Consider the experience a few years ago of applicants for firefighting jobs in Halifax:

> A total of 94 applicants for firefighting jobs in Halifax were told that they would be removed from the primary eligibility list at the end of the current year because there were not enough minority applicants. All of the applicants were white males except for two women and two black men. There has been an employment equity program since 1999 and the recruiting service used outreach programs to try to increase the number of minority applicants. New applicants to the fire service may end up paying close to $1,000 for such things as an application fee, an aptitude test, an integrity interview, a physical agility test, and a polygraph test. The various tests had fees ranging from $50 to $350. In addition to the costs of the application, there was considerable criticism of the polygraph test, which asked candidates such questions as whether they had ever thought about committing suicide or had sex with animals.[97]

Figure 4-7 shows the areas where a firm must make changes if inclusion initiatives are to succeed. Mere verbal support of system and policy changes is unlikely to produce tangible results. Linking inclusion initiatives to business goals and incorporating diversity goals into performance criteria (reflected in salaries) ensures the accountability of managers for inclusion.

> A survey revealed that only about 12 percent of organizations have a clearly defined policy aimed at integrating Internationally Educated Professionals (IEPs). About 46 percent of participants reported that

FIGURE 4-7

Systems and Practices Requiring Modification during a Diversity and Inclusion Effort

- Recruitment and selection processes and criteria
- Orientation
- Work assignments
- Performance management
- Reward systems
- Employee communication systems
- Training
- Career and management development policies and programs
- Employee counselling practices
- Benefits policy
- Group and team practices
- Leadership skills and practices
- Job descriptions and specifications

the number of IEPs being hired has increased over the past 10 years. The major barriers to integrating IEPs include language (93 percent), recognition of foreign credentials (84 percent), cultural barriers (78 percent), and lack of Canadian work experience (61 percent).[98]

Changes in internal systems and procedures must be communicated to all members. Information should be provided on what changes will occur, what the likely results will be, how important these changes are for the success of the organization, accomplishments until this point, and responses to questions related to diversity initiatives. More on employee communication strategies is discussed in Chapter 11.

> For a long time, Canada Post had a very stable and homogenous workforce. Over time, the organization attempted to enhance its diversity by recruiting more women, Indigenous persons, and African-Canadians into its workforce. Today, women account for about 50 percent of its employees, and 33.3 percent of senior managerial positions are held by women.

Targeted initiatives such as the Progressive Aboriginal Relations Program helped the organization to attract more Indigenous persons into its workforce. Members of visible minorities and persons with disabilities account for more than 20 percent of its workforce. To widely communicate its commitment to diversity, Canada Post runs special events such as celebrations around Aboriginal Day or Black History month.[99]

Unless the firm monitors the progress of the diversity and inclusion effort on a systematic basis, corrective actions may not follow. Monitoring will also ensure that quantitative and qualitative indices of change are available to the management, the union, and the workforce. These results should be widely communicated and the gaps between targets and accomplishments publicized along with the proposed corrective actions. Indices such as number of hires, promotions, absenteeism, turnover, salary levels, grievances, harassment complaints, and so on, are useful for gauging progress, but should not be used exclusively since qualitative responses from employees may convey other dimensions of work climate and the intensity of employee feelings. More progressive organizations make use of **diversity and inclusion audits** on a regular basis to uncover the underlying dimensions, causes, and progress-to-date on diversity management matters. Prompt follow-up actions to accelerate accomplishments are necessary and should be planned in consultation with the senior managers and the unions to ensure success.

diversity and inclusion audits Audits to uncover underlying dimensions, causes, interdependencies, and progress-to-date on diversity and inclusion matters.

Current Industry Practices

More progressive employers have adopted a variety of policies and practices to create an inclusive culture that welcomes everyone irrespective of their sex/gender, colour, and religious or other beliefs. The approaches to diversity and inclusion are as varied as organizations. The choice of specific mechanisms should be made after a careful consideration of the unique challenges and constraints facing an organization:

> A study by the Royal Bank of Canada of 64 major Canadian organizations revealed that almost 90 percent of participants indicated that they strongly believe that diverse and inclusive teams make better decisions while 66 percent strongly agree and 20 percent agree that leveraging diverse backgrounds and individuals is fundamental to their organizational performance. A bit over half of respondents indicated that they use

scorecards to track annual diversity performance, about 60 percent train executives and managers on how to manage diverse teams, 55 percent publicly communicate how the organization is progressing in meeting diversity and inclusion goals, and a bit over 40 percent hold leaders accountable for diversity and inclusion results.[100]

Diversity and Inclusion Training Programs

Managers and lower-level supervisors need to learn new skills that will enable them to manage and motivate a diverse workforce. Often, outside experts are invited to provide **diversity and inclusion training programs** in organizations. Indeed, in many firms this is one of the first actions taken to implement diversity management. Such training programs help to cre-ate awareness of the bottom-line impact of diversity manage-ment and the role of managers, supervisors, and co-workers in creating a work climate that is comfortable for all employ-ees, irrespective of their differences.

diversity and inclusion training programs Training programs aimed at importing new skills to motivate and manage a diverse and inclusive workforce.

Experts suggest two types of training: awareness train-ing and skill-building training. **Awareness training** focuses on creating an understanding of the need for managing and valuing diversity and inclusion. It is also meant to increase participants' self-awareness of diversity- and inclusion-related issues, such as stereotyping and cross-cultural insensitivity.

awareness training Training employees to develop their understand-ing of the need to manage and value diversity.

Once individuals develop an awareness, they can then monitor their feelings, reactions, and so on, and make conscious decisions about their behaviour, often resulting in improved inter-personal communication. **Skill-building training** edu-cates employees on specific cultural differences and how to respond to differences in the workplace. Often awareness and skill-building train-ing are combined.

skill-building training Training employees in interpersonal skills to correctly respond to cul-tural differences at the workplace.

In the long run, it is therefore more practical, although more difficult, to focus on *process training*; that is, supervisors and employees have to learn about diversity. Participants in a process-oriented diversity training pro-gram develop an understanding of how management style, the interpersonal communication process, teamwork, and other managerial issues are affected by diversity. After such a training program, participants may not have all the answers, but they will have plenty of questions.

Mentoring Programs

Some firms encourage **mentoring programs** where women or members of vis-ible minorities and other disadvantaged groups are encouraged to work with a senior manager who acts as a friend, philosopher, and guide in achieving career success within the firm.

mentoring programs Programs encouraging members of disadvantaged groups (e.g., women) to work with a senior man-ager who acts like a friend and guide in achieving career success.

Mentors may be identified formally or informally. Organizations can bring greater predictability into diversity outcomes by establishing formal mentoring systems since they result in greater tangible results and accountability on the part of both mentors and proteges.

One large Canadian bank lists all relevant details of its senior managers on its website. All new hires are encour-aged to select someone from the list and contact him or her on a regular basis for receiving helpful hints for day-to-day performance and long-term career advice. Both the mentor and the protege are encouraged to submit reports of their deliberations to the bank.

Alternate Work Arrangements

Often, removal of negative factors can enhance employee performance and career growth. This is especially so in the case of women who have multiple and conflict-ing role demands from work and family, or older work-ers who find the traditional work arrangements diffi-cult. Several **alternate work arrangements** such as flex-ible work hours, telecom-muting, extended leave, job sharing, et cetera, have been used in the past to accommo-date the unique needs of employee groups. These arrange-ments are discussed in more detail in Chapter 3.

alternate work arrangements Nontraditional work arrangements (e.g., flex-time, telecommuting) that provide more flexibility to employees while meeting organizational goals.

Apprenticeships

Apprenticeships are similar to mentoring except that they relate to junior-level or tech-nical jobs and often involve working with prospective employees before they for-mally join the organization. Such programs are particularly useful to attract members of visible minorities, women,

apprenticeships A form of on-the-job training in which junior employees learn a trade from an experienced person.

people with disabilities, and other disadvantaged group members to nontraditional jobs within the firm:

> Temisan Boyo, a native of Nigeria with an interest in law, was pretty sure she would not want to work for a major corporate law firm like Blake, Cassels and Graydon. Boyo stated that she thought it would be "very white, very male, very formal, and very unaccepting of things that were not part of the status quo." However, Boyo became the recipient of an Equity & Diversity Pre-Law Internship at Blakes and she found out that the firm was very flexible and more diverse than she had expected. Blakes is involved in several other initiatives, such as their Indigenous Summer School program, and supports a number of affinity groups, including Women@Blakes, Pride@Blakes, and the Diversity and Inclusion Network.[101]

Support Groups

Employees belonging to racial or other groups that are under-represented in the organization may often feel lonely and uncomfortable at the workplace. Sometimes, this might be simply a feeling of loneliness and distance from mainstream workers. In other instances, the new employee may even face hostility from other members of the work group, especially when others perceive that the employee's minority status resulted in preferential treatment during hiring. Co-worker hostility is more likely to happen when a visible minority employee (or woman) is hired for a job that is nontraditional for that group. Often the result is employee alienation, which in turn results in high turnover.

To overcome this problem, one organization formed **support groups** that are designed to provide a nurturing climate for employees who may otherwise feel unwanted or shut out. Socialization in such groups enabled the newcomer not only to share concerns and problems but also to assimilate the organization's culture faster.

support groups Groups of employees who provide emotional support to a new employee who shares a common attribute with the group (e.g., racial or ethnic membership).

Communication Standards

Several organizations have established **communication standards**—formal protocols for internal messages and communication to avoid offending members of different sex/gender, racial, ethnic, age, or other groups.

communication standards Formal protocols for internal communications within an organization to eliminate sex/gender, racial, age, or other biases in communications.

There is considerable interest in and focus on diversity and inclusion in Canadian industry. However, resistance to diversity and inclusion may emerge from employee groups, unions, work supervisors, and managers. Employee groups and unions fear the emergence of new systems that may bring in hiring quotas, employment and promotion criteria that result in reverse discrimination policies, and lowering of power, status, and rewards. Some managers and supervisors share several of the same concerns and may also fear that the new procedures will alter internal systems and performance standards and reduce autonomy. In some instances, the resistance may originate from misperceptions, lack of understanding of the need for change, prevailing stereotypes, and even rumours about negative outcomes associated with diversity and inclusion implementation elsewhere.

SUMMARY

Government is a significant variable that strongly shapes the role of human resource management. It influences human resources through laws governing the employment relationship. The application of the Charter of Rights and Freedoms was awaited with high expectations from both labour and management. However, its impact on the human resource management field has been mixed.

The two sources of equal employment laws are the federal and provincial human rights statutes. The *Canadian Human Rights Act* applies to federal government departments and agencies, Crown corporations, and businesses and industries under federal jurisdiction, such as banks, airlines, and railway companies. Areas not under federal jurisdiction are protected by provincial human rights laws. Each of Canada's provinces and territories has its own antidiscrimination laws that are broadly similar to the federal law.

To eliminate past discrimination and ensure future compliance, many organizations have developed employment equity programs. The programs identify areas of past and present discrimination, develop affirmative goals, and design remedial, active, and preventive programs.

To actively promote the employment of women, Indigenous people, persons with a disability, and members of a visible minority, the federal government introduced the *Employment Equity Act,* which requires employers with 100 or more employees under federal jurisdiction to develop plans and timetables for the employment of these groups. It also requires annual reports that have to be submitted to the Canadian Employment and Immigration Commission.

Workplace diversity includes important human characteristics that influence an employee's values, perceptions of self and others, behaviours, and interpretation of events around him or her. Diversity, at a minimum, includes age, ethnicity and culture, sex/gender, race, religion, sexual orientation, and mental and physical capabilities.

Many organizations are moving toward creating a diverse and inclusive organizational culture. This involves creating work practices and an environment where all employees are valued and included regardless of their differences. Current policies, systems, practices, rules, and procedures have to be examined (and perhaps modified or eliminated) in terms of their appropriateness for a diverse and inclusive workforce. The progress of the diversity and inclusion effort has to be monitored on a systematic basis, and corrective actions must be taken.

TERMS FOR REVIEW

alternate work arrangements 135
apprenticeships 135
awareness training 135
bona fide occupational requirement (BFOR) 108
Canadian Charter of Rights and Freedoms 106
Canadian Human Rights Act 107
Canadian Human Rights Commission (CHRC) 111
communication standards 136
concentration 126
core dimensions of diversity 128
diversity and inclusion audits 134
diversity and inclusion training programs 135
duty to accommodate 112
Employment Equity Act 124
employment equity programs 125
glass ceiling 130

harassment 119
managing diversity 131
mentoring programs 135
natural justice 127
old boys' network 129
provincial human rights laws 107
reasonable accommodation 117
regulations 106
secondary dimensions of diversity 129
sexual harassment 120
skill-building training 135
stereotyping 129
support groups 136
systemic discrimination 111
underutilization 126
workplace diversity 128

SELF-ASSESSMENT EXERCISE

How Knowledgeable Are You about Human Resource Legal Issues and Diversity and Inclusion?

1.	Men are prohibited from filing sexual harassment complaints.	T	F
2.	The Bank of Nova Scotia falls under the jurisdiction of the federal *Canadian Human Rights Act.*	T	F
3.	Minimum height requirements are considered systemic discrimination.	T	F
4.	The "duty to accommodate" means that an employer has to accommodate employees even if it involves "undue hardship."	T	F
5.	Mandatory retirement is permitted in most provinces.	T	F
6.	It is illegal to ask a candidate whether he or she has been convicted of a crime, unless it is job-related.	T	F
7.	Drug dependency can be interpreted as a disability.	T	F
8.	If a supervisor harasses an employee, the employer can be held liable.	T	F
9.	The term "old boys' network" has now been changed to "diversity network" to include women.	T	F
10.	The percentage of minorities in Canadian companies is now typically similar to their percentage in the population.	T	F

SCORING

If you answered statements 1, 4, 5, 9, 10 as False you get one point each. All other statements are True, resulting again in one point each.

Scores of 8–10: Very good! Congratulations on a job well done.

Scores 5–7: You made it, but barely. It would be advisable for you to go over the chapter text again.

Scores of less than 5: Are you sure you read the chapter?

REVIEW AND DISCUSSION QUESTIONS

1. Suppose that during your first job interview after graduation you are asked, "Why should a company have an employment equity program?" How would you respond?

2. List the major prohibitions of the *Canadian Human Rights Act*.

3. Since a human resource department is not a legal department, what role does it play in the area of equal employment law?

4. Suppose that you are told that your first duty as a human resource specialist is to construct an employment equity program. What would you do? What types of information would you seek?

5. What conditions would have to be met before you could bring suit against an employer who discriminated against you because of your sex?

6. A job candidate answers yes to the question of whether she is a smoker. She is well qualified, but you decide not to hire her. Does she have legal recourse?

7. Why is diversity and inclusion important for an organization today?

8. How would you go about creating a diversity and inclusion program?

CRITICAL THINKING QUESTIONS

1. If you are a supervisor in a bank and an employee demands to be allowed to miss work on Fridays for religious reasons, what would you do? Under what circumstances would you have to let the employee have time off? Under what circumstances could you prohibit it?

2. You have a job opening for a warehouse helper, a position that sometimes requires heavy lifting, up to 50 kilograms. A woman applies for the job and claims that she is able to do the work. She looks rather petite, and you are afraid that she might hurt herself. When

you deny her the job, she threatens to complain to the Human Rights Commission. What do you do?

3. Choose an organization that you are familiar with. Are any of its rules, practices, or policies likely to be found undesirable by its female, minority, or older employees? Why?

4. If 40 percent of your employees are women, but if women account for only 2 percent of the executive group and 4 percent of the managerial group, what steps will you take to improve the status of women in your organization?

ETHICS QUESTION

A Weighty Issue*

Most countries do not prohibit discrimination based on a job candidate's weight. For instance, in the United States, 49 of 50 states do not include weight as a prohibited

ground of discrimination. Jackson Jefferson III is the managing partner of a long-established public relations firm. According to Jackson, a person's looks and image are of major importance when hiring a new employee: "Our clients have certain expectations and we need to meet them. If a person is overweight, there is no place for him or her in our firm. Also, piercings and tattoos are not acceptable." Jill Andrew, co-founder of the Body Confidence Canada Awards, argues that people are discriminated against based on several personal characteristics such as height, weight, facial features, and hair loss, and such individuals are "often not placed in front positions or do not travel to represent the company."

Should employers be able to discriminate against people based on personal characteristics?

---

* Based on Vander Wier, M. (2017, January 23), Weight discrimination goes up for debate in Manitoba legislature, *Canadian HR Reporter* , pp. 1, 8.

RESEARCH EXERCISE

1. Canadian Human Rights Commission (https://www.chrc-ccdp.gc.ca/index.html)

   a. Find and summarize three cases decided last year in favour of employers and three cases decided in favour of employees.

   b. What are the implications of the latest case decisions on gay rights for human resource managers?

2. Canadian Public Health Association (https://www.cpha.ca/)

   a. Go to the HIV/AIDS Information Centre and give a summary of the resources available to organizations to inform them about AIDS.

3. Pay Equity Commission of Ontario (http://www.payequity.gov.on.ca/Pages/default.aspx)

   a. How is progress in the pay equity process monitored?

4. Select any two industries and calculate the percentage of women and members of visible minorities and other disadvantaged groups who are employed in these sectors. What are the implications for diversity management practices in organizations in these sectors? (Hint: You may begin your research with the websites of Statistics Canada, Employment and Social Development Canada, and Industry Canada.)

INCIDENT 4-1

Is Climbing the Ladder (Carrying Shingles) an Essential Job Requirement?

Matt Martino operates a roofing business in a small town. Most of his clients are homeowners but he also does some work for small commercial enterprises. Matt typically has three other employees who work alongside him on the roofing jobs. One of Matt's employees recently quit and Matt is looking for a replacement. In addition to checking out a job candidate's résumé and conducting an interview, Matt has each applicant show that he or she can climb a ladder ("Had one guy who was scared of heights") and carry a bundle of shingles up the ladder to the roof ("This is essential if my business is to remain competitive. It is pretty standard for the industry").

One job applicant, Catherine Silva, had no problem climbing the ladder but didn't even try to carry a bundle of shingles up to the roof. In Silva's words, "I know I am a really good roofer and made it past the résumé and interview. But I also know that I cannot physically carry a full bundle of shingles up a ladder, and even if I could, I don't think it is safe. On my other jobs, we used a laddervator."

DISCUSSION QUESTIONS

1. Is it acceptable for Matt to not hire Catherine because she can't carry the shingles to the roof?

2. Does the "duty to accommodate" apply in this case?

EXERCISE 4-1

Carver Jewellery Company

Carver Jewellery Company Ltd. has the following workforce composition:

Job Classes	Male	Female	White	Black	Asian	Indigenous
Executive	9	1	10	0	0	0
Management	71	9	79	0	1	0
Salaried/commission	43	31	74	0	0	0
Hourly paid	24	164	168	10	8	2

An analysis of the local labour force from which Carver draws its employees is as follows:

Male	Female	White	Black	Asian	Indigenous
53 percent	47 percent	84 percent	8 percent	3 percent	5 percent

On the basis of this information:

1. Identify which job classes at Carver exhibit underutilization.

2. Identify which job classes at Carver exhibit concentration.

WE CONNECTIONS: DIVERSITY AND INCLUSION

Heard It through the Grapevine

Anna knocked softly on the open door, and asked, "Do you have a minute? I wanted to tell you about something. To be honest, it may be nothing, but I'm not sure."

Charlotte quickly pushed the Save button on her laptop and sat back in her chair. "Actually, your timing is pretty good. I could use a break from my screen. Come on in."

Anna came in and sat down. "I was hoping you would say something like that."

Charlotte frowned. "Are you having trouble figuring out that benefit stuff I asked you to do?"

Anna shook her head. "No. Well, yes. I am having some trouble with that, but I think I can figure it out. This is about something different. I went out to lunch today with my friend Sarah from accounting. We wanted to check out the new Thai place that opened in that plaza up the street. Well, she invited a couple other people, so there were four of us from the company."

Charlotte said, "Yeah, I know you eat lunch with Sarah a lot. Who were the other two?"

Anna shuffled uncomfortably in her chair. "I don't know if I should say. I'll call them P and M for now, if that's okay. I just don't know if I should identify them. Let me tell you what was said, and you can tell me if you think I should give their names or not."

Charlotte looked uneasy. "Uh-oh. I don't like the sound of this. Something tells me this is not going to be a story about how good the food was."

Discrimination? Harassment?

Anna chuckled, and said, "You're right about that." She jumped up and quickly shut the door. "Now, I don't know P and M that well. We don't usually hang out. I can say that they are programmers that have both been with the company for a couple of years, and they work for different project managers. The thing is that both of them seem to think they have been treated badly at this company because they are women. They think they have been victims of discrimination and maybe even sexual harassment."

Charlotte gasped, and said, a little loudly, "What? That can't be right! WEC has a great track record when it comes to equity. We both know that we hire and promote based on merit. You don't believe that we are unfair to women, do you? For goodness sakes, one of our founders is a woman!"

Anna shook her head, and said hurriedly, "I'm not saying I agree with it. I am just telling you what I heard. I didn't mean to upset you. Should I have kept this to myself?"

You Had to Be There

Taking a breath, Charlotte softened her tone. "No. I'm so sorry. I was just caught off guard. Please tell me what they said. If there is a problem, then I need to know."

Anna replied, "Okay. I'll tell you what I heard. P is the only woman on her team, and she is the only person in her work group that is not invited to go for drinks after work on Fridays. She said that one of the guys on the team said that his girlfriend was jealous and didn't want him hanging out with other girls after work, and it wasn't personal, but it would be best if P didn't come very often. She had said okay to avoid any trouble. She told me she didn't really want to go to the bar every time, but after a few occurrences it made her feel left out when they would be laughing over private jokes that originated in the bar. She was trying to just concentrate on her work, but a couple of weeks ago her boss put together a sub-team to do a certain part of the new project, and he didn't pick her even though it was something she had done before. When she asked him why, he said that he tried to pick a group that got along really well since they would be working a lot of long hours. So now it seems that the fact that she isn't really close friends with these guys is hurting her career."

Lonely Hearts Need Not Apply

Charlotte said, "And what about the other person?"

Anna replied, "M has a different story. She dated someone from here a few times last year. It didn't work out, but since then there have been three or four different guys who have asked her out. One of them was a manager, though not her manager. She turned them all down, but she is tired of everyone treating work like a singles bar. She wishes the company would do something to let everyone know they should just focus on work, not romance."

Anna sat back in her chair, and added, "Those are the main points. I should say that they didn't tell me this stuff because I work in HR. This seemed like just normal lunchtime venting. But I thought it might be something I should let you know about. Was I right? Do you think this might be discrimination or harassment?"

DISCUSSION QUESTIONS

1. Assess Charlotte's reaction to the information brought to her by Anna. Do you think that this was an ideal response? Is there a more effective way that she could have responded?

2. Would the situation with P be considered discrimination or harassment? What about the situation with M?

3. If Charlotte wants to talk to either of the two women, how should she approach them?

4. Charlotte mentions that she believes the company "has a great track record when it comes to equity." What evidence is she considering?

5. Imagine that you are a consultant advising Charlotte on building an inclusive work environment. How would you go about creating a diversity and inclusion audit for WEC?

In the next installment of the WE Connections story (at the end of Chapter 5), leaders discuss how to approach recruiting and selecting for an important new role.

CASE STUDY

Metro School District

Born at the Wrong Time?

Julio Ramirez sat forward at his desk and pondered the latest contract he taken in his human resource management consultancy. He been contracted by the Metro School District to provide some outside advisory on the selection of kids into a workshop, which had led to a series of complaints by parents. Julio reviewed the facts of the case.

The Leadership Forum (a professional group made up of community business leaders) had agreed to sponsor 100 boys and 100 girls to participate in a two-day "Peer Leaders Workshop." The workshop was designed to encourage students to assume peer leadership roles at school and was open to all students in the 11-year-old age group (that is, all children who would be 11 years of age between January 1 and December 31 of the current year). Almost all of the students selected were in grade 6. Each child attending the workshop received a T-shirt, a backpack, and educational materials on leadership.

Based on class size, each teacher was asked to select a specified number of students to attend the workshop. A few parents whose children were not chosen for the workshop asked for some information about the leadership program and were provided with the following information from the Metro School District.

There are 1,000 boys and 1,000 girls in the appropriate age category throughout the school district. Since 100 boys and 100 girls were selected for the workshop, 900 boys and 900 girls were not chosen by their teacher. As observed in Table 1, for the 100 boys and 100 girls selected to the program, a greater percentage of children are born earlier in the year (i.e., January to March group and April to June group). In other words, of the 100 boys selected for the workshop, 44 were born in the January to March quartile while only 5 boys were born in the October to December quartile. Similarly, 41 girls from the January to March quartile were chosen compared to only 7 girls born in the October to December category.

When we examine the breakdown of birthdays for all of the children (the 1,000 boys and 1,000 girls), it is about the same across the four quartiles presented below (that is, about 25% of boys and 25% of girls were born in each of the four quartiles). Some research on education and sports in Canada and other countries across various age groups has shown a trend of favouring the older children within the age group when selecting participants for academic and sports activities.

Several of the parents reviewed this data and complained that the Metro School District was discriminating against younger children (those born later in the year) when selecting participants for the Peer Leaders Workshop because so few of the younger children were selected. From what Julio was told, there is no evidence indicating that the teachers knew the birth dates of the children when selecting them for the peer leadership program. Interviews with the teachers confirmed that selection was made based on each teacher's overall assessment of each child.

DISCUSSION QUESTIONS

1. If you were in Julio's position, would you suggest that this is discrimination?

2. What steps should Julio recommend to mitigate the relative age effect form of discrimination within the organization?

3. Would an organization be able to immediately rectify an age effect? Why or why not?

Note: For a further understanding of the issue, look up the topic "the relative age effect."

TABLE 1

Children Selected for Workshop Birth Date and Sex

	January/March	April/June	July/September	October/December
Boys Peer Leader Group	44% (44)	36% (36)	15% (15)	5% (5)
Girls Peer Leader Group	41% (41)	34% (34)	18% (18)	7% (7)

* Note that both percentages and actual numbers of students are provided.

CHAPTER 5

Recruitment

To ensure organizations are consistently attracting top professionals, they must establish nimble and comprehensive hiring processes capable of successfully evolving with current market conditions and limited candidate supply.

GREG SCILEPPI[1]

LEARNING OBJECTIVES

After studying this chapter, you should be able to:

LO1 Explain the strategic importance of the recruitment function.

LO2 Discuss the constraints faced in a typical recruitment process.

LO3 Describe the two most common methods of applying for a job.

LO4 Identify the appropriate recruiting methods for different types of jobs.

LO5 Explain how to generate effective recruitment advertisements.

LO6 Describe how to choose among the recruitment sources.

LO7 List key measures for evaluating the effectiveness of the recruitment function.

Finding new employees for the organization is a continuing challenge for most human resource departments. Sometimes the need for new workers is known well in advance because of detailed human resource plans. At other times, the human resource department is faced with urgent requests for replacements that must be filled as quickly as possible. In either case, finding qualified applicants is a key activity, as seen in the following example:

Consulting giant Accenture Inc. is a leading employer in Canada with about 3,800 employees. Globally, Accenture hired approximately 70,000 employees in 2011, including about 1,000 new workers in Canada. With this fast-paced growth, Accenture faces one of the biggest human resource challenges: "attracting and retaining the best and brightest."[2]

Recruitment is the process of finding and attracting capable individuals to apply for employment and to accept a job offer if or when one is made to them. **Selection** involves identifying candidates from the pool of applicants who best meet

recruitment The process of finding and attracting capable applicants to apply for employment and accept job offers that are extended to them.

selection The identification of candidates from a pool of recruits who best meet job requirements, using tools such as application blanks, tests, and interviews.

job requirements using tools such as application blanks, tests, and interviews. The recruitment process begins with generating a pool of applicants, continues during selection while decisions are made among applicants to choose the best one, and then extends after selection decisions have been made to convince candidates who have been made an offer to accept the job.[3]

Recruitment includes all activities by an organization that affect an applicant's decision to apply for and to accept a position. These can be activities that the organization *purposefully* engages in to persuade applicants to want to work for them (such as recruitment websites), or *unintentional* activities or occurrences (such as the length of time between when an applicant applies for the job and when he or she hears about an interview; or public relations fiascos, such as the British Petroleum oil spill in the Gulf Coast in 2010[4]) that may affect applicant attraction to the organization.[5]

Recruiting is a two-way street: It is a matching process between firms with jobs and individuals seeking jobs. The organization is trying to entice highly qualified people to consider working for it. Meanwhile, applicants are trying to learn about what it would be like to work for the organization. Work is a large part of most people's days and can have a substantial impact on their well-being. How the organization treats individuals from the moment they first learn about it right through to a job offer being extended to them can impact whether or not they will choose to work

there. Recruiting then segues into newcomer socialization, covered in Chapter 7.

Responsibility for recruitment usually belongs to the human resource department. This responsibility is important because the quality of an organization's human resources depends on the quality of its recruits. In organizations that recruit almost continuously, human resource departments will have dedicated recruitment specialists.

As Figure 5-1 illustrates, recruitment can be done only after the identification of job openings through human resource planning or requests by managers. As mentioned in Chapter 3, advanced knowledge of job openings allows the recruiter to be proactive.

After identifying openings, the recruiter learns what each job requires by reviewing job analysis information, particularly the job descriptions and specifications, and speaking with the requesting manager. This information tells the recruiter the characteristics of both the jobs and the future job incumbents. Knowing the job's requirements helps recruiters to choose methods of finding the right number and type of applicants.

Typically, most recruiters use more than one recruitment method to find suitable candidates for vacant job positions. Common recruitment methods include recruitment advertisements and postings on websites and job boards; school, college, and university campus visits; contacts with professional and labour associations; and use of government agencies, such as Employment and Social Development

FIGURE 5-1

An Overview of the Recruitment Process

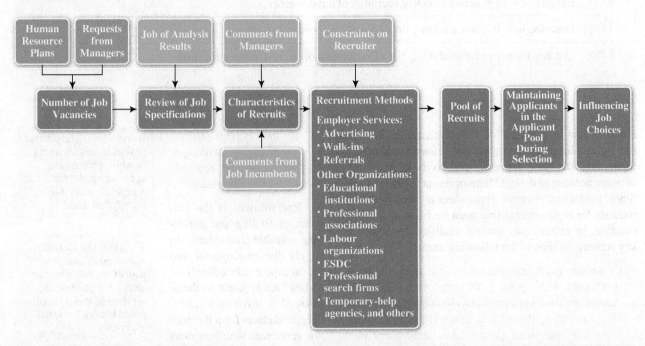

Canada (ESDC). Sometimes, to attract high-quality applicants a recruiter may have to use unconventional procedures, as the following example shows:

> Inspector Kevin McQuiggin from the Vancouver Police Department recognized that it was getting harder and harder to recruit IT talent to the force. In the past, the VPD averaged about a thousand applications a year from traditional recruitment sources, such as job fairs, newspaper ads, and word of mouth. In this new era, attracting tech-savvy applicants who will need to complete the two–three years of training to get up to speed and then stick around for the long haul is a rising challenge for police forces around the world. To alleviate the hiring crunch and attract a technologically adept crowd, McQuiggin held a recruiting seminar in Second Life, a three-dimensional virtual world with millions of people around the globe participating through their avatars. The first VPD recruitment session was hosted by VPD avatars made in the images of the VPD real-life recruiters. It was attended by 30 avatars and produced four applications.[6]

Recruitment involves far more than just getting people to apply for jobs, and success in recruitment is not simply measured by the number of applications received. The right type of applicants is far more important than the number of applicants. And remember that recruiting efforts should not end when the applicant pool is created, but should continue until the successful candidates have accepted the firm's offers of employment. The following section discusses the strategic importance of the recruitment function.

LO1 Strategic Importance of the Recruitment Function

In the recent past, recruitment has gained considerable attention among practitioners as well as in the media. Recruiting can be challenging because of a variety of factors, including an aging population, which results in a large number of retirements; stiff competition for talent; growth in the Canadian economy; and rising compensation and aspiration levels of new entrants. Over the 2015–2024 period, growth in Canada's economy is anticipated to create about 1.45 million new non-student jobs and a further 4.5 million positions to fill due to retirements, deaths, and emigration. Over the longer term, positions freed due to replacement demand will generate an even higher share of total job openings.[7] Front-line positions such as clerks and sales are the easiest to fill, whereas executives, skilled trades, and high-tech jobs are the toughest for recruiters to fill. Health-related occupations, applied sciences, and some trades and construction occupations have the strongest shortage pressures.

Today, recruitment of human resources has a significant impact on the organization and its strategic success. The most important HR and organizational activities affected by recruitment are examined below.

Gaining Competitive Advantage from Human Resources

Successful firms recognize that today, more than ever before, human resources spell the difference between success and failure. Despite the existence of state-of-the-art human resource systems and procedures, poorly qualified and motivated recruits often prove extremely costly to firms. In contrast, in today's global knowledge economy, the presence of highly skilled and motivated workers can be a real **competitive advantage**.

> **competitive advantage**
> An advantage that exists when the firm is able to deliver the same value and benefits as competitors but at a lower cost (cost advantage), or when the firm is able to deliver unique value or benefits that exceed those of competing products (differentiation advantage).

Experience working in a foreign country is considered a major asset by many employers. As one executive recruiter noted, "an international assignment on your CV gives you an edge over competitors because it shows breadth of experience and adaptability."[8] In one survey of 6,000 employees, 75 percent of the respondents considered foreign work credentials "essential" or "extremely useful."[9] However, managers with foreign country experience are also hard to come by. Only about 37 percent of 2,700 executives surveyed stated that they would consider taking an overseas assignment. This makes people with foreign work experience extremely valuable, which in turn makes recruiting them difficult.

Further, if applicants lack the necessary skills or aptitudes, or both, considerable additional resources may have to be invested into selection, training and development, employee communication systems, and employee relations practices. A small pool of recruits also poses a major challenge to the selection procedure (which will be discussed in Chapter 6).

Reaping the Benefits of Diversity

Many Canadian firms recognize the vitality and competitive advantage that often accompanies a diverse workforce. Further, as discussed in Chapter 4, if the firm's workforce does not reflect the larger labour market composition, the firm may be asked to pursue an employment equity program to correct imbalances. Progressive employers monitor their environments continuously and adjust their recruitment strategies to deal with the emerging trends in a proactive manner. Faced with acute competition for valuable human resources, some employers are forming partnerships with social agencies and community associations to help them with their recruiting:

> As a group, people with disabilities make up about 11 percent of the population ages 25 to 64 in Canada[10] and offer a major source for highly qualified employees for a variety of jobs. Organizations like the Solutions Learning Centre in Nova Scotia and EmployAbilities in Edmonton have been successful in placing people with disabilities in a number of organizations.

Hiring from a larger, diverse pool of candidates offers a greater choice of job applicants to the firm. A diverse workforce also offers greater flexibility and additional capabilities in some instances. It reflects an organization's commitment to broader social goals and projects a better image of the firm to clients and other constituents.

Focusing on Employee Development

When recruiting (especially for middle- and upper-level jobs), a firm has a choice: it can either develop and promote internal candidates or hire from outside. The strategic choice of internal versus external recruitment has profound implications for an organization.

Figure 5-2 lists some of the advantages and weaknesses of internal versus external recruiting. Needless to say, the specific strategy that the firm chooses has major

---

FIGURE 5-2

Internal versus External Recruiting

Internal Recruiting

Advantages

- Employee is familiar with the organization and its culture.
- Employee is "known" to the firm; the fit of this individual to the organization will be known as well.
- Recruiting from within improves workforce morale and motivation.
- Information about employee performance is known in addition to scores on selection tests; this improves the organization's ability to predict the person's success in the new job.

Weaknesses

- Internal recruiting can lead to internal rivalry and competition for higher positions; it can also reduce interpersonal and interdepartmental co-operation.
- No "new blood" is brought into the system, which can prevent creative solutions from emerging.
- It can lead to poor morale (leading to possible turnover) of employees who were not promoted.
- Offering counselling, training, and development to employees who vied for, but did not get, the promotion may be expensive.
- Performance evaluation records are only relevant to the extent that the promotion job is similar to the employee's current job.

External Recruiting

Advantages

- The organization is able to acquire skills or knowledge that may not be currently available within.
- Newer ideas and novel ways of solving problems may emerge.

Weaknesses

- Newcomers may not fit in with the organization and into its present culture.
- Newcomers take a longer time to learn about the organization's culture, policies, and practices.
- Usually, hiring from the outside is more expensive.
- External recruiting may lead to lowered morale and motivation levels of current employees, who don't see any career growth possibilities within the firm.

SOURCES: M. Krakel, and A. Schottner (2012), "Internal labor markets and worker rents," *Journal of Economic Behavior & Organization, 84,* pp. 491–509; C. R. McConnell (2010), "Management recruiting: Inside versus outside," *Health Care Manager, 29,* Jan–March, pp. 1–3.

implications for recruitment and salary costs, employee morale, and organizational innovation and change. One additional consideration is that, typically, promoting an employee will generate a job opening somewhere else in the organization. The internal promotion of a supervisor to a manager position results in a supervisor opening, which may in turn be filled by the internal promotion of a front-line worker. The front-line worker position may need to be filled by recruiting externally.

Investing Resources into Recruitment

The decision about the total recruitment budget affects the quality of recruits and the overall effectiveness of recruitment activity. Note that the costs of recruitment are not simply the hiring costs (such as the costs of advertisement, recruiter's travel, and so on). Often the costs of a bad hire may not be translatable into monetary terms as there is no accurate way of measuring the number of lost customers or resources due to delays and inefficient handling of a situation. Furthermore, inappropriate recruits often leave the organization, causing significant additional costs to hire and train replacements. Often such costs are not apparent. However, some organizations, such as NCR, have recognized the importance of the recruitment function and have found innovative ways to recruit qualified persons and reduce recruitment costs.

> NCR, a global Fortune 500 company, produces point-of-sale terminals, automated teller machines, cheque-processing systems, and bar-code scanners and is one of the largest providers of IT maintenance support services. It maintains its competitive edge by hiring employees at the entry level, retaining them, and promoting from within. Its Graduate Gateway program provides recent graduates with experience working in four key business areas during a two-year professional rotation program. Graduates gain experience in technical acumen, project management, business strategy, and leadership to prepare them for a successful career at NCR. The company actively seeks a competitive advantage through its employees by hiring top people and creating a work climate where they are highly productive.[11]

Other investments into the recruiting process include selecting and training recruiters. When selecting recruiters, friendliness or personableness, knowledge of the job, organization, career-related issues, and enthusiasm are important characteristics.[12] Choices must also be made about whether recruiters should be HR professionals, line managers, or co-workers. HR professionals may be knowledgeable about career paths and the organization but lack understanding of specific job details. Line managers, on the other hand, may know details of the job and company but not necessarily career development opportunities. And co-workers may understand the job very well but not necessarily the

organization or career paths to the same extent as HR professionals. Depending on the recruiter's areas of expertise, training may be needed for interviewing and interpersonal skills, job analysis, laws and regulations, and marketing and sales for creating advertisements and being persuasive to candidates.[13]

Key issues in the context of evaluating the effectiveness of the recruitment function and its contribution to organizational success will be discussed in a later section in this chapter. But first, it is important to recognize the several constraints a recruiter faces.

LO2   Constraints on Recruitment

A successful recruiter must be sensitive to the constraints on the recruitment process. These limits arise from the organization, the recruiter, and the external environment. Although the emphasis may vary from situation to situation, the next section describes the most common constraints, summarized in Figure 5-3:

Organizational Policies

Organizational policies can constrain the recruiter. Policies seek to achieve uniformity, economies, public relations benefits, and other objectives unrelated to recruiting. Four policies that have implications for recruitment are highlighted below.

> **organizational policies**
> Internal policies that affect recruitment, such as "promote-from-within" policies.

1. Promote-from-within Policies

As already pointed out, promote-from-within policies are formulated to give present employees the first opportunity for job openings and to facilitate their career growth. These policies are widespread. Searching for candidates internally versus external searching significantly impacts how recruiting is conducted. For instance, will recruitment ads be placed in the newspaper or posted in the staff lunchroom? Moreover, the content of the job postings will be different: Substantially less information will be needed about the organization for internal as opposed to external candidates, and internal candidates may have a better sense of what a job entails than will an external applicant.

Bypassing current employees to hire from outside can lead to employee dissatisfaction and turnover. On the other hand, providing opportunities for movement among positions may encourage people to join and stay with a firm, as shown in the following Facebook example:

> At Facebook, where the workforce numbers about 19,000, the company prides itself on its flat organizational structure and open and transparent culture. All employees engage in leadership development activities and move across teams and into management

FIGURE 5-3

Constraints on Recruiting

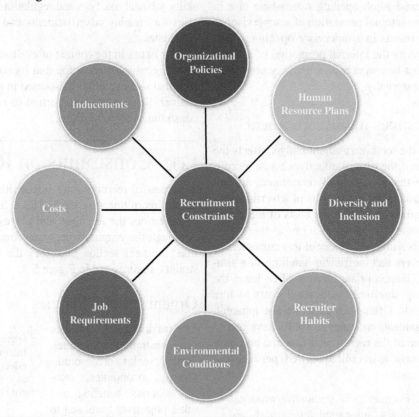

positions as their leadership skills grow. Although they may not have managed teams before, Facebook encourages development of millenials to grow into leadership positions.[14]

2. Compensation Policies

A common constraint faced by recruiters is pay policies. Organizations with human resource departments usually establish pay ranges for different jobs. These pay ranges aim to attract new staff while maintaining the viability of the organization. Factors such as minimum wage requirements can impact the benefits or hours offered, along with product and service prices, as shown in the following Tim Hortons example:

> Several provinces in Canada, including Ontario, B.C., and Alberta, have recently undergone significant increases to minimum wage. To pay for the increases, employers have implemented changes, such as reducing hiring plans, raising prices, delaying expansion plans, cutting back hours, or reducing employee benefits. When Tim Hortons franchisees cut paid breaks and restructured medical benefits to reduce the financial impact of the minimum wage

jump in Ontario, rallies were staged to boycott the chain, using the slogan #NoTimmiesTuesday.[15]

Along with setting pay ranges to attract new hires, HR departments must also consider the compensation offered to current staff and managers. As minimum wage goes up, wage compression is experienced by employees making just higher than minimum wage. Compensation policies may address the ripple effect.

3. Employment Status Policies

Some companies have policies restricting the hiring of part-time and temporary employees. Although there is growing interest in hiring these types of workers, several unionized settings have limitations against hiring part-time, temporary, and contract workers, which can cause recruiters to reject all but those seeking full-time work. Likewise, policies against hiring employees who "moonlight" by having second jobs also inhibit recruiters. Prohibitions against holding extra jobs are intended to ensure a rested workforce.

4. International Hiring Policies

Policies in some countries, including Canada, may also require foreign job openings to be staffed with local citizens. The use of foreign nationals, however, does reduce relocation expenses, lessens the likelihood of nationalization, and, if top jobs are held by local citizens, minimizes charges of economic exploitation. Moreover, unlike relocated employees, foreign nationals are more apt to be involved in the local community and understand local customs and business practices.

Human Resource Plans

The **human resource plan** is another factor recruiters consider. Through skills inventories and promotion ladders, the plan outlines which jobs should be filled by recruiting externally and which ones should be filled internally. Having such a plan helps recruiters because it summarizes future recruiting needs. This foresight can lead to economies in recruiting:

> **human resource plan** A firm's overall plan to fill existing and future vacancies, including decisions on whether to fill internally or to recruit from outside.

> At Facebook, only about 25 percent of managers are hired into the company from outside. They try to maintain a ratio of 70–30 homegrown to hired-in talent, although the ratio in some areas, such as engineering, is as high as 90–10.[16]

Diversity and Inclusion Programs

Where diversity and inclusion programs exist, recruitment must also take these programs into account. As we saw in Chapter 4, employers cannot discriminate against people with physical disabilities unless the disability would prevent the person from doing the job after reasonable accommodation by the employer. Proactive employers, such as the Vancouver International Airport, use innovative recruitment programs to tap the skills of a diverse workforce:

> Results of a Statistics Canada survey show that compared to nondisabled co-workers, 90 percent of people with disabilities did as well as or better at their jobs, 86 percent rated average or better in attendance, and retention rates were 72 percent higher. Although most required no workplace accommodations (or if required they were generally inexpensive and tax-deductible),making work spaces and facilities more accessible for people with physical disabilities could lift economic activity in Canada by $16.8 billion by 2030.[17] There are about 300,000 workers in British Columbia with disabilities, of whom 34,000 have college diplomas, 30,000 have trade certificates, and 28,000 have university degrees, yet people with disabilities are three times more likely to be unemployed than those without disabilities. Recognizing these facts and wanting to reflect the communities it serves, the Vancouver International Airport (YVR) began actively recruiting people with disabilities to their "barrier-free" workplace. Now an entrenched hiring practice, YVR considers disability issues when designing and planning for new facilities and renovations, and staff understanding of disabilities creates a better travel experience for customers, as well.[18]

Recruiter Habits

A recruiter's past success can lead to habits. While **recruiter habits** can eliminate time-consuming deliberations that reach the same answers, they may also perpetuate past mistakes or obscure more effective alternatives. So although recruiters need positive and negative feedback, they must guard against self-imposed constraints.

> **recruiter habits** The propensity of a recruiter to rely on methods, systems, or behaviours that led to past recruitment success.

> At Economical Insurance, headquartered in Waterloo, Ontario, the results of the annual employee engagement survey showed a proud, highly satisfied, and loyal workforce. But comments in the survey revealed that the employees were all very much the same. Delving further into diversity, they found that hiring leaders were unconsciously selecting new employees who fit a particular profile, which is known as "unconscious bias." Focusing on diversity and inclusion helped to prepare the company to expand operations to four continents in the following five years.[19]

Environmental Conditions

External conditions strongly influence recruitment. Changes in the labour market and the challenges mentioned in Chapter 1 affect recruiting. The unemployment rate, the pace of the economy, shortages in specific skills, the size of the labour force, labour laws, and the recruiting activities of other employers—all of these factors affect the recruiter's efforts.

> Faced with a labour market that had a severe shortage of experienced drivers, Coastal Pacific Xpress, a Surrey, British Columbia–based long-haul trucking firm, increased the pay of its owner-operators by 45 percent in four months to attract more recruits.[20]

Although these factors are considered in human resource planning, the economic environment can change quickly after the plan is finalized. To be sure that the plan's economic assumptions remain valid, recruiters can check three fast-changing measures.

1. Leading Economic Indicators

Statistics Canada routinely publishes the direction of the leading indicators. The economic indices suggest the future course of the national economy. If these indices signal a sudden downturn in the economy, recruiting plans may have to be modified. Other agencies, such as ESDC, Innovation, Science and Economic Development Canada, The World Bank, and the International Monetary Fund, also publish information that is of great interest to national and international organizations.

2. Predicted versus Actual Sales

Because human resource plans are partially based upon the firm's predicted sales, variations between actual and predicted sales may indicate that these plans also are inaccurate. Thus, recruiting efforts may need to be changed accordingly.

3. Employment Statistics

Statistics Canada routinely reports various employment statistics. Periodically, it produces reports on the state of employment in different industry sectors. ESDC also produces an occupational projection system for 292 occupational groupings covering the entire Canadian workforce, which is updated every two years.[21]

Employers can also monitor competition for specific job groups by looking at job postings in the region, nation, or internationally depending on the market pertaining to their business. Tighter competition for applicants may require more vigorous recruiting. When business conditions decline, an opposite approach is called for, as the following example illustrates:

> After almost two decades of uninterrupted growth during which the workforce doubled, BuildForce projects construction activity to plateau from 2018 to 2027.[22] Although human resource plans in this sector may have called for recruitment efforts, these are now being revised to include layoffs or more modest recruitment plans.

Job Requirements

Of course, the requirements of each job are a constraint. Highly specialized workers, for example, are more difficult to find than unskilled ones. Recruiters learn of a job's demands from the requesting manager's comments and from job analysis information. Job analysis information is especially useful because it reveals the important characteristics of the job and of applicants. Knowledge of a job's requirements allows the recruiter to choose the best way to find recruits, given the constraints under which the recruiter must operate.

"Find the best and most experienced applicant you can" is often a constraint that is imposed on recruiters as though it were a job requirement. At first, this demand seems reasonable: All managers want to have the best and most experienced people working for them. But several potential problems exist with this innocent-sounding request.

One problem in seeking out the "best and most experienced" applicant is cost. People with greater experience usually command higher salaries than less experienced people. If a high level of experience is not truly necessary, the recruit may become bored soon after being hired. Moreover, if the human resource department cannot show that a high degree of experience is needed, then experience may be an artificial requirement that discriminates against some applicants. Another point about experience is worth remembering: For some people in some jobs, 10 years of experience is another way of saying 1 year of experience repeated 10 times. Someone with 10 years of experience may not be any better qualified than an applicant with only 1 year.

Costs

Like all other members of an organization, recruiters must also operate within budgets. The **costs** of identifying and attracting recruits are an ever-present limitation:

> **costs** Expenses related to attracting recruits.

> Home Depot sought to hire 6,000 sales associates into full-time, part-time, and seasonal positions across the country for the 2016 spring season. It used a centralized recruitment model to recruit for its 182 stores. The central location built the recruitment plan, organized career events across the county, and led advertising efforts with aggregators such as Indeed, Simply Hired, Google, Workopolis, and Facebook. Then a recruiter responsible for about 10 to 12 stores in each district provided additional support for booking and scheduling interviews.[23]

Careful human resource planning and forethought by recruiters can minimize recruiting expenses. For example, recruiting for several job openings simultaneously may reduce the cost per recruit. Proactive human resource management actions go far in achieving this objective.

Inducements

The recruiter is very much like a marketer—he or she is selling the company as a potential place of work to all eligible recruits. As with any marketing effort, **inducements** may be necessary to stimulate a potential recruit's interest. The growing global marketplace means that workers are also mobile, and attracting them may require unconventional incentives:

> **inducements** Monetary, nonmonetary, or even intangible incentives used by a firm to attract recruits.

> Nurses at Health Canada are offered up to a $4,500 inducement for working in remote and isolated Indigenous communities.[24] Recent tech company

signing bonuses averaged $45,708 at Facebook, $41,340 at Amazon, and $20,191 at Microsoft.[25]

Not all inducements are monetary or even tangible. Flextime, high quality of life, and other initiatives can be potential selling points for a firm; in some instances, certain items (such as flextime) can also be a constraint if all major employers are using them. In such an instance, a firm needs to meet the prevailing standards. Inducements may be a response to overcoming other limitations faced by the recruiter:

> The fast-food industry, which employs a large percentage of young workers, typically experiences high employee turnover. To reduce turnover and thereby its recruiting costs, McDonald's introduced an educational assistance program. Employees can be reimbursed up to $5,250 per year in eligible expenses for grades C and above.[26]

More recently, several employers have been using nontraditional benefits to attract and retain their employees:

> Some of the benefits offered today include fitness centre memberships, reimbursement of professional membership fees and course fees, on-site vaccination programs and daycare centres, employee mental health insurance, retiree health care benefits, financial planning assistance, and on-site parking. Companies such as Google provide free legal advice, dog-walking, free cafeterias, and extra time off when employees have a baby.[27]

The key in all cases is to understand the needs and motivations of the target recruits and offer a set of inducements that appeal to them.

LO3 Applying for a Job

Traditionally, job seekers formally apply for a job by either submitting their résumé or completing a job application. The **résumé** (or curriculum vitae, or CV) is a brief summary of the applicant's background. It typically includes a one-to two-page summary of the applicant's education, work experience, personal contact information, work goals, and related skills.

> **résumé** A brief voluntary listing of an applicant's work experience, education, personal data, and other information relevant to the job.

In the case of unsolicited applications, the résumé is the first piece of information about an applicant that a recruiter will see, and it will be used to determine whether the applicant is worthy of further consideration. This makes the résumé a vital part of a job search for any person. To help them sift through a large pile of résumés, many recruiters,

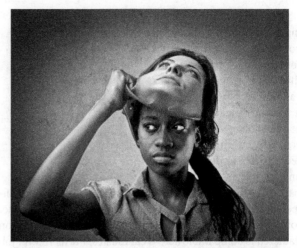

© Ollyy/Shutterstock

Up to 40 percent of minority applicants may engage in "résumé whitening." This may include changing their name on their résumé to a more anglicized name, or excluding experience related to an ethnic group or organization. Applicants are less likely to whiten their application when the organization they are applying to is considered to be pro-diversity.[28] What are some ways diversity and inclusion could be promoted during the recruitment process?

such as Home Depot and TD Canada Trust, will scan paper résumés into an **applicant tracking system** or accept résumés electronically. They will then use résumé screening software to filter through and score the résumés according to key education and job requirements:

> **applicant tracking system (ATS)** A database of potential candidates that enables a good match between job requirements and applicant characteristics and also enlarges the recruitment pool.

> MCI Telecommunications and Disneyland Resorts use computer scanning to take advantage of the large number of résumés they receive. Recruiters can search the database of résumés for candidates with specific qualifications. Thus, job requirements such as "needs significant selling experience" and "should know French" can immediately be matched with applicant characteristics. The search reveals the number of résumés that meet the required criteria. If the number is too large or too small, the recruiter can change the required qualifications (e.g., if a search for candidates who have had 10 years of work experience yields only five résumés, the recruiter can change the search criterion to 7 years of experience). Once the program finds a manageable number of applicants, the recruiter can view the résumés or résumé summaries online and eliminate any that are not appropriate.

The second way of formally applying for a job is by completing a **job application form**. Many people think that completing a job application form after submitting a résumé is redundant. Not so! The job application form collects information about recruits in a uniform manner and, hence, is an important

> **job application form**
> A company's form that is completed by a job applicant, indicating the applicant's contact information, education, prior employment, references, special skills, and other details pertaining to the position.

part of all recruitment efforts. Even when recruits volunteer detailed information about themselves on a résumé, job applications are often required so that the information gathered is comparable across candidates. Furthermore, job application forms outline the information that the recruiters would like to have for each applicant and may make indicators such as education credentials and gaps in employment history more readily apparent.

Each human resource department generally designs its own form. Nevertheless, certain common features exist. Figure 5-4 provides a typical example of an application form and its major divisions.

Name and Address

Most application forms begin with a request for personal data. Name, address, and contact information are nearly universal. But requests for some personal data—such as place of birth, marital status, number of dependants, sex, race, religion, or national origin—may lead to charges of discrimination. An unsuccessful applicant may conclude that rejection was motivated by discrimination when these types of personal data are sought. Likewise, when applications solicit information about health, height, weight, disabilities that relate to the job, major illnesses, and claims for injuries, the burden of proof that such questions are job related falls on the employer.

Employment Status

Some questions on the application form concern the applicant's employment objective and availability. Included here are questions about the position sought, willingness to accept other positions, date available for work, salary or wages desired, and acceptability of part-time and full-time work schedules. This information helps a recruiter match the applicant's objective and the organization's needs. It may also cue the recruiter to be sensitive about an applicant's current employment status. Often applicants who are currently employed will not have their current place of employment contacted for a reference until they are close to receiving a job offer so that if they are not successful in obtaining the new job, their current employer does not know they were looking for an alternative.

Education and Skills

The education and skills section of the application form is designed to uncover the job seeker's abilities. Traditionally, education has been a major criterion in evaluating job seekers. Educational attainment does imply certain abilities and is therefore a common request on virtually all applications. Questions about specific skills are also used to judge prospective employees. More than any other part of the application form, the skills section reveals the suitability of a candidate for a particular job.

Work History

Job seekers must frequently list their past jobs. From this information, a recruiter can tell whether the applicant has hopped from job to job or has been a long-service employee. A quick review of the stated job title, duties, responsibilities, and ending pay also shows whether the candidate is a potentially capable applicant. If this information does not coincide with what the recruiter expects to see, the candidate may have exaggerated job titles, duties, responsibilities, or pay.

References

Besides the traditional references from friends or previous employers, applications may ask for other "reference-like" information. Questions may explore the job seeker's criminal record, credit history, friends and relatives who work for the employer, or previous employment with the organization. Information about criminal record, credit history, and whether the applicant has friends or relatives who work for the company may be important considerations if the job involves sensitive information, cash, or other valuables. Job-relatedness must be substantiated if these criteria disproportionately discriminate against some protected groups. Previous employment with the organization means there are records of the applicant's performance.

Signature Line

Candidates are usually required to sign and date their applications. Adjacent to the signature line, a blanket authorization commonly appears. This authorization allows the employer to check references; verify medical, criminal, or financial records; and undertake any other necessary investigations. Another common provision of the signature line is a statement that the applicant affirms the information in the application to be true and accurate as far as is known. Although many people give this clause little thought, falsification of an application form or a résumé is grounds for discharge (or worse) in most organizations:

From celebrity chef Robert Irvine's claims of having designed Charles and Diana's wedding cake, to George O'Leary's lies about playing college football

FIGURE 5-4

A Typical Application Form

Application for Employment

Personal Data

1. Name _____

2. Address _____

3. Phone number _____

4. Email address _____

Employment Status

4. Type of employment sought: Full-time _____ Part-time _____ Permanent _____
   Temporary _____

5. Job or position sought _____

6. Date of availability, if hired _____

7. Are you willing to accept other employment if the position you seek is unavailable?
   Yes _____ No _____

8. Approximate wages/salary desired $ _____ per month

Education and Work History

9. Circle the highest grade or years completed.

   9 10 11 12 13   1 2 3 4   1 2 3 4
   High School   University   Graduate School

10. Please provide the following information about your education.
    (Include only vocational schools, colleges, and universities.)

    a. School name _____ Degree(s) or diploma _____
       School address _____
       Date of admission _____ Date of completion _____
    b. School name _____ Degree(s) or diploma _____
       School address _____
       Date of admission _____ Date of completion _____

11. Please describe your work skills. (Include experience with machines, tools, and equipment, and other skills you possess.)

Work History
Beginning with your most recent or current employer, please provide the following information about each employer. (If additional space is needed, please use an additional sheet.)

12. a. Employer _____ Dates of employment _____
       Employer's address _____
       Job title _____ Supervisor's name _____
       Job duties _____
       Starting pay _____ Ending pay _____

(Continued)

Application for Employment

b.   Employer _____ Dates of employment _____

Employer's address _____

Job title _____ Supervisor's name _____

Job duties _____

Starting pay _____ Ending pay _____

References

In the space provided, list three references who are not members of your family.

13. a.   Name _____ Contact Information _____

Name _____ Contact Information _____

Name _____ Contact Information _____

14. Please feel free to add any other information you think should be considered in evaluating your application.

By my signature on this application, I:

a.   Authorize the verification of the above information and any other necessary inquiries that may be needed to determine my suitability for employment.

b.   Affirm that the above information is true to the best of my knowledge.

Applicant's Signature _____ Date _____

---

when named head coach at Notre Dame, to Scott Thompson's fabrication of a computer science degree as CEO of Yahoo, famous examples of résumé fraud abound. Consequences of falsifying information on a résumé range from losing a job and public humiliation to jail time.[29]

LO4   Recruitment Methods

Recruiters have many options to let job seekers know about job opportunities at a company. In most instances, recruiters will tend to use several methods at the same time in their search for applicants.

Walk-ins and Write-ins

Walk-ins are job seekers who arrive at the human resource department seeking to drop off their résumé or to complete a job application form. **Write-ins** are those who send a written inquiry by either mailing in their résumé or completing a job application online. Indeed, today, a significant percentage of human resource managers prefer to receive résumés and job applications electronically because of the ease of storage and retrieval.[30] Suitable résumés and applications are typically kept in an active file until an appropriate opening

> **walk-ins/write-ins** Job seekers who arrive at or write to the organization in search of a job without prior referrals and not in response to a specific ad.

occurs or until the application is too old to be considered valid—usually six months. Larger firms transfer information collected like this into their overall human resource information systems.

Employee Referrals

Present employees may refer job seekers to the human resource department. **Employee referrals** have several unique advantages. First, employees with hard-to-find job skills may know others who do the same work.

> **employee referrals** Recommendations by present employees to the recruiter about possible job applicants for a position.

RBC and KPMG were chosen as two of Canada's Top 100 Employers for 2012 (and again each year since), in part because of their employee referral programs. RBC offers referral bonuses of up to $1,500 for some positions, with KPMG's referral bonuses reaching up to $5,000.[31]

Second, new recruits already know something about the organization from those employees who referred them. Thus, referred applicants may be more strongly attracted to the organization than are walk-ins. Third, employees tend to refer friends whom they identified through personal networking. These persons are likely to have similar work habits and work attitudes. Even if work values are different, these candidates may have a strong desire to

© Callahan/Shutterstock

There are 350,000 Canadians now living in Silicon Valley.[32] Canadian tech founders move to the valley just as aspiring actors move to Hollywood. How can tech companies in Canada retain other tech employees and rising future stars?

work hard so that they do not let down the person who recommended them.

> Referrals may account for only 7 percent of applicants, but they may account for 40 percent of new hires, according to Applicant Tracking System provider Jobvite.[33]

Employee referrals are an excellent legal recruitment technique. However, the major problem with this recruiting method is that it tends to maintain the status quo in terms of race, religion, sex, and other features of the employer's workforce, which may lack diversity.

LO5 Advertising

Advertising is an extremely common, effective method of seeking recruits. Since it can reach a wider audience than employee referrals or unsolicited walk-ins, many recruiters use it as a key part of their efforts. **Ads** describe the job and the benefits, identify the employer, and tell those who are interested how to apply. They are the most familiar form of employment advertising. For highly specialized recruits, ads may be placed in professional journals or specific locations with high concentrations of people with the desired skills.

ads Advertisements in a newspaper, magazine, and so on, that solicit job applicants for a position.

Ads have some significant drawbacks, however. They may lead to thousands of job seekers for one popular job opening, many of whom may not be qualified for the position.[34] Often the ideal recruits are already employed and not reading job ads. Finally, secretly advertising for a

recruit to replace a current employee cannot easily be done with traditional ads.

These problems are avoided with **blind ads**. A blind ad does not identify the employer. Interested applicants are told to send their résumé to a post office box or to a noncorporate email account.

blind ads Job ads that do not identify the employer.

The cost of most advertising is determined by the size of the advertisement (in general, larger ads cost more), and the size of the distribution of the advertisement (ads that are circulated to more people generally cost more than ads reaching fewer people). They may also be produced using various media. Radio and small print ads are typically the least expensive, followed by recruitment brochures and billboards, with television advertising as the most expensive form of recruiting. Typically, television advertising is only used for large hiring campaigns with a national focus. For instance, the Canadian Forces ran a TV ad campaign when it was looking to hire 30,000 recruits during one summer.

Because most readers will be travelling in a vehicle, the amount of information that can be conveyed on a billboard is limited. Another limitation of this approach is that it generally requires considerable lead time to prepare a sign. In deciding whether to use a billboard, the recruiter should consider the type of job to be advertised. If it is a job for which the firm is continuously recruiting, it may be worthwhile to have a billboard in visible locations.[35]

Transit advertising involves placing posters in buses, commuter trains, and subway stations. By and large these are only used by employers who have difficulty filling positions using traditional methods. Transit job advertising is relatively inexpensive. If it is placed in a specific geographic location (such as a particular bus stop), it allows an organization to target its advertising to a specific demographic or even ethnic group. If placed in a bus or train, a job advertisement can be seen by thousands of people each week (or even day). In order to make it easy to respond, the organization should attach QR codes or physical coupons that can be torn off with information on how to apply.

Regardless of the advertising media, applicants prefer to learn basics about the job, including hours of work, location, wages, and benefits, from the advertisement itself.[36] In addition, job ads must present information about the job in a way that effectively portrays a message about the job, work environment, management style, organizational climate, and future growth potential. This cannot be done if the ad contains information that explains only what responsibilities the job includes, who may be qualified, where the company is located, and how and when to apply.

Recruiters must also determine whether to portray the job only in an attractive manner so that applicants are enticed to apply for and accept the job, or whether to also include potential negative aspects of the job. Realistic recruitment messages portray the job and organization as it really is by including both positive and negative aspects.

This "tell it like it is" philosophy may lead some applicants to decide not to apply, but applicants who choose to apply and eventually accept job offers may be more committed to the organization and leave less frequently; they may be better able to cope with job demands; and they may avoid the disappointment of finding out negative aspects after they've accepted the job.[37] Consider the following example of a realistic message:

> In New York, the Administration for Children's Services implemented realistic ads in 500 subway cars. One of its sales pitches was "Wanted: Men and women willing to walk into strange buildings in dangerous neighbourhoods, be screamed at by unhinged individuals—perhaps in a language you do not understand—and, on occasion, forcibly remove a child from the custody of parents because the alternative could have tragic consequences." It also emphasized the importance of the position: "Our job is to keep children safe. You have to be able to walk into

someone's home and get them to talk to you. You have to cope with unknown and troubling situations, and figure out the truth. It's all about how to protect a child. It's tough—but it's worth it." The first month after the ads were up and running, inquiries were up about 200 percent.[38]

The choice of whether to use an attractive or a realistic message may depend on the labour market and particular requirements of the job. If applicants are hard to find, then enticing prospects with an attractive message is likely best. And if there are lots of potential applicants, then having some applicants self-select out of the applicant pool by using a realistic message will leave recruiters with fewer applicants to sort through.

Recent research has found that providing high-information messages is particularly important when the employer has an unfavourable reputation.[39] Figure 5-5 lists some of the information contained in good job ads, along with other desirable attributes.

FIGURE 5-5

Attributes of Good Job Ads

Good job ads, in general, seem to have several common characteristics, such as the following:

1. They attract attention!
2. They address the audience and use a language that the applicant finds comfortable.
3. They use short sentences and familiar words that are action oriented.
4. They contain all relevant information about the job and the firm, including the following:
   - Job title
   - Working conditions
   - A clear description of the job
   - Training offered
   - Organizational and work culture
   - Major skills, competencies, and educational requirements
   - Career and personal development possibilities
   - Location of the job
   - Salary, benefits, and other incentives
   - Travel and other requirements
   - Company selling points
5. They sequence the content logically and in an engaging manner.
6. They respect provisions of human rights and other laws and the dignity of the readers.
7. They do not use sexist, racist, or otherwise unacceptable language. Even the use of adjectives that are normally associated with males or whites may be unacceptable to other groups (e.g., use of adjectives such as *assertive, dominant, aggressive,* etc., usually connote male sex roles while terms such as *compassionate, gentle,* and *sympathetic* signify female sex roles).[40]
8. They stand out from other advertisements with good copy layout, visual balance, visual tension, and colour contrast.
9. Their size and presentation should be cost-effective compared with other recruitment methods and considering size and location of target audience.
10. They should make a favourable projection of corporate image and activities without boasting or making unsupported claims.

As illustrated, there are many decisions to be made about recruitment advertising. Regardless of the media and the message, the layout, design, and copy of an advertisement should reflect the image and character of the company and departments that are being represented.[41] This includes dimensions such as the size of the organization, the degree of decentralization seen in the firm, the degree of dynamism and progressive policies typical of the unit, and so on. In addition, an ad should emphasize the nature of the organization and the benefits of the package that it offers to attract the applications of qualified people but, at the same time, be specific enough to screen out the wrong persons.

Internet Recruiting

Internet recruiting is one of the most important tools used to match jobs with candidates—whether one is a recruiting firm or a job applicant. There are three major reasons for this. First, the Internet offers a cost-effective distribution of information to over 100 countries and millions of users, and its information is accessible day and night. Second, by specifying the exact qualifications and job skills needed, the time necessary to weed out unsuitable job candidates is minimized. Indeed, the applicants themselves may, on the basis of information supplied, decide not to apply for unsuitable positions. This also adds to the recruiting process the important attribute of timeliness. Third, Internet recruiting is relatively inexpensive. Compared to the commissions to be paid to an executive search firm or the travel expenses of a campus recruiter, the cost of putting an ad on the Internet is minimal, making it an attractive method for many organizations.

Internet recruiting has taken several forms. There are job board sites where job seekers can post their résumés and recruiters can post their job opportunities. Further, most organizations now have a Careers section on their corporate website that can be accessed in two clicks or less from their home pages.[42] Careers pages often contain detailed information about job opportunities; wages and benefits; the organization; and, increasingly, employee testimonials about what it is like to work at the company.

Safeway Canada worked with an HR and marketing consulting firm to create the Safeway Jobpod website. The site allows prospective applicants to visit links that appear like buttons on an iPhone. The site includes Generation Y video hosts and information on topics including student programs and educational reimbursement, different types of career opportunities at Safeway, what to expect on the first day, a calculator to help prospective applicants figure out how long it will take them to earn various amounts of money, and, of course, a button to apply for jobs.

Other firms, including Google and Lego, include virtual office tours.[43] The City of Edmonton reports that it receives half of all applications via mobile devices, and it has introduced a series of podcasts to answer prospective recruits' questions.[44]

To improve upon how résumés are searched on its job board site, Monster launched Power Résumé. Employers can use this product to search out job seekers with particular qualifications; the software then rates job seekers out of 10 and distills their résumés down to a short summary with education, skills, and years of experience that can be stacked side-by-side for easy comparison. Workopolis, an online career resource with job postings from across Canada, distributes its job postings automatically on Twitter.[45] With over 30,000 new résumés posted each month, Workopolis offers employers Workopolis TV as a creative way to sell themselves to potential recruits, featuring career advice and employers talking about what makes their companies great places to work as they highlight available positions.[46]

Spotlight *on* ETHICS

Facing Recruitment Dilemmas

Like many other HR activities, recruitment often raises ethical dilemmas and questions. Consider the following situations. Do you believe that there are ethical issues here? Rate each item on a five-point scale with these anchors:

1. Very unethical

2. Somewhat unethical

3. Can't decide

4. Somewhat ethical

5. Very ethical

What values, beliefs, or other arguments justify your conclusion?

1. A fire at a competing plant has caused a sudden but short-term increase in demand

(Continued)

for your product until your competitor reopens. You need an additional manager to help meet the demand. Your plant is located in a somewhat remote place devoid of many urban conveniences. You know that this is only a temporary position, but if you publicize it as such, you are unlikely to attract competent candidates. In your advertisements and during the job interviews, you decide not to make any statements about the short-term nature of the position. You will not make any false statements but also will not divulge that the position is going to be available for only about six months.

2. Of late, your firm, a designer clothing firm, has not been very successful in coming out with many innovative designs. If you do not make a breakthrough in the immediate future, the possibility exists that your firm may go under. You meet with your competitor's chief designer and offer him an $8,000 raise in an effort to attract him to your firm and turn around your fortunes.

3. You are examining the job applications of eight applicants for a receptionist position at your day spa. This person will be the first point of contact for people coming into your spa. You would prefer to interview only three candidates and are considering looking at public posts on social media to whittle down your list.

4. Your medical device firm is considering development of a new product but you want to know more about your competitor's patent applications before investing more money into development. While you do not intend to infringe your competitor's patents, a good knowledge of the intricacies of its patent applications and future product plans could give you a head start in the next phase of development. You offer a very attractive salary and a share of profits emerging from the new product to your competitor's star programmer if she'll join your firm. You are hopeful that when she joins your firm, she will be able to tell you secrets of your competitor's success and future plans.

One caution with recruiting on the Internet is that some Canadians, in particular those with less education and those who are older, may not access the Internet.[47] Further, since the Internet opens up recruiting to a global audience, great care has to be taken when designing ads and choosing hiring procedures.

Although many countries use English as their major language for business, there are vast differences in English usage across countries. For example, several words and expressions used in North America are alien to people in Hong Kong, Australia, or India, although many applicants in those countries are fluent in English. Many symbols and graphics also have vastly different meanings in different countries. For example, a thumbs-up gesture meant to signal a positive thought would be seen as obscene in Sicily.[48] Job applicants in Holland and France expect that employers will ask them about personal details such as gender, age, and marital status, although such questions are illegal in Canada.

For some suggestions on how to recruit on the Internet, see the "Spotlight on HRM" that follows.

Spotlight *on* HRM

Recruiting on the Web

Effective recruiting online is dependent on the care and planning behind the strategy. This means that the message and tone conveyed can affect not only recruitment effectiveness but also the company's public image. Some of the suggestions for improving a firm's success with recruiting online are as follows:

1. *Make your postings attractive:* In the past, print media costs and space constraints have forced recruiters to use brief job descriptions. Online job postings can be longer and more informative, visually more exciting, and interactive. Because the website has to compete for attention from surfers, it is important that the website be attention-grabbing, be easy to navigate, and have self-contained information. Researchers are now experimenting with how to tailor web-based

recruitment based on individual applicant preferences.[49]

2. *Use hyperlinks:* Using eye-tracking software and surveys, and having participants explain their thoughts while viewing websites, one study found that applicants pay more attention to information presented as hyperlinks in text than information presented as part of graphics or navigation tools. Content, site design, and communication features including social interaction with the website were all important. Information about the job opening, the organization, and geographic location should be obvious and easily accessible. Content found in text and hyperlinked information may be more important than posting lots of information on pretty graphics.[50]

3. *Highlight your organization's corporate social performance on web recruitment materials:* Researchers recently found that presenting information about the organization's community involvement (including philanthropic efforts and employees' volunteerism efforts) and, to a lesser extent, pro-environmentalism (policies and procedures supporting eco-friendliness and sustainability) produced higher anticipated pride in working for a company and fit between the company's values and their own.[51] Diversity and inclusion information on web materials has also been found to increase viewing time and to attract minority applicants.[52]

4. *Publish your web address on everything:* Make sure that your URL is included in your traditional ads in newspapers, in marketing information, and in public relations notices; with published material for college, university, or trade school markets; on social media; and on all other corporate communication devices. Continue to look for unconventional recruitment outlets: Even when you announce job openings in less conventional locations (e.g., in a minority language newspaper), include your URL in your message.

5. *Use specialized recruitment websites:* Today, a plethora of recruitment sites specialize in different kinds of personnel. By advertising on specialized websites, you are likely to target specific markets, such as the following:

   - Teachers (http://ww1.recruitingteachers.org/)
   - Fire and police personnel (https://iosolutions.com/)
   - Engineers (https://engineeringjobs.org/)
   - Information technology personnel (https://www.jobserve.com/ca/en/Job-Search/)
   - Oil and gas industry personnel (https://www.careersinoilandgas.com/)
   - Home-based workers (https://www.hea-employment.com/)
   - Hospitality workers (https://www.hcareers.ca/)

6. *Target the websites in the province or territory where the job is:* Employment and Social Development Canada (ESDC) can give you a breakdown of applicants in each province for a specific job. There are also specialized websites for each province (e.g., Government of Alberta recruitment at https://www.alberta.ca/alberta-public-service-jobs.aspx).

7. *When national recruitment efforts fail, consider attracting foreign nationals:* Once again, there are many choices in terms of recruitment websites, including the following:

   - Australia (https://www.seek.com.au/)
   - United Kingdom (http://www.topjobs.co.uk/)
   - Philippines (https://www.pniinternational-corp.com/)

8. *Post the recruitment ad in online newsgroups:* Most are free. Because newsgroups continuously update materials, you will need to periodically reinsert your ad. This also gives you an opportunity to revise your ad. One popular newsgroup is can.jobs. Following are some other interesting websites (some originating in the United States):

   - CareerBuilder.com
   - Career Magazine (http://www.thecareermag.com/index.html)
   - MonsterTrak (https://www.monster.com/internships-entry-level-college-jobs.aspx?wt.mc_n=monstertrak)

No matter where the ad is listed, it should contain all key words likely to be used by a firm's recruits.

9. *Take advantage of special online advertisement offers:* Advertise your openings with popular online newspapers and magazines as their websites receive high traffic.

(Continued)

10. *List your ad with all major web-based job banks (including ESDC's) and various career sites to send applicants to you, such as the following:*

    * Workopolis (https://www.workopolis.com/en/)
    * Monster (https://www.monster.ca/)
    * Indeed (https://www.indeed.ca/)

11. *Remove the ad as soon as the position is filled:* If the recruitment is for a one-time position, the advertisement should be removed as soon as the position is no longer available. The site should also indicate the period of time during which applications are kept active.

12. *Choose software carefully:* Software that scans résumés should be keyed for pertinent, job-relevant words. A periodic review of the "screened out" applications will indicate whether the software is systematically deleting applications from protected employment groups.

Social Media

To leverage technology, recruiting has also expanded to mobile devices. iPhone and Android have applications that allow job seekers to search and apply for jobs through their smartphones. Many organizations are also on Facebook, where the average user is age 32, and LinkedIn, where the average user is 37 years old.[53]

Social media can be used by recruiters in two primary ways. First, recruiters can post their opportunities and seek applicants using tools such as LinkedIn and Google+. While LinkedIn may have a greater number of users, it has limitations in terms of the conversations that can take place, and few comments are made despite many postings by "thought leaders." Google+, on the other hand, may allow for greater engagement, targeted audience networking, creation of a brand page, and help with directing traffic to the business from search engines, but there are currently fewer users. Some social media experts advocate that recruiters should leverage multiple tools and keep abreast of emerging ones; others recommend that recruiters need to know which tools their prospective recruits are using and focus their recruiting efforts on using those same tools.[54]

Second, recruiters may seek information about candidates and prospective candidates through social networking sites, such as Facebook, Twitter, blogs, wikis, online discussion boards, Google Groups, Tumblr, and video- and photo-sharing sites such as YouTube and Snapchat. While recruiters may be able to learn more about applicants from these sites, much of what they learn may be unrelated to the job. For instance, information on these sites may relate to protected status, such as age, gender, religion, race, political affiliation, national origin, disabilities, or sexual orientation. Furthermore, the information on these sites is not verified, and the profile accessed may be for the wrong person (that is, someone who has the same name as the applicant).[55]

Figure 5-6 shows that, across job levels, the use of social media for recruiting has gone up over the past few years.

FIGURE 5-6

Job Levels Recruited via Social Media

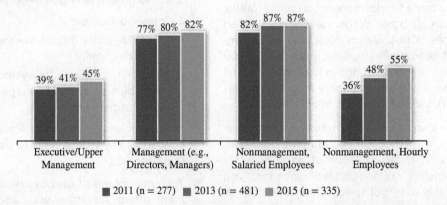

2011 (n = 277)　2013 (n = 481)　2015 (n = 335)

SOURCE: Reprinted from p.14, "Using Social Media for Talent Acquisition" (2017, September 20), with permission of the Society for Human Resource Management (SHRM). © SHRM 2017. All rights reserved.

Recall that recruiting includes all activities that may intentionally or unintentionally affect candidates' likelihood of applying for and accepting a job offer at a firm. The use of social media by employees of the firm may impact how candidates view an organization. Many organizations today are grappling with whether social media should be restricted to only those organizational functions that may need to use it (such as marketing, media relations, and HR), or whether they should promote its use by all employees. Regardless, HR may be involved with other functions (e.g., legal, marketing) in creating a social media use policy. An example of the social media guidelines by one progressive firm is reproduced in Figure 5-7.

FIGURE 5-7

The Current and Official "IBM Social Computing Guidelines"

Introduction

Responsible engagement in innovation and dialogue

Whether or not an IBMer chooses to create or participate in a blog, wiki, online social network or any other form of online publishing or discussion is his or her own decision. However, emerging online collaboration platforms are fundamentally changing the way IBMers work and engage with each other, clients and partners.

IBM is increasingly exploring how online discourse through social computing can empower IBMers as global professionals, innovators and citizens. These individual interactions represent a new model: not mass communications, but masses of communicators.

Therefore, it is very much in IBM's interest—and, we believe, in each IBMer's own—to be aware of and participate in this sphere of information, interaction and idea exchange:

To learn: As an innovation-based company, we believe in the importance of open exchange and learning—between IBM and its clients, and among the many constituents of our emerging business and societal ecosystem. The rapidly growing phenomenon of user-generated web content—blogging, social web-applications and networking—are emerging important arenas for that kind of engagement and learning.

To contribute: IBM—as a business, as an innovator and as a corporate citizen—makes important contributions to the world, to the future of business and technology, and to public dialogue on a broad range of societal issues. As our business activities increasingly focus on the provision of transformational insight and high-value innovation—whether to business clients or those in the public, educational or health sectors—it becomes increasingly important for IBM and IBMers to share with the world the exciting things we're learning and doing, and to learn from others.

In 1997, IBM recommended that its employees get out onto the Internet—at a time when many companies were seeking to restrict their employees' Internet access. In 2005, the company made a strategic decision to embrace the blogosphere and to encourage IBMers to participate. We continue to advocate IBMers' responsible involvement today in this rapidly growing space of relationship, learning and collaboration.

IBM Social Computing Guidelines: Executive Summary

1. Know and follow IBM's Business Conduct Guidelines.
2. IBMers are personally responsible for the content they publish on blogs, wikis or any other form of user-generated media. Be mindful that what you publish will be public for a long time—protect your privacy.
3. Identify yourself—name and, when relevant, role at IBM—when you discuss IBM or IBM-related matters. And write in the first person. You must make it clear that you are speaking for yourself and not on behalf of IBM.
4. If you publish content to any website outside of IBM and it has something to do with work you do or subjects associated with IBM, use a disclaimer such as this: "The postings on this site are my own and don't necessarily represent IBM's positions, strategies or opinions."
5. Respect copyright, fair use and financial disclosure laws.
6. Don't provide IBM's or another's confidential or other proprietary information. Ask permission to publish or report on conversations that are meant to be private or internal to IBM.
7. Don't cite or reference clients, partners or suppliers without their approval. When you do make a reference, where possible link back to the source.
8. Respect your audience. Don't use ethnic slurs, personal insults, obscenity, or engage in any conduct that would not be acceptable in IBM's workplace. You should also show proper consideration for others' privacy and for topics that may be considered objectionable or inflammatory—such as politics and religion.

(Continued)

9. Find out who else is blogging or publishing on the topic, and cite them.

10. Be aware of your association with IBM in online social networks. If you identify yourself as an IBMer, ensure your profile and related content is consistent with how you wish to present yourself with colleagues and clients.

11. Don't pick fights, be the first to correct your own mistakes, and don't alter previous posts without indicating that you have done so.

12. Try to add value. Provide worthwhile information and perspective. IBM's brand is best represented by its people and what you publish may reflect on IBM's brand.

Reprint Courtesy of International Business Machines Corporation, © International Business Machines Corporation.

Employment and Social Development Canada

Employment and Social Development Canada (ESDC) is the department of the Government of Canada responsible for developing, managing, and delivering social programs and services. The Skills and Employment branch provides programs and initiatives that do the following:

> **Employment and Social Development Canada (ESDC)** Federal department that provides programs and services for employers and present and potential employees.

- Promote skills development, labour market participation and inclusiveness, and labour market efficiency
- Address the employment and skills needs of those facing employment barriers, and contribute to lifelong learning and building a skilled, inclusive labour force
- Support an efficient labour market, including the labour market integration of recent immigrants, the entry of temporary foreign workers, the mobility of workers across Canada, and the dissemination of labour market information

Further information about this fourth-largest department of the Canadian government is available on the ESDC website (https://www.canada.ca/en/employment-social-development.html).

ESDC's mission is to build a stronger and more competitive Canada, to support Canadians in making choices that help them live productive and rewarding lives, and to improve Canadians' quality of life. Service Canada offers single-window access to a wide range of Government of Canada programs and services for citizens (including several of those from ESDC) through more than 600 points of service located across the country, call centres, and the Internet. In addition, ESDC offers specific programs and activities, including the Jobs and the Workplace webpages and the Job Bank.[56]

Jobs and the Workplace

The Jobs and the Workplace pages (https://www.canada.ca/en/services/jobs.html) are designed to help Canadians find work, explore skills and training possibilities, make career decisions, plan for retirement, and apply for temporary financial assistance. On these pages, job seekers can explore job descriptions, examine wage rates and skills requirements, and find training and job opportunities. The information can be sorted by occupation and also within specific geographical regions. The site was designed to help Canadians choose career paths, explore educational options, and prepare for job searches and interviews. For employers, the site offers information on hiring and retaining workers, labour market information, advice on human resource management tools, and government program and regulatory information.

The Job Bank

The Job Bank provides a comprehensive database of thousands of jobs and work opportunities available across Canada. When an employer has a job opening, the human resource department voluntarily notifies ESDC of the job and its requirements, which are then posted at the website. Here, prospective employees can scan the job openings and discuss any vacancy with one of the counsellors available. When an applicant expresses interest in a particular job, counsellors interview that person. Over 40,000 employers use the services to advertise full-time, part-time, and summer job opportunities.[57]

Private Employment Agencies

Private employment agencies, now present in every major metropolitan area, arose to help employers find capable applicants. Placement firms take an employer's request for recruits and then solicit job seekers, usually through advertising or from walk-ins. Candidates are matched with employer requests and then told to report to the employer's human resource department. The matching process conducted by private agencies varies widely. Some placement services carefully screen applicants for a client. Others simply provide a stream of applicants and let the client's human resource department do most of the screening.

Use of a private employment agency may be necessary when the employer needs only a few people and on a temporary or irregular basis. Also, when the employer has a critical need to fill a position quickly this method can be very useful. In times of tight labour markets, it may be necessary to attract individuals who are already employed on a part-time basis. Private employment agencies can achieve this more cost-effectively, especially if the employer has limited experience in the local labour market.

In many provinces, it is either illegal for private employment agencies to charge applicants a fee for placement, or the fees charged are regulated. Most fees are paid by the agencies' clients—that is, the prospective employers. The fees commonly equal either 10 percent of the first year's salary or one month's wages, but the amount may vary with the volume of business provided by the client and the type of employee sought.

Professional Search Firms

Professional search firms are much more specialized than placement agencies. Search firms usually recruit only specific types of human resources for a fee paid by the employer. For example, some search firms specialize in executive talent, while others use their expertise to find technical and scientific personnel. Perhaps the most significant difference between search firms and placement agencies is their approach. Placement agencies hope to attract applicants through advertising, but search firms actively seek out recruits from among the employees of other companies. Although they may advertise, direct contact is their primary tool for locating and attracting prospective recruits:

> **professional search firms** Agencies that, for a fee, recruit specialized personnel for a company.

The Interlake-Eastern Regional Health Authority has hired a professional search firm to help fill physician vacancies in Eastern Manitoba. The region has relied on international medical grads to fill its openings, but most leave following two- or four-year commitments and after successfully passing examinations to allow them to practise anywhere in Canada. The focus of the professional search firm is to recruit physicians who will want to remain in the communities.[58]

There are a couple of advantages to using professional search firms. First, search firms have in-depth experience that many human resource departments lack. Second, search firms are often willing to undertake actions that an employer would not, such as calling a competitor. Some human resource professionals consider search firms' practice of "stealing" or "raiding" candidates from among their clients' competitors to be unethical, and refer to them as "headhunters."[59]

What is the reason for the popularity of executive search firms? Professional search firms may have greater understanding of niche requirements in particular industries, cost less per recruit, have access to candidates integrated into specific industries as well as to passive job seekers, and result in an overall higher success rate in recruiting the right quality personnel.[60]

> Executive search has typically followed a set formula: "Typically, when a firm wins an engagement, it spends several months defining the candidate criteria, quietly reaching out to leaders worldwide, compiling a short list, interviewing and investigating candidates, then acting as a hush-hush go-between for the client and the top prospects." The network of contacts for the search firm was incredibly important. Now, through LinkedIn and other social media, corporate HR managers can easily find and contact prospects themselves. Organizations like RBC are now posting vice-president positions on LinkedIn.[61]

When choosing a search firm, care must be taken to test the "fit" between the firm and the client organization. Checking the firm's recruiting record and its reputation is very important. The larger firms can be quite expensive, often charging 25 to 33 percent of the candidate's gross starting salary as fees (not inclusive of other expenses).[62] Some of the factors that should be considered in evaluating a recruiting firm include the firm's size, staff qualifications, ability to meet time requirements, financial soundness, proven validity of the testing/selection instruments and practices, technological savvy, and provision of measurable results from previous contracts (track record and acceptable references).

Educational Institutions

For entry-level openings, **educational institutions** and **alumni associations** are another common source of recruits. Counsellors and teachers often provide recruiters with leads to desirable candidates in high schools. Many universities, community colleges, and technical schools offer their current students and alumni placement assistance. This assistance helps employers and graduates to meet and discuss employment opportunities and the applicant's interest.

> **educational institutions** High schools, technical schools, community colleges, and universities where applicants for job positions are sought.
>
> **alumni associations** Associations of alumni of schools, colleges, or other training facilities.

> Loblaw traditionally sent five to seven recruiters for two- to four-day recruitment drives to pharmacy

schools at nine campuses across Canada. The company introduced a video interview to "meet" candidates and ask them screening questions (especially, the locations where they were interested in working) before on-campus interview offers were extended. The cloud-based system allowed busy students to complete their video responses from any device. Loblaw recruiters were able to screen, short-list, rank, comment on, and share their responses in about 4 minutes per interview as compared to 30 minutes spent face-to-face interviewing. Fewer on-campus interviews then saved the company both time and money on the recruiting process, and resulted in no fewer applications.[63]

Past research studies indicate that students desire campus recruiters to be well informed, honest, and skilled. The title and age of the recruiter, and even whether the recruiter is an alumnus of the same institution, may also be important factors in creating a favourable impression on recruits.[64] Some other characteristics of successful campus recruiters are shown in Figure 5-8. However, not many recruiters are successful in getting the best talent during their campus visits. The recruitment cycle is getting shorter each year with top candidates often snapped up the September before they graduate. The National Association of Colleges and Employers (NACE) offers a number of suggestions on best practices for campus recruitment programs.[65]

Increasingly, organizations find that summer internships and co-operative education programs, where students alternate between study and work terms, significantly facilitate college and university recruitment efforts.

Summer internships are particularly popular in large companies such as Procter & Gamble, Aetna Life Insurance, and Manitoba Liquor and Lotteries Corporation; however, even smaller organizations find that hiring students to complete summer projects helps them to identify qualified, motivated, and informed recruits for permanent placement.

During their work terms, students are exposed to the organization and gain a clear idea of what to expect from the firm should they later join as full-time employees. Such "informed" recruits are less likely to leave the firm soon

© Benny Marty/Alamy Stock Photo

The Building Opportunities for Leadership and Development (BOLD) Internship Program is a paid summer internship for rising undergraduate students interested in technology and full-time opportunities at Google. The program is designed to expose historically under-represented students to career opportunities in the industry. What are the pros and cons of focusing the program on under-represented students?

FIGURE 5-8

A Profile of an Ideal Recruiter

- Hires for specific positions rather than looking for future recruits without any clear idea about job vacancies
- Possesses considerable knowledge about the firm and the job position
- Discusses strengths and limitations of the firm knowledgeably
- Never exaggerates or oversells the employer
- Studies the student's résumé carefully before the interview and asks specific questions
- Validly assesses the student's awareness of and interest in the job and the company
- Asks thought-provoking questions to measure the student's knowledge on relevant job matters
- Expresses interest in the student as an individual
- Is upbeat about the company and his or her own role in the firm
- Displays good interpersonal skills and appears polite and sincere
- Follows up promptly with feedback and evaluation
- Is professional and ethical in demeanour

after they are hired. Employers can also assess the students' abilities, attitudes, and performance without incurring any significant costs.[66]

Universities that provide business administration programs aimed at senior- and middle-level managers (such as executive MBA programs) are also a valuable source for recruiting managers. Keeping tapped into the alumni associations of schools, colleges, and even prior employees can also be an excellent source for hiring experienced technical and managerial staff.[67]

Professional Associations and Labour Organizations

Recruiters find that professional associations also can be a source of job seekers. Many associations conduct placement activities to help new and experienced professionals get jobs; some have publications that accept classified advertisements. Professionals who belong to the appropriate associations are considered more likely to remain informed of the latest developments in their field, and so this channel of recruitment may lead to higher quality applicants. Another advantage of this source of applicants is that it helps recruiters zero in on specific specialties, particularly in hard-to-fill technical areas.

When recruiters want people with trade skills, local labour organizations have rosters of those people who are looking for employment. The local union of plumbers, for example, keeps a list of plumbers who are seeking jobs. In the construction industry, many contractors often hire on a per-project basis. A union hiring hall is a convenient channel for attracting large numbers of pretrained recruits for new projects.

Canadian Forces

The Canadian Armed Forces trains personnel in almost every profession imaginable, from trades to medical professionals to culinary arts. A veteran who joined the forces at 18 may be eligible for a full CF pension at 43, and some may seek to transition into a civilian career. Some veterans, such as those who have been trained as mechanics, welders, or pilots, have hard-to-find skills. Human resource departments that need skills similar to those found in the military often find nearby military installations a valuable source of recruits.

Military jets have the highest performing engines on the planet, and disc-braking systems were developed for military aircraft. Audi's veteran hiring program recognizes the transferability of the skills gained working with adjusting and replacing disc brakes during military service to their high-performance car engines.[68]

Temporary-Help Agencies

Most large cities have **temporary-help agencies** that can respond quickly to an employer's need for help. These agencies do not provide recruits. Instead, they are a source of supplemental workers. The temporary workers actually work for the agency and are "on loan" to the requesting employer. For temporary jobs—during vacations, peak seasons, illnesses, and so on—these agencies can be a better alternative than recruiting new workers for short periods of employment. Besides handling the recruiting and bookkeeping tasks caused by new employees, these agencies can often provide clerical and secretarial talent on short notice, sometimes within less than a day. And when the temporary shortage is over, there is no need to lay off surplus workers because "temporaries" work for the agency, not the company.[69] Occasionally, temporary workers are recruited to become permanent employees.

> **temporary-help agencies**
> Agencies that provide supplemental workers for temporary vacancies caused by employee leave, sickness, etc.

With over 40 locations in Canada, Adecco employs over 9,000 temporary Associates in Canada each day.[70] Adecco provides a pool of workers employed by the agency who can be loaned to local organizations for particular lengths of time. For instance, Adecco may lend one of its associates to Cirque du Soleil in Montreal while its regular employee is on maternity leave. Once that job ends, the associate returns to Adecco awaiting the next firm. The associate may then go to Nespresso for a three- to six-month contract.

Departing Employees

An often overlooked source of recruits is among departing employees. These workers might gladly stay if they could rearrange their schedules or change the number of hours worked. Family responsibilities, health conditions, or other circumstances may lead a worker to quit when a transfer to a part-time job could retain valuable skills and training. Even if part-time work is not a solution, a temporary leave of absence may satisfy the employee and some future recruiting need of the employer.

An employee who leaves a company to pursue another job or venture and is later rehired is known as a "boomerang employee." As competition for top talent has intensified, the number of boomerang employees has grown vastly. A company such as Ernst & Young LLP, a Toronto-based accounting firm, actively cultivates a continuing connection with its past employees. Former employees have access to webcasts sponsored by E&Y that discuss developments in the accounting field. A newsletter is sent a couple of times a year and several social events are held for former staff. When people leave the firm, they are even given a password to access the website, which includes a directory of current and former employees, details of what former employees are doing, and a place to post résumés. Encouraging former employees to reconsider E&Y is definitely one of the objectives of such efforts, according to a director of E&Y.[71]

A **buy-back** occurs when an employee resigns to take another job and the original employer outbids the new job offer or renegotiates the terms of the employee's job contract. Consider this anecdote from Patty McCord from her time as the chief talent officer at Netflix:

> **buy-back** A method of convincing an employee who is about to resign to stay in the employ of the organization, typically by offering an increased wage or salary.

During a time when Netflix was losing employees to exorbitant offers by their competitors, Patty learned that Google had offered one of her employees almost twice his salary to go and work for it. As a key employee, his manager wanted to make a counteroffer to retain his employment. Patty describes a heated debate about whether Netflix would and could meet the new salary. In the end, she realized that this employee's unique work on a personalization technology made him one of only a few in the world with that expertise, giving him a whole new market value. In the end, Netflix doubled the salaries not just of that employee, but of everyone on that team.[72]

Even when the authority to enter into a bidding war exists, the manager may discover that other workers expect similar raises. Many HR practitioners are averse to this approach because of its ethical implications. Employees may also reject a buy-back attempt because of the ethical issue raised by not reporting to a job that has already been accepted.

Job Fairs

Attending **job fairs** can pay rich dividends to recruiters who are looking for specialized talents or a number of personnel. Over the years, budgetary constraints and the emergence of Internet recruitment have resulted in a decline in the popularity of job fairs. However, even today, there are examples of striking successes:

> **job fairs** Trade-show-style fairs with many employers showcasing their companies and jobs to potential recruits.

The job fair organized by the University of Waterloo, Wilfrid Laurier University, Conestoga College, and University of Guelph has tripled in size of attendees since it was first organized a quarter century ago. The 2018 event was expected to attract over 200 companies and 2,500 to 3,000 students, making it the largest job fair in Canada.[73]

Some job fairs are scheduled one year in advance; hence, employers should plan well ahead. More recently, it has also become popular to give out "swag," such as pens, notepads, USB sticks, and water bottles to visitors to promote the organization.[74]

Contract Workers

As discussed in Chapter 3, a very large segment of our labour market is composed of contract workers. Contract workers are useful when the work is of limited duration so the firm can avoid fixed salary commitments; the employer pays a flat fee for the employees (and is not responsible for benefits). Contract workers, often, are compensated on the basis of task completion and hence need less supervision. Often, they also require lower training costs, making this an attractive proposition.

> More organizations employ contract workers now than ever before. In many organizations, the proportion of the staff who are on contract is 7 to 10 percent, and two-thirds of HR professionals in a Canadian survey have seen an increase in the number of contract workers in the past five years. Reasons for the increase may include ability to better balance work–life needs, not being tied to a single employer, and the increasingly project-based nature of work.[75]

Contract workers may not always be committed to the goals and philosophy of the organization, however. Because these workers are not part of an organization's regular workforce, they do not benefit from the statutory protections offered by various provincial employment laws. The contracting firm is also not responsible for remitting Canada Pension Plan premiums or withholding income tax. However, determining whether an individual is an independent contractor or an employee is not as easy as it appears. Courts and arbitrators have been increasingly monitoring contractual agreements to ensure that the employer is not using the independent contractor relationship to avoid its statutory and common law obligations.[76] Accordingly, it is important for the contracting parties to understand their rights and obligations.

Recruitment Abroad

With the growing labour shortages in Canada, many employers are looking abroad to secure skilled, hard-to-find employees.

> Many high-tech and software companies today look at India as a major source of highly skilled

programmers. Some of the software manufacturers have gone as far as locating their operations in Indian cities, such as Bangalore and Hyderabad, while others have formed partnerships with Indian firms that periodically send their own staff to North America on a contract basis.

Indeed, Canada has been recruiting a large number of skilled workers from other countries. Figure 5-9 shows the

© FINDLAY KEMBER/AFP/Getty Images.

Many Canadian high-tech companies and accounting firms are taking advantage of India's low labour costs and highly skilled programmers and accountants, thus displacing local workers. What proportion of jobs should Canada export?

origins of 148,181 economic immigrants who entered the country in 2013. With an aging domestic workforce and a predicted shortage of technical and highly skilled employees, foreign nationals may become an important source of our workforce.

Foreign workers, especially those from developing countries, may be less expensive (at least initially). Relocation expenses may have to be paid in some instances, however, which can significantly add to the total cost. Firms hiring from abroad will need to train new recruits to adapt to local and organizational culture. The process of getting employment visas may also be time-consuming.

LO6 Choosing Recruitment Sources

With all of the options available for sourcing potential applicants, how does a recruiter choose which method(s) to use? The choice of recruiting method may be assisted by answering the following six questions:[77]

1. *How many recruits are needed*? Some sources, such as advertising, will produce larger numbers of applicants whereas others are used when small numbers of recruits are needed (e.g., employment agencies).

2. *What is the skill level required*? If there is a high level of skill or experience required for the job, niche

FIGURE 5-9

Origins of Canada's Skilled Immigrants, 2015

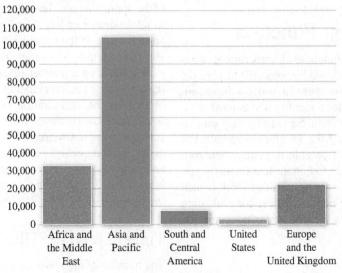

SOURCE: Chart prepared by the authors based on the data reported in Citizenship and Immigration Canada (2015), "Immigration overview: Permanent residents" by category and source area, https://open.canada.ca/data/en/dataset/2fbb56bd-eae7-4582-af7d-a197d185fc93?_ga=2.96482975 .1678281054.1518800815-781687463.1495736649

recruiting might be needed, for instance by approaching a professional association or using a professional search firm.

3. *What sources are available in that industry and geographic region?* Not all sources are available in all areas (e.g., a rural area might not have a temporary-help agency).

4. *What has worked in the past?* Tracking over time how well certain sources have worked may guide future recruitment efforts. For example, if advertising on an Internet job board has produced more applicants who have turned out to be good performers in the past than a community newspaper, the recruiter may choose to advertise new postings on the same job board.

5. *How much is the budget?* The budget will determine the methods the recruiter can afford to use. For instance, transit advertising may be too expensive to use for filling a single position.

6. *Are there labour agreements in place that specify recruitment options?* Collective agreements in place at the organization may obligate the recruiter to rely on internal versus external recruiting, and to use specific recruitment sources.

In competitive recruitment environments, recruiters will often employ multiple methods and then track each method to see the number of applicants, the quality of applicants, the number who eventually accept and perform the job well, and even retention rates. Producing a good system for tracking recruitment success saves time and effort down the road and can have a substantial impact on the organization's bottom line.

LO7 Evaluating the Recruitment Function

Like most other important functions, the recruiting activity in an organization should also be subjected to periodic evaluation. Typically, the recruitment process is expensive. Unless efforts are made to identify and control these costs, the potential benefits from the activity may end up being lower than the costs. Like all other corporate HR functions, recruiters will not be able to justify their own efforts unless these contribute to bottom-line financial performance. Recruitment also reflects a firm's overall human resource strategy. The more popular indices for evaluating the effectiveness of a firm's recruiting strategies are discussed below.

Cost per Hire

The dollar cost per person recruited is one possible measure of the effectiveness of the recruiting function. The costs should include not only the direct costs (e.g., recruiters' salaries, costs of advertisement, consultants' fees, and so on), but also apportioned costs and overheads (e.g., time of operating personnel, stationery, rent). However, often cost data are either not collected at all or are not interpreted so as to facilitate the evaluation of recruiting. Cost data collected from previous recruiting activities could serve as useful benchmarks for comparison.

Quality of Hires and Cost

A major criticism of using a simple dollar cost per hire as a measure of effectiveness is that it ignores the quality of the people hired. The performance, absenteeism, and motivation levels of employees recruited from one source (or using one media) may differ from those of other sources.

> Recruits selected through advertisements in professional journals and professional conventions may have qualitatively superior performance compared to those who were selected through campus recruitment efforts.

The number and quality of résumés and job applications received gives an indication of the overall effectiveness of a recruitment method or source.

Offers–Applicants Ratio

A somewhat better index is the ratio between the number of job offers extended and the total number of applicants calculated for each recruitment method or media. Even if a recruiting source brings in better-quality résumés, this may not be translated finally to job offers; an offers–applicants ratio gives a better picture of the overall quality of the applicant pool. The ratio of number of offers accepted to total number of job offers extended to applicants gives an indication of the overall effectiveness of the recruiting. However, caution is in order. The acceptance of a job offer is dependent on a number of extraneous variables, including the labour market situation, the compensation package offered by the organization and its competitors, and the firm's location. However, when used judiciously, this measure can point out weaknesses, such as lack of professionalism and long delays in the recruiting process, that could encourage a prospective employee to go elsewhere. This is particularly true for good candidates, who may receive multiple job offers from employers.

Time Lapsed per Hire

The number of days, weeks, or months taken to fill a position provides yet another measure of the effectiveness of the recruitment system. Clearly, a firm that takes a week to fill a position when the industry average is 10 days or two weeks is, in comparison, more efficient. Several external

FIGURE 5-10

Popular Measures Used for Evaluating Effectiveness of Recruitment Function

1. Total number of applications received

2. Time required to get applications

3. Time elapsed before filling positions

4. Costs per hire

5. Ratio of offers extended to number of applicants

6. Ratio of offers accepted to number of offers extended

7. Ratio of number of qualified applicants to total number of applicants

8. Performance rating of hires

9. Turnover of hires

and uncontrollable factors (including the nature of the job, labour market conditions, and location) affect the time for recruiting. However, the time lapsed from when people apply to when they find out that they got the job has increased in Canada from an average of 12 days in 2010 to 22.1 days in 2014 (compared to 22.9 days in the U.S., 31.9 days in France, and 27.9 days in Australia) based on a survey of 340,250 people (14,600 Canadians).[78]

Figure 5-10 shows some of the more popular measures used to evaluate the recruiting function. Naturally, many of these measures are influenced by a firm's selection, training, and compensation systems. Indeed, an evaluation system that explicitly considers various factors related to the selection process and that contains job performance information (including tenure and value of job to the organization) may be very useful in several organizational settings. The next chapter will look at the various steps involved in the selection of personnel from the pool of applicants identified during recruiting.

SUMMARY

Recruitment is the process of finding and attracting capable applicants for employment. Then, once the top candidates have been selected, recruiters seek to convince applicants to say "yes" to the job offer. Before recruiters can solicit applicants, they should be aware of organizational policies, human resource plans, employment equity plans, recruiter habits, environmental conditions, and the requirements of the job.

At the recruiter's disposal are a variety of methods to find and attract job seekers. Employer sources include walk-ins, write-ins, employee referrals, the Internet, and direct solicitations through ads and other forms of advertisement. Applicants can be found through referrals from Employment and Social Development Canada offices, private placement agencies, or search firms. Of course, recruits can be found through a variety of institutions, such as educational, professional, and labour organizations; the military; and government training programs. Some firms have reported success in converting temporary employees into permanent ones, on a full- or part-time basis, and in inducing departing employees to remain. Job fairs may inform prospective applicants about multiple companies and available positions and prompt them to submit applications.

The choice of sources used will depend on the quality and quantity of recruits needed, available sources, past

successes with the source, the recruiting budget, and labour agreements. Over time, recruiters can track the success of each of their recruitment sources to guide them in future recruitment processes.

Applicants formally apply to organizations by submitting completed application forms or résumés. Application forms seek a variety of answers from recruits, including personal, employment, educational, and work history information. Questions may be asked about memberships, awards, and personal interests. References are usually solicited on the application form as well.

Like all other human resource functions, the recruitment activity also needs to be evaluated for its degree of effectiveness and efficiency. This is to ensure that the recruitment function achieves both organizational and individual objectives. A number of indices for evaluating the recruitment activity were suggested in this chapter. Bear in mind that all of these indices are affected by a firm's selection, training, compensation, and general human resource–related policies. With a pool of recruits and the information contained in completed application forms, the human resource department is now ready to assist line managers in the process of selecting new employees.

TERMS FOR REVIEW

ads 155
alumni associations 163
applicant tracking system (ATS) 151
blind ads 155
buy-back 166
competitive advantage 145
costs 150
educational institutions 163
employee referrals 154
Employment and Social Development Canada
(ESDC) 162
human resource plan 149

inducements 150
job application form 152
job fairs 166
organizational policies 147
professional search firms 163
recruiter habits 149
recruitment 143
résumé 151
selection 143
temporary-help agencies 165
walk-ins/write-ins 154

SELF-ASSESSMENT EXERCISE

How Do You Recruit Employers?

Just as organizations have to recruit potential employees, most individuals also need to scan their environments for potential employers. Take this simple self-test to see how you go about collecting information about your future employers. Answer all questions on a five-point scale of strongly agree (SA), agree (A), undecided (U), disagree (D), and strongly disagree (SD).

Statement	Strongly Agree	Agree	Undecided	Disagree	Strongly Disagree
1. I have a clear idea of the type of job I want and the general competencies it requires.					
2. Looking at online job ads is a waste of time; most jobs are filled even before they are advertised anyway.					
3. I frequently look at job ads in newspapers circulating in the region I am interested in.					
4. I rarely (if ever) look at the annual reports of the firms where I would like to work in the future.					
5. I use social media to tell all my friends and acquaintances who work in the industry or profession that I am looking for a job in that field.					
6. I do not have a clear idea of the region or the industry where I want to work.					
7. I regularly look online to find out more about possible job openings in the industry or occupation I am interested in.					
8. I don't watch TV news or read newspapers.					
9. I keep in touch with my school and college friends, and network with them at social or professional events.					
10. In general, I never talk to others about their experiences in job hunting.					

SCORING

For the odd-numbered statements, give yourself a score of 5, 4, 3, 2, and 1 for SA, A, U, D, and SD, respectively. For the even-numbered statements, give a score of 1, 2, 3, 4, and 5 for SA, A, U, D, and SD, respectively. Add up all scores.

Your total score can lie anywhere from 10 to 50 in this exercise. If your score is 40 or above, you are doing a good job of keeping yourself abreast of the events in the job market. If you got a lower score, you may want to do some of the things indicated above. Getting the right job takes a lot of effort and time, and you have to begin efforts in that direction today!

REVIEW AND DISCUSSION QUESTIONS

1. What background information should a recruiter have before beginning to recruit job seekers?

2. Give three examples of how organizational policies affect the recruitment process. Explain how these influence a recruiter's actions.

3. Under what circumstances would a blind ad be a useful recruiting technique?

4. "If a job application form omits important questions, needed information about recruits will not be available. But if a needless question is asked, the information can be ignored by the recruiter without any other complications." Do you agree or disagree with this statement? Why?

5. Suppose your employer asks you, the human resource manager, to justify the relatively large recruiting budget that you have been historically assigned. What arguments would you provide? What indices or measures would you provide to show that your recruitment is cost effective?

CRITICAL THINKING QUESTIONS

1. After months of insufficient recognition (and two years without a raise), you accept an offer from another firm that involves a $2,000-a-year raise. When you tell your boss that you are resigning, you are told how crucial you are to the business and are offered a raise of $2,500 per year. What do you do? Why? What problems might exist if you accept the buy-back?

2. Suppose you are a manager who has just accepted the resignation of a crucial employee. After you send your request for a replacement to the human resource department, how could you help the recruiter do a more effective job?

3. If at your company the regular university recruiter became ill and you were assigned to recruit at six universities in two weeks, what information would you need before leaving on the trip?

4. In small businesses, managers usually handle their own recruiting. What methods would you use in the following situations? Why?

   a. The regular janitor is going on vacation for three weeks.

   b. Your office assistant, who manages all appointments and handles all filing in your office, has the flu and won't be in the office for two days.

   c. Two more salespeople are needed: one for local customers and one to open a sales office in Victoria, British Columbia.

   d. Your only chemist is retiring and must be replaced with a highly skilled person.

   e. Your only computer programmer/analyst plans to go on a three-week leave to India to visit his sick mother next week. If his mother's health turns for the worse, he may be delayed by another week or two.

5. You are the human resource manager in a large auto-assembly unit employing 2,000 semiskilled and skilled employees. Each year, you recruit dozens of full-time and part-time workers. Recently, the vice-president (Finance) pointed out that recruitment costs in your firm are increasing steadily. She has proposed a freeze in the recruitment budget. What kind of information will you provide in an effort to change her mind on the matter?

ETHICS QUESTION

Consider how you might respond in the following situation:

You are interviewing for a position you are really excited about with a well-regarded employer in your field. The recruiter seems friendly and informative and very interested in you as a candidate. At the end of the interview, the recruiter asks you if you are married and if you have children.

1. How would you respond to the recruiter?

2. Would you follow up with the recruiter or with the organization about the inappropriate questions? Why or why not?

3. Would your responses to the previous two questions be different if the position you were applying for was in HR versus another field? Why or why not?

RESEARCH EXERCISE

Choose any two Internet recruiting sites. Select advertisements for two different job positions in each site (i.e., four in all). Compare their features and strengths. Do you expect different types of recruits to respond to these advertisements and sites? Why? Which of the four advertisements that you chose is the best? Which is the worst? Why? What suggestions do you have to enhance the effectiveness of poor ads? Report your findings to the class.

INCIDENT 5-1

Dronexx Electronics Expansion

Dronexx Electronics developed a revolutionary method of drone fast-food delivery that could pick up orders from a fast-food location and keep the warm food warm and the cold food cold until delivery at a specified GPS address up to 8 km away depending on the size of the order. The head of research and development, Guy Jiang, estimated that Dronexx Electronics could become a supplier to every fast-food chain in the world. The future success of the company seemed to hang on securing the broadest possible patents to cover the still-secret technology.

The human resource director, Jackson Huang, recommended that Jiang become a project leader in charge of developing and filing the necessary patent information. Jiang and Huang developed a list of specialists who would be needed to rush the patent applications through the final stages of development and the patent application process. Most of the needed skills were found among Dronexx Electronics' present employees. However, after a preliminary review of skills inventories and staffing levels, a list of priority recruits was developed. It required the following:

- An experienced patent lawyer with a strong background in electronics technology

- A patent lawyer who was familiar with the ins and outs of the patent process and the patent office in Hull, Quebec

- Twelve engineers and software developers: three electronics engineers with prototype development experience, four full-stack programmers, and five junior programmers

- An office manager

Jiang and Huang wanted these 15 people recruited as promptly as possible.

DISCUSSION QUESTIONS

1. Assuming you are given the responsibility of recruiting these needed employees, what channels would you use to find and attract each type of recruit sought?

2. What other actions should the human resource department take now that there is the possibility of rapid expansion?

WE CONNECTIONS: RECRUITMENT FOR A KEY POSITION

End-of-Day Check-in

Alex and Selina, the co-founders of WEC, sat huddled at the round table in Alex's office. They often met there toward the end of the day to update each other on what was happening in the organization. Sometimes, especially when there were lots of problems, the meeting could stretch until midnight. On this day, the news was mostly good. New projects kept rolling in, quarterly profits were higher than expected, and the company's reputation seemed to be getting stronger. Indeed, the company continued to grow and prosper. However, they both knew that they could take nothing for granted. There were plenty of examples of promising companies that had fallen apart when their leaders got complacent. They were determined that was not going to happen to them.

More HR Bench Strength

It was past 7:00 p.m. when Selina said, "Listen, maybe I had better go. I'm getting kind of hungry."

Alex looked out the window and noticed the increasingly darkening skies. He said, "You're right, it is getting late. Time for one more thing?" When she nodded, he continued, "I have been thinking for some time that we need to invest a little more in the people management side of our business. We've had a couple of key people leave, and I'm worried that we might not have enough control over our HR strategy."

Selina looked up in surprise: "I thought that was one of the reasons why we hired Charlotte. She has training in that kind of thing, and she is pretty 'on the ball,' in my opinion."

Alex fidgeted with one of the stress balls that littered his office. Some part of him always had to be moving. He said, "Charlotte is great, but right now, all her time goes to putting out fires. We need to start being proactive, and I think we need some deeper bench strength. I was thinking we should hire an HR manager. You know, someone who doesn't just wait for us to tell them what to do. Someone seasoned who can help us figure out what strategies we should be following. In other words, I'm concerned that Charlotte is a good follower, but I think we need more of a leader in this area." Although he wanted to keep talking, he paused to let Selina consider his words.

A few moments later she responded: "I can see how that might be helpful, but are you sure Charlotte wouldn't be capable of doing more if we gave her the chance?"

Leaning forward to shut off his laptop, Alex shrugged his shoulders. "Maybe she would be able to grow into the job, but I don't think we have time to wait and find out. We need someone soon. And the good news is that I may

have already found the right person. When I was in that golf tournament last month, the organizers mixed up the teams as a networking thing. I ended up sharing a cart with a woman named Rebecca Ali. She works in HR at a major department store, though I can't remember which one. She has over 10 years of experience, and I really liked her. She was telling me that she creates a recruitment binder for every new job complete with onboarding materials, job ads, position profiles, compensation and benefits information. . . . And she was a fabulous golfer. I am sure I can find her through a quick Google search. Why don't we bring her in for an interview? I think she would be perfect!"

Let's Not Be Hasty

Shaking her head, Selina said, "I don't know, Alex. I don't have a good handle on what exactly you're looking for in this position. I don't want to be hasty."

Alex stood up and paced around his office. "Come on, Selina. I've got a good feeling about this person. You know I'm a great judge of character. Think about how nice it would be if we could fill this position with the very first candidate we see!"

Selina laughed at Alex's enthusiasm. She was always amazed at his ability to jump into things with both feet. However, she knew that sometimes he jumped too fast and got burned. She said, "Let me sleep on it, Alex. I don't want to make any big decisions when it's late and I'm hungry. We'll talk tomorrow. Okay?" She grabbed her things from the table and started to make her way out.

He nodded and said with a smile, "Okay, Selina. Fair enough. But mark my words. You're going to love Rebecca when you finally meet her!"

DISCUSSION QUESTIONS

1. What are the advantages and disadvantages of recruiting internally versus externally for the HR manager position? Should WEC consider both internal and external candidates for the HR manager position?

2. What do you think of Alex's plan to hire the person he met at the golf tournament? If you were to give him some advice on how to recruit for an HR manager, what would you say? Write down a list of steps for Alex to follow.

3. What are the best recruitment methods for finding qualified applicants for the HR manager position?

In the next installment of the WE Connections story (at the end of Chapter 6), a candidate is brought in for a job interview during the selection process.

CASE STUDY

Crown and Bull Pub

Screening Job Applicants Based on Applications and Social Media

Jessica Eagles worked as the day manager of Crown and Bull Public House. The pub was seeking to hire a new daytime server and two new night servers in anticipation of a busy summer patio season and summer vacations by current staff. To advertise the position, Jessica posted signs at the front entrance of the pub, added the openings to the pub's Facebook page, and posted the openings on Indeed.ca.

At the closing date for applications, they had received 20 applications and résumés. From her first review of the applicants, 6 could be immediately rejected for various reasons: The application was incomplete, the applicant was not local, the applicant was in high school and not old enough to serve alcohol, or the applicant's preferred start date was not until the fall.

With the remaining 14 applications, Jessica made a scoring guide based on the qualities and experience required for the position. She and the night manager, Ryder Dawson, planned to review the applications and identify the six to eight candidates they wanted to interview. After the interviews, their plan was to make the hiring decisions for both the daytime and night positions jointly.

Jessica thoroughly reviewed all 14 applications and used the scoring guide. She made some notes for each candidate to justify her ratings. When Jessica and Ryder met to discuss the applications, Ryder said that he had already identified whom they should interview. He revealed that he had rejected all of the male applicants, stating that the bar needed only "hot females" as servers and that males should stay behind the bar. He had met three of the female candidates previously and stated that Jessica should trust him that two of the candidates would not be people they would

want to work with but that one would be terrific. For the candidates he didn't know, he had gone onto Facebook and looked at their profiles. He was excited to note that most of the applicants had open profiles so he was able to readily see lots of pictures of them and read their posts, but that for the ones with private profiles, he had just befriended them and all but one (now on his rejected list) had accepted his friend requests.

According to Ryder, there were four candidates who were "super hot," and he dismissed others for being overweight, not pretty, or not the type of person they would want to work at the bar. Jessica was shocked at Ryder's approach to hiring new staff.

DISCUSSION QUESTIONS

1. What potential problems do you foresee with Ryder's approach to hiring?

2. Is it reasonable to use information from previous personal interactions during screening? Why or why not?

3. Should male candidates automatically be rejected from the server positions? Why or why not?

4. Are assessments of candidate attractiveness relevant? Discuss.

5. What would you do if you were in Jessica's place? How would you approach the conversation with Ryder about the screening process? How might you bring the scoring criteria into the conversation?

6. Would you use the information that Ryder has found on social media to supplement the applications, or ignore it? Justify your decision.

CHAPTER 6

Selection

> Employers hire based on results, not on what you were responsible for, and they use the results or accomplishments to predict your future performance, what might be possible, in a similar role.
>
> DAISY WRIGHT[1]

LEARNING OBJECTIVES

After studying this chapter, you should be able to:

LO1   Explain the strategic significance of the selection function.

LO2   Describe the various steps in the selection process.

LO3   Discuss the types and usefulness of applicant screening tools in selecting employees.

LO4   Explain the role of employment tests in the selection process, and discuss the types of employment tests.

LO5   Discuss the major approaches to test validation.

LO6   Outline the various steps in conducting an employment interview.

LO7   Describe how to evaluate the effectiveness of the selection process.

Once a pool of suitable applicants is created through recruiting, the process of selecting applicants begins. Consider the hiring process at Unilever, maker of products including Dove soap and Axe deodorant:[2]

By posting recruitment ads on Facebook and through career-advice sites like WayUp and Muse, Unilever enables applicants to apply for its entry-level jobs and internships in just a few clicks. The company's software completes application forms for candidates by pulling information from their LinkedIn profiles, which it then uses to screen out about half of the applicants. Candidates are then asked to play 12 short online games designed to assess skills such as short-term memory and concentration under time pressure. The top third then complete a video interview through HireVue on how they would respond to various business challenges. Artificial intelligence tools scan the interviews and use data from facial expressions, speed of responses, and vocabulary to make further screening decisions. The top 20 percent of candidates make it through to a face-to-face interview, at which point 80 percent are extended offers.

Although many employers do not use such elaborate screening devices, all but the smallest employers put applicants through a variety of steps called the **selection process**. The selection process is a series of specific steps used to decide which recruits should be hired. The process begins when recruits

> **selection process** A series of specific steps used by an employer to decide which recruits should be hired.

apply for employment and ends with the hiring decision. And recall from Chapter 5 that the recruitment process continues during the selection process as recruiters try to maintain applicant interest in the organization while selection is occurring, and then convince chosen applicants to accept a job offer if one is presented to them. The steps in between match the employment needs of the applicant and the organization.

LO1 Strategic Significance of the Selection Function

In many human resource departments, recruiting and selection are combined and called the *employment function*, or simply *recruiting*. In very small firms, the owner-manager typically does the hiring. In larger departments, human resource managers or employment managers handle these duties. Whatever the title, in most firms hiring is associated closely with the human resource department.

A proper selection process is integral to the strategic success of firms. Below, we discuss the more critical dimensions of an organization's strategy that are affected by this function.

Successful Execution of Organization's Strategy Depends on Calibre of Employees

An organization's overall effectiveness and success depends on the quality and calibre of the employees it hires. Poor selection practices also result in the HR department's not meeting the objectives specified in Chapter 1. In turn, an organization's mission and overall strategy affect the selection process and place major constraints on the human resource manager when selecting employees. This is because the skills and qualifications of the new hires need to closely match the organization's culture and strategic requirements, as the following example illustrates:

> A study of 243 small businesses found that firms have 7.5 percent higher revenue growth, 6.1 percent higher profit growth, and 17.1 percent lower turnover when they focus on attracting, finding, and selecting employees who fit the organization's culture and values. When person–organization fit is integrated with a self-management strategy—as opposed

to a controlling management strategy—within a family-like work atmosphere, retail firms had 74.7 percent lower turnover, low-skilled services had 57.9 percent lower turnover, and manufacturing firms watched 19.4 percent fewer employees walk out the door.[3]

An Organization's Selection Decisions Must Reflect Job Requirements

As we saw in Chapter 2, the results of job analysis help an organization to identify job duties, specifications, and performance standards. A mismatch between these and the selection criteria will not only result in poor hires but will also expose the organization to possible lawsuits from job applicants who believe that they have been discriminated against.

> Gian Singha was an immigrant from India who was fluent in four languages, including English; held post-graduate degrees, including a Ph.D. from Germany in environmental science; and was a co-author of two books and numerous research papers. He applied for a mid-level position as a regulatory officer with the Land and Water Board of the Mackenzie Valley He scored among the highest of the 12 applicants the Board chose to interview. Yet, to his shock a few days later, he was told that his application had been rejected because he was overqualified. The Board felt that he would become bored with the job's routine nature and would quit prematurely. Mr. Singha complained to the Canadian Human Rights Tribunal, and, in a groundbreaking decision, the Tribunal ruled that the Board's action discriminated against Mr. Singha and visible minority immigrants in general. Mr. Singha was awarded damages and, more significantly, the Board was ordered to cease using any hiring policies that would automatically disqualify visible minority immigrants on the grounds that they are overqualified.[4]

Today, the employer is required to show that the tools used for selecting employees are reliable and valid. "Feelings" or myths, as in the above case, are not valid arguments. This means that performance-based job descriptions and valid selection tools are necessary in the context of selection.

Selection Strategy Must Be Well Integrated with Organizational Priorities

As seen in Chapter 1, organizations differ in their strategic posture. Organizational characteristics—including such factors as product lines, market share, and culture—vary widely and are dynamic in nature. As a firm grows, different selection priorities start to emerge:

> A startup business typically has a few product lines and places heavy emphasis on entrepreneurship. In contrast, a multinational organization with operations in several different countries and cultures worries about achieving control over operations while providing adequate autonomy to local operations. An aging or declining organization needs to emphasize renewal if it is to survive. The type of employees sought are also somewhat different in each instance. A new organization may attempt to hire entrepreneurial managers, whereas a mature organization needs managers who can continually search for economies of scale and implement efficient systems. In contrast, a declining organization may seek managers who can cut costs, generate revenues, rebuild the organization, and turn it around.

The specific needs of an organization are determined by a variety of factors (and not merely by its stage in the life cycle); however, an organization's stage in the life cycle provides a starting point in linking an organization's overall needs and its selection strategy.

Selection Strategy Must Recognize Organizational Constraints

All organizations have finite resources. This means that the systems employed for the selection of human resources should be cost-effective. The selection process is not an end; it is a means through which the organization achieves its objectives. Most organizations impose some limits, such as budgets and policies. Although higher budgets may refine selection procedures, hiring costs should not be so high as to impede organizational effectiveness.

The firm's policies may expand existing challenges or simply add more constraints. Policies toward workforce diversity and inclusion reinforce external prohibitions, for example. Internal decrees may exceed legal demands from outside. For example, policies to hire ex-convicts further societal objectives but are not legally required. Such internal policies add still another challenge for employment specialists.

Selection Strategy Must Adapt to Labour Market Realities

It is important to have a qualified pool of recruits from which to select applicants. But some jobs are so hard to fill that there are few applicants per opening.

> For example, notwithstanding current low oil prices and the devastating fires of 2016, Fort McMurray in Alberta has experienced shortages in many jobs related to the oil and gas sector, including drilling coordinators/production managers, land agents/purchasing agents, geologists and geophysicists, mining engineers, industrial electricians, and heavy-duty equipment mechanics. Companies looking for these types of workers will face an unfavourable selection ratio. Shortages in one area of the country impact other areas in Canada as well, as favourable incentives may prompt workers from other areas to move for employment.[5]

A **selection ratio** is the relationship between the number of applicants hired and the total number of applicants available. A selection ratio such as 1:25 (compared to a selection ratio of 1:2) means that there is a large number of applicants from which to select. In many instances a selection ratio such as 1:3 or 1:5 also means a low quality of recruits. The ratio is computed as follows:

selection ratio The ratio of the number of applicants hired to the total number of applicants available.

$$\frac{\text{Number of applicants hired}}{\text{Total number of applicants}} = \text{Selection ratio}$$

Job ads that emphasize what the organization can supply to meet an applicant's needs, such as skill variety, opportunities for advancement, and autonomy (as opposed to ads that focus on job requirements), may increase both the number and quality of applicants.[6] According to one of the study's authors, Dr. Derek Chapman, "Weaker applicants, they'll apply for whatever jobs are available. Strong applicants can pick and choose among the ones they choose to apply for and, as a result, they're looking for job ads that stand out to them . . . the ones that emphasized what the company can do for them, rather than a list of what the job requirements are."[7]

The number of applicants for a position is also partially dependent on a firm's salary and benefit package compared to others in the industry. Industry information can be secured from Statistics Canada, Employment and Social Development Canada, or other associations.

Figure 6-1 summarizes the key factors that influence and are affected by a firm's selection strategy. As can be seen, selection affects virtually all major human resource functions within the organization. Moreover, an organization's policies on other matters (e.g., compensation levels, training) also have an impact on selection strategy, at least in the long term. This fact is indicated by the dotted arrow in Figure 6-1.

This chapter introduces various tools at the disposal of human resource managers in formulating an effective selection strategy. The next section begins the discussion by outlining major steps in the selection of human resources.

Spotlight *on* ETHICS

Selection Practices Must Be Ethical

An organization's selection strategy should be ethical. Because employment specialists strongly influence the hiring decision, those decisions are shaped by their ethics. Consider the following situations and rate them as ethical or unethical. If unethical, what actions would you take to achieve the goals while at the same time maintaining high ethical standards? Compare your answers with those of others. Do you see any differences? What accounts for the differences?

You are the human resource manager in a medium-sized firm and report to the director of human resources. Your boss gives you a lot of discretion in decision making and, in general, you are very happy with your job. However, more recently, the following three events have caused you some concern:

1. You are told to find "some positions" in the company for some of the executives' children for the coming summer months. You feel that disobeying the order may affect your career. However, you wonder whether hiring some of them would be an admission

that you selected people based on criteria other than merit.

2. An executive search firm, which your firm had hired in the past year to do a routine job search, has given you an expensive watch as a Christmas gift. Even a casual glance shows you that the watch is worth over $750. You wonder whether accepting it puts you under a moral obligation to the firm and taints your future decisions when hiring search firms. While you have no problems with the service provided by the firm, the firm is neither the best service provider in the industry or region nor the cheapest.

3. You have a minority applicant who does not score as highly on a selection test as the other two non-minority applicants, although all three perform well on the interview. You are concerned about perceptions of discrimination if you select one of the majority applicants. You also know that the firm could use a minority hire.

FIGURE 6-1

Relationship between Selection Strategy and Other Organizational Variables

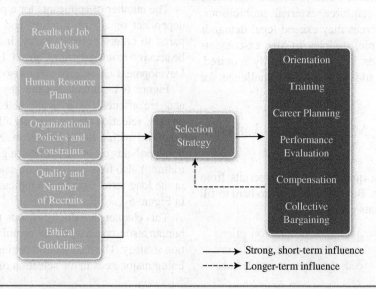

Results of Job Analysis

Human Resource Plans

Organizational Policies and Constraints

Quality and Number of Recruits

Ethical Guidelines

Selection Strategy

Orientation

Training

Career Planning

Performance Evaluation

Compensation

Collective Bargaining

⟶ Strong, short-term influence

------▸ Longer-term influence

LO2 Steps in the Selection of Human Resources

The selection process is a series of steps that applicants pass through. The process can be facilitated using tools such as an Applicant Tracking System. Simplicity should not be achieved, however, at the cost of lower effectiveness. Consider this:

> Using an Applicant Tracking System can greatly reduce the selection workload by automating résumé screening using keyword searches, tracking communications with each candidate, scheduling interviews, managing candidate ratings by multiple interviewers, and even making biased assessments of interviewers' judgments.[8] However, when you are rejecting a significant proportion of applicants without human oversight, top candidates may be erroneously screened out as well. Periodic auditing of the screened-out candidates can help to determine if suitable candidates are being rejected.[9]

To ensure quality hiring, human resource departments commonly use the sequence of steps shown in Figure 6-2. Note that these steps reflect considerable variation from one organization to the next. For example, in small organizations the hiring decision could be based on a single interview by the owner or manager. Further, depending on the unique constraints facing an organization, some of the stages may be combined or their sequence altered. For instance, for internal applicants there is seldom a need to verify references from outsiders or do a medical evaluation. As another example, some employers find it useful to introduce a realistic job preview at an earlier stage to save the time and expense of administering tests and interviews for applicants who are unlikely to fit the position. In most organizations, a medical evaluation, if done at all, is carried out only after a hiring decision is made. In such cases, the job offer is conditional on the applicant's satisfactorily completing the medical evaluation. Notably, an applicant may also be rejected at any step in the process.

The type of selection procedure used by an organization depends on a variety of factors, including the organization's size, the stage of its growth (e.g., new versus established for some time), and the jobs involved. There are also variations across industries. For example, use of honesty tests and checks for bondability are seen in the Canadian retail industry, but not in the education sector.

The Canadian Workplace and Employee Survey reported that 79 percent of employees were given an interview, 10 percent were given a test of job-related knowledge, and 9 percent were given a personality test.[10] Other past surveys of employers indicate that letters of reference and weighted application blanks are most popular for the selection of white-collar professional workers whereas biographical information blanks are more frequently used

FIGURE 6-2

Steps in the Selection Process

NOTE: The above sequence is likely to show some variation across organizations. Not all firms go through all of the above steps or in the above sequence. In general, an applicant who is disqualified on a step does not advance to the next step.

for white-collar nonprofessional jobs. Personality tests are popular for selecting middle-management employees, and aptitude tests are most common for white-collar nonprofessional jobs. Whereas 64 percent of organizations use a knowledge test for middle management positions, only 18 percent use a written test for nonmanagement roles.[11]

Step 1: Preliminary Reception of Applicants

Job applicants may make initial contact either in person or in writing. When applicants "walk in," a preliminary interview—typically with a representative of the human resource department or the store manager, in the case of a very small firm—is often granted as a courtesy. This "courtesy interview," as it is sometimes called, is unlikely to be as rigorous as otherwise, but it does attempt to screen out obvious "misfits" (e.g., someone who is not willing to travel but is interested in a salesperson's job with the firm requiring considerable travel). Such courtesy interviews are also an important part of good employer branding by the firm, as information conveyed during these meetings and the professionalism displayed by the HR manager during this early encounter may have lasting implications for its future recruitment and marketing success.[12] Candidates applying in writing are often sent a polite letter of acknowledgement. If the applicant looks promising (either on the basis of the initial letter or the courtesy interview), he or she is typically asked to complete a formal application form.

LO3 Step 2: Applicant Screening

At the applicant screening stage, the organization will have received a number of résumés or completed job application forms. The purpose of the screening stage is to remove from further consideration those applicants who do not meet either the education or experience qualifications required for the job. More fine-grained assessments of applicant qualities and their match to job specifications will be made during the later testing stages of the selection process; the goal of screening is merely to whittle the applicant pool down to only those applicants who meet minimum qualifications.

Résumés and job application forms, which were introduced in Chapter 5, can both be useful tools to screen out applicants who do not meet minimum specifications for a job. As discussed in Chapter 5, an application form may have additional utility over résumés when care is taken in crafting the form.

One might suspect that some aspects of a person's background (e.g., years of education, previous experience in similar positions) would have a greater relationship to job success than some other factors (e.g., number of part-time jobs held while in school). A **weighted application blank** (WAB) technique provides a means of identifying which of these aspects reliably distinguish groups of satisfactory and unsatisfactory job incumbents.[13] Weights are assigned in accordance with the predictive power of each item so that a total "success score" can be calculated for each job applicant.

> **weighted application blank (WAB)** A job application form in which various items are given differential weights to reflect their relationship to criterion measures.

An office equipment firm in Toronto was seeking to lower its turnover rate. Over time, the firm observed that salespeople in the firm with university degrees were less likely to turn over than sales staff with post-secondary diplomas or no post-secondary education. Furthermore, as number of years of sales experience went up, turnover rates decreased. The firm implemented a weighting scale to score the education and experience sections of their job applications. Using a scoring system on the education portion of 4 points for university degrees, 2 points for post-secondary diplomas, and 1 point for high school diplomas, and scores of 8 points for four or more years of sales experience, 5 points for two or three years of sales experience, and 2 points for one year or less of sales experience, the firm calculated a total score for each application. The firm identified a success score of 5 for applicants to continue in the selection process.

WABs have been found to be useful in predicting a number of different indicators (including job performance, turnover, absenteeism, and accident rates). They are cost-effective and may be particularly valuable for job positions where a large number of applicants apply for a few positions; however, they do not provide any insight into why relationships exist

Spotlight *on* ETHICS

Anonymous Job Applications in Canada

A policy introduced by the Ontario Human Rights Commission in July 2013 stated that requiring a job applicant to have "Canadian experience" is a form of discrimination. Ratna Omidvar, the president of Maytree Foundation, a nonprofit Toronto-based organization aimed at reducing poverty in Canada and enhancing diversity and leadership development, is encouraging Canadian organizations to consider anonymous job applications as an avenue toward bias-free hiring. By minimizing subjective reactions elicited from sex, name, and immigrant status, anonymous applications may produce a more diverse set of applicants for employment testing. Germany has piloted anonymous applications at freight company DHL, cosmetics company L'Oréal, and consumer goods giant Proctor & Gamble Company. Ecommerce retailer mydays has continued with anonymous job applications following a pilot. What are the pros and cons of anonymous job applications in Canada?

SOURCE: Based on Catherine Skrzypinski (2013), "Will anonymous job applications end hiring discrimination in Canada?" Society for Human Resource Management, http://www.shrm.org/hrdisciplines/global/articles/pages/anonymous-job-applications-canada.aspx.

(for instance, why might higher education be associated with greater absenteeism?).[14]

Another applicant screening tool that is increasingly being used is the **biographical information blank (BIB)**, also referred to as "biodata." The BIB is a questionnaire that applicants complete relating to their personal history and life

> **biographical information blank (BIB)** A type of application blank that uses a multiple-choice format to measure a job candidate's education, experiences, opinions, attitudes, and interests.

experiences, such as their hobbies, family relations, accomplishments, values, reactions to stressful and disappointing experiences, and leisure-time pursuits. The items may range from early childhood to educational experiences to work experiences or current hobbies and relationships. Although primary emphasis is on past behaviours as a predictor of future behaviour, BIBs frequently also look at present behaviours and attitudes. Actual items from Google's BIB are available in this *New York Times* article (https://www.nytimes.com/2007/01/03/technology/03google.html), and some sample items are presented in Figure 6-3.

FIGURE 6-3

Sample Biographical Information Blank Items

1. What is the level of supervision that you prefer?

   a. None
   b. Minimal
   c. Moderate
   d. Fairly close
   e. Very close

2. How many of your family members have been/are currently members of law enforcement?

   a. none
   b. one
   c. two
   d. three
   e. four or more

3. How many hours each week do you spend doing each of the following:

   a. _____ Music
   b. _____ Reading books and magazines
   c. _____ Socializing with friends
   d. _____ Watching TV
   e. _____ Home improvement projects
   f. _____ Outdoor activities

4. How many friends did you have in high school compared to other people?

   a. _____ Fewer
   b. _____ More
   c. _____ About the same

5. When faced with disappointment in your life, what is your typical reaction?

   a. Quietly reflect on the situation
   b. Talk to a friend or spouse
   c. Exercise or take a walk
   d. Try to forget about it
   e. Release your anger on something

6. In the last four years, how many employers have you had?

   a. more than 5
   b. 3 to 5
   c. 2
   d. 1
   e. 0

The items on the BIB are differentially weighted according to how well they separate high from low performers. For instance, a company might identify that the leaders in its organization were all leaders in various roles in their communities (as sport team captains, or through Girl Guides or Scouts). The company might also find that its employees who prefer to spend time with other people are more successful on the job than employees who prefer watching TV or reading books. More points would be granted on the BIB for candidates who have been in leadership positions in their communities and who prefer spending time with other people as opposed to independent activities. Cut-off scores are then developed, with only those applications reaching the minimum score proceeding to the next stages of the selection process.

> To search for talent among over 100,000 job applications received each month, Google has job applicants complete an online BIB. Google's algorithm calculates a score for each applicant between 0 and 100 to predict how well the applicant will fit into its free-wheeling and competitive culture.[15]

There are several considerations when determining whether or not to use a BIB. First, the items must not adversely affect any protected groups of Canadians (for instance, an item asking about whether someone has been a sports team captain may unintentionally discriminate against people with physical disabilities), and the items must be job-related. Second, BIB questions may be viewed by applicants as invasive and may have the unintended effect of turning off well-qualified applicants. Third, responses to BIB questions are not easily verifiable and, thus, they can be faked by applicants. And fourth, typically BIBs will have to be developed for each organization; rarely do commercially available BIBs exist that will suit organizations' specific needs.[16]

Properly developed WABs and BIBs have been found to be useful in several occupations, including life insurance agents, sales clerks, engineers, research scientists, and architects. Reviews of studies that used biographical information as predictors of job success showed that over various occupations, the average validity was about 0.35.[17] Given this, carefully designed application blanks (especially in WAB and BIB format) seem to hold considerable potential as a selection tool.

Whatever the type of application form used, information given in an application form or résumé may contain elements of embellishment and even outright fabrication. Indeed, in recent years, "résumé fraud" (as it is called) has become a major concern of recruiters.

> A newly hired chief administrative officer of the City of Waterloo was fired because he had not disclosed critical information about his problems on a previous job. In a survey of 300 executive recruiters, it was found that "reasons for leaving prior jobs" was the item that was fabricated most, closely followed by "results and accomplishments on past jobs." Past salary, job responsibilities, education, dates of employment, and job titles were other major items where the candidates provided false information.[18]

This means that application forms and résumés have to be carefully analyzed for inconsistencies and checked against information coming from other sources, such as references or background checks. In the case of several jobs, key KSAs (knowledge, skills, and abilities) are also assessed through standardized and validated tests. The following section discusses the use of employment tests to assess the key competencies required for a job.

LO4 Step 3: Administration of Employment Tests

Employment tests are useful for obtaining relatively objective information that can be compared with information pertaining to other applicants and present jobholders. **Employment tests** are devices that assess the match between applicants and job requirements. Some are written tests; others are exercises that simulate work conditions. A math test for a bookkeeper is an example of a written test, and a manual-dexterity test for an assembly worker is an example of a simulation exercise.

employment tests
Devices that assess the probable match between applicants and job requirements.

Ultimately, through selection testing the aim is to identify people who are likely to perform well on the job. There are many options available, including purchasing an already established test or making a new test specific to

© John Fedele/Getty Images

Biographical information blanks often contain questions relating to a candidate's early life experiences, e.g., hobbies and interests. How would you feel if asked these types of questions when applying for a job?

the organization. With all of the options available, how do we choose which test(s) to use? The use of tests should be guided by their reliability and validity. These are discussed in some detail below.

LO5 Reliability and Validity of Selection Tests

Testing became popular on a large scale during the First World War, when intelligence tests were given to army recruits. During the following 60 years, tests were developed for a wide range of employment uses, but many of these tests were assumed to be valid without sufficient proof. (For a discussion on testing and assessment, visit the American Psychological Association at https://www.apa.org/science/programs/testing/index.)

For a test to be useful, it must meet the twin criteria of reliability and validity.

Reliability

Reliability means that the test yields consistent results. For example, a test of manual dexterity for assembly workers should give a similar score each time the same person takes the test. If the

> **reliability** A selection device's ability to yield consistent results over repeated measures; also, internal consistency of a device or measure.

results vary widely with each retest because good scores depend on luck, the test is not reliable.

Reliability of a test may become low for a variety of reasons, including the following:

- The test questions may be hard to understand or ambiguous, thus resulting in different test takers reading different meanings into the same question or sentence. It is also possible that the same person may interpret a question differently on different occasions because of poor test construction.
- The test questions may be so hard or boring that the examinee loses all interest and begins to respond almost randomly or erratically.
- External factors (e.g., noise, smell), events (e.g., war), or personal characteristics (e.g., being ill at the time of test taking) may result in random errors.

Being aware of the above factors help the test maker to avoid them and improve reliability. However, high reliability alone does not ensure that a test is in fact valid or useful.

> If a clock gains exactly five minutes each day, the time is predictable; it will be five minutes late after the first day, ten minutes late after the second day, and so on. However, the clock is still not an accurate device. Without knowing the number of days the clock ran uncorrected, we will not be able to predict the correct time.

Validity

Validity asks the question, "Is the test accurately measuring what it is purported to measure?"

In the context of selection tests, validity requires that the test scores significantly

> **validity** A key attribute of a selection device that indicates its accuracy and relationship to job-relevant criteria.

relate to job performance or some other relevant criterion. The stronger the relationship between test results and performance, the more effective the test is as a selection tool. When scores and performance are unrelated, the test is invalid and should not be used for selection:

> At Dial Corp., a strength test for entry-level production jobs led to a disproportionate number of female candidates being rejected. Prior to the use of the test, 46 percent of hires were women, but after the use of the test, only 15 percent of hires were women. Dial defended the test, noting there were now fewer injuries to hired workers. Expert testimony established that the test was considerably more difficult than the job and that the reduction in injuries had started two years before the test was implemented.[19]

When tests are not reliable, they are also not valid since they are not measuring the trait or competency with any degree of consistency. But the mere fact that the test is reliable does not ensure validity:

> As in our earlier clock example, the clock is reliable (it gains five minutes each day) but not valid (it does not tell the correct time).

To ensure that its tests are valid, human resource departments should conduct *validation studies*. These studies compare test results with performance of traits needed to perform the job. Figure 6-4 summarizes the most common approaches to validation.

To ensure that selection tests are valid and reliable, over time organizations seek to accumulate evidence from both the empirical and rational approaches. Is it a lot of work to accumulate validity and reliability evidence? Yes! However, when an invalid test rejects people of a particular race, sex, religion, or national origin, it violates the *Canadian Human Rights Act* or related provincial legislation.[20] Evidence is necessary to know the test is not producing **differential validity**. When differential validity exists, a test may be valid for a large group (for instance, white male applicants) but

> **differential validity** Test validation process aimed at discovering the validity of a test for various subgroups, e.g., females and members of visible minorities.

not for subgroups of minorities or women. The test should predict job performance (or absenteeism or counterproductive work behaviours) equally as well for multiple

FIGURE 6-4

An Explanation of Common Approaches to Test Validation

Empirical Approaches

Empirical approaches to test validation attempt to relate test scores with a job-related criterion, usually performance. If the test actually measures a job-related criterion, the test and the criterion exhibit a positive correlation between 0 and 1.0. The higher the correlation, the better the match.

- *Predictive validity* is determined by giving a test to a group of applicants. After these applicants have been hired and have mastered the job reasonably well, their performance is measured. This measurement and the test score are then correlated.

- *Concurrent validity* allows the human resource department to test present employees and correlate these scores with measures of their performance. This approach does not require the delay between hiring and mastery of the job.

Rational Approaches

When the number of subjects is too low to have a reasonable sample of people to test, rational approaches are used. These approaches are considered inferior to empirical techniques but are acceptable validation strategies when empirical approaches are not feasible.

- *Content validity* is assumed to exist when the test contains an adequate and representative sample of items from the domain of the construct that it is attempting to measure. For example, a vocabulary test should contain a representative sample of words contained in an unabridged dictionary. If all the words in a test contain only words beginning with *m* or *q*, or if they are all four-letter words containing the letter *e*, the test is not content-valid.

- *Construct validity* is established by showing that the test measures the construct and only the construct under consideration. For example, an intelligence test should measure intelligence, not simply a person's reading ability or memory. Establishing construct validity is the most difficult form of test validation because it can be done only over time by comparing the outcomes of the test with the outcomes of other tests and measures. For instance, the construct validity of a test on job stress may be established by comparing the scores on the test with other measures of stress or predicted outcomes of stress. Such a relationship is established over time and by using theoretical arguments.

subgroups, such as women and minorities. Yet even when tests have been validated, the type of validation used is still important. Faulty procedures, no matter how well intentioned, cannot be relied on to prove a test's validity.

To assist in the collection of reliability and validity evidence, employment tests will have a test manual. The manual will contain information on the exact purpose of a test, its design, the directions for its administration, and its applications, and it should be reviewed before a test is used. The manual also reports the test's reliability and the results of validation efforts by the test designer. Today, many tests have been validated on large populations. Organizations may rely on—or generalize—the reliability and validity information contained within the manual to guide their selection test choices for their applicant pool and job.[21] This is called **validity generalization**— applying validity results amassed from many individual validity studies to guide test choices for a current organization and job.

validity generalization
Using validity evidence accumulated for other jobs or applicant populations to guide employment test choices until local validation study results can be acquired.

But human resource specialists should conduct their own studies (called "local validation studies") to make sure a particular test is valid for its planned use. The HR specialist should be also aware of the confounding effects of situational variables on a job applicant's performance on a specific test.

Types of Tests

There is a wide variety of employment tests. Common categories of employment tests in Canada include personality, ability, knowledge, performance, and integrity tests. Within each category, there are a number of tests and test publishers. Each type of test has a different purpose. Application forms, WABs, BIBs, and references discussed earlier may also be considered forms of employment tests and are most commonly used for broad screening of applicants (as opposed to making more fine-grained differentiations as with the tests described below). Figure 6-5 lists examples and a brief explanation of some of the employment-related tests by category along with the approximate frequency of use, cost, reliability, and validity of the testing category.

FIGURE 6-5

Evaluation and Examples of Employment-Related Tests

Name	Application	Cost	Reliability	Validity
Personality Tests		Low	High	Moderate
NEO-PI-R	Measures the Big 5 Personality Factors in 12–99-year-olds			
HEXACO	Measures six factors of personality, including honesty/humility			
16 PF	Measures personality and is used to provide vocational guidance, hiring, and promotion recommendations			
Hogan Personality Inventory	Measures normal personality and is used to predict job performance			
Ability Tests		Low	High	High
Wonderlic Contemporary Cognitive Ability Test	General mental ability; how easily individuals can be trained, how well they can adjust and solve problems on the job, and how well-satisfied they are likely to be with the demands of the job			
General Aptitude Test Battery	Nine distinct aptitudes, including: general learning ability; verbal aptitude; numerical aptitude; spatial aptitude; form perception; clerical perception; motor coordination; finger dexterity; manual dexterity			
Minnesota Clerical Test	Clerical ability; perceptual speed and accuracy			
MacQuarrie Test for Mechanical Ability	Aptitude for acquiring manipulative skills, including space relations, speed of decision and movement, hand–eye coordination, muscular control, and visual acuity			
Knowledge Tests		Moderate	High	High
How to Supervise?	Measures knowledge of supervisory practices			
Leadership Opinion Questionnaire	Measures knowledge of leadership consideration and structure practices			
Performance Tests		High	High	High
Stromberg Dexterity Test	Measures physical coordination			
Revised Minnesota Paper Form Board Test	Measures spatial visualization			
B-PAD	Situational judgment test assessing behavioural responses to video scenarios			
Job Simulation Tests, Assessment Centres	Measures a sample of "on the job" demands			
Integrity Tests		Low	High	Moderate
Stanton Survey	Measures honesty and integrity			
Reid Report	Measures attitudes and behaviours associated with high levels of integrity and responsible work habits			

SOURCE: Created by the authors based on: H. Heneman III, T. Judge, V. Smith, and R. Summers (2010), *Staffing Organizations* (2nd Canadian ed.); SHRM Research, 2005 Weekly Survey.

Personality Tests

Personality tests measure personality or temperament. Personalities are thought to be stable traits for individuals. That is, they do not change depending on the

> **personality tests** Questionnaires designed to reveal aspects of an individual's character or temperament.

circumstances or context the person happens to be in at a particular moment but, rather, are relatively constant over time. Early personality testing in an employment context used personality inventories that were developed to help diagnose psychological abnormalities. It is little wonder that an inventory such as the Minnesota Multiphasic Personality Inventory, which is designed to diagnose various psychoses (using items such as "I sometimes feel as though my limbs are falling off"), was not well-received in an employment context.

More recent personality tests have been designed with psychologically normal, working people in mind. Many of these inventories have centred on the "Big 5 Personality Factors," which include conscientiousness, agreeableness, neuroticism/emotional stability, openness to experience, and extraversion. A convenient acronym to help with remembering the Big 5 is CANOE.

> Of the Big 5 Personality Factors, conscientiousness (e.g., achievement-oriented, persistent, and organized) has the highest correlation to job performance. The personality factors have all been found to predict job performance in some occupations, in particular when work is unstructured and employees have discretion to make decisions.[22] For instance, extraversion (e.g., to seek and interact easily with others, likeable) may predict performance in occupations involving social interactions, such as sales,[23] and extraversion and openness to experience (e.g., imaginative, intellectually curious) may predict training readiness and training success.[24] Although agreeableness (e.g., co-operative, eagerness to help) has shown some promise as a predictor of job performance, one can imagine that having an agreeable bill collector or police officer might not be the best choice!

Scores on personality tests have been linked to ratings of job performance, training performance, absenteeism, and counterproductive work behaviours. One concern with personality testing, however, is the potential for applicants to fake their responses. For instance, it is unlikely—even if the trait does not describe them—that candidates will respond with disagreement to the item "*I am a hard worker.*"[25]

Ability Tests

Ability tests aim to predict which job applicants have the skills, knowledge, and ability to do the job. Many

> **ability tests** Tests that assess an applicant's capacity or aptitude to function in a certain way.

different types of tests have been developed to measure specific human abilities and aptitudes, with some of the most common measuring cognitive ability (or intelligence) and specific physical abilities, such as finger or manual dexterity and visual skills.

Cognitive ability tests were first adopted during the First World War: The Army Alpha test was used to match recruits with various abilities to different military positions. For instance, high scorers on the Army Alpha test may have been made airplane pilots, and low scorers became infantry. More recently, paper-and-pencil or computerized versions of general cognitive ability tests are used to assess memory, reasoning, and verbal and mathematical abilities. Cognitive ability tests are one of the strongest predictors of job performance in many occupations (with an average predictive validity of $r = 0.50$),[26] in particular for highly complex jobs (such as managers and engineers). Following is an example of how a test of cognitive ability quickly and inexpensively helps to select applicants:

> The National Football League (NFL) has used the Wonderlic Contemporary Cognitive Ability Test to test its potential recruits since 1968. Along with tests of their football skill, the NFL administers the 12-minute Wonderlic test, at a cost of about $4 per test, to all prospects. Scores on the Wonderlic are out of 50 with an average score of 21 in the population. The NFL has average scores for each position ranging from 24 for quarterbacks and 26 for offensive tackles to 17 for wide receivers and fullbacks. Lower than average scores for a position may flag the applicant as potentially not able to meet the cognitive demands of the game.[27]

There is one serious potential issue with cognitive ability tests. There are racial differences in scores on cognitive ability tests disadvantaging blacks and Latinos compared to whites.[28] One strategy for selection specialists is to include measures without differential validity along with measures of cognitive ability to both allow good prediction of performance and minimize racial biases.

Knowledge Tests

Knowledge tests measure a person's information or knowledge about job requirements. Arithmetic tests for an accountant, knowledge of

> **knowledge tests** Tests that measure a person's information or knowledge.

tax laws for a tax specialist, and a weather test for a pilot are examples of knowledge tests. Human resource specialists must be able to demonstrate that the knowledge is needed to perform the job.

Performance Tests

Performance tests (or work samples) measure the ability

> **performance tests** Tests that measure the ability of job applicants to perform specific components of the job for which they are to be hired.

of applicants to do some parts of the work for which they are to be hired. A typing test for administrative assistants or a driving test for cab or truck drivers are obvious examples of performance tests.

Validity is often assumed when the test includes a representative sample of the work the applicant is to do when hired. The closer the demands of the test are to the demands of the job, the higher the test's fidelity and the better the test will be at predicting performance on the job.

One variation of performance tests is called a **situational judgment test**. In situational judgment tests, applicants are placed into hypothetical job scenarios and asked to select a behavioural response from among a list of alternative courses of action. Their responses are then rated on their demonstration of problem solving and interpersonal skills. Situational judgment tests have been found to predict job performance moderately well ($r = 0.34$),[29] and they are relatively inexpensive compared to other performance tests. A sample of situational judgment test items is found in Figure 6-6.

> **situational judgment test** A test that places applicants in hypothetical scenarios and asks them to indicate how they would respond from a list of alternatives.

A second variation of performance tests for identifying managerial potential is an assessment centre (see Chapter 8).

As one example, to assess the people skills of applicants to many police and fire departments in Canada and the U.S., many candidates take the Behavioral Personnel Assessment Device (B-PAD). B-PAD presents eight videos depicting scenarios that might be encountered on the job, and candidates indicate how they would respond in each situation.[30]

Currently, assessment centres are used mostly at larger organizations, such as Rio Tinto Alcan, Manitoba Liquor and Lotteries Corporation, and Verizon, and are increasing in popularity in several municipal, provincial, and federal government units as well. They are usually conducted over a period of a few days at a location physically removed from the job site. During this time, multiple assessors, who may include psychologists and managers, will typically estimate the strengths, weaknesses, and potential of each attendee. They will then pool their estimates to arrive at some conclusion about each member of the group being assessed.

Assessment centres (ACs) use several methods of assessment, including written tests, job simulations, in-basket exercises, projective tests, interviews, personality inventories, and/or leaderless group discussions. Typically, the tests are used to measure intellectual ability, work orientation, and career orientation. Leaderless group discussions, role-playing, and in-basket exercises measure an applicant's administrative skills. However, ACs do more than simply test applicants. Through the use of multiple

---

FIGURE 6-6

Sample Situational Judgment Test Items

1. You are currently working on several tasks, all of which are pressing. Your supervisor asks you to work on another assignment with an immediate deadline. She asks you to phone companies to obtain financial data. The list of companies is long and not yet complete. You would . . .

   a. Describe the pressing deadlines in which you are already involved and ask your supervisor to assign the new task to a less busy colleague.

   b. Complete those assignments on which you are already working, then concentrate on phoning the companies.

   c. Work on your other assignments and begin phoning companies only when you receive a complete list.

   d. Immediately phone the companies currently listed, then continue working on your other assignments; make the other phone calls as you are notified of company names.

2. You have just prepared a report that you have checked and rechecked for accuracy. It was sent to your communications group for assistance with formatting and creating some charts and figures to visualize the data. Before you attend a meeting at which you will submit your report, you review the formatted version and note many serious errors. You would . . .

   a. Show the original and the formatted version to the communications person and demand that the errors be changed before the meeting.

   b. Present the report at the meeting, point out the errors, and state they were due to the communications group.

   c. Present the errors to the communications person, ask him to make the corrections, and explain to individuals at the meeting that your report is still being formatted.

   d. Present your report at the meeting and make no mention of the errors but notify attendees of corrections after the meeting.

SOURCE: Adapted by the authors from Elaine D. Pulakos (2005), "Selection assessment methods: A guide to implementing formal assessments to build a high-quality workforce," Society for Human Resource Management (SHRM).

assessment techniques and multiple assessors (or panel judges), ACs are able to predict a candidate's future job behaviour, managerial potential, and training needs. In recent years, the AC technique has become increasingly popular for nonsupervisory and skilled labour as well.

Candidates for managerial and executive jobs may participate in ACs lasting up to several days, involving a combination of individual testing and evaluation and group-based exercises. The result is a profile of each applicant's strengths and weaknesses. For instance, the AC used by KPMG starts with an e-tray exercise based on fictional emails. The same information then carries through into a written exercise. Next is a group exercise that includes a group presentation of their findings. There is then a 10-minute individual presentation to a partner, who asks questions, followed by a partner interview.[31]

Research studies evaluating the validity of the assessment centre technique have reported positive conclusions, by and large, indicating a median 0.40 correlation coefficient between AC ratings and criteria such as career progress, salary advances, supervisor ratings, and evaluations of potential progress.[32]

Performance tests are increasingly being conducted using **computer-interactive performance tests**. During the tests, applicants' abilities, such as reaction time, ability to concentrate, ability to work under different time pressures, perceptual speed, spatial visualization, and so on, are measured. Candidates' reactions to the simulation, both mental (e.g., comprehension, coding, calculation) and motor (e.g., keying speed, accuracy) are assessed.[33] One computer-interactive test that many business students interested in pursuing an MBA will encounter is the Graduate Management Admission Test (or GMAT). Sample questions are depicted in Figure 6-7.

computer-interactive performance tests Performance tests using computer simulations that can measure skills, comprehension, spatial visualization, judgment, etc.

FIGURE 6-7

Sample Questions from a Computer-Interactive Test

1. You are the human resource manager in our firm. At 8 a.m., when you walk into your office, you find the following email messages on your computer:

    Sharon (your colleague): Can we start our meeting at 10? It should take two hours to get the Job Evaluation briefing sharpened up. As planned, we should be able to do the presentation in 90 minutes leaving 30 minutes for questions.

    Chan (a manager): Can we meet for, say, one hour—no, make that one and a half hours—today? It is urgent. I am free any time between 9:30 and 12 and after 3 p.m.

    Andre (your boss): Can you interview a job candidate this morning? She is in town only this morning; so you will have to meet her between 9 and 10:30 a.m. She looks really good for the position we advertised. So I would not want to miss this opportunity.

    Jim (your secretary): Just to let you know that the Job Evaluation briefing to the staff is now moved up. It is going to be at 1 p.m. and not at 2 p.m. The message came in only as I was leaving the office at 6 p.m. Didn't want to call you at home and inform.

    What is the earliest time you can meet with Chan?

    a. 9:30

    b. 3

    c. 4:30

    d. 12:30

    e. not possible today

2. Dog food should not include products containing gluten, such as wheat or barley. A study found that dogs fed *Farmer's Delight*—a brand consisting of 50% meat product—developed serious intestinal issues as well as general malaise, whereas those fed *Call of the Wild*—a brand consisting of 100% meat products—developed none of these symptoms. Which of the following, if true, most strengthens the argument above?

    a. *Farmer's Delight* brand contains only organic meat products of the highest quality.

    b. Veterinarians are now strongly recommending that gluten be removed from most animal diets.

    c. The meat products used in the two brands of dog food were identical.

    d. In similar studies using dog food brands containing only 10% wheat, dogs did not develop intestinal symptoms or malaise.

    e. The type of wheat used in dog food does not contain more gluten than other types of wheat.

Integrity Tests

Integrity tests, also called honesty tests, measure an applicant's honesty and trustworthiness. These tests are of great interest to employers for two reasons: First, if the candidate is not honest in filling out the job application form and in his or her answers during the job interview, much of the information collected to assess the applicant's suitability for the position is useless; second, all employers desire employees whom they can trust.

> **integrity tests**
> Employment tests that measure an applicant's honesty and trustworthiness.

> Each year, cargo theft (stealing merchandise and reselling it) costs the Canadian economy about $5 billion.[34] And a significant amount of this theft is done by employees through "shrinkage." According to the Retail Council of Canada, the average employee steals $2,500 before being caught, in comparison with an average customer theft worth $185.[35] To overcome the problem, Canadian businesses have been doing more personal reference checks, honesty tests, credit and bondability assessments, and multiple interviews to screen out undesirable employees.

Early integrity testing attempts used polygraphs, or lie detector tests. Use of lie detector tests for the purpose of employment is prohibited in some provinces (e.g., Ontario) under the *Employment Standards Act*.[36] Two types of written integrity tests are now typically used because of their ease of use and inexpensiveness (typically available at less than $20 per administration). With overt tests, applicants are asked direct questions about past thefts. With non-overt tests, applicants are asked to respond to questions about their risk-taking behaviours (such as driving cars over the speed limit and sky-diving), and their attitudes toward dishonest behaviours.

> To assess the validity of one integrity test, 50 percent of the applicants were given the Stanton Survey, while the other half were not. Of the applicants, 37 percent of those not tested were later dismissed for theft whereas only 22.6 percent of those tested with the Stanton Survey were dismissed for the same reason. The number of policy violators in the untested group was 10.4 percent compared to 1.5 percent in the tested group. The average loss from the untested group was approximately $208 higher compared to the tested group.[37]

When confronted by direct questions, many individuals are not likely to openly admit theft. Are dishonest applicants likely to be honest about their dishonesty? In a meta-analysis of 104 studies, overt integrity tests have been found to predict job performance with a validity coefficient of 0.14, and to predict counterproductive behaviours

(including theft, accidents, disciplinary problems, and absenteeism) with a validity of 0.38. Non-overt tests predict with an average validity coefficient of 0.18 for job performance, and 0.27 for counterproductive behaviours.[38] This indicates that integrity tests are better predictors of counterproductive behaviours than of job performance.

Integrity tests present human resource specialists with an inherent dilemma. On the one hand, these methods offer some additional screening tools to better ensure an optimal workforce. On the other hand, such tests are subject to errors: Some honest applicants will be misclassified as having low integrity. Also, to many applicants and employees, these tests are an invasion of their privacy.[39]

Besides specific cautions associated with individual tests, human resource specialists should realize that testing is not always feasible. Even when tests can be developed or bought, their cost may not be justified for jobs that have low selection ratios or that are seldom filled. Examples include technical, professional, and managerial jobs. Even when feasible, the use of tests must be flexible. They need not always be the first or last step in the selection process. Instead, human resource experts use tests during the selection process at the point they deem appropriate. Consider the comments of an experienced human resource manager of a large chain of grocery stores:

> Many human resource managers in other industries use testing only after other steps in the selection process. In the grocery business you must test first. Why waste time interviewing a grocery clerk who doesn't know that three for 88 cents is 30 cents apiece? Besides, when we take applications on Tuesdays, we may have 300 of them. Interviews would take 75 hours a week, and my staff consists of a clerk and myself. But through testing, we can test the entire group in an hour. Then we interview only those who score well.

Lastly, employment tests are only one of several techniques used in the selection process because they are limited to factors that can be easily tested and validated. Other items, not measurable through testing, may be equally important.

Step 4: Employment Interview(s)

The immediate supervisor is ultimately responsible for newly hired workers. Since that responsibility is ever-present, supervisors should have input into the final hiring decision. The supervisor is often better able to evaluate the applicant's technical abilities than is the human resource department. Likewise, the immediate supervisor can often answer the interviewee's specific job-related questions with greater precision.

When supervisors make the final decision, the role of the human resource department is to provide the supervisor with the best applicants available. From these three or four applicants, the supervisor decides whom to hire. Some organizations leave the final hiring decision to the human resource department, especially when applicants are hired into a training program instead of for a specific job.

In larger organizations, it is also common for the applicant to be interviewed by several persons (especially for supervisory and managerial positions), either consecutively or during a panel interview. The immediate work supervisor may still have considerable influence on the final decision; however, the "satisfactory" candidate also will have to satisfy larger organizational requirements and fit well with the culture of the organization.

Regardless of who has the final hiring authority, the personal commitment of supervisors is generally higher when they participate in the selection process. When the supervisor recommends hiring an individual, he or she has made a psychological commitment to assist the new employee. If the candidate turns out to be unsatisfactory, the supervisor is then more likely to accept some of the responsibility for failure.

Because interviewing is a critical step in the selection process, this will be discussed in some detail in a later section in this chapter.

Step 5: Realistic Job Previews

Often, the supervisory interview is supplemented with a realistic job preview. A **realistic job preview (RJP)** allows the potential employee to understand the job setting before the hiring decision is made—often by showing him or her the type of work, equipment, and working conditions involved.

> **realistic job preview (RJP)** Involves showing the candidate the type of work, equipment, and working conditions involved in the job before the hiring decision is final.

Unmet expectations about a job contribute to initial job dissatisfaction. The RJP attempts to prevent job dissatisfaction by giving the newcomer an insight into the job. RJPs indicate the positive or favourable aspects of the job along with negative and neutral aspects. Recently hired employees who have had an RJP are less likely to be shocked by the job or the job setting on the first day they report to work. Two writers concluded the following:

> The RJP functions very much like a medical vaccination. . . . The typical medical vaccination injects one with a small, weakened dose of germs, so that one's body can develop a natural resistance to that disease. The RJP functions similarly by presenting job candidates with a small dose of "organizational reality." And, like the medical vaccination, the RJP is probably much less effective after a person has already entered a new organization.[40]

Previous research has found that RJPs help to lower turnover, improve performance, increase job satisfaction,

and generate greater trust of the organization, which may be due to perceptions of organizational honesty.[41]

> Applicants to CIBC can experience what it is like to work in the call centre during an online RJP. Within an hour, applicants can see what the job is like in terms of repetition, supervision, and the potential for them to deal with rude or unpleasant customers.[42]

The adverse effect of RJPs may be that more candidates will decline job offers when the working conditions do not appear appealing. Many RJPs may also focus unduly on extrinsic and job-context factors rather than on job content (or intrinsic) factors. Also, RJPs are no substitute for continuous monitoring of working conditions and in-depth job analysis. Informing job applicants about unpleasant working conditions may increase the probability that they will remain on the job once hired; however, they are unlikely to be any more satisfied with the job than those who were not told and did not leave. This means that only a conscious and continuous effort at improving "irritants" at the workplace (i.e., job redesign) is a real, long-term solution.

Step 6: Verification of References

What type of person is the applicant? Is the applicant a good, reliable worker? To answer these questions, employment specialists use references. Many professionals have a skeptical attitude toward references, however. *Personal references*—those that attest to the applicant's sound character—are usually provided by friends or family. Their objectivity and candour are certainly questionable. When a reference is in writing, the author usually emphasizes only positive points. Thus, personal references are not commonly used.

Employment references differ from personal references because they discuss the applicant's work history. Many human resource specialists doubt the usefulness of these references because

> **employment references** Evaluations of an employee's past work performance and job-relevant behaviours provided by past employers.

references may not be completely candid, especially with negative information (see Figure 6-8). Further, many managers do not seek the right information or ask the right questions while checking references.

Often, many employment references are little more than confirmation of prior employment. Many employers are concerned about the risk of possible legal action by past employees who were not given positive references. In some cases, references provide only basic information to protect themselves (e.g., simply stating that a person worked for them in the past in a certain capacity during specific dates). This lack of candour has caused some human resource specialists to omit this step entirely from the selection process. Other specialists have substituted phone inquiries for written references, hoping that voice inflections or hesitation

FIGURE 6-8

Percentage of Professionals and Applicants Describing Dishonest Employment References

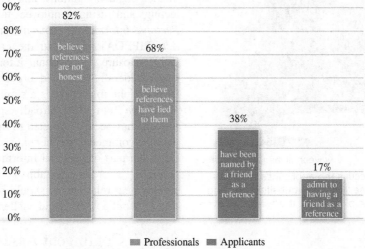

SOURCE: Chart prepared by the authors based on Vander Wier, M., Dishonest references test recruitment (2018, January 2), *Canadian HR Reporter.*

over blunt questions may tip off the interviewer to underlying problems.

Lack of candour in **reference letters** may be due to a variety of reasons, including fear of legal reprisal, legal requirements (as

> **reference letters** Written evaluations of a person's job-relevant skills, past experience, and work-relevant attitudes.

in the United States) to show reference letters to an applicant, desire to get rid of an employee, and reluctance to pass judgment on a fellow human being. Given this state of affairs, an employer can get to the truth about a potential employee's character and work performance in a number of ways. Some of the possible strategies are shown in Figure 6-9.

FIGURE 6-9

How to Get the Truth Out of References

Use the phone: Most references are more likely to be honest over the phone or in person than in a formal letter or email.

Seek information on job-related behaviour: Ask for details on job behaviours, such as tardiness and absenteeism, rather than on personality traits, such as ambition and intelligence, which are hard to evaluate reliably.

Ask direct questions: As questions such as "Would you rehire this employee now?" or "How is this person's behaviour in a group setting?" and listen for how the referee responds, including hesitations such as "ahh, umm."

Combine references with other predictors: Reference letters are no substitute for application blanks, tests, and interviews.

Use credible sources only: Former work supervisors are, typically, the most useful reference sources. Letters from acquaintances and friends are usually worthless for predicting future job success.

Note frequency of job changes: A person who has not stayed in any organization for more than a few months may be either an extremely successful employee or a problem employee. Persons who have been moving laterally across organizations without any apparent change in job challenge, rewards, or working conditions should be carefully watched.

Watch out for phrases with hidden meanings: Most references do not blatantly lie; they simply don't tell the whole truth. A person who is described as "deeply committed to family and friends" may be someone who will not work beyond five o'clock; an "individualist" may be a person who cannot work with others.

SOURCE: Adapted and summarized from Pamela Babcock (2004), "It takes more than a reference check to weed out liars," Advice for Supervisors from the Society for Human Resource Management; Vander Wier, Marcel (2018, January 2), "Dishonest references test recruitment," *Canadian HR Reporter.*

© wavebreakmedia/Shutterstock

Employment references discuss the applicant's work history. Some employers refuse to answer questions relating to former employees on the phone. Are there ways to overcome this?

More recently, several firms have begun to include a background investigation as part of their selection process. Some applicants exaggerate their skills, education, and/or past work experience. While virtually every qualification listed on an application form or résumé can be verified, the cost of doing so may be prohibitive, especially for smaller employers. Some large organizations today use the services of specialized agencies to conduct background checks:

> BackCheck, one of Canada's leading pre-employment background check and employment verification organizations, screened over a half-million Canadians during the 2008 and 2009 recession, and placed "red flags" on between 25 and 50 percent of those screened. In the decade since, they have contacted over 100,000 employers and every educational institution in Canada. Their database and process enable them to respond to customer background check needs quickly and with high completion rates.[43]

Another emerging trend is the use of social networking websites, such as Facebook, to learn more about the applicant's interests and behaviours. Although this practice has been outlawed in Germany[44] and caution has been advised in Alberta,[45] its use has not been tested legally yet in Canada:

> Several recruiters check applicants' backgrounds through search results on Google and other search engines. They can also access social networking sites, such as Facebook, Twitter, or LinkedIn, to learn more about an applicant's position on morality, drugs, sex, and various social phenomena as well as to gather personal profiles that indicate age, sex, race, ethnicity, political affiliation, etc. Although it is illegal to use any of the latter in making a hiring decision, hiring decisions based on behaviours and

self-stated opinions and other posted material may not be considered discriminatory.[46]

Whatever the approach, employers should be aware of their legal obligations, and abide by them, when collecting and using employee information. The federal *Personal Information Protection and Electronic Document Act* (PIPEDA) applies to the collection, use, retention, and disclosure of "personal information" about employees in federally regulated organizations. In Alberta and British Columbia, there is a similar *Personal Information Protection Act* (PIPA). Broadly speaking, "personal information" has been interpreted to include all opinions, evaluations, comments, social status, and disciplinary actions. Only that part of personal information that is "reasonably required" in order to establish, manage, or terminate an employment relationship should be collected or disseminated to avoid possible legal challenges.[47]

Step 7: Contingent Assessments

The selection process may include a contingent assessment. This occurs when a candidate has been selected and will receive a job offer provided he or she passes the contingent assessment. Although any type of selection method can be used contingently (for instance, a taxi company may verify a driving record before offering a driving position, and a security company may conduct a background check before offering a job to a new officer), drug testing and medical evaluations should be used exclusively as contingent methods for legal purposes.

Normally, a **medical evaluation** is a health checklist that asks the applicant to indicate health and accident information. The questionnaire is sometimes supplemented with a physical examination or physical fitness test conducted by a physician or at a clinic. The medical or physical evaluation may

medical evaluation
Assessment of physical and/or mental health of an applicant through self-reports and/or medical examination by a preferred physician.

- entitle the employer to lower health or life insurance rates for company-paid insurance;
- be required by provincial or local health officials, particularly in food-handling operations where communicable diseases are a danger;
- be useful to evaluate whether the applicant can handle the physical or mental stress of a job; and/or
- prevent injuries to workers susceptible to, for instance, musculoskeletal disorders and reduce time off for workers who are screened but then get hurt.[48]

One caution with physical testing is that it must relate to bona fide occupational requirements of the job. If an 85-pound object can be lifted by two people or assisted by equipment, then lifting that amount of weight is not a requirement. If the employer wants a medical or physical evaluation, it may be scheduled *after* the hiring decision. Medical examinations are usually conducted only if the job requires a clearly determined level of physical effort or other abilities (e.g., ability to climb poles). Even here, an applicant can be rejected only if reasonable accommodations cannot be made to allow the person to perform the job. Consider this example:

> Post Consumer Brands, makers of Shreddies and Shredded Wheat, decided to implement post-offer physical testing at its facility in Niagara Falls, Ontario. The functional fitness testing identifies candidates who would not have the strength or endurance to do the job. If a candidate fails the test, which about 25 percent of candidates do, the job offer is rescinded. This type of testing can only be implemented if there is evidence of previous injuries on the job; Post had a case of an injury that cost U.S. $700,000 in Workers' Compensation costs. The tests relate only to specific physical requirements for specific jobs. Advances in equipment would allow candidates who did not pass to try again, and candidates can retest in six months. The cost of the testing is between $100 and $200 per test. The result for Post was a reduction in Workers' Compensation costs of 81 percent, a decrease in lost days and restricted days, and a safety record with no injuries to workers with less than three years on the job for one year.[49]

In summary, medical and physical examinations should be conducted only when they are absolutely necessary. The testing should be conducted by qualified professionals and the results analyzed in a competent laboratory. There should be procedures for the physician or clinic to review the test results with the employee concerned, and all health assessment information should remain exclusively with the examining physician and separate from the employee's human resources file.

One noteworthy exception to the trend of fewer medical evaluations is **drug tests**. Increases in mortality rates, accidents, theft, and poor performance affect the employer's economic performance. The drug user's performance may also carry negative consequences for customers or fellow employees. For instance, substance abuse was identified as the number one workplace concern by both workers and managers in the Ontario sawmill industry.[50] Through the analysis of urine, hair, or blood samples, laboratories are able to screen for the presence of drugs. Although professional and amateur intercollegiate athletes have been tested for many years to assure the absence of steroids and stimulants, the popularity of such tests in work organizations has been more recent.

drug tests Tests that determine whether a job applicant uses marijuana, cocaine, or other drugs.

In 2012, 78.4 percent of Canadians reported drinking, with 8.2 percent of males and 2.0 percent of females reporting frequent heavy drinking. Marijuana use was reported by 10.2 percent of Canadian adults in 2012, with heaviest usage on the east and west coasts, and 2 percent of Canadians reported using an illicit drug other than cannabis (e.g., heroin, cocaine, crystal meth).[51] Workplace substance abuse is estimated to cost Canadian employers $39.8 billion annually.[52] TD Canada Trust, Imperial Oil Limited, and Transport Canada are among organizations that use drug testing in Canada.

Given these figures, it is not surprising that some companies are advocating the use of drug tests.

Drug dependence is considered to be a disability, and no Canadian is to be discriminated against on the basis of a disability, according to the *Canadian Charter of Human Rights and Freedoms*. This means that, today, an employer must delicately balance the individual rights of the employee against risk of liability and lack of safety at the workplace. Notably, the issue of whether casual or recreational users are protected under human rights legislation is still a matter of debate. However, several court cases have found that only dependent drug users have a disability and are accorded protection under human rights laws.[53] The Canadian Human Rights Commission has

© Tim Masters/Shutterstock

Alcohol, recreational drugs, and prescription drugs can impair employee performance and lead to major workplace accidents. Should organizations abolish alcohol and drug usage during work hours?

decreed that the following types of pre-employment testing are permissible:[54]

1. When an individual discloses an existing or recent history of drug or alcohol abuse

2. Where a pre-employment medical exam provides the physician with reasonable cause to believe that an individual may be abusing drugs or alcohol and therefore may become impaired on the job

3. For drivers of commercial bus and truck operations

However, employers cannot automatically withdraw offers of employment from candidates who fail alcohol or drug tests without offering accommodation. Canadian employers owe drug-dependent workers accommodation to the point that (a) the accommodation would alter the nature of or viability of the enterprise, or (b) notwithstanding the accommodation efforts, there are serious health or safety risks to workers or members of the public. A relationship or rational connection between the drug or alcohol testing and job performance is an important component of any lawful drug or alcohol testing policy.

In *Chiasson v. Kellogg Brown & Root (Canada) Co.*, a construction company terminated a new employee who failed a mandatory pre-employment drug test. The Alberta Court of Appeal upheld the employer's policy on the belief that such testing legitimately perceives that employees who are drug users are a safety risk in an already dangerous workplace. The court also pointed out that the effects of marijuana can linger for several days.[55]

However, because most drug tests do not yield accurate data on current impairment or usage level and may be unreliable, even the pursuit of a productive, safe workplace may not justify universal, mandatory drug testing. If the testing policy is a bona fide occupational requirement of the job, particularly in a safety-sensitive job position, an employer might have better luck defending it as policy.[56]

Related to substance abuse policies, many employers may have to revise their workplace drug and alcohol policies to meet the legalization of recreational cannabis in 2018. Some suggestions about how to build a policy that includes protocols for multiple substances can be found in this article: https://www.hrreporter.com/workplace-health-and-wellness/34393-managing-marijuana/.[57]

Step 8: Hiring Decision

Whether made by the supervisor or the human resource department, the final hiring decision marks the end of the selection process. When a single predictor such as a job interview is used, the decision is simple: Whoever had the best interview performance is typically selected. However, when multiple predictors such as tests, interviews, and reference checks are used, the decision process becomes more complex. A brief discussion on the decision process is attempted in the following section.

Tradeoffs among Predictors

Alternate approaches to combine the scores on different predictors exist. Three popular approaches are the subjective approach, multiple cut-off approach, and compensatory approach.

Subjective Approach

In the **subjective approach**, also referred to as the clinical approach, the decision maker looks at the scores received by the various applicants on predictors, subjectively evaluates all of the information, and comes to an overall judgment.

> **subjective approach** An approach where the decision maker looks at the scores received by the various applicants on predictors, subjectively evaluates all of the information, and comes to an overall judgment.

Three finalists for a marketing position received the following scores in a sales aptitude test and in the job interview, both scored out of a maximum of 100 points.

Candidate A: Sales Aptitude Test = 80, Interview = 50
Candidate B: Sales Aptitude Test = 40, Interview = 80
Candidate C: Sales Aptitude Test = 70, Interview = 70

The decision maker who looks at the above data may choose Candidate A if she believes that sales aptitude scores of the individual are the most critical in predicting future performance.[58]

It should be noted that another decision maker who looks at the same data may come to a different conclusion, especially if that person believes that interview performance is more important than aptitude. In that instance, Candidate B would be chosen. Similarly, a decision maker who believes that both are equally important and that a high score on one dimension does not compensate for a low score on another may come out with a totally different conclusion—namely, Candidate C. It is precisely the judgmental nature of the decision that causes confusion and potential problems. Decisions are based on gut feelings and may be hard to justify in the event of human rights complaints.

Multiple Cut-off Approach

In a **multiple cut-off approach**, cut-off scores are set for each predictor and each applicant is evaluated on a pass–fail basis. Applicants are rejected if any one of their predictor scores fall below a set minimum score.

> **multiple cut-off approach** An approach where scores are set for each predictor and each applicant is evaluated on a pass–fail basis.

In the above example, if the employer has set a cut-off score of 60 for the test and 60 for interview scores, only Candidate C would qualify.

It is easy for managers to understand this approach, making the acceptance levels for this approach high. However, under this method, the deficiency in one predictor cannot be compensated by superior performance on another. The organization may reject a number of applicants who may be actually qualified to do the job. This can, in turn, result in poor public relations and possible legal challenges.

Compensatory Approach

In a **compensatory approach**, a higher score on a predictor may compensate for a low score on another. Predictors are assumed to be additive and to compensate for one another (in our above example, performing well on the test compensates for a relatively poorer performance on the interview). The applicant with the highest total score will be selected for the position.

> **compensatory approach**
> An approach where a higher score on a predictor may compensate a low score on another.

During selection, some organizations use a sequential elimination process called the *multiple hurdles approach,* where an applicant has to pass a predictor satisfactorily before he or she can proceed to the next predictor.

In this example, under the multiple hurdles approach, only those who achieve a satisfactory score in the sales aptitude test will be interviewed. Thus, if the organization has set up a minimum test score of 60 as satisfactory, then only Candidates A and C will be interviewed.

The multiple hurdles approach is particularly relevant to organizations when some of the predictors used are expensive (e.g., an expensive assessment centre evaluation, inviting job applicants from abroad). In such instances, by keeping these predictors in the latter half of the selection process, the firm is able to screen out candidates who are unlikely to meet organizational needs and thereby save considerable resources. However, the underlying assumption here (as in the case of the multiple cut-off model) is that a high score on one predictor does not compensate for a low score on another predictor. But, unlike in the case of other models, with multiple hurdles as soon as an applicant receives a lower than desired score on a predictor, he or she shall be removed from further consideration and will not proceed to the next stage.

After Selection

Once selected, the successful candidate must be contacted immediately. Having a good employment contract is a must in most instances. When drawing up the employment contract, particular attention should be paid to the following areas:[59]

- *Specify probationary period if applicable.* A common misunderstanding is that all new employees are automatically subject to a probationary period, which is not the case.

- *Clearly specify start date and terms of employment.* In today's competitive labour market, employees move frequently from one job to another. If the employment contract does not specify the start date, under certain circumstances the employers may find themselves competing for the employee's service with a previous employer (especially if the required notice was not given by the employee).

- *Specify reasonable restrictive covenants.* Confidentiality of information and noncompete clauses should be specific, reasonable, and explicit.

- *Ensure that termination procedures are legally enforceable.* Ensure that termination procedures, if specified in the contract, meet the provincial minimum employment standards. (For information on employment law in Canada, visit Canadian Employment Law Today at https://www.employment-lawtoday.com/).

Dispositioning of Applicants

Throughout the selection process, there will be applicants the organization no longer wishes to pursue. The organization's decision should be communicated to these applicants at the earliest possible opportunity. From a public relations standpoint, unsuccessful applicants should be notified that they were not selected. However, the increased use of technology in the recruitment function has resulted in large volumes of job seekers applying for positions, making such a policy impractical. Several employers advise their applicants that only successful ones will be contacted. While this relieves the employer of the responsibility to contact all applicants, it still may not be advisable from a public relations point of view. It is also important to pay careful attention to the wording of the rejection letter. The wording should be positive, and the reason offered for rejection should not be offensive or reduce the self-esteem of the applicant.

Employment specialists may also want to consider rejected applicants for other openings, since these applicants have already expressed an interest in the firm and may have gone through various stages of the selection process. Informing the applicants of such an action enhances public goodwill. Even if no openings are immediately available, applications of candidates with potential who were not hired should be kept on file for future openings. Retaining these applications can also be useful if the employer is charged with employment discrimination.

The job applications of those hired should be carefully preserved as well. This not only enables the human resource department to update its HR information system (HRIS) but also helps HR to learn about the source of its applicants. Information on sex, race, and age of employees helps the human resource department assess the extent of underutilization and concentration (referred to in Chapter 4) and to take necessary corrective action proactively.

If some recruits prove unsatisfactory after they are hired, human resource specialists may be able to reconstruct the selection process beginning with the application. In their reconstruction, they may uncover invalid tests, improperly conducted interviews, or other flaws in the selection process.

The newly hired employee should be treated with respect and consideration. An employer does not get a second chance to make a good first impression with a new hire. The new hire's supervisor or co-worker should call the person a few days before the start date. Sending a welcome note to the entire family may be appropriate in some instances, especially if the employee's family is moving from another location. The time and place that the new hire should report on arrival should be clearly communicated. Some of the unwritten rules (such as dress code) should also be communicated so that the new hire does not arrive formally dressed on casual Friday, for example. A detailed orientation should follow upon arrival. More on orientation and job placement will be discussed in the next chapter.

LO6 Employment Interview

The **employment interview** is a formal, in-depth conversation conducted to evaluate the applicant's acceptability. Employment interviews are the most widely used selection technique and can be adapted across levels of management and employees. They allow a two-way exchange of information: Interviewers learn about the applicant and the applicant learns about the employer. Validity coefficients for unstructured interviews are only about 0.37 but are as high as 0.59 when they are highly structured.[60] Reasons for the popularity of interviews include the following:

> **employment interview**
> A formal, in-depth, face-to-face, or, more recently, a phone or video conference between an employer and a job applicant to assess the appropriateness of the applicant for the job under consideration.

- An interview allows a personal impression. Besides assessing a candidate's ability to perform well on the job, an interviewer can also assess a candidate's fit with the team.
- An interview offers the firm an opportunity to sell a job to a candidate. In high-demand areas such as engineering and business administration, "selling" the company to top candidates assumes great importance. Typically, the employment policies, compensation, flexible work arrangements, career and development opportunities, and overall quality of work life are highlighted in an effort to convince top applicants to choose the firm.

- An interview offers the organization an opportunity to answer the candidate's questions regarding the job, career opportunities, and company policies.

High reliability means that the interpretation of the interview results should not vary from interviewer to interviewer. In reality, it is common for different interviewers to form different opinions. Reliability is improved when identical questions are asked, when interviewers are trained to record responses systematically, and when a scoring guide is provided to gauge the calibre of responses.

The Canadian federal government is among a growing number of employers who are using blind assessments of résumés to determine lists of candidates to interview, aiming to increase diversity and inclusion of minority candidates. They are tracking the number of newcomers who get to the interview stage and the number who are ultimately hired to assess where roadblocks may be to newcomer employment within the federal government.[61]

Interviewers should take care to not let biases associated with protected grounds affect their candidate ratings and should make no references to protected grounds in conversations about hiring or interview notes about candidates.[62]

Carefully structured interviews based on a thorough job analysis are more useful and valid than unstructured interviews that dwell on applicant opinions about topics not directly related to the job.[63] Also, interviews that probe what the applicant has actually done in the past in situations similar to those described in the job analysis may be better predictors of future performance.

The following pages introduce you to types of interviews and the interview process. After this, the discussion turns to some of the common errors made by interviewers and interviewees that you should recognize and avoid during interviews.

Types of Interviews

Interviews are commonly conducted between the applicant and one or more interviewers on a one-to-one basis. A **panel interview** occurs when all interviewers meet with an applicant at the same time. This allows all interviewers to evaluate the individual(s) on the same questions and answers.

> **panel interview** An interview using several interviewers with one applicant.

Whether a one-to-one or panel interview, there are different interview formats that depend on the type of questions that are asked. Questions can be unstructured, or they may be types of structured questions, including behavioural description and situational. Figure 6-10 compares these different formats. Most commonly, interviews will consist of a combination of question types.

FIGURE 6-10

FIGURE 6-10

Different Question Formats in Interviews

Interview Format	Types of Questions	Useful Applications
Unstructured	Few if any planned questions. Questions are made up during the interview.	Useful when trying to help interviewees solve personal problems or understand why they are not right for a job.
Structured	A predetermined checklist of questions, asked of all applicants.	Useful for valid results, especially when dealing with large numbers of applicants.
1. Behavioural Description	Questions are limited to actual past behaviours. Evaluation is on the solution and the approach of the applicant.	Useful to understand applicant's past work behaviour and abilities under specific work situations.
2. Situational	Questions focus on important situations likely to arise on the job and what the applicant would do in such situations.	Useful for understanding the applicant's behavioural propensities.
3. Stress-Producing	A series of harsh, rapid-fire questions intended to upset the applicant.	Useful for stressful jobs, such as handling complaints.

Unstructured Interviews

As the summary in Figure 6-10 indicates, **unstructured interviews** allow human resource specialists to develop questions as the interview proceeds. The interviewer goes into topic areas as they arise, and the end result is more like a friendly conversation. Unfortunately, this unstructured method lacks the reliability of a structured interview because each applicant is asked a different series of questions. Even worse, this approach may overlook key areas of the applicant's skills or background.

unstructured interviews Interviews using few if any planned questions to enable the interviewer to pursue, in depth, the applicant's responses.

Structured Interviews

Structured interviews rely on a predetermined set of questions. The questions are developed before the interview begins and the same questions are asked of every applicant. Candidate responses are compared to a list of potential responses and scored according to a predetermined scoring guide. This approach improves the reliability of the interview process, but it does not allow the interviewer to follow up on interesting or unusual responses. Here, the end result is an interview that may seem quite

structured interviews Interviews wherein a predetermined checklist of questions usually asked of all applicants is used.

mechanical to all concerned. The rigid format may even convey a lack of interest to applicants who are used to more flexible interviews. Situational and behavioural description interviews (discussed below) are two more useful forms of structured interviews.

A survey of 300 human resource practitioners in Canada reveals that 78 percent prepare questions in advance, although 75.4 percent also add new questions during the interview. Only 12.6 percent of respondents use a rating scale. About 85.7 percent of respondents reported using behavioural questions most or all of the time, and 84.7 percent reported taking notes on candidate responses.[64]

Another survey of 592 interviewers from more than 500 Canadian and international organizations showed that trained interviewers are more standardized and formalized in their evaluation processes. They employ more sophisticated questioning strategies and are more consistent in their questioning practices. The study also identified four key factors to a structured interview: evaluation standardization, question consistency, question sophistication, and rapport building.[65]

Behavioural description interviews attempt to find out how job applicants responded to specific work situations in the past. They

behavioural description interviews Interviews that attempt to find out how job applicants responded to specific work situations in the past.

are based on the principle that the best predictor of people's future behaviour is their past behaviour in a similar circumstance. This is especially so if the behaviour being considered occurred recently and, in addition, is of a long-enduring nature. The questions posed to the candidate could be along these lines:

> To assess conflict resolution: "Tell me about the most serious disagreement that you have had with a co-worker in the past and how you dealt with it."
>
> To assess motivation: "Tell me about a time in your last job (or in your present job) when you were asked to take on new duties and responsibilities even if they didn't appear in your job description and how you dealt with it."
>
> To assess decision-making ability: "Tell me about the most unpopular decision you made on your last job."

The work situations chosen should be relevant to the job for which the applicant is under consideration. For instance, practically everyone who has worked in retail sales for any considerable length of time has had to deal with an angry customer. People who have worked in an office would have faced a situation where they had to do something outside of their regular job duties.

Choosing *typical* situations such as the above is important when designing behavioural description questions. Figure 6-11 depicts a behavioural description interview question and a scoring key for the interviewer to use. Typically, the interviewer(s) would record the candidate's responses

to each question, and then compare that response to the responses on the scoring guide. A numerical score is then given for each question, and the sum or scores for all questions produces a total interview score. The total interview score is then used to make comparisons across candidates.

Situational interviews attempt to assess a job applicant's likely future response to specific situations, which may or may not have been faced by the applicant in the past. In this type of interview, the interviewer describes situations that are likely to arise on the job and are important for effective job performance and then asks the job applicant what he or she would do in such situations. Here, the "behavioural intentions" of the applicant are being assessed (unlike statements of actual behaviour in behavioural description interviews). For the purpose of interview questions, real events that describe either effective or ineffective work behaviour (called "critical incidents") are identified. These are situations faced or actions taken by actual workers on the job and may be gathered from past or present employees, supervisors, clients, and others who come into contact with the person doing the job. When it is not practical to collect such incidents, the interviewer may do a comparative analysis by considering the most effective and most ineffective employees in the same position. Whatever the approach, the focus is on

> **situational interviews**
> Interviews that attempt to assess a job applicant's likely future response to specific situations, which may or may not have been faced by the applicant in the past.

FIGURE 6-11

Sample Behavioural Description Interview Question and Rating Criteria

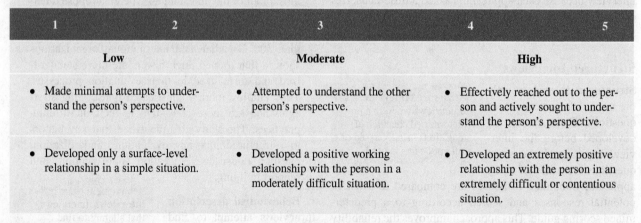

Tell me about a time when you were able to establish rapport with someone when the situation made it difficult to do so. What were the circumstances? What did you do? What were the results?

1	2	3	4	5
Low		**Moderate**		**High**
• Made minimal attempts to understand the person's perspective.		• Attempted to understand the other person's perspective.		• Effectively reached out to the person and actively sought to understand the person's perspective.
• Developed only a surface-level relationship in a simple situation.		• Developed a positive working relationship with the person in a moderately difficult situation.		• Developed an extremely positive relationship with the person in an extremely difficult or contentious situation.

FIGURE 6-12

Stages in a Typical Employment Interview

getting information on relevant job behaviour during the employment interview:

> For example, an organization that attempts to hire managers who must maintain tight cost controls may ask applicants to imagine themselves in a work situation where they faced escalating costs. The applicants' description of what they would do in that situation (e.g., co-operating with others to reduce costs, initiating own action plans to reduce costs, or seeking boss's advice on the matter) would be noted during the interview and evaluated against a pre-set scoring guide.

Behaviour description and situational interviews are highly job-related because they reflect the job applicant's behavioural intentions and the critical behaviours needed for successful job performance. The following steps are recommended to improve the overall validity of an interview method:

1. Conduct a job analysis and develop critical incidents.
2. Select criteria for job success based on the results of the job analysis.
3. Select one or more incidents that indicate a specific performance criterion (for example, cost-consciousness in the previous illustration).
4. Turn each critical incident into a situational or behavioral description question.

5. Develop a scoring guide to facilitate agreement among interviewers on what constitutes a good, acceptable, or unacceptable response to each question.
6. Evaluate the validity of the instrument and implement.

The Interview Process

The five stages of a typical employment interview are listed in Figure 6-12. These **stages of an interview** are interviewer preparation, creation of rapport, information exchange, termination, and evaluation. Regardless of the type of interview used, each of these steps must occur for a successful interview to result. They are discussed briefly to illustrate how the actual interview process develops.

stages of an interview
Key phases in an employment interview: interview preparation, creation of rapport, information exchange, termination, and evaluation.

Stage 1: Interviewer Preparation

Obviously, before the interview begins, the interviewer needs to prepare. In addition to preparing interview questions, the interviewers must consider what questions the applicant is likely to ask. Because the interview is used to persuade top applicants to accept subsequent job offers, the interviewer needs to be able to explain job duties, performance standards, pay, benefits, and other areas of interest.

A list of typical questions asked by recruiters and other interviewers appears in Figure 6-13. Note that several of

FIGURE 6-13

Popular Employment Interview Questions and Suggested Modifications

Popular Interview Questions	Suggested Modifications
1. Why do you want to work for our organization?	1. How do your skills and career goals match with our organizational activities?
2. What are your hobbies?	2. How do your hobbies/spare-time activities add to your value as an employee in this organization?
3. Describe your last job.	3. What were your duties in the last job? What measures of success or failure were employed? How did you fare on those criteria?

(Continued)

Popular Interview Questions	Suggested Modifications
4. Tell me about a project you did recently.	4. Tell me about a project you were involved in, in the recent past. What was your role in the project? How might the skills and competencies you acquired on the project be used in the present position?
5. What was your favourite subject in school/college/university?	5. What was your favourite subject in school/college/university? Can you relate the subject matter to this job or other jobs that you might hold here?
6. Do you have any geographical preferences?	6. This job requires approximately two days of travel each month and periodic (typically, once in three years) relocations. Are there any factors that will prevent you from meeting this requirement?
7. What was your favourite sport at school/college/university?	7. Were you involved in any extracurricular activities at school/college/university? Do you think that the activity provided you with specific competencies that might be relevant for the present job?
8. Have you played any team sports?	8. Your ability to work in a team is critical for success in this position. Can you describe your work in a team that faced a conflict? How was the conflict resolved? What role did you play in the resolution of the conflict?

these questions, while popular, are of questionable predictive power in assessing the applicant's future work performance. Further, under the law, questions relating to sex, family status, race, etc., are prohibited. As can be seen from the list, these questions are intended to give the interviewer some insight into the applicant's interests, attitudes, and background. The same figure provides modified versions of the same questions that provide greater insights into an applicant's strengths and attitudes. Specific or technical questions are added to the list according to the type of job opening. These questions should be designed to assess specific tasks, duties, and competencies identified in the job analysis.

Spotlight *on* HRM

Video Interviews

Although interviews provide rich, face-to-face information, they are expensive to conduct—particularly if the interviewer(s) or applicant(s) have to travel to a single location. Apart from travel, subsistence, and lodging costs, there are additional soft or invisible costs, such as lost time during travel.

To reduce time and monetary expenses, employers are increasingly turning to video interviews. Video interviewing options include live conversations using Google Hangouts, Skype, or a video interview provider; or recorded interviews, where a candidate receives a list of questions and records his or her answers to send to the hiring manager. Some recorded interviews allow candidates to re-record their responses until they are satisfied with each response before submitting while others allow only one take to respond to each question.

Although face-to-face interviews are still preferred by most employers, video interviews are increasingly being used. Assessing the quality of the answers and not the quality of the videography is an important key.[66] One study found that interviewers may attribute candidate pauses or lacklustre responses to the technology as opposed to the candidate.[67] Both employers and candidates indicate that using video interviewing affords a wider pool of prospective employers and candidates in a smaller time commitment.

Video interviews are still quite new for most organizations, and many managers may not be comfortable with the process and equipment. Thus, interviewer training on the technology is a must. The equipment should be tested before the interview starts to allow for a smooth interview process for both the candidate and interviewer(s).

The future of video interviews seems bright as technology continues to improve and candidates and interviewers become attuned to interviews being conducted without being in the same location.

SOURCES: Robert Waghorn (2011, November), "Internet puts new spin on traditional career fair," *Canadian HR Reporter, 24,* p. 20; Roy Maurer (2015, March 5), "Video Interviews help address long-term unemployment," SHRM, http://www.shrm.org/hrdisciplines/staffingmanagement/articles/pages/video-interviews-long-term-unemployment.aspx; Dave Imbrogno (2015, October 15), "Are you ready for your close up? Video interviewing grows in popularity," *HR.BLR.com,* hr.blr.com/HR-news/Staffing-Training/Recruiting/Video-interviewing-grows-in-popularity/

Before interviewing can begin, careful construction of interview questions designed to assess tasks, duties, and competencies identified in the job analysis is required along with an accompanying scoring guide for strong and weak responses to each question. Interview development may be done jointly between line management and HR specialists. Prior to the interview, interviewers should review scoring guide materials, the interview protocol (such as procedures for meeting the candidate, assigning interview questions to particular interviewers in the case of a panel interview, deciding who will answer candidate questions), and standard statements to tell the candidate, such as interview length, next stages in the selection process, and timeline for communicating the hiring decision. Before the interview, interviewers should also review the application form and/or résumé before each candidate arrives.

Given the importance of interviewer preparation and skills in determining the overall effectiveness of the interview (as a selection tool), several organizations have begun to train their managers in interview techniques. Large companies often train their interviewers in matters such as human rights legislation and techniques to get more information from job candidates.[68] Interviewers should also be trained to link interview questions tightly to job analysis results, to use a variety of questions, to ask the same questions of each candidate, and to anchor the rating scales for scoring answers with examples and illustrations.[69]

Stage 2: Creation of Rapport

Often the interviewer is one of the first representatives of the company with whom the applicant has an opportunity to talk. A strong and lasting impression of the company is likely to be formed at this stage. If the interviewer does not show courtesy to the applicant, that impression is certain to be negative.

Once the interview begins, the burden is on the interviewer to establish a relaxed rapport with the recruit. Without a relaxed rapport, the interviewer may not get a clear picture of the applicant's potential. Rapport is aided by beginning the interview on time and starting with nonthreatening questions such as, "Did you find parking all right?" At the same time, the interviewer may use body language to help relax the applicant. A smile, a handshake, relaxed posture, and moving paperwork aside all communicate without words; such nonverbal communications maintain rapport throughout the interview session. The interviewer has to act as the perfect host or hostess, greet the candidate with a warm smile showing him or her into the office, make small talk, and reduce the candidate's nervousness by initiating friendly conversation. Only in a relationship of mutual trust and comfort will a candidate talk freely. By projecting an image of confidence, competence, and concern, especially in the early stages of the interview, an interviewer can create trust.

Stage 3: Information Exchange

The heart of the interview process is the exchange of information. To help establish rapport, some interviewers may begin by asking the applicant if he or she has any questions. This establishes two-way communication and lets the interviewer begin to judge the recruit by the type of questions asked. Consider the following dialogue. Which response creates the most favourable impression?

Interviewer: Well, let's start with any questions you may have.

Applicant 1: I don't have any questions.

Applicant 2: I have several questions. How much does the job pay? Will I get two weeks' vacation at the end of the first year?

Applicant 3: What will the responsibilities be? I am hoping to find a job that offers me challenges now and career potential down the road.

Each response creates a different impression on the interviewer. But only Applicant 3 appears concerned about the job. The other two applicants appear to be either unconcerned or interested only in what benefits they will receive.

In general, an interviewer will ask questions worded to learn as much as possible. Questions that begin with *how, what, why, compare, describe, expand,* or "Could you tell me more about . . ." are likely to solicit an open response, while questions that can be answered with a simple yes or no do not give the interviewer much insight. Specific questions and areas of interest to an interviewer are suggested in Figure 6-13.

Stage 4: Termination of Interview

As the list of questions dwindles or available time ends, the interviewer must draw the session to a close. It is important to set candidate expectations at the start of the interview. For instance, state the number of questions, the total interview time, and when the candidate will be allowed to ask questions (first, throughout, or at the end of the interview). Nonverbal communication can also be useful. Sitting erect, turning toward the door, or glancing at a watch or clock all clue the applicant that the end is near. Some interviewers terminate the interview by asking, "Do you have any final questions?" At this point, the interviewer informs the applicant of the next step in the interview process, which may be to wait for a call or email.

Stage 5: Evaluation

Immediately after the interview ends, the interviewer should record the candidate's specific answers onto the scoring guide and note the candidate's general questions.

© Shutterstock/bluedog studio

Both applicants and interviewers anticipate a selection interview. Would it seem unusual to you to get a job without having had an interview?

Interviewer Errors

Caution must be exercised to avoid some common **interviewer errors**, summarized in Figure 6-14, that

> **interviewer errors**
> Mistakes like biases and domination that reduce the validity and usefulness of the job interview.

FIGURE 6-14

Typical Interviewer Errors

Halo Effect

Interviewers who use limited information about an applicant to bias their evaluation of that person's other characteristics are subject to the halo effect. In other words, some information about the candidate plays a disproportionate part in the final evaluation of the candidate.

Examples:

- An applicant who has a pleasant smile and firm handshake is considered a leading candidate before the interview begins.
- An applicant who wears blue jeans to the interview is rejected in the interviewer's mind.

Leading Questions

Interviewers who "telegraph" the desired answer by the way they frame their questions are using leading questions.

Examples:

- "Do you think you'll like this work?"
- "Do you agree that profits are necessary?"

Stereotypes

Interviewers who harbour prejudice against specific groups are exhibiting a personal bias based on stereotypical thinking.

Examples:

- "I prefer salespersons who are tall."
- "Accountants are not outgoing people."

Interviewer Domination

Interviewers who use the interview to oversell the applicant, brag about their successes, or carry on a social conversation instead of an interview are guilty of interviewer domination.

Examples:

- Spending the entire interview telling the applicant about the company plans or benefits.
- Using the interview to tell the applicant how important the interviewer's job is.

Contrast Errors

When interviewers compare candidates to those who came before instead of to an objective standard.

Examples:

- "This candidate did a better job responding to this question than that guy did yesterday."
- "Of the three candidates we've seen, I like the second one best. I wonder how the next candidate will compare?"

decrease the effectiveness of the interview. When the applicant is judged based on interviewer errors or other personal biases, it reduces the validity and reliability of the interview, and the results of the interview are misinterpreted. Applicants are accepted or rejected for reasons that may bear no relation to their potential performance. Biased interviews merely waste organizational resources and the applicant's time. Figure 6-15 summarizes some major dos and don'ts in the employment interview.

Interviewee Errors

Interviewees make errors too. Some **interviewee errors** may be to cover job-related weaknesses. Others may emerge from simple nervousness. Although interviewers—especially those in the human resource department—may conduct hundreds of job interviews in a year, most applicants never experience that many in a lifetime. Common interview mistakes made by job candidates

interviewee errors Interviewee mistakes, such as boasting, not listening, or not being prepared, that reduce the validity and usefulness of an interview.

include playing games, talking too much, boasting, not listening, and being unprepared.

Playing games—for example, acting nonchalant—is often taken at face value: The candidate is not interested. The candidate may be excited or nervous and talk too much, especially about irrelevant topics such as sports or the weather. Instead, applicants should stick to the subject at hand.

Likewise, boasting also is a common mistake. Applicants need to "sell themselves," but credential distortion—even if just "embellishment"—about responsibilities and accomplishments or simply bragging too much can turn off the interviewer's interest. Failure to listen may result from anxiety about the interview. Unfortunately, it usually means missing the interviewer's questions and failing to maintain rapport. And, of course, being unprepared means asking poorly thought-out questions and even conveying a lack of interest, neither of which is likely to land the job being sought.

A recent survey of 400 hiring managers in Canada revealed that interviewers are prone to making snap judgments about applicants within the first 5 minutes (51 percent of interviewers) or 15 minutes (89 percent of interviewers). These quick

---

FIGURE 6-15

Some Dos and Don'ts of Conducting Employment Interviews

Do:

1. Collect only job-related information and not information on general personality traits.
2. Concentrate on securing information about the applicant's past job behaviour.
3. Use several interviewers (to interview each candidate) to increase the reliability of the interview process.
4. Treat all interviewees equally and impartially.
5. Have a checklist of questions to ask each job applicant.
6. Attempt to create a relaxed setting by asking easy, nonthreatening questions first and showing support to the applicant.
7. Provide job-related information to the candidate.
8. Compare your evaluation of each candidate with other interviewers and find out why discrepancies exist.
9. Compare the candidate's responses to objective standards (e.g., scoring guides).

Do Not:

1. Attempt to predict personality traits from a single interview.
2. Be guided by initial impressions (or nonverbal cues) and generalize them to all relevant work and nonwork behaviour of the applicant.
3. Allow your evaluation of the candidate's job performance to be influenced by a single characteristic (such as how well the applicant dresses).
4. Be tempted to make snap judgments of the candidate early in the interview, thus locking out further information.
5. Ask leading questions that communicate the correct or desired answer to the applicant (e.g., "Do you believe that women workers should be treated equally with males?").
6. Exhibit personal biases ("In my experience, good sales managers are all talkative").
7. Dominate the interview; rather, use the interview to collect relevant information about the candidate.
8. Compare the candidates to each other. Compare them to a standard instead.

decisions are often made on the basis of the applicant's body language, such as not making eye contact or not smiling, fidgeting or displaying bad posture, playing with hair or face, or having a handshake that is too firm or too soft.[70]

LO7 Evaluating the Selection

How do you know whether the selection procedures in your organization are effective? How can you evaluate whether they achieved your organization's goals? Even if the procedures are effective (namely, they achieve the objective of hiring the right candidates), are they efficient and worth the costs and trouble?

The final outcome of the selection process is the people who are hired. Productive employees are the best evidence of an effective selection process. Some of the questions to ask in this context are as follows:

1. Are the superiors and peers of new hires indicating dissatisfaction with them?
2. Is the selection process too expensive?
3. Are the hiring criteria and practices showing too much variation across even similar jobs and regions?
4. Are the training costs of newer employees increasing?
5. Do managers spend too much time managing new hires?
6. Are the grievances, absenteeism, and turnover inordinately high?

To evaluate both new employees and the selection process requires feedback. Feedback on successful employees is sometimes hard to find, but feedback on failures is ample. It can include displeased supervisors, growing employee turnover and absenteeism, poor performance, low employee satisfaction, union activity, and legal suits.

The ultimate utility of a selection procedure is decided by looking at the quality and productivity of the workforce hired and the costs incurred in the process. The costs include not only the out-of-pocket costs (such as costs of testing, interviewing, postage, and stationery), but also the costs associated with errors in the decisions made. If the wrong candidate is hired or promoted, the costs are particularly high. However, an exhaustive look at all costs (actual and potential) associated with a selection system may be very difficult in real life. Appendix A to this chapter describes a procedure to assess the utility of the selection system.

SUMMARY

The selection process depends heavily upon inputs such as job analysis, human resource plans, and recruits. These inputs are used within the challenges of the external environment, ethics, and guidelines established by the organization.

The selection process then takes recruits and puts them through a series of steps to evaluate their potential. These steps vary from organization to organization and from one job opening to another. In general, the selection procedure will determine whether applicants meet broad criteria based on résumés, job applications, or biographical information blanks. Candidates who pass screening move onto tests (e.g., personality tests, ability tests, knowledge tests, performance tests, or integrity tests) and/or interviews for more specific job qualifications. Significant preparation is required to prepare structured interview questions and scoring materials, and to ensure a smooth interview process for interviewers and candidates.

Some employers will use a realistic job preview (RJP) to depict positive and negative aspects of the job and work environment. After considerable expense and effort to recruit and select employees, the use of RJPs seems well advised as a means of reducing turnover among new employees. The applicant's references are often verified, and, in some occupations, physical or drug testing may be required as a contingent assessment. The use of all tests must be empirically justifiable or the employer risks human rights violation charges.

The supervisor's role should include participation in the selection process, usually through provision of valid job-relevant information and an interview with job candidates. Through participation, the supervisor is more likely to be committed to the new worker's success.

Like all other human resource functions, the costs and benefits of the selection process also have to be compared periodically to evaluate the utility of various predictors. However, this is a complex activity, often requiring fairly advanced mathematical skills. Notwithstanding, all human resource management systems have to implement evaluation studies to maintain their effectiveness and efficiency.

TERMS FOR REVIEW

ability tests 186
behavioural description interviews 197
biographical information blank (BIB) 181

compensatory approach 195
computer-interactive performance tests 188
differential validity 183

SELF-ASSESSMENT EXERCISE

How Do You Fare As an Interviewee?

This short test helps you assess your behaviours as a job applicant in the context of job interviews. Indicate your behaviours on a scale of "Always," "Often," "Sometimes," and "Never." Do not omit any statements.

Statement	Always	Often	Sometimes	Never
1. Before attending an interview, I gather as much information about the employer as possible by consulting annual reports, Internet searching, and/or talking to knowledgeable persons.				
2. During many interviews, I indicate how another employer has expressed interest in hiring me at this time.				
3. I carefully study the job responsibilities involved in the position and link my own competencies and training to each one of them before going for an interview.				
4. During the interview, I make sure that I talk a lot, even if that means I have to use "fillers" such as sports news or jokes.				
5. During the interview, I always maintain my composure and try to project a positive, can-do attitude.				
6. I often "sell" myself to the interviewer by mildly exaggerating my past accomplishments or work responsibilities.				
7. I utilize a part of the interview time to find out more about the job and focus on how I can contribute to its success.				
8. When the interviewer asks me, "Do you have any questions?" my typical response is, "Not really, thank you."				
9. I follow up the interview with a thank-you email that also highlights my continuing interest in the position.				
10. At times during an interview, I flatter the interviewer and/or the employing organization. After all, is there a person out there who does not like flattery?				

SCORING

For the odd-numbered statements, give yourself a score of 4, 3, 2, and 1 for Always, Often, Sometimes, and Never, respectively. For the even-numbered statements, reverse the scoring. Now add up the scores for all 10 statements.

The total score may range anywhere from 10 to 40. If your score is 34 or above, you are currently doing well and have a general awareness of what is required for a successful interview. Scores below 20 require that you pay serious attention to developing interview skills.

REVIEW AND DISCUSSION QUESTIONS

1. What is the strategic importance of the selection function for an organization?

2. List and briefly discuss the various steps in the selection process.

3. What are the five stages of the employment interview? What specific actions should you, as an interviewer, take to conduct a proper interview?

4. What are the different types of validity? If you want to validate a new dexterity test (which measures physical coordination) for workers in an assembly plant, how will you go about it?

5. What attributes of behavioural description and situational interviews make them appear more promising than unstructured interview formats?

6. What is a weighted application blank? How is it different from a traditional application form?

CRITICAL THINKING QUESTIONS

1. Suppose you are an employment specialist. Would you expect to have a large or small selection ratio for each of the following job openings?

   a. Janitors

   b. Nuclear engineers with five years' experience designing nuclear reactors

   c. Pharmacists

   d. Software programmers

   e. Elementary schoolteachers in the Yukon

   f. Elementary schoolteachers in Ontario

   What are the implications for human resource managers?

2. If a human resource manager asked you to streamline the firm's selection process for hourly paid workers, which steps described in this chapter would you eliminate? Why?

3. A Canadian university has been experiencing a high student dropout rate in recent years. One calculation showed that although the first-year enrollment in commerce courses increased from 650 to 980 students in the last four years, the dropout rate for first-year students has worsened from 9 percent to 15 percent. The university has been using uniform admission standards during the years and has not made any significant changes in the grading or instructional procedures. Based on what you've learned in this course until this point, what recommendations would you make to the university to improve its retention rates? Why?

4. If you are hired as a consultant to evaluate the selection process for salespersons in a large car dealership in the Toronto area, what kind of information will you collect?

5. Assume you are hired to improve the interview process used by a large real estate organization when it hires sales and customer service representatives. When suggesting improvements, what factors will you focus on? What steps will you recommend to check whether your suggestions indeed result in better hires in the future?

6. Suppose you are approached by the human resource department in a large insurance firm that routinely hires dozens of clerical workers. Of the various types of tests discussed in the text, which would you recommend? What are the steps you will suggest to validate the test(s) you recommended?

ETHICS QUESTION

You are the human resource manager in a large chain of grocery stores about to hire a new shipper/receiver. Because of a local economic slowdown, you have received a large number of applications for the position. Mike, one of the applicants, is a nephew of your neighbour Mercy, a real estate agent. One day while you were working on your lawn, Mercy approached you and conveyed to you how "nice it would be to see Mike settled in a stable job like the one in your store." Mercy knows that you are on the lookout for a new, larger house right now. During the conversation, she indicated that she will find one for you without charging you any commission. You looked at

Mike's application and found him to have minimum qualifications necessary for the position. However, there are a large number of candidates who have better qualifications and experience. You know that your employer is making some major strategic changes now that will enhance the information needs of the firm significantly.

What considerations will you have in making the decision? What would you do right now?

RESEARCH EXERCISE

Using the Employment and Social Development Canada website and others, estimate the demand (and supply where available) of pharmacists, software programmers, accountants, salespersons, and financial analysts in Canada. What selection ratios do they indicate? What are the implications for human resource managers employed in the relevant sectors?

INCIDENT 6-1

A Selection Decision at Empire Inc.

At Empire Inc. the turnover rate is very high among assembly workers. Supervisors in the production department have told the human resource department that they do not have time to conduct a supervisory interview with the large number of applicants who are processed to fill assembly-line openings. As a result, the human resource department's employment specialists make the final hiring decisions. The profiles of three typical applicants are presented below.

The nature of the assembly jobs is rather simple. Training seldom takes more than an hour or two. Most people master the job and achieve an acceptable level of production during the second full day on the job. The tasks involve very little physical or mental effort. The employment test is valid, but has only a weak relationship between scores and actual performance.

	Applicant A	Applicant B	Applicant C
Years of Experience	4	8	1
Education	1 year of university	Finished grade 8	High school diploma
Age	24	43	32
Test Score	77/100	74/100	82/100
Medical Evaluation	OK	OK	OK
Performance Evaluation	Very good	Excellent	Fair/good (last job)
Work History	Limited data	Stable	Stable
Ranking by:			
Interviewer 1	1	2	3
Interviewer 2	3	2	1
Apparent Eagerness	Moderate	Strong	Weak
Availability	4 weeks	2 weeks	Immediately

DISCUSSION QUESTIONS

1. What information would you consider irrelevant in the preceding selection profiles?

2. Are there any changes you would recommend in the selection process?

3. Which of the three candidates would you select, given the limited knowledge you possess? Why?

WE CONNECTIONS: THE SELECTION PROCESS

Selecting a New HR Manager

Rebecca Ali was impressed as she looked around the lobby of WEC. The company seemed to be doing well. The room was spacious and the decor was clearly selected by a professional decorator. She was glad she had come.

When she was first contacted by Alex, the CEO, it took a moment before she remembered meeting him at that golf tournament the month before. He had let her know that his company was looking for an HR manager and he wanted to see if she was interested in the position. Although she was pretty happy with her job at the head office of a major department store, she thought it wouldn't hurt to hear him out.

The Tour

A few minutes later, Alex entered the lobby and smiled when he saw her. She stood up and they shook hands. He said, "Thank you so much for coming in, Rebecca. It's so nice to see you again. Follow me. I'll give you a tour."

As they walked through the building, Alex explained the different departments and the types of projects they took on. Rebecca wasn't able to fully grasp what services they offered, but she nodded amiably as he talked. They also chatted with several employees along the way. Half an hour later they finally made their way into Alex's office, and she said, "You have a great set-up here, Alex. You must be very proud."

The Interview Begins

He chuckled, as they sat down. "I am very fond of this place. And that's why I wanted to talk to you, Rebecca. We have an HR specialist, but I think we need someone more like you. A person who can take charge of the people issues."

She nodded. "I do have a lot of HR experience. I started out as a salesperson, but I eventually moved into an administrative role in HR, and then a managerial one. I think I've seen it all."

Alex replied, "That's what I thought. Do you think you could handle being an HR manager here?"

Rebecca paused, then said, "I am sure I could, because I've never hit an HR challenge that I couldn't handle. But I wonder if you have a job description that I could see."

Alex began to shuffle the papers on his desk. "I have one here somewhere. I asked Charlotte to draw one up. Ah, here it is!" He handed her a piece of paper.

She noticed that it was very brief. In essence, it noted that the HR manager would be in charge of developing and implementing policies and procedures for recruitment and selection, performance management, health and safety,

compensation, reward systems, training and development, HR planning, and employee relations. Rebecca was not sure what to say. She did not have experience developing policies in many of these areas. While she was indeed an HR manager, she had focused mostly on recruiting and hiring activities for the department store.

Just then there was a knock on the door, and they both looked up. Selina stepped into the office, and said, "I hope I'm not intruding."

Alex jumped up, and said, "Of course not. Thanks so much for dropping in. Please let me introduce you to Rebecca Ali. She's the person I was telling you about." The two women smiled and shook hands, and they all sat down.

Selina asked, "How is the interview going so far?"

Alex replied, "It's going great. I've shown her around and I gave her a copy of the job description. Now that you're here, I can start asking some tough questions."

"Tough" Questions

Reading from a sheet he had prepared, he asked Rebecca a number of questions, including the following: (1) What are your greatest strengths and weaknesses? (2) Why are you interested in working for WEC? (3) What would a perfect day be like for you? (4) If you could have one superpower, what would it be? Selina took careful notes on Rebecca's responses.

Finally, Selina had a chance to address Rebecca. She said, "Rebecca, I noticed on your résumé that you have only worked for one company since you finished college. What do you think the main differences will be between retail and a software firm?"

Rebecca mulled over the question. She had a feeling that Selina was harder to impress than Alex. Finally, she replied, "I'm sure there will be differences, but people are people. At the end of the day, they really all want the same things."

Alex smiled broadly, and nodded. He said, "That's very true! Excellent point, Rebecca. It is going to be great to have a real people expert teaching us about this stuff."

Twenty minutes later, Selina had finished her questions, and Rebecca had promised to send them a list of three references. As Rebecca walked out of the lobby toward her car, she was feeling very pleased with how the meeting had gone. She thought to herself, *"Wow. I think I'm going to have a new job. This is amazing!"*

DISCUSSION QUESTIONS

1. What are the selection process steps that WEC is using for the HR manager position? Be sure to describe each step.

2. Imagine that you are a consultant to WEC. Provide the company with a better selection process for the HR manager position.

3. To counter the lack of depth of the questions from Alex, develop two behavioural description interview questions and two situational interview questions that Alex or Selina could ask of an HR manager candidate.

4. At this point, should Alex and Selina hire Rebecca? Explain why or why not.

In the next installment of the WE Connections story (at the end of Chapter 7), HR staff consider how to best train and onboard a new employee.

CASE STUDY

Trajectory Investments

Evaluating the Selection Process in a New Region

Trajectory Investments had expanded its investment services rapidly into foreign markets over the last four years. Although it had given careful attention to developing and honing its selection processes in its North American locations, Jackson gave a sigh as he received feedback from the company's Pacific Rim Region HR lead. Gang Lim's latest email summarized that only 50 percent of the new financial services advisors in his region were considered "satisfactory" by their managers. Jackson sat back, acknowledging that the hiring process that had worked successfully in North America for the last 10 years simply wasn't effective in producing the same results in the Pacific Rim.

Jackson had been involved with the project team that had developed the selection process for financial services advisors in North America at its inception. At the time, Trajectory had brought in Right Fit Consulting to help build the steps. The process, essentially, was that applicants completed an online application, which was then given an auto-assessment score. The score was based on the applicant's education and experience. Applicants meeting a minimum score of 50 were invited to participate in an on-site assessment at an assessment centre. North American applicants were referred to a local branch of Talent Assessors Inc., where they completed assessment centre exercises in mixed groups, including people who had applied to other positions in other organizations. These exercises included a leaderless group discussion, a situational judgment test, and a financial services aptitude test; Trajectory was then provided with an overall assessment centre score for each candidate.

Candidates scoring above 70 were invited for an interview with Trajectory HR personnel as well as with the applicant's prospective manager. Jackson recalled the careful attention that the team had paid to developing a solid structured interview with both behaviour description and situational questions based on critical incidents. He was proud of the integrity of the scoring guide and the thoughtful instructions that would add reliability and validity to the interview process. At the conclusion of each interview, the HR person and prospective supervisor would each complete independent scores for the candidate, and then would meet to discuss their assessments. Successful candidates were then offered the job.

HR had been collecting information about the performance of the hires made since the implementation of the hiring process. Scores on the interviews and indications of whether the hire was ultimately successful at performing the financial services advisor job (as evaluated by the hire's manager as part of the annual performance evaluation process) were tracked. Jackson pulled up the latest report on the rates of success of hires from the North American operations (see Table 1). Based on the success of previous applicants and the number of applications typically received, Trajectory focused on hiring applicants who scored 80 and higher on the interview.

When the company first began expansion into the Pacific Rim, Jackson had recommended that financial services advisors be hired using the same process that had been honed in North America. A few adjustments were needed, however. First, the application screening tool was not available in all countries. Strict censorship policies in China made the online screening application that Trajectory used in North America inaccessible for Chinese applicants. As a result, for the Pacific Rim region, the screening assessment was considered optional. When applicants were able to successfully log onto the tool, their scores were used, but applicants were able to move onto the assessment centre stage even if they didn't complete the job application. As Jackson reflected on the process now, he knew that it would be possible for applicants to get through to later stages without the desired financial education and experience that Trajectory desired.

As for the assessment centre, Jackson admitted that there, too, the company had cut some corners. There was not a network of firms offering assessment centre services in all major centres where Trajectory was in operation in

> ## TABLE 1
>
> Interview Score Distributions and Subsequent Evaluations of Performance as Successful and Unsuccessful for Trajectory's North American Operations
>
> | | Number of People Receiving This Interview Score | Number of People with Successful Performance | Number of People with Unsuccessful Performance |
> |---|---|---|---|
> | 10 | 3 | — | 3 |
> | 20 | 5 | — | 5 |
> | 30 | 10 | — | 10 |
> | 40 | 12 | 2 | 10 |
> | 50 | 14 | 5 | 9 |
> | 60 | 13 | 6 | 7 |
> | 70 | 15 | 9 | 6 |
> | 80 | 13 | 13 | — |
> | 90 | 8 | 8 | — |
> | 100 | 7 | 7 | — |
> | **Total** | 100 | 50 | 50 |

the Pacific Rim as there was in North America through its partnership with Talent Assessors. Gang Lim had established relationships with local assessment centres in the cities of their major operations, but he had expressed that there was not a standardized process used by each of the firms. Some firms would run applicants through the assessment centre individually, which Jackson knew meant that they couldn't be running a leaderless group discussion. In short, ratings from one assessment centre location were not necessarily equitably comparable to assessments from other locations. Jackson rubbed his temples to ease the headache beginning to form behind his eyes.

Next, Jackson considered the interview process used in the Pacific Rim. He believed that this North American tool would have some validity in the Pacific Rim. Looking at Table 1, he reflected again on the success of financial services advisors on the job and their interview performance from the North American data. He wondered if the company should complete a similar table for the Pacific Rim region, or whether the problems with the selection process required a deeper look.

DISCUSSION QUESTIONS

1. If the numbers in Table 1 were true for operations in the Pacific Rim, how many people would Gang Lim have to interview to get 50 successful employees who have

   a. a score of 60 or higher on the test?

   b. a score of 70 or higher on the test?

2. What suggestions do you have for Jackson and Gang Lim about amendments they could make to the existing hiring process in the Pacific Rim that could improve the success of hires?

3. How would you go about designing a selection process for the Pacific Rim operations from scratch?

4. Is it important to have similar hiring processes for different regions of the same company? Why or why not?

5. What additional programs could you put into place in the Pacific Rim to help improve the success of newly hired financial services advisors?

APPENDIX A

Utility Analysis

The utility of a selection procedure should be assessed only after considering a number of factors. The more important ones among these are (1) the validity of the predictor; (2) the variability in job performance; (3) the selection ratio; (4) the base rate of job success; and (5) selection costs.

1. VALIDITY OF THE PREDICTOR

Different predictors have differing validity coefficients. One study by Hunter and Hunter[71] showed that predictors such as tests and assessment centres had average validities in the range of 0.43 to 0.54, while others such as reference checks (0.26) and interviews (0.14) were much lower. Of course, when choosing between predictors with equal validity, the cost of the predictor becomes an important consideration; however, as one writer noted, the trade-off between the cost of a predictor and its validity should almost always be resolved in favour of validity.[72] This is because the potential cost of an error in the course of the test is extremely high.

2. VARIABILITY IN JOB PERFORMANCE

A useful measure of a job's value to the organization is the variability of job performance for a job expressed in dollar terms. For some jobs, the differences in performance ranges (example: "outstanding" to "totally incompetent") have relatively little effect in terms of dollar value to the organization. For example, the variability of performance of a receptionist or window cleaner is relatively less significant to the organization than that of a production planner or marketing manager. Thus, a "good" receptionist may contribute, say, $6,000 over his or her salary and benefits to the organization, while a "poor" one may cost the firm, say, $2,000 in terms of lost sales because of disgruntled customers who have had bad experiences when paying visits to the organization. In the case of a marketing manager, the effects of outcomes may be far more serious. A good marketing manager may contribute $500,000 above his or her salary and benefits, while a poor one may cost the firm $200,000 in lost sales or decreased market share. The variability in performance in dollar terms for the receptionist is about $8,000; for the marketing manager's position, the corresponding figure may be $700,000. The statistical index used for computing this type of variability is the standard deviation of performance. Hunter and Schmidt's[73] research led them to conclude that a "40 percent rule" prevails for most common job positions—namely, the variability in job performance is typically 40 percent of the average annual salary of a position. Clearly, in the above example, an organization is more likely to spend $5,000 on

improving the selection procedures for its marketing manager than for its receptionist.

3. SELECTION RATIO

As already mentioned in this chapter, a large selection ratio (such as 1:25) means that the firm can afford to be choosy, while a small ratio of 1:2 does not give the organization much freedom to make selection decisions. On the one hand, a ratio such as 1:25 means that a large number of applicants must be tested and screened (thus adding to the selection costs). On the other hand, it also means that only the "cream" of the applicant "crop" will be selected, thus implying that even a predictor with relatively low validity can be employed.

4. BASE RATE OF JOB SUCCESS

The base rate denotes the relative incidence of any given attribute or behaviour in the total population.[74] If 70 percent of the people between 22 and 40 years old are married, then the base rate for marriage for that segment of the society is 70. A low base rate of job success in an organization indicates that few employees reach an acceptable level of job performance. Typically, base rates of success tend to be high for easy and simple jobs. For complex jobs requiring many skills and years of training, the base rates tend to be lower. Generally, the usefulness of a selection procedure increases when it is able to increase the base rate of success for a job. If the base rate is already high, at 80 or 90, it is very difficult to find a predictor that will improve on it as the typical validity coefficients for various predictors currently in use range from 0.15 to 0.60.

5. SELECTION COSTS

Selection costs may be actual or potential. Actual costs include costs of administering standardized tests, collecting and processing biographical blanks, conducting employment interviews, and offering money and other benefits to job candidates who are selected. The potential costs include cost of selection errors, as when the wrong person is hired for a job. The benefits of a selection process should also be defined broadly to include not only current benefits but also likely future events (e.g., potential of an employee to hold additional responsibility).

Clearly, a thorough evaluation of all the above variables is a complex and difficult task. In the past, several writers have offered somewhat different algorithms and formulas to assess the usefulness of the selection procedure.[75] One formula suggested to calculate the utility of the selection procedure is as follows:[76]

$P = (N) \times (T) \times (C) \times (S) \times (Z)$ where

P = increase in productivity in dollars

N = number of persons hired

T = average job tenure in years of those hired

C = the correlation between a selection predictor and job performance (or validity coefficient)

S = variability in job performance (measured by standard deviation of job performance in dollars, roughly 40 percent of annual wage)[77]

Z = the average predictor score of those selected (in standard score form)

As an illustration, consider the job position of marketing manager in a consumer goods organization.

Let us assume that the organization used an assessment centre technique (which had an estimated validity of 0.6) to hire 10 managers who are paid a salary of $80,000 each year. Further, let us assume that each manager will stay with the organization for five years. Assuming an average predictor score (standardized) of 1.4, it can be shown that the assessment centre procedure would increase productivity by $1.344 million over five years, or an average of $268,800 each year of its tenure.

Utility analysis such as the above has been successfully used in a number of organizations and different work settings.[78] It should be noted that utility analysis does not require reducing all selection-decision outcomes to a dollar figure; indeed, what is more important may be identifying all possible outcomes of a decision and weighing their relative importance systematically.[79] The factors identified earlier in this section (namely, selection ratio, base rate of success, and so on) interact; hence they must be considered together. For example, typically the utility is higher with a low base rate of job success or when the variability in job performance is high. However, given identical base rates of job success, different selection ratios can make a major difference in the context of selection. For example, it can be mathematically shown that with a base rate of 50 percent and a validity coefficient of 0.40, a selection ratio of 70 percent will yield 58 percent successful employees. Keeping the other things the same, if the selection ratio is changed to 40 percent, the proportion of successful employees climbs to 66 percent, while for a 10 percent selection ratio the corresponding figure is a whopping 78 percent.[80] Such interdependence among the relevant selection variables makes utility analysis a complex procedure, indeed. Yet its contribution to an effective human resource management system should not be underestimated.

PART 4

Placing, Developing, and Evaluating Human Resources

New employees need to know what is expected of them and what their responsibilities are, and they have to be trained properly to carry out these responsibilities effectively. A savvy employer will provide a career path for each employee and will provide opportunities to develop employees to their fullest potential. Also, employees need feedback on their performance to experience job satisfaction or to find out where they can improve. The next two chapters are about employee development and evaluation. As a student, you need to understand the human resource department's role in these activities. They affect you, whether you work in a human resource department or elsewhere in the organization. Understanding these activities will assist you to be a better employee or manager.

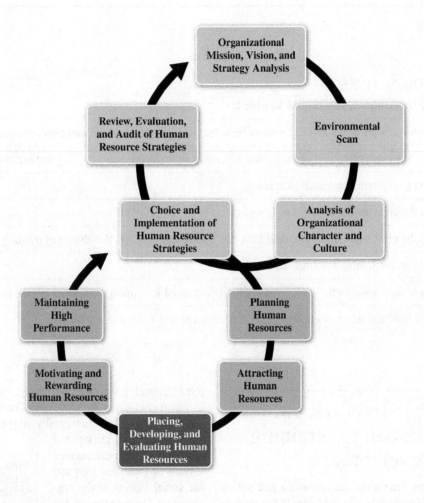

CHAPTER 7

Onboarding, Training and Development, and Career Planning

Research and conventional wisdom both suggest that employees get about 90 days to prove themselves in a new job. The faster new hires feel welcome and prepared for their jobs, the faster they will be able to successfully contribute to the firm's mission.

TALYA BAUER[1]

LEARNING OBJECTIVES

After studying this chapter, you should be able to:

LO1   Explain the key purposes and differences between onboarding, training, and development.

LO2   Describe the orientation and socialization aspects of onboarding and why they are important.

LO3   Describe the systems approach to training.

LO4   Explain different approaches to needs analysis.

LO5   Explain the principles of learning and how this knowledge impacts the choice of training programs.

LO6   Define strategic human resource development.

LO7   Discuss how to assess whether learning actually occurred in training and development programs.

LO8   Describe how human resource departments encourage and assist career planning.

LO1   Strategic Importance of Onboarding, Training, and Development

Given the significant time spent on recruiting and selecting the best possible candidate, the next step in the process is to ensure that the organization uses its talent resources effectively. That means extending a warm welcome to the new hire; helping the employee to understand the organizational mission, vision, values, and how to do his or her job effectively; and communicating ways for the new hire to make continued contributions. The term **onboarding** is used to describe the strategically aligned process of helping new hires adjust quickly and smoothly to the performance aspects of their new jobs and the social aspects of the organization. Once on the job, the gap between employee performance and the job's characteristics and demands may require training. Furthermore,

> **onboarding** The process of integrating and acculturating new employees into the organization and providing them with the tools, resources, and knowledge to become successful and productive.

employees may need development to meet the firm's future strategic objectives.

The onboarding, training, and development functions seek to socialize the new hire to the organization, match what the employee can do with job demands, and tap employee potential for future job roles, all while meeting the employee's career objectives. Although these efforts are time consuming and expensive, they reduce employee turnover, help new employees to be productive sooner, and contribute to overall employee satisfaction.[2]

Successful organizations manage the knowledge held by their workforces and have advanced capacity to learn, adapt, and change in response to their environment. **Knowledge management** can be defined as the process of capturing, distributing, and effectively using knowledge.[3] To do this, HR has a role in facilitating knowledge acquisition, knowledge sharing between employees, and knowledge retention when employees leave or retire from the organization. The goal of the **human resource development (HRD)** function, also referred to as the *training, organizational development,* or *employee development function,* is to establish learning interventions that will enable individuals within organizations to optimally perform current and future jobs.

knowledge management
The process of capturing, distributing, and effectively using knowledge.

human resource development (HRD)
A function of human resource management that integrates the use of onboarding, training, and employee and career development efforts to improve individual, group, and organizational effectiveness.

Especially for quality-oriented, high-performing companies, onboarding, training, and development are critical parts of a firm's overall long-range strategy. An example is EllisDon, one of the winners of Canada's Top 100 Employers to work for:

EllisDon believes that knowledge is a vital resource and must be captured. At the same time, it recognizes that its employees have a thirst for knowledge. EllisDon has bridged these two needs by developing the EllisDon University (EDU). EDU is an in-house training program offering a variety of courses and programs for all employees, ranging from financial management to conflict resolution to Leadership in Environmental and Energy Design (LEED) certification. At EllisDon, employees receive tuition subsidies for courses related to their position and subsidies for professional accreditations. Also available are in-house training programs, online training programs, online employee skills inventories, formal mentoring programs, and career planning services.[4]

In 2016–17, the average amount of money spent on training per employee across industries and organizational size was $889, or 1.39 percent of payroll in Canada.[5] Small organizations with fewer than 500 people tend to spend more on training per employee than medium and large employers. However, large employers may be able to offer more training hours for the same cost due to economies of scale.[6] The average number of hours of training offered each year to employees in Canada is 32.[7] Sectors such as health/pharmaceuticals and technology spend more on average on training and development than sectors such as manufacturing. Onboarding, training, and development dollars are highly correlated with the economy, with greater spending when the economy is strong and sharp cuts to these budgets at the first signs of economic slowdowns.[8] Critics report that Canada has chronically underinvested in job training relative to other nations in the world and that we need to make our training programs more agile and current, with streamlined access.[9]

Whereas the focus of onboarding is clear (i.e., targeted toward new hires), the terms *training* and *development* are often used interchangeably despite several important differences. **Training** prepares people to do their *present* job. It is oriented for the short term to focus on the skills required to perform

training Planned activities aimed to provide employees with enhanced skills to perform their current jobs.

the immediate job or to improve performance of a current job or task. Because of its focus on improving current job performance, training efforts may be prioritized for employees who are not currently performing well.[10] Little benefit may come from providing training to employees who are performing well in their current roles.

Development, on the other hand, prepares employees for *future* jobs. Development efforts may focus on building specific skills but also on competencies for future job roles. It is more about expanding an employee's potential through various learning processes so that that individual can, at some

development Planned activities aimed at providing employees with enhanced skills and competencies for the future.

point, assume a future role. Development may be ongoing and occur through many learning experiences. Although some organizations may seek to develop all employees, others will focus development efforts on those employees determined to have the greatest potential.[11] Figure 7-1 highlights the differences between training and development.

This distinction between training and development is primarily one of intent, with training focusing on the present job and development focusing on the future contributions that an employee will make. The *benefits of training* extend throughout a person's entire career and help develop that person for future responsibilities.

FIGURE 7-1

Differentiating Training and Development

	Training	Development
Time frame	Short term—immediate	Mid- to long term
Focus of activity	Current job—skill development	Future roles and responsibilities, competency development, multiple learning experiences
Who are the participants?	Individuals new to their roles and employees who are underperforming	Individuals who are high performers in their current roles, and those deemed to have future role potential
Goal	Enhance skills in current job	Optimize potential—future developmental/growth opportunities
Examples of methods used	Programmed instruction, role plays, job shadowing, simulation, self-study	Coaching, counselling, mentoring, conferences, case study, simulations, job rotations

The first part of this chapter discusses the concept of onboarding and the key steps involved in the orientation process. The next part discusses the training and development functions and explains how human resource departments support the learning management framework. Finally, the chapter will address how the organization is able to assist employees to develop a progressive career plan.

LO2 Onboarding

Almost a quarter of employees experience some type of career transition each year, and half of new hires leave an organization within the first four months.[12] Canada's employee turnover rate is the fourth highest globally, according to a recent study.[13] To mitigate new employees' feelings of disappointment with their new job and organization, HR professionals must engage and onboard new employees.[14]

Onboarding includes orientation, socialization, and training and development activities. Over 45 percent of firms start their onboarding process when they deliver a job offer,[15] and the process may last throughout the employee's first year.[16] The purpose of these programs is to help employees feel welcome, build relationships with peers and experienced workers, understand the organization's culture, and leverage the skills and talent that a new hire brings.

For the new hire, the onboarding process builds knowledge of the organization at the individual, department, and job level. It is a commitment on the part of an organization to fully integrate employees into an organization. Figure 7-2 provides a comprehensive onboarding model that illustrates the strategic focus of onboarding.

Strategic Importance of Onboarding

If done properly, onboarding can serve several strategic purposes, including the following.

Reduce Employee Turnover

When employees decide to join a firm, they have expectations: If they contribute in a certain way they will receive certain rewards as a result. If these expectations are not managed properly, employees will likely feel dissatisfied and want to leave the organization. As a general rule, turnover costs for first-line employees are between 0.16 and 0.25 times annual salaries; for management employees, between 1 and 1.5 times; and for executives, over double the annual salary.[17] For a large firm, a few thousand dollars may seem inconsequential; but if thousands of employees leave every year, the costs can quickly escalate into millions, as shown in the following example:

At the Royal Bank of Canada, the annual turnover averages 5 percent of its workforce. Compared to the national turnover rate of 16 percent[18] this may look quite reasonable. However, the size of the bank's workforce warrants action to reduce the turnover rate. With a workforce of about 81,000, this means that approximately 4,000 employees leave the bank annually.[19]

When experienced, long-service employees quit, the loss may be incalculable because of the training, knowledge, and skills these workers take with them. Effective onboarding involves managing and meeting employee expectations.

Onboarding Model

ONBOARDING JOURNEY MAP

At Booz Allen, YOU are the organizations' greatest investment. During your first year, you will build relevant skills, have opportunity and choice to forge your own path, and be shown appreciation for your contribution.

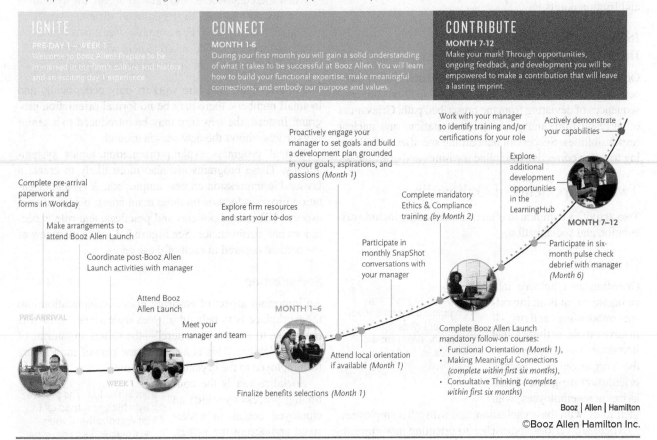

IGNITE	CONNECT	CONTRIBUTE
PRE-DAY 1 – WEEK 1	**MONTH 1-6**	**MONTH 7-12**
Welcome to Booz Allen! Prepare to be immersed in the firm's culture and history and an exciting day 1 experience.	During your first month you will gain a solid understanding of what it takes to be successful at Booz Allen. You will learn how to build your functional expertise, make meaningful connections, and embody our purpose and values.	Make your mark! Through opportunities, ongoing feedback, and development you will be empowered to make a contribution that will leave a lasting imprint.

Complete pre-arrival paperwork and forms in Workday

Make arrangements to attend Booz Allen Launch

Coordinate post-Booz Allen Launch activities with manager

Attend Booz Allen Launch

Meet your manager and team

PRE-ARRIVAL

WEEK 1

Explore firm resources and start your to-dos

Finalize benefits selections *(Month 1)*

Attend local orientation if available *(Month 1)*

MONTH 1–6

Proactively engage your manager to set goals and build a development plan grounded in your goals, aspirations, and passions *(Month 1)*

Participate in monthly SnapShot conversations with your manager

Complete mandatory Ethics & Compliance training *(by Month 2)*

Complete Booz Allen Launch mandatory follow-on courses:
• Functional Orientation *(Month 1)*,
• Making Meaningful Connections *(complete within first six months)*,
• Consultative Thinking *(complete within first six months)*

Work with your manager to identify training and/or certifications for your role

Explore additional development opportunities in the LearningHub

MONTH 7–12

Participate in six-month pulse check debrief with manager *(Month 6)*

Actively demonstrate your capabilities

Booz | Allen | Hamilton

©Booz Allen Hamilton Inc.

Reduce Errors and Save Time

Typically, new employees are less efficient than experienced employees.[20] This factor, combined with other additional costs involved in getting a new employee started (e.g., supervisor's time and attention), makes the **startup costs** of new employees significant. Well-onboarded employees know exactly what is expected of them and are less likely to make mistakes.

> **startup costs** The additional costs associated with a new employee because the new employee is typically less efficient than an experienced worker; the new worker also requires additional supervisory time.

Develop Clear Job and Organizational Expectations

For some jobs, the duties and job expectations are clear. However, for a majority of other jobs, this is simply not the case. There are no clear-cut lists of "desirable" behaviours,

outcomes, and attitudes. Most new employees would like to know what it takes to survive and get ahead in an organization. In the absence of clear guidelines from their employer, they may have to find answers to their questions informally through the grapevine and by chatting with others. Unfortunately, in the latter instance, there is no guarantee that they will find the right answers. Effective onboarding is necessary to properly inform employees what the organization expects of them and what they can expect in return.[21]

Attain Acceptable Job Performance Levels Faster

Spelling out expected job performance standards at the beginning eliminates uncertainty about what is expected on the job, as shown in the following example:

> Employees of companies with longer onboarding programs gain full proficiency 34 percent faster than those with shorter onboarding programs—a difference of four months.[22]

Reduce Employee Anxiety and Increase Organizational Stability

New employees will experience less stress if an organization communicates with new employees openly, clarifies their roles, and familiarizes them with organizational objectives. Communicating policies and regulations to new employees early on clearly reduces undesirable behaviour and friction points.

Reduce Instances of Corrective Discipline Measures and Grievances

Onboarding activities clarify the rights and duties of employees, outline disciplinary regulations, and spell out the consequences of deviating from the prescribed path. Grievances often result from ambiguous job expectations and unclear responsibilities. Successful onboarding specifies both, leading to fewer corrective discipline measures and grievances.

Two Components of Onboarding

Two activities common to effective onboarding include orientation and socialization.

Orientation

Orienting an employee into an organization is an important onboarding activity. It involves those activities that introduce the employee to the organization. Formal **orientation programs** familiarize new employees with their roles, with the organization, and with other employees.

> **orientation programs**
> Programs that familiarize new employees with their roles, the organization, its policies, and other employees.

There are various approaches to orienting new employees. Some organizations conduct orientation on an individual basis, although group orientation programs are used in larger organizations and firms where several employees are hired at the same time. Some organizations assign new hires a *buddy* or *sponsor* who is available to answer any questions they may have and to direct the employee to the appropriate resources.

Cloud-based customer intelligence company Vision Critical uses a buddy system that helps new employees go through onboarding seamlessly. Along with offerings including a four-day leadership program, ringing a cowbell on the sales floor when a deal closes, wheeling out free beer carts, and giving away hockey tickets and flight passes, the buddy system is part of Vision Critical's acclaimed engagement strategy.[23]

The delivery of orientation programs is varied. Some are delivered through the company intranet and others through a combination of online and face-to-face delivery. The length of time devoted to orientation also varies considerably depending on the size of the organization. Consider EllisDon's orientation program:

EllisDon, a large Canadian construction and project management firm, launched an online orientation program. A thousand employees across Canada can now access the system anytime, anywhere, and proceed through the program at their own pace. The orientation system starts with an automatic welcome message that is sent to the new hire's new company email. Then the employee is told how to access the system and review the various modules at different stages within the first year. For example, week two's module for managers is designed to help with information specific to assist them in managing their team.[24]

For employers that hire workers only occasionally and in small numbers, there may be no formal orientation program. Instead, the new hire may be introduced to a senior worker who shows the new person around.

Formal programs explain orientation topics systematically. These programs are also more likely to create a favourable impression on new employees. A typical orientation program focuses on three main areas: organizational aspects, HR-related policies and practices, and role expectations and performance. See Figure 7-3 for an overview of the content covered in each of these areas.

Socialization

An important aspect of ensuring effective integration into the workplace is to help employees understand "what it is really like to work around here"—the values and norms of the organization. This is an important part of introducing the employee to the organization culture.

Socialization is the continuing process by which an employee begins to understand and accept the values, norms, and beliefs held by others in the organization. New employees need to know, accept, and demonstrate behaviours that the organization views as desirable.

> **socialization** The process by which people adapt to an organization through learning and accepting the values, norms, and beliefs held by others in the organization.

During socialization, new hires are expected to build new relationships with their co-workers, get to know and understand the style and personality of their boss and co-workers, and understand the values espoused by the organization. What the employee learns is dependent on the his or her social skills and efforts and the willingness of others to form a relationship with the newcomer.[25]

Socialization involves turning outsiders into insiders and helping the newcomer learn how to effectively fit into the organization. There are formal and informal ways in which employees learn about these norms and values. For example, in some organizations executives meet new hires and discuss the values that are important to the organization and the type of behaviour expected. Some organizations have recognition systems in place, which reinforce and reward employees for demonstrating valued organizational norms. Other socialization techniques are

FIGURE 7-3

Topics Often Covered in Employee Orientation Programs

Organizational Issues

History of employer	Product line or services provided
Organizational structure	Customers and competitors
Names and titles of key executives	Overview of production process
Employee's title and department	Company policies and rules
Layout of physical facilities	Disciplinary regulations
Probationary period	Safety procedures and enforcement
Tour of the locations	Code of conduct

HR-Related Topics

Pay scales and paydays	Employee benefits
Vacations and holidays	Insurance, retirement, employer-provided services
Training and education benefits	EAP services and counselling

Role Expectations and Performance

Job location	Overview of job
Job tasks	Job objectives and accountabilities
Job safety requirements	Relationship to other jobs
	Internal and external customers

much less formal or leverage technology, as the following example shows:

> Roots Canada is taking advantage of its position as a global business to spread its efficiencies across a number of provinces through a new learning management system. The new HR learning system has quickened the onboarding process and trained employees more consistently across all retail locations. Consistent training and a career framework model are two ways that Roots aims to keep its employees loyal to its brand.[26]

Consider the example of an employee being told that the hours of work are 9 a.m. to 5 p.m. but noticing after the first few weeks that no one in the department ever leaves before 6:30 p.m. Although a policy is developed, the actions may be more representative of the culture than the words. During socialization, observing the language, behaviours, dress, and other artifacts at the workplace will provide new hires with many clues on the expected behaviours and norms.

To ensure that orientation and socialization activities are effective, the HR department may seek to gather reactions to such activities and assess the new hires' attitudes (e.g., overall satisfaction with the organization and the job, work motivation, and so on) and behaviours (e.g., labour turnover, ability to carry out roles effectively, spontaneity visible in job performance, and so on). Tracking the extent

to which onboarding materials are accessed as well as cost–benefit studies on orientation and socialization activities should be carried out continually.

In summary, the onboarding process, with related orientation and socialization activities, helps new hires to understand the social, technical, and cultural aspects of the workplace. As new employees are accepted, they become part of the social fabric of the organization. Orientation and socialization programs help speed up the onboarding process and benefit both the employee and the organization.

LO3 Training

Training is an investment in human capital. Canadian companies have to compete in a global economy and in a fast-changing business environment. This requires a workforce with the capability to respond quickly and reliably to new challenges. Below are some examples of how the evolving global economy impacts training requirements:

- Competing globally against companies from countries with low wage levels has forced many Canadian companies to flatten their organizational structure and to reduce the number of employees. A flatter organization—with fewer managers and supervisors—requires employees who are able to schedule their work, manage their team, and do their own quality control. Greater flexibility requires multiskilled (or cross-trained) employees who perform diverse tasks.

- Multiskilled employees prefer to be paid according to their competencies, not jobs performed. This requires a match to the company's compensation and performance appraisal systems. Multiskilled employees have to keep up-to-date on their skills and continue a lifelong learning process. The organizational environment must foster and support this concept.

- Many immigrants come to Canada annually, mostly from Asian countries.[27] This makes it essential that organizations understand the specific training needs of these new arrivals and learn to work with colleagues who hold different cultural values. Other forms of individual differences (e.g., sexual orientation, gender identity) add to the diversity in Canadian workplaces. Diversity and inclusion training helps to alert supervisors and employees to stereotypes and prejudices.

- Changing information technology and mobile technology applications, innovative multimedia training methods, and job-specific technologies require fresh skills, necessitating novel training programs and strategies.

The Training System

An effective training program benefits employees and the organization. Some of the benefits for the employees are skill improvement, self-development and stronger self-confidence, more effective handling of stress and conflicts, and a sense of growth. For the organization, the benefits may include improved profitability through higher productivity, improved morale, better corporate image, lower costs, stronger identification with corporate goals, and fewer demands for managing poor performers, including involuntary turnover.[28]

To develop an effective training program, human resource specialists and managers must assess the needs, objectives, content, and learning principles associated with training. Figure 7-4 shows a training systems approach that describes the sequence of events to be followed before training begins.

LO4 Needs Assessment

To get maximum benefit from training expenditures, HRD must concentrate on those people and situations that can benefit most from such training. **Needs assessment** diagnoses present problems and environmental challenges that can be met through training, or the future challenges to be met through long-term development.

> **needs assessment**
> A diagnosis that presents problems and future challenges that can be met through training or development.

Sometimes a change in the organization's strategy can create a need for training. For example, new products or services usually require employees to learn new procedures. Sales personnel, programmers, and production workers have to be trained to produce, sell, and service a new product line. Training can also be used when high accident rates, low morale and motivation, or other problems are diagnosed.

Regardless of these challenges, needs assessment must consider each person. Needs may be determined by the HRD function, by supervisors, or through self-nomination. HRD specialists may find weaknesses among those who are hired or promoted. Supervisors are another source of recommendations for training. However, supervisors may suggest training to banish troublemakers, "hide" surplus employees who are temporarily expendable, or reward good workers. Because these are not valid reasons for training, the HRD specialists often review supervisory recommendations. Likewise, HR may also review self-nominations to determine whether training is actually needed.

FIGURE 7-4

A Training Systems Approach: Preliminary Steps in Preparing a Training Program

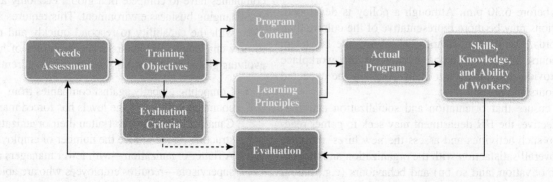

Trainers are alert to other sources of information that may indicate a need for training. Production records, quality control reports, grievances, safety reports, absenteeism and turnover statistics, and exit interviews may indicate problems that should be addressed through training and development efforts. Training needs may also become apparent from career planning and development discussions or performance appraisal reviews, which will be discussed in Chapter 8. Regardless of how needs assessment takes place, it is important because the success of the remaining steps in Figure 7-4 depends on an accurate assessment. If the trainer's assessment of needs is incorrect, training objectives and program content will not match.

Training Objectives

An evaluation of training needs results in training objectives. These statements serve as the standard against which individual performance and the program can be measured. These objectives should state the following:

- Desired behaviour
- Conditions under which training is to occur
- Acceptable performance criteria

Training objectives for an airline reservation agent might be stated as follows:

1. Provide flight information to call-in customers within 30 seconds.
2. Complete a one-city, round-trip reservation in 120 seconds after all information is obtained from the customer.

Objectives such as these give the trainer and the trainee specific goals that can be used by both to evaluate their

© PJF Military Collection/Alamy Stock Photo

Soldiers in the armed forces go through intensive and vigorous training exercises with clear training objectives. To what extent can the knowledge needed in the armed forces be taught in classrooms, via digital learning sources, or in simulations? Can some skills and knowledge only be learned through field experience?

success. If these objectives are not met, failure gives the human resource department feedback on the program and the participants.

Program Content

The program's content is shaped by the needs assessment and the learning objectives. This content may seek to teach specific skills, provide needed knowledge, or try to influence attitudes. Whatever the content, the program must meet the needs of the organization and the participants. If company goals are not furthered, resources are wasted. Similarly, participants must view the content as relevant to their needs, or their motivation to learn may be low.

LO5   Learning Principles

Perhaps the best way to understand learning is through the use of a **learning curve**, pictured in Figure 7-5. As the curve illustrates, learning takes place in bursts (from points A to B) and in plateaus (from points B to C). Trainers have two goals related to the shape of each employee's curve. First, they want it to reach a satisfactory level of performance, shown as a dashed line in the figure. Second, they want the curve to get to that level as quickly as possible.

> **learning curve** A visual representation of the rate at which one learns given material.

Although the rate at which an individual learns depends upon the person, the use of various learning principles helps speed up the learning process. **Learning principles** are guidelines to the ways that people learn most effectively. The more they are included in training, the more effective training is likely to be.

> **learning principles** Guidelines to the ways people learn most effectively.

FIGURE 7-5

A Typical Learning Curve

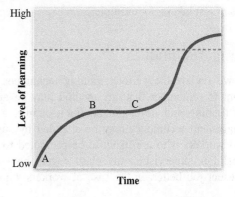

The principles are participation, repetition, relevance, transference, and feedback.

- *Participation.* Learning is usually quicker and more long-lasting when the learner can participate actively. As a result of participation, we learn more quickly and retain that learning longer. For example, once they have learned, most people never forget how to ride a bicycle or drive a car.

- *Repetition.* Although it is seldom fun, repetition apparently etches a pattern into our memory. Studying for an examination, for example, involves memorization of key ideas to be recalled during the test. Likewise, most people learned the alphabet and the multiplication tables by repetition.

- *Relevance.* Learning is helped when the material to be learned is meaningful. For example, trainers usually explain the overall purpose of a job to trainees before explaining specific tasks. This explanation allows the worker to see the relevance of each task and the importance of following the given procedures.

- *Transference.* **Transference** is the application of training to actual job situations. The closer the demands of the training program match the demands of the job, the faster a person learns to master the job. For example, pilots are usually trained in flight simulators because the simulators very closely resemble the actual cockpit and flight characteristics of the plane. The close match between the simulator and the plane allows the trainee to quickly transfer the learning in the simulator to actual flight conditions.

> **transference**
> Applicability of training to job situations; evaluated by how readily the trainee can transfer the learning to his or her job.

- *Feedback.* Feedback gives learners information on their progress. With feedback, motivated learners can adjust their behaviour to achieve the quickest possible learning curve. Without feedback, learners cannot gauge their progress and may become discouraged. Test grades are feedback on the study habits of test takers, for example.

Training Techniques

Before we review the various training techniques, it is important to remember that any method may be applied to both training and development. For example, a class on management techniques may be attended by supervisors and workers who are likely to be promoted to those positions. For supervisors, the class covers how to do their present job better. In the case of workers who have no management responsibilities, the classes are intended to develop them into supervisors. The classroom instruction would be identical for both groups, but with two different purposes: training for supervisors and development for workers.

In selecting a particular training technique, there are several trade-offs. That is, no one technique is always best; the choice of method depends upon the following:

1. Cost-effectiveness
2. Desired program content
3. Appropriateness of the facilities
4. Trainee preferences and capabilities
5. Trainer preferences and capabilities
6. Learning principles

The importance of these six trade-offs depends upon the situation. For example, cost-effectiveness may be a minor factor when training an airline pilot in emergency manoeuvres. Trainee preferences may be very important to certain employee demographics. For example, the Millennial and X generations may be more savvy with social networking than members of other generations. Mobile learning technologies may be better suited for this demographic than for broader demographics.[29]

Equally as important as the type of technique is the delivery of that technique. Today many organizations are using digital learning platforms, apps, and learning management systems to deliver the content online in various types of formats. These formats can be a combination with some face-to-face training and some online training; they can be delivered solely online, all online, or as a hybrid (partially online and partially in class), which may be most effective.[30] They can be suited for mobile technology (e.g., smartphones or tablets) or created in a virtual reality/augmented reality format.

On-the-Job Training

On-the-job training (OJT) is received directly on the job and is used primarily to teach workers how to do their present job. A trainer, supervisor, or co-worker serves as the instructor. This method includes each of the five learning principles (participation, repetition, relevance, transference, and feedback) in a series of carefully planned steps.

First, the participant receives an overview of the job, its purpose, and the desired outcomes, which emphasize the relevance of the training. Then the trainer demonstrates the job to provide the employee with a model to copy. Since the employee is being shown the actions the job actually requires, the training is transferable. Next, the employee is allowed to mimic the trainer's example. Demonstrations by the trainer and practice by the trainee are repeated until the job is mastered by the trainee. Repeated demonstrations and practice provide the advantage of repetition and feedback. This training can be delivered digitally where appropriate. Common digital methods include instructional videos and interactive simulations. Finally, the employee performs the job without supervision, although the trainer may visit the employee periodically to see if there are any lingering questions.

Job Rotation

As discussed in Chapter 2, to cross-train employees in a variety of jobs some trainers will move the trainee from job to job. Besides giving workers variety in their jobs, **cross-training** helps the organization when vacations, absences, and resignations occur. Learner participation and high job transferability are the learning advantages to job rotation.

> **cross-training** Training employees to perform operations in areas other than their assigned jobs.

Apprenticeships and Coaching

Apprenticeships, discussed in Chapter 4, involve learning from a more experienced employee or employees. Most tradespeople, such as plumbers, carpenters, and chefs, are trained through formal apprenticeship programs. Assistantships and internships are similar to apprenticeships. These approaches use high levels of participation by the trainee and have high transferability to the job.

Coaching is similar to apprenticeship in that the coach attempts to provide a model for the trainee to copy. Most companies use some coaching, especially for leadership development. Coaching tends to be less formal than an apprenticeship program because there are few formal classroom sessions, and the coaching is provided when needed rather than as part of a carefully planned program. More than half of all coaches come from outside the organization[31] with the remainder typically being supervisors and management. Participation, feedback, and job transference are likely to be high in this form of learning.

Off-the-Job Training

Lectures and Video Presentations

Lectures and other off-the-job techniques tend to rely more heavily on communications than on modelling, which is used in on-the-job programs. These approaches are applied in both training and development. Presenting a lecture is a popular approach because it offers relative economy and a meaningful organization of materials. However, participation, feedback, transference, and repetition are often low. Feedback and participation can be improved when discussion is permitted after the lecture. The lecture can be delivered digitally or face-to-face. Instructor-led classroom learning remains the dominant delivery method for formal learning in Canada with 48 percent of all training taking this form.[32]

Job Labs and Simulations

So that training does not disrupt normal operations, some organizations use job lab training or simulations. Separate areas or vestibules are set up with the same kind of equipment that will be used on the job. This arrangement allows transference, repetition, and participation. The meaningful organization of materials and feedback are also possible:

> At the corporate training facilities of Best Western, the job lab duplicates a typical motel room, a typical front desk, and a typical restaurant kitchen. This allows trainees to practise housekeeping, front-desk service, and kitchen skills without disrupting the operations of any one property. More recently, Best Western has invested in virtual reality training at select properties, and reports tangible boosts in guest satisfaction.[33]

Simulation exercises involve a mechanical simulator that replicates the major features of the work situation. Driving simulators used in driver's education programs are an example. This training method is similar to job lab training, except that the simulator more often provides instantaneous feedback on performance.

Role-Playing

Role-playing is a method that forces trainees to assume different identities. Role-plays are commonly used in sales training for dealing with difficult customers and to enhance communication. For example, a male worker and a female supervisor may trade roles. The result? Usually participants exaggerate each other's behaviour. Ideally, they both get to see themselves as others see them. This technique seeks to change attitudes of trainees (such as racial understanding) and help them develop interpersonal skills. Although participation and feedback are present, the inclusion of other learning principles depends on the situation.

> **role-playing** A training technique that requires trainees to assume different identities in order to learn how others feel under different circumstances.

> The RCMP in British Columbia used role-playing exercises to reduce tensions between members of the force who are of Caucasian and Indian (mainly Sikh) origin. Friction between members of the different cultures on the force had caused breakdowns in communications. The role-playing exercises required a small number of members of the two groups to assume the role of the other race. Through these exercises and subsequent discussions, members of the different cultural groups were able to learn how their behaviour and attitudes affected each other. As a variation on role-playing, the RCMP in Regina recently posted job ads for contract scenario actors to assist in their Cadet training.[34]

Case Study

By studying a case, trainees learn about real or hypothetical circumstances and the actions others took under those circumstances. Besides learning from the content of the case, trainees can develop decision-making skills. When cases are meaningful and similar to work-related situations, there is some transference. There also is the advantage of participation through discussion of the case. Feedback and repetition, however, are usually lacking. This technique is most effective for developing problem-solving skills.

Self-Study and Programmed Learning

Carefully planned instructional materials can be used to train and develop employees. These are particularly useful when employees are dispersed geographically or when learning requires little interaction. Self-study techniques range from manuals to prerecorded videos or webcasts. The learning in this case is more knowledge-based and the employees learn at their own pace.

Programmed learning materials are another form of self-study. Commonly, these are printed booklets or online systems similar to the Connect and LearnSmart technology that accompany this textbook. These materials contain a series of questions and answers. After a question is read, the answer can be uncovered immediately. If the reader is correct, he or she proceeds. If incorrect, the reader is directed to review accompanying materials. Programmed materials provide learning participation, repetition, relevance, and feedback.

Digital Learning

Most of the above techniques can be delivered digitally. The terms *Web-based training, virtual education,* and *elearning* all refer to the same concept: training or education delivered digitally. An intranet is a private and internal business network that enables employees to share information, collaborate, and improve their communications within an organization. Advantages of an intranet over the Internet include allowing for self-pacing, the storing of individual progress, the organizational ability to track progress and training completion, the central updating of materials, and the ensuring of secure content.

Singapore's United Overseas Bank has over 500 offices in 19 countries. The bank has initiated a digital training program called "i-learn." It is a virtual campus that has internally developed best practices. It also interfaces with external specialists and a suite of elearning modules created around key workplace skills.[35]

In a recent survey, 79 percent of training leaders indicated that offering multiple training modalities is vital to their success. For instance, creating training information that can be accessed via mobile apps and digitally and also through job aids and simulations will help employees consume the training information and drive behaviour change.[36] There are many different options when providing digital delivery:

Self-paced portal: The program may be accessed via a portal (e.g., Sharepoint) and the user interacts with only one specific program.

Performance support: Trainees may have access to various databases, online tools, and discussion forums that help them work through the training material.

Synchronous: Trainees and trainers meet at a predetermined time. Demonstrations are displayed to the class with real-time access.

Asynchronous: Here, trainees and trainers interact using email, chat, and discussion forums. Class materials are posted on a bulletin board or by uploading lecture notes. It is accessible anytime, but trainees and the trainer are not necessarily present at the same time. Applications such as Illuminate allow students to interact with the trainer with discussions recorded in an audio file so that the student can replay the content at another time.

© VirTra, Inc.

Trainees using virtual reality equipment train in a three-dimensional environment. In the system pictured above, trainees use their real weapons, modified with lasers, and can deploy supplemental equipment like TASERS® and mace. They'll be asked to explain their choices after the simulation ends. What types of jobs might virtual reality technology be useful for?

Virtual reality/augmented reality also has application to training. Using realistic three-dimensional visual impressions of the actual work environment, it allows trainees to respond to job requirements as though they worked on the job. It also allows companies to prepare trainees for job experiences that normally would involve high costs (e.g., flying an airplane), have the risk of costly damage to equipment (e.g., landing a helicopter on a deck), or have the potential for injuries to the trainee (e.g., armed police situations).[37]

> **virtual reality/augmented reality** Use of modern computer technology to create a 3D environment.

Simulation provides real-time interactions, and a trainee can simulate using many different modes: sensory, tactile, audio, and so on. However, while simulation deals with certain aspects of the job, virtual reality can augment real aspects of the job with artificial ones. The trainee works in a three-dimensional space and is able to interact with and manipulate objects in real time.

> Wal-Mart uses virtual reality to aid training its managers and specialists. The simulations range from recreating Black Friday crowds to placing managers behind deli counters to inspect for issues such as food contamination.
>
> KFC provides a virtual reality (VR) experience that terrifies and entertains while teaching serious business.[38] View the trailer for this VR training experience that no KFC employee is likely to forget.

Popular Digital Tools

There are several simple yet powerful tools that have been developed to facilitate the acquisition of learning. Some of these tools merely assist learning while others encourage collaboration and enable the learner to contribute to an existing knowledge base:

Blogs: Created by an individual or an organization, training **blogs** may contain comments, graphics, and videos, and are often interactive, allowing trainees to post comments on the material displayed. Some companies use blogs to enhance communication and its corporate culture, others for training and development purposes. The advantage of a blog is that trainees can choose the material they want to study.

> **blogs** Web logs—online journals, diaries, or serials published by a person or group of people.

RSS (Rich Site Summary): RSS is a format for delivering regularly changing Web content. Many news-related sites, blogs, and other online publishers syndicate their content as an RSS feed to whoever subscribes to it. It saves time by allowing users to retrieve the latest information from several sites without having to visit individual sites or rely on a newsletter.

Webcasts: Trainers can use this form of multimedia publishing to include audio or video clips that are automatically delivered to organization members or subscribers. Subscribers can then hand-pick the material they want to observe and have future episodes sent to their device without taking any further action. Webcasting is becoming increasingly popular in education. It enables students and instructors to share information with anyone at any time. An absent student can download the webcast of the missed lesson. It can be a tool for instructors or administrators to communicate curriculum, assignments, and other information. Instructors can record team discussions and interviews and use it even with embedded slides.

> Computer storage leader DellEMC produces 5–10 webcasts in a week for its employees. Using an RSS feed, employees subscribe to their favourite casts and can listen to them while travelling to client meetings.[39]

Wikis: Hawaiian for "quick," a **wiki** is a webpage with information available to everyone that also allows the reader to contribute to or change the information content. The collaborative encyclopedia Wikipedia is one of the best-known wikis. Wikis are used in business to create intranets and knowledge management systems.

> **wiki** A type of server program that allows multiple users to contribute to a website.

Social Networking Websites: Organizations are using social networks for information exchange, training and development, enhancing corporate culture, and motivating employees. Consider the following examples to illustrate how companies are developing their employees with digital sources and social networking:

> Global Knowledge, a leader in business and IT training, in conjunction with Deloitte, a leading professional services firm, was awarded gold honours by the Canadian Society for Training and Development (CSTD) for their Managers 1 and 2 programs. These programs are designed to prepare the new managers to increase their confidence and capability. The program offers originality, instructional design, virtual class elearning, self-paced elearning, live labs, and a knowledge centre that includes webinars, blogs, mobile apps, and special reports. The programs focus on the day-to-day realities that new managers face and provide them with the tools to manage these situations using technology.[40]

Spotlight *on* HRM

Using MOOCs in Corporate Training

Given the popularity of using massive open online courses (MOOCs) in higher education, it is no wonder that training executives and chief learning officers are excited about their potential in corporate settings.

MOOCs at AT&T

In 2013 AT&T partnered with MOOC-provider Udacity Inc. and Georgia Tech University to create one of the first accredited degree programs using the MOOC teaching model. With significantly lower tuition costs than an on-campus master's degree and tuition covered by the company, more than 200 AT&T employees have registered in the MOOC format Master's in Computer Science program.

The company needs more skilled software and network engineers to meet its evolving business in wireless, cloud-based products and services, and MOOCs can deliver leading-edge knowledge in those areas. AT&T senior vice president of human resources, Scott Smith, said, "The MOOCs are a complement to the training we deliver internally, and they enable employees to access content 24/7 in ways that fit their work schedules and lifestyles. The format gives us a way to provide additional learning that in some cases may be too expensive to do internally, or when we may not have the instructors or content that a Georgia Tech or Udacity can offer."

Corporate MOOC Design

The key to MOOC success in the corporate domain may rest with motivated learners and MOOC design. Corporate learners may not seek to complete full courses, but rather seek information to address a specific issue or problem they are facing at work. Learners will engage in the MOOC for only the portions providing the knowledge they seek. In organizations where MOOC completion is desired, some companies may provide "badges" for corporate profiles (e.g., AT&T) or certificates (Yahoo).

Funding from the Bill & Melinda Gates Foundation has been provided to create new MOOC models for business. The focus is on bringing the best instruction from academia in leadership development and STEM skills—science, technology, engineering, and math—to the workplace. The goal is to close the gap between critical STEM skills needed by their workforces and the skills new college graduates have.

Open University in the United Kingdom is pioneering a structure with promise for corporate settings as well. Through their design, it is possible to have trainees attend a MOOC with 10,000 people, but engage the dialogue and peer collaboration behind a company's firewall with only the people from that company participating. The assessment and collaboration are done inside the company's walls with the course instructions shared across many companies.

Business MOOCs will continue to evolve as corporate trainers take the best aspects of MOOCs from the post-secondary setting and innovate for corporate training effectiveness.

MOOCs and Nanodegrees: As discussed in the Spotlight on HRM, MOOCs and other digital learning courses are changing the nature of training options. Companies such as Lynda.com (purchased by LinkedIn for $1.5 billion in 2015[41]) and Udacity (founded by the same founder as Google X, of famed projects including the self-driving car and Google Glass) are revolutionizing education for aspiring learners around the globe.[42] For instance, at Udacity, trainees can earn nanodegrees in Flying Cars and Autonomous Flight, Robotics Software Engineering, and VR Development. Although MOOCs started out as free education sources, other digital learning offerings charge course-based fees.

Benefits and Challenges of Digital Learning

Advances in digital learning offerings have increased the options available to HR specialists for training and development of their workforces. When deciding upon delivery, specialists have options that range from developing custom programs in house, to tailoring off-the-shelf programs, to determining outside offerings in which to enroll their staff. In addition to delivery modalities, there has been a fundamental shift in understanding how people learn from a one-size-fits-all approach toward a more individual, learner-centred approach, where the learning materials can be adjusted to the learner's needs and preferences. The ability to provide "just-in-time" training or information allows the learner to learn when it is convenient and to target the instruction to what the learner needs to know, when he or she needs to know it. Digital training can offer the learner significant flexibility in terms of pace of content and various media-rich options. Advances in EDTech applications and platforms are sure to bring even greater options in the near future.[43]

Figure 7-6 shows adoption rates of new technologies in training by large Canadian firms. Notably, there are some trends in the types of training across sectors. IT/telecom companies use MOOCs more often than other sectors. Gamification—the use of rules, competition, and teamwork to encourage engagement by mimicking games—is most heavily used in the services sector.[44]

LO6 Employee Development

Employee development helps to prepare the employee to assume greater responsibilities and authority, often in formal leadership positions. Its focus is on developing competencies and skills that will enable the employee to be successful in a future role in the organization. Employee development does not always entail learning something new; the focus can also be on taking what the employee has already learned and applying it in innovative ways or to new levels of mastery.[45]

Many development programs focus on developing competencies, defined in Chapter 2. A competency approach allows management and employees to pinpoint unique personal and organizational characteristics that make the company successful in achieving a competitive advantage. For example, key competencies for a manager would be demonstrating a "results oriented" approach and development of coaching skills, and key competencies for HR professionals would be demonstrating that they are a "trusted adviser" and exhibit "strategic orientation." An advantage of using the competency framework is the opportunity for employees to understand what competencies are needed to get to the next level or to perform in a way that adds value to the business.

The Conference Board of Canada developed an "Employability Skills Profile," listing critical skills required for success in current and future jobs in three different areas: fundamental skills, personal management skills, and teamwork skills (see Figure 7-7). This document identifies for students and educators what skills and competencies are critical for employers today. It signals to educators to build awareness, practice, and evaluation of these skills into their programs so the students are ready

---

FIGURE 7-6

Use of Technologies by Large Canadian Firms

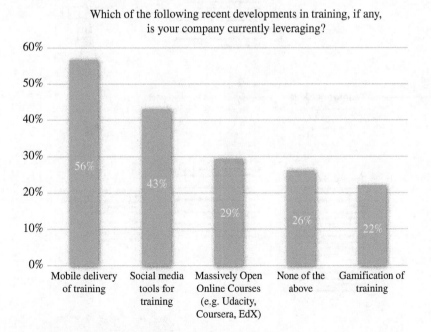

Which of the following recent developments in training, if any, is your company currently leveraging?

Mobile delivery of training	Social media tools for training	Massively Open Online Courses (e.g. Udacity, Coursera, EdX)	None of the above	Gamification of training
56%	43%	29%	26%	22%

SOURCE: Aon Hewitt (2016, March), "Developing Canada's future workforce: A survey of large private-sector employers."

FIGURE 7-7

Employability Skills Profile: The Critical Skills Required of the Canadian Workforce

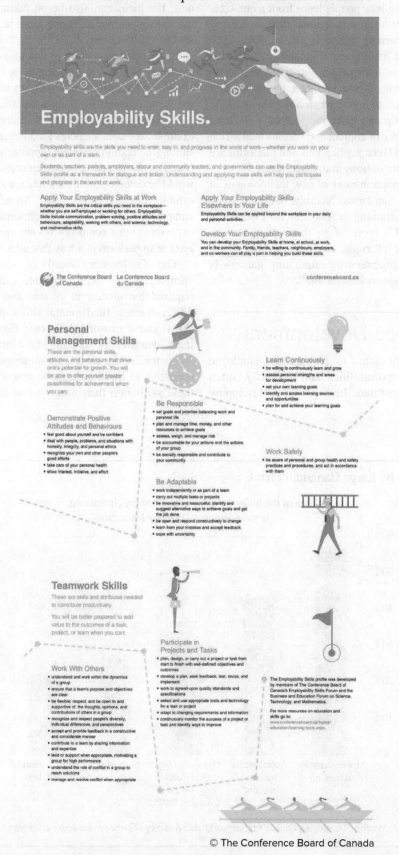

© The Conference Board of Canada

for the workforce. Notably, emphasis is placed on interpersonal skills, such as communication and working with others, but also on the ability to think and learn, two crucial requirements for the future of more complex jobs.

Strategic Human Resource Development—Linking Employee Development to Business Strategy

Strategic human resource development is the identification of essential job skills and the management of employees' learning for the long-range future in relation to explicit corporate and business strategies.[46] Sixty-three percent of Canadian executives agree that having talent management processes closely linked to business strategy is critical to help an organization achieve its goals.[47]

> **strategic human resource development** The identification of needed skills and active management of employees' learning in relation to corporate strategies.

To prepare a pool of developed employees to meet future organizational challenges and opportunities, many organizations will focus a segment of their HR department on talent development, or establish a specific talent management group tasked with this responsibility. There may be specific policies and practices developed to manage employees with high and/or critical levels of talent (e.g., knowledge, skills, and abilities) that add value to the organization.[48] Managing development of future talent requires senior leaders to commit financial resources to talent development, even if there is no short-term payoff. Talent development makes good business sense, as these activities contribute to the creation of a robust and diverse talent pool from which the organization can draw when resources are needed. Research has indicated that organizations that invest in their employees' development have higher performance (including profitability, productivity, and lower costs) and higher retention, and employees themselves experience greater job satisfaction and commitment to the organization.[49]

One of the key development decisions is deciding which employees to develop. Some organizations have focused on developing employees deemed to have high future potential from primarily within the management ranks or in key positions. For instance, one strategy is to develop the top 10 percent of employees deemed to have the highest potential.[50] Other organizations have spread development efforts more broadly by giving all employees a little development rather than focusing all development money into extensive development of only a few. There are advantages and disadvantages to both approaches. Those receiving development may anticipate compensation benefits to accompany their expanding breadth of skills and expect future promotions. With fewer positions available at higher ranks, more people developed may mean more disappointed employees when compensation and promotion expectations are not met.

On the other hand, some employees may emerge as having high future potential only following development efforts. Other key factors include talent shortages (i.e., putting development into hard-to-fill positions) and retention of high performers. Talent managers must balance these considerations when determining with top management which employees to develop.[51]

Steps to Create Employee Development Plans

There are several steps to consider when developing an employee development plan, as outlined below:

1. *Assess employees' needs.* The first step toward creating a plan is to understand the employees' interests and the type of work they are most interested in doing. To obtain information about employees' needs, HR managers have access to several sources. An employee's performance appraisal is one; using an assessment centre that would provide interest and ability testing is another. A third is engaging the employee in a career planning discussion, as will be discussed later in this chapter.

2. *Link competencies and skills to business goals.* Organizations seek to develop employees in accord with their business goals. In other words, the organization should benefit from the development. For example, if the organization seeks to implement a new system, and an employee has good project management skills and wants to develop them in a larger scope, then the organization will be interested in helping to develop such skills. Typically, an objective is written and measurable terms specified. For example, "Ashlyn needs to learn to manage projects greater than $1 million in revenue by the first quarter of next year."

3. *Identify learning and development activities.* This relates to which activities and learning methods the organization chooses to offer. To choose applicable methods, the HR or talent manager must consider the type of development that would be appropriate.

4. *Determine resources.* This step focuses on who will be involved, what the costs will be, how much time should be set aside, and what support is needed to ensure success.

5. *Identify barriers.* As with any plan there may be obstacles. Consideration must be given to any hurdles that the employee may face and how best to manage them.[52]

Developmental Strategies—Identifying Learning and Development Activities

The types of development activities to offer will depend on whether the areas to develop are cognitive, behavioural, or environmental in nature.[53] Figure 7-8 describes examples of instruments and programs that are used in each developmental strategy.

Training and Development Strategies

Strategies	Definition	Instruments/Programs
Cognitive	Being concerned with altering thoughts and ideas (knowledge, new processes)	Articles, lectures, videos, university courses, management seminars
Behavioural	Attempting to change behaviour (e.g., management/interpersonal style)	Role-playing, behaviour modelling, sensitivity training, outdoor adventures, team building, mentoring, coaching
Environmental	Strategies to change attitudes and values	Job rotation, the learning organization, temporary assignments, employee exchange programs, project team, internal consulting, cross-cultural management training, diversity and inclusion training

The *cognitive strategy* is part of the ongoing information-sharing process necessary in an organization, the adaptable skills needed in a fast-changing business environment. Cognitive development implies constant learning and upgrading. However, methods used in the cognitive strategy tend to be relatively passive: lectures, seminars, and academic education. This approach fulfills at least part of the definition of employee development: It adds to the value of the person by increasing his or her knowledge and expertise. However, it does little to change a person's behaviour, attitudes, and values—important elements of an employee's development. Unfortunately, this seems to be the dominant strategy in employee development.

The ideal organizational setting continuously reinforces desirable behaviour, the second of the development strategies. Desirable behaviour includes the appropriate management style (modelled after top management and being part of the corporate culture), proper leadership style (strongly influenced by the CEO), type of communication, conflict resolution, and interaction with customers.

Behavioural strategies aim at making individuals more competent in interacting with their environment, for example, with colleagues, subordinates, or customers. Some common instruments or programs used in this strategy are outlined below:

- *Behaviour modelling* teaches a desired behaviour effectively by providing the trainee with a vivid and detailed display of desirable behaviour by a manager (the model), often with strong social reinforcement.

- *Sensitivity/mindfulness training* is considered a very effective method for making managers more aware of the impact of their own behaviour on others or to prepare them for more effective interactions with staff in foreign subsidiaries or joint ventures.[54]

To increase their gender and racial diversity, Google has put more than 60,000 of its employees around the world through unconscious bias training. Their goal is to make people aware of the negative and positive stereotypes they hold in their subconscious. Take a look at the training at https://www.businessinsider.com/google-unconscious-bias-training-presentation-2015-12

- *Team building* helps team members to diagnose group processes and devise solutions to problems. There are many different types of team-building exercises. Using team-related activities that take place outdoors or in the wilderness are popular (e.g., mountain climbing, whitewater rafting, even surviving in a jungle). The objective is to develop a strong team spirit and to help people learn how to maximize their strengths and stretch their potential.[55]

© Pixtal/AGE Fotostock

Many companies are sending their employees on outdoor exercises to build teamwork and trust. How can whitewater rafting, go-carting, or rock-climbing develop employees and increase trust in a team?

- *Mentoring* involves establishing a close relationship with a boss or someone more experienced who takes a personal interest in the employee's career and who guides and sponsors it. The person being mentored is less experienced than the mentee but not necessarily younger. There are formal and informal relationships that can exist. Formal mentorships are established by the organization, typically by HR, and there is a formal process as to who is assigned to a mentor. Informal mentor arrangements are spontaneous and arise due to the common interests of both parties.

Zynga, developer of some of the world's most popular social games, including FarmVille and CSR Racing 2, has made mentoring an integral part of its development process. Hires start with onboarding mentoring, transition into mentoring that promotes workplace flexibility and career progress, and then become mentors themselves. It's a perpetual cycle of knowledge transfer with great outcomes for the company.

The *environmental approach* is concerned with providing the organizational setting in which employees can thrive and develop. Here is an example of how effective this approach can be:

The Great Little Box Company (GLBC) began in 1982 as a small enterprise with seven employees in Vancouver, British Columbia, but has grown into one of the largest folding carton plants in western Canada. What made the company so successful? Robert Meggy, the owner, says, "Everything we do has to be by people who are well motivated. I see it in the bottom line for us. Turnover is very low. If you've got people who enjoy working together, they don't leave."

Robert's "people first" approach includes improving teamwork and boosting morale by applying the principles of open-book management. It is designed to get employees involved in running the company. At monthly meetings, management shares all corporate and financial information. In the beginning, Robert had to explain what a balance sheet was and the implications of a high or low income-to-debt ratio. He wants every employee to know how the company is doing and why. "Everyone works together to reach the same target," says maintenance manager Philip Lim. "The company cares about the employees and, in turn, the employees care about the company."[56] It will come as no surprise that GLBC was chosen again in 2018 to be among Canada's 100 Top Employers.

The environmental approach seems to be the most promising developmental strategy. It involves a variety of methods, such as the following:

- *Job rotation* is extremely useful in offering employees exposure to different business areas and gaining

fresh perspectives on existing roles as employees are rotated through.

Sun Life Financial's Rotational Leadership Development Program gives graduates the opportunity to rotate through three different roles over a three-year period, in Toronto, Montreal, and Waterloo, Ontario. According to Sandy Delamere, vice-president of HR, "By placing new graduates in a rotation program, we knew we would be able to accelerate their development and build the kind of leaders we need to fill key roles in the future. We wanted to offer our participants a journey so they could explore different roles, business units and functions—all with the hope that they could eventually be in a role best-suited for them as an individual."[57]

- *The learning organization* creates a knowledge network where employees can share ideas and learn more about content that is important to their development.

- *Temporary assignments* allow management trainees to gain valuable special experiences they could not have had in one job (e.g., a salesperson assigned for a period of time to the engineering department to assist in the development of a saleable product).

- *Employee exchange programs* have been implemented by companies such as Bell Canada, IBM, and Xerox, and the federal government of Canada. Usually, a manager takes a one-year leave (either paid or unpaid, depending on the arrangement with the host organization, with the stipulation that the exchange manager does not lose money) and joins another organization. The manager, the host, and the parent organization all tend to gain from this experience.

- *Project teams* bring employees together from different functional areas to work on a project or solve a particular problem for the set duration. For example, when IBM developed the personal computer, it put together a project team whose members were independent from their functional units. This strategy allows for a highly concentrated effort.[58]

- *Internal consulting (or troubleshooting assignments)* allows organizational needs and individual development needs to be combined simultaneously. For example, an expert in management information systems may assist the human resource department in developing a human resource information system, not only enhancing the effectiveness of the department but also gaining valuable personal experience.

- *Lateral transfer* is the movement of an employee from one position to another in the same class but under another supervisor or in another department. It can also refer to the movement of an employee to a position in a different class that has the same level of duties, responsibility, and salary.

- *Job redefinition/reclassification* allows management—with the consent of the job incumbent—to change an employee's job responsibilities, often to avoid a layoff.

- *Cross-cultural management training* prepares employees to work in a different cultural environment.

- *Diversity and inclusion training* deals specifically with removing employment barriers and improving work environments for people from four designated groups: women, people with disabilities, Indigenous peoples, and visible minorities. More broadly, inclusion training teaches skills and provides knowledge about how to make all workers feel included and valued within a workplace, regardless of their individual differences. This also includes gender identity and sexual orientation in addition to the four designated groups. A focus on inclusion, the deliberate act of welcoming diversity, is relatively new compared to diversity training and is becoming the focus of such training (for a more detailed discussion, see Chapter 4).

LO7 Evaluation of Training and Development

Did Learning Actually Take Place?

Training and development serve as transformational processes. Untrained employees are transformed into capable workers, and present workers may be trained to assume new responsibilities. To verify the program's success, human resource managers increasingly demand that training activities be evaluated systematically.

A lack of evaluation may be the most serious flaw in most training efforts. Simply stated, human resource professionals too seldom ask, "Did the program achieve the objectives established for it?"

They often assume it had value because the content seemed important. Or trainers may rely on the evaluation of trainees who comment on how enjoyable the experience was for them but who cannot yet determine how valuable it is.

To determine whether the training was successful there are four types of evaluation criteria that can be used to assess training outcomes:[59]

1. *Reaction.* Also known as the happiness or smile sheet, participant reactions are the most widely used criteria in training evaluation. The usual question asked is, "How satisfied are you with the program?" or "Would you recommend it to a colleague?" This measure evaluates the setup of the program, but not its effectiveness. However, it can provide valuable information for the organizers of programs as to the proper training environment, seating arrangement, satisfaction with training facilities, food, and accommodation.

2. *Knowledge/Skill.* Consider the learning aspect—what skills and knowledge were acquired? To evaluate whether knowledge/skills were acquired, a popular method is to give trainees a test at the end of a training program. There are inherent problems with this method. We do not know whether a high score was because the training was effective, or whether the trainees were already experienced and knew the material beforehand, in which case they did not need the training in the first place.

A more effective approach is the pre-test/post-test design, in which the instructor applies tests at the beginning and at the end of the training program to measure first the precondition (baseline characteristic) of the participants and then the outcome:

$$O \qquad T \qquad O$$
(observation/   (training)   (repeat observation/
test)   test)

3. *Behaviour.* Here we look at the "actions" of an employee to assess behavioural change. For example, if the employee is expected to learn to be more collaborative, do the individuals who interact with this employee observe this change? For the measurement of behaviour change, self-reports and observations by others are used (e.g., neutral observers, superiors, peers, subordinates, or customers). Supervisor observation of behaviour change is more effective, but this approach has an inherent weakness. It is usually the supervisor who sends the employee to the training program and, because of this, is less likely to admit that he or she made an error in judgment.

4. *Organizational Results.* Organizational results would be ideal measurements were it not for the difficulty in determining the cause–effect relationship between training programs and organizational results. The time difference between a training program and the availability of reports on organizational results can be many months. Who is then to say whether it was the training program or some other event that caused the results?

The ideal training evaluation would use evidence on each of these four criteria to determine training effectiveness.

Another approach to evaluating the effectiveness of a training program is to use a cost–benefit analysis. A training investment should be treated like any other investment decision and be subject to a **cost–benefit analysis**. Such an analysis assesses the cost-effectiveness of a project or program. It also assists a trainer or talent manager in demonstrating the contribution the training or department makes to the organization's profit.

cost–benefit analysis Analysis undertaken to assess the cost-effectiveness of a project or program.

Contributions to profit can be made through increasing revenues or by decreasing expenditures, according to this formula:

$$\text{Revenue} - \text{Costs} = \text{Profit}$$

Spotlight *on* ETHICS

Was It Really That Good?

A training specialist is asked by his human resource manager to give her an assessment of the effectiveness of the company's training programs for a report to the president, who wants to know "how much bang we get for our training buck." The HR manager was a benefits officer prior to her promotion and knows little about training techniques and evaluation; the president has a sales background. The programs are usually offered in a nearby resort hotel very much liked by the trainees.

So far, the training specialist has assessed training outcomes through reaction measurements because they were cheap and easy to do, and, more importantly, they tended to be very positive. He suspects that the positive results were largely based on the relaxing hotel environment, but he is sure that the HR manager and the president would be quite happy with this kind of feedback.

Please comment.

Training and development can contribute to increased revenue by improving the performance of revenue-producing employees, by increasing output or by reducing production costs, or by both. If training is used to increase productivity, training costs have to be included in the pricing of the product. Figure 7-9 presents factors associated with

FIGURE 7-9

Training Costs and Benefits

Activities	Costs
Needs analysis	Labour: consultant, clerical staff
Program development	Labour: consultants and programmers, clerical staff Materials: office material, videography, digital tool creation Equipment rental Other potential costs: travel, accommodation, per diem expenses
Course delivery	Equipment Room rental Food Trainers' salaries Trainees' salaries Lost production
Program evaluation	Evaluator's fee Travel and accommodation (assuming external evaluator) Overhead costs: staff and clerical support, office

Examples of Financial Benefits Derived after Training
Increased productivity (widgets/hr or $/hr)
Reduced labour costs ($/hr or per year)
Reduced error rate ($/hr or per year)
Higher sales ($/year)
Reduced accident rate (days lost, reduced absenteeism in $)

different training activities. It should be mentioned that companies, depending on the industry, spend between 1.7 to 6 percent of their payroll expenditures on training.[60]

LO8 Career Planning and Development

Linked with employee development are career planning and career management. To be ready for career opportunities, successful people develop career plans and then take action to achieve their plans. As shown in the following example, meeting employees' career development objectives can alleviate other organizational concerns, such as retention:

> IBM was losing employees due to the perception that there were not enough career advancement opportunities. Management devised a plan to create a more formal and consistent way of providing people with new skills and connecting them to business opportunities within IBM through a job bank, called "Blue Opportunities." The program was designed to electronically connect employees through a system with direct employee and manager feedback. Employees were able to learn about opportunities by shadowing other employees as they performed their jobs anywhere in the world and by speaking with them virtually about their work or with the manager of a department.[61]

Career Planning and Development Overview

Career planning and development refers to the process through which individuals become more aware of their interests, needs, and motivations in terms of their job life, and engage in activities in pursuit of a career. **Career management** is a series of formal and less formal activities designed and managed by the organization to influence the career development of one or more employees.[62] Well-planned and managed careers tend to result in greater job satisfaction and career commitment. A well-designed career development system effectively taps a firm's resources and is effective in matching an individual's skills with organizational needs. This matching is an important concept from an employee

career planning and development The process through which someone becomes aware of his or her interests and needs, motivations, etc., in terms of a career, and engages in a lifelong series of activities in pursuit of that career.

career management A series of formal and less formal activities designed and managed by the organization to influence the career development of one or more employees.

FIGURE 7-10

A Model of Career Development

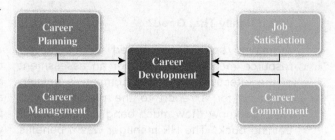

commitment and engagement perspective, as is shown in the relational diagram in Figure 7-10.[63] When employers encourage career planning, employees are more likely to set goals. In turn, these goals may motivate employees to pursue further education, training, or other career development activities. These activities then improve the value of employees to the organization and give the human resource department a larger pool of qualified applicants from which to fill internal job openings.

Individual Career Development

In past decades, employees expected that if they were loyal and hard-working, their employer would "take care of them." While there are some employee–employer relationships that will span an employee's full career, it is also common now to see the employer and employee meet each other's needs for the moment, with neither one making long-term commitments. This may look like a series of permanent jobs, or even a series of short-term contracts (i.e., the so-called "gig economy").[64] Many employers recognize that employees are focused on and committed to their personal growth, which may be within the firm or at another employer in the future. The trend is geared toward having employees create a career portfolio—one that illustrates not just promotions, but also horizontal or lateral movement and the ability to enhance one's skills and competencies through job rotations, projects, volunteering, and other activities.[65]

The starting point for career development is the individual employee, who is responsible for transforming his or her career path by playing an active role in managing a career. Once a personal commitment has been made, there are several actions that employees typically take to direct their personal development:

- *Demonstrate exceptional job performance.* The most effective action an employee can undertake is good job performance. When performance is substandard, even modest career goals are usually unattainable because low performers are quickly excluded from promotion considerations.

- *Increase visibility and exposure within the organization.* Being known—and held in high regard— by those who decide on promotion and other career opportunities make an employee more likely to be considered for an advancement. It used to be considered that putting in "face time" (or hours in the workplace visible to others) was required to obtain exposure. Indeed, Yahoo decided in 2013 to drop its work from home policy in favour of more time at the office.[66] However, several reports suggest that visibility and exposure may best be attained through strong performance results shared with colleagues and bosses rather than merely face time at the workplace.[67]

- *Leave the organization to seek a better job.* Some employees—perhaps young professionals in particular—change employers as part of a conscious career strategy. Also called "job hopping," changing employers every few years often comes with a promotion, a pay increase, and a new experience; however, it may also indicate low commitment and be a warning sign to future employers. While astute managers and professionals formerly used this technique sparingly to avoid a "job hopper" stigma, a recent survey by Accountemps suggests that especially younger Canadian workers believe the benefits of changing jobs every few years may outweigh the potential bad reputation.[68]

- *Seek mentors, sponsors, and coaches.* A **mentor** is someone who offers informal career advice. If the mentor can nominate the employee for career development activities, such as training programs, transfers, or promotion, the mentor becomes a **sponsor**, someone in the organization who can create career development opportunities for others. *Coaching* was discussed earlier in this chapter in connection with apprenticeship training and is common with corporate executives. All workers from entrepreneurs to new hires to the recently retired may benefit from using coaches to move into new careers, to prepare for promotion, to refocus, or to refine communication or leadership skills.

> **mentor** Someone who offers informed career guidance and support on a regular basis.

> **sponsor** A person in an organization who can create career development opportunities for others.

- *Seek growth opportunities.* By working on a project, volunteering to run a United Way campaign, sitting on a board of directors for an agency, or entering into a management development program, individuals may advance their career.

How Do Employees Measure Career Success?

Being satisfied with one's career encompasses both objective and subjective criteria, such as promotions, status, salary, the development of new skills, work–life balance, challenge, and purpose.[69] Researchers have determined that there are four general outcome measures that employees use to evaluate success: advancement, learning, employability, and the evidence of positive psychological factors.[70]

- *Advancement* refers to the ability to gain a sense of power or status, the ability to develop a positive reputation and achieve a sense of autonomy and entrepreneurship.

- *Learning* refers to the acquisition of new skills and competencies that individuals value and see as important in their development.

- *Employability* relates to being able to make money to survive and have the applicable experiences so that obtaining meaningful work will be possible.

- *Psychological factors* include focusing on internal motivational drivers, such as recognition, self-esteem, engagement, satisfaction, and self-actualization.

Consider how this Proctor and Gamble employee defines career success after attending a course from the company's business school in Massimiliano, Italy:

> "When I was selected for the EFS (European Financial Seminar), I took for granted that I would have had fun, met a group of outstanding international students, and had the opportunity to take a close peek at the work of P&G employees. Well, all this happened. That definitely makes the EFS one of the most valuable experiences I have had so far in my whole life. From the number of resources and amount of time the company spent for the organization of the event, I could see how P&G values talent and looks after its reputation as an employer—we could closely feel the firm's commitment to making us live an unforgettable experience. To conclude, I would suggest even to the most skeptical student to apply for the EFS 2010—the risk–reward profile is nothing, but attractive!"[71]

Note that these outcomes are not necessarily important to everyone in equal measure. Nor do all employees possess the same expectations regarding what organizations offer in terms of career planning programs. Employees value these programs in varying degrees, based on their contextual and interpersonal characteristics. The next section will address some of these factors affecting career choice.

Factors Affecting Individual Career Choices

When determining career aspirations and direction, individual values, attitudes, and abilities may vary along eight anchors (see Figure 7-11).[72]

FIGURE 7-11

Eight Career Anchors

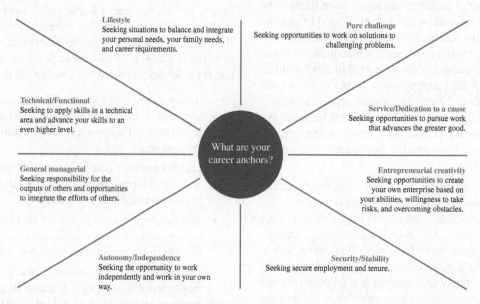

SOURCE: Based on Edgar Schein and John Van Maanen (2013), *Career Anchors: The Changing Nature of Work and Careers Self Assessment* (4th ed.), Wiley. Visualization downloaded from Telos Partners: http://www.telospartners.com/accelerating-talent-success-2/

Researchers have found that everyone has a propensity toward one or more of these elements. When considering what type of developmental opportunities to offer to an employee, it is important for HR to recognize and pay attention to individual differences in anchors and personality types, and to offer employee development opportunities that match. Below are three examples of individual differences and examples of how HR professionals can offer career experiences to match.

Social or Environmental Concern

Some individuals especially value social or environmental concerns (i.e., the dedication to a cause anchor). For instance, a recent study indicated that 61 percent of Millennials see themselves as accountable for making a difference in the world, and 78 percent feel that their employer should join them.[73] Companies may meet their employees' career objectives by echoing their social or environmental concerns, as shown in the following example:

> Patagonia recognized how important ecological and environmental concerns are to some workers when it established an employee internship program. Through the program, employees can leave their jobs for up to one month to work for the environmental group of their choice. This program will pay employees' salaries and benefits while they're gone, and environmental groups worldwide get them for free.[74]

Work–Life Balance

While some employees are happy to put in long hours at the workplace, more and more workers are seeking a balance between their home and work lives; their anchor is lifestyle. Offering development opportunities that maintain work–life balance will be important when choosing development activities for lifestyle-focused employees. Read what Deon Harris, key account manager at Concord National Prairies has to say about work–life balance:

> "Concord National allows me to maintain a great work/life balance. I thoroughly enjoy the culture that allows you the independence to make decisions and in many ways act as an entrepreneur. The management group operates in a very open and honest atmosphere, are always available to answer questions and offer insight when needed. I am made to feel like an important part of the team and treated with respect. What more could you ask for!!"[75]

Personality–Job Fit

One career development model developed back in the 1960s and still relevant today identified individual occupational preferences based on personality types. The Holland Codes model suggests that certain personality types may be well-suited for particular occupations.[76] For example, if someone was outgoing, extroverted, co-operative, and liked people then occupations such as teacher, social worker, clergy, or sales representative might fit. If a personality was more analytical, reflective, curious, and precise, a more applicable occupation might be an investigator, dentist, or systems analyst. In addition to understanding their anchors, career counsellors use this theory to augment their discussions with their clients to help individuals think through what type of work would be the best fit with their personalities. Also known as the RIASEC model (as is shown in Figure 7-12), the types are: Realistic, Investigative, Artistic, Social, Enterprising, and Conventional.

Savvy HR professionals will seek to match employee personality with the personality characteristics of the occupation on specific career paths.

Human Resource Departments and Career Management

As mentioned earlier, career management refers to the programs, processes, and assistance provided by the organization to optimize employees' opportunity for success in their careers.[77] It is the HR department's role to ensure that the applicable processes and practices are developed.

HR managers encourage career development in a number of ways: They encourage management support; they devise communication plans that incorporate HR tools to raise awareness of career options, provide education to employees about career opportunities, and offer career counselling services; they establish and maintain HR-related processes

---

FIGURE 7-12

The RIASEC Model

SOURCE: Based on the work of Holland, J. (1973), *Making Vocational Choices: A Theory of Careers,* Prentice-Hall.

that align with career planning efforts; and they utilize technology effectively to facilitate employees' developmental processes.

Encourage Management Commitment and Support

If a manager does not value development, then employees will receive little reinforcement for their efforts. In addition, efforts by the human resource department to encourage career development have little impact unless supported by managers. Ideally, this effort is advanced by the practice of evaluating managers on their ability to develop their subordinates:

> The Ford Motor Company has made it part of its performance appraisal for managers that they are assessed on how well they succeeded in developing a successor for themselves. The company is aware of the danger that if the "successors" have to wait too

long for a promotion, they will look for opportunities elsewhere. However, the company has the experience that many of those who move return later with significantly more knowledge.[78]

Devise Communication Plans through HR Tools to Raise Awareness of Career Options

Workshops/Seminars

Conducting workshops and seminars on career planning increases employee interest by pointing out the key concepts associated with career planning. Workshops help the employee set career goals, identify career paths, and uncover specific career development activities. These educational activities may be supplemented by information on career planning and establishing a career planning record for employees to review and discuss with their managers and mentors. See Figure 7-13 for an example of a career planning record to see how one company connects its career discussions to its

---

FIGURE 7-13

Career Planning Record

Employee's Name: Date Record Initiated:

Job Title:

Personal Development Assessment

List at least two major strengths:

List the two most important skills that require additional development in order to contribute effectively in the desired job or to attain future career goals:

Career Planning Goals

A. No Career Development Activity Required: no change; focus on existing level of job requirements.

B. Job Enrichment: current position, more variety through assignments, joining task forces, etc.

C. Job Enlargement: current position, more accountability, complexity.

D. Secondment: temporary move to another position.

E. Lateral Transfer: permanent move to another position at the existing band and level of accountability.

F. Promotion: increased level of accountability and authority to next higher band.

	Goals: Now–12 months	(indicate A–F)
	13–24 months	(indicate A–F)
	Over 24 months	(indicate A–F)

Development Plan

(Indicate the specific development plans or career moves required within the next two years.) Specific plans / career actions:

Timing:

Further Comment:

(List anything about your qualifications, aspirations, needs that you would like to add to this Career Planning Record.)

planning efforts. This record can be reviewed once a year, facilitating career planning discussions.

Job Posting

Offering an internal job posting process and ensuring that job descriptions and specifications are accurately documented and are easily accessible can be helpful to employees who are thinking about their next move.

Career Paths

HR professionals create career paths and link these paths to the type of training required to move to the next step. They ensure that these paths are available for employees to view and encourage discussion with employees about applicable paths to follow. Career paths are a valuable information source to help employees understand "what their next step" might be in their area of interest.

Career Counselling

Offering career counselling to employees is another way that HR helps to raise awareness of options. Some organizations have onsite counsellors, whereas other organizations outsource this function. Counsellors will help employees establish career goals and find appropriate career paths. They will inform employees of changes that may affect their career choices and help them explore the various opportunities that exist. The counsellor may simply be someone who has the employee's interests in mind and provides the specific job-related information, or she may be more active in terms of helping an employee by offering options such as seeking training for new skills, accepting special assignments, rotating jobs, making lateral moves, taking sabbaticals, or even making a career change.

In addition, the counsellor may help employees discover their interests by administering and interpreting aptitude and skill tests. Examples including the *Kuder Preference Record* and the *Strong Interest Inventory* are useful for guiding people into occupations likely to be of interest. Other tests are also available to measure individual abilities and interests in specific types of work. But to be truly successful, career counsellors must get employees to assess themselves and their environment. See Figure 7-14 to view a self-interest inventory. In addition, career counsellors may create a career development record to help employees track and document their career planning efforts (as is seen in Figure 7-13).

FIGURE 7-14

A Self-Inventory for Career Planning

	Low				High
Work Interests and Aptitudes	1	2	3	4	5
Physical work (fixing, building, using hands)	1	2	3	4	5
Written work (writing, reading, using words)	1	2	3	4	5
Oral work (talking, giving speeches, using words)	1	2	3	4	5
Quantitative work (calculating, doing accounting, using numbers)	1	2	3	4	5
Visual work (watching, inspecting, using eyes)	1	2	3	4	5
Interpersonal work (counselling, interviewing)	1	2	3	4	5
Creative work (inventing, designing, ideas)	1	2	3	4	5
Analytical work (doing research, solving problems)	1	2	3	4	5
Managerial work (initiating, directing, coordinating)	1	2	3	4	5

(continued)

	Low				High
Work Interests and Aptitudes	1	2	3	4	5
Clerical work (keeping records)	1	2	3	4	5
Outdoor work (farming, travelling, doing athletics)	1	2	3	4	5
Mechanical work (repairing, fixing, tinkering)	1	2	3	4	5

Work Skills and Abilities List below specialized skills, unique personal assets, enjoyable experiences, and major accomplishments. Then check the skills and abilities required.	Physical	Written	Oral	Quantitative	Visual	Interpersonal	Creative	Analytical	Managerial	Clerical	Outdoor	Mechanical
1.												
2.												
3.												
4.												
5.												

Align HR Processes to Facilitate Career Planning

There are several HR-related processes that contribute to employee development. Some of the processes are succession planning, human resource planning, training and development, and performance management.

Succession Planning

It is the responsibility of the human resource department to engage in **succession planning**—that is, to ensure that there are a sufficient number of candidates for key positions ready to take over if an unexpected vacancy occurs, be it because of someone leaving the company, sickness, or death.

> **succession planning** The process of making long-range management development plans to fill human resource needs.

A number of years ago, a small plane with seven executives of a Calgary-based oil company on a flight to New York crashed, killing all seven and the crew. It was a catastrophic event for the company, but the company survived because it had a sufficient number of trained managers ready. This event is oft-cited in numerous industries when engaging in succession planning efforts—and in designing corporate travel policies.

As the example shows, having well-developed employees ready to take on critical responsibilities in case of an emergency can be crucial for the survival of a company.

Human Resource Planning

Designing a robust planning process that considers a number of different programs to balance demand and supply is important for helping individuals plan their careers. Organizations that plan effectively will greatly contribute to the career planning efforts of its employees as the opportunities to move into different roles will be transparent and communicated in a timely fashion.

Training and Development Function

As discussed throughout this chapter, the relationship between training and development is highly interdependent. Aligning the needs of the employee with the organizational needs and managing the talent within an organization is critical for sustainability.

Performance Management

A well-run performance management program is critical to ensuring that employees receive effective feedback with respect to their performance. An integral component of these programs is to ensure a tight link between performance feedback, employee development, and career planning efforts. This information is invaluable in terms of helping the employees understand their strengths and areas of development and what they must do to enhance their value to the organization. Chapter 8 discusses the performance management process in greater detail.

Use Technology to Support Career Planning Efforts

Technology now plays a significant role in career planning and career development. Robust enterprise-wide applications have career planning modules where organizations are able to place their career paths online through a secure portal. They can create default career paths and design individual plans for employees. Employees can see what type of training would be required to move up to the next level and what development activities are required as well as a suggested time for how long it would take to build these skills.

An alternative to offering in-house career counselling is to use an intranet for career counselling purposes.

> The Bank of Montreal has an extensive career planning site allowing prospective and current employees to browse through six areas of work, including sales and service, technology, analytics, customer support, digital, and corporate functions. There are employee testimonials and videos available for each area designed to help people find their perfect fit at BMO along with detailed career opportunities.[79]

Many organizations are using various forms of technology to engage employees in career planning. For instance, Deloitte uses webcasts of existing employees who "tell their story about what they do" and ask the viewers to "consider where they might fit."

As a result of HR's active involvement in career planning, the contribution that HR makes toward employee engagement and satisfaction and to overall talent management can be evidenced in several ways. Active career planning does the following:

- *Develops promotable employees.* Career planning helps to develop internal supplies of promotable talent.
- *Lowers turnover.* The increased attention to and concern for individual careers generates more organizational loyalty and therefore lower employee turnover.
- *Furthers employee growth.* Career plans and goals motivate employees to grow and develop.
- *Reduces hoarding.* Without career planning, it is easier for managers to hoard key subordinates. Career planning causes employees, managers, and the human resource department to become aware of employee qualifications.
- *Satisfies employee needs.* With less hoarding and improved growth opportunities for employees, individual needs for recognition and accomplishment are more readily satisfied, and self-esteem is boosted.
- *Assists organizations meet legal requirements such as employment equity plans.* Career planning can help members of protected employee groups prepare for more important jobs.
- *Taps employee potential.* Career planning encourages employees to tap more of their potential abilities because they have specific career goals.
- *Optimizes organizational potential.* This helps create a talent pipeline, a pool of talent that ensures that organizations have the needed skills when and where they need their respective human resources.

SUMMARY

After workers are selected, they are seldom ready to perform successfully. They must be integrated into the social and work environment of the organization through onboarding. Orientation programs help a worker begin this socialization process. The organization benefits because training time and costs are lowered, employee satisfaction is higher, and initial turnover is lower.

Training is an essential part of an organization's short-term strategy, ensuring that employees have the skills and knowledge they need to perform their current roles well. If a company wants to thrive in a competitive global environment, it requires an efficient and flexible workforce that is adaptable to fast-changing technologies and new approaches to doing business. Employee development programs are a key component in building a long-range strategy. Canadian managers also have to learn to manage a diverse workforce and create an inclusive work environment for all employees. Flatter organizations necessitate new skills for employees, who have to shoulder more responsibilities. This, in turn, leads to greater emphasis on employees' competencies, resulting in the need for lifelong learning.

The training process begins with an assessment of training needs. Specific training objectives can then be set. These objectives give direction to the training program and serve to evaluate the training program at its completion. The content of the program depends upon the training objectives. The design of the training should consider such learning principles as participation, repetition, relevance, transference, and feedback.

Different development strategies may be employed, at the cognitive, behavioural, and environmental levels, with the cognitive method being the least promising and the environmental method the most promising approach.

Once training and development programs are completed, it is essential that they be evaluated. Without evaluation, a company does not know what it gets in return for its training and development investment.

Career planning and development are offered by some (mostly large) organizations in the form of career education, information, and counselling. But the primary responsibility for career planning and development rests with the individual employee. The planning process enables employees to identify career goals and the paths to those goals. Then, through developmental activities, the workers seek ways to improve themselves and further their career goals.

Career planning does not guarantee success. But without it, employees are seldom ready for career opportunities that arise. Because of this, their career progress may be slowed and the human resource department may be unable to fill openings internally.

TERMS FOR REVIEW

blogs 225
career management 234
career planning and development 234
cost–benefit analysis 232
cross-training 223
development 215
human resource development (HRD) 215
knowledge management 215
learning curve 221
learning principles 221
mentor 235
needs assessment 220

onboarding 214
orientation programs 218
role-playing 223
socialization 218
sponsor 235
startup costs 217
strategic human resource development 229
succession planning 240
training 215
transference 222
virtual reality/augmented reality 225
wiki 225

SELF-ASSESSMENT EXERCISE

Test Your Knowledge of Onboarding, Training and Development, and Career Planning

1. Because of the importance of managing a diverse and inclusive workforce, most Canadian managers have been trained in this type of management.   T   F

2. Training programs focus on skill development.   T   F

3. A training needs assessment includes learning principles.   T   F

4. Training focuses on management skills; development focuses on interpersonal skills.   T   F

5. Strategic human resource development focuses on training future executives.   T   F

6. Coaching is mainly used in team building.   T   F

7. Virtual reality training uses a real-time approach.   T   F

8. A *knowledge worker* is defined as an employee who has scored at least 60 percent on a knowledge test.   T   F

9. One type of training evaluation is called "Training and Development Audit."   T   F

10. A person's career plan requires an environmental assessment.   T   F

SCORING

If you marked statements 2, 3, 7, and 10 as *True,* give yourself one point for each. If you marked statements 1, 4, 5, 6, 8, and 9 as *False,* give yourself one point for each.

Scores of 8–10: Very good! You seem to have a good understanding of the concepts. Congratulations.

Scores of 5–7: Okay, that keeps you in the running, but you may want to reread the chapter to improve your score.

Scores of less than 5: It may be advisable for you to spend more time studying the concepts and their application.

REVIEW AND DISCUSSION QUESTIONS

1. "If employees are properly selected, there should be no need for an orientation program or training." Do you agree or disagree? Why?

2. What are the organizational and employee benefits that result from a comprehensive onboarding process?

3. For each of the following occupations, which training techniques do you recommend? Why?
   a. A cashier in a grocery store
   b. A welder
   c. An assembly-line worker
   d. An inexperienced supervisor

4. Assume you were hired to manage a research department. After a few weeks, you noticed that some researchers were more effective than others and that the less effective ones received little recognition from their more productive counterparts. What forms of training would you consider for both groups?

5. What is the purpose of a cost–benefit analysis?

6. Discuss why a linkage between an organization's human resource development needs and its mission and strategy is so important.

7. Explain the differences between the cognitive, behavioural, and environmental approaches to strategic employee development.

8. Why should a human resource department be concerned about career planning, especially when employee plans may conflict with the organization's objectives? What advantages does a human resource department expect to receive from assisting career planning?

9. Suppose you are in a management training position after completing university. Your career goal is not very clear, but you would like to become a top manager in your firm. What type of information would you seek from the human resource department to help you develop your career plan?

10. Why is employee feedback an important element of any organization's attempt to encourage career development?

11. Suppose a hard-working and loyal employee is passed over for promotion. What would you tell this person?

CRITICAL THINKING QUESTIONS

1. Before you entered your college or university, you had certain ideas about what your values and expectations would be as a student. How did the institution's socialization process change those values and expectations?

2. Your company is desperately looking for a systems analyst. You know that your competitor invested heavily in training and has a highly competent systems analyst, who indicated to you privately that she would switch if you paid her $10,000 more. Your boss thinks

that this is a bargain and tells you, "Get her!" It surely would hurt the competitor. What issues does this raise?

3. You are the training and development manager. Your president calls you in and tells you that the employee development budget has to be cut because of the company's financial situation. What arguments can you use to persuade your boss that development money is well spent?

ETHICS QUESTION

1. **Onboarding:** You are about to give an orientation session to new employees and you plan to stress ethical behaviour as outlined in a company brochure. You

know that company executives have recently been convicted in a foreign country of bribing government officials. Will you mention this?

2. Training: During a training program, which requires taking tests to measure progress, you notice that one of the participants, who struggled in some early tests, suddenly submits tests without mistakes. She is a probationary employee. You notice too that she is dating a staff member in your department, who has access to the test solutions. What do you plan to do?

3. Development: Should employees who are to retire soon have access to development programs, if they so desire? Please comment.

4. Career planning: You are the HR manager and one of your staff members asks you for career advice on this company. She wants to get ahead and is willing to take courses fitting your company's special needs. You have strongly encouraged such moves in the past. You know that the company is not doing well in its market and has probably less than a year to survive. How will you advise her?

RESEARCH EXERCISE

ONBOARDING

1. Trello (https://trello.com/)

   a. Examine the blog by Lauren Moon on new employee onboarding at Trello available here: https://blog.trello.com/new-employee-onboarding-best-practices-for-new-hires. Do you think it is comprehensive?

   b. What are some of the major components covered?

EMPLOYEE ORIENTATION

1. Robert Bacal of Bacal & Associates (http://work911 .com/articles/orient.htm)

   a. In this quick guide to employee orientation, what does Bacal have to say about the outcomes of an effective orientation program?

   b. What different types of orientation programs does he describe? How do they differ?

TRAINING AND DEVELOPMENT

1. Employment and Social Development Canada (ESDC) (https://www.canada.ca/en/employment-social-development.html)

   Explore the "Training" link. Give an overview of what types of career and training resources are available from the Government of Canada. Which ones would be relevant for you? Why?

2. The Job Bank (https://www.jobbank.gc.ca/ skillsandknowledge?action=search_form)

   Within the Job Bank, explore careers that match your skills and knowledge. Do the career options the Job Bank suggests based on your skills and knowledge sound appealing to you?

CAREER

1. Career Planning (https://www.thebalancecareers.com/ self-assessment-4161888)

   Explore the self-assessments, including the interest inventory and personality type tests.

   a. Do you agree with the results/recommendations?

   b. Assume that you want to pursue a career in accounting. What steps will you follow?

2. Another Career Self-Assessment Instrument (https:// profile.keirsey.com/#/b2c/assessment/start)

   Do the self-assessment. Do you agree with the results?

WE CONNECTIONS: TRAINING AND ONBOARDING A NEW EMPLOYEE

Final Few Issues of the Day

It was 7:00 p.m., and most of the staff had left for the day, leaving many work spaces dark and quiet. In the HR department, Rebecca and Charlotte, an HR specialist, sat together in Rebecca's office, talking quietly as they reviewed a few final issues.

Rebecca had been hired as the company's first HR manager three months before and quickly realized that there

was a lot to learn about working in the technology industry. She was grateful to have Charlotte's help as she attempted to develop and implement a comprehensive HR strategy for WEC—one that would add value to the company as it grew.

If she was being honest, Charlotte would have admitted that when Rebecca was hired, she had been more than a little annoyed that she had not been promoted to the HR manager position herself. However, after working with

Rebecca for a few months, she realized that it was for the best. Rebecca was better able to manage all of the competing demands that came into the department, and she had a lot of good HR knowledge that she was open to sharing. Even with the long hours, Charlotte's job had become more enjoyable, and she felt she was developing professionally at a faster pace than when she had been on her own, trying to figure things out as she went along.

How Are We Going to Train Her?

This night, they had finally decided on their preferred candidate for the open receptionist position, a woman named Polly Modi. Charlotte made a note to call her the next day to make the offer. Thinking they were done, she began to gather up her papers, but Rebecca said, "Wait a minute. How are we going to train the new receptionist? How did you do it the last time?"

Charlotte shrugged, and said, "We usually just have somebody sit with the hire for part of the first day to show her how the phones work and how to do the administrative tasks. Anna and Mario DeJulio are the back-up receptionists. We would usually just see which of them is available that day, and send that person over to do it."

Rebecca frowned as she sat back in her chair, and said, "I wonder if that's sufficient. I really like all of the people who work reception, but I've noticed that there is real variability in the service, depending on who is working. For instance, some people answer the phone after one or two rings, and others wait for up to four or five. The script changes depending on who answers the phone—some start with their name, others with the company name, or something else. Sometimes visitors get greeted with enthusiasm, sometimes not. Even the prioritization of the admin tasks seems to differ across employees. I know the last receptionist was not considered that strong before she quit. Maybe part of that was because she didn't get a lot of good training. It might be a good idea to get a little more structured when it comes to training new receptionists."

"Hmmmm. It *would* be great to know that everyone is starting with the same information. The receptionist position seems to have a fair bit of turnover. It seems the good ones get promoted, and the bad ones find another job somewhere else," Charlotte responded. She added, "What did you have in mind?"

Rebecca tapped her pen on the table as she thought about it. After a few moments, she said, "I think that this is an important, front-line position, and we should figure out a way to make sure every person working that front desk has a shared vision of how it should be run. We should develop a standard training process so that everybody gets the same training, no matter who happens to be free to train that day. And we will have to take the time to make sure it is actually working."

Charlotte nodded, and began to make some notes.

Helping Employees Hit the Ground Running

Rubbing her forehead to relieve the tension she felt there, Rebecca added, "While we're at it, let's talk about the onboarding process. I know what it was like for me when I started at WEC. I signed my offer from Alex, then I didn't hear anything from the company until my start day. When I arrived, I waited in the lobby for maybe half an hour before Alex had time to come and get me. He showed me around and introduced me to everyone who was at their desk, although I remember losing track of names after the fifth or sixth person. Then he dropped me off with you, and you had me sign a bunch of benefit and payroll forms. Eventually, I was kind of left alone in this office. I remember feeling a little lost. I remember asking you a lot of questions in the weeks that followed. But, still, it probably took me a month before I began to feel comfortable."

After taking a sip of her lukewarm coffee, she continued, "We need a plan to train new people and get them onboarded effectively. We need people to connect to us right away and we want them to start contributing as soon as possible. This company is trying to grow, and we have to do more to help new employees hit the ground running. Let's figure out what we're going to do."

DISCUSSION QUESTIONS

1. Outline an onboarding plan for the new receptionist. What information would the new hire need to know? Who should be involved? What should the timeline be? How would you store and refine the onboarding information so it is used in the future?

2. Develop a training plan for the receptionist position. What training techniques would you incorporate, considering aspects such as cost-effectiveness, content, and learning principles?

3. Develop a plan so that Rebecca and Charlotte can evaluate the effectiveness of the training. Consider how you would measure knowledge, reaction, learning, and results.

In the next installment of the WE Connections story (at the end of Chapter 8), a project manager conducts a performance appraisal.

CASE STUDY

Calico Industrial Furniture

A New Career Planning Initiative

Walking from his bus station to the Calico Industrial Furniture headquarters in Saskatoon, Jayson was excited. Today was the day he would start work on the company's new career planning initiative. Jayson had been with Calico for almost a year-and-a-half. He and the talent team had just wrapped the company's second annual performance evaluation process since he began. During the first annual performance review, Jayson had been still relatively new, both to Calico and to the field of human resource management. Having graduated from the University of Saskatchewan with a Bachelor of Commerce just the month before he started, Calico was his first job as an HR professional. He had observed the first review process and noted that several employees seemed to have questions about next opportunities that might be available for them at Calico. During the most recent performance evaluation process, Jayson had assisted managers from each of the organization's 12 departments with the process, and sat in personally on about 30 evaluation interviews between managers and their staff.

Over his time at Calico and from his participation in the performance review process, Jayson had come to realize that the company did not have career planning and employee development as part of its HR processes. Staff members would attend their performance review, which was tied to administrative outcomes including bonuses and the Calico employee stock option purchase plan. Performance reviews were also meant to be an important piece of data the organization considered in internal promotions of staff. However, there wasn't a mechanism in place for employees to communicate about their career goals and objectives while working for Calico. And there wasn't a process in place for managers to respond to employee career development requests.

Jayson had observed that the managers of the various departments handled staff career goals differently. For instance, Andrew in Supply Chain and Logistics had had some retirements in his department over the last 18 months, and he had transitioned people from his own team into new, higher roles. Chelsea in Customer Growth and Mikhail in Customer Service had actually swapped two employees in lateral positions who had each expressed the desire to try out roles in the other department for a two-year term. There may have been some career planning conversations taking place in other departments as well, but Jayson knew the company could benefit from introducing these conversations more formally and adding some structure to ensure they were offered to all employees.

As he got to his desk, Jayson opened up a fresh Word document and prepared to start crafting the plan for a new career planning initiative. While the obvious starting point would be to dive right in on drafting a career planning guide for each employee to complete, Jayson knew that rolling out this initiative would involve many more steps. He began brainstorming some of the aspects that he would have to determine. Ten minutes later, his list included the following: (a) *People:* Who would have to be involved in the initiative development process (e.g., senior leadership, managers from all departments, focus groups of staff from each area?), at what points in the development of the initiative should different people be involved, and in what capacities? (b) *Timing:* When should the career planning initiative be offered (at the same time as the performance review, or perhaps on the six-month opposite annual cycle)? (c) *Delivery:* What would the career planning process entail (e.g., would employees complete a form and submit it to their managers before a planning conversation or would HR handle the process)? (d) *Connections:* How would the initiative connect to other HR processes, such as the Calico Learn-to-Lead and tuition reimbursement programs? (e) *Action steps:* What action steps would Calico be willing to introduce to meet the career planning goals that employees identify? Jayson took a brief pause in his writing. He knew that there would be more points for consideration than he had come up with already.

As he re-read the list he had compiled so far, Jayson realized that there could be some policy implications for the company associated with this new initiative. For instance, would the company be interested in establishing a hire-from-within policy if promotions were identified as career goals coming out of the career planning process? Could the company formalize the type of temporary lateral transition that the two employees in Chelsea and Mikhail's departments had currently engaged in? Jayson also recognized that while his gut feeling was that employees wanted some career planning assistance, he really didn't have any data to back up his assertion. He knew that the range of careers available at Calico had surprised him when he began working there. For instance, Calico had a department devoted to analytics, where employees implemented latest practices in e-commerce and used big data to discover inefficiencies in their supply chain and to examine the value of marketing campaigns. And Calico had a department called Creative/UX, for which the talent team had assisted in hiring for positions called imagery applications senior associate and associate photography project manager. The Category

Management department addressed strategic goals ranging from catalogue expansion and promotions to supplier negotiations. With operations now spread across five cities in Canada, there was a tremendous range of career options available at Calico. Were employees at Calico interested in exploring their career objectives and goals and learning more about opportunities, and were senior executives as interested in investing in this process as Jayson was?

Jayson knew the career planning initiative was hardly going to be completed in one day, but he was surprised at how involved it might turn out to be. It struck him that he should call a good friend and experienced HR colleague for some advice. He reached for the phone.

DISCUSSION QUESTIONS

Your phone rings and it's your friend Jayson calling for your thoughts on his career planning initiative.

1. You know that employees have different goals in terms of advancement, learning, employability, and various psychological factors they will be seeking through their careers. What tools might you suggest for Jayson to look into that might guide his employees in determining what the important factors are to each of them?

2. Jayson has identified that he will need buy-in to create and launch Calico's career planning initiative. Identify some stages that will have to take place in the development of the career planning initiative and list who from the organization he will need to involve in each stage.

3. What advice would you have for Jayson on the delivery of the career planning initiative? (a) Should it be held at the same time or opposite to the performance evaluation process, once annually or more often? (b) Who should be responsible for the career planning initiative: managers or the talent team? (c) Who should have access to the employees' completed career planning forms?

CHAPTER 8

Performance Management

"In business, the idea of measuring what you are doing, picking the measurements that count like customer satisfaction and performance . . . you thrive on that."

BILL GATES[1]

LEARNING OBJECTIVES

After studying this chapter, you should be able to:

LO1	Discuss how managing employee performance relates to achieving organizational goals.
LO2	Describe the various purposes of performance appraisals.
LO3	Describe the commonly used comparative and noncomparative appraisal methods.
LO4	Discuss the advantages and disadvantages of the various raters of performance appraisal information.
LO5	Describe the guidelines for effective performance evaluation interviews.
LO6	Explain how talent management uses information about employee performance and potential to guide employee decisions.
LO7	Outline steps to creating a performance improvement plan.

LO1 Introduction to Performance Management

A comprehensive **performance management**[2] system involves much more than just **performance appraisal**. To achieve the organization's strategic objectives, individual employees need to meet their individual performance goals. In combination, employees meeting their individual goals all contribute to an organization's achieving its objectives. When any employee does not play his or her role, the organization will not perform at its best.

Here the human resource function has the potential of having an enormous influence through the development and maintenance of a sound performance management program. This requires that human resource professionals run performance management strategically—to align each employee's performance management plan with the strategy for the organization— whether the strategic focus of the organization is safe working, competitive pricing, high quality, or exemplary customer service. It

performance management The continuing process of identifying, measuring, and developing the performance of individuals and teams and aligning performance with the strategic goals of the organization.

performance appraisal The process by which organizations evaluate employee job performance over a period of time.

also requires industry experts to be involved in determining the indicators of performance.[3] The ideal performance management system provides incentives for employees to concentrate on improving things that contribute most to value creation, ranging from hiring the right people to producing high-quality goods or services to using the most effective training and development programs. The examples below illustrate issues when the measurement of performance does not align with good business strategy:

> When Britain's ambulance service began measuring response times, call centres falsified their data. Ambulances were arriving at emergency scenes before their calls were logged. Also in health care, when the success rate of surgeons was recorded, some surgeons turned away tricky cases to keep their success rates high, a process known as "creaming."[4]
>
> A U.S. phone company took over local phone operations in the Dominican Republic and implemented repair goals for repair crews. It soon became apparent that the repair crews were sabotaging the phones of their friends and families to increase their number of repair calls to meet the performance goals.[5]

These measurements were simple but hardly appropriate. No doubt actual response times, responses to tricky surgical cases, and effectively repairing phones that were legitimately broken would have been more effective. The next example shows a strong link between performance and corporate strategy:

> At Microsoft, three inputs determine a single performance rating for each employee: (a) what employees did during the year versus their commitments and goals as compared to the achievements of their peers, (b) the behaviour used to achieve their results as provided in feedback from peers and managers, and (c) employees' proven capabilities based on their work inputs plus their long-term performance record. The single rating triggers increases in merit pay, bonuses, and restricted stock units, with the size linked to job family and discipline. The company can target its compensation investment to critical positions and disciplines, such as engineering research and development, which are most significant in the company's success. Employees are able to see how their compensation would shift based on different performance ratings through the interactive intranet portal. When this performance management system with a clear line of sight between performance and pay was implemented, the quality of conversations about performance expectations went up, as did pay satisfaction.[6]

This example shows how incentives can be used to reinforce performance that matches desired business strategy. Business strategy, performance management, and compensation systems should be carefully linked.

Performance Management System Goals

Organizations concerned with running an efficient and effective performance management system will try to achieve the following objectives:

- Transform organizational objectives into clearly understood, measurable outcomes that define success and are shared with stakeholders in and outside the organization.

- Provide instruments for measuring, managing, and improving the overall health and success of the organization.

- Include measures of quality, cost, speed, customer service, and employee satisfaction, motivation, and skills to provide an in-depth, predictive performance management system.

- Provide forward-looking strategic partnership between top and middle management and employees.

Sound performance management programs make clear the connection between company goals and employee objectives and work plans, as well as criteria for success.[7] One approach is to have organizational goals cascade into refined goals and expectations at the unit, team, and individual levels. With this approach, high-level executives will develop goals for their division that align with the organizational goals. Then, mid-level managers will develop unit goals to meet the division goals, followed by managers developing team goals to meet the unit goals, and so on until the goals are cascaded down to individuals.[8] The left side of Figure 8-1 shows the cascade approach to setting performance goals.

Although cascading goals are used to ensure line of sight between organizational objectives and individual work, they can be time-consuming to set up (each level

FIGURE 8-1

Cascading versus Linking Up Approaches to Aligning Organizational and Individual Performance Goals

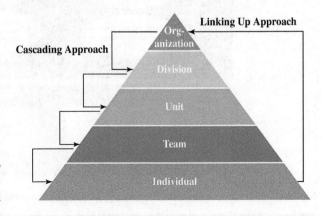

is dependent on the level above to complete its goals in a timely manner), and they risk being distorted down the chain until the individual goal no longer contributes to the organizational goal. In the "linking up" approach, each unit and employee clearly links their goals to the organization's objectives (see the right side of Figure 8-1). The linking up approach may be faster than the cascading approach, and it allows for a more direct line of sight between the individual's goals and the organization's objectives, which may produce more meaningful and clearer goals.[9] In either approach, the goal is for performance management plans to provide clarity for what is expected of the employee and how the work of the employee contributes to the overall functioning of the organization.

To assess the performance of the overall organization, one popular system—the **balanced scorecard**—integrates financial measures with other key performance indicators around customer satisfaction; internal organizational processes; and organizational growth, learning, and innovation.[10] The performance measures, targets, and initiatives for each of these areas all align with the organization's vision and mission to ensure that all aspects of the organization are moving forward together. Figure 8-2 provides an example of a balanced scorecard.

Human resources play a critical part in an organization's performance, of course. HR has direct links to innovation and learning, but it also influences customer

> **balanced scorecard** An integrated organizational performance measuring approach that looks at organizational learning and innovation, financial management, internal operations, and customer management.

FIGURE 8-2

A Balanced Scorecard Example

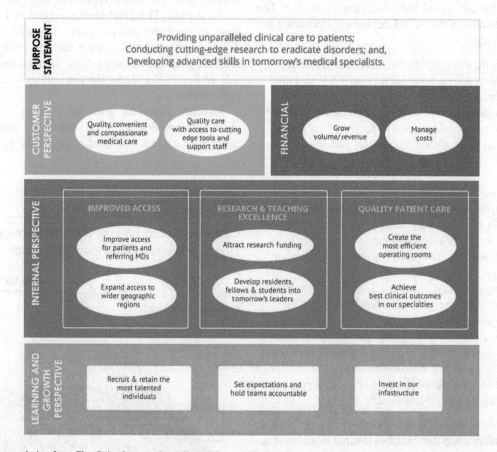

Hospital Strategy Map
* Strategy Map is Modified for Educational Purposes
To care for our patients and their families as if they were our own

PURPOSE STATEMENT
Providing unparalleled clinical care to patients;
Conducting cutting-edge research to eradicate disorders; and,
Developing advanced skills in tomorrow's medical specialists.

CUSTOMER PERSPECTIVE
- Quality, convenient and compassionate medical care
- Quality care with access to cutting edge tools and support staff

FINANCIAL
- Grow volume/revenue
- Manage costs

INTERNAL PERSPECTIVE

IMPROVED ACCESS
- Improve access for patients and referring MDs
- Expand access to wider geographic regions

RESEARCH & TEACHING EXCELLENCE
- Attract research funding
- Develop residents, fellows & students into tomorrow's leaders

QUALITY PATIENT CARE
- Create the most efficient operating rooms
- Achieve best clinical outcomes in our specialties

LEARNING AND GROWTH PERSPECTIVE
- Recruit & retain the most talented individuals
- Set expectations and hold teams accountable
- Invest in our infrastructure

Reprinted with permission from ClearPoint Strategy, https://www.clearpointstrategy.com

satisfaction, quality improvement programs, and other internal processes. Variations of the balanced scorecard have been developed to focus on particular HR functions, including the HR scorecard and the leadership scorecard. Designed to align HR's twin imperatives of cost control and value creation, the HR scorecard aims to identify HR deliverables, align HR systems through the use of high-performance work systems, align the HR system with the organizational strategy, and identify HR efficiency measures.[11] In short, the HR scorecard tracks how well the HR function as a whole is meeting the organization's objectives.

LO2 Performance Appraisal Purpose

Just as the engineering department is concerned with designing equipment, the maintenance department is concerned with running equipment, and manufacturing is concerned with turning out a quality product at minimal cost, the human resource department should be concerned with identifying what the people in engineering, maintenance, and manufacturing must do (*behaviour*) to be proficient in their respective functions. Similarly, the HR department should determine what top management must do to implement the strategic plan once it has been formulated.

> Whereas some people may groan during performance appraisal season, it may be surprising that a recent Ceridian Canada survey reports that 71 percent of the 800 respondents said that their review made them feel valued, and 91 percent felt that their performance appraisal process met or exceeded their expectations. However, only 51 percent reported that the performance reviews provided a clear path for the future.[12]

Although almost all organizations (99 percent) assess employee performance,[13] the purpose of or intended use of the performance appraisals vary, and the intended uses will impact how the process is designed and executed. The uses of performance appraisals are outlined in Figure 8-3.

Administrative Purpose

One of the primary purposes of the performance appraisal process is to guide administrative decisions. Stronger performers may receive pay raises and promotions while weaker performers may be transferred or terminated. The ratings and comments made on performance appraisals provide necessary documentation to justify HR decisions.[14]

Feedback and Performance Improvement

Performance appraisals may also serve an informational purpose to tell employees how they are performing on the aspects of their job. As well, they are a communication

Uses of Performance Appraisals

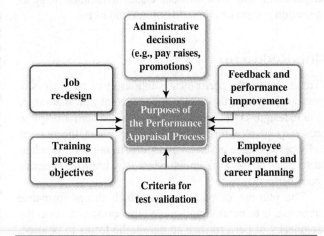

tool for managers to use to inform employees about performance expectations.

Employee Development and Career Planning

Performance appraisals with a development focus are useful tools for managers to use to coach employees for performance improvement on an ongoing basis. They are also useful to guide discussions about areas of strength and weakness for the employee, which may trigger training and development enrollment and inform longer-term career planning (see Chapter 7). When employee development is the goal, the performance appraisal may not include numeric ratings of performance. The focus is on ongoing immediate feedback, coaching and support, and forward-looking direction with the goal of employee engagement over control and oversight.[15]

Criteria for Test Validation

As discussed in Chapter 6, the effectiveness of selection tests may be validated against performance ratings. Stronger performers on selection tests should perform better on performance evaluations. To this end, performance appraisals become evidence in the event of litigation.

Training Program Objectives

In addition to identifying individual training needs for specific employees when they are not performing well in specific areas, performance appraisals provide insights into the effectiveness of other aspects of the HR system. For instance, if multiple employees have weak performance in a particular area, the training program offered may be insufficient or require an adjustment to meet the organization's needs. If poor performance is widespread, the HR department may have broader issues associated with its selection system or promotion of internal hires.

Job Redesign

Trends across the performance appraisals of employees in various jobs may also be a useful source of information for job redesign. Observing poor performance across employees may prompt further conversations about the reasons why performance is suffering. Efforts to improve job characteristics or the work environment may improve systemic poor performance.[16]

The purpose or purposes for which the performance appraisal is to be used will guide other decisions about the frequency of performance appraisal, the forms to be used, who completes the evaluations, and so on, which are discussed next.

The Performance Appraisal Process

Figure 8-4 shows an overview of the performance appraisal process. First, pertinent performance-related criteria must be identified, performance against those criteria is measured, and then feedback is given to employees and the HR department. Based on that feedback, the employee will continue in his or her job, and performance will be measured again following the next review period.

The HR department usually develops performance appraisals for employees in all departments. This centralization is meant to ensure uniformity. With uniformity in design and implementation, results are more likely to be comparable among similar groups of employees. Although the HR department may develop different approaches for managers and non-managers, uniformity within each group is needed to ensure useful results.

The appraisal should create an accurate picture of an individual's job performance by measuring performance-related criteria. To achieve this goal, appraisal systems should be job-related, be practical, have standards, and use dependable measures.[17] *Job-related* means that the appraisal evaluates critical behaviours that constitute job success. If the evaluation is not job-related, it is invalid and probably unreliable. Without validity and reliability, the system may discriminate in violation of antidiscrimination laws. Even when discrimination does not occur, appraisals are inaccurate and useless if they are not job-related, such as if an assessment of a manager's performance is based on whether the manager has a university degree. Validity and reliability evidence (discussed in Chapter 6) will be essential for any court challenge of performance criteria—for example, in case of a wrongful dismissal suit in which the employee's performance is an issue.

In addition, a job-related approach also must be *practical*. A practical system is one that, first of all, is understood by evaluators and employees; a complicated, impractical approach may cause resentment and non-use. The confusion can lead to inaccuracies that reduce the effectiveness of the appraisal. An example of a simple and practical approach would be to judge an employee's performance on production—for example, number of widgets.

FIGURE 8-4

The Performance Appraisal Process

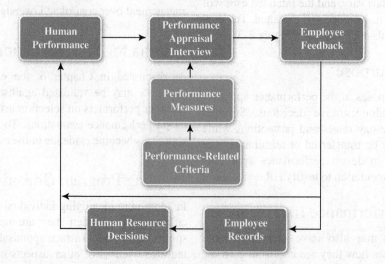

Performance evaluation requires **performance standards**—benchmarks against which performance is measured. To be effective, they should relate to the desired results of each job; they cannot be set arbitrarily. Knowledge of these standards is collected through job analysis. As discussed in Chapter 2, job analysis uncovers specific performance criteria by analyzing the performance of existing employees.

performance standards
The benchmarks against which performance is measured.

From the duties and standards listed in the job description, the analyst can decide which behaviours are critical and should be evaluated. If this information is lacking or unclear, standards may be developed from observation of the job or discussion with the immediate supervisor.

Performance evaluation also requires dependable **performance measures**, the ratings used to evaluate performance. To be useful, they must *be easy to use, be reliable,* and *report on the critical behaviours* that determine performance. For example, a call centre supervisor must observe the following in each representative:

performance measures
The ratings used to evaluate employee performance.

- *Use of company procedures*—following the appropriate script, verifying customer identity, and following company rules and regulations
- *Phone etiquette*—speaking clearly and courteously, staying calm even when customers do not
- *Accuracy*—providing accurate answers to customer questions and offering complementary service options to meet customer needs

Such observations can be made either directly or indirectly. *Direct observation* occurs when the rater actually sees the performance. *Indirect observation* occurs when the rater can evaluate only substitutes for actual performance. For example, a supervisor's monitoring of a representative's calls is direct observation; a written test on company procedures for handling calls from difficult customers is indirect observation. Likewise, hearing a report about performance from a second-hand source is another form of indirect observation.[18] Indirect observations are usually less accurate because they evaluate substitutes for actual performance.

Another dimension of performance measures is whether they are objective or subjective. *Objective* performance measures are those indications of job performance that are verifiable by others: for example, the average length of calls to solve customers' problems. The results are objective and verifiable. Usually, objective measures are quantitative. They typically include items such as gross units produced, net units approved by quality control, scrap rates, response time, number of customer complaints, or some other mathematically precise measure of performance. Objective measures are not available in all jobs, however. For instance, how would you objectively measure the performance of many white-collar jobs? A measure of minutes sitting at a computer or number of keystrokes would not give a very good indication of performance!

Subjective performance measures are those ratings that are based on opinion or perception. Usually, such measures are the rater's personal opinions, but they may be subject to biases, which will be discussed later in the chapter. When subjective measures are also indirect, accuracy becomes even lower. For example, measurement of a representative's phone etiquette is done subjectively because supervisors must use their personal opinions of good or bad manners. Accuracy is likely to be even lower when the rater uses an indirect measure, such as a test of phone etiquette or another employee's second-hand account of the employee's phone etiquette. Whenever possible, human resource specialists prefer objective and direct measures of performance.

Considerations for Designing an Effective Performance Appraisal Process

Once the purpose of the performance appraisal is established (e.g., administrative decisions versus employee development) and the appraisal system is linked to organizational objectives, a series of other considerations needs to be thought through. These include setting performance targets that are acceptable and achievable, determining the type of rating method and format, deciding whom to have involved in the process and training of the raters, providing performance appraisal feedback, and following up on the appraisal results. Further discussion of these considerations is presented next.

© Rob Daly/OJO Images/Getty Images.

Performance feedback is crucial for the motivation of employees. Ongoing feedback is also ideal for another motivational tool. Which one? (*Hint:* Setting . . .)

Performance Targets

Best practices suggest that the HR department should use information from the job analysis and collaborate with both management and employees to develop performance criteria. Input into system development significantly increases the probability of acceptance of the system by both management and employees. It gives employees a feeling of ownership. It is true that employees hired after a system has been installed will not have had input into it, but the knowledge that it was developed with the input of those who are rated by it will make it more acceptable.[19]

Once the performance criteria for a job have been established, it is time to identify acceptable performance standards. Performance standards may relate to *quality* (how well the objective has been achieved), *quantity* (how much, how many, and how often), and *time* (due dates, adherence to schedule, cycle times, and so on). If standards are set unilaterally by management, they risk becoming "management's standards" and may get little commitment from employees. This does not mean that employees should set their own performance standards but, rather, that the standards should be set with the employees to gain their commitment. It may be necessary for a manager to start out with a lower standard for a new employee until he or she has developed some experience and more self-confidence. Here, the manager's coaching skills become crucial, as do open communication, trust, and support by colleagues.[20] Characteristics of good performance standards are shown in Figure 8-5.

Goals or performance targets should also be set. Goals derive from the strategic business plans of the organization, operationalized at the department level by the manager. It is the responsibility of the manager, as coach and counsellor, to set goals that the employee sees as achievable.

© Rob Daly/OJO Images/Getty Images.

A maître d', a server, and a wine steward all do restaurant-related work, but each of their performance evaluations uses different criteria. Do you recognize some criteria that they may have in common?

Characteristics of Good Performance Standards

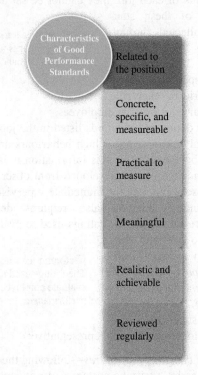

Characteristics of Good Performance Standards

- Related to the position
- Concrete, specific, and measureable
- Practical to measure
- Meaningful
- Realistic and achievable
- Reviewed regularly

SOURCE: Based on Aguinis, Herman (2012), *Performance Management* (3rd ed.), Pearson.

Studies have consistently found that when supervisors set specific goals, performance improves twice as much as when they set general goals.[21] Increasingly, supervisors and employees set goals together at the beginning of the appraisal period and establish a *performance management plan,* also known as a PMP. Then, after the review period (and, hopefully, after ongoing feedback and dialogue between the supervisor and employee), they meet again to review the employee's progress against the goals set forth in the PMP.

LO3 Comparative and Noncomparative Evaluation Methods

Performance appraisal systems can use different types of evaluation methods. For ease of discussion, we have grouped these methods into those that focus on comparisons between employees and noncomparative methods. The forms that raters complete to evaluate the performance of employees depend on whether employees are compared to each other or only to performance standards and targets.

Comparative Evaluation Methods

Comparative evaluation methods compare one person's performance with that of co-workers. Usually, comparative evaluations are conducted by the manager. They are useful for deciding merit pay increases, promotions, and organizational rewards because they can result in a ranking of employees from best to worst. The most common forms of comparative evaluations are the ranking method and forced distributions. Although these methods are practical and easily standardized, they offer little job-related feedback.

> **comparative evaluation methods** A collection of different methods that compare one person's performance with that of co-workers.

Ranking Method

The **ranking method** has the rater place each employee in order from best to worst. All the HR department knows is that certain employees are better than others. It does not know by how much. The employee ranked second may be almost as good as the one who was first or considerably worse. This method is subject to the halo and recency effects (discussed later in this chapter) although rankings by two or more raters can be averaged to help reduce biases. Its advantages include ease of administration and explanation.

> **ranking method** A method of evaluating employees that ranks them from best to worst on some trait.

Forced Distributions

Forced distributions require raters to sort employees into different classifications. Usually a certain proportion must be put in each category. Figure 8-6 shows how a rater may classify 10 subordinates, and Figure 8-7 shows these ratings plotted in a typical bell curve. As with the ranking method, relative differences among employees are unknown, but this method does overcome the biases of central tendency, leniency, and strictness. Some workers and supervisors strongly dislike this method because employees are often rated lower than they or their supervisor/rater thinks is correct because the HR department's forced distribution requires some employees to be rated low.

A famous example of a forced distribution is the "Vitality Curve" used by GE under its legendary CEO Jack ("Neutron Bomb") Welch:

> Jack Welch insisted that all managers categorize their employees into categories of "Top 20," "The Vital 70," and "Bottom 10" and that the latter be fired every year, regardless of actual performance. It is understandable that many managers strongly resisted this demand, but they had no choice. It should be noted that under Jack Welch's reign, GE had over 400,000 employees.[22]

HR departments may use comparative methods, such as forced distributions along a bell curve, to inform compensation decisions, wherein the top performers are granted bonuses or higher raises than average performers. Top performers may be offered development opportunities, recognition, or promotions. The weakest performers may be targeted for dismissal, remedial training, or performance improvement plans.[23]

> **forced distributions** A method of evaluating employees that requires raters to categorize employees.

FIGURE 8-6

The Forced Distribution Method of Appraisal of 10 Subordinates

Captone Fisheries Ltd. Forced Distribution Rating				
Classification: Overall Performance				
Lowest 10% of Subordinates	**Next 20% of Subordinates**	**Middle 40% of Subordinates**	**Next 20% of Subordinates**	**Best 10% of Subordinates**
A. Wilson	G. Carrs	B. Xe	K. McDougal	W. Vasilopolo
	M. Lopez	X. Chen	S. Savasriram	
		C. Grant		
		T. Valley		

FIGURE 8-7

Plotting Performance onto the Bell Curve

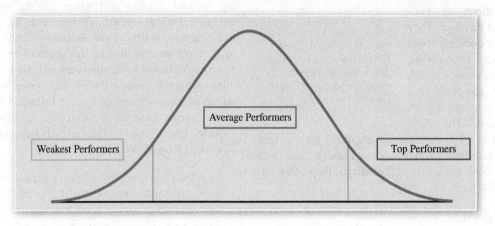

Noncomparative Evaluation Methods

Noncomparative evaluation methods, as the name implies, do not compare one employee against another but use scales or reports with performance criteria developed by supervisors or a committee. These methods include rating scales, behaviourally anchored rating scales, performance tests and observations, and management by objectives.

> **noncomparative evaluation methods** Appraisal methods that evaluate an employee's performance according to preset data, and not by comparing one person's performance with that of co-workers.

Rating Scales

Perhaps the oldest and most widely used form of performance appraisal is the **rating scale**, which requires the rater to provide a subjective evaluation of an individual's performance along a scale from low to high. An example appears in Figure 8-8. As the figure indicates, the evaluation is subjective in nature. Although subordinates or peers may use it, the immediate supervisor usually completes the form.

> **rating scale** A scale that requires the rater to provide a subjective evaluation of an individual's performance.

FIGURE 8-8

A Sample of a Rating Scale for Performance Evaluation

NutriGrow Organic Foods
Instructions: For the following performance factors, please indicate your rating and the basis for your evaluation.
Employee's Name _____ Department _____
Rater's Name _____ Date _____
Rating Definitions and Score Points
5 Outstanding (clearly superior performance)
4 Very good (exceeds expectations)
3 Good (meets expectations)
2 Marginal (needs improvement)
1 Poor (unsatisfactory)

Factors	Score	Comments
1. Dependability (reliability of employee)	_____	
2. Initiative (willingness to take action)	_____	
3. Overall output (productivity of employee)	_____	
4. Attendance (overall attendance, punctuality)	_____	
. . .		
. . .		
. . .		
20. Quality of work (accuracy, thoroughness, etc.)	_____	
Total	_____	

The form is completed by checking the most appropriate response for each performance factor. Responses may be given numerical values to enable an average score to be computed and compared for each employee. The advantages of this method are that it is inexpensive to develop and administer, raters need little training or time to complete the form, and it can be applied to a large number of employees.

This method has a number of disadvantages, however. A rater's biases are likely to be reflected in a subjective instrument of this type. Specific performance criteria might be omitted to make the form applicable to a variety of jobs. For example, "maintenance of equipment" might be left off because it applies to only a few workers. But for some employees, that item may be the most important part of the job. These omissions tend to limit specific feedback. Also, descriptive evaluations are subject to individual interpretations that vary widely. And when specific performance criteria are hard to identify, the form may rely on irrelevant personality variables that dilute the meaning of the evaluation. The result is a standardized form and procedure that are not always job-related.

To combat some of the criticisms that have been levied against rating scales, proponents now advocate for streamlined rating scales: specifically, by limiting the number of performance ratings to only those that are critical to job performance and using a simplified rating scale,[24] such as the one presented in Figure 8-9.

Behaviourally Anchored Rating Scales

Behaviourally anchored rating scales (BARS) attempt to reduce the subjectivity and biases of subjective performance measures. From descriptions of effective and ineffective performance provided by employees, peers, and supervisors, job analysts or knowledgeable employees group these examples into performance-related categories, such as employee knowledge, customer relations, and the like. Then, specific examples of these behaviours are placed along a scale (usually from 1 to 7).

Actual behaviours for a bank branch manager are illustrated on the rating scale shown in Figure 8-10. Since the positions on the scale are described in terms of job-related behaviour, an objective evaluation along the scale is more likely. The form also cites specific behaviours that can be used to provide performance feedback to employees. The BARS are job-related, practical, and standardized for similar jobs. But the rater's personal biases may still cause ratings to be high or low, although the specific behaviours that "anchor" the scale provide some criteria to guide the sincere rater. If the rater collects specific incidents during the rating period, the evaluation is apt to be more accurate and more legally defensible, besides being a more effective counselling tool. One serious limitation of BARS is that they only look at a limited number of performance categories, such as customer relations or team management. Also, each of these categories has only a limited number of specific behaviours. To improve the effectiveness of this approach when it comes time to counsel the employee, it is important that supervisors maintain records of performance events that occurred throughout the rating period.

behaviourally anchored rating scales (BARS) Evaluation tools that rate employees along a rating scale by means of specific behaviour examples on the scale.

FIGURE 8-9

A Simplified Rating Scale Example

Unacceptable — Failed to meet technical quality standards; work was incomplete, poorly conceived, error ridden or not well targeted; work performed unsatisfactorily or in an unresponsive manner.

Successful — Products and services met expectations, were complete, well targeted and understandable; work performed was responsive and competent.

Outstanding — Surpassed quality standards and expectations; products were thorough, error-free, ideally targeted and maximally responsive to needs.

FIGURE 8-10

Behaviourally Anchored Rating Scale for Bank Branch Manager

Team Management		Bank of Ontario
Outstanding Performance	—7—	Can be expected to praise publicly for tasks completed well, and constructively criticizes in private those individuals who have produced less than adequate results.
Good Performance	—6—	Can be expected to show great confidence in subordinates, and openly displays this with the result that they develop to meet expectations.
Fairly Good Performance	—5—	Can be expected to ensure that employee HR records are kept right up to date, that reports are written on time, and that salary reviews are not overlooked.
Acceptable Performance	—4—	Can be expected to admit a personal mistake, thus showing that he or she is human too.
Fairly Poor Performance	—3—	Can be expected to make "surprise" performance appraisals of subordinates.
Poor Performance	—2—	Can be expected not to support decisions made by a subordinate (makes exceptions to rules).
Extremely Poor Performance	—1—	Can be expected not to accept responsibility for errors and to pass blame to subordinates.

A slightly different, and less common, method is the *Behaviour Observation Scale (BOS)*. Like BARS, BOS uses critical incidents. Instead of making a judgment about whether a specific job behaviour is expected to occur, however, it measures the frequency of the observed behaviours with scales ranging from high to low.

Performance Tests and Observations

With a limited number of jobs, performance appraisal may be based upon a test of knowledge or skills. The test may be of the paper-and-pencil variety or an actual demonstration of skills. The test must be reliable and valid to be useful. For the method to be job-related, observations should be made under circumstances likely to be encountered. Practicality may suffer when the cost of test development is high:

> Pilots of all major airlines are subject to evaluation by airline raters and Transport Canada. Evaluations of flying ability are usually made both in a flight simulator and while being observed during an actual flight. The evaluation is based on how well the pilot follows prescribed flight procedures and safety rules. Although this approach is expensive, public safety makes it practical, as well as job-related and standardized.

The above approaches evaluate past performance; they examine what the employee's behaviours have been over the previous performance appraisal period. The next approach evaluates employee potential for future performance with the focus on setting future performance goals.

Management-by-Objectives Approach

The heart of the **management-by-objectives (MBO) approach** is that each employee and superior jointly establish performance goals for the future.[25] Ideally, these goals are mutually agreed upon and objectively measurable. If both conditions are met, employees are apt to be more motivated to achieve the goal, as they have participated in setting it. Moreover, they can periodically adjust their behaviour to ensure attainment of an objective if they can measure their progress toward the objective. But to adjust their efforts, performance feedback must be available on a regular basis.

When future objectives are set, employees gain the motivational benefit of a specific target to organize and direct their efforts. Objectives also help the employee and supervisor discuss specific developmental needs of the employee. When done correctly, performance discussions focus on the job's objectives and not personality variables. Biases are reduced to the extent that goal attainment can be measured objectively.

In practice, some challenges with MBO programs include objectives that are too ambitious or too narrow. The result is frustrated employees or overlooked areas of performance. For example, employees may set objectives that are measured by quantity rather than quality because quality, while it may be equally important, is often more difficult to measure. When employees and managers do focus on subjectively measured objectives, special care is needed to ensure that biases do not distort the manager's evaluation. Figure 8-11 shows the annual assessment of the performance of a salesperson, using an MBO approach. The Spotlight on HRM provides an example of the successful implementation of an MBO process at Agilent Technologies.

management-by-objectives (MBO) approach Requires an employee and superior to jointly establish performance goals for the future; employees are subsequently evaluated on how well they have obtained these objectives.

FIGURE 8-11

MBO Evaluation Report for a Salesperson

Objectives Set	Period Objective	Accomplishments	Variance
1. Number of sales calls	85	98	−15%
2. Number of new customers	10	8	−20%
3. Sales of Dulcha product line	2,500	3,100	+24%
4. Sales of Salmy product line	1,500	1,350	−10%
5. Customer complaints	10	22	+120%
6. Number of training courses taken	5	3	−40%
7. Number of monthly reports on time	12	11	−8%

Spotlight *on* HRM

Management by Objectives at Agilent Technologies

With 18,500 employees in 110 countries, test and measurement giant Agilent Technologies (the now wholly independent former test and measurement division of Hewlett Packard) has values including dedication to innovation; trust, respect, and teamwork; uncompromising integrity; speed, focus, and accountability to meet customer needs; and a culture of performance drawing on the full range of its employees' skills and aspirations. However, its pay practices and training tools were not having the desired impact. Facing high turnover, the need to increase employee engagement and plan for employee development, and, most importantly, to make HR a strategic decision-making partner, Agilent developed a management-by-objectives performance management system. Its purpose is to give employees freedom to do their work in the manner that suits them, make them responsible and accountable for their objectives and results, and create visibility for how their individual work contributes to the objectives of the organization.

The MBO process at Agilent involves four steps:

Step 1: Define the Measures of Success

The broad measures of success at Agilent reside in four quadrants: Customer Satisfaction (create loyal customers); Employees, Leadership, and Culture (speed to opportunity); Financial (leverage the operating model); and Markets (accelerate profitable growth). These four quadrants are further subdivided to set priorities for each group, business unit, and department within a performance plan defining individual priority objectives and development. Following this step, employee deliverables are clear, as is their link to achieving organizational objectives.

Step 2: Quarterly MAPS Process

The objective of MAPS (short for My Accountability and Performance Standards) is to ensure that employees are crystal-clear about what is expected of them, where they stand, and what their manager is doing to support their development. The focus is on open dialogue on areas where employees are performing well and

where they need to improve. Jointly determined goals are documented and uploaded onto the MAPS website for future reference. Function-wide reports are also published to share and increase accountability. The entire process is transparent, providing clarity and ownership of the objectives.

Step 3: HR Analytics

Quarterly meetings are held between HR and the function leads to discuss the function's HR data. Data points discussed include rank and level turnover data; a compensation ratio (calculated as the average of the employee's actual pay divided by the pay range mid-point of the job grade); percentage of employees below the minimum compensation ratio; comparison of turnover/pay between new, existing, and exited employees; and employees on a corrective action plan. These meetings help function leads understand and own the HR data in their departments. HR's role is then to help them with tools, consultation, and brainstorming, and to partner with them on creating and executing programs. This process helps the function leads to make prudent HR decisions, such as distribution of wages, and provides information to HR that can be used to improve business processes or inform policy changes.

Step 4: Leadership Audit Survey

The purpose of the Leadership Audit Survey is to provide feedback from employees to each manager through a twice-annual survey of all Agilent employees. The survey measures four aspects of employee engagement: customer orientation (to surpass customer expectations); speed and decisiveness (for addressing conflicts and making decisions); risk taking (to allow employees freedom to take informed risks); and engagement (through feedback and clear links between their performance and the performance of Agilent as a whole). The survey provides leaders with feedback and allows managers with perfect scores to share their stories with managers who are not doing as well to help them learn and improve performance. Development support is provided to managers requiring improvement.

Agilent has recognized the importance of paying employees well to keep them engaged, happy, and motivated. It also provides intangible motivators like work/life flexibility where employees are able to work from home once a week. The company's philosophy is to manage by objectives and not by the number of hours in the office. It also believes in differentiation with feedback and letting employees know where they stand with respect to their performance.

Since adopting MBO, turnover has dropped significantly below market, they have best-in-class engagement scores, industry recognition through awards such as a top 10 Great Place to Work, and a successful culture of differentiation within the company.

SOURCE: Excerpts taken and adapted from: SHRM Case Studies on HR Best Practices, "Agilent technologies—measures for excellence" (2012), https://www.shrm.org/hr-today/trends-and-forecasting/research-and-surveys/Documents/SHRMIndiaBestworkplaces.pdf.

LO4 Raters and Rater Training

When evaluating employee performance, significant consideration is given to who should be conducting the evaluation and to training the raters.

Multiple Sources for Performance Ratings

Should ratings be made by the employee's supervisor or other potential raters as well? Although the HR department usually designs the appraisal system, it seldom does the actual evaluation of performance. Although the employee's immediate supervisor participates in the evaluation 95 percent of the time,[26] managers are not the only source of information about employee performance. Other sources including employees themselves, peers, direct reports/subordinates, and customers may be able to provide feedback on different aspects of the job, given that every contributor probably has a different focus.[27]

Pictured in Figure 8-12, the **360-degree performance appraisal**, or "multi-source feedback," is now used by more than 85 percent of Fortune 500 companies.[28] Advantages of 360-degree systems include improved feedback from more sources, team development, reduced discrimination risk, improved customer service, and enhanced training needs assessment.[29]

> **360-degree performance appraisal** Combination of self, peer, supervisor, and subordinate performance evaluation.

Self-Appraisals

Getting employees to conduct a self-appraisal can be a useful evaluation technique if the goal of evaluation is to further self-development. The onus is on employees to recall and document the work they have performed over the

FIGURE 8-12

360-Degree Performance Appraisals

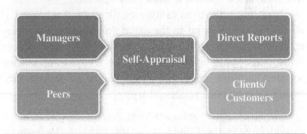

appraisal period and to highlight major accomplishments. Self-perceptions of performance are often higher than perceptions of other sources, however, so managers need to be prepared to provide clear reasoning for the differences in ratings.[30] Through self-evaluations, employees are also given the opportunity to identify areas for improvement, which can help managers identify what they might be able to do to eliminate roadblocks and obstacles.

Peer Appraisals

Peers may have unique opportunities to observe employees' interpersonal, collaboration, and influence skills. They may also observe other employees' typical performance, such as when they are not on their "best behaviour" because their boss is present. There are multiple benefits to including peer appraisals into multi-rater feedback, including encouraging recognition, facilitating accountability for performance improvement, increasing the accuracy of ratings, and surfacing hidden talent when peers observe behaviors such as team leadership or networking skills.[31]

Direct Report Appraisals

Many employees are in a good position to evaluate the performance of their supervisors. No one is in a better position to assess how a supervisor provides praise or feedback, autonomy, and guidance to an employee than the employee him- or herself.[32] More and more organizations are including direct report appraisals, or upward feedback, in their performance appraisal systems. Direct report appraisals may help to identify potential leadership or management issues, and are valuable for developmental (more than administrative) purposes. Many direct reports may be concerned about providing feedback and ratings to their supervisors for fear of potential retribution if their responses are identified. However, direct report and peer ratings of supervisors are typically comparable, and, thus, there may not be significant rating inflation despite these concerns.

Customers

Customers or clients may provide another useful source of performance feedback. Customer complaints or compliments, customer feedback surveys, or asking valued clients to evaluate their employee contact can all provide informative feedback as part of a multi-rater system.

Using multiple sources may confirm an assessment if all or a majority point in the same direction, or they may raise a caution flag if the assessments by difference sources are at odds. While many organizations across Canada have adopted multiple raters into their performance appraisal systems, here is one success story:

> The Greater Toronto Airports Authority (GTAA), which operates Canada's busiest airport (Pearson handled about 41 million passengers in 2017), needed to align its human resources with its customer-centric strategy. Over a two-year period, HR completed 360-degree feedback sessions with all 1,200 employees. They were able to address the identified shortcomings in how staff related to its customers through their core competency training. The result was more consistent and effective leadership at the GTAA.[33]

Not everybody shares the enthusiasm about the 360-degree approach. The approach is better suited for employee development purposes (i.e., to improve performance) as opposed to administrative decisions (e.g., to determine pay raises and promotions)[34] and can sap morale, harm motivation, and enable disenfranchised employees to sabotage performance feedback to others if careful attention is not paid to their development.[35] For instance, consideration must be given to how rating sources with different perspectives on the employee's performance are integrated and how to preserve anonymity yet provide specific feedback.

Rater Training

Regardless of who the raters are going to be, they will all need some training regarding the performance appraisal system. They will need to learn the purpose of the performance evaluations and understand how they align with the organization's strategy. Some HR departments provide raters with a rater's handbook that describes guidelines for conducting the evaluation or for providing ratees with feedback. Key terms, such as "shows initiative" or "provides leadership," may also be defined in the handbook.

Raters also need to be trained in observation techniques and categorization skills (e.g., the use of diaries or critical incidents and how to group job behaviours or apply organizational performance standards). Frame-of-reference (FOR) training aims at improving these skills.[36] Rater training will often include information about potential rating errors (e.g., the halo effect, leniency) and the ways to minimize them. Figure 8-13 provides a summary of rating errors.

Although rater error training used to form a large component of rater training, the newer trend is training on how to make valid judgments on the basis of relatively complex information.[37] Likewise, all rating sources, including employees, will typically receive training.[38] Finally, rater training may include information on how to conduct the evaluation interview.

LO5 Evaluation Interviews

Once the performance appraisal has been completed and integrated, the results must then be communicated with the employee. This feedback process is called the *evaluation interview*. **Evaluation interviews** provide employees with feedback about their past performance or future potential. The evaluator may provide this feedback through several approaches: tell and sell, tell and listen, and problem solving. The *tell-and-sell approach* reviews the employee's performance and tries to convince the employee to perform better. It is best used on new employees. The *tell-and-listen approach* allows the employee to explain reasons, excuses, and defensive feelings about performance. It attempts to overcome these reactions by counselling the employee on how to perform better. The *problem-solving approach* identifies problems that are interfering with employee performance. Then, through training, coaching, or counselling, efforts are made to remove these deficiencies, often by setting goals for future performance.

Regardless of which approach is used to give employees feedback, the guidelines listed in Figure 8-14 can help make the performance review session more effective.[39] The intent of these suggestions is to make the interview a positive, performance-improving dialogue. By stressing desirable aspects of employee performance, the evaluator

> **evaluation interviews** Performance review sessions that give employees feedback about their past performance or future potential.

FIGURE 8-13

Common Rater Errors

Error Type	Description	Example
Halo	A favourable opinion of employee performance in one category skews ratings across multiple categories	Friendship and favourable impression of social skill leads to a rating of high productivity despite low quantity and quality
Central Tendency	Reluctance to give very poor or excellent ratings, instead placing ratings near the centre of the rating scale	Not giving out any ratings of 1 or 7 on a 7-point scale to any employees
Leniency	Raters are too easy in evaluating employee performance	All employees are rated as "above average"
Strictness	Raters are too harsh in evaluating employee performance	All employees are rated as "below average"
Personal Prejudice	A rater's dislike for a person or group distorts his or her ratings	Giving ratings to female welders that are all lower than ratings given to male welders (notwithstanding welding performance)
Recency Effect	Ratings are strongly affected by the employee's most recent actions	Just last week, an average nurse happened to save a patient's life, and his performance is praised despite average performance over the last year
Contrast Errors	Raters compare employees to each other rather than to a performance standard	Everyone's performance is compared to Javier, who is the best, and Wen, who is the worst, instead of to the performance standards described as low, moderate, and high.

FIGURE 8-14

Guidelines for Effective Performance Evaluation Interviews

1. *Emphasize* positive aspects of employee performance.
2. *Tell* each employee that the evaluation session is to improve performance, not to discipline.
3. *Provide* immediate positive and developmental feedback in a private location, and explicitly state that you are providing the employee with performance feedback.
4. *Review* performance formally at least annually and more frequently for new employees or those who are performing poorly. Ongoing and regular feedback is optimal.
5. *Make* criticisms specific, not general and vague.
6. *Focus* criticisms on performance, not on personality characteristics.
7. *Stay* calm and do not argue with the person being evaluated.
8. *Identify* specific actions the employee can take to improve performance, and discuss the manager's role in supporting future development and career planning.
9. *Emphasize* the evaluator's willingness to assist the employee's efforts and to improve performance.
10. *End* the evaluation session by stressing the positive aspects of the employee's performance and reviewing plans to improve performance.

Spotlight *on* ETHICS

On Probation

You have recently been hired as a supervisor and accepted a six-month probationary period. You have earned a Certificate in Human Resource Management from a well-known university. Your arrival coincides with performance appraisal time in the company. You quickly realize that the currently used appraisal instrument is of little value because it consists mainly of subjective measures. The appraisal instrument is the brain-child of the CEO, who is very proud of "his baby," as he explained when he hired you. One of the tasks given to you is the training of supervisors in assessing performance. You know that any training with this instrument is a waste of time, but if you criticize it, there is a danger that you will not survive the probationary period. What will you do?

can give the employee renewed confidence in his or her ability to perform satisfactorily. This positive approach also enables the employee to keep desirable and undesirable performance in perspective because it prevents the individual from feeling that performance review sessions are entirely negative. When negative comments are made, they focus on work performance and not the individual's personality. Specific rather than vague generalities and examples of the employee's shortcomings are used so that the individual knows exactly what behaviours need to be changed. The review session concludes by focusing on actions that the employee can take to improve areas of poor performance. In that concluding discussion, the evaluator usually offers to provide whatever assistance the employee needs to overcome the deficiencies discussed.

Having managers provide guidance and feedback is not only linked to employee performance, but also has a significant impact on employee engagement.[40]

Frequency of Feedback

Most performance appraisals that form the basis for administrative decisions, such as pay raises and promotions, take place once a year. When the purpose of the performance appraisal is to communicate performance expectations and provide course correction feedback, ideally performance feedback would be given by the supervisor immediately after effective or ineffective job behaviour was observed. However, this is challenging in many organizational settings where both employee and supervisor are busy completing their job tasks, and may not be nearby when performance events occur. When the performance appraisal is intended for employee development, feedback sessions on a monthly, quarterly, or at least twice-yearly basis is typical. Feedback provided as an ongoing activity in real time as it occurs is most useful to help employees develop and realize their full potential.[41] Notably, when the employee has received unsatisfactory performance reviews and the employee and manager are engaged in a performance improvement process, the appraisal and feedback loop may be weekly or even daily.

A survey across Western Canadian employers in 2016 revealed that 56 percent perform annual performance reviews, another 16 percent perform reviews more often, and 8 percent do not perform reviews at all. The remaining 19 percent conduct either formal or informal ongoing performance coaching. Smaller firms were more likely to engage in coaching, and the public sector was more likely to engage in formal annual reviews.[42]

LO6 Talent Management

Within the human resource management field, one recent development is a focus on talent management. As discussed in Chapter 7, talent management involves identifying and developing specific individuals within the organization who are seen as having high potential. The concept comes from recognizing that employees who are *top performers* are not necessarily the people with the *highest potential* for working in key organizational positions or areas, or for moving up in the organization.

One tool for conversing about the development opportunities that could be provided to employees who might have high potential within an organization is the 9-box grid.[43] Figure 8-15 shows an example of a 9-box grid. Employees are plotted into the grid according to both their performance in their current job and ratings of their potential for future positions. Employees categorized into the "future star," "consistent star," and "current star" boxes may be targeted for specific developmental opportunities. Opportunities granted may include (a) specific work assignments designed to give them the opportunity to grow their skills in a particular area, such as a key

FIGURE 8-15

A 9-Box Grid Depicting Performance by Potential

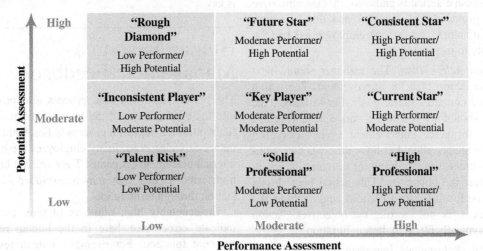

business unit or overseas assignment (often referred to as "stretch assignments"); (b) educational opportunities, such as advanced degree or certificate programs, or organization-specific leadership or other training opportunities; and/or (c) inclusion in events or mentor activities that will give the employee visibility and access to senior employees of the organization.[44]

Many global organizations, such as Pepsi Co., Citi, and SC Johnson, and Canadian organizations,[45] including National Bank in Montreal, Xerox Canada, and TD Bank Group, now have a talent management department or talent management group within their HR department.[46] Many times, employees will receive evaluations of potential along with ratings of performance. Both cues can be used by the HR department to inform their decisions, such as development and compensation.

LO7 Establishing a Performance Improvement Plan

Appraisals without consequences lose their effectiveness very quickly. Employees as well as supervisors have to see that appraisal results are taken seriously by management

and are followed up on. If there are administrative consequences of the appraisal, such as pay raises or bonuses, they should follow in a reasonably tight time frame.[47] Likewise, if the performance appraisal has indicated that the employee is not meeting acceptable performance standards, a plan needs to be put in place to bring performance up to acceptable levels. There are multiple reasons for poor performance, such as insufficient or inadequate training, unclear job expectations, or roadblocks preventing effective performance. A *performance improvement plan* (PIP) is an effective way of giving employees struggling to meet performance standards the opportunity to succeed, while still holding them accountable for past performance.

Figure 8-16 summarizes six steps for creating a PIP, and these are described below:[48]

1. *Getting Started.* The first step for establishing a PIP is to document the employee's current performance and the areas that require improvement. This documentation should include the main performance issues expressed specifically and objectively using facts, examples, and patterns of performance concerns.

   Important questions for the supervisor to address in advance include ensuring that the performance

FIGURE 8-16

The Performance Improvement Plan Process

Getting Started → Develop an Action Plan → Review the Performance Improvement Plan → Meet with the Employee → Follow Up → PIP Conclusion

expectations set were clear; that the employee has the tools, resources, and skills necessary to be successful; that the background information needed to document the performance deficit is gathered; that the employee has been provided with feedback and that it is non-personal in nature; and that the employee has had the opportunity to respond.[49]

2. *Develop an Action Plan.* The manager should next develop an action plan for improvement. The action plan should contain specific goals. For instance, "the employee should not be late for work once during this 90-day performance improvement cycle." For each goal, the manager should contemplate whether additional resources, time, training, or coaching is necessary to meet the objectives. This action plan should help set performance expectations and include the consequences for not meeting the objectives. Action plans are typically 60 or 90 days in duration.[50]

3. *Review the Performance Improvement Plan.* Before meeting with the employee, the manager should seek assistance from the HR department or other knowledgeable professionals. The HR department should ensure that the plan is clear, specific, unemotional, and attainable within the set time frame. This is an important step in the event that the employee does not meet the performance improvement objectives and may proceed *toward termination.*

4. *Meet with the Employee.* When meeting with the employee, the manager should clearly lay out the areas for improvement and the action plan. Following the employee's feedback and input, the action plan may need some modification. After the changes are implemented, both the manager and employee should sign the PIP.

5. *Follow Up.* Regular follow-up meetings on a weekly or bi-weekly basis should be set for the manager and employee. These meetings should discuss any potential roadblocks encountered and required tools or training, and provide the opportunity for the employee to ask questions or to seek guidance or clarification.

6. *PIP Conclusion.* Following the PIP period, if the employee was able to meet the objectives, then the PIP is closed and the employee continues employment. If the employee was unable to improve and meet the objectives in the plan, then the employer should close the PIP and terminate employment. If the employee did improve a bit but perhaps did not quite meet performance expectations set out in the PIP, there are several options. First, the employer may agree to extend the PIP for another few weeks or months. Second, the employer may seek to revise the objectives, believing in retrospect that the objectives were too challenging or not within the employee's control. In this case, the employer may end the PIP or extend the PIP period. Third, the employer may terminate employment because the standards simply were not met.

When terminating an employee for not meeting performance expectations, documentation is critical. Engaging the HR department to ensure proper processes are followed is key.

Human Resource Management Feedback

The performance appraisal process also provides insight into the effectiveness of the human resource management function. If the appraisal process indicates that poor performance is widespread, many employees are excluded from internal placement decisions. They will not be promoted or transferred. In fact, they may be excluded from the organization through termination.

Unacceptably high numbers of poor performers may indicate errors elsewhere in the human resource management function. For example, human resource development may be failing to fulfill career plans because the people who are hired during the selection process are poorly screened. Or the human resource plan may be in error because the job analysis information is wrong or the employment equity plan seeks the wrong objectives. Likewise, the human resource department may be failing to respond to the challenges of the external environment or effective job design. Sometimes, the human resource function is pursuing the wrong objectives. Or the appraisal system itself may be faulty because of management resistance, incorrect performance standards or measures, or a lack of constructive feedback.

Finally, focusing on future performance targets allows the human resource department to provide feedback to employees as to the status of their career progression. If an employee's performance is inadequate, the cause has to be investigated. If it is a lack of skill or experience, the necessary improvements have to be made part of the goals discussed with the employee. Ideally, a step-by-step plan will be the outcome of the interview process.

Legal Aspects of Performance Appraisal

A performance appraisal form is a legal document. The implication is that raters have to be careful to use only performance criteria that are relevant to the job. In a court challenge, for example, where an employee loses a job as a result of inadequate job performance, the human resource manager has to prove that the job-related performance criteria used were *valid* and were used *consistently.* Nonrelevant criteria can be avoided if performance standards are established through a thorough job analysis and recorded in a job description.

It is also a legal requirement that a reasonable time frame be set for performance improvement.[51] The length of time would depend on the job. While it may be reasonable to expect an office clerk to improve his or her performance within a few weeks or months, it might take a manager a year or more to show improvement.

Well-documented performance shortcomings and documentation maintained through the performance improvement plan process will be key to establishing that dismissal was not wrongful.[52]

SUMMARY

Performance management is an ongoing process that integrates an organization's vision with performance objectives and performance measurements. Performance appraisal is a critical part of a performance management system. There are multiple purposes for which performance appraisals might be used, and the purposes will influence the choice of performance evaluation method used. Different methods will compare employee performance to performance of other employees, or to established performance standards. Standards are based on job-related criteria that best determine successful job performance.

Multiple raters may be used to gather information and feedback on the employee's performance, including managers, peers, customers/clients, direct reports, and the employee him/herself. The raters require training to ensure that they will contribute effectively to the performance management system. Once ratings are integrated into a completed appraisal, an evaluation interview with the employee is held.

Administrative consequences of performance appraisals, such as pay raises or bonuses, should be paid shortly after the evaluation interview. If a performance improvement plan is necessary, it should be initiated as soon as the inadequate performance level is described to the employee. Performance appraisals also provide feedback to the HR department about its performance. HR specialists need to be keenly aware that poor performance, especially when it is widespread, may reflect problems with previous HR management activities that are malfunctioning.

TERMS FOR REVIEW

360-degree performance appraisal 261
balanced scorecard 250
behaviourally anchored rating scales (BARS) 257
comparative evaluation methods 255
evaluation interviews 262
forced distributions 255
management-by-objectives (MBO) approach 259

noncomparative evaluation methods 256
performance appraisal 248
performance management 248
performance measures 253
performance standards 253
ranking method 255
rating scale 256

SELF-ASSESSMENT EXERCISE

Performance Appraisal as a Crucial Management Skill

1. Performance appraisal includes assessing managerial attitudes.		T	F
2. One application of performance appraisals is to discipline employees.		T	F
3. One of the key elements of a performance appraisal system is a training needs analysis.		T	F
4. Effective performance standards are determined through a survey to ensure employee input.		T	F
5. The halo effect occurs when raters are too easy on employees in evaluating their performance.		T	F

(continued)

6. The reliability of a performance appraisal instrument is the most crucial characteristic.   T   F

7. Because of potential personal biases, performance appraisal results cannot be used in courts.   T   F

8. A weighted checklist weighs the performance evaluation made by a department head higher than that of   T   F
   a direct supervisor.

9. The critical incident method uses employee self-reports of critical events that employees experience on   T   F
   the job.

10. Self-appraisal is the preferred performance appraisal method for executives.   T   F

SCORING
Of course, you realized that all of the above statements are false. If not, it is advisable to reread the sections where the mistake originated.

REVIEW AND DISCUSSION QUESTIONS

1. Discuss the differences between performance management and performance appraisal.

2. Explain why Agilent is a good example of effective performance management. What did management do to make it one of the great employers?

3. What are the purposes of performance appraisals?

4. Suppose that a company for which you work uses a rating scale. The items on the scale are generally personality characteristics. What criticisms would you have of this method?

5. If you were asked to recommend a replacement for the rating scale, what actions would you take before selecting another appraisal technique?

6. Why are direct and objective measures of performance usually considered superior to indirect and subjective measures?

7. If your organization were to use subjective measures to evaluate employee performance, what instructions

would you give evaluators about the biases they may encounter?

8. Describe how you would conduct a typical performance evaluation interview.

9. How do the results of performance appraisals affect other human resource management activities?

10. Describe the characteristics of a 360-degree performance appraisal.

11. In what ways is the linking up approach a useful performance management process?

12. What is the relationship between a performance appraisal system and a selection system?

13. Explain how you would go about establishing a performance improvement plan?

14. Explain the legal aspect of a performance appraisal system. Under what circumstances could it become a crucial document?

CRITICAL THINKING QUESTIONS

1. If the dean of your faculty asked you to serve on a committee to develop a performance appraisal system for evaluating the faculty, what performance criteria would you identify? Of these criteria, which ones do you think are most likely to determine the faculty members' success at your school? What standards would you recommend to the dean, regardless of the specific evaluation instrument selected?

2. Your organization has dismissed an employee for not performing up to par. She sues the company for

unjust dismissal, claiming that the company's performance appraisal instrument is not a valid assessment tool, since no woman had served on the committee responsible for developing it. Are you able to persuade a judge that, despite the fact that no woman served on the committee, your appraisal instrument is a valid one?

3. Can one performance appraisal instrument be used for all levels in an organization—that is, executives, middle managers, and employees? Why or why not?

ETHICS QUESTION

You are a branch manager, and one of your supervisors is a good friend of yours, the friendship going back to your high school years. His normally average performance has been deteriorating over the last two years, mainly because of his sick wife, a situation that causes him to miss many working days. He also has five children. You know that money is a big issue for him, and if you give him above-average performance ratings he would receive significant bonuses.

Discuss the ethical issues involved.

RESEARCH EXERCISE

1. 360-Degree Performance Appraisal (http://performance-appraisals.org/faq/index360.htm)

   What are the strengths and weaknesses of a 360-degree performance appraisal? Would you be comfortable using it if you were a manager? Why or why not?

2. Matthew Effect (http://www.performance-appraisal.com/bias.htm)

   What is the Matthew Effect in performance appraisals? Where does the name come from? Can it be avoided? How?

3. "Ten Stupid Things Managers Do to Screw Up Performance Appraisals" (http://performance-appraisals.org/Bacalsappraisalarticles/articles/stupman.htm)

   Are the 10 "stupid" things some managers do based on research, or do they represent the personal opinion of the author? How valid are they? If they are valid, are there remedies?

4. "Seven Stupid Things Employees Do to Screw Up Performance Appraisals" (http://performance-appraisals.org/Bacalsappraisalarticles/articles/stupemp.htm)

   In what way are these seven "stupid" things different from the ten "stupid" things managers do (see above)? Who would initiate remedies?

INCIDENT 8-1

The Malfunctioning Regional Human Resource Department

For one month, the corporate human resource department of Universal Insurance Ltd. had two specialists review the operations of their regional human resource department in Vancouver. The review of the regional office centred on the department's human resource information base. A brief summary of their findings listed the following observations:

- Each employee's performance appraisal showed little change from the previous year. Poor performers rated poor year in and year out.

- Nearly 70 percent of the appraisals were not initialled by the employee even though company policy required employees to do so after they had discussed their review with the rater.

- Of those employees who initialled the evaluations, several commented that the work standards were irrelevant and unfair.

- A survey of past employees conducted by corporate office specialists revealed that 35 percent of them believed performance feedback was too infrequent.

- Another 30 percent complained about the lack of advancement opportunities because most openings were filled from outside, and no one had ever told these workers they were unpromotable.

The corporate and regional human resource directors were dismayed by the findings. Each thought the problems facing the regional office were different.

DISCUSSION QUESTIONS

1. What do you think is the major problem with the performance appraisal process in the regional office?

2. What problems do you think exist with the regional office's (a) job analysis information, (b) human resource planning, (c) training and development, and (d) career planning?

EXERCISE 8-1

Developing a Performance Appraisal System

Time: one hour. Form groups of five to six. Assume that your group is the Faculty Evaluation Committee assigned the task to assess the performance of the course instructor.

1. Define at least three performance criteria for the instructor.
2. How would you measure them so that the results would be useful for a tenure and promotion decision?

3. Which type of instrument or method do you suggest? Why?
4. Who should be the appraisers?
5. Time permitting, compare the results in your group with those of another group.

WE CONNECTIONS: PERFORMANCE MANAGEMENT

Performance Appraisal Meeting

Project Manager Oliver Caine skimmed his notes as he waited for Ben Robins to come to the meeting room. He hoped Ben would arrive soon, as he wanted to get the conversation finished quickly. He had a lot of other people to get through. It was performance appraisal season, and Oliver had to sit down with each of his seven software engineers, just as he had done the year before. Oliver had promised the HR people that he would hand in the forms by Friday, which had seemed like a good idea three weeks ago when he had agreed to it. Unfortunately, there had been some unexpected issues with his project in the meantime so now he had to squeeze all of the performance management activities into a couple of days.

Ben walked into the conference room, and smiled as he said, "Hi, Oliver. I hope I didn't keep you waiting."

Oliver replied, "No, I was a little early. Come on in and sit down. Let's get this performance appraisal done."

Smiling good-naturedly, Ben shrugged and chuckled as he said, "Sounds good to me. Just tell me how great I am and I'll get out of your hair."

Ben shut the door and slid into a chair, looking expectantly at Oliver to begin.

Performance Feedback

Glancing down at the performance appraisal form (see Table 1) he was in the process of hastily completing, Oliver said, "Ben, I see that you have been with us for just over seven months, and you have been working with me for the last four. Generally, I can say that you have been doing a good job. You have always handed in your work on time, and people seem to like you. There are some areas that

need improving, however. Let me tell you what you need to work on. First, I've noticed you coming in late a couple of times. That's never a good idea, especially for a junior person. Please do what you can to cut that out."

Leaning forward in his chair, Ben looked startled as he said, "Well, okay. I guess it's true I was late on two mornings, but that's because I've been having some car trouble this month. You know that I work late most nights, sometimes till 11:00 p.m. And I've never taken a sick day. I can't believe that being 10 minutes late twice is at the top of your list. That really doesn't seem to be significant in my mind."

Looking uncomfortable, Oliver replied, "You don't need to get so upset, Ben. I'm trying to help you here. And actually, this reminds me of another area that needs improvement. You seem to get upset too easily. Come to think of it, I've seen you react strongly to things that people say in our project meetings. I wish you would make more of an effort to stay calm and reasonable."

Shaking his head, Ben said, "Excuse me? I honestly don't know what you are talking about. I have never gotten upset in a project meeting! I may have defended an idea, but that's it. Can you give me an example of a time when you think this happened?"

Oliver sighed, and shook his head. He said, "No, I don't have an exact date or anything, but I know I've seen it, and on more than one occasion. It seems silly to argue about this. Why would I lie?"

Eyes flashing, Ben replied quietly with his teeth clenched, "I'm not saying that you are a liar, Oliver. I'm simply disagreeing with what you're saying. You're just wrong."

Oliver shook his head impatiently. "Well, I think you're the one who is wrong. But, we're getting off track here.

TABLE 1

WEC Performance Appraisal Form

WEC Performance Appraisal Form

Employee Name _____

Employee Role _____

Supervisor Name _____

Appraisal Period _____ to _____

Performance Contributions:

Please indicate three areas where the employee performed well:

1. _____
2. _____
3. _____

Performance Improvement:

Please indicate three areas for suggested performance improvement:

1. _____
2. _____
3. _____

Circle the rating corresponding to the employee's performance over the appraisal period:

1	2	3	4	5
Unsatisfactory	Improvement needed	Meets expectations	Exceeds expectations	Exceptional
Performance was consistently below expectations in most *essential* areas of responsibility, and/or reasonable progress toward critical goals was not made. Significant improvement is needed in one or more areas. A performance improvement plan or separation agreement is attached.	Performance did not *consistently* meet expectations. Performance failed to meet expectations in one or more *essential* areas of responsibility, and/or one or more critical goals were not met. A performance improvement plan to improve performance must be attached, including timelines to measure progress.	Performance consistently met expectations in all *essential* areas of responsibility, at times possibly exceeding expectations, and the quality of overall work was very good. The most critical annual goals were met.	Performance consistently exceeded expectations in all *essential* areas of responsibility, and the quality of overall work was excellent. Annual goals were met.	Performance far exceeded expectations due to exceptionally high quality of work in all *essential* areas of responsibility, resulting in superior quality work. A major goal or project was completed, or an exceptional or unique contribution was made to the organization. This rating is achievable but given infrequently.

Signatures:

Employee _____

Supervisor _____

Evaluation Date _____

I'm just telling you what I've seen. If you want to improve, you'll be more open to listening to feedback. Oh, actually, that's great." Oliver wrote quickly on his paper, and continued. "Let's actually put the listening to criticism thing as something you need to do better. There! That's good. Now we have three areas for improvement so I can fill out this form properly. We'll list punctuality, staying calm, and accepting criticism as areas that you need to work on. I was having trouble thinking of three weaknesses, but now I think we're set."

Ben sat speechless, unsure what to say.

The Overall Rating

Oliver put down his pen, and said, "On the bright side, I am rating you at 'meets expectations.' You'll be happy to know that you are aligned with all of the other engineers on this project. Good job! While each of you has strengths and weaknesses, I'm happy to say that everyone is doing fine overall. I'm sure you'll agree that we have a very good team."

What About Scott?

Finally finding his voice, Ben said, "Wait. We're all rated the same? What about Scott Browski? That guy is a walking disaster. We all spend time fixing his mistakes because he can't do anything right. And if you care so much about punctuality, maybe you've noticed that he is late at least once a week."

Annoyed, Oliver said, "Woah. Calm down, Ben. There's no need to come down so hard on Scott. He may not be perfect, but the customers love him. He is just the most easy-going guy. If we get behind schedule, we just send him out to 'make nice' and no one gets upset. We couldn't get by without him. Besides, I only gave him a rating of 'meets expectations' as well."

Jumping out of his chair, Ben replied, "This makes no sense! Scott is the reason we get behind schedule! If he weren't here we wouldn't *need* anyone to kiss up to the customer."

Oliver held out his hands in a calming gesture, and said, "You're getting upset again, Ben. What's with that? Didn't we just agree that you were going to work on that problem? Please. Have a seat. I think we're just about done. You just need to sign these forms for me saying that we had this meeting." Oliver held out his pen to Ben, who seemed unsure how to react.

DISCUSSION QUESTIONS

1. Which rater biases does Oliver seem to be displaying?

2. Using the guidelines for effective performance evaluation interviews (Figure 8-14), develop a plan for what Oliver should do to improve his ability to conduct more effective performance appraisal interviews.

3. Examining the performance appraisal form in Table 1, what recommendations would you have for its improvement?

In the next installment of the WE Connections story (at the end of Chapter 9), HR staff mull over their compensation strategy when some employees express dissatisfaction with the equity of the company's system.

CASE STUDY

Start Up Central

Performance Appraisal Issues

Jocelyn took a deep breath and took another look at the clock. It was 5:45 p.m. and still no Melvin. Start Up Central was running its fifth session in the eight-week Hatchery program from 6:00 p.m. until 8:00 p.m., and Melvin was scheduled to facilitate the session. The front door bells jingled and two more keen entrepreneurs entered the collision space for the reception before the session. They hung up their coats and headed toward the coffee and snack station, joining the other entrepreneurs gathered in anticipation of tonight's session. The event calendar indicated they should expect representatives from 12 early-stage companies, although Jocelyn knew from experience that others might decide to show up at the last minute. Tonight was their practice pitch event and all representatives would get the opportunity to spend three minutes describing their business opportunity to the mock investors in the room and receive feedback on their performance. The entrepreneurs had been generating their business canvases and crafting their pitch decks in the weeks since the Hatchery program had begun. On the final night just three weeks from tonight, they would be pitching their business opportunities to an angel investment crowd in the greater Toronto area.

Back when Start Up Central was just getting off the ground, Jocelyn had led the Hatchery program herself. She was the inaugural executive director of Start Up Central, which was founded by a group of serial entrepreneurs in the Toronto area. The group had put seed money into Start Up Central with a view to developing new entrepreneurs in a boot camp type fashion. Jocelyn herself had built a social marketing company that had been acquired by Forbes four years ago. With a successful experience building and then exiting a startup herself, she found the executive director role filled her desire to give back to the community by connecting new entrepreneurs with the various resources they needed to make their business dreams come true. Building Start Up Central and setting new entrepreneurs up for success was more than a job to Jocelyn, it had become her life's work.

But there was a reason she had hired Melvin to now shoulder some of the Start Up Central workload. Jocelyn had been at her desk since before 8 a.m. that morning. She had met with their advisory group over lunch, provided input on a panel to the Ontario provincial government about their Young Entrepreneurs program, and placed calls to secure business advisors for the next round of the Hatchery program beginning in the fall. When Jocelyn had decided to bring on an entrepreneur-in-residence (EiR), Melvin had come strongly recommended by one of the advisors on the Start Up Central advisory group. When she had met with him, he exuded confidence and was credible in the EiR role. He had been a serial entrepreneur for 10 years, but was still "relatable" to the new entrepreneur crowd. In Jocelyn's experience, the distance between start-up hopefuls and some of the successful entrepreneurs in the greater Toronto area was perceived as vast. As well, the travel and commitment schedules of many of the super successful entrepreneurs meant they weren't available for eight Wednesdays in a row to help with the Hatchery program. Through his EiR

role, Melvin was still able to be engaged in his own start-up ventures, but he received a stipend from Start Up Central to act as an advisor one-on-one to the start-up companies in their programs and to attend their events. Jocelyn thought that the $50,000 per year stipend they were paying him was at least enough to get him to show up for the Hatchery program as the lead facilitator.

Jocelyn pushed back her chair and sighed. She stood up and grabbed her suit jacket, prepared to go out and lead tonight's practice pitch event. She put a smile on her face and tried to leave her frustration with Melvin behind as she went out to greet the budding entrepreneurs.

DISCUSSION QUESTIONS

1. Are there any differences between Melvin as an entrepreneur-in-residence with a stipend as compared to an employee of Start Up Central? Discuss.

2. As Jocelyn, how would you handle Melvin's absence? How would you ensure that Melvin has clear performance expectations?

3. If this was Melvin's third unexplained absence as compared to his first, how would you set up a set of steps to ensure performance improvement?

4. Is absence a reason for just cause dismissal? Explain the documentation and steps you would have to take to dismiss Melvin for just cause.

PART 5

Motivating and Rewarding Human Resources

Employees have to be compensated for their performance fairly and equitably. The human resource department assists managers in assessing the how much employees should be paid in terms of direct compensation—wages, bonuses, commissions and so forth—as well as indirect compensation through employee benefits. It is also one of

the responsibilities of a human resource manager to create a motivating job environment.

Each of these topics is discussed in Part 5. They are important management tools for human resource specialists and managers alike. Regardless of your job, you will find that these tools are helpful ways to ensure effective performance.

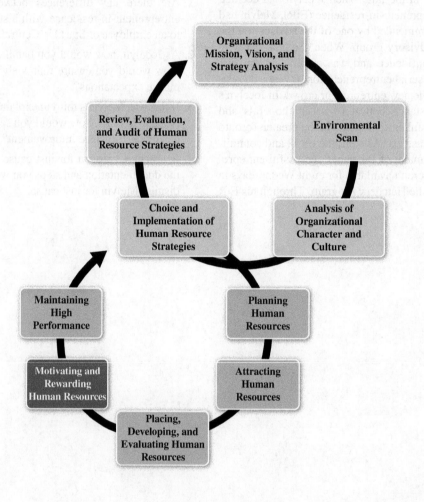

Organizational Mission, Vision, and Strategy Analysis

Environmental Scan

Analysis of Organizational Character and Culture

Planning Human Resources

Attracting Human Resources

Placing, Developing, and Evaluating Human Resources

Motivating and Rewarding Human Resources

Maintaining High Performance

Choice and Implementation of Human Resource Strategies

Review, Evaluation, and Audit of Human Resource Strategies

CHAPTER 9

Compensation Management

When determining appropriate levels of compensation, management must determine if the employee turnover rate is too low, too high, or just right. If turnover rate is high enough to adversely impact the entity's performance, then employee compensation is probably too low.

JASON CHAFFETZ[1]

LEARNING OBJECTIVES

After studying this chapter, you should be able to:

LO1   Explain the objectives of effective compensation management.

LO2   Describe what a compensation philosophy is and why organizations need one.

LO3   Describe how direct compensation is determined through job evaluation and market pricing methods.

LO4   Discuss skill-based approaches to pay.

LO5   Describe the various forms of individual incentive and group or team-based variable pay systems.

LO6   Define *total rewards*.

LO7   Explain the differences between "equal pay for equal work" and "equal pay for work of equal value."

LO8   Describe advantages and disadvantages of pay secrecy.

The human resource group is responsible for the development, implementation, and administration of compensation systems, which tie rewards to the achievement of company objectives. Direct compensation is the wages paid by employers to employees in exchange for the work they do. In addition to wages or salary, direct compensation includes variable pay, such as bonuses, commissions, and stocks paid as short- or long-term incentives. Indirect compensation in the form of employee benefits and services is discussed in Chapter 10.

Compensation systems aim to pay workers for the jobs they do and incentivize them through enhancing motivation and job satisfaction. It would be rare to find employees in any job who would claim that they are overpaid (at least not directly to their managers!). Much more commonly, employees will evaluate whether they are adequately paid or underpaid. When compensation is perceived to be inadequate, the firm may lose employees and will incur costs to recruit, select, train, and develop replacements. Even if workers do not quit when they are unhappy with their pay, they may become dissatisfied with the company.

Perceptions of fair and adequate pay are based on *absolute* and *relative* levels of pay. When the total, or absolute, amount of pay is too low, employees cannot meet their physiological or security needs. In industrial societies, the absolute level of pay usually is high enough to meet these basic needs, at least minimally. A more common source of dissatisfaction centres on relative pay. For instance, employees might compare their salary with that of other employees in relation to experience and the duties and responsibilities required. More duties and experience and higher levels of responsibility bring expectations of higher relative pay.

Wages and salary, known as base pay, form the foundation of compensation systems because they establish the standard of living for employees.[2] This chapter outlines how to determine wage and salary ranges for jobs based on job evaluations, external market comparisons, and by the skills and knowledge employees hold. The chapter also discusses multiple forms of variable pay, which is paid contingent on factors such as employees' performance and retention. Also central to compensation management, a total compensation approach, pay equity, and pay secrecy are discussed in this chapter.

LO1 Objectives of Compensation Management

When determining rates of wages and salaries to pay employees, effective compensation strives to achieve **internal equity** and **external equity.** Internal equity requires that pay be related to the relative worth of jobs. That is, within an organization, jobs of similar value should get similar pay. Jobs that have a higher worth to the organization and/or require more skill or knowledge to complete are paid more. Likewise, jobs that have less worth to the organization or require less skill or knowledge are paid less. The focus is on comparing jobs and skills within the organization in terms of their relative contributions to the organization's objectives. External equity involves paying workers at a rate perceived to be fair compared to what the market pays. In short, it involves comparing what one firm's employees are being paid relative to employees in similar jobs employed by competitors.

The objectives sought through effective compensation management include the following:

- *Acquire qualified personnel.* Compensation needs to be high enough to attract applicants. Companies compete in the labour market, so pay levels must respond to the supply and demand of workers. But sometimes a premium wage rate is needed to attract applicants who are already employed in other firms.

- *Retain present employees.* To prevent employee turnover, pay must be kept competitive with that of other employers. Additionally, employees will compare their duties and responsibilities and the pay they receive relative to others in the organization, and they expect to be compensated more when they are providing higher value.

- *Reward desired behaviour.* Pay should reinforce desired behaviours. Good performance, experience, loyalty, new responsibilities, and other behaviours can be rewarded through an effective compensation plan.

- *Control costs.* A rational compensation program helps an organization to obtain and retain its workforce at a reasonable cost. Paying employees is typically the largest expense line for the employer. Without a systematic wage and salary structure, the organization might overpay or underpay its employees.

- *Comply with legal regulations.* As with other aspects of human resource management, wage and salary management must comply with applicable provincial or federal regulations. A sound pay program ensures adherence to all government regulations, such as minimum wage, overtime, and vacation provisions that affect employee compensation.

These objectives can sometimes conflict. For instance, base pay must comply with minimum wage provisions across the country and be attractive enough to gain and keep workers. But organizations must also provide their goods and services at prices low enough that consumers will buy them. Finding the balance between these objectives is addressed through the firm's compensation philosophy, discussed next.

internal equity Perceived equity of a pay system across different jobs within an organization.

external equity Perceived fairness in pay relative to what other employers are paying for the same type of work.

Determining Direct Compensation

Figure 9-1 depicts the major phases of compensation management. The first step in determining the wages and salary for a job is to establish the firm's compensation philosophy with the objectives listed above in mind.

LO2 Phase 1: Establishing the Compensation Philosophy

A compensation philosophy is a guiding principle for how the organization manages compensation. Simply put, a strong compensation philosophy ties an organization's

FIGURE 9-1

Major Phases of Compensation Management

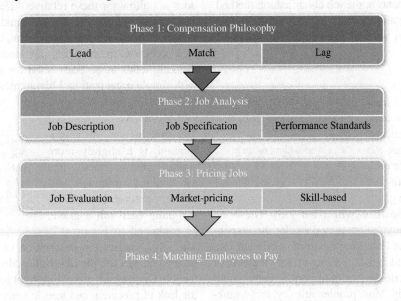

mission, core business, operating strategies, and competitive outlook to the pay it provides it employees.[3] Organizations may set lead, match, or lag compensation philosophies,[4] as illustrated in the examples below.

> With a *lead* strategy, a company pays rates that are higher than the relative marketplace. For instance, a high-tech company with a core strategy to attract and retain top talent in the tech industry to outpace its competitors may adopt a strategy of leading the market with its total compensation package. Google has followed a lead strategy with paying its employees more than other high tech firms.[5]
>
> In a *match* strategy, a company matches the market by paying comparable rates to the relative marketplace. For instance, one retail store may choose to match the pay of other retailers in the same mall.
>
> A company with a *lag* strategy will pay rates lower than those of the relative marketplace. For example, a warehouse with low turnover in a remote community with a large labour pool may set a compensation strategy to control costs and offer compensation valued at less than it would be in a highly competitive community.

The compensation philosophy will be determined by HR in conjunction with management buy-in and input to understand supply, demand, and labour market issues in the organization, and the operational and legal ramifications surrounding compensation.

Phase 2: Reviewing the Job Analysis

It will come as no surprise that to determine fair pay for jobs, the second step is to understand the elements of the job and the skills needed to conduct the job, which comes from examining job analysis information. As discussed in Chapter 2, job analyses produce job descriptions, job specifications, and performance standards, which describe the tasks and skills associated with jobs in the organizations. Compensation specialists review the job analysis data to compare jobs for internal equity and to identify comparable jobs at other organizations to make external equity assessments.

LO3 Phase 3: Pricing Jobs

The third phase of the compensation process is to price the worth of each job. Three approaches to pricing jobs are discussed next: job evaluation, market-pricing, and skill-based evaluation.

Job Evaluation

Job evaluations are systematic procedures to determine the relative worth or value of jobs. Although evaluations take several different approaches, each one considers the duties, responsibilities,

> **job evaluations**
> Systematic processes of assessing job content and ranking jobs according to a consistent set of job characteristics and worker traits.

and working conditions of the job. The purpose of job evaluation is to identify which jobs should be paid more than others. The simplest form of job evaluation is a job ranking, with modest improvements in the job classification method. The more popular and valid approach to job evaluation, however, is the point system, which is the focus of the discussion below.

Job Ranking

The simplest albeit least precise method of job evaluation is **job ranking**. Specialists review the job analysis information for each job. Then each job is ranked subjectively according to its importance in comparison with other jobs. These are overall rankings, although raters may consider the responsibility, skill, effort, and working conditions of each job. One challenge with rankings is that important elements of some jobs may be overlooked or unimportant items could be weighted too heavily. Most problematically, these rankings do not differentiate the relative importance of jobs. For example, the job of clerk might be ranked as 1, the front store manager might get a 2, and the district manager

> **job ranking** A form of job evaluation in which jobs are ranked subjectively according to their overall worth to the organization.

might rank as a 3. But the front store manager might be three times as important as the clerk and half as important as the job of district manager. The job ranking approach does not allow for these relative differences between jobs. Pay scales based on these broad rankings ensure that more important jobs are paid more. But because the rankings lack precision, the resulting pay levels may be inaccurate. Ranking tends to be best suited for smaller organizations with simple organizational hierarchies.[6]

Job Grading

Job grading, or job classification, is a slightly more sophisticated method than job ranking, although still not very precise. It works by assigning each job a grade, as explained in Figure 9-2.

> **job grading** A form of job evaluation that assigns jobs to predetermined job classifications according to their relative worth to the organization.

The job classification description in the figure that most nearly matches the job description determines the grade of the job. Once again, more important jobs are paid more. But the lack of precision can lead to inaccurate pay levels. The largest user of this approach has been the Public Service Commission of Canada, which employ over a half-million Canadians in occupations such as Correctional Services,

FIGURE 9-2

A Job Classification Schedule for Use with the Job Grading Method

Job Classification Schedule	
Directions: To determine appropriate job grade, match job classification description with job description.	
Job Grade	**Job Classification Description**
I	Work is simple and highly repetitive, done under close supervision, requiring minimal training and little responsibility or initiative. *Examples:* Janitor, file clerk
II	Work is simple and repetitive, done under close supervision, requiring some training or skill. Employee is expected to assume responsibility or exhibit initiative only rarely. *Examples:* Administrative assistant I, machine cleaner
III	Work is simple, with little variation, done under general supervision. Training or skill required. Employee has minimal responsibilities and must take some initiative to perform satisfactorily. *Examples:* Parts expediter, machine oiler, administrative assistant II
IV	Work is moderately complex, with some variation, done under general supervision. High level of skill required. Employee is responsible for equipment or safety; regularly exhibits initiative. *Examples:* Machine operator I, tool-and-die apprentice
V	Work is complex, varied, done under general supervision. Advanced skill level required. Employee is responsible for equipment and safety; shows high degree of initiative. *Examples:* Machine operator II, tool-and-die journeyman

Border Services, and Architecture and Town Planning across the country. The Public Service is gradually replacing this approach with more sophisticated methods.

Point System

The **point system** evaluates the critical—also called compensable—factors of each job, determines different levels or degrees for each factor, and allocates points to each level. Although this quantitative system is more difficult to develop initially, it is more precise than other

> **point system** A form of job evaluation that assesses the relative importance of the job's key factors in order to arrive at the relative worth of jobs.

methods because it can handle critical factors in more detail. It is usually done by a job evaluation committee or a compensation analyst. In most cases, organizations use a system that has predetermined job factors and assigned points to each factor. This system requires six steps to implement.

Step 1: Determine Compensable Factors Figure 9-3 shows how the factor of responsibility can be broken down into the following components:

- Safety of others
- Equipment and materials
- Assisting trainees
- Product/service quality

FIGURE 9-3

Point System Matrix

Critical Factors	Levels or Degrees				Factor Points
	I	II	III	IV	
1. Responsibility (weight 40%)					**400**
Subfactors:					
a. Safety of others	20	80	140	200	
b. Equipment and materials	8	24	56	80	
c. Assisting trainees	8	24	56	80	
d. Product/service quality	4	16	28	40	
2. Skill (weight 30%)					**300**
Subfactors:					
a. Experience	18	72	126	180	
b. Education/training	12	48	84	120	
3. Effort (weight 20%)					**200**
Subfactors:					
a. Physical	8	32	56	80	
b. Mental	12	48	84	120	
4. Working conditions (weight 10%)					**100**
Subfactors:					
a. Unpleasant conditions	3	12	21	30	
b. Hazards	7	28	49	70	
				Total points	**1,000**

Step 2: Determine Levels (Or Degrees) of Factors Because the extent of responsibility or other factors may vary from job to job, the point system creates several levels (or degrees) associated with each factor. Figure 9-3 shows four levels, although more or fewer may be used. These levels help analysts to reward different degrees of responsibility, skills, and other critical factors.

Step 3: Allocate Points to Subfactors With the factors listed down one side and the levels placed across the top, as in Figure 9-3, the result is a point system matrix. Points are then assigned to each subfactor to reflect their relative importance. Analysts start with Level IV and weight each subfactor with the number of points they think it deserves. This allocation allows them to give very precise weights to each element of the job. For example, if assisting trainees is twice as important as product/service quality, it is assigned twice as many points: 80 versus 40.

A detailed calculation of the data in Figure 9-3 is provided in Appendix A at the end of this chapter.

Step 4: Allocate Points to Levels (Degrees) Once the points for each job element are satisfactory under column IV, analysts allocate points across each row to reflect the importance of the different levels. Usually equal point differences are used, but analysts or job evaluation committees may decide to use variable differences. See Appendix A at the end of this chapter for a calculation of equal differences.

Step 5: Develop the Point Manual The point manual contains a written explanation of each job element, as shown in Figure 9-4 for responsibility of equipment and materials. It also defines what is expected for the four levels (degrees) of each subfactor. This information is needed to assign jobs to their appropriate level.

Step 6: Apply the Point System When the point matrix and manual are ready, the relative value of each job can be determined. This process is subjective. It requires specialists to compare job descriptions with the point manual for each subfactor. The match between the job description and the point manual statement reveals the level and points for each subfactor of every job. Once completed, the points for each subfactor are added to find the total number of points for the job. An example of this matching process for Machine Operator I appears below:

> The job description of Machine Operator I states this: "[O]perator is responsible for performing preventive maintenance (such as cleaning, oiling, and adjusting belts) and repairs." The sample point manual excerpt in Figure 9-4 states this: "Level III: . . . performs preventive maintenance and repairs. . . ." Because the job description and the point manual match at Level III, the points for the equipment subfactor are 55. Repeating this matching process for each subfactor yields the total points for the job of Machine Operator I.

Once the total points for each job have been decided, the jobs are all rank ordered. As with the job ranking and job grading systems, this relative ranking should be reviewed by department managers to ensure that it is appropriate.

As can be seen from the six steps for creating a point system, it is complex and therefore it is rare that a company develops a system from scratch. Large organizations often

---

FIGURE 9-4

Point Manual Description of "Responsibility: Equipment and Materials"

1. **Responsibility . . .**

   b. *Equipment and Materials.* Each employee is responsible for conserving the company's equipment and materials. This includes reporting malfunctioning equipment or defective materials, keeping equipment and materials cleaned or in proper order, and maintaining, repairing, or modifying equipment and materials according to individual job duties. The company recognizes that the degree of responsibility for equipment and materials varies widely throughout the organization.

Level I.	Employee reports malfunctioning equipment or defective materials to immediate superior.
Level II.	Employee maintains the appearance of equipment or order of materials and has responsibility for the security of such equipment or materials.
Level III.	Employee performs preventive maintenance and repairs on equipment or corrects defects in materials.
Level IV.	Employee makes replacement and purchasing decisions and is in control of the "equipment and materials" factor.

Spotlight *on* ETHICS

Job Evaluation

You are the human resource director of a large grocery chain. As part of a restructuring of its compensation system, and to comply with pay equity legislation, the company has recently switched from the job ranking system to the point system. You are chairing the Job Evaluation Committee, which is ready to allocate points to the cashier job category, the largest category in the company. The discussion so far has focused on how many points to allocate to the responsibility factor, and the committee is essentially split 50–50 on the numbers. As it so happened, there are three women and three men on the committee. The women argue that cashiers have the same responsibility as the accounting clerks, who are all male, in the office. The male members of the committee, on the other hand, disagree, suggesting that a cashier's responsibility

is to balance the cash register, not accounts, a more difficult task. You seem to have the deciding vote. The dilemma from your point of view is that all the cashiers are women while the three accounting clerks are all male. In your assessment you agree that the accounting clerks carry a higher responsibility and deserve more points. If you support the male members of the committee you are pretty sure that the cashiers will launch a pay equity grievance, usually a costly and time-consuming affair. If you agree with the female members it means cashiers will fall into a higher pay category, increasing payroll expenses significantly. You know very well that the competition in the food market is fierce, with low profit margins (2 to 3 percent). A pay increase would have a direct impact on the bottom line. What do you do?

modify standard approaches to create unique in-house variations. Perhaps most commonly, firms will engage a firm specializing in compensation to help them to establish their pay systems. One well-known consulting firm specializing in job evaluation is Korn Ferry:

> The Korn Ferry Hay Guide Chart—Profile Method—is widely used with global recognition.[7] This proprietary method evaluates each job on three factors: (a) the value that is created by the job (accountability), (b) how the value is created (problem solving), and (c) what the job requirements are that an employee must meet to deliver the value (know-how). The group uses its expandable guide charts to ensure that the job evaluations fit their client's business, operating model, organization structure, and culture. Korn Ferry provides direct comparisons with the reward strategies of other organizations across their global total compensation databases, which helps to benchmark jobs and increase confidence in their job evaluation results.[8]

Market-Based Pay Structures

The job evaluation techniques discussed above all result in a ranking of jobs based upon their relative worth. They assure internal equity, that is, jobs that are worth more will be paid more within an organization. But how much should be paid? What constitutes *external equity*? Market-pricing focuses on external competitiveness—how much organizations should pay for jobs based on what their competitors are offering for similar work.

To determine a fair rate of compensation, most firms rely on **wage and salary surveys**, which discover what other employers in the same labour market are paying for specific key jobs. The *labour market*— the area from which the employer recruits—is generally the local community; however, firms may have to compete for some workers in a wider market. Consider how the president of one large university viewed the market:

wage and salary surveys Studies of the wages and salaries paid by other organizations within the employer's labour market.

> Our labour market depends on the type of position we are trying to fill. For the hourly paid jobs, such as facilities maintenance, student services, and administrative assistants, the labour market is the surrounding metropolitan community. When we hire professors, our labour market is Canada. We have to compete with universities in other provinces to get the type of faculty member we seek. When we have the funds to hire a distinguished professor, our labour market is the whole world.

Sources of Compensation Data

Wage and salary data are benchmarks against which analysts compare compensation levels. Sources for this information include the following:

- Employment and Social Development Canada
- Canadian Human Resource Centres
- Employee trade and professional associations
- Consulting companies

The major challenge of market pricing is matching jobs within the organization to those reported in the survey. Simply matching job titles may be misleading: Federal, provincial, and association job descriptions using the same title may be considerably different. Compensation specialists will also have to decide whether to use industry-specific comparables or all-industry data, and whether to use only data from organizations of similar revenue size across all levels of positions. One professional group suggests that HR should look for comparables beyond their specific industry, and should include the last employer of their new hires and companies that their employees go to when they leave.[9] Data from wage and salary surveys needs to be aged to a common point in time. This means projecting forward the salary rates from older surveys to account for salary movement in the interim. Survey data older than two years is likely too old and has lost market reliability.[10]

Once all comparables for a job within the identified labour market are known, the compensation specialist can see the range of direct compensation paid by competitors. In conjunction with comparables across all jobs, with job evaluation rankings for internal equity, and with consideration of the compensation philosophy, the HR group can determine the percentiles they are going to pay:

- *Matching the market.* Targeting the fiftieth percentile means the organization will pay at the middle of all organizations with similar positions. Fifty percent of competitors would pay more for the same job, and 50 percent would pay less.
- *Market leader.* Organizations targeting a market leader position typically aim for paying at the seventy-fifth percentile, meaning 75 percent of competitors will pay less for the same job. When competing for employees with specialized skill sets in a tight labour market, as Google was in the earlier example, a market leader position makes sense.
- *Market lag.* Paying at the twenty-fifth percentile, where only 25 percent of firms pay less for comparable jobs, is a market lag position. This strategy may suit loose labour markets as in the earlier warehouse example. Organizations with strong variable compensation or benefits programs may also opt for a market lag position.[11]

Often, organizations will integrate job evaluation and market-based pricing to settle on base pay that achieves both internal equity and external equity. Notably, the use of market pricing has gone up with 9 out of 10 organizations using it to some degree and 50 percent relying on it exclusively. The point-factor approach to job evaluation is now only used by 20 percent of firms.[12]

LO4 Skill-Based Pay

Both the job evaluation and the market-pricing methods focus on paying for the *job* done. An alternative method is to pay employees based on the *skills or knowledge* they have. **Skill- or knowledge-based pay** can reward the employee based on depth (gaining greater expertise in existing skills), breadth (increases in the employee's range of skills), and self-management (gaining higher level management-type skills, such as budgeting, training, planning, and so forth). Figure 9-5 depicts two different forms that skill-based pay systems may take.

> **skill- or knowledge-based pay** A pay system based on the employee's mastery of skills or knowledge (in contrast to the more common job-based pay).

As pictured in the purple circle labelled A in Figure 9-5, depth-oriented plans pay employees for gaining greater experience on existing skills. Employees in these systems gain specialized skills, and, as their mastery of those skills goes up, their pay goes up as well. Pay systems based on depth of skill have been around since the Middle Ages and are commonly seen in the skilled trades (e.g., carpenter, boilermaker, millwright), where workers move over their careers from apprentice to journeyman to master craftsman.[13] Depth-based pay is also used for professors who move from assistant to associate to full professor ranks over the course of their careers.

Depth-based pay systems are seen in white collar careers, where there is a dual career ladder. As shown in Figure 9-6, one branch of the career ladder leads from technical practice into management levels, whereas the second branch recognizes achievement of skill levels. Dual career ladders are common in aerospace, pharmaceuticals, and high technology.[14]

FIGURE 9-5

Two Forms of Skill-Based Pay Systems

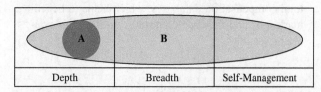

| Depth | Breadth | Self-Management |

SOURCE: Adapted from Gerald Ledford, Jr., and Herbert Heneman III (2011, June), "Skill-Based Pay," *SHRM-SIOP White Paper Series,* http://www.siop.org/SIOP-SHRM/SIOP_SHRM_Skill_Based_Pay.pdf

FIGURE 9-6

Dual Career Ladder Example

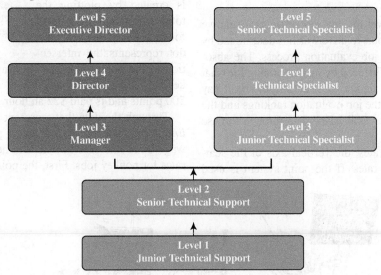

Information technology employees join the organization at Level 1 and earn promotions to Level 2. Future promotions after Level 2 will be into either a management branch, pictured on the left, or technical branch, pictured on the right. Both branches are valued by the organization. The branch on the right provides pay based on skill depth.

Within the blue oval labelled B in Figure 9-5, the goal is to reward a balance between skill breadth, depth, and self-management skills. This type of skill-based system pays employees for their flexibility to do different jobs in the organization, to conduct simple and more complex tasks, and to work with few or no supervisors. These systems are most common in manufacturing, but also occur in call centres, help desks, and processing centres for banks and insurance services.[15] Employees who can flexibly work in multiple capacities for the organization are rewarded with higher levels of pay, as can be seen in the example below:

> Shell Canada's Brockville Lubricants plant employs 85 people and is the largest blender and packager of passenger-car motor oils in Canada. Products bearing the Shell, Quaker State, and Penzoil brands are produced in this ultramodern plant. Missing are the traditional foremen and supervisors who tell people what to do and how to do it. Every worker, or team operator, is a supervisor of sorts. Operators must master all the jobs within his or her team, plus at least one skill in two other groups. Pay is based on a number of defined skills. The impact on pay when this new plant and pay system was introduced was significant. The average salary increased by 22 percent, and some employees almost doubled their income.[16]

The greatest advantage of skill-based pay is the flexibility of the workforce. This includes filling in after turnovers and covering for absences and when other employees are in training or meetings. Also, if a company's production or service process is changing frequently, it is desirable to have a highly trained workforce that can adapt smoothly to changes. The rise of lean systems and trends such as cross-training, self-inspection, shorter life cycles of products, the increasing demand for product customization, and the need to respond quickly to market changes mean that this type of skill-based pay system is likely to grow in popularity in the future.[17] Below is an example in which a highly skilled workforce made a major difference:

> Johnson & Johnson implemented a skill-based pay system for a plant that makes Tylenol. As a result of the Tylenol poisoning tragedy, J&J decided to completely redo its packaging of Tylenol to add greater safety. The skill-based plant quickly installed the new technology needed and got back into production. Not so with its sister plant, which was a traditional, job-based seniority-driven plant. Seniority rights and traditional pay grades got in the way of people's flexibility in adapting to the new technology.[18]

Skill-based pay systems tend to generate higher pay rates. This does not mean total wage costs have to be higher; if the organization can make better use of its people, total costs can be significantly lower.[19]

Phase 4: Matching Employees to Pay

The final step in the compensation process includes integrating the data on pricing jobs obtained from job evaluations, market-pricing, and/or skill-based approaches to match pay to employees. This involves establishing the appropriate pay level for each job and grouping the different pay levels into a structure that can be managed effectively.

Pay Levels

The appropriate pay level for any job reflects its relative and absolute worth. A job's relative worth is determined by its ranking through the job evaluation process. The absolute worth of a job is influenced by market pricing for what the labour market pays similar jobs. Setting the right pay level means combining the job evaluation rankings and the survey wage rates and/or skill-based data through the use of a scattergram.

As Figure 9-7 illustrates, the vertical axis of the scattergram shows the pay rates. If the point system is used to determine the ranking of jobs, the horizontal axis is in points. The scattergram is created by plotting the total points and wage level for each **key job**. Thus, each dot represents the intersection of the point value and the wage rate for a particular key job. For example, key Job A in Figure 9-7 is worth 500 points and is paid $22 an hour.

Through the dots that represent key jobs, a *wage-trend line* is drawn as close to as many points as possible. The wage-trend line uses two steps to help determine the wage rates for nonkey jobs. First, the point value for the nonkey

> **key job** A job that is common in the organization and in a labour market (e.g., janitors, drivers, secretaries) and that is used to determine pay scales.

Brian Gable/The Globe and Mail. Reprinted with permission from The Globe and Mail/ CP Images

FIGURE 9-7

The Development of a Wage-Trend Line

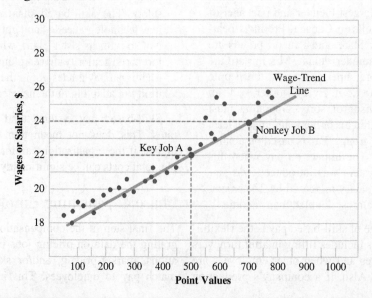

job is located on the horizontal axis. Second, a line is traced vertically to the wage-trend line, then horizontally to the dollar scale. The amount on the vertical scale is the appropriate wage rate for the nonkey job. For example, nonkey Job B is worth 700 points. By tracing a vertical line up to the wage-trend line and then horizontally to the vertical (dollar) scale, Figure 9-7 shows that the appropriate wage rate for Job B is $24 per hour.

The Compensation Structure

A medium-sized organization with 2,000 workers and 325 separately identifiable jobs would present the wage and salary analyst with complex problems. The existence of 325 separate wage rates would be meaningless because the differences in wages between each job might be no more than a few cents.

Compensation analysts find it more convenient to lump jobs together into job classes. In the job grade approach, jobs are already grouped into predetermined categories. With other methods, the grouping is done by creating job grades based on the previous ranking, pay, or points. In the point system, for example, classifications are based on point ranges: 0 to 100, 101 to 150, 151 to 200, and so forth. This grouping causes the wage-trend line to be replaced with a series of ascending dashes, as shown in Figure 9-8. Thus, all jobs in the same class receive the same wage rate. A job valued at 105 points, for example, is paid the same as a job with 145 points. Having too many grades defeats the purpose of grouping; having too few groupings results in workers with jobs of widely varying importance receiving the same pay.

The problem with flat rates for each job class is that exceptional performance is not rewarded. To give a worker a merit increase requires moving the employee into a higher job class. This upsets the entire balance of internal equity developed through job evaluations. To solve these problems, most firms use rate ranges for each class.

A **rate range** is simply a pay range for each job class.

> **rate range** A pay range for each job class.

For example, suppose that the wage-trend line indicates that $24 is the average hourly rate for a particular job class. Every employee in that class gets $24, if a flat rate is paid. With a rate range of $3 for each class, a marginal performer can be paid $21 at the bottom of the range, as indicated in Figure 9-9. Then, an average performer is placed at the midpoint in the rate range, or $24. When performance appraisals indicate above-average performance, the employee may be given a **merit raise** of, say, $1.00 per hour for the exceptional performance. If this performance continues, another merit raise of $1.00 can be granted. Once the employee reaches the top of the rate range, no more wage increases will be forthcoming. Either a promotion or a general across-the-board pay raise needs to occur for this worker's wage to exceed $27. An across-the-board increase moves the entire wage-trend line upward.

> **merit raise** A pay increase given to individual workers according to an evaluation of their performance.

As new jobs are created, the wage and salary section performs a job evaluation. From this evaluation, the new job is assigned to an appropriate job class. If the rate ranges are used, the new employee will start at the bottom of the range and receive raises, where appropriate, to the top of the rate range.

Challenges Affecting Compensation

Even the most rational methods of determining pay must be tempered by several challenges. The implications of these contingencies may cause wage and salary analysts to make further adjustments to employee compensation.

FIGURE 9-8

The Impact of Job Classes on the Wage-Trend Line

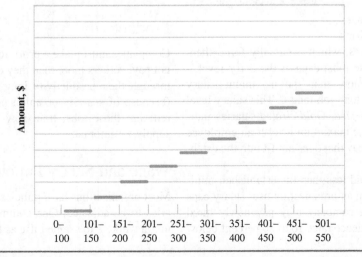

0– 100	101– 150	151– 200	201– 250	251– 300	301– 350	351– 400	401– 450	451– 500	501– 550	

FIGURE 9-9

Varying Wage Ranges for Job

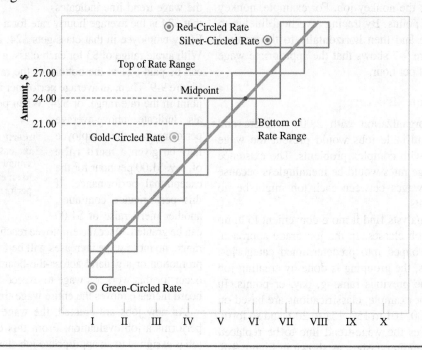

Prevailing Wage Rates

Some jobs must be paid more than is indicated by their relative worth because of market forces. For instance, data scientists are currently in short supply.[20] Fitting these jobs onto a wage-trend line would result in a wage rate below their prevailing wage rate. Because demand outstrips supply, market forces cause wage rates for these specialists to rise above their relative worth when compared with other jobs. Firms that need these talents are forced to pay a premium. Diagrammatically, these rates appear on a wage chart as a **red-circled rate**, as seen in Figure 9-9. The term arises from the practice of marking out-of-line rates with a red circle on the chart. Some shortages become so serious that firms offer huge hiring bonuses, which eventually force them to raise salaries for these jobs, even at the entry level.[21] Some companies pay more than the maximum salary level to employees with long job tenure. This salary level appears then as *silver-circled. Gold-circled* salaries indicate payments beyond the maximum level if an employee receives a special merit pay that does not fit into the established range.

Some jobs may be paid less than the established minimum. This happens when an organization uses salary caps (limits). For example, a company may pay newly hired employees with no experience rates 10 to 20 percent below

> **red-circled rate** A rate of pay higher than the contractual, or formerly established, rate for the job.

the pay minimum until they have "learned the ropes." This level is *green-circled.*

Union Power

When unions represent a portion of the workforce, they may be able to use their power to obtain wage rates out of proportion to their relative worth. For example, wage and salary studies may determine that $20 an hour is appropriate for a truck driver. But if the union insists on $22, the human resource department may believe paying the higher rate is less expensive than a strike. Sometimes the union controls most or all of a particular skill, such as carpentry or plumbing. This enables the union actually to raise the prevailing rate for those jobs.

Productivity

Companies must make a profit to survive. A company cannot pay workers more than they contribute back to the firm through their productivity long term. When this happens (because of scarcity or union power), companies usually redesign those jobs, train new workers to increase their supply, or automate.

Wage and Salary Policies

Most organizations have policies that cause wages and salaries to be adjusted. One common policy is to give nonunion workers the same raise as that received by unionized

© Design Pics/Don Hammond

Electricians belong to a dominant union, which is why their wage rates are so high. Is it justified to pay an electrician double—or close to double—what a carpenter makes?

workers. Some companies have automatic cost-of-living clauses that give employees automatic raises when the Statistics Canada cost-of-living index increases. Raises or policies that increase employee compensation move the wage-trend line upward.

A useful index for salary administrators is the **compa-ratio**, an indicator of how the salary of an employee relates to the midpoint of the relevant pay grade.[22] A compa-ratio of above or below 1 shows that the individual's salary is above or below the midpoint of the pay grade. The pay-grade midpoint can be viewed as a benchmark for salary decision criteria, such as performance, tenure, and experience. Ideally, the majority of employee pay rates would have room to go up within the pay grade.[23] The formula for the individual compa-ratio is as follows:

> **compa-ratio** An index that indicates how an individual's or a group's salary relates to the midpoint of their relevant pay grades.

$$\text{Compa-ratio} = \frac{\text{Salary of the employee}}{\text{Midpoint of the pay grade}}$$

Also of interest to salary administrators is the compa-ratio for groups. A ratio above 1 indicates that a large number of employees are bunched at the top of the pay grade (top-heavy). A ratio below 1 may be caused by many new employees or may be an indication of high turnover. The formula for the group compa-ratio is as follows:

$$\text{Group Compa-ratio} = \frac{\text{Average of salaries paid}}{\text{Midpoint of the pay grade}}$$

Employment Standards and Labour Codes

Canada is a nation of wage-earners. What people earn bears a direct relationship to the economy and general welfare of the population. The federal government and each provincial government have established *employment standards* that regulate the rights, restrictions, and obligations of nonunionized workers and employers in Canada. (Labour Codes, which apply to unionized workers, are discussed below.) The federal employment standards apply to works in federally regulated occupations, such as banking, media, and transportation, that cross provincial boundaries, and all other employees are governed by the employment standards of their respective province. The provisions in the legislation covers such things as the following:

- Minimum wage
- Annual vacations and other types of leave
- Public (statutory) holidays
- Hours of work, including standard hours, overtime, and emergency requirements
- Staff records

The minimum wage provisions require employers to pay at least a minimum hourly rate of pay regardless of the worth of the job. When the minimum is increased by law, it may mean adjusting upward the wages of those who already earn above the minimum. If those just above minimum wage do not also get raises, wage differentials will be squeezed together. This is called *wage compression.*[24] The current minimum-wage rates at the provincial and federal levels can be found at http://srv116.services.gc.ca/dimt-wid/sm-mw/rpt1.aspx?lang=eng. The rates shown are typical for persons 18 years of age and over.

While minimum wages are intended to create a minimum standard of living to protect the health and well-being of employees, some argue that minimum-wage regulations increase the cost of production in Canada. Increases in minimum wages are usually accompanied by increases in unemployment figures of low-skilled and young persons in the workforce. It is also pointed out by some that continual increases in minimum-wage rates may actually contribute to the inflationary trends in the economy.[25]

In terms of overtime, for every covered job, the organization must pay one-and-a-half times the employee's regular pay rate for all hours over a stipulated maximum number per day or per week. Executive, administrative, professional, and other employees are exempt from the overtime provisions.

The employment standards also furnish information relating to hours of work, general holidays, annual vacation, and conditions of employment. Accurate records are also to be kept, for example, on maternity leave and severance pay relating to all affected employees. This is to ensure that all provisions of the legislation relating to such things as minimum wages, maximum weekly hours, and overtime payments are strictly adhered to by each employer. Further information defining the employment standards in a particular jurisdiction can be found at http://www.workplace .ca/laws/index.html.

In parallel to the employment standards guiding nonunionized employment, federal and provincial *labour laws* regulate the rights, restrictions, and obligations of trade unions, workers, and employers in Canada. These labour codes guide industrial relations (such as collective bargaining, dispute resolution, strikes and lockouts), occupational health and safety, and federal labour standards. In a union context, the specific conditions of employment are guided by the collective agreement between the union and management. The union-management framework is the topic of Chapter 13. Of note, about 94 percent of employees fall under provincial legislation, with 6 percent covered by the Canada Labour Code.[26]

LO5   Variable Pay

There is strong evidence that the prevalence and variety of variable pay programs at Canadian companies is on the rise. One recent report suggests that 74 percent of Canadian companies now use variable pay, with that number rising to 82 percent of top-performing companies and 85 percent of enterprise companies.[27] WorldatWork reports that variable pay plans were used by 88 percent of organizations in 2016.[28] Figure 9-10 shows the frequency with which various types of variable pay programs are used by companies around the world.

The objectives of variable pay are (1) to improve business performance through efficient and productive employee behaviour, (2) to keep compensation competitive, and (3) to enhance employee recruitment, engagement, retention, and employer branding.[29] The advantage of the variable compensation approach is that it provides employees with incentives linked to performance. Unlike merit pay, it can incorporate the performance of individuals, groups, business units, and corporate financial and stock price performances. The cost advantage of a variable pay plan to the organization is that the award must be re-earned every year and does not permanently increase base salary.

Variable pay systems provide the clearest link between pay and performance or productivity. (*Performance* is the accomplishment of assigned tasks; *productivity* is the measure of output.) **Incentive pay** offered through variable pay systems is directly linked to an employee's performance or productivity. Employees who work under

> **incentive pay**
> Compensation that is directly tied to an employee's performance, productivity, or both.

FIGURE 9-10

Types of Variable Pay Plans Used Around the World

	Profit Sharing	Performance Sharing (based on other financial or nonfinancial goals)	Individual Incentives (other than sales incentives)	Bonuses (e.g., sign-on, retention)	Recognition (e.g., spot award)
United States/ Canada	19%	65%	52%	80%	73%
Africa	16%	66%	43%	66%	59%
Asia-Pacific	13%	67%	53%	68%	64%
Eastern Europe	14%	66%	56%	66%	64%
Western Europe	16%	67%	52%	71%	64%
Middle East	14%	61%	45%	73%	67%
Latin America	19%	64%	57%	68%	62%

a financial incentive system find that their performance (productivity) determines, in whole or in part, their income. A typical example of an incentive pay is a salesperson's commission. The more the salesperson sells, the more he or she earns.

The HR function has a significant role in the design and implementation of incentive compensation programs, including the following:[30]

- Surveying employees about the incentives they value
- Explaining how incentives work, and the level of performance necessary to achieve the benefit
- Checking in with employees regularly to gauge their satisfaction with the incentive plan
- Interviewing employees who are leaving the organization to determine if the incentive plan had anything to do with their exit decision
- Keeping upper-level management aware of how the incentive plan is working

One of the most significant benefits of financial incentives is that better performance is reinforced on a regular basis. Unlike raises and promotions, the reinforcement is generally quick and frequent—usually with each paycheque. Since the worker sees the results of the desired behaviour quickly, that behaviour is more likely to continue. The employer wins because wages are given in proportion to performance, not for the indirect measure of time worked. And if employees are motivated by the system to expand their output, recruiting expenses for additional employees and capital outlays for new workstations are minimized. A switch from hourly to direct incentive pay can be quite dramatic:

> At Safelite Glass Corporation, the changeover from hourly pay to incentive pay led to an increase in productivity of 44 percent per worker. Incentive pay induced (1) higher output per worker, (2) lower quitting rates among the highest output workers, and (3) the company's ability to hire more productive workers.[31]

Offsetting these advantages are some potential challenges. The administration of an incentive system can be complex. As with any control system, standards have to be established and results measured. For many jobs, the standards and measures are too imprecise or too costly to develop. This means that the incentive system may result in inequities. Some incentive systems require less effort than other systems that pay the same. Sometimes, workers make more than their supervisors, who are on salary. Another problem is that the employee may not achieve the standard because of uncontrollable forces, such as work delays or machine breakdowns.

Variable pay programs tend to focus efforts on only one aspect (output, sales, or stock prices), sometimes to the exclusion of other dimensions (quality, service, and long-term objectives). Some of the more common individual incentive plans, team or group-based incentive plans, and employee ownership and profit sharing systems are outlined below.

Individual Incentive Plans

There are multiple forms that individual incentive plans can take. In general, these pay plans reward the accomplishment of specific results. Typically, the amount of the reward is tied to expected results from the outset so that employees know what their compensation will be for particular levels of performance. Common individual incentive plans include piecework, production bonuses, sales commission, discretionary bonuses, and spot awards.

Piecework

Piecework is an incentive system that compensates the worker for each unit of output. Daily or weekly pay is determined by multiplying the output in units times the piece rate per unit. For example, in agricultural labour, workers are often paid a specific amount per bushel of produce picked. Piecework does not always mean higher productivity, however. Group norms may have a more significant impact if peer pressure works against higher productivity. And in many jobs, it may be difficult to measure the person's productive contribution (e.g., receptionist), or the employee may not be able to control the rate of output (e.g., an assembly-line worker).

> **piecework** A type of incentive system that compensates workers for each unit of output.

Production Bonuses

Production bonuses are incentives paid to workers for exceeding a specified level of output. They are used in conjunction with a base wage rate or salary. Under one approach, the employee receives a predetermined salary or wage. Through extra effort that results in output above the standard, the base compensation is supplemented by a bonus, usually figured at a given rate for each unit of production over the standard. A variation rewards the employee for saving time. For example, if the standard time for replacing an automobile transmission is four hours and the mechanic does it in three, the mechanic may be paid for four hours. Through taking on an additional task during the fourth hour, the organization can service more vehicles and the employee is compensated for his or her speedy work.

> **production bonuses** A type of incentive system that provides employees with additional compensation when they surpass stated production goals.

A third method combines production bonuses with piecework by compensating workers on an hourly basis, plus an incentive payment for each unit produced. In some cases, the employee may get a higher piece rate once a minimum number of units are produced. For example, the employee may be paid $15 an hour plus $0.30 per unit for the first 30 units each day. Beginning with unit 31, the production bonus may become $0.50.

Commissions

Commission is commonly paid in sales jobs. The salesperson may be paid a percentage of the selling price or a flat amount for each unit sold. Organizations often tie commission rates to sales quotas.[32] Salespeople meeting the highest quotas will be paid the highest commission rates, with those meeting lower targets paid lesser commission rates. For instance, salespeople may receive 10 percent commission on each unit sold up to the tenth one, and 20 percent commission on each unit sold thereafter. The salesperson is motivated to sell more units to make more money. Another approach is to tie commission rates to revenue goals. The goal may be to sell, say, $100,000 worth of goods with a higher commission rate paid for each dollar of goods sold over that amount.

When no base compensation is paid, the salesperson's total earnings come from commissions. Real estate agents and car salespeople are often paid this form of straight commission. Variations on straight commission plans include combining commissions with base wages, as one example below depicts:

> EchoSign, a software as a service company, initially based its compensation plan on a high quota, base salary, and low commissions. Problems with the system included poor retention, the relatively low commission did not inspire reps to spend time serving their customers once signed, and the mediocre reps were being paid too much while the best reps were not making enough. The company redesigned its compensation structure so that it included a competitive base salary, but reps had to cover their base salary with their sales before bonuses would kick in. After covering their base salary, they would make twice the rate of commission. The company also inspired reps to take care of their customers by paying them on receipt of payment as opposed to at contract E-signing. New reps became highly motivated to perform at their peak performance watching the top performers driving their M6 convertibles. Mediocre reps voluntarily left the organization.[33]

Discretionary Bonus Plans

With discretionary bonus plans, employees are paid base wages and then are paid a bonus at the discretion of management. When these bonuses are paid on the basis of performance, management will typically determine the size of the total bonus pool and then allocate amounts to individuals after a performance period. The top employees may receive bonus amounts commonly around 10 percent of their base salary. Employees who did not meet performance expectations will get no bonus. A related form of discretionary bonus is pay-at-risk. Employees can earn the additional amount or percentage of their wages that is pay-at-risk provided they meet specific targets.

Other discretionary bonuses may be paid as sign-on bonuses to prompt new employees to join and stay at the organization. These are one-time payments made at the start of employment, ranging from cash amounts of $5,000 to $10,000 most commonly, or as a percentage of salary.[34] Such bonuses often make the sought-after new employee's salary more affordable for the organization.

> Sign-on bonuses aim to increase the length of time that employees will stay at an organization. However, similar-sized sign-on bonuses show the relationship with tenure not to be strong. For instance, Tesla Motors, Pandora, and Spotify all had average sign-on bonuses around $20,000 and employees stayed about two years. Microsoft had a similar-sized sign-on bonus and employees stayed, on average, 44 months. Hewlett Packard Enterprise paid an average of only $8,265 and employees stayed about 3.5 years.[35]

Other bonuses may be paid as retention bonuses. With retention bonuses, employees who are still working for the organization after the stipulated period of time will receive a lump-sum bonus. These are common with overseas employment, where the organization has invested a lot of money in moving the employee (and potentially his or her family as well). Employees may be paid the retention bonus when they hit three- or five-year time points. They are also used when companies are going through transitions, such as a merger. Companies in difficult situations may pay retention bonuses to have existing employees see them through their tough times.[36] One criticism of retention bonuses is that employees may stay just for the money and not because they are committed and engaged.

> Amid negative news and RCMP investigations, SNC-Lavalin paid cash rewards of 50 percent of salary to key employees to keep them from leaving the "sinking ship."[37]

Spot Awards

Spot awards recognize special contributions as they occur. Employees may receive spot awards for a project or task, generally accomplished in a short period.[38] These types of recognition awards can range from gift certificates and thank-you notes to paid time off to cash awards or salary increments unrelated to annual merit increases. Their aim is to acknowledge the employee's noteworthy contribution and reinforce the behaviours and values. Spot awards that are given to the deserving employee publicly have higher status than private ones. While thank-you notes and celebrations can be valued, it is fair to say that "good old-fashioned cash" is still one of the best incentives.[39]

Team (or Group) Incentive Plans

Several plans have been developed to provide incentives based on the performance of a group or work team. These programs often are used when measurable output is the result of group effort and it is difficult to separate individual contributions.

Team Results

Under team-based pay plans, employee bonuses and salary increases are based on a team's overall results and typically shared equally. There can be a number of advantages in a team-based pay system. For example, in project teams, many jobs are interrelated; that is, they depend on each other for making progress. A team approach tends to foster group cohesion and organizational commitment. Communication in cohesive teams tends to be more open, and decision making can be more effective if a consensus approach is in the team's interest. Team-based pay often includes rewards for developing better interpersonal skills to improve co-operation and incentives for cross-training.

There can also be disadvantages to team-based pay systems. If team cohesiveness is not strong, a "freeloader effect" may take place. As in any group, individual contributions to team goals vary. Some put in more effort; others, less. If these differences are significant and the high performers do not receive satisfaction for their input, they may cut back their contributions. Usually, however, high-input members get their satisfaction from being recognized as team leaders or higher status members, for example as experts or specialists. Another potential drawback is social pressure on high performers to lower their input to avoid drawing management's attention to the low performers. This issue will most likely occur in a hostile management–union environment. It is also possible that the team approach may be too effective, resulting in competition between teams and undesirable consequences, such as hoarding of resources or withholding of important information.

Production Incentive Plans

Production incentive plans allow groups of workers to receive bonuses for exceeding predetermined levels of output. They tend to be short-range and related to very specific production goals. A work team may be offered a bonus for exceeding predetermined production levels, or it may receive a per-unit incentive that results in a group piece rate.

Profit-Sharing and Ownership Plans

Apart from individual incentive and team-based incentives, organizations may also compensate employees through profit-sharing plans and employee stock ownership plans.

Profit-Sharing Plans

A **profit-sharing plan** shares company profits with the workers. When the organization is profitable, the employer shares profits with all, or a participating group of, employees. The amounts paid are given to a trustee and invested for the benefit of all of the beneficiaries of the plan. Profitability, however, is not always related to employee performance: A recession or new competitors may impact whether or not the company makes money. Furthermore, it is often difficult for employees to perceive their efforts as making much difference. Some companies further reduce the effectiveness of the incentive by diverting the employees' share of profits into retirement plans. Thus, the immediate reinforcement value of the incentive is reduced because the incentive is delayed. However, when these plans work well they can have a dramatic impact on the organization because profit-sharing plans can create a sense of trust and a feeling of common fate among workers and management.

> **profit-sharing plan**
> A system whereby an employer pays compensation or benefits to employees, usually on an annual basis, in addition to their regular wage, on the basis of the profits of the company.

How effective are profit-sharing plans in motivating employees? The evidence is not that clear-cut. Profitable companies with profit-sharing plans also tend to have open and two-way communication between management and employees. In addition, managers in these companies tend to have participative management styles, resulting in a supportive and satisfying work environment.[40] Although companies with profit-sharing plans tend to be more profitable, it is by no means certain that the plan is the cause of increased profitability.[41] As usual, many factors play a role.

Employee Stock Ownership Plans (ESOPs)

Employee stock ownership plans (ESOPs) have become very popular in North America and Europe. One study indicates that 28 million U.S. employees participating in 11,000 employee ownership plans own 8 percent of corporate equity in the U.S. In Europe, 85 percent of publicly traded firms have employee stock ownership plans with 10 million employees in Europe holding some form of company stock.[42] Many Canadian firms, such as WestJet and Golder Associates, have adopted ESOPs. Unlike the more traditional profit-sharing plans, ESOPs give employees genuine ownership and voting power when it comes to major decisions relating to the company's future.

Beau's, the largest independent producer of organic beer in Canada, plans to maintain its independence from large breweries by handing ownership over to its employees. Around 4 to 5 percent of the company was offered to employees during the first year of the ESOP. Employees could spend up to 2 percent of their salary buying shares in the company. Future-year share offerings will depend on how much the Beauchesne family decides to put up for sale. Other craft breweries in the area have been acquired by Labatt Breweries of Canada. The ESOP plan was adopted to maintain legacy and protect workers from layoffs in the event of an acquisition.[43]

In addition to motivating employees and improving their productivity, some Canadian employers are using ESOPs as a succession planning tool and to transition out of their business.[44] Viive Tamm, president of Toronto-based advertising and branding agency Tamm Communications, is using an ESOP as her exit strategy. She is selling 49 percent of the business to her employees, aiming for the company to flourish as workers take on ownership. Over time, she plans to sell the remainder of the company to employees.[45]

Although some stock-ownership plans vest shares to employees as compensation for their work, a variation on this is offering the employee a stock option. Stock-option plans grant employees the right to buy a certain amount of company shares at a predetermined price for a certain period of time. With stock options, the employees are not granted stocks automatically but, rather, are given the opportunity to buy-in to the company over time.

LO6 Total Reward Model

In the past few years we have seen the increased popularity of a **total reward model**, also known as a total compensation approach in the compensation field. Total compensation is everything that the company provides an employee in exchange for working. It includes base wages, variable pay, perks and on-site amenities, status/recognition, as well as benefits, discussed in Chapter 10. The total compensation package that an employee receives is the sum total of all of the components of the system. Figure 9-11 lists 13 components that may be included

> **total reward model**
> Inclusion of everything employees value in an employment relationship.

FIGURE 9-11

Components of a Total Reward System

1.	Compensation	Wages, commissions, and bonuses
2.	Benefits	Vacations, health insurance
3.	Social interaction	Friendly workplace
4.	Security	Stable, consistent position and rewards
5.	Status/recognition	Respect, prominence
6.	Work variety	Opportunity to experience different things
7.	Workload	Right amount of work (not too much, not too little)
8.	Work importance	Is work valued by society?
9.	Authority/control/autonomy	Ability to influence others; control own destiny
10.	Advancement	Chance to get ahead
11.	Feedback	Receive information helping to improve performance
12.	Work conditions	Hazard free
13.	Development opportunity	Formal and informal training to learn new knowledge/skills/abilities

SOURCE: George T. Milkovich, Jerry M. Newman, Nina Cole, and Margaret Yap (2013), *Compensation* (4th Canadian ed.), Toronto: McGraw-Hill Ryerson, p. 224. Used with permission.

in a total compensation valuation. Of note, not all of the components have a dollar value associated with them. For instance, onsite daycare and casual dress codes may add to an employee's total compensation valuation through savings in time, worry, and stress.[46]

Studies have shown that companies with total rewards approaches enjoy easier recruitment of high-quality staff, reduced costs because of lower turnover, higher employee performance, and an enhanced reputation as an employer of choice.[47]

A related trend in compensation plans is to allow employees to choose their rewards.[48] Not all of the components of the total reward system will be equally valued be all employees. For instance, those without dogs may not find as much value in an ability to bring pets to work, nor will those with grown or no children find value in the onsite daycare offerings. Some employees will prefer cash and others will prefer additional vacation time. Some compensation systems are now being designed to offer tailor-made packages to boost satisfaction and meet multiple sets of needs.[49]

LO7 Pay Equity

As first mentioned in Chapter 4, an important issue in compensation management and equal opportunity is **equal pay for work of equal value**, the concept that jobs of comparable worth to the organization should be equally paid (referred to as **pay equity**). The idea goes beyond **equal pay for equal work** (referred to as *equal pay*), which requires an employer to pay men and women the same wage or salary when they do the same work.

The pay equity concept, and legislation stemming from the *Canadian Human Rights Act*, makes it illegal to discriminate on the basis of job value (or content). For example, if a nurse and an electrician both received approximately the same number of job evaluation points under the point system, they would have to be paid the same wage or salary, regardless of market conditions. This approach to compensation is sought by governments as a means of eliminating the historical gap between the income of men and women, which

> **equal pay for work of equal value** The principle of equal pay for men and women in jobs with comparable content; based on criteria of skill, effort, responsibility, and working conditions; part of the *Canadian Human Rights Act*.
>
> **pay equity** A policy to eliminate the gap between the income of men and women, ensuring that salary ranges correspond to value of work performed.
>
> **equal pay for equal work** The principle or policy of equal rates of pay for all employees in an establishment performing the same kind and amount of work, regardless of sex, race, or other characteristics of individual workers not related to ability or performance.

results in women in Canada earning about 87 percent as much as men.[50] This gap exists in part because women have traditionally found work in lower paying occupations, such as teaching, retailing, nursing, and secretarial work.

> Tesco supermarket is embroiled in the employment tribunal process under claims that female shop workers should get the same wages as male warehouse staff. Currently, the shopworkers are paid about $5 less per hour than the warehouse staff.[51]

It should be emphasized, however, that the above-mentioned figure of 87 percent as the earning gap between men and women is misleading, although it is widely used by proponents of equal pay to point to the discrimination in pay against women. This figure emerges if one compares all men and women wage-earners regardless of job tenure and skill level. However, women have greater career interruptions during which their male colleagues may have obtained training and advancement opportunities. By using comparable groups, the pay gap decreases to between 5 to 10 percent, depending on the group studied.[52] For example, the income of single women aged 35 to 44 was 94.5 percent of that earned by men of the same age. If one looks only at the most educated members of that age group—single females with a university degree—women actually made 6 percent more than their male counterparts. Taking all of the above factors into account, a gap of between 5 and 10 percent still exists that is not explained.

One contributing factor to the gap may be in the form of differential pay to permanent full-time jobs versus part-time and casual jobs. A recent arbitration decision in Ontario saw a wage increase for casual workers, who were mostly female, to make their wages the same as full-time workers, who were mostly men:

> An arbitration decision compelled the Liquor Control Board of Ontario (LCBO) to pay casual workers the same wages as full-time workers. The casual workers performed essentially the same work as the full-time workers but were paid $2 to $7 per hour less. Of the casual workers, the "vast majority" are female.[53]

Although the casual category is frequently used to justify a pay difference, it becomes an issues of unequal pay if one of those jobs is gendered. Notably, a job is gender-dominated if, depending on jurisdiction, 60 to 70 percent of the job occupants are from one sex. There is no evidence that there is a conspiracy among entrepreneurs and managers to keep the wages of female-dominated jobs down.

What makes the issue of equal pay for work of equal value very tricky is the lack of any generally acceptable definition of "equal value" and how it can be measured. The definition offered in the guidelines issued by the Canadian Human Rights Commission is not of much help:

> "Value of work is the value which the work performed by an employee in a given establishment

Jupiterimages/Stockbyte/Thinkstock

In 2015–16, nearly 1,900 women in Canada received more than $6.8 million in compensation adjustments following workplace investigations of pay inequity.[54]

represents in relation to the value of work of another employee, or group of employees, the value being determined on the basis of approved criteria, without the wage market or negotiated wage rates being taken into account."[55]

The "approved criteria" referred to above are skill, effort, responsibility, and working conditions. These criteria will be considered together; that is, they will form a composite measure. This does not mean that employees must be paid the same salary, even if their jobs are considered equal. The equal wage guidelines define seven "reasonable factors" that can justify differences in wages:

1. Different performance ratings (ratings must be based on a formal appraisal system and be brought to the attention of each employee)
2. Seniority (based on length of service)
3. Red-circling (because of job re-evaluation)
4. Rehabilitation assignment (e.g., after lengthy absence because of sickness)
5. Demotion pay procedures (because of unsatisfactory work performance, or reassignment because of labour force surplus)
6. Procedure of phased-in wage reductions
7. Temporary training positions

These factors justify a difference in wages only if they are applied consistently and equitably. It must be clearly demonstrable that existing wage differences are not based on sex.

Where does this leave the human resource manager? A human resource manager has to make sure that the company's pay system is in line with the province's or the federal government's legislation. An overview of pay equity in various Canadian jurisdictions can be found at http://www.payequity.gov.on.ca/Pages/default.aspx. The Spotlight on HRM provides a series of suggestions to examine pay equity and then act on inequities identified.

Spotlight *on* HRM

What Can Employers Do to Address Gender Pay Inequity?
By John Schwarz

Executives can begin by gaining a high-level understanding of the state of gender equity at their organizations. Some simple metrics to start with include metrics such as "female ratio" (looking at the percentage of total head count that are female) by department, role or location, and in hiring pipelines.

Next, executives should dig deeper to find out if pay and performance ratings are unbiased for men and women. Compa-ratio is a classic compensation calculation that indicates how close a person's base pay is to the pay level midpoint for the role they perform. The best practice for ensuring pay equity is a well-designed, individual compensation plan that takes into consideration job difficulty, education and training requirements, experience and performance.

If women have a lower than average compa-ratio, then it is likely pay decisions are not being made equitably. Similarly, understanding the proportion of employees who receive each level of performance rating, and then comparing this to the proportion of each rating for female employees, will uncover if performance ratings are handed out in an unbiased manner.

To address the manager divide and increase the representation of women in manager roles, companies need to measure not only promotions by gender, but also the nature of the promotions—by role, department or location—and analyze if the percentage of women promoted to or holding manager positions is lower than the percentage of men promoted to or holding manager positions.

Lastly, executives need to take steps to correct gender inequity, starting with their processes for hiring and promotion. One idea is to implement the Rooney Rule—for every open manager position, consider "at least one woman and one underrepresented minority" in the slate of candidates.

Originally implemented by the National Football League (NFL) and named after Pittsburgh Steelers chair Dan Rooney, the Rooney Rule sought to increase the opportunities for minorities to hold NFL head coaching positions.

Executives can also consider blind screening of resumés (removing names or other gender identifiers from resumés) when selecting applicants for interviews.

It is important to note that even with these policies in place, society must be willing to give women a reasonable job experience credit for time spent raising children, and promote women to enter management ranks at the same rate as men.

Without these changes, the pay gap inside a given profession is likely to remain.

SOURCE: John Schwarz (2017, October 16), "Best practices for gender pay equity," *Canadian HR Reporter.*

Although much of the focus of pay equity is about gender, racial wage disparities also exist. A recent study found that white men are paid more than black men, despite similar educational attainment and family backgrounds.[56]

Not only is pay equity a human right, it also makes good business sense. The pay equity process helps organizations and employees accurately see the value of all jobs in the organization, identify potential biases, and removed barriers to engagement and productivity. Workplaces that establish pay equity have a recruitment advance, lower turnover, and better organizational and financial performance.[57]

The gender pay gap represents $18 billion in foregone income per year, according to a 2016 analysis by Deloitte.[58] Imagine the economic impact through additional taxes paid and consumer spending if the gap were eliminated. From societal and economic perspectives, pay equity makes good sense.

LO8 Pay Secrecy

Pay secrecy is a touchy topic. Many employers prefer not to publish salary levels to avoid having to defend their pay decisions. If a pay policy is indefensible, disclosure may cause significant dissatisfaction among employees. Research has shown that employees generally prefer secrecy about individual salaries but favour disclosure of pay ranges and pay policies.[59] Figure 9-12 shows the advantages and disadvantages of insisting on secrecy.

> **pay secrecy** A management policy not to discuss or publish individual salaries.

According to Edward Lawler, founder and director of the Center for Effective Organizations, pay secrecy has two major effects: (1) It lowers the pay satisfaction of employees and (2) it reduces employees' motivation to perform.[60] It is practically unavoidable that employees will talk about

FIGURE 9-12

Advantages and Disadvantages of Pay Secrecy

Advantages	Disadvantages
Most employees prefer to have their pay kept secret	May generate distrust in the pay system
Gives managers greater freedom	Employees may perceive that there is no relationship between pay and performance
Covers up inequities in the internal pay structure	

and compare salaries. On the basis of rumours and speculations, employees tend to overestimate the salaries of their colleagues, causing feelings of unfairness, inequity, and resentment. Pay secrecy also prevents employees from perceiving the connection between their performance and their pay.

When it comes to asking about salary histories during hiring, some U.S. jurisdictions are currently prohibiting employers from asking about salary history in an effort to improve pay equity. However, WorldatWork suggests that employers should have access to all relevant employment information to determine fair compensation—including a candidate's total rewards history. WorldatWork rationalizes that compensation should then be tied to specific job requirements and market pricing to determine the rate of pay for a job.[61]

International Pay

"Think globally, act locally!" has become a popular part of business strategies of international companies. For HR managers, this policy has become quite a challenge. Traditionally, when companies went international, they imposed the "home-country system" on their overseas operations, which often led to quite serious discrepancies in

HR policies. For example, it was possible that a Canadian middle manager in a Canadian subsidiary in Japan could be earning $150,000 (with generous "overseas benefits") while the Japanese counterpart, having the same job title and responsibilities, might be paid a quarter of the expatriate's salary—surely a cause for friction.

An integrated "global" strategy requires a common framework but not a one-size-fits-all solution, which is quite a challenge when it comes to pay. Global enterprises aim to preserve national cultural differences while maintaining organizational values that allow the application of a global strategy. For example, these companies hire employees on the basis of their expertise, not nationality. A Japanese employee may work for a Canadian company in Germany. The Japanese employee would be expected to adapt to the German culture, while maintaining his Japanese values. The company, in turn, would have developed a corporate culture, policies, and strategies that would allow it to do business in any country of the world.[62] Compensation philosophies will play a crucial role in the effectiveness of the organization.

Among organizations with multinational operations, 47 percent adopt the same pay programs internationally, although flexibility is provided to countries or regions to make some adaptations to corporate programs or to install some small local pay initiatives.[63]

SUMMARY

Employee compensation, if properly administered, can be an effective tool to improve employee performance, motivation, and satisfaction. Mismanaged pay programs can lead to high turnover and absenteeism, more grievances, poor performance, and job dissatisfaction.

For compensation to be appropriate, it must be internally and externally equitable. The organization must first establish a compensation philosophy to determine whether it will lead, match, or lag its market competitors. Referring to job analysis data and with their compensation philosophy in hand, organizations can begin the process of pricing jobs. Jobs are priced within an organization through job evaluation techniques. This assures internal equity. Wage and salary surveys are used to determine external equity by comparing what similar jobs are paid by competitors. A third approach is to value employee pay according to the knowledge and skills held by the employee. With knowledge of the relative worth of jobs and external pay levels, each job can be properly priced with pay matched to individuals within the organization.

Determining compensation rates is affected by multiple factors, including union power, the productivity of workers,

and government constraints on pay. Pay equity legislation requires "equal pay for work of equal value," which requires employers to compare the content of jobs when determining pay scales and to pay equal wages for jobs of comparable value.

Variable pay offers incentives to employees to reach peak performance or meet other desired behaviours. Individual incentives, such as commission and discretionary bonuses, relate pay to productivity. Group or team-based incentive plans, such as a bonus for reaching a production target, aim to inspire high team performance. Profit sharing plans and employee stock ownership plans share the company's profits with workers and may inspire loyalty through ownership in the company.

A total rewards model aims to examine all forms of compensation provided to an employee, including base wages, variable pay, and benefits and services. The next chapter describes the range of benefits and services offered by employers.

TERMS FOR REVIEW

compa-ratio 287
equal pay for equal work 293
equal pay for work of equal value 293
external equity 276
incentive pay 288
internal equity 276
job evaluations 277
job grading 278
job ranking 278
key job 284
merit raise 285

pay equity 293
pay secrecy 295
piecework 289
point system 279
production bonuses 289
profit-sharing plan 291
rate range 285
red-circled rate 286
skill- or knowledge-based pay 282
total reward model 292
wage and salary surveys 281

SELF-ASSESSMENT EXERCISE

Examining Compensation Issues

1. One objective of compensation administration is to ensure administrative efficiency.	T	F
2. Job evaluation committees set wage and salary policies.	T	F
3. Job ranking is a superior evaluation method because it compares jobs directly.	T	F
4. The labour market for salary surveys is generally considered to be the local community.	T	F
5. Unions insist that nonunionized employees do not receive the same increases as union members.	T	F
6. Under no circumstances can an employee legally be paid less than minimum wage.	T	F
7. The pay equity concept specifies that women are paid the same as men for the same work.	T	F
8. The wage gap between males and females is between 5 and 10 percent for comparable groups.	T	F
9. Profit-sharing plans are ideal instruments for motivating employees.	T	F
10. The variable pay concept emphasizes a linkage between pay and performance.	T	F

SCORING

If you answered statements 2, 3, 5, 7, and 9 as false, you get one point each. All other statements are true, resulting again in one point each.

Scores of 8–10: Very good! Congratulations.

Scores of 5–7: You made it, but barely. It is advisable that you go over the chapter text again.

REVIEW AND DISCUSSION QUESTIONS

1. What is the difference between absolute and relative pay?

2. Why is job analysis information, discussed in Chapter 2, necessary before job evaluations can be performed?

3. Suppose that when you interview new employees, you ask them what they think is a fair wage or salary. If you hire them, you pay them that amount as long as it is reasonable and not below minimum wage laws. What problems might you expect?

4. Assume that your company has a properly conducted compensation program. If a group of employees asks you why they receive different hourly pay rates even though they perform the same job, how would you respond?

5. Why is the point system superior to the other job evaluation systems? Discuss the advantages and disadvantages of the system.

6. If you are told to find out what competitors in your area are paying their employees, how would you get this information without conducting a wage and salary survey?

7. Even after jobs are first priced using a wage-trend line, what other challenges may cause you to adjust some rates upward?

8. Since variable pay gives employees feedback for good performance and relates pay to performance, why do most companies pay wages and salaries instead of variable pay?

9. Explain the difference between "equal pay for equal work" and "equal pay for work of equal value," and the implications of the difference for a human resource manager.

10. Under what circumstances are pay differentials justified?

11. Why is it so important to explain to employees the performance–reward relationship?

12. In what ways does the total reward model differ from the regular compensation approach?

CRITICAL THINKING QUESTIONS

1. Suppose that you manage a small business with 30 employees. You discover that some people are much more motivated by money and others are more motivated by security. Is it possible to satisfy the needs of both groups? What difficulties may arise?

2. "Money is a strong motivator" and "In surveys on what employees want from their job, money ranks low." How can you reconcile these two statements?

3. Obviously, profit-sharing plans are not an option as an incentive plan in nonprofit and government organizations. Can you think of incentive plans that would fulfill a similar function?

4. "Minimum wages increase unemployment." Please comment on this statement often made by many economists. Do you agree?

5. How should an HR manager find out what employees value as rewards? Is it acceptable to ask employees directly? Discuss. Are other methods preferable? Which ones? Why?

ETHICS QUESTION

The issue of the wage gap between the sexes has been discussed for decades, and pay equity legislation is supposed to take care of it. However, Statistics Canada reports that there is still a gap of about 13 percent in average salaries across jobs and provinces. It has been argued that women will never achieve pay equity because their role in society often requires them to interrupt a career, have children, and stay home to bring them up. How ethical is it to expect women to make this sacrifice and then pay for it in terms of lower average compensation?

RESEARCH EXERCISE

1. National Center for Employee Ownership (U.S.) (https://www.nceo.org/)

   a. What are the characteristics of an effective employee ownership plan? What steps should be followed in its development?

   b. Research seems to indicate that employee ownership plans have a different effectiveness depending on the size of the company. Try to determine what the relationship of the effect is to size and why there may be a difference in effectiveness.

2. An interactive program on employee ownership (https://www.nceo.org/pages/interactive.cgi?nextpage=1)

   Take the demonstration training program.

3. The Conference Board of Canada (https://www.conferenceboard.ca/)

   What different types of information are available to Canadian managers regarding incentive plans?

4. Gainsharing: Different types of plans: at HR.com and at Quality Digest.com

   Summarize the research studies on the effectiveness of gainsharing programs.

INCIDENT 9-1

Compensation Administration at Reynolds Plastic Products

The family-owned Reynolds Plastic Products Co. in London, Ontario, was recently purchased by a much larger company, International Plastics Ltd. When the human resource director of International Plastics, Hans Himmelman, looked at Reynolds Plastic compensation policies, he became concerned that some of them were questionable and in some cases actually seemed to violate the law. When he asked the plant manager, an engineer, who also acted as an HR manager, how he determined pay rates, the manager explained that he would ask applicants what they had earned in their previous job and just add 25 or 50 cents to this amount, depending on their job experience. To make matters worse, two recently hired ethnic minority machinists complained that they were paid less for the same work than their nonminority colleagues. The machine shop supervisor disputed their claim, asserting that the nonminority employees had more work experience and deserved higher pay. Himmelman also discovered that productivity in the subsidiary was lower than in other plants of International Plastics. An HR consultant was hired to assess the compensation system of the Reynolds Plastic subsidiary. The key points of her report are summarized below:

- Executives in the past have received an annual bonus determined by the owner at his discretion.
- Wages for hourly employees ranged from $16.00 per hour for employees during their probationary period to $28.00 per hour for the more skilled or experienced ones.
- The amount of overtime paid by Reynolds was very modest; overtime was paid for all hours over 180 per month.
- The wage rates for different workers varied widely even on the same job; those employees who were not visible minorities received approximately 18 percent more than those workers who were.

- Visible minority employees were paid 10 to 20 percent less in all job categories.
- On highly technical jobs, the firm paid a rate of 20 percent above the prevailing wage rate for these jobs. All other jobs were paid an average of 15 percent below the prevailing rate.
- Production workers were eligible for a $200 draw each month if there were no accidents during the month.
- Sales personnel were paid a commission and received a $200 bonus for every new customer.
- Whenever sales went up 10 percent, all the hourly employees got a day off with pay or could work one day at the double-time rate.
- Turnover averaged a modest 12 percent. However, in technical jobs turnover was less than 2 percent; in nontechnical jobs turnover was nearly 20 percent.
- Absenteeism followed the same pattern.

DISCUSSION QUESTIONS

1. What laws were probably being violated?
2. What problems do you see with the incentives for (a) executives? (b) production workers? (c) salespeople? (d) hourly employees?
3. Himmelman read about new approaches to pay policies such as variable pay and profit sharing, and he wondered whether either one would be a suitable solution for the subsidiary, especially profit sharing to increase low productivity. How would you advise him?
4. Develop a step-by-step plan of actions you would take and the order in which you would undertake them if you were made human resource director of the Reynolds subsidiary.

EXERCISE 9-1

A Realistic Job Evaluation Simulation

Form groups of three to five. (Three students may need approximately 20 minutes, five students about 45 minutes for the exercise.)

Use the following rules:

1. Have each student choose a job he or she is familiar with (ideally, a job description would be available but

is not essential). The jobs should be different but from a single organization (e.g., hospital, school, manufacturing plant).

2. Use the table below to record numbers.

Critical Factors	Job 1	Job 2	Job 3	Job 4	Job 5

1. Responsibility
   a. Safety of others
   b. Equipment and materials
   c. Assisting trainees
   d. Product/service quality

2. Skill
   a. Experience
   b. Education/training

3. Effort
   a. Physical
   b. Mental

4. Working conditions
   a. Unpleasant conditions
   b. Hazards

3. Using Figure 9-3, find consensus in your group in choosing the most appropriate point level for each job.

   Example: For the job of a janitor, what level of responsibility for the safety of others (critical factor) is appropriate? Probably not a high one, so a good choice might be Level I, 25 points. For a bus driver or an emergency room nurse, the appropriate choice might be Level IV, or 100 points.

4. Choose one of the above jobs, called a "key job"—a well-known job, ideally common in many organizations (e.g., secretary, accountant, tool-and-die maker in the manufacturing industry, and so on). Conduct a simulated wage survey. In this exercise it is sufficient to take an educated guess on what the key job is paid in the job market.

   It does not matter whether you choose an hourly wage or a monthly or annual salary, but it must be the same for each job.

5. Calculate the pay coefficient by dividing the estimated wage by the point total of the key job, according to the following formula:

$$\text{Pay coefficient (pc)} = \frac{\text{Wage of Key jobs}}{\text{Point total for key jobs}} = \frac{\$}{\text{Point}}$$

6. Multiply all job point totals by the pay coefficient. The results are the wages/salaries for all the above jobs. (In reality, this procedure would have to be done by the job evaluation committee for all jobs in the organization, often in the hundreds.)

COMMENT

This exercise is a fairly realistic simulation of what is going on in a job evaluation committee. In all probability, the opinions in your group were diverse when it came to determining the level for each job. The results, of course, are not realistic, since the point table has been created artificially and not by a job evaluation committee and the pay level of the key job has been estimated by you. Nevertheless, this exercise should give you a good feel for the job evaluation process, using the point method. It also demonstrates the need to choose members of the committee who are knowledgeable about the jobs in the organization and are trained in the application of the point method. One more point: Up to the wage survey, money was not part of the discussion, only points.

WE CONNECTIONS: COMPENSATION

Money Matters

Rebecca, the HR manager, left the conference room with Abdul Syed, and walked with him toward the entrance to the department. There she stopped, shook his hand, smiled, and said, "Thank you for talking to me, Abdul. I really appreciate it. We all wish you the best of luck. Please stay in touch."

Abdul nodded and walked toward his office. As Rebecca returned to her office, she gestured for Charlotte, the HR specialist, to join her.

Exit Interview Results

As she sat down in Rebecca's office, Charlotte said, "How did the exit interview go?"

Rebecca sat down behind her desk and slipped off her shoes. She was feeling a little worried. She said, "Not great. I mean he was really open, but the news is bad. The compensation problem might be even bigger than we thought."

"Uh oh," said Charlotte with a grimace. "What did he say?"

Looking at her notes, Rebecca replied, "He said he decided to leave when he found out Abigail Desai, the new accountant, was getting paid $13,000 a year more than him."

Charlotte gasped, "How did he find that out? Salaries are supposed to be confidential!"

Shrugging, Rebecca said, "They always find out, Charlotte. You can count on it. No matter what we say, people will talk. Salaries never stay fully confidential."

Charlotte countered, "Still, I don't get why he's mad. She *should* make more than him. Abdul's job as a financial coordinator is important, but Abigail is an accountant and that job has some serious responsibilities. That's why that job requires a lot more education and certification. Plus, she has a master's degree! That has to count for something. On top of all that, she is really good at her job. She has worked for some pretty progressive tech companies. I know she has brought in some great ideas even in the short time she's been here."

Tempting Employees Away

Continuing, Charlotte said, "I was talking to her boss about this just last week. He was asking what the process was to increase her salary when she finishes her probationary period. She is so good that he is afraid he's going to lose her to another company. Apparently, she was seen having lunch with some people in suits, and the rumour is that it was an interview."

Rebecca groaned. "Don't tell me that! We can't have another person lured away. Alex would lose his mind. From what I can tell he's still reeling from losing that project manager named Jake a few months back. He brought me in at least partly to stop this sort of thing from happening. But first let's get back to Abdul and his problem with Abigail. I don't know if he knew about her master's degree. He just noticed that their jobs are somewhat similar but she makes a lot more money even though he has been here longer. That really didn't seem fair to him. And he mentioned that his new job pays a lot more than what he was getting here. The scary part is, if he starts telling people that, I wouldn't be surprised if more people start considering other options."

Underwhelming Pay

Looking troubled, Charlotte replied, "I don't want to add fuel to the fire, but while you were meeting with Abdul I was making some calls. I just had our two top candidates for that software position turn me down. Both of them said we weren't offering as much as they were hoping for. Could it be that we don't pay well? That seems weird to me. I've heard some people say that we are very generous."

"*Both* those candidates said no?" Rebecca asked, her voice heavy with disbelief. "It took forever to find them. Let's look at upping the offer."

Charlotte replied, "The offers were already a little above what we usually start people out at. But I guess we can do it if you think that's a good idea."

Rebecca sat back in her chair and gazed out the window, as she said, "Let me think for a minute. This is a tough one. Talk about being stuck between a rock and a hard place. If we don't go higher, we won't be able to hire good people. But if we do go higher, the people we already have will feel like they are getting the short end of the stick. I'm honestly not sure what to do next."

"What if we're focused on the wrong thing?" Charlotte thought out loud, and then continued, "What if we should be looking at other ways to pay people that won't make salary comparisons between old and new employees a problem?"

Rebecca picked up Charlotte's conversation thread and said, "Charlotte, that's it! We should be looking at options like hiring bonuses and retention bonuses. One-time payments that won't be ongoing increases in our staffing costs."

Now caught up in their brainstorming and happy to use some of her HR education, Charlotte replied, "And we could look into variable pay options to reward our strong performers. We need to think beyond just salary to keep the employees we've got happy *and* bring on some more top talent."

DISCUSSION QUESTIONS

1. Based on what you know about the company so far, what compensation philosophy is WEC using?

2. How can WEC use job evaluations to determine base pay levels? Which job evaluation method should it use and how should that method be designed and implemented?

3. What forms of variable pay do you think would be useful for Charlotte and Rebecca to consider implementing? Why?

4. What can be done in the future to help ensure that WEC is perceived as having both internal and external equity?

In the next installment of the WE Connections story (at the end of Chapter 10), the HR manager tries to convince her boss that they need to beef up their benefit program in order to keep employees satisfied.

CASE STUDY

Greener Environmental Services, Inc.

Flexible Benefit Program

Raj Chandra looked over the auditor's report for the company's financials from the last year. It was official: Greener Environmental Services had weathered the tough economic times and was finally back in the black. Nearly 10 years ago, Raj had left his position as an incident commander for Shell Canada to launch his own environmental consulting firm. Raj founded Greener with the vision of comprehensive environmental assessments pre-disturbance and remediation strategies that would renew the environment back to its pre-disturbance state.

In the decade since its inception, both the number of people and the range of environmental services offered by Greener had grown. Greener's current suite of offerings included comprehensive environmental services from environmental site, risk, and pre-disturbance assessments to monitoring, reclamation, and remediation services. Although most staff had environmental backgrounds (including environmental technology, environmental science and engineering, soil science and wetlands ecology), Greener also employed equipment operators, project managers, accounting/billings, and a small office staff. Lagging economic slowdowns for its mining and energy customers had significantly diminished the Phase I and Phase II environmental site assessment and pre-disturbance assessment aspects of their business. While the soil and groundwater monitoring and remediation services related to potash mining had remained reasonably strong, Raj and Greener had faced some fiscal challenges over the past three years.

Raj sat back in his chair and thought about the employees who had been with the company during the past few tough years. Raj knew they would be relieved to see confirmation that the company was at a turnaround. It was not hard to recall memories of an all-staff meeting he had held 18 months ago to lay out the company's financial situation to employees. He had asked employees to stick with the company based on projections for economic recovery of their customers in the energy sector. As their customers returned to new projects, Greener would be hired to conduct environmental assessment work. Rather than cut any staff from the assessment side of the business and focus only on the profitable monitoring branch, Raj had convinced Greener's investors that the assessment side would see recovery and growth. He had proposed that rather

than lay staff off only to rehire them later as the company rebuilt, they should keep everyone on staff. However, Raj had implemented a salary freeze across all employees. Staff in the slow assessments areas had been asked to assist with business development and sales to drum up business, and to assist staff on monitoring and mining remediation projects.

It had now been three years since Greener staff had seen a pay raise, and Raj knew that he would have to invest some of the company's recovered profits in direct pay. Having met with his chief financial officer last week, Raj and Natalia Wong had determined that 4 percent of revenue should be invested in employee compensation.

The question Raj was now facing was whether to implement a flat increase across all Greener staff or to differentially reward some key contributors. Raj wondered if even though the salary freeze had been implemented evenly across all employees, he would have to provide equal raises to all staff. He really wanted to channel some of the hard-won funds toward a few of his assessment staff who had really added value on the monitoring and mining remediation projects, even though the projects weren't in their focal areas of expertise. Furthermore, Raj knew that the mining remediation and monitoring groups had sought-after skill sets. These areas had been busy throughout the slowdown and would be key to revenue generating projects for Greener over the next few years. While Raj was pleased that the overall compensation news would finally be good news, he needed an effective compensation distribution plan.

DISCUSSION QUESTIONS

1. What are the pros and cons of providing even increases in base pay to all Greener staff?

2. What type(s) of variable pay might Raj want to consider? Which staff should be eligible for the variable pay plans?

3. What proportion of the 4 percent of revenue that Greener has available should be allocated to base pay increases versus variable pay? Justify your decision.

4. What recommendations would you have for Raj on how to communicate with Greener employees about the changes to their base pay and/or variable pay?

APPENDIX A

Calculation of Data in Point System Matrix (Replication of Figure 9-3)

Critical Factors	Levels or Degrees				Factor Points
	I	II	III	IV	
1. **Responsibility (weight 40%)**					**400**
Subfactors:					
a. Safety of others	20	80	140	200	
b. Equipment and materials	8	24	56	80	
c. Assisting trainees	8	24	56	80	
d. Product/service quality	4	16	28	40	
2. **Skill (weight 30%)**					**300**
Subfactors:					
a. Experience	18	72	126	180	
b. Education/training	12	48	84	120	
3. **Effort (weight 20%)**					**200**
Subfactors:					
a. Physical	8	32	56	80	
b. Mental	12	48	84	120	
4. **Working conditions (weight 10%)**					**100**
Subfactors:					
a. Unpleasant conditions	3	12	21	30	
b. Hazards	7	28	49	70	
			Total points		**1,000**

STEP 1. DETERMINE TOTAL POINT MATRIX NUMBER

Determining how many points to be used for allocation purposes is a personal choice. A rule of thumb is the number of compensable factors times 250. Another formula takes the highest paid job and divides its wage rate by the wage rate of the lowest paid job times 100. For example, if the president is paid $200,000 and the lowest job is $20,000, the result is 10 ($200,000 ÷ $20,000). Multiplying by 100 results in a total of 1,000 points for the point system. (For convenience, numbers are rounded.)

STEP 2. DETERMINE INDIVIDUAL FACTOR WEIGHTS

This decision is made by the Job Evaluation Committee. In this example the committee decided on the following weight distribution:

Responsibility	40%
Skill	30%
Effort	20%
Working condition	10%
	100%

Multiplying 1,000 points by the weights results in:

Responsibility	400 points
Skill	300
Effort	200
Working conditions	100

STEP 3. DETERMINE SUBFACTOR WEIGHTS AND ALLOCATION OF SUBFACTOR POINTS

Again, the job evaluation committee has to decide the weight of each subfactor.

Responsibility

Safety of others	50%
Equipment and materials	20%
Assisting trainees	20%
Product/service quality	10%

Skill

Experience	60%
Education/training	40%

Effort

Physical	40%
Mental	60%

Working conditions

Unpleasant conditions	30%
Hazards	70%

Now the factor points are multiplied by the subfactor weights. We will use only the first factor, responsibility, for this example.

Safety of others:	400 points × 50% = 200 points
Equipment and materials:	400 points × 20% = 80 points
Assisting trainees:	400 points × 20% = 80 points
Product/service quality:	400 points × 10% = 40 points

The highest subfactor points are always given to the highest level, in this case IV. The lowest-level point value is calculated by the formula: Subfactor weight × Factor weight.

Safety of others:	50% × 40% = 20 points
Equipment and materials:	20% × 40% = 8 points
Assisting trainees:	20% × 40% = 8 points
Product/service quality:	10% × 40% = 4 points

STEP 4. DETERMINE INCREMENTS BETWEEN LEVELS

This is calculated by the formula:

$$\text{(Highest level points} - \text{Lowest level points)}/\text{(Number of levels} - 1).$$

For subfactor "Safety of others," this means:

$$\frac{200 - 20}{4 - 1} = \frac{180}{3} = 60 \text{ points}$$

The steps are 20, 80, 140, 200 (see table at beginning of this Appendix). This assumes equal distance between levels. However, if the job evaluation committee feels that this does not reflect reality, it is free to determine the point differences between levels. *What is important is that employees perceive this judgment to be fair.*

CHAPTER 10

Employee Benefits and Services

"Take care of your employees. They'll take care of your business."

SIR RICHARD BRANSON[1]

LEARNING OBJECTIVES

After studying this chapter, you should be able to:

LO1   Describe the objectives of indirect compensation.

LO2   Explain how government furthers employee security and which major Canadian laws relate to it.

LO3   Discuss the voluntary benefits organizations may provide to their employees.

LO4   Describe the major types of pension plans.

LO5   Discuss the benefits and services that are likely to become more common in the future.

LO6   Describe the costs of employee benefits and ways to control them.

LO7   Explain the implications of employee benefits for human resource management.

Many people think of compensation as pay. In addition to direct compensation in the form of pay, most employers offer benefits and services. Benefits and services are *indirect compensation* because they are usually extended as a condition of employment and are not directly related to performance. They include insurance (health, dental, vision, life, disability, accidental death and dismemberment), income security (unemployment insurance, pension contributions, and worker's compensation), and time off (vacations, paid leave, and scheduling benefits), in addition to educational, financial, and social services.

The value of benefits and services has gone up over time relative to direct pay, and they are an increasingly important part of the total compensation package used to attract, motivate, and keep key employees. Some employers even

go so far as to tailor-make benefit packages for individual employees to satisfy their special needs.

To explain the broad scope of benefits and services, this chapter discusses the objectives of indirect compensation. We follow this with an examination of legally required benefits. The chapter concludes with a description of voluntary benefit programs.

Benefits and Corporate Strategy

Benefit programs have become a significant part of a company's compensation system, ranging between 1.25 and 1.4 times salary.[2] This means that when we talk about an employee's annual salary of $50,000 we are really talking about between $62,500 and $70,000 in actual payroll expenses for the company. What once were called "fringe benefits" are not "fringe" anymore.

Benefit policies can have a significant impact on the issue of attracting and retaining key and high-performing employees. Benefits will not replace performance incentives as motivators, but—especially for older employees—health and pension benefits can make a great difference in corporate loyalty.

Making benefits an important part of the company's compensation strategy has paid off tremendously for Husky Injection Molding Systems Ltd. in Bolton, Ontario. The firm spends more than $4 million a year on its 2,800 employees at a time when most companies are considering cutting back. However, Husky managers say that the program more than pays for itself in higher productivity and, ultimately, lower costs.

Husky's voluntary turnover rate is about 15 percent, or 5 percent below the industry average. Absenteeism averages 4 days a year in contrast with an industry average of 7.3 days. And injury claims are 1.2 for every 200,000 hours worked, against an industry average of 5.8.

In addition to an above market retirement savings plan and market competitive group benefits, Husky offers a fitness and wellness centre; intramural sports activities; an on-site cafeteria; and clean, state-of-the-art manufacturing facilities with outstanding safety records.[3]

It is clear from this example that benefits can be a critical part of a company's staffing strategy.

LO1 The Role of Indirect Compensation

Employee benefits and services seek to satisfy several objectives. These include societal, organizational, and employee objectives.

Societal Objectives

Industrial societies have changed from rural nations of independent farmers and small businesses to urban nations of interdependent wage earners. This interdependence was illustrated forcefully by the mass unemployment of the Great Depression of the 1930s. Since that time, industrial societies have sought group solutions to societal problems.

To solve social problems and provide security for interdependent wage earners, governments rely on the support of employers. Through favourable tax treatment, employees can receive most benefits tax-free, while employers can deduct the cost of benefits as a regular business expense.

Today, benefits and services give many employees financial security against illness, disability, and retirement. These outlays by employers are a major and growing cost of doing business that help to fulfill an essential societal objective.

Organizational Objectives

What do employers gain for these large outlays for benefits? Companies must offer some benefits if they are to be able to recruit successfully in the labour market. If a company did not offer retirement plans and paid vacations, recruits and present employees would work for competitors who did offer these forms of indirect compensation. Similarly, many employees will stay with a company because they do not want to give up benefits, so employee turnover is lowered. For example, employees may stay to save pension credits or their rights to the extended vacations that typically come with greater seniority.

Vacations, along with holidays and rest breaks, help employees reduce fatigue and may enhance productivity during the hours the employees do work. Similarly, retirement, health care, and disability benefits may allow workers to be more productive by freeing them from concern about medical and retirement costs. Likewise, if these benefits were not available to employees, they might elect to form a union and collectively bargain with the employer. (Although collective action is legal, many nonunion employers prefer to remain nonunion.) Therefore, it is accurate to state that indirect compensation may do the following:

- Reduce fatigue.
- Discourage labour unrest.
- Satisfy employee objectives.
- Aid recruitment.
- Reduce turnover.
- Minimize overtime costs.

Employee Objectives

Employees usually seek employer-provided benefits and services because of lower costs and availability. For example, company insurance benefits are usually less expensive because the employer may pay some or all of the costs. Even when workers must pay the entire premium, rates are often lower because group plans save the insurer the administrative and selling costs of many individual policies. With group plans, the insurer also can reduce the adverse selection of insuring just those who need the insurance. Actuaries—the specialists who compute insurance rates—can factor these savings into lower premiums for policyholders.

For some employees, the primary objective may be to obtain benefits and services—especially supplementary health and life insurance. Without employer-provided insurance, these policies may not be obtainable if the employee has a pre-existing medical condition.

The objectives of society, organizations, and employees have encouraged rapid growth of benefits and services. There are two types of benefits and services: those that are legally required and those that an employer voluntarily gives. This chapter will focus first on the required type.

LO2 Legally Required Benefits

Legally required benefits and services are imposed upon organizations by the government; employers must comply with the law and its procedures. Most of these benefits and services are designed to help employees. In general, government seeks to ensure minimum levels of financial security for the nation's workforce. Figure 10-1 shows that the objective of providing financial security is to ease the monetary burdens of retirement, death, long-term disability, and unemployment. The loss of income from these causes is cushioned by the security provisions. The financial problems of *involuntary unemployment* are lessened by unemployment compensation. And job-related injuries and death are compensated under workers' compensation laws. None of these programs fully reimburses the affected workers; nevertheless, each worker does get a financial base to which additional protection can be added.

Legally required benefits and services are important to the human resource department for two reasons. First, top management holds the human resource department responsible for meeting these legal obligations. If the department is to meet this responsibility, it must ensure that the firm is in compliance with the law. Second, if the obligations are improperly handled, the result can be severe fines and more taxes. None of these outcomes contributes to the organization's objectives.

Financial Security

Most Canadians are financially dependent on their monthly paycheques. Only about 16 percent of the population is self-employed;[4] most others work for another person or organization. To protect the well-being of society, governmental regulations on retirement plans, employment insurance, disability compensation, and health care are imperative. The major legal provisions concerning the above matters will be discussed below. Note that in Canada (unlike in the United States or in some other Western countries), many of these regulations are provincially administered. To suit the specific work environments, many of these statutes and provisions vary from province to province.

The Canada Pension Plan (CPP), the Quebec Pension Plan (QPP), and the Public Service Pension Plan (PSPP)

The **Canada Pension Plan (CPP)** (Quebec Pension Plan in the province of Quebec and the Public Service Pension Plan for federal employees) is a mandatory plan for all self-employed persons and employees in Canada. CPP, as well as the QPP and PSPP, are **contributory plans**—that is, both the employer and the employee pay part of the costs.

> **Canada Pension Plan (CPP)** A mandatory, contributory, and portable pension plan applicable to all employees and self-employed persons in Canada. Public service employees have their own pension plan, the Public Service Pension Plan (PSPP), but it is coordinated with the Canada Pension Plan.

> **contributory plans** Benefits that require the employer to contribute to the cost of the benefit.

FIGURE 10-1

Sources of Financial Protection for Workers

Protection for Workers	Sources of Protection	Legislating Government
Fair remuneration	Minimum-wage acts	Federal and provincial
Retirement	Canada Pension Plan	Federal (except in Quebec)
Involuntary unemployment	Employment Insurance	Federal
Industrial accidents	Workers' compensation acts	Federal and provincial
Medical care	Health insurance plans	Provincial
Child sustenance	Family allowances	Federal

Portability clauses are applicable to the plans in Canada, meaning that pension rights are not affected by changes of job or residence. The plans are also tied to cost-of-living changes.

> **portability clauses**
> Clauses that allow accumulated pension rights to be transferred to another employer when an employee changes employers.

Government-determined formulas calculate the amount of the contribution toward CPP (or QPP or PSPP) that an employee will make based on the amount of her or his paycheque with an annual maximum. The employer withholds this amount from the paycheque and remits the employee's contribution along with an equal contribution from the employer to the Canada Revenue Agency (CRA). At age 65 (or age 60 with reduced benefits), the employee will receive a monthly pension benefit. There are also provisions for disability benefits if an employee becomes unable to work and death benefits to provide for the surviving spouse and children. Since 1999, both common-law relationships and same-sex relationships are treated equally to spousal relationships under federal law.

The latest information about amendments to the CPP can be found at Employment and Social Development Canada (https://www.canada.ca/en/employment-social-development/services/pension/reports.html).

Employment Insurance (EI)

Employment Insurance (EI) helps to alleviate people's financial problems during the transition from one job

> **Employment Insurance (EI)** A program to help alleviate the financial problems of workers in Canada during the transition from one job to another.

to another. Most salaried and hourly workers who are employed for a minimum number of hours, depending on regional unemployment rates, are covered by EI. Employers withhold a contribution to EI from the employee's paycheque up to an annual maximum and remit this along with their own contribution (which is 1.4 times the size) to CRA. If employees lose their job through no fault of their own (for instance, due to a shortage of work or seasonal or mass lay-offs), they will receive a monthly payment from EI while they are looking for work. Information about eligibility and amount an individual would receive through EI is available at the Government of Canada website (https://www.canada.ca/en/services/benefits/ei.html). An estimate is that individuals could receive 55 percent of their previous earnings up to a maximum insurable salary of $55,000.

Starting in 2009, self-employed people could register for EI for maternity, parental, adoption, medical, and compassionate-care benefits.

Workers' Compensation Acts

All provinces and the territories have some act (usually called *Workers' Compensation Act* or *Ordinance*) that entitles workers to **workers' compensation** in the event of personal injury by accident during their regular

> **workers' compensation**
> Compensation payable by employers collectively for injuries sustained by workers in the course of their employment.

work. The industries covered by the act are classified into groups according to their special hazards, and all employers in each group are collectively liable for payment of compensation to all workers employed in that group. All

Spotlight *on* ETHICS

Trust Betrayed

You are the HR manager of a medium-sized, family-owned company. You discovered that a long-time, trusted employee, a purchasing officer, had been embezzling company funds for several years to the tune of close to $20,000. It was found out only because she went on vacation and a replacement had taken over her job for that time. She was known to be hard-working, and it had been the first vacation she had taken in many years. You and all the staff had always admired her dedication and commitment to the company. The company owner did not want to press charges because of her length of service and because, in his opinion, the loss was not that significant. He also blamed himself for not installing more effective controls. The purchase officer's excuse was that she had had a bad divorce and that her

husband did not provide sufficient support for her and her children to continue their lifestyle.

When you wanted to dismiss her for cause, she cried and asked you to consider her situation and think of her children. She asked whether you could give as the official reason for her leaving the company a company reorganization and elimination of her job so that she would be able to collect EI benefits and have a better chance to find another job. There has been a precedent for this, when the owner did not press charges against an employee who had stolen company property and who had been officially "laid off for lack of work" and had been receiving unemployment benefits. You feel sorry for her, as she has ruined her life and career, and you think of her children. What are you going to do?

employers makes an annual contribution to workers' compensation as a percentage of their total annual payroll figures. However, an employer can also be charged a higher rate of contribution if there are many workers' compensation claims.

Health Insurance Plans

Canada's health and medical insurance, also referred to as simply **health insurance**, is provided by provincial governments with assistance from the federal government. Much of the cost of Canada's universal health-care system is paid for by taxes collected at the federal level. Detailed explanations of health insurance plans in all provinces can be found at the Government of Canada website (https://www.canada.ca/en/immigration-refugees-citizenship/services/new-immigrants/new-life-canada/health-care-card.html).

> **health insurance** Health and medical insurance provided by provincial governments with assistance from the federal government.

Employers may opt to provide extended health plans that cover costs for prescription medications, dental care, and so forth, for their employees. These supplementary health plans are discussed in this chapter under "Voluntary Benefits."

Holidays and Vacations

Vacations are usually based on the employee's length of service, but federal and provincial laws specify a two-week (in Saskatchewan, three-week) minimum vacation entitlement. In some regions, this increases to three weeks (in Saskatchewan, four) after five, six, or ten years of service. Holidays are also federally and provincially regulated. A listing of federal and provincial holidays can be found at https://www.statutoryholidays.com/.

LO3 Voluntary Benefits

In addition to the legally required benefits that employers must provide to employees, many offer an additional series of benefits voluntarily. These include insurance benefits, income security, retirement security, paid time-off benefits, and employee services.

Insurance Benefits

Insurance benefits spread the financial risks encountered by employees and their families. These risks are shared by pooling funds in the form of insurance premiums. Then, when an insured risk occurs, the covered employees or their families are compensated.

Life Insurance

Life insurance is almost universally offered by Canadian companies for their employees.[5] There are two types of plans. Under the first, the deceased's family receives a lump sum payment. Under the second, the family receives a generally lower lump sum than in the first case, plus a survivor's pension payable to the deceased's spouse for life. Employers generally pay the cost of these life insurance plans. Coverage is commonly based on the employee's pay, often 100 or 200 percent of annual pay. Optional expanded coverage is usually available if the employee chooses to pay for it.

Health-Related Insurance

All Canadian citizens—and landed immigrants—are covered by provincial health care programs. For this reason, employers in Canada offer only supplementary health insurance plans. This is in contrast to the United States, where health insurance is the most common form of benefit.[6]

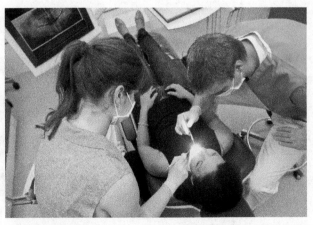

© Halfpoint/Shutterstock

Workers' compensation covers a wide variety of benefits, but the law stipulates that workers cannot sue their employers in case of injury. Is this just?

© Anderson Ross/Getty Images.

Dental insurance is a common benefit offered by many companies to their employees, but it is a voluntary one. Should it be mandatory?

Extended health insurance will pay for expenses that government plans do not fully cover. These plans may cover costs for prescription medications, dental care, paramedical expenses (for instance, physiotherapy, massage therapy, chiropractic), ambulance services, vision care, and travel insurance. In many cases, the cost of health and dental premiums is shared between the employer and the employee, and there may be annual maximums set for each category of coverage. Figure 10-2 shows the percentage of Canadian organizations providing various forms of health coverage.

Disability Insurance

If an employee misses a few days because of illness, it is usually not crucial from a financial point of view since most employers grant paid sick leave for a limited time. It becomes more of a problem when an employee becomes disabled for a longer period of time or even permanently. Many Canadian companies offer short-term and long-term disability plans.

A **short-term disability plan** typically involves crediting or allocating a certain number of days to an employee, to be used as sick leave for nonoccupational accidents or illnesses. Sick leave credits may be cumulative or noncumulative. A plan is cumulative if insured credits earned during one year may be trans-

> **short-term disability plan** A benefit plan crediting a number of days to be used as sick leave.

ferred to the following year; it is noncumulative when the employee's entitlement is reviewed on a yearly basis or after each illness.

For workers who are disabled for a prolonged time, employers offer some form of **long-term disability insurance**. Such plans generally have a long waiting period (six months is very common), and they pay the employee a smaller amount (usually 50 or 60 percent) of the employee's working income. Under most plans, these payments, if necessary, are made until the normal retirement age is reached.

> **long-term disability insurance** A benefit plan providing the employee with an income in the case of long-term illness or injury.

Income Security Benefits

In addition to insurance, there are noninsurance benefits that enhance employee security. These benefits seek to ensure an income before and after retirement.

Employment Income Security

Discharges or layoffs may entail severe economic consequences for an employee; the impact, however, can be cushioned by employer-provided benefits. If employees have not been given at least two weeks' notice, and if the dismissal was not for just cause, according to the

---

FIGURE 10-2

Percent of Employers Offering Forms of Health Coverage

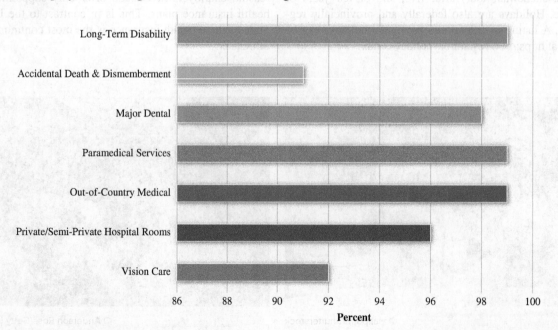

SOURCE: "Providing Employee Benefits Continues to be a Significant Cost for Employers" (2015, November 9), *The Conference Board of Canada.*

Canada Labour Code they are entitled to severance pay equal to two weeks' regular wages. For executives, who usually work on a contract basis, **severance pay** can reach six months' or a year's compensation.

> **severance pay** Payment to a worker upon permanent separation from a company.

Layoffs may be eased by accrued vacation pay. A few companies go so far as to provide a **guaranteed annual wage (GAW)**. These plans assure the worker of receiving some minimum amount of work or pay. For example, employees may be promised a minimum of 1,500 hours of work or pay a year (compare this with the "normal" 52 forty-hour weeks for a total of 2,080 hours). Some employers guarantee 30 hours per week. Even on layoff, the employees draw some income.

> **guaranteed annual wage (GAW)** A benefits plan by which an employer assures employees that they will receive a minimum annual income regardless of layoffs or a lack of work.

The auto industry is a leader in another method, **supplemental unemployment benefits (SUB)**. When employees are out of work, employment insurance benefits are supplemented by the employer from monies previously paid to the SUB fund. This assures covered employees an income almost equal to their previous earnings for as long as the SUB fund remains solvent.

> **supplemental unemployment benefits (SUB)** Private plans providing compensation for wage loss to laid-off workers.

LO4 Retirement Security

Retirement plans were originally designed to reward long-service employees. Through employer generosity and union pressure, retirement plans have grown in scope and coverage so that in Canada the average firm spends 4.95 percent of its total payroll costs on legally required payments (CPP/QPP, EI, and workers' compensation) alone.[7] On average, employers contribute 60 percent of the money invested in pension plans, and employees contribute 40 percent.[8]

As of 2015, 37.8 percent of all Canadian employees are covered by Registered Pension Plans (RPP), so called because they have to be registered with Revenue Canada for preferential tax considerations.[9] Most plans take into account benefits received from the CPP. (See the discussion in the latter part of this chapter.) The two most common forms of pension plans are defined benefits (DB) and defined contribution (DC) plans.

Defined Benefits (DB) Plans

With a **defined benefits (DB) plan**, upon retirement the employee receives a fixed dollar amount as a pension, depending on age and length of service. For instance, employees may receive 2 percent of their highest annual salary for each year of service they worked for the employer. Many employees and unions prefer DB plans because of their predictable outcomes. These type of plans are strictly regulated by the *Employee Retirement Income Security Act.* The advantage for employees is that they know in advance what their retirement benefits will be. For the employer the advantage is that by providing a predictable, guaranteed benefit at retirement that is valued by workers, such a plan can promote worker loyalty and help retain valuable workers. However, these plans can be costly for both employees and employers to fund given that they specify the amount of income the employee is to receive at retirement. If the investments do not perform well, higher contributions are needed to make up the benefit the employee is to receive.

> **defined benefits (DB) plan** A benefits plan whose benefits are defined by a formula based on age and length of service, with the employer assuming responsibility for funding.

About 67 percent of the employees in Canada who have a pension plan have a DB type. However, the number of DB pension plans has gone down from 90 percent in the 1980s due to their costliness.[10]

Defined Contribution (DC) Plans

When the employer and employee contribute to a pension plan, it is called a **defined contribution (DC) plan**; if only the employer makes the contributions, it is called a *noncontributory plan.* In a *contributory plan,* the employee makes a commitment to make regular payments, which are matched by the employer. A typical arrangement would be that the employee allows monthly or weekly deductions from his or her salary, say 5 percent, and the employer either matches this or makes a higher contribution, up to a specific level. These amounts are usually invested in secure funds. After the employee's retirement the money is used to purchase an annuity or may be invested in other approved financial arrangements that pay a regular income to the retiree. The amount that the retiree receives depends entirely on how well the investments did. DC plans make up 18 percent of all RPPs in Canada.[11]

> **defined contribution (DC) plan** A benefits plan based on amounts contributed by the employer and the employee, with the final pension depending on amounts contributed, investment income, and economic conditions at retirement.

Two significant problems have developed in the administration of pension plans. *First,* some employers go out of business, leaving the pension plan unfunded or only partially funded, as seen in this example:

> Although DB plans are thought to be certain retirement funds, when Sears Canada went bankrupt in

2017, many employees were shocked to learn that they would only be receiving 81 percent of the value of their pension plans as part of of the company's insolvency problem. The other 19 percent is "up in the air," to be figured out over the next five years. Employees need to be sure that the pension plans are not underfunded before they count on them as retirement income.[12]

Second, some companies minimize their pension costs by having very long vesting periods. **Vesting** gives workers the right to pension benefits even if they leave the company. Employees who quit or are fired before the vesting period has passed, however, often have no pension rights or are entitled only to receive their contributions to the plan but not the employer's matched contributions or the investment returns earned during employment.

> **vesting** A provision in employer-provided retirement plans that gives workers the right to a pension after a specified number of years of service.

The **Pension Benefits Standards Act** regulates pension plans and requires that pension funds be held in trust for members and that the funds not be held under the complete custody and control of either the employer or the employees. To accomplish this, the funding of a private pension plan must be carried out by an insurance company, a trust, or a corporate pension society, or be administered by the government.

> **Pension Benefits Standards Act** A federal act regulating pension plans in industries under the jurisdiction of the Government of Canada.

Paid Time-Off Benefits

Time periods during which the employee is not working but is getting paid are the result of time-off benefits. Time-off benefits include legal (such as statutory holidays and vacation) and voluntary benefits (such as wash-up time). Although these benefits may seem minor, according to one survey they were the costliest major category, making up 16 percent of gross annual payroll.[13]

On-the-Job Breaks

Some of the most common forms of time-off benefits are those found on the job. Examples include rest breaks, meal breaks, and wash-up time. Taking a break from the physical and mental effort of a job may in fact increase productivity. The major problem for human resource and line managers is the tendency of employees to stretch these time-off periods:

> When one human resource manager was confronted by a supervisor with the problem of stretched breaks, she suggested a simple solution. Each employee was assigned a specific break time—from 9:15 to 9:30 a.m., or 9:30 to 9:45 a.m., for example—but could

not leave for break until the preceding employee returned. Since each clerk was anxious to go on break, the peer group policed the length of breaks and the stretched breaks ended.

Paid Sick Leave

Absences from work are unavoidable. Today, most companies pay workers when they are absent for medical reasons by granting a limited number of days of sick leave per year. Unfortunately, this is one of the most abused benefits; many workers take the attitude that these are simply extra days off. If the human resource policies prohibit employees from crediting unused sick leave to next year's account, absences increase near the end of the year. To minimize abuses, some companies require medical verification of illness or pay employees for unused sick leave.

A few firms avoid the abuse question by granting "personal leave days." This approach allows an employee to skip work for any reason and get paid, up to a specified number of days per year. Sick leave banks allow employees to "borrow" extra days above the specified number when they use up their individual allocation. Then, when they earn additional days, the days are repaid to the sick leave bank.

Holidays and Vacations

As mentioned under federally and provincially regulated holidays and vacation days, most employers grant vacation days beyond the minimum required number, depending on tenure. Policies for vacations vary widely. Some companies allow employees to use vacation days a few at a time. Other companies insist that the worker take the vacation all at once. A few employers actually close down during designated periods and require vacations to be taken during this period. Still other companies negate the reason for vacations completely by allowing employees to work and then receive vacation pay as a bonus.

Employee Services

Some companies go beyond pay and traditional benefits. They also provide educational, financial, and social services for their employees.

Educational Assistance

Tuition refund programs are among the more common employer services. These programs partially or completely reimburse employees for furthering their education. They may be limited only to courses that are related to the employees job, or the employer may reimburse workers for any educational expenditure. In the future, more companies may follow the lead of Kimberly-Clark Corporation in the United States:

> Kimberly-Clark created an educational savings account for employees and their dependants. The company gives employees credits for each year of

service. Then, when an employee or dependant wants to go to college, he or she can be partially reimbursed from the educational savings account established by the company.

Financial Services

Probably the oldest service is employee discount plans. These programs, common among retail stores and consumer goods manufacturers, allow workers to buy products from the company at a discount.

Another common financial perk is providing employees with a smartphone and paying for the monthly expenses. Employees may enjoy not having to pay for a personal phone and data plan, and employers benefit from easy access to employees even when they are not at work and during nonwork hours. But company policies are varied in whether the employee is allowed to use the device for personal as well as work purposes. Issues associated with privacy when using a corporate device for personal use abound. Some companies are using a variation to provide employees with mobile access to circumvent the privacy issue, as seen below:

> VMware ended the distribution of corporate phones, instead choosing to provide subsidies for their employees' personal devices, assuming they would be used, at least in part, for business purposes. Employees get their privacy, and the company gets

the value of having their employees access work from their mobiles along with cost savings.[14]

Stock purchase programs are another financial service. These plans enable employees to buy company stock, usually through payroll deductions. In some stock purchase programs, employee outlays may be matched by company contributions. Another financial service offered in some organizations is financial well-being, as shown in the Spotlight on HRM.

Social Services

Employers provide a wide range of social services. At one extreme are simple interest groups, such as bowling leagues and softball teams; at the other are comprehensive **employee assistance programs (EAPs)** designed to assist employees with personal problems. EAPs may provide assistance with child care or transportation, with individual and group counselling, with employee quarrels, with family disputes, or may even assist managers in dealing with employee complaints.

employee assistance programs (EAPs) Comprehensive company programs that seek to help employees and their family members overcome personal and work-related problems.

EAPs are becoming more common. Human resource managers realize that employee problems affect company performance through productivity losses and on-the-job

Spotlight *on* HRM

Four Steps to Building a Successful Financial Wellness Program
By Linda Lewis-Daly

With studies showing high levels of employee stress about their finances that's translating into lost productivity, absenteeism or health issues, the time is right for financial wellness programs in the workplace.

There's an opportunity for employers to step in and offer much-needed guidance, but they could (and should) be helping workers with far more than the basic advice about where to put their retirement contributions. Employees need help navigating day-to-day money issues, such as student loan repayment, managing credit card debt, saving for a down payment and building emergency funds. And older workers fret they may outlive their retirement savings—assuming they have any in the first place.

Just like supporting employees' physical or mental health, the first step to improving their financial well-being is through awareness, education and supports. Here are four considerations to build a financial wellness strategy:

1. **Commit to financial well-being**

   Organizations that believe they have a responsibility to educate their employees on financial issues tend to have more successful programs. Most workplace wellness programs offer seminars or lunchtime sessions on topics such as physical activity, nutrition and managing stress. Adding seminars about financial health may be the first step to helping employees understand concepts

(Continued)

like budgeting or the difference between registered retirement savings plans, registered education savings plans and tax-free savings accounts.

2. Offer varied topics and methods

Workplaces with successful programs provide education on multiple topics, including savings, debt repayment, investments, mortgages, insurance, spending, wills, health care in retirement and pre-retirement financial planning.

Employers can offer financial wellness training through a variety of formats, including personal consultation services, classes and workshops, online resources, workbooks and calculators. Employers can partner with and leverage relationships with third-party subject experts, such as their financial institution or employee assistance program provider.

3. Target programs to employee needs

Information is more effective if it resonates with the learner. While that seems obvious, many employers use generalized communication strategies to reach diverse team members. With five generations in the

workforce, employers will have greater success with customized educational programs that vary according to age or income level.

4. Offer financial counselling

When we think of employee assistance programs, we immediately think of mental-health or crisis-counselling services. Yet employee assistance programs can offer a wide variety of personal counselling supports, from nutritional coaching to financial advice. Personalized financial counselling is an emerging support tool because counsellors can readily adapt to different types of employees in highly diverse workforces.

When introducing financial wellness supports in the workplace, some companies worry about backlash or lawsuits from employees or retirees over advice that didn't generate profits. For employees, there's the very real concern about privacy.

But the benefits far outweigh the risks. In addition to increased productivity and lower absenteeism, a more holistic financial wellness program can help with employee attraction and retention. Above all, the goodwill employers generate from offering financial counsel to employees struggling with personal finance stresses is worthwhile.

SOURCE: © Linda Lewis-Daly (2018, April 2), *Benefits Canada*, http://www.benefitscanada.com/benefits/health-wellness/four-steps-to-building-a-successful-financial-wellness-program-111508

injuries.[15] Employer services that can lessen these problems by addressing mental health problems, substance abuse, and so forth, offer potential dividends in employee performance, loyalty, and reduced turnover.

Relocation programs are the support in dollars or services a company provides to its transferred or new employees. At minimum, this benefit includes payment for moving expenses. Some employees receive fully paid house-hunting trips with their spouse to the new location before the move, subsidized home mortgages, placement assistance for working spouses, and even family counselling to reduce the stress of the move.

Employee assistance programs have traditionally involved personal interaction; especially if they were concerned with counselling services, face-to-face communication was important. However, with technology advances

relocation programs Company-sponsored benefits that assist employees who must move in connection with their job.

employers can respond to their employees' needs not only faster, but also more effectively and efficiently. The scope of possibilities is vast: opportunities for live chat rooms, one-on-one video counselling, group-help bulletin boards, and online self-help applications are only the tip of the iceberg. The goal of online assistance programs is not to replace counselling, but mostly to provide an enhancement to services already offered.[16] Additional assistance activities are discussed in Chapter 11 in connection with counselling.

LO5 Flexible Benefits and Emerging Services

Flexible Benefits

Many benefits packages were originally designed with a "one size fits all" approach in which employees had little discretion over benefits that would particularly suit their individual needs. For example, pension and maternity benefits usually were granted to all workers equally regardless of age and family status. This uniformity failed to recognize individual differences and wishes. Admittedly, uniformity leads to administrative and actuarial economies; but when employees receive benefits they neither want nor need, these economies are questionable.

In many organizations, offering only one benefits package has given way to flexible benefits programs. **Flexible benefits programs,** also known as *cafeteria benefit programs,* allow employees to select benefits and services that match their individual needs. Workers are provided a benefit and services account with a

> **flexible benefits programs** Programs that allow employees to select the mix of benefits and services that will answer their individual needs. Also known as cafeteria benefit programs.

specified number of dollars in the account. Through deductions from this account, employees shop for specific benefits from among those offered by the employer. The types and prices of benefits are provided to each employee in the form of a cost sheet that describes each benefit. In Canada, in 2015, the average cost of employee benefits not including pensions or paid time off (e.g., vacation, holidays, parental leave) was $8,330 per full-time equivalent.[17] Figure 10-3 illustrates how two employees may select their package of benefits and services for the coming year based on the $8,330 average.

Although the approach shown in Figure 10-3 creates additional administrative costs and an obligation for the human resource department to advise employees, there are several advantages. The main advantage is employee participation. Through participation, employees come to understand exactly what benefits the employer is offering,

FIGURE 10-3

Hypothetical Benefit Selection of Two Different Workers

	Worker A	Worker B
	27, married woman with one child. Husband in graduate school.	56, married male. Spouse does not have a benefits package.
Paramedical services (massage, physio, chiro, etc.)	$ 1000	$ 1500
Dental care	$ 890	$ 1090
Extended health care (e.g., prescription drug coverage, out-of-province)	$ 1035	$ 760
Optional life insurance ($100,000)	$ 235	$ 300
Spousal life insurance ($50,000)	$ 250	$ 0
Long-term disability insurance	$ 300	$ 0
Short-term disability insurance	$ 1,270	$ 305
Accidental death & dismemberment	$ 200	$ 200
Vision care	$ 250	$ 360
Concierge services	$ 1,200	$ 200
Employee assistance plan	$ 400	$ 200
Wellness spending account	$ 1,300	$ 3,415
Total	$ 8,330	$ 8,330

and employees can better match their benefits with their needs. In Canada, in 2015, 29 percent of organizations offered flexible benefits plans, with 71 percent offering traditional benefits plans.[18]

Flexible benefits, until recently, have offered the usual choices of better long-term disability insurance, dental or vision care, prescription drug coverage, life insurance, group legal services, etc., but it has become more common that employers offer the opportunity to "purchase" more vacation. Some companies also allow employees to sell back their vacation time for extra money.[19]

Emerging Services

One emerging trend is to offer employees a health spending account. Employees can use the credits in their health spending account toward eligible medical and dental expenses not covered by the extended health coverage. The services are paid with nontaxable dollars on a broad range of medical expenses in accordance with the *Income Tax Act.* Examples include deductibles, orthodontic procedures, glasses or contacts purchases, dietitians, and acupuncturists. Six in ten Canadian organizations had health spending accounts in place as of 2014, with an average of $943 per eligible employee.[20]

A related trend is employee wellness accounts. Credits in a wellness account can be spent toward proactive health and a broad range of wellness domains. For instance, gym memberships, fitness equipment and activities and even purchasing a canoe, financial planning, education courses, or a big screen TV—anything that benefits the employee's wellness and health—may be eligible; however, dollars in wellness accounts are taxable benefits.

Another emerging trend is to offer concierge services, where employees may seek a broad variety of services limited only by what's legal, ethical, and within imagination. These types of services may include free laundry, backup child care, or dog walking services. One concierge service even aims to use artificial intelligence (AI) to predict what services an employee might be potentially interested in:

> Through John Paul concierge services, a leader in innovative loyalty programs, employees can obtain access to a huge variety of concierge services from event ticketing, dry-cleaning pickup, or home repair services. Depending on the company's selection of loyalty program, on-site concierges may be available or employees may be able to access 24/7 chatbots offering personalized service. John Paul has recently introduced AI to predict client behaviour and provide personalized solutions and suggestions for ultimate employee satisfaction.[21]

While benefits used to be reserved for full-time employees, part-time employees are now offered benefits by 93 percent of Canadian organizations.[22] Most require part-time employees to work a minimum of 20 hours per week to qualify.

© IT Stock Free.

Child care, with the employer providing either full or partially subsidized care facilities and staff, is an extended benefit for employees. What advantages does this benefit offer to workers?

LO6 Management of Voluntary Benefit and Service Programs

Administration of increasingly complex benefits packages is a major challenge for human resource management. The administrative burden is significantly eased by technology designed to handle flexible benefits enrollment and communication. Many companies rely on the web administration of their health plan providers, such as Blue Cross Canada, as seen in the example below:

> Blue Cross Canada offers health spending account administration services for companies with flexible benefit plans. It saves these companies the headaches of administering the plans and claims to be cheaper than if the company managed the plan on its own.[23]

One challenge for HR groups is effectively communicating about benefits to workers. Ignorance about the mix of benefits often lead to pressure from employees for more benefits to meet their needs. For example, older workers may request improved retirement plans, while younger workers seek improved insurance coverage of dependants. Often the result is a proliferation of benefits and increased employer costs. These costs, which represented 15.1 percent of an employer's gross annual payroll in 1953, escalated to about 40 percent in 2010.[24] Still, employees' ignorance and confusion can lead to complaints and dissatisfaction about their benefit package.

One remedy to poorly understood benefit packages is to increase employee awareness, usually through publicity. Publicizing benefits often includes orientation sessions for new employees as new benefits are introduced, and online notices with links to benefit resources as regular parts of company communications and annually during benefit allocation season. Some tips for effectively communicating employee benefits include sending benefits communications home to spouses as well as to employees, providing access through QR codes and smartphone apps, and anticipating that HR will have to communicate a benefit fact 19 times before it is understood and accepted.[25]

LO7 Implications for Human Resource Management

Change in the field of employee benefits has been dramatic over the last decade. Retirement plans have been and are under constant legal review, tax reforms have added complexity, and health care policies have changed and their expenses have gone up. All of this has added to the responsibilities of the human resource professional.

The implications of financial security plans for human resource departments are several. First, human resource managers should make sure that the firm adheres to all provisions relating to minimum wages and pension deductions. For example, the *Canada Labour Code* requires every employer to furnish, from time to time, information relating to employee wages, hours of work, general holidays, annual vacations, and conditions of employment. As well, the Canada Labour Standards Regulations require that each employee's social insurance number, sex, and occupational classification be recorded and kept ready for inspection. Accurate records of maternity leave, overtime, and termination should also be maintained.

Second, to avoid duplication, human resource managers need to consider CPP (or QPP or PSPP) and other benefits available to employees when designing their firm's own benefit and service plans. In many provinces, some of the items included in private group insurance plans are already covered under the workers' compensation and health insurance plans.

Third, human resource specialists need to be concerned about reducing accidents in order to lower the cost of workers' compensation. These costs are directly related to the claims made against the company by employees. The more that must be paid to these employees, the greater the cost. Yet even aside from cost considerations, many managers feel a moral obligation to provide a safe working environment.

To keep ballooning benefits costs under control, employers may want to consider the following measures:[26]

- Reducing prescription drug coverage to 80 percent from 100 percent

- Introducing a combined maximum amount of coverage across all paramedical services (e.g., massage, physio, chiropractic) rather than separate maximums for each service

- Stopping out-of-country medical coverage for personal travel, or setting a 30-day limit or a dollar maximum

- Investigating whether six-month dental checkups are necessary anymore, keeping in mind that many dental plans were designed in prefluoride days

- Where available, encouraging generic drug substitution, multi-tiered formularies, and case management for specialty or high-cost medications, possibly in order to save 12 percent per employee[27]

- Encouraging employees to seek pharmacies with lower dispensing fees and to request several months of refills at a time

- Introducing a health care spending account to allow employees to focus their benefit dollars and forego coverage across all domains

- Embracing proactive health maintenance apps and care for employees

Given the trends outlined above, it will be critical for top management in general and the human resource manager in particular to adopt a total compensation approach when decisions have to be made relating to pay. Organizations cannot afford to treat employee benefits and services as being independent of direct compensation, especially since they are growing at twice the pace of wages and salaries.

Retention

The issue was raised earlier as to what role benefits play in retaining employees. **Retention** of key employees has become a major issue, especially in high-tech companies.[28] Several studies have shown that innovative and flexible benefit plans are very effective tools in attracting and retaining highly skilled staff.[29]

retention A company's ability to keep employees.

Benefit Audit

Often, the administration of benefit plans still leaves room for improvement. One approach that readily identifies inefficiencies is a **benefit audit**. It usually consists of two components: a claims audit, which examines claims and claim trends, and an organization audit, which examines the efficiency and effectiveness of handling employee benefits within the employer organization, including dealings with an insurer or third-party administrator.

benefit audit A system to control the efficiency of a benefit program.

A benefit audit enables employers to do the following:

- Identify opportunities for financial and human resource savings.

- Ensure that insurers or third-party administrators are doing a good job.

- Exert effective control over their benefits area.

- Identify who is in control of the benefits budget.

- Check how their employee claiming habits compare against other Canadian employers.

Tax Application to Benefits

GST and GST/HST apply to some benefits, but not to others. Generally, GST/HST has to be paid on the following benefits:

- Company cars (if also used for private purposes)
- Car operating costs
- Tax return preparation
- Short-term residential accommodation
- Holiday trips within continental North America
- Frequent flyer points
- Financial counselling
- Parking

Not affected are awards, health benefits, stock options, low-interest or no-interest loans, tuition fees, child care, a Christmas turkey, and gifts under $100.

Benefits and Strategy Implications

As outlined in Chapter 1, management has to look at the long-term objectives of the organization and match these with organizational conditions to create the necessary environment for reaching the objectives. Specifically, the following steps have to be taken:

- Define the organization's objectives.
- Link the human resource department's objectives with those of the organization.
- Assess the needs of the employees.
- Assess the legal requirements to ensure that laws are followed.
- Compare the company's benefits with those of the competition.
- Make sure the benefits are valued by the employees.
- Conduct an annual benefit audit.

It is important for human resource managers to integrate benefits into the wage and salary package. This compensation package has to fulfill both short- and long-term goals. The short-term goals, for example, high motivation and productivity, are usually satisfied with merit pay and incentive systems that reward high performers. A common long-term goal is to retain good employees, an objective that can be achieved by a valued pension or a profit-sharing plan. Another strategy may address the need for downsizing by using an appropriate severance package. These are just a few items contributing toward a comprehensive pay strategy.[30]

SUMMARY

Employee benefits and services are the fastest-growing component of compensation. The Canadian government has instituted compulsory programs that provide citizens with certain benefits and services. Financial security is achieved partially through such benefits as the Canada Pension Plan (or QPP or PSPP), employment insurance, and workers' compensation. The CPP provides income at retirement or upon disability. It also provides the family members of a deceased worker with a death benefit and a survivor's annuity, under certain conditions.

Employment insurance pays the worker a modest income to reduce the hardships of losing a job. These payments go to employees who are involuntarily separated from their jobs. Payments last until the worker finds suitable employment or until the worker receives the maximum number of payments permitted by the government.

Workers' compensation pays employees who are injured in the course of their employment. The payments are made to prevent the employee from having to sue to be compensated for injuries. If an employee dies, benefits are paid to the employee's survivors.

Whereas the provincial governments provide basic health coverage to Canadians, most organizations also provide extended health and dental coverage to their employees and their families. Additional forms of voluntary benefits include insurance, security, and time-off benefits. Employee services encompass educational, financial, and social programs. To accommodate diverse needs, many employers are now offering flexible benefits programs and other forms of health spending accounts. However, a major issue is ballooning benefits costs.

To ensure that benefits are meeting the needs of employees and at a reasonable cost, employers should be conducting an annual benefit audit, consisting of a claims and an organization audit. The audit examines the efficiency and effectiveness of handling employee benefits, including insurers and third-party administrators.

TERMS FOR REVIEW

benefit audit 317
Canada Pension Plan (CPP) 307
contributory plans 307
defined benefits (DB) plan 311
defined contribution (DC) plan 311
employee assistance programs (EAPs) 313
Employment Insurance (EI) 308
flexible benefits programs 315
guaranteed annual wage (GAW) 311
health insurance 309

long-term disability insurance 310
Pension Benefits Standards Act 312
portability clauses 308
relocation programs 314
retention 317
severance pay 311
short-term disability plan 310
supplemental unemployment benefits (SUB) 311
vesting 312
workers' compensation 308

SELF-ASSESSMENT EXERCISE

Understanding Benefits

Benefits tend to be neglected when it comes to considerations of labour costs, but with the average benefits package in Canada now being close to 35 percent of payroll, HR managers are well advised to pay special attention to the management of benefits. Test yourself on your expertise.

1. If the current trend continues, soon benefits will make up over one-half of most firms' payroll.   T   F

2. Vacations, along with holidays and rest breaks to reduce fatigue and enhance productivity, are part of employees' objectives.   T   F

3. Salaried, hourly paid, and self-employed persons are eligible for unemployment benefits.   T   F

4. In Canada, as in the U.S., health insurance is the most common form of insurance coverage.   T   F

5. Vesting gives workers the right to pension benefits even if they leave the company.   T   F

6. Meal breaks, rest breaks, wash-up time, sick leave, holidays, and vacations make up the costliest major category of benefits.   T   F

7. Cafeteria benefits allow employees free meals.   T   F

8. Benefits play a major role in retaining employees.   T   F

9. Benefits cannot be taxed.   T   F

10. Benefits and services are the fastest-growing component of compensation.   T   F

SCORING

If you marked statements 1, 5, 6, 8, and 10 as true, give yourself one point each. The remaining statements are false.

Scores of 8–10: Very good! Congratulations for your thorough understanding of the content in this chapter.

Scores of 5–7: Well . . . it's okay, but rereading this chapter could help you do better.

Scores of less than 5: Oops . . . add this chapter to your reading list again.

REVIEW AND DISCUSSION QUESTIONS

1. Why has government been interested in providing financial security to workers through laws? What areas do you think are likely to receive government attention in the future to ensure employee financial security?

2. Some people believe that Employment Insurance has, over a period of time, worked against workers rather than for them. What is your opinion of Employment Insurance? Why?

3. Suppose a friend of yours contracted lead poisoning on the job. What sources of income could this person rely on while recovering during the next two months? What if it took two years for your friend to recover? Are other sources of income available?

4. Besides retirement income, what other benefits are provided through the Canada Pension Plan?

5. What changes should be made to the Employment Insurance program to address its present weaknesses?

6. How would you design a benefits package for a diverse group of workers?

7. Briefly describe the benefits that an organization might give employees to provide them with greater financial security.

8. How would you reduce the cost of benefits to the employer without reducing coverage for employees?

9. What are the common problems you would expect to find with the benefits and services program of a large company?

10. If you were asked to increase employee awareness of benefits, what actions would you take without changing the way the company provides benefits? If you could change the entire benefit program, what other methods would you use to increase employee awareness?

CRITICAL THINKING QUESTIONS

1. Suppose you are asked to explain why employees are better off receiving pay and benefits rather than just getting larger paycheques that include the monetary value of benefits. What arguments would you use?

2. For each of the following groups of employees, what types of problems are likely to occur if a company goes from a five-day, 40-hour week to a four-day, 40-hour week: (a) working mothers, (b) labourers, (c) customer service employees?

3. Should companies pay educational assistance? Assume that a company is paying for a degree in information technology. What if a competitor offers a higher salary to the successful graduate? How could you make sure the company's investment remains in the organization?

ETHICS QUESTION

It is quite common for fish-processing companies in the Atlantic provinces to allow employees to work the number of weeks required to qualify for Employment Insurance (EI), then lay them off and hire other family members to let them qualify for EI. Discuss the ethical issues involved.

RESEARCH EXERCISE

1. What are the key features of defined benefit and defined contribution pension plans? (See the Ontario Securities Commission at https://www.getsmarteraboutmoney.ca/plan-manage/retirement-planning/pension-savings-plans/2-main-types-of-pension-plan/.)

2. What are the advantages of a flexible benefit plan? (See Benefits Canada at https://www.benefitscanada.com/benefits/health-benefits/so-you-think-you-want-a-flex-plan-48671.)

3. Employee assistance programs have become very popular with small and large companies. Give some good reasons for the introduction of an EAP. Look at this website: https://www.benefits.org/coverage/health-care/employee-assistance.

4. What are the eligibility criteria for the Employment Insurance program (https://www.canada.ca/en/services/benefits/ei/ei-regular-benefit.html)? Give details.

INCIDENT 10-1

Soap Producers and Distributors Ltd.

Soap Producers and Distributors Ltd. faced an employee turnover problem. The company's annual turnover rate was nearly 20 percent among technical and white-collar workers. Among hourly paid employees, the rate was nearly 30 percent.

Wage and salary surveys repeatedly showed that the company's pay levels were 10 to 11 percent above those of comparable jobs in the labour market. The benefits program was not as impressive, but management thought it was competitive. Employees received supplementary health and life insurance, paid vacations and holidays, and a holiday bonus of $1,000.

Although some employees complained about the company's benefits, complaints varied widely and no one benefit or lack of benefit seemed to be the key issue.

To make Soap Producers and Distributors' problems worse, they operated in a tight labour market, which meant jobs sometimes took weeks to fill. To hire specialized workers almost always meant recruiting them from other cities and paying their moving expenses.

DISCUSSION QUESTIONS

1. What additions do you think should be made to the company's benefits program? (Hint: What is missing?)

2. What problems in the incident might be solved by a cafeteria approach? Think of specific interest groups.

3. To overcome the company's recruitment problems, what other changes do you suggest? What are the trends in benefits programs?

WE CONNECTIONS: EMPLOYEE BENEFITS AND SERVICES

Expanding the Benefits Plan

"You have *got* to be kidding me!" Alex struggled to keep his voice from rising. "Haven't I given enough? Do you think I'm made of money?"

Rebecca stood up and quietly closed Alex's office door. She figured there was no need for everyone to hear this argument. As she sat back down in her chair, she attempted to sound calm although she was feeling a bit nervous. Alex often got excited, but on this day he seemed especially agitated. This was not a good sign.

She said, "I'm sorry. I am simply trying to look at every part of the employee experience. I know that the changes we've made to the compensation program are going to be expensive, but there's more that needs to be done."

Alex took a deep breath to steady himself before he responded. "I thought if we did some work on the compensation issues then our employees would be satisfied. Now you're telling me that we need to revamp the benefits program, too? We already have great benefits. Why do we need more?"

Choosing her words carefully, Rebecca said, "We have indeed made some major strides in improving our compensation system, and I know the employees have responded well. But, as I told you before, money is not enough. We have to work on the whole system to keep our employees

engaged and motivated. There are a number of facets for a strategic human resources plan, and the compensation system is just one. Benefits are another. We got some pretty clear indicators from our benefits audit and I think some adjustments are in order. Do you want to hear what I'm thinking, or should I come back another day? Or maybe we should ask Selina to join us. She can help us determine what's reasonable." Rebecca liked the idea of bringing in Selina, a person who was known for being analytical and even-tempered.

Alex shook his head. "Let me hear what you have to say. I don't want to wait. We can loop in Selina later."

Modern Benefits and Services

Rebecca nodded, gathering her courage to forge ahead. She knew it might be a bumpy ride. She said, "Well, right now we have a pretty good benefits plan. It covers dental, prescription drugs, life insurance, and educational assistance. This is all fine, but, to be honest, it's kind of the bare minimum. Employees these days, especially in this industry, expect more. As you know, some of our employees have worked at other tech companies, or they have friends who work at other progressive companies. Naturally, there are some comparisons being drawn across workplaces. When that happens, I'm afraid we seem to usually be on the low side of the equation. Through the benefits audit, it became clear that our employees are aware that we are not in line with the marketplace."

Rebecca could see that Alex was about to interrupt her, so she put up a hand and continued, "I know what you're going to ask. They are asking for things like a games room, Friday sundae parties, and napping pods, for starters."

Shaking his head from side to side, Alex said, "Napping pods? They want to nap at work? Now I know you're joking." He looked around the room. "Did you set up a camera in here, Rebecca? Is this a practical joke? Why would I want people to nap at work? I want people to work at work!" He threw his hands up in the air, exasperated.

Rebecca waited a beat before she responded. She had been afraid he was going to react this way. Alex thought everyone should love working as much as he did.

She said, "Maybe the napping pods are not a good idea for us. I don't know about that. What I do know is we want our employees to feel that we are giving them an overall pay and benefits plan that is as good as or better than what they'll get at other companies. We really need to look at

expanding our plan so that you and Selina think it's reasonable, and employees think it is fair compared to what others are getting. We don't have to go with every suggestion that comes our way. There are lots of options out there. The good news is that some of them don't cost a lot of money. But we do need to beef up our benefits plan if we want to stay competitive. Let's be strategic about this!"

DISCUSSION QUESTIONS

1. Design an expanded benefits plan for WEC. Consider paid time-off benefits, employee services, as well as emerging services and trends.

2. Explain how your outlined plan could impact the organization in both the short and long term.

3. What steps does Rebecca need to take to implement the expanded benefits plan that you have designed?

In the next installment of the WE Connections story (at the end of Chapter 11), an underperforming employee is profiled, introducing a consideration of the company's employee relations approach.

CASE STUDY

Aptech Medical Laboratories

Flexible Benefit Program

Sara Ipsides, senior vice-president HR, sat across the meeting room table from Bennett Fox, Aptech Medical Laboratories' CEO. Bennett had called Sara to a meeting to discuss the lab's benefit expenses. Both came prepared with copies of their recent annual financial statement. The report indicated that the lab's benefit expenses had reached almost 40 percent of the company's total payroll. Bennett also produced benchmark data from a survey that showed that the health sector average was closer to 30 percent.

"Sara, why are our benefits expenses are so much higher than those of our competitors?" he asked.

Sara was prepared for the question. Over the past two-and-a-half years, Sara had made some purposeful increases in the health benefits offered to staff across their medical laboratories. Specifically, she had worked with their health insurance provider to add a health care spending account in the amount of $1,000 per employee in an effort to add some flexibility to the company's otherwise uniform benefits offerings. In addition, and with executive and board of director approval, Aptech had implemented a health benefits program for all part-time staff working 20 hours per week or more. Sara had also diligently read communications from the health insurance provider announcing that

the cost of offering the same coverage in terms of health, dental, and travel insurance was rising at a rate faster than inflation. In short, some of the higher benefits expense was due to increases in benefits offered to staff, some was due to offering benefits to staff that previously had not qualified for the company's benefits package, and the remainder was due to escalating costs from its health insurance provider.

As she looked at the benchmark data that Bennett passed across the table, Sara pointed out that the data Bennett was referring to had assessed the health sector as a whole, not just medical laboratories, and that the sector included medical equipment manufacturers. Medical equipment manufacturers typically had much lower benefit levels than laboratories—which, by and large, had benefit expenses similar to those of Aptech. Undeniably, however, Aptech certainly occupied the high end of the scale.

Bennett wondered whether these expenses were really justified. "Where is the payoff?" he asked.

Sara had no problem defending the laboratories' benefits outlays. She pointed out that Aptech had the lowest turnover rate among large medical laboratories—nearly 2 percent lower than any other—and that every employee engagement survey showed that Aptech staff felt that the lab was a very good place to work; job satisfaction and engagement were high. In particular, because the company's diagnostic and imaging staff was largely female with nearly half working 20 to 30 hours per week, Sara felt strongly that providing health insurance benefits to its part-time staff was a huge retention incentive and the right thing to do. She also mentioned that Aptech was able to recruit top-flight new hires. She was convinced that the lab's generous benefits package contributed significantly to this level of satisfaction.

She concluded her explanation by saying, "Bennett, look at the level of customer satisfaction. We beat out every other lab company on this measure. I am sure the reason is that happy employees mean happy customers. And there is the main payoff."

Bennett appreciated Sara's explanation. He always had been proud when he saw the results of Aptech's employee engagement surveys. There was no doubt that people liked to work for Aptech. "Still," he wondered, "are there ways to cut the expenses without doing too much damage to employee satisfaction?"

Sara agreed to look into that matter and to make suggestions regarding more efficient methods of delivering benefits services.

Sara headed back to her office, logged onto Aptech's intranet, and created a new file folder she named Benefits Audit and Changes. She had been keeping current on trends for benefits offerings and knew that some organizations were reducing the amount of coverage they offered, or increasing employee deductibles. Sarah thought that she could probably work with Aptech's health insurance provider to come up with a list of potential cost saving changes. However, Sara also wanted to be sure that the company did not cut benefits that would endanger employee attachment to it. She would need some employee input into coverage reductions. Sara realized it had been a couple of years since Aptech's last benefits audit. It was time to take a fulsome look.

Additional Information

The lab's benefits package included supplementary health and life insurance, child care, elder care, a prescription payment plan, an EAP, educational support in the form of tuition reimbursements, and financial advising. It was also possible to purchase more vacation time pro-rated based on the employee's salary. These benefits were standard to all employees across the labs who worked 20 or more hours per week. There was also the new health care spending account in the amount of $1,000 per employee, which added some flexibility and responded to staff requests for coverage for massage, vision care, and physiotherapy and chiropractor expenses. The health insurance provider, Magenta Providers Cross, managed all of Aptech's benefits, and employees were able to access their benefits resources through its website.

DISCUSSION QUESTIONS

1. What are the steps that Sara will need to take to conduct a benefits audit?

2. What are some suggestions you would have for Sara on how to save money on the benefits package? In addition to reducing benefits coverage or increasing employee deductibles across all staff, what other options could Sara explore?

3. As part of the audit process, Sara will gather information relating to employees' understanding of the company's current benefits offerings. How might information about staff understanding of current benefits be useful in her decisions on where to make cuts?

4. What recommendations would you have for Sara about how to communicate the changes in the benefits package once they are determined? Discuss whether you think staff should be involved in the process of changing the benefits package.

5. One option could be to retract the benefits package offering to part-time staff. What are the pros and cons of this strategy?

Maintaining High Performance

An organization's culture and working environment has an effect on the motivation and job satisfaction of its employees. To maintain good relationships, an effective communication process is essential. Good interpersonal relations also require appropriate and fair discipline procedures. Workplace safety is also very important. Managing in a union environment requires familiarity

with the legal requirements in dealing with unions, the collective bargaining process, and administration of the collective agreement.

The three chapters in Part 6 discuss ways to create a positive work environment, maintain proper discipline, ensure a safe workforce, and deal with union management issues.

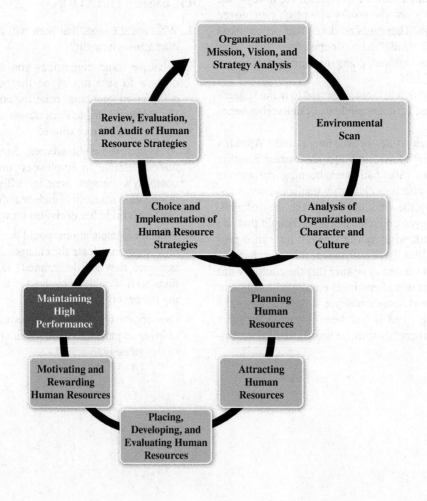

CHAPTER 11

Managing Employee Relations

> When people are financially invested, they want a return. When people are emotionally invested, they want to contribute.
>
> SIMON SINEK[1]

LEARNING OBJECTIVES

After studying this chapter, you should be able to:

LO1 Discuss the importance of downward and upward communication in organizational settings.

LO2 Define employee counselling and the major types of counselling.

LO3 Describe how progressive discipline and wrongful dismissal work.

LO4 Explain the different techniques available to improve the quality of work life.

LO5 Outline the major issues relating to downsizing the workforce and their implications for strategic human resource management.

In many ways, this entire book is about employee relations. How well the human resource department handles human resource planning, placement, training and development, evaluation, and compensation largely determines the state of employee relations. Even when these activities are performed properly, solid employee relations demand careful attention to organizational communication, employee counselling, discipline, and management of work groups. In addition, a number of organizations are becoming high-involvement workplaces that emphasize human resource management.

A number of employees express frustration with their employer and their manager/supervisor. In a study of Canadian employees, only 15 percent reported having jobs with both clear feedback and a significant impact (that is, the work is important). Almost 25 percent of employees indicated that their job had both little recognition and

low satisfaction. According to study author Paul Fairlie, "Engagement, commitment, and performance are important, but these are outputs. They don't happen unless employees view their work as meaningful."[2]

A *Canadian HR Reporter* survey on problem managers revealed that 46 percent of respondents viewed problem managers as a big problem and 27 percent reported that they are a huge problem. More than half of the respondents said that one in ten managers is a problem manager. The survey identified what types of behaviours create the most problems: inappropriate comments (74 percent), showing favouritism (70 percent), failing to follow due process (63 percent), treating employees in a disrespectful manner (62 percent), and bullying or intimidation (57 percent). About 35 percent of participants indicated that their organization tolerates just about anything if the manager delivers results, while about 14 percent reported little tolerance for managerial misbehaviour. Only about 17 percent of respondents stated that they were able to get problem managers to change their behaviour most of the time.[3]

Although the focus of this chapter is on employee relations, an effective organization also pays considerable attention to relationships among workers. Several human resource initiatives, such as policies on workplace and sexual harassment, conflict resolution procedures, and employee involvement programs, play an important role in enhancing human relations.

Strategic Importance of Employee Relations Practices

"Employee relations" is a complex blend of organizational culture, human resource practices, and individual perceptions. Virtually everything the human resource department does affects employee relations, directly or indirectly. But many human resource activities (such as recruitment, selection, and benefits administration) go largely unnoticed by employees. Other important human resource functions affect employees only periodically, as in the case of performance appraisal and salary review sessions. This necessitates ongoing activities to foster good employer–employee relations.

Why are employee relations practices important? At least four major reasons can be offered:

1. *Good employee relations practices improve productivity.* Employee productivity is significantly affected by two factors: ability and attitude. Ability is simply whether the employee is able to perform the job. Ability is influenced by such things as training, education, innate aptitude, tools, and work environments. Attitude, on the other hand, refers to an individual's willingness to perform the job. Attitude is affected by myriad factors, such as level of motivation, job satisfaction, and commitment to work. Good employee relations practices help improve both the ability and attitude of the employee. The result is an improvement in employee productivity:

   A University of Melbourne (Australia) study suggests that tweeting or using Facebook during office hours may actually increase employee productivity. The study indicates that employees who use the Internet for personal reasons while working are about 9 percent more productive than those who do not. According to the study author, Brent Coker, "People need to zone out a bit to get their concentration back. Short and unobtrusive breaks, such as a quick surf of the Internet, enables the mind to rest itself."[4]

2. *Good employee relations ensure implementation of organizational strategies.* In Chapter 1, the importance of the role that human resource activities play in achieving organizational goals was discussed. Good employee relations practices ensure that organizational goals and strategies are properly communicated and that the employees are committed to achieving them.

3. *Good employee relations practices reduce employment costs.* When concern for and interest in employees becomes part of the overall organizational culture, significant cost savings can emerge in terms of reduced absenteeism and turnover. Good employee relations practices also give employers a recruiting advantage as most job applicants prefer to work for an organization that treats them fairly and offers them a challenging job with potential for career growth.

4. *Good employee relations help employees grow and develop.* As discussed in Chapter 1, an important goal of human resource departments today is to help employees achieve their personal goals. A keen interest in the employee's work-related and career goals not only brings benefits to the organization (in terms of improved employee morale, loyalty, improved productivity, ready availability of skilled personnel within), but also helps it meet its social objectives.

A study by CareerBuilder indicated that just under 60 percent of employees are satisfied at work but about 20 percent plan to change jobs by the following year. Individuals planning to stay with a company reported that it was because they like the people they work with (54 percent), and they are satisfied with their benefits (49 percent) and salary (43 percent). Among workers who were very dissatisfied, almost 60 percent indicated a desire to change jobs. The sources of dissatisfaction included concerns over salary (66 percent), a feeling of not being valued (65 percent), limited advancement opportunities (45 percent), a lack of work–life balance (39 percent), and a poor opinion of their supervisor or manager's performance (37 percent).[5]

As Figure 11-1 shows, there are five major components of effective employee relations: communication, counselling, discipline, rights, and involvement. Each of these will be discussed in some detail in this chapter. In addition, a section of the chapter will address the issues of employee retention, job security, and organizational downsizing.

LO1 Effective Employee Communication

Information about the organization, its environment, its products and services, and its people is essential to management and employees. Without information, managers cannot make effective decisions about markets or resources, particularly human resources. Likewise, insufficient information may cause stress and dissatisfaction among employees. Moreover, effective communication is an essential component of learning organizations.

FIGURE 11-1

Five Key Dimensions of Employee Relations

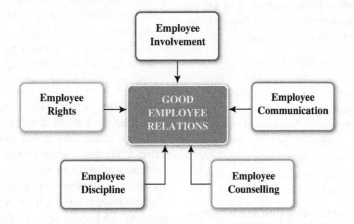

The need for information is met through an organization's communication system. In small or less-sophisticated firms, communication may be informal, but in large multibillion-dollar enterprises, specialists may serve as employee communications directors or as chief information officers.

Most organizations use a blend of formal, systematically designed communication efforts and informal ad hoc arrangements. For convenience, most of these approaches can be divided into *downward communication systems,* which exist to get information to employees, and *upward communication systems,* which exist to obtain information from employees.

A global study of more than 3,800 employees by Dell and Intel revealed that about 62 percent of employees perceived that their job could be made easier with the assistance of artificial intelligence. However, about 44 percent of employees felt that their workplace was not smart enough while 41 percent said it was as smart as they wanted it to be. There is still considerable reliance on desktops and landlines at many organizations. About half of respondents worked remotely at least a few times a week. While 57 percent preferred face-to-face communication, about 51 percent believed that better communication technology and remote teams would make face-to-face communication obsolete. In addition, just over 70 percent reported that workplaces are more collaborative now than in the past.[6]

Downward Communication Systems

Human resource professionals try to facilitate an open, two-way flow of information, although often messages are of the top-down variety. **Downward communication** is information that begins at some point in the organization and proceeds down the organizational hierarchy to inform or influence others. Top-down methods are necessary for decision makers to have their decisions carried out. These communications also help give employees knowledge about the organization and feedback on how their efforts are perceived.

downward communication
Information that begins at some point in the organization and feeds down the organization hierarchy to inform or influence others.

A Quantum Workplace survey indicated that communicating human resource initiatives organization-wide was perceived as the top HR challenge. The study also found that almost 80 percent of employers rely on emails from management for most communication, 76 percent use all-company meetings, and 75 percent use manager and worker one-on-one discussions.[7]

Organizations use a variety of downward communication methods because multiple channels are more likely to overcome barriers and reach the intended receivers. For example, limiting messages to email or text messaging may exclude large numbers of employees. Some common examples of downward communication approaches include in-house publications, information booklets, employee bulletins, prerecorded messages, email, and jobholder reports and meetings.

An OfficeTeam study revealed that the majority of workers (62 percent) believed it is appropriate to connect with co-workers on Facebook, followed by Twitter (52 percent), Instagram (45 percent), and Snapchat (33 percent). Senior managers tended to be less supportive of connecting with co-workers on social media with 54 percent agreeing it is appropriate to connect with co-workers on Facebook, followed by Twitter (34 percent), Instagram (34 percent), and Snapchat (29 percent).[8]

In-House Publications and Prerecorded Messages

Many organizations publish internal magazines, newspapers, or information booklets for employees (in hard copy or electronic formats or both). Their purpose is to inform employees about current developments and to foster a long-term understanding about objectives and missions:

> At Air Canada, keeping employees in the loop is critical. In addition to a daily newsletter of current information and a weekly newsletter from the chief operating officer, the organization also has a monthly magazine, *Horizons,* to keep the almost 27,000 employees worldwide in touch. Employees can also check out a Yammer social networking site that addresses such topics as flight issues and offers ideas to the company on a page titled "Creative Juices."[9]

Human resource departments often distribute information on various subjects to employees. For instance, an employee handbook is often given to new employees to inform them about regulations and benefits. It is important that the information in employee handbooks be updated regularly and carefully reviewed—in some instances, information contained in employee handbooks has been used by former employees in litigation against the organization.

Information on specialized subjects relating to human resource activities, such as suggestion programs, employee assistance programs, occupational health and safety, wage incentives, retirement, and fringe benefits is also frequently provided, often as online publications. Also, a number of organizations develop internal video programs for employees to access.

Electronic Communication

Using email as a means of communicating with employees is taken for granted in many organizations. However, email may not be appropriate for all types of communication:

> Aesthetician Crystal Bell of Kelowna, British Columbia, checked her Facebook account one morning as she was getting ready for work and discovered that she had been terminated (cybersacked). Bell, who had only been employed for two weeks, showed up for work because she thought her employer was kidding. According to Bell, "It is not the human way to go. I think that using any kind of texting or emailing to let people go is a coward's way out." Ruth Haag, author of *Hiring and Firing,* states that "doing an email is quickest and easiest but people forget that it is the most public way to communicate because it can be around the world in minutes and you're looking like a jerk for firing someone that way."[10]

In addition, more and more employers are using intranets (internal communications systems that function like a smaller version of the World Wide Web). Denis Zenkin, an E2.0 expert, calls intranets and HR a "perfect match":

Zenkin identifies several uses of an intranet by HR specialists, including information dissemination of HR documents and collection of employee information, HR transactions (use of eforms), training (such as a slideshow, video, or text embedded in a wiki), collection of feedback information (such as surveys and blog posts), community building (for example, tracking birthdays and organizing special events), performance management, and recruitment.[11]

Firms use intranets for a variety of purposes, ranging from tracking benefit enrollments to providing copies of employee handbooks, policy manuals, and company newsletters.[12] Human resource departments have found intranet communication to be particularly effective as a means of updating handbooks and manuals and in eliminating some of the administrative burden associated with forms management. Examples of ways that human resource departments use intranets include creating an electronic employee directory, setting up training registration information, using electronic pay stubs, updating employee accounts, mapping performance achievements, managing succession planning, and creating discussion groups.[13]

With intranet communication, the traditional top-down communication system is altered, with communication opportunities extended to a much larger group of employees. However, the use of technology needs to be carefully managed. Although more than half of North American organizations report having a self-service HR portal, another 20 percent of organizations are working to develop one. Of those with employee portals, more than 6 in 10 assess the portals to be at least somewhat effective.[14] Still, technology can be a very valuable tool:

> Some organizations are using "assistive technology" (software and/or hardware) to help both individuals with disabilities and nondisabled employees. In addition to the continuing development of established technologies, new apps for use on smartphones and tables are increasing productivity for employees with sensory or motor impairments. For example, next generation screen readers (such as Window-Eyes) can read the screen content to employees and provide speech and Braille output. Similarly, technology aimed at assisting motor skill impairments range from speech recognition software to physical assistance, such as the X-Ar (an exoskeletal arm that supports an employee's natural range of motion). A drywaller who had rotator cuff surgery, for example, could use the tool to hold up his or her arm for more extended periods of time.[15]

Many employers have developed policies on Internet usage. Among the issues to consider are the restriction of the Internet to business purposes, the right of employers to monitor employee usage of the Internet, and specific prohibitions (relating to such concerns as copyright, distribution of viruses, or the posting or downloading of material that is threatening, abusive, defamatory, or obscene). In addition, firms must be concerned about hackers obtaining confidential company and employee data.

A seven-step plan to protect the organization from the misuse of electronic communications includes (1) developing and implementing a policy addressing electronic communications; (2) being aware of legal issues and limitations associated with monitoring electronic communications; (3) training employees and managers concerning the policy; (4) encouraging prompt reporting of policy violations and immediately addressing all complaints; (5) understanding your system; (6) examining the available tools for controlling Internet access; and (7) developing a policy for telecommuting.[16]

People between the ages of 18 and 24 receive about 110 text messages a day, and most Millennials (83 percent) open such messages within 90 seconds. One study showed that the rate of errors after hearing or feeling a text alert was the same as actually opening the message; the error rate increased by 23 percent after receiving a text compared to 28 percent after receiving a phone call. A CareerBuilder study showed that cellphone use and texting was the largest productivity killer at the workplace.[17] Still, some employers are encouraging the use of electronic communication:

> Shannon Boudjema, a business manager for marketing communications firm Bond Brand Loyalty, posted a message on Twitter asking for help in finding research on young consumers. On returning to work the next day, she had received dozens of tweets. Bond Brand Loyalty is encouraging employees to find ways to use social networking to help the company. While several Canadian companies block access to instant messaging (IM) and social networking sites, other employers believe that using such sites can increase productivity and employee value.[18]

How often do Canadians use the web? New evidence from Statistics Canada showed that over 90 percent of Canadians over the age of 15 use the Internet at least a couple of times each month. Internet usage has grown dramatically over the past three years for older individuals (81 percent usage for people aged 65 to 74 and 50 percent for those over 75 years of age). The benefits of using technology include helping communicate with others (77 percent), saving time (52 percent), helping to make more informed decisions (52 percent), and helping to be more creative (36 percent). There was some concern about the use of technology and work–life balance, with 68 percent indicating some level of satisfaction with work–life balance (down from 78 percent eight years earlier).[19]

An issue that has caused some concern for employers revolves around employee blogs (web logs). From an organizational perspective, employers are worried about employees leaking confidential information about the company (intentionally or unintentionally), hurting the

organization's reputation, describing the business in a negative way, or exposing the employer to potential liability. Rather than simply trying to ban employees from blogging, some organizations are developing a blogging policy; typical guidelines include writing in the first person (using *I*) to make it clear that the views are not those of the company, being aware of the responsibilities with respect to corporate information, and adhering to professional standards.[20]

Workplace social media policies are gaining more and more attention as employers become increasingly concerned about employee abuse of social media at work to the detriment of the brand and image of the organization. A recent study on professionalism in the workplace indicated that about half of HR professionals believed that IT abuses had increased over the past five years, with about two-thirds indicating problems with excess tweeting and Facebook use.[21]

Social Media and the Use of Mobile Devices

An issue for human resource professionals is the growing use of social media by employees. Canadian professionals report spending almost three-quarters of an hour a day using their mobile devices for nonwork activities, and employees also admit spending around 40 minutes a day on personal tasks (for a total of almost seven hours weekly on tasks not related to the job). Workers in the 18 to 34 age group tend to spend the most time on nonwork activities, and 35 percent of employees use personal devices at work to check sites banned by their employer.[22] Is banning social media use associated with improved productivity?

> In 2016, 100,000 computers used by civil servants in Singapore were disconnected from the Internet with the goal of increasing security. However, research by the Pew Centre suggests that banning social media use may not increase productivity. While employees indicate that the top two reasons for using social media are taking a mental break from work (34 percent) and connecting with family and friends (27 percent), other important reasons include fostering professional connections (24 percent), solving work-related problems (20 percent), and seeking answers to work-related queries from other people (12 percent).[23]

A major concern with the increased use of mobile devices, such as laptops and tablets, is the security of networks and data. Experts are calling for good mobility management as part of an enterprise security management system. Concerns include protecting precious data from attacks and human error and meeting ongoing changes to privacy laws. From an HR perspective, it is critical that employees are aware of policies addressing the use of mobile devices; while about 95 percent of large organizations report having a policy on usage, only about 30 percent of employees are aware of such policies.[24] However, not everyone wants to be connected:

An OfficeTeam study of executives revealed that 71 percent of participants were uncomfortable being "friended" by their boss on Facebook, 66 percent did not want to be Facebook friends with people they managed, and 63 percent did not want to connect on Facebook with their clients.[25]

A recent BMO Report revealed that 45 percent of small business owners have a social media account and three-quarters understand how social media works. Main uses of social media include promoting products or services (35 percent), communicating with customers (22 percent), and finding prospective customers (20 percent). Almost two-thirds plan to make major changes/investments in their online presence.[26]

With the growth in the use of social media comes a dramatic increase in social media hacking. According to Mark Nunnikhoven, VP of cloud and emerging technologies at Trend Micro in Ottawa, social media hacking "usually comes down to financial gain. Over the last two or three years, cybercrime has shifted to be a big business, so this is organized criminals who are in it for profit." Being hacked has several consequences for organizations, including damage to a brand's reputation, declining employee engagement, and a loss of trust by customers.[27]

A study of executives revealed that 33 percent of respondents reported having a social media policy, 40 percent were considering developing a policy or had other related policies, and 27 percent had no policy or plans to develop one. While 71 percent of participants indicated that their company was concerned about risks associated with social media, only 36 percent provided any type of social media training. The four biggest concerns were damage to the employer brand, disclosure of confidential or proprietary information, corporate identity theft, and legal/regulatory and compliance violations. Almost 60 percent of organizations did not have a social media risk assessment plan in place.[28]

With increased reliance on social media and concern by organizations about their reputation, more and more employers are hiring a chief reputation officer. Most employers do not have anyone directly responsible for reputation management with the expertise to address issues related to the reputation of the business.[29] Having individuals or departments address reputation issues on an ad hoc basis may result in inconsistent application of policies by employees who may not have proper training in reputation management.

The growth in cloud-based tools provides new challenges for organizations with particular impacts on information sharing, meetings, and communication throughout the organization. Among the issues for human resource professionals are social communication (such as integrating social networking capabilities, blogs, wikis and activity feeds), unified communication (for instance, instant messaging; conferencing; Enterprise Voice capabilities

using PC, browser, and mobile devices), rich communication services (such as audio/video calling and rich online meetings), and accessible software (for instance, being able to access PowerPoint or Excel from a mobile device or browser).[30]

Some employers are using social media in creative and innovative ways to communicate with employees:

ICBC, an auto-insurance Crown corporation with 5,400 employees, has been using social media in a fairly intensive way over the past few years. According to Len Posniak, VP of Human Resources, "Every morning we are using Twitter to promote any positions that we are having difficulty filling. And it's very inexpensive to use so it's a good way of getting our message out there. We want people to be able to speak across the company and through levels of the management structure."[31]

However, employers need to be aware that social media must be used responsibly. There is an increasing trend among employers meeting a new job candidate or client to Google the person or check the individual out on Facebook, Twitter, or other social networking sites. There are risks to using social media to check an individual's background, however. The information may not be accurate or up-to-date, or you might be obtaining information about the wrong person. Employers need consent to collect certain information under privacy laws, and collecting information pertaining to an individual's background (age, sex, race, etc.) may make the organization susceptible to a claim of discrimination by the individual. Under the privacy guidelines, simply viewing the information is considered collection.[32]

Information Sharing and Open-Book Management

Some employers provide reports to employees about the organization's economic performance. The reasoning is that economic information is as important to employees as it is to shareholders. The report is often presented in the same style as the annual report, except that it shows how the annual economic results affect workers. The release of the report may be followed by meetings that are organized and conducted in the same way as shareholder meetings. Top management attends the meetings, and all employees are invited. Management formally presents the report, and employees are invited to question management and make proposals in the same way that owners do in stockholder meetings. These meetings improve communication and give jobholders a stronger feeling of belonging.

While many companies believe that the firm's financial performance and budget goals are not the business of employees, some firms have adopted an approach of sharing such information with employees (for example, a Statistics Canada study indicates that about 36 percent of employers follow a practice of sharing information with workers.[33] Using *open-book management,* some firms are making employees assume more responsibility for the firm's success. The basic concepts involve educating employees about how the firm earns profits, giving workers a stake in the performance of the business, and providing feedback on how the company is doing.

Some actions by organizations to improve communications internally and to enhance the link between employees and the organization (and its customers or clients) include the following:

- Conducting more research/employee surveys to understand employee attitudes toward communication and what is working (and not working)
- Issuing "total rewards" communication that addresses the numerous benefits of working for the employer
- Providing performance-oriented communication that outlines performance standards for employees and the effect of employee performance on the organization and its customers
- Offering communications training for managers and employees
- Regularly reviewing or auditing the communication system[34]

Should employees be required to respond to email around the clock? A recent collective agreement in France contained a provision that addressed the issue, limiting employee obligations to respond to emails sent after 6:00 p.m. Among the concerns associated with after-hours emails are demands by employees for overtime pay, allegations of harassment, higher error rates if people are tired, and increased employee stress and burnout. In response to such concerns, Edelman Canada's Toronto office established a "7 to 7 rule" prohibiting emails outside of the hours of 7:00 a.m. to 7:00 p.m.[35]

Upward Communication Systems

Perhaps no area of communication is more in need of improvement in most organizations than upward communication. **Upward communication** consists of information initiated by people who seek to inform or influence those higher up in the organization's hierarchy. The cornerstone of all such messages is the employee and the supervisor. When a free flow of information travels between an employee and the supervisor, informal day-to-day communication is often sufficient for most situations. If open communication does not exist, or exists only for a limited range of issues, other approaches are needed.

upward communication Communication that begins in the organization and proceeds up the hierarchy to inform or influence others.

How do organizations create open, upward communication? No universal formula exists—the type of approach used may vary depending on the situation. However, one common element in many organizations is a genuine concern for employee well-being combined with meaningful opportunities for ideas to flow up the organization's hierarchy. Some of the more common upward communication channels include the grapevine, HR management and technology, in-house complaint procedures, manager–employee meetings, suggestion systems, and attitude survey feedback.

Grapevine

Grapevine communication is an informal system that arises spontaneously from the social interaction of people in the organization. It is the people-to-people system that arises naturally from human desires to make friends and share ideas. For instance, two employees chatting at the water cooler about their problems with a supervisor is a grapevine communication.

grapevine communication Informal communication within an organization that arises from normal social interaction.

The grapevine provides a large amount of useful off-the-record feedback from employees. There are many opportunities for feedback because human resource specialists are in regular contact with employees as they discuss benefits, counsel employees, and perform other functions. Employees feel somewhat free to talk with human resource specialists since the occupation of human resource management is oriented toward helping people, and human resource specialists do not directly supervise employees in other departments. Some of the types of grapevine feedback that come to the human resource department include information about employee problems, the quality of labour–management relations, important grievance issues, areas of job dissatisfaction, difficulties with supervisors, and acceptance by employees of changes within the organization. However, the Internet and the use of social media are changing how employees communicate:

Social networking used to involve gossip around the water cooler or lunchroom chats. However, sites like Facebook, YouTube, and Twitter have changed the rules. HR professionals need to be aware of the new social media and the rights of both employers and employees relating to the use of electronic social networking. What an employee posts online could constitute discrimination, bullying, or harassment. In addition, an employee could intentionally or inadvertently divulge private company information. What about employees posting information outside of regular work hours? If the employer can show that its legitimate business interests are affected by the material posted by the employee, the employee may be liable and subject to discipline.[36]

© Leon/Getty Images.

An informal gathering around the water cooler or coffee station is one method by which employees exchange information but also gossip and rumours. What can management do to curtail rumours?

Human Resource Management and Technology

Although the issue of electronic communication has been discussed in detail earlier in the chapter, it is important to recognize that email, intranets, social media, and discussion groups are also very useful in facilitating upward communication. Again, the importance of issues such as security of use, monitoring of employee messages, rules of conduct, and the need for a policy on email and Internet usage must be emphasized.[37]

Using workplace surveillance is not new, but technological advances let employers monitor employee actions in detail. Consider talent management company Crossover, where photos of employees (even those working remotely) are taken every 10 minutes using its productivity tool WorkSmart. Screenshots of employee work stations in combination with other data such as app use and keystrokes are used to calculate productivity scores for employees. Other employers can monitor activities such as web-use patterns, text messages and emails, screenshots, social media posts, and private messaging apps, and examine trends and deviations in use.[38]

Having a record of email communications may be helpful to a party involved in litigation—in the case described below, an examination of email messages may be more helpful to the dismissed employee:

During a wrongful dismissal trial in which a CIBC portfolio manager was terminated after a margin-related glitch cost his clients $35 million, a judge ordered that the approximately 3,500 emails in the employee's account should be made available by CIBC to his lawyers. The judge stated that the emails could aid the court in determining whether trades made by the employee were properly authorized by CIBC.[39]

More and more organizations are implementing human resource management systems (HRMS). This is not surprising considering that mastering HR technology has recently been identified as one of the five competency domains for human resource management (along with business knowledge, HR delivery, strategic contribution, and personal credibility).[40] Still, many HRMS are being used for maintaining employee records rather than for strategic human resource issues and communication purposes.[41]

HR departments and professionals are using cloud computing for a wide range of tasks and activities, including payroll administration, employee communication and self-service applications, and employee file and records management. For example, Toronto marketing firm Ariad's movement to the cloud resulted in cost savings and efficiencies and streamlined HR activities, and provided management and employees with ready access to HR information and employment data.[42]

While a lot of focus on the use of social media has been on the concern for abuse, social media may prove to be a valuable tool for HR professionals. Some of the benefits cited include mentoring (such as one-to-many, using blogs; or many-to-many, using forums), performance management (and the provision of timely feedback), leadership (transparency and visibility), e-recruiting (trying to attract both active and passive candidates), and communications (timely messages, information, and feedback to employees and customers).[43]

An issue that is beginning to impact employers is the growing use of "wearables" at the workplace. Wearables include activity monitors (which can track an individual's body behaviour), head-mounted displays (such as Google Glass and GoPro), and smart watches. Associated with such devices are key questions relating to privacy. For example, while a device that monitors employee health conditions may allow an employer to improve productivity, reduce injuries, and enhance employee wellness, there are major issues relating to employee privacy and concerns over hacking and data theft, who can access the data, and the use of the information against a current or prospective employee:[44]

An employee-tracking system patented by Amazon involves workers wearing a wristband on each arm.

The devices are being promoted as a way to track and manage inventory and use ultrasonic pulses to link inventory modules with an employee's hands. However, there is concern that the devices could be used to track an employee's every move, such as when the person rests, goes to the bathroom, and slows down. Also, the data could be used to compare workers and assess performance.[45]

In-House Complaint Procedures

How does an employee solve a problem if the supervisor is not willing to discuss it? In some organizations, the employee has no other option except to talk with the supervisor's superior. Although that may seem reasonable, most people in organizations are very reluctant to do that because they do not want to create negative feelings between themselves and their supervisor. To lessen the burden of "going over the supervisor's head," some organizations have installed **in-house complaint procedures**.

> **in-house complaint procedures** Formal methods through which an employee can register a complaint.

In-house complaint procedures are formal methods through which an employee can register a complaint. Normally these procedures are operated by the human resource department and require the employee to submit the complaint in writing. Then, an employee relations specialist investigates the complaint and advises the employee of the results. In some companies, the employee's name is known only by the employee relations investigator. However, if a supervisor is questioned about the issue, it may be obvious who filed the complaint.

In recent years, there has been growing interest in *alternative dispute resolution* (ADR) programs. The goal of ADR is to resolve disputes in a timely, cost-effective manner. Some types of ADR programs include the following:

1. An **open-door policy** in which an employee is encouraged to meet with his or her supervisor or another member of management to resolve workplace conflict.

> **open-door policy** A company policy that encourages employees to address their problems to higher levels of management.

2. A *peer review panel,* or ombudsperson, who hears an employee's presentation of the problem and makes recommendations. While the composition of the peer review panel may vary, a typical structure involves two individuals from a similar job classification as the employee and one management representative. It is estimated that about 90 percent of disputes getting to peer review are settled at this level.

3. *Mediation,* in which a neutral third party meets with the parties and tries to resolve the issue. Although the mediator cannot impose a settlement, his or her involvement is often instrumental in resolving the conflict.

4. *Arbitration,* in which a neutral third party hears both parties' views of the case and makes a binding decision. While arbitration is common in unionized environments, it is also becoming more popular as a means of resolving disputes in nonunion settings.[46]

The previous two decades have seen considerable growth in the presence of a grievance system for nonunion employees. A nonunion grievance procedure can be defined as one that is in writing, guarantees employees the right to present complaints to management, and is communicated to employees.[47] For example, a study of Canadian firms revealed that about 31 percent had a grievance procedure for nonunion employees, with the typical procedure consisting of a three- or four-step process.[48] In setting up a nonunion grievance procedure, several issues exist. Some questions to consider are as follows:

- What subjects may be grieved? For example, can disciplinary actions be grieved?
- Are all nonunion employees eligible to participate in the procedure?
- Are employees protected from retaliation if they use the procedure?
- Must the grievance be filed in writing? Are there time limits for employee filing and management response?
- How many steps will the grievance procedure contain? Can an employee bypass his or her supervisor? What are the specific steps in the procedure?
- Does the employee have the right to be present throughout the procedure? Can the employee have someone else (such as another employee, human resource staff member, lawyer) present the case? Can the employee call witnesses?
- What is the final step in the procedure? For instance, who ultimately resolves the issue? Some options include a senior line manager, HR professional, a panel (which can be comprised of just managers, managers and employees, or just employees), or outside arbitration.[49]

Manager–Employee Meetings

Closely related to in-house complaint procedures are meetings between managers and groups of employees to discuss complaints, suggestions, opinions, or questions. These meetings may begin with some information sharing by management to inform the group about developments in the company. However, the primary purpose of these meetings is to encourage upward communication, often with several levels of employees and lower-level management in attendance at the same time. Attendance at such meetings varies according to how the meetings are planned. In small facilities, it may be possible to get all the employees together annually or semi-annually; however, this does not reduce the need to keep in touch with employees on a regular basis. In some organizations, there is a growing focus on virtual meetings. Depending on the employer structure, different meeting formats may be needed:

> One major bank's Open Meeting Program arranges meetings of about a dozen employees at a time. Meetings are held with different groups until at least one in five employees from each department attends. Employees are selected randomly and may decline to participate if they wish. A human resource specialist coordinates each meeting and develops the group report on a newsprint sheet in open discussions with the group. No employee names are used in the report, which becomes the basis of action plans with management. The program is repeated annually, and it has significantly improved upward communication.

Does an employer have the right to record performance review or disciplinary meetings? Invariably, there is the need to balance employer rights to operate with employee rights to privacy. Calgary lawyer Tim Mitchell notes that in a number of recent cases, employers engaging in nonconsensual recording of employee meetings have been prevented from using the evidence or ordered to refrain from continuing the practice.[50]

Suggestion Systems

Suggestion systems are formal methods for generating, evaluating, and implementing employee ideas. All three of these elements are crucial to a successful suggestion system.

> **suggestion systems** Formal methods of generating, evaluating, and implementing employee ideas.

A successful suggestion system begins with the employee's idea and possibly a discussion with the supervisor. The suggestion system office or committee evaluates the idea, and the decision is communicated to the employee. If it is considered a good idea, implementation follows, with the employee receiving recognition and usually some award (often awards are equal to about 10 percent of the first year's savings from the suggestion).

Although most suggestion systems pay employees a percentage of the first-year savings, some companies pay a flat dollar amount in order to minimize the need for precision in evaluating the suggestion's exact dollar savings. This approach means that employees receive feedback about their suggestions much faster. In addition, organizations that place a higher focus on teamwork may need to revamp their suggestion system program to reflect a group contribution. For suggestion systems to work, management must provide prompt and fair assessment of the ideas, supervisors must be trained to encourage employee

suggestions, and top management must actively support the program.

While suggestion systems can work in government, there is some evidence that they are harder to implement because management changes when a new administration takes over. This results in variations in the types of suggestions that are made.[51]

Employee Attitude/Opinion Surveys

What do employees think about the organization? Do they have problems or concerns? How engaged are the employees? Do they understand the human resource department's benefit plan? Compensation program? Career planning efforts? Answers to these and many other questions can make a useful addition to the human resource department's information system.

An **employee attitude/opinion survey** is a systematic method of determining what employees think about their organization. While surveys may be conducted through face-to-face interviews, they are usually done through questionnaires that employees complete anonymously. Many organizations are now using web technology to conduct employee surveys.

> **employee attitude/opinion survey** A systematic method of determining what employees think of their organization.

An employee survey typically seeks to learn what employees think about working conditions, supervision, human resource policies, and other organizational issues. New programs or special concerns to management also may be a source of questions. The resulting information can be used to evaluate specific concerns, such as how individual managers are perceived by their employees.

Attitude/opinion surveys can be a frustrating experience for employees if they do not receive any information on the survey results. Therefore, a summary of the survey results should be provided to employees for their reaction. In addition, employees need to see that the survey findings result in problems being solved. Feedback of the results and action on the problem areas make survey feedback a powerful communication tool.

LO2 Employee Counselling

Counselling is the discussion of a problem with an employee, with the general objective of helping that employee resolve the issue or cope with the situation so that he or she can become more effective both at work and away from the workplace:

> **counselling** The discussion of a problem with an employee, with the general objective of helping that employee resolve the issue or cope with the situation so that he or she can become more effective.

> One company has a program available to employees and their families that covers both personal and

work-related problems. The company maintains a 24-hour hotline and uses both company counsellors and community agencies. The service is strictly confidential. An average of 750 employees use the service each month. Many successes have been reported, although the program is unable to solve every employee problem. A study of alcoholic employees reported a remarkable 85 percent reduction in lost work hours, a 47 percent reduction in sick leave, and a 72 percent reduction in sickness and accident benefit payments. In a survey, 93 percent of the employees reported that they believe that counselling is a worthwhile service.

Some firms advise managers to avoid giving personal advice to employees that is not related to the job because the managers are not professionally qualified to do so. There is a chance that they will give inappropriate or wrong advice that aggravates an employee's problem. A growing number of organizations have formal arrangements with outside professional counselling agencies to help their employees.

Employee Assistance Programs

Organizations may establish an employee assistance program (EAP) to assist employees with personal problems (such as family or marital difficulties, substance abuse, or stress) that may be affecting their performance at work.

While a number of employees may prefer a face-to-face meeting with an EAP counsellor, there is a substantial growth in digital EAPs (such as chat messaging, e-counselling, video counselling, and mobile apps). Privacy, security, and quality issues are obviously important, but digital EAPs allow workers to get assistance around the clock from local and remote locations.[52] However, online services are not appropriate for every case; rather, they represent one of a number of alternative approaches to providing EAP services.

LO3 Employee Discipline

Even after counselling, there are instances where an employee's behaviour remains inappropriately disruptive or performance is unacceptable. Under these circumstances, discipline is needed. **Discipline** is management action to encourage compliance with organization standards. It is a type of action that seeks to inform employees about organizational expectations and change worker attitudes and behaviour.

> **discipline** Management action to encourage compliance with organization standards.

There are two types of discipline: preventive and corrective.

Preventive Discipline

Preventive discipline is action taken prior to an infraction to encourage employees to follow standards and rules. The basic objective is to encourage self-discipline among employees. In this way, employees maintain their own discipline, rather than having management impose it.

> **preventive discipline** Action taken prior to an infraction to encourage employees to follow standards and rules.

Management has the responsibility for building a climate of preventive discipline. If employees do not know what standards are expected, their conduct is likely to be erratic or misdirected. Employees will better support standards that they have helped to create.

The human resource department has a major responsibility for preventive discipline. For example, it develops programs to manage absenteeism and employee grievances. It communicates standards to employees and encourages employees to follow them. It also provides training programs to explain the reasons behind standards and to build a positive spirit of self-discipline.

Corrective Discipline

Corrective discipline is an action that follows a rule infraction. It seeks to discourage further infractions so that future acts are in compliance with standards. Typically the corrective action is a penalty of some type and is called a *disciplinary action.* Examples are a warning or suspension without pay. The objectives of disciplinary action are as follows:

> **corrective discipline** Discipline that follows a rule infraction.

- To reform the offender
- To deter others from similar actions
- To maintain consistent, effective group standards

The objectives of disciplinary action are positive, educational, and corrective. The goal is to improve the future rather than punish past acts. The corrective disciplinary interview often follows a "sandwich model," which means that a corrective comment is sandwiched between two positive comments in order to make the corrective comment more acceptable. An example: "Your attendance is excellent, Jason (a positive comment), but your late return from coffee breaks disrupts our repair operations (negative). Otherwise, your work is among the best in our department (positive)." The supervisor then focuses on ways in which the two of them can work together to correct the problem. However, corrective discipline is frequently not used or not used properly. Many managers receive little or no training in addressing employee discipline or in the consequences if the disciplinary process is not managed effectively.

Restrictions on Discipline

The ability to discipline may be restricted by union contracts and government legislation. Corrective discipline is an especially sensitive subject with unions, who may see it as an area where employees need protection from unreasonable management authority. In addition, the union wants to show employees that the union leadership cares for their interests.

Government legislation makes it illegal for an employer to discipline a worker who is asserting rights protected by law. For example, an employee cannot be disciplined or dismissed for union activities (the right to participate in union activities is protected under labour relations statutes) or for refusing to perform work that is hazardous, unsafe, or unlawful. Other employment restrictions may also apply, depending on the circumstances and the laws of the provinces concerned.

Due process for discipline may be required of the employer by courts of law, arbitrators, and labour unions. **Due process** means that established rules and procedures for disciplinary action need to be followed and that employees are provided an opportunity to respond to allegations or complaints made against them.[53] It is the human resource department's responsibility to ensure that all parties in a disciplinary action follow the proper rules and procedures so that due process will be used.

> **due process** In a disciplinary situation, following proper, established rules and procedures and giving employees the opportunity to respond to allegations.

If a disciplinary action is challenged, the human resource department must have sufficient documentation to support the action; therefore, human resource policy should require proper documentation for all employer disciplinary actions.

Proper documentation should be specific, beginning with the date, time, and location of an incident. It should also describe the nature of the undesirable performance or behaviour and how it relates to job and organizational performance. Specific rules and regulations that relate to the incident must be identified. Documentation should include what the manager said to the employee and how the employee responded, including specific words and actions. If there were witnesses, they should be identified. All documentation must be recorded promptly, when the incident is still fresh in the memories of the parties. The evidence recorded should be objective, that is, based on observations, not on impressions.

A useful guide for corrective discipline is the **hot-stove rule**. The hot-stove rule states that disciplinary action should have the same characteristics as the penalty a person receives from

> **hot-stove rule** The principle that disciplinary action should be like what happens when you touch a hot stove: It is with warning, immediate, consistent, and impersonal.

touching a hot stove: Discipline should be with warning, immediate, consistent, and impersonal.

Progressive Discipline

Most employers apply a policy of **progressive discipline**, which means that there are stronger penalties for repeated offences. The purpose of this is to give an employee an opportunity to take corrective action before more serious penalties are applied. Progressive discipline also gives management time to work with an employee to help correct infractions:

> **progressive discipline** The use of stronger and stronger penalties for repeated offences.

> When Margaret Stoner had two unauthorized absences, the human resource department provided counselling. It also arranged for her to join a ride pool that allowed her to leave home 30 minutes later than with public transportation. Eventually, her unauthorized absences stopped.

A typical progressive discipline system is shown in Figure 11-2. The first infraction leads to a verbal reprimand by the supervisor. The next infraction leads to a written reprimand, with a record placed in the file. Further infractions result in stronger discipline, leading finally to discharge. Usually, the human resource department becomes involved at the third step or earlier to ensure that company policy is applied consistently in all departments.

It is essential that employers document efforts made to help employees. One possible program involves four steps:

1. Clearly indicate in writing the nature of the problem and the impact of the employee's performance or conduct on the organization.

2. Provide the employee with a clear and unequivocal warning that failure to improve behaviour will result in discipline (up to and including termination).

FIGURE 11-2

A Progressive Discipline System

1. Verbal reprimand by supervisor
2. Written reprimand, with a record in file
3. One- to three-day suspension from work
4. Suspension for one week or longer
5. Discharge for cause

3. Establish through progressive discipline that the employee's performance was still unacceptable despite repeated warnings.

4. Demonstrate that discipline was applied in a fair and consistent manner.[54]

Some progressive systems allow minor offences to be removed from the employee's record after a period of time (typically between one and five years). However, serious offences, such as fighting or theft, are usually not dealt with by means of progressive discipline. An employee who commits these offences may be discharged on the first offence.

In some organizations, lawyers play an important role in the disciplinary process while in others they are consulted after a problem arises. More than one-quarter of HR professionals view their lawyer or legal team as a strategic partner while 46 percent use lawyers only for transactional assistance. A *Canadian HR Reporter* survey indicated that lawyers are most likely to be consulted for certain issues, such as terminations (87 percent), wrongful dismissal lawsuits (40 percent), employment contracts and hiring (37 percent), accommodation and return to work (32 percent), and harassment claims (31 percent).[55]

Positive Discipline

Instead of using punishment to discipline employees, some organizations employ an approach called *positive discipline,* which involves an acceptance on the part of the employee that a problem exists, an acknowledgement by the employee that he or she must assume responsibility for the behaviour, and the use of a problem-solving approach to resolve the problem. The key steps in using positive discipline are as follows:

1. Focus on the specific problem rather than on the employee's attitude or personality.

2. Gain agreement with the employee that a performance problem exists and that the employee is responsible for changing his or her behaviour.

3. Approach discipline as a problem-solving process.

4. Document suggested changes or commitments by the employee.

5. Follow up to ensure that the employee is living up to his or her commitments and to reduce the likelihood of having to take more severe action.[56]

Dismissal

The ultimate disciplinary action is dismissal, which is separation from the employer. Michael Wilson, former CEO of Agrium (now Nutrien) notes the following:

"Building a new culture also means you get rid of people who aren't prepared to accept best practices and move toward that. You cannot afford to have a naysayer on the team. If someone's not in support, you have to take them out of the company."[57]

A nonunion employer who does not have just cause for dismissing an employee may be sued for **wrongful dismissal**. Consider the experience of one small business:

> **wrongful dismissal**
> The termination of an employee without just cause or without giving the employee reasonable notice or compensation in lieu of notice.

The owner of a small business with 18 employees terminated a manager who had been with the firm for 22 years. Although there was no documented evidence to support his claim, the owner said that the manager's performance had been slipping over the past few years. Shortly after being released, the employee contacted an employment lawyer and the parties settled out of court for in excess of $100,000. The business owner had never heard of the law of wrongful dismissal, and the settlement put the business in jeopardy.

The law of wrongful dismissal is very complicated, and human resource professionals without considerable expertise in this area are advised to seek prudent legal advice. Note that the dismissal of unionized employees (slightly less than 30 percent of the nonagricultural workforce) is governed by the provisions of the collective agreement, and the remedy exists with the grievance arbitration process (see Chapter 13). Save for a few exceptions, an employer can terminate a nonunion employee at any time if just cause exists; however, in the absence of just cause, the employer is usually obligated to give the former employee "reasonable notice" or compensation in lieu of notice.

All provinces and the federal jurisdiction have employment standards legislation providing minimum periods of notice for employees terminated without cause. The amount of advance notice an employer is required to give an individual is dependent on the employee's length of service with the employer, and some jurisdictions have specific notice periods that apply if the employer engages in a mass layoff or termination. However, the provisions under employment standards legislation are statutory *minimums,* and the amount of reasonable notice awarded by the courts frequently exceeds such provisions.

> One human resource manager indicated that the company's practice was to provide the minimum notice provisions under employment standards legislation if terminating an employee. The reason for this approach was simply that the manager was uninformed about the law of wrongful dismissal.

Three jurisdictions (federal, Quebec, and Nova Scotia) provide an alternative forum for some wrongfully dismissed employees meeting specified period of service requirements (ten years in Nova Scotia, five years in Quebec, and one year for the federal jurisdiction). While the provisions of the statutes vary, the thrust of the legislation is to permit employees to bring their cases to an adjudication process in which the adjudicator may order reinstatement and damages if sufficient cause for dismissal does not exist. The specifics of the legislation are quite detailed, and legal assistance is advised.

Determining Just Cause

Cause for dismissal under common law includes any act by the employee that could have serious negative effects on the operation or reputation of the organization. This typically includes incompetence and employee misconduct (such as fraud, drunkenness, dishonesty, insubordination, or refusal to obey reasonable orders). The onus for proving the existence of **just cause** is on the employer.[58] Ideally, there is a carefully planned termination interview to ensure that the separation is as positive and constructive as possible—the Supreme Court of Canada has ruled that an employer must act in a way that demonstrates good faith and fair dealing in the dismissal of employees.[59]

> **just cause** Legal grounds for termination, such as employee misconduct or incompetence.

While an employer may terminate an employee at any time if just cause exists, the courts' interpretation of what constitutes just cause for dismissal is often much different from managers' perceptions of cause. Although employers argued just cause for dismissal in 44 percent of wrongful dismissal cases over a 15-year period, the court found that just cause existed in only 37 percent of the decisions—in other words, while employers often believe just cause was present, this belief is frequently not supported by the courts.[60] However, some recent decisions suggest that the pendulum has swung back toward the employer side.[61] Note that in many instances, cases are settled out of court:

> An executive of the Nova Scotia Liquor Corporation was terminated after eight months of service. The employer asserted that the individual did not fit in and failed to get along with other executives. The former employee was given a severance package that included six months' pay and a bonus (for a total compensation package of $62,000).[62]

When considering federally regulated employees, the Supreme Court of Canada in *Wilson v. Atomic Energy of Canada* held that there is an onus on employers to provide reasons why dismissal is appropriate and that employment contracts giving the employer the right to terminate without just cause are unenforceable. In addition, even if an employee is provided with notice and given severance, this will not prevent the individual from claiming unjust dismissal under the *Canada Labour Code*.[63]

Incompetent Work Performance

When considering dismissal on the basis of incompetence, the employment contract contains an implied warranty that the employee is "reasonably competent" and able to perform the work for which the person was hired. If the employee proves to be incompetent, the employer may dismiss the employee on the basis of just cause.

However, employers and the courts often differ in their assessment with respect to cause involving dismissal for incompetence. Employers were able to establish employee incompetence in less than 25 percent of the cases in which they argued just cause for termination on the basis of incompetence—establishing cause on the grounds of incompetence is not easy (see Figure 11-3).

> Kathleen Fisher, who had worked at Lakeland Mills Ltd. for 18 years, informed company president Keith

---

FIGURE 11-3

Requirements in Dismissing an Incompetent Employee

1. The employer must provide reasonable, objective standards of performance in a clear and understandable manner.

2. The employee must fail to meet those standards.

3. The employer must have given the employee a clear and unequivocal warning that she or he has failed to meet the standards, including particulars to the specific deficiency.

4. The warning must clearly indicate the employee will be dismissed if she or he fails to meet the requisite standards.

SOURCE: Andrew Treash (2011, September 26), "Terminating underperforming employees a delicate act," *Canadian HR Reporter*, p. 26. Reprinted by permission of Canadian HR Reporter. © Copyright Thomson Reuters Canada Ltd. (2015), Toronto, Ontario, 1-800-387-5164. http://www.hrreporter.com

Anderson of her intention to stay with the company upon turning 65 years of age. Anderson responded, "You can stay with our company for as long as you wish." A year later, the office manager wanted to replace Fisher with someone who was more versatile. In addition to her accounting position, Fisher was asked to back up the shipping clerk—the job required certain computer skills that Fisher did not have, but she expressed a desire to acquire the necessary skills. The company then argued that her performance was not up to standards and that it was going to hire someone to take over part of her accounting work unless she retired. Fisher resigned and sued for constructive dismissal. The BC Court agreed that Fisher was wrongfully dismissed and awarded her 10 months' severance with bonus and benefits.[64]

The employer must establish *real* incompetence, an inability to carry out job duties, or substandard work performance that fails to improve even after the employee has been put on notice that his or her performance is not adequate. Performance standards must be nondiscriminatory, reasonable, and applied fairly, while warnings must clearly describe what constitutes acceptable performance and what specific actions the employee should take to improve performance. Merely giving an employee average or substandard ratings is not enough. Also, the employer should make it clear to the employee that his or her job is at risk if performance does not improve. A single incident of incompetence will rarely justify dismissal, especially if the incident is a single blemish on an otherwise clean work record.

Employee Misconduct

The courts have repeatedly found that an allegation of employee misconduct must be decided with reference to the unique factors of each case. Four classes of misconduct identified in the case law include (1) unfaithful service to the employer; (2) misconduct of a general nature; (3) theft, fraud, or dishonesty; and (4) willful disobedience of a reasonable and lawful order.

Acts of unfaithful service, such as conspiracy and competition against the employer or serious conflict of interest, are generally regarded as being in that class of misconduct justifying immediate dismissal. The employer's case is relatively straightforward when there is an intent on the part of the employee to commit an act of unfaithful service and the threat of loss to the employer is real.

What about cases involving drug or alcohol abuse; abuse of co-workers, clients, or customers; or improper activity outside the workplace? In determining whether the misconduct is sufficient to justify dismissal, the courts consider both the nature of the misconduct and the employee's position within the organization. A serious act of misconduct may justify immediate discharge. In addition, employees in senior management or in positions of trust (such as a teacher) may be held to higher standards of conduct regarding misconduct both at and away from the workplace.

> Consider the following case and decide if there is cause for dismissal. The case involved two Research in Motion (now BlackBerry) vice-presidents who became drunk and disorderly on an Air Canada flight from Beijing to Toronto. Their behaviour became so bad that flight attendants and passengers had to subdue the two men, one of whom even chewed through his plastic handcuffs. The men received suspended sentences, one year probation, and a requirement that each pay about $35,000 to Air Canada. In this case, RIM fired the two executives.[65]

Theft, fraud, and dishonesty are among the most serious grounds for dismissal because they call into question the honesty and integrity of the employee. Depending on the circumstances, a single isolated act of theft, dishonesty, or fraud may justify dismissal, but the court carefully reviews any explanation for the employee's behaviour. Employers may be justified in worrying about employee theft and fraud:

> A survey of almost 3,500 employees in the United States, United Kingdom, and Australia revealed that 22 percent of American, 29 percent of Australian, and 48 percent of British workers with access to employer or client confidential data would feel comfortable doing something (intentionally or accidentally) with that data, and 10 percent of American, 12 percent of Australian, and 27 percent of British workers reported that they would be willing to forward the data to a nonemployee.[66]

Willful disobedience (which may include absenteeism, tardiness, or a breach of rules or policy) is considered to constitute a repudiation of the employment contract. An employee who refuses to obey the lawful and reasonable order of the employer is in breach of the employment contract. However, disobedience must be seen to be willful or deliberate; petty disagreements and personality conflicts usually do not amount to cause. Furthermore, a reasonable excuse for disobedience will negate the intent required for cause.[67]

A survey on employee misconduct by ClearView revealed that 42 percent of Canadian workers have witnessed incidents of misconduct. Among the violations were misuse of company property (28 percent); harm to other employees (25 percent); privacy violations (17 percent); fraud (17 percent); conflict of interest (13 percent); environmental violations (12 percent); and bribery, corruption, or both (9 percent). However, 48 percent of employees witnessing misconduct did not report it due to such reasons as a lack of faith that an investigation would be conducted properly (69 percent), a perception that disciplinary measures would not be consistently applied (66 percent), or a fear of retaliation or negative consequences (23 percent).[68]

Business or Economic Reasons

Contrary to the impressions of many managers, courts have consistently held that terminating an employee because of business or economic factors is not just cause for dismissal because such factors are not related to the employee's behaviour. It is critical that employers seeking to dismiss employees due to declining demand or as a result of an organizational downsizing ensure that terminated employees are provided with reasonable notice or appropriate compensation. It is advisable to seek legal assistance to review the process and compensation or severance package offered to terminated employees.

Constructive Dismissal

Rather than terminate an employee, an employer may decide to change the individual's job in such a way that the employee decides to quit. A major change in the employment terms that results in an employee's resigning may be considered as **constructive dismissal**. Some examples of constructive dismissal include a significant change in job function, a demotion, a demand for an employee's resignation, or a forced transfer.[69] The law relating to constructive dismissal is technical in nature, and human resource professionals are advised to seek legal advice prior to changing a major term of an employment contract. Consider the case of a manager at Sobeys:

> Debbie Gillis, a 47-year-old food experience manager, started with the company as a teenage cashier and worked her way up to a management position at head office. As part of a restructuring, her position was eliminated, but the company made it clear that it wanted to retain her as an employee and presented her with two job alternatives—an assistant store manager position or a demo-coordinator. Both positions paid less money than her original job, but the company agreed, for the first year, to pay a lump sum equal to the salary differential and maintain her current vacation and benefits. Gillis believed that both positions represented a demotion and, after coming to work for part of a day, went home and did not return. She sued for constructive dismissal. The court held that while the demo-coordinator position represented a demotion, the assistant store manager job did not as it involved working with more employees, more responsibilities, and a competitive but lower salary. Even though the salary was lower, the opportunities for further advancement were strong and the court held that Gillis had not been constructively dismissed.[70]

In its 2015 decision in *Potter v. New Brunswick Legal Aid Services Commission,* the Supreme Court of Canada

constructive dismissal
A major change in the terms of the employment contract that results in an employee's resigning.

identified two branches of constructive dismissal (a single act by the employer that breaches an essential term of the contract or a series of acts that, in combination, show that the employer no longer wants to be bound by the employment contract). The court made it clear that an administrative suspension cannot be justified if there is no basic communication with the employee or no reason for suspension is given. The court also underscored the importance of an employer's acting in good faith in dealing with an employee and that this requires being honest, forthright, candid, and reasonable.[71]

Reasonable Notice

An employer that does not have just cause for dismissal must provide a dismissed employee with "reasonable notice" or compensation (typically salary, benefits, and reasonable job search expenses) in lieu of notice. While several managers believe that the organization need only provide the minimum notice period outlined under employment standards legislation, these provisions are only minimums and courts may (and frequently do) award much greater notice periods. Further, establishing just cause at common law does not mean that an employer will also always have sufficient cause under provincial labour or employment standards legislation to avoid providing minimum statutory severance.[72]

The major factors used to predict notice include the following:

- *The former employee's age, length of service, salary, and occupational status:* On average, older employees, long-service employees, more highly paid employees, and employees occupying more senior positions in the organization tend to receive higher periods of notice. However, the character of employment variable (an employee's position and responsibilities) has come under criticism in recent case law.

- *An attempt to mitigate losses:* Employees who are terminated must make reasonable efforts to find similar alternative employment.

- *A less favourable labour market:* When alternative employment opportunities are limited, courts tend to award greater notice periods.

While each case is settled based on its own particular facts, some guidelines relating to wrongful dismissal have been developed. However, these are only guidelines to provide some guidance to students relating to wrongful dismissal awards. Based on the guidelines, an employee in a clerical/blue-collar position will receive about two weeks' notice (or compensation in lieu of notice) for each year of service; an employee in a supervisory or lower-level management position will receive three weeks' notice (or compensation) for each year of service; and senior management and professional employees will receive one month's notice (or compensation) for each year of service. In the past, it has been rare (but not unheard of) for notice periods to exceed 24 months.[73]

The law firm of Samfiru Tumarkin has developed an app (see https://www.severancepaycalculator.com/) to calculate severance pay. The app looks at factors such as an employee's union status, age, salary, length of service, and type of job to give an estimate of severance.

Do employees have to give notice? Although labour standards legislation may require an employee to provide notice of resignation, the period is typically a week or two. However, if any employee fails to provide reasonable notice of resignation (or the notice provided in the employment contract), the employer may sue for damages (such as lost business or costs of recruiting another employee) arising from the contractual breach.[74] Consider the following case:

> Sebastien Marineau-Mes, an executive with BlackBerry, signed a contract with the company. Among the terms of the agreement was a provision providing for the right to resign at any time upon providing six months' prior written notice and the obligation to provide active service during the notice period. Marineau-Mes wasn't happy at BlackBerry and decided to join Apple without giving the six months' notice. An Ontario court held that the notice period was reasonable and the contract was binding, thus requiring Marineau-Mes to satisfy the terms of the agreement.[75]

An employer has the right to provide "working notice" and have employees continue working during the notice period. The Target withdrawal from Canada included a minimum of 16 weeks' compensation to employees. However, the company had employees continue working for at least some of the notice period and then receive payment from a $70 million trust fund as a top-up or pay in lieu of notice. An employee refusing to work would have been viewed as having resigned and would not have been entitled to additional compensation. Having employees work during the notice period may be cost effective but often results in lower morale, reduced productivity, and sometimes even sabotage.[76]

The "Wallace Effect"

The 1997 decision of the Supreme Court of Canada in *Wallace v. United Grain Growers* has led to the awarding of extended periods of notice in a number of wrongful dismissal cases in which the employer was found to have terminated an employee in bad faith. In the *Wallace* case, the court ruled that the employer had dismissed Wallace in "bad faith" and thus added an additional 9 months onto a reasonable notice award of 15 months. However, as MacKillop, Nieuland, and Ferris-Miles observe, the trend in recent decisions has been to close the floodgates relating to punitive damage claims.[77]

In the *Honda Canada v. Keays* case, the Supreme Court of Canada addressed the issue of *Wallace* damages. Employment lawyer Stuart Rudner noted the following:

> The Supreme Court of Canada completely revamped the manner in which bad-faith damages are calculated. The court replaced the notice extension with a compensatory approach that appears to require the employee to prove not only that the employer acted in bad faith but that the employee actually suffered damages as a result. The court also determined that punitive damages are restricted to advertent wrongful acts that are so malicious and outrageous that they are deserving of punishment on their own.[78]

Managing the Dismissal

There are several guidelines to follow in dismissing an employee:

- Prepare for the interview and conduct a rehearsal.
- Conduct the interview in private.
- Consider the dismissal process from the employee's perspective and ask, "How would I like to be treated in such a situation?"
- Get to the point. Some experts suggest that you convey the message of termination within the first few sentences.
- Select the time and place. Experts often suggest a meeting in the morning and during the middle of the week.
- Have any necessary information ready (such as a severance package and outplacement counselling assistance).
- Notify others in the organization and ensure that the individual's duties are covered.
- In some instances, special security arrangements may be necessary.
- Discuss the process with other colleagues who have had to terminate employees.[79]

For an example of how *not* to dismiss an employee, consider the following case:

> Gail Galea joined Walmart Canada in 2002 as a district-manager-in-training and was ultimately promoted to vice-president of General Merchandising. In 2010, Galea was removed from her role and given different responsibilities and one month later was transferred from the senior management team to a supporting position. Later in the year, her performance was rated lower so that she was not eligible for promotion, her personal effects were moved to another office, and in November 2010 she was offered either a position below her experience or a

severance package. Ten days later, she was terminated, and 11 months later her benefits were cut off (even though she had signed a noncompete agreement assuring her of two years severance if she was dismissed without just cause). Galea sued Walmart for the remaining severance and punitive and moral damages. The Ontario Superior Court awarded her more than $1.6 million, including $750,000 in moral and punitive damages. According to Galea's lawyer Natalie MacDonald, "This is about how not to dismiss an employee. This is about how not to embarrass and humiliate an employee, and how an organization must conduct itself throughout as appropriate."[80]

Should employers specify a notice period in employment contracts? As lawyer Tim Mitchell points out, this practice is not without its dangers and any attempt to limit the notice period to statutory minimum periods outlined in employment or labour standards legislation must be based on clear and unambiguous language. According to Mitchell, it is essential to recognize "the importance of careful drafting in an employment contract and the importance of reviewing the contract periodically, particularly where some change has occurred. The providing of a specific notice entitlement is a dangerous practice based on the jurisprudence."[81]

What should an employer do when terminating an employee who may be potentially violent? Among the suggestions are trying to identify the high-risk worker (What are the common characteristics of such individuals? Are there warning signs?), protecting the organization and employees during and after the termination, protecting the intellectual property of the employer, and tracking or monitoring the social media and communication activities of the former employee immediately after the dismissal.[82]

What if an employee reveals terms of a confidential settlement? In a recent decision, the Ontario Divisional Court upheld a decision of an arbitrator who had ordered Jan Wong, a former reporter with *The Globe and Mail,* to pay back a settlement of $209,912 to the paper after she disclosed some of the confidential terms of the settlement in a book. Ms. Wong wrote about her experiences in her 2012 memoir but the court did not support her argument that it was acceptable to discuss the settlement as long as she did not reveal the actual settlement amount.[83]

Employee Rights

Employee rights refer to those rights desired by employees relating to working conditions and job security. Some of these rights are protected under law, others under the collective agreement with the union (if one exists), and yet others may be listed in the letter of appointment given to the employee at the time of hiring. Regardless of whether these rights are recorded in writing or currently protected by law and agreements, they have a significant impact on the human resource management activities of an organization. Progressive human resource managers recognize this and strive to provide fair and equitable working conditions that help the employee to maintain dignity on the job. Would you be willing to have a computer chip implanted in your body? Consider the following:

Three Market Square, a Wisconsin technology company, is giving employees the opportunity to have a chip about the size of a grain of rice injected between their thumb and index finger. The majority of workers have volunteered to have the chip implanted and will be able to do any task using RFID technology, such as paying for food in the cafeteria or swiping to enter a building, by simply waving their hand. The company says the chip does not have GPS tracking ability but security experts worry about issues such as hacking or using the data for more invasive purposes, such as monitoring employee breaks.[84]

Are employees becoming more litigious? What are the implications for human resource professionals? A *Canadian HR Reporter* survey revealed that 84 percent of 533 participants believe that competence in dealing with litigation has become somewhat or much more important for HR professionals in the past five years. About 70 percent of respondents perceived that employees are becoming somewhat or much more litigious compared to five years ago, and almost 69 percent believe that when in court, the playing field is slanted in favour of the employee. The issues that are most problematic include wrongful dismissal (68 percent), termination and severance pay (58 percent), human rights issues (54 percent), and reasonable accommodation (31 percent). As Robert Smith, managing partner of Injury Management Solutions, observes, once a legal action has started, it is imperative that HR gather witness statements and all of the appropriate documentation as soon as possible—the longer the delay, the less likely HR will get the true story.[85]

Right to Privacy

Employer concerns about employee privacy rights mean that many employers are careful to collect only job-related information at the point of hiring. There is an increasing realization among employers that collecting nonwork information is an unnecessary intrusion into the private lives of job applicants. Even when such additional information is not considered illegal, many employers feel that such an action constitutes a moral violation of workers' rights.

In Saanich, British Columbia, the privacy commissioner, Elizabeth Denman, ruled that employees' privacy rights were violated when the organization installed employee monitoring software. The mayor of Saanich, Richard Atwell, initiated the complaint and refused to use his work computer until the

Spotlight *on* HRM

You're Fired

"You're fired." Real estate tycoon and current United States president Donald Trump used the catch phrase when he hosted *The Apprentice,* a reality show where individuals competed for the ultimate prize of being Trump's apprentice.

Contestants were put into teams. Winners received a prize while the losers earned a trip to the boardroom to explain why they had lost. Every week, at least one person was "fired."

In Trump's termination process, he and two of his advisors confronted the contestants, pummelling each of them with questions about their performance. He sent the contestants out while he deliberated about who would be terminated. The contestants returned to the boardroom where he handed down his decision, listing all of the reasons why he was about to terminate one of them. The drama and the tension built until he made his final choice.

While this made for good television, it is not a great way to terminate someone's employment. If employers in Canada were to adopt Trump's method, they would undoubtedly be on the hook for significant damages. Trump's television terminations were often insensitive and callous, making the employee's firing much more difficult than it needed to be.

Trump's 10 Biggest Termination Mistakes

In the course of his terminations, Trump committed a number of serious mistakes. Here's a look at 10 of the most serious errors Trump made that should never be emulated in a Canadian workplace:

- The person being terminated is brought into a boardroom where she is with her peers and is terminated in front of her peers, not in private with Trump.

- She is terminated not only in front of her peers, but also with two of Trump's advisors watching, thereby creating a firing-squad-like atmosphere, rather than simply being in front of one advisor and Trump.

- Prior to the termination, all of the team members know that one of the select group being pulled into the boardroom will be terminated, instead of the termination being kept confidential among only senior management.

- The person being terminated is advised of all the things she did wrong but is never given a warning and the chance to correct the behaviour before being fired.

- She is terminated for cause where there is likely no legal cause for her termination.

- She is not provided with what she is entitled to under applicable employment standards legislation.

- She is terminated without reasonable notice of the termination or compensation in lieu of notice pursuant to the employer's obligation under the common law.

- She is not provided with a letter of reference, outplacement counselling, or anything that will assist her in the transition to new employment.

- She may have been enticed to leave secure employment to be "employed" with Trump, which would increase Trump's liability when firing her.

- An employee terminated in this manner would likely be entitled to significant Wallace damages. That's because she was ostracized in front of her peers and Trump's advisors, terminated with cause when there was no cause, and made to feel worthless. This is exactly what the Supreme Court of Canada warned against in its decision in *Wallace v. United Grain Growers Ltd.*

If any of the contestants on *The Apprentice* had been actual employees and had sued for wrongful dismissal, it is likely that each would be successful in a claim for *Wallace* damages. A court would likely not hesitate in lengthening the notice period because of Trump's actions. In fact, a firing handled like Trump's television ones may even result in a successful claim for mental distress damages.

(Continued)

Steps Employers Should Take

To avoid creating a scenario like the ones in Trump's boardroom on *The Apprentice,* it is recommended that employers do the following:

- *Keep the termination confidential:* Ensure the termination is known only to those terminating the employee or those involved in the decision.

- *Keep the termination small:* Bring the person being terminated into a room without anyone else except another senior manager as a witness. Never terminate someone in front of her colleagues.

- *Do not allege cause:* If an employer does not have cause, it should not allege it.

- *Do not list:* Don't get into a long list of what the employee has already done wrong.

- *Have a severance package ready:* Have a package ready for the employee, including provision of entitlements pursuant to employment standards legislation and under the common law.

- *Provide transitional assistance:* If the employee is not terminated for cause, consider providing transitional assistance to find another job, including a letter of reference and outplacement counselling.

- *Know the person's employment history:* The employer should have accounted for this person's particular circumstances, especially what happened before she was hired. If the employee was lured away from secure employment, take that into account.

- *Be sensitive:* Being fired is one of the most difficult things for an individual to hear and it is usually a major blow to self-esteem. Those doing the firing should remember the golden rule and treat the worker as they would want to be treated in a similar circumstance.

The Apprentice was only a television show, but if Trump's methods are emulated by employers, it will cause them significant grief. When terminating someone's employment, all the employer has to do is act in good faith and not make the termination more difficult than need be.

SOURCE: Adapted from Natalie C. MacDonald (2005, January 31), "Great television doesn't translate into great policy," *Canadian HR Reporter,* pp. R4 and R9. Reprinted by permission of Canadian HR Reporter. © Copyright Thomson Reuters Canada Ltd. (2018), Toronto, Ontario, 1-800-387-5164. http://www.hrreporter.com.

---

software was removed. According to Denman, "The district can only collect personal information that is directly related to and necessary for the protection of the IT systems. An employee's every stroke and email, or screen captures of computing activities at 30-second intervals clearly exceeds that purpose and is not authorized by privacy law."[86]

A number of recent high-profile cases have demonstrated that the lines between workplace and private rights are blurring and conduct away from the workplace may lead to discipline or dismissal. The Supreme Court of Canada, in *Bhasin v. Hrynew,* imposed an obligation on both employers and employees to deal with each other honestly and in good faith. As lawyer David Whitten notes, "Employees should always be mindful that comments and postings on the Internet are permanent and publicly accessible. Therefore, they really need to consider whether the content they post is appropriate by asking 'would an employer care?'"[87]

The *Personal Information Protection and Electronic Documents Act* (PIPEDA) came into force in January 2004 in every province without its own privacy legislation. The aims of the legislation include requiring organizations to hold personal information about individuals in a responsible manner, permitting individuals to access and correct personal information, and allowing individuals control over the handling of information about them (see Figure 11-4).

What is personal information? As defined in PIPEDA, personal information is "factual information, recorded or not, about an individual." Under PIPEDA and provincial privacy legislation, information should be kept only as long as required for the purpose for which it was intended. The main problems with information security often revolve around security expertise and responsibility for security, poor enforcement of policies and procedures, outdated security software, and poor hiring (about 70 percent of identity theft occurs at the workplace).

The privacy commissioner held that Health Canada violated privacy laws by disclosing personal health information of more than 40,000 Canadians. In November of 2013, Health Canada sent notices in oversized envelopes to individuals outlining changes to the Marijuana Medical Access Plan (MMAP). The return address included the words "Health

FIGURE 11-4

The 10 Principles of the *Personal Information Protection and Electronic Documents Act*

Principle 1: Accountability

An organization is responsible for personal information under its control and shall designate an individual or individuals who are accountable for the organization's compliance with the following principles.

Principle 2: Identifying Purposes

The purposes for which personal information is collected shall be identified by the organization at or before the time the information is collected.

Principle 3: Consent

The knowledge and consent of the individual are required for the collection, use, or disclosure of personal information, except where inappropriate.

Principle 4: Limiting Collection

The collection of personal information shall be limited to that which is necessary for the purposes identified by the organization. Information shall be collected by fair and lawful means.

Principle 5: Limiting Use, Disclosure, and Retention

Personal information shall not be used or disclosed for purposes other than those for which it was collected, except with the consent of the individual or as required by law. Personal information shall be retained only as long as necessary for the fulfillment of those purposes.

Principle 6: Accuracy

Personal information shall be as accurate, complete, and up-to-date as is necessary for the purposes for which it is to be used.

Principle 7: Safeguards

Personal information shall be protected by security safeguards appropriate to the sensitivity of the information.

Principle 8: Openness

An organization shall make readily available to individuals specific information about its policies and practices relating to the management of personal information.

Principle 9: Individual Access

Upon request, an individual shall be informed of the existence, use, and disclosure of his or her personal information and shall be given access to that information. An individual shall be able to challenge the accuracy and completeness of the information and have it amended as appropriate.

Principle 10: Challenging Compliance

An individual shall be able to address a challenge concerning compliance with the above principles to the designated individual or individuals accountable for the organization's compliance.

SOURCE: Adapted from Office of the Privacy Commissioner of Canada, Privacy Principles, http://www.priv.gc.ca.

Canada—Marijuana Medical Access Plan." More than 300 individuals complained to the privacy commissioner, who concluded that Health Canada had mishandled patients' personal information.[88]

Some Canadian health insurance firms are starting to focus on pharmacogenetics (examining how genetics affect how a person reacts to medication) as an approach to addressing disability and mental illness cases. Although genetic information can be easily obtained from a saliva sample or cheek swab, there are privacy concerns. While the results are confidential and the employee is supposed to have control relating to the use of personal information, genetic information could also reveal other information about the health of an employee, and there is always a fear that the data could be used for other nonapproved purposes.[89]

In an article to celebrate Data Privacy Day (January 28), federal privacy commissioner Daniel Therrien stated that about one-third of the PIPEDA complaints to his office involve small businesses with fewer than 100 employees. In a recent poll, more than 50 percent of participants indicated they would do business with an organization specifically because it does not collect personal data, but only 16 percent perceive that employers take their obligation to protect personal information very seriously. According to Therrien, firms should limit the information they collect to what is necessary for delivering the product or service, and should make it clear why such information is needed (through a privacy policy). The most common complaints involve the use and disclosure of personal information for purposes other than specified or an employee's accessing a person's file without authorization. A survey by Therrien's office revealed that 55 percent of companies do not have a privacy policy and 67 percent do not have policies or procedures designed to assess the privacy implications of new products, services, and technologies.[90]

Privacy in the workplace is becoming an extremely sensitive issue, and HR professionals must be aware of the legal and ethical challenges surrounding it. For example, there is a difference of opinion about an employer's examining an employee's social media activity:

The Maryland Department of Public Safety and Correctional Services recently asked a corrections officer returning to work, after being on a leave of absence due to the death of his mother, to turn over his Facebook username and password as a condition of being reinstated to his job. The department subsequently decided to suspend the practice for 45 days as it looked into the implications of its actions. Similarly, Justin Bassett, during the course of an employment interview, was asked for his Facebook login information when the interviewer couldn't see his private profile when she went to his Facebook page. Bassett refused and decided to withdraw from the job search because he didn't want to work for a company that would track personal employee information. Jurisdictions in the United States and Canada have made it illegal or are considering making it illegal to ask for private employee passwords.[91]

The Supreme Court of Canada is immersed in the privacy debate. The case of *R. v. Cole* involved a charge of possession of child pornography when a computer technician performing maintenance on a teacher's computer found a hidden folder containing nude pictures of an underage female student. The court held that employees may have a reasonable, but limited, expectation of privacy in their work computer, but the court did not specifically address employer monitoring of employee computers. In *R. v. Telus Communications,* the court found that text messages are considered private communications, and in *R. v. Vu,* the court ruled that police must have specific authorization in a search warrant to search data in a computer. These cases are quite complex, and HR professionals are advised to seek legal advice in developing and administering privacy policies at work.[92]

Employers need to balance employee privacy rights with operational requirements. Advice to employers includes that they do the following: (1) communicate to employees what personal information will be collected, used, and disclosed, and for what purposes; (2) disclose to employees the use of any recording or surveillance and that the information can be used for specific purposes, such as safety or discipline; (3) develop a clear, written policy and communicate it to employees if the employer is going to monitor employees. The policy, which should be signed by employees, needs to explain that employees should not have any expectation of privacy and that the information may be used by the employer for performance, conduct, and workplace security monitoring.[93]

Colleen Colwell, a commercial manager with Cornerstone Properties, had been employed with the company for more than seven years when she discovered that a hidden camera had been installed in the ceiling of her office a year earlier. Her boss, VP of Finance Trent Krauel, asserted that the camera was used to detect theft by maintenance staff. Colwell sought medical attention because she felt emotionally violated and psychologically distraught. Krauel insisted he had a legal right to install the camera and did not owe Colwell an apology. Ultimately, Colwell resigned and sued for wrongful dismissal. The court concluded that the secret installation of the camera, Krauel's unwillingness to apologize, his assertion of a right to install the camera without advising Colwell, and his preposterous explanation of the reason for installing the camera made it impossible for Colwell to stay in her job. While employers may have the right to install cameras in the workplace, the right is limited by the need to exercise it in good faith and fair dealing.[94]

Canada introduced anti-spam legislation that came into effect on July 1, 2014, and on January 1, 2015, new rules came into effect that made it illegal to install programs, such as malware, on someone's computer without consent. The definition of spam is "any electronic commercial message sent without the express or implied consent of the recipient." The legislation had major implications for businesses that now needed to obtain consent from members of the public before sending a message. There was concern that the legislation is particularly problematic for small businesses that may be unaware of the legislation and lack the expertise or resources to comply with the law. From an HR perspective, it may be necessary to develop a policy to address the legislation or amend an existing social media policy as well as provide training for employees to make sure that they understand their rights and responsibilities.[95]

Using GPS tracking and surveillance, the City of Hamilton discovered that a group of city workers were visiting coffee shops, having downtime at home, and running personal errands on company time. As a result, 29 employees were dismissed and two were suspended for 30 days. According to lawyer Daniel Michaluk, when it comes to GPS devices, employers have prevailed for the most part. On the other hand, video surveillance can collect more sensitive information, and one-half of the arbitrators in Ontario will ask employers to justify its use. For major investigations, HR rarely handles the issue itself.[96]

The need for training on privacy is critical. The Office of the Privacy Commissioner of Canada, which oversees PIPEDA, asserts that organizations should provide training for both management and front-line workers. Although training should vary depending on the organization, Rick Shields, an Ottawa-based privacy lawyer, suggests that the training should include some background information on privacy, the meaning of key terms and key privacy concepts, the organization's activities with regard to privacy, a review of policies and procedures, introduction to the employer's privacy officer or team, and a highlighting of each person's role and responsibilities relating to privacy.[97]

Right to Fair Treatment

Earlier in this book we saw that an individual's age, race, sex/gender, religion, physical disability, and so on, should not be considered when hiring unless it is a *bona fide job requirement*. As previously noted, an employer has an obligation to make reasonable accommodation to meet employee needs. The right of employees to fair treatment requires that these principles govern the actual work once the applicants are hired. Thus, employees have the right not to be discriminated against in all employment decisions (such as compensation, training, and promotion issues) as well as the right to work in a safe and harassment-free environment. In a split decision, the Supreme Court of Canada held that an Irving Oil policy providing for random alcohol testing of unionized employees in "safety-sensitive positions" is not justified in the absence of evidence that there was a problem with alcohol use at work. The court concluded that Irving was only able to cite eight alcohol-related incidents over a decade-and-a-half; thus, there was insufficient evidence of a serious enough problem to warrant an invasion of union workers' privacy in the absence of consent by the union.[98]

Proactive employers continuously monitor working conditions through employee surveys, open-door policies,

and the presence of grievance committees. They also initiate new programs and policies to meet the changing needs of the workforce. However, not all employers respect employee rights:

Migrant workers in British Columbia are being tracked using wearable devices and scanning stations at the end of fruit and vegetable rows. When a box is full, it is scanned and at lunchtime, the names of workers who are in red are posted on a large screen. If their productivity doesn't improve, they are at risk of being sent back home.[99]

Cannabis Legalization

Not surprisingly, employers are concerned about the workplace implications now that cannabis is legal (as of October 17, 2018). A Health Canada survey showed that 28 percent of Canadians consider smoking marijuana occasionally for nonmedicinal purposes to be socially acceptable. Among employer concerns are a lack of product knowledge, the unavailability of an accurate and reliable test of impairment, and concern over cannabis use by people in safety-sensitive positions.[100]

According to Jason Fleming, director of HR at MedReleaf, it is important to distinguish between recreational and medical cannabis. If an employee requires medical cannabis for treatment, the employer may need to accommodate, using options such as medical leave or an alternative work assignment. As Fleming notes, "No employer will have to tolerate impairment at work." Lawyer Robert Weir believes that there is legal risk in having a blanket, zero-tolerance policy on cannabis use, but the employer has the right to prohibit alcohol and drug use while an employee is working. Similarly, banning employees from coming to work while impaired is fair. Implications for HR professionals include developing a policy on cannabis use, training employees and supervisors on best practices, and seeking the assistance of occupational therapists and legal professionals.[101]

Commentators are suggesting that principles from past legal decisions are applicable to drug and alcohol cases. For instance, in the case of *Stewart v. Elk Valley Coal Company,* the company had a drug and alcohol policy that required employees to disclose any addictions prior to any drug- or alcohol-related incident. In addition, while an employee disclosing an addiction would be provided with treatment, failure to disclose could lead to termination. The employee, who worked in a safety-sensitive position at the mine, failed to disclose an addiction to cocaine, was involved in an accident at work, subsequently tested positive for cocaine, and was dismissed. The Supreme Court of Canada upheld the initial decision of the Alberta Human Rights Tribunal, which concluded that the dismissal was justified because the employee was terminated for being in breach of the company policy and not because of an addiction.[102]

LO7 Employee Involvement

To increase employee productivity and satisfaction, human resource departments often attempt to improve the satisfaction of employees at the workplace. Most of the approaches to employee involvement focus on the increased participation of workers. The quality of an employee's life while at work is affected by many factors, including the quality of supervision, working conditions, pay and benefits, and an interesting and rewarding job:

> A survey conducted during the global financial crisis indicated that 89 percent of employers introduced strategies to try to improve employee morale. What were companies doing? About 49 percent reported increasing the frequency and quality of communication, 28 percent provided additional professional development opportunities, 25 percent gave additional financial rewards, 20 percent enhanced employee recognition programs, and 20 percent conducted additional team-building activities.[103]

Does morale really matter? A Sirota study found that companies with high morale (seventy-fifth percentile or higher) outperformed their competitors by 368 percent with regard to year-over-year stock returns (15.1 percent improvement in stock price for high-morale companies versus 4.1 percent for competitors). Not surprisingly, companies with low morale (below the twenty-fifth percentile) were about 166 percent below their industry counterparts.[104]

A popular method used to improve the quality of work life is employee involvement. *Employee involvement* (EI) consists of a variety of systematic methods that empower employees to participate in the decisions that affect them and their relationship with the organization. Through EI, employees feel a sense of responsibility or even "ownership" of decisions in which they participate. To be successful, however, EI must be more than just a systematic approach; it must become part of the organization's culture and management philosophy.[105] Today, some North American organizations provide employees with considerable involvement in the decision-making process.

EI is based on two important principles. First, individuals tend to support systems or decisions that they helped to make. For example, if an employee was actively involved in developing a new credit collection procedure, then this individual is more likely to ensure that the new procedure is carried out correctly. Second, employees who actually perform a task know more about it than anyone else, including their supervisor. Asking for information from employees who actually perform the job can provide insights not available from their supervisors or outside experts.

A recent report showed a strong link between best practices in human resource management and stronger performance on such outcomes as faster revenue growth and higher stock prices. Some of the best practices included spending significant amounts of time on nurturing talent and leadership, encouraging leaders to support employee engagement, and succession planning. The study also showed a positive relationship between having certified HR professionals and better business performance.[106]

While it has been argued that employee loyalty is an outdated concept (and a recent study by Bain and Company revealed that less than half of employees believe that their organization deserves their loyalty), there is evidence that employee loyalty does matter. The following is from Fred Reichheld, author of *Loyalty Rules:*

> "For the average company, loyalty is dying. Of course, this means that the average company is dying. Employees spend half their waking hours working at a company that they don't really believe in. The key to success is building mutually beneficial relationships, a give and take in which employees are offered opportunities to grow, learn, and make money—but only if they contribute to custom value creation and the bottom line."[107]

Employee Involvement Interventions

A number of different interventions have been used to increase employee involvement and improve overall employee satisfaction at work.

Self-Directed Work Teams or Groups

A common approach to EI is **self-directed work teams or groups**. Self-directed work teams are teams of workers without a formal, company-appointed supervisor who decide among themselves matters traditionally handled by a supervisor. These groups of workers typically decide daily work assignments, the use of job rotation, orientation for new employees, training, and production schedules. Some groups even handle recruitment, selection, and discipline.

> **self-directed work teams or groups** Teams of workers without a formal, employer-appointed supervisor who decide among themselves most matters traditionally handled by a supervisor.

Some observers are critical of the increased focus on innovation and workplace teams. In a number of organizations, managers "stress the system" by speeding up the line, cutting the number of employees or machines, or having workers take on more tasks (at times through "multiskilling"). Under such systems, workers may be required to act like machines. While management by stress may help in raising productivity (at least over the short term), workers often experience considerable personal stress and a sense of being "dehumanized."[108]

How is technology shaping how teams operate? A study of U.S. and Canadian employers revealed that about 23 percent use virtual teams and 57 percent are planning on using more virtual teams (defined as "employees from different functions of an organization distributed across disparate locations and between companies"). About 72 percent of respondents cite cost savings as a major reason for the use of virtual teams. Concerning HR's role, major issues include the need for more training relating to virtual teams, the requirement of additional communication (particularly cross-cultural), and time zone and distance concerns.[109]

High-Involvement Work Practices

There is growing evidence that human resource management practices do matter and are related to organizational performance. In one study, **high-involvement work practices** were related to lower turnover, higher productivity, and improved financial performance. In another study, "low road" practices (such as use of short-term contracts, low levels of training, little commitment to job security, and low levels of HR sophistication) were negatively associated

> **high-involvement work practices** A set of human resource practices aimed at increasing employee performance.

with corporate performance while "high road" practices (characterized by high-commitment human resource management) were strongly related to a high level of organizational performance. The thrust of the work in this area has been away from focusing on any single human resource practice in favour of studying systems or bundles of practices and the strategic impact of human resource management on organizational performance. In addition, a growing number of researchers are examining employee perceptions of high-involvement work systems and the roles that workers play in both low- and high-involvement workplaces.[110]

AON's *Trends in Global Employee Engagement* 2018 study of more than 1,000 companies globally revealed that about 65 percent of employees were engaged (and Canada's score was about 69 percent). About 14 percent of workers worldwide were actively disengaged, and a further 21 percent were passively engaged. The three key drivers (in order) were rewards and recognition, senior leadership, and career opportunities.[111]

What does this mean for human resource management? The human resource function must focus on business-level outcomes and problems, become a strategic core competency with the ability to understand the human capital dimension of the organization's major business priorities, and develop a systems perspective of human resource management.[112] Seven practices of successful organizations are (1) a focus on employment security, (2) selective hiring, (3) self-managed teams and decentralization of accountability and responsibility as basic elements of organizational design, (4) comparatively high compensation contingent on organizational performance, (5) extensive training, (6) the reduction of status differentials, and (7) the sharing of information with employees.[113]

To what extent are Canadian organizations pursuing high-involvement workplace strategies? The results of one study are presented in Figure 11-5. A survey of more

© Stuart O'Sullivan/Getty Images.

Quality circles involve a small group of employee volunteers with a common leader who meet regularly to identify and solve work-related problems. Why the emphasis on volunteers?

than 600 Canadian workplaces found that 50 percent had problem-solving groups, just over one-quarter had a total quality management (or similar) program, and just under 40 percent had training in EI. About 70 percent reported having project teams.

Employee Self-Service

Although employee self-service was a fairly new concept a decade ago, a growing number of organizations are introducing self-service as a means of reducing the amount of administrative work performed by human resource professionals.

Currently, human resource activities that can be addressed by employee self-service have been divided into two groups:[114]

- *Productivity applications.* This includes *management of personal data, retirement plans,* and *health and benefits management.* In addition, productivity applications for managers may include the use of management reports and approval applications. For example, an employee seeking an approval to participate in a training program could request such an approval electronically and the process could be set up to route the request by email to the appropriate manager.

- *Strategic applications.* This includes *online recruitment and skills management applications.* By way of example, there are a growing number of programs designed to increase management productivity and free up time for more strategic initiatives.

While employee self-service applications are becoming more common in larger companies, it is expected that their use will increase noticeably in the next five years.

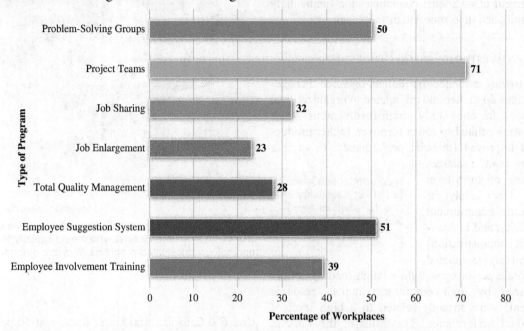

FIGURE 11-5

Employee Involvement Programs in Canadian Organizations

SOURCE: Terry H. Wagar (2009), *Human Resource Management and Workplace Change,* Saint Mary's University.

Spotlight *on* ETHICS

The High-Involvement Workplace Dilemma

Consider the following situation and make a note of your answer on a separate sheet of paper.

You are a human resource management associate at a manufacturing company with just under 800 employees. You report to the human resource manager who, in turn, reports to the vice-president of human resource management. Neither you nor the manager is part of the senior executive team. Your most recent project involves an assessment of whether your organization should incorporate a high-involvement workplace strategy.

A few days ago, the following memo appeared (by mistake) in your email inbox:

All members of the senior executive team:

As you are aware, we are carefully considering the implementation of a high-involvement workplace system. The key to making this project succeed is to get employee buy-in. I have had chats with some other friends in our industry, and the gist of what they are saying

is that if we sell this right, we can really save ourselves on labour costs. One company set up workplace teams and rewarded employees for coming up with labour-saving ideas—nine months later, the firm was able to cut almost 20 percent of the workforce. I figure we can follow a similar approach and will be able to get rid of between 125 and 150 jobs. Of course, we can't let the employees find out about this.

Maggie Pool (Vice-President of Human Resources)

You are unsure what you should do in this situation. On one hand, it is not illegal for a company to reduce the size of its workforce. On the other hand, both you and the human resource manager believe that the organization is interested in considering a high-involvement strategy as a way of increasing employer performance and employee satisfaction (not as a tool for reducing labour costs and cutting jobs).

LO5 Job Security, Downsizing, and Employee Retention

No-Layoff Policies

In the past, loyal, hardworking employees could expect a secure job in return for dedicated work for the organization. However, this is no longer the case and the traditional psychological contract (the unwritten commitments between employers and employees) has been radically rewritten.[115] This new employment relationship has been described as follows:

> You're expendable. We don't want to fire you, but we will if we have to. Competition is brutal, so we must redesign the way we work to do more with less. Sorry, that's just the way it is. And one more thing—you're invaluable. . . . We're depending on you to be innovative, risk-taking, and committed to our goals.[116]

Contrary to the downsizing trend of the 1990s, some organizations are developing no-layoff policies. These firms are using such policies as part of an integrated system of progressive HR practices—the idea is that employees who have job security are more receptive to change, more likely to be innovative and suggest changes that will improve the organization, and are more willing to "go the extra mile."

Organizational Downsizing

In many organizations, lifetime employment has been replaced by job insecurity. To give a few examples that downsizing is by no means a thing of the past, in late 2017, Sears Canada announced that it was closing all of its Canadian stores. As well, a swap of newspapers between Postmedia and Torstar led to the closure of 36 community newspapers. In early 2018, Yellow Pages cut about 500 jobs across the country.[117]

Downsizing may be defined as "a deliberate organizational decision to reduce the workforce that is intended to improve organizational performance."[118] It has also been described as a set of activities undertaken on the part of management and designed to improve organizational efficiency, productivity, and/or competitiveness.[119] It is possible to identify three types of downsizing strategies:

> **downsizing** Reducing employment to improve efficiency, productivity, and competitiveness.

1. *Workforce Reduction.* This is a short-term strategy focused on cutting the number of employees through programs such as attrition, early retirement or voluntary severance incentive packages, or layoffs.

2. *Work Redesign.* This strategy takes somewhat longer to implement and requires that organizations critically examine the work processes and evaluate whether specific functions, products, or services should be changed or eliminated.

3. *Systematic Change.* This is a long-term strategy requiring a change in the culture and attitudes and values of employees with the ongoing goal of reducing costs and improving quality. This strategy takes a long time to implement, and thus the benefits only accrue over time.[120]

While firms frequently believe that downsizing will enhance organizational performance, study after study shows that "following a downsizing, surviving employees become narrow-minded, self-absorbed, and risk averse. Morale sinks, productivity drops, and survivors distrust management."[121] Employee responses can be severe:

> At HMV, an employee hijacked the firm's Twitter account and gave live updates about the termination, including "There are over 60 of us being fired at once! Mass execution, of loyal employees who love the brand."[122]

In addition, there is growing evidence that firms engaging in downsizing do not perform better financially—the bulk of the research indicates that the stock price of downsized firms often declines after a layoff announcement is made.[123]

© Ariel Skelley/Getty Images.

Downsizing and layoffs often cause a drop in employee morale and lower productivity. What are the ways to avoid these consequences or at least to reduce the negative impact?

Downsizing efforts often fail to meet organizational objectives. This is not surprising, considering that many workforce reductions are carried out with little strategic planning or consideration of the costs to the individuals and employer. Frequently, cutting jobs is a short-term response to a much more serious problem. In several instances, little attention is given to carefully examining and resolving critical human resource issues.

In April of 2014, Liat Honey, a married mother of two children, showed up at the Cobequid Children's Centre where she had worked for two years to find that the doors were locked and she was out of work. In addition to the need to fight for wages and vacation pay she was due, Liat was devastated by the loss of her job. In her words: "I was very, very angry, and I was very depressed. I was crying for literally two months. Now I am doing a lot better, but I was very angry that they didn't let us know. I understand businesses go down, but why wouldn't they tell us before, to give us time to plan?"[124]

While downsizing may be an appropriate strategic response for some organizations, it is not a "quick fix" remedy. Before implementing such a program, it is critical to carefully consider the decision, plan the process, and assess the consequences from the perspectives of the organization, the customer, the "survivors" (those employees that remain), and the victims (those that lose their jobs).

Don Walker has more than 33 years in the forest industry. However, in the summer of 2008, he lost his job as a hydraulic log loader when his employer closed down. Walker says he has taken all he can and no longer has the will to pull himself back up after losing his job. He is running out of money and suffering from depression. "I've been beaten down my whole life and pulled myself back up off the ground so many times, but I just don't give a damn anymore. There are zero prospects—I've applied everywhere."[125]

Of those organizations that engage in the workforce-reduction stage of downsizing, many ignore the critical elements of redesigning the organization and implementing cultural change.[126] One organization had planned to contract out the maintenance of vehicles to local garages. While huge savings were projected, several of the local garages did not have repair bays big enough to accommodate the vehicles, and the hoists were not strong enough to support the trucks. From a best practices perspective, six key principles deserve attention:

1. Change should be initiated from the top but requires hands-on involvement from all employees.
2. Workforce reduction must be selective in application and long term in emphasis.
3. There is a need to pay special attention both to those who lose their jobs and to the survivors who remain with the organization.
4. It is critical that decision makers identify precisely where redundancies, excess costs, and inefficiencies exist and attack those specific areas.
5. Downsizing should result in the formation of small semi-autonomous organizations within the broader organization.
6. Downsizing must be a proactive strategy focused on increasing performance.[127]

Human resource professionals have an important role to play in downsizing efforts and should be involved in the strategic process. HR people are often in a good position to advise on the impact of restructuring an organization (from a variety of perspectives, including work groups, teams, departments, and individuals) to maximize productivity and retain quality performers. Similarly, HR can develop skill inventories and planning charts to evaluate the effects on human resource needs and projected capabilities.

Organizational changes such as downsizing, restructuring and job redesign are associated with greater stress with about 40 percent of employees reporting that such changes had negatively affected their health and 46 percent reporting that they or a co-worker had taken more time off as a result of workplace change.[128]

Moreover, in light of the compelling evidence that most downsizings have dramatically negative impacts on those who survive, human resource experts can assist in co-ordinating and communicating the downsizing decision. There is growing evidence that effective communication can reduce some of the negative consequences associated with downsizing:[129]

A number of employers are developing social media policies and limiting who can speak to the media, but experts agree it is not possible to prevent all employees and former workers from accessing social media. However, Professor Aneil Mishra provides an excellent example of effectively handling a downsizing—when retailer Zappos had to lay off about 8 percent of its staff, its CEO sent an email to employees explaining why layoffs were necessary and describing the severance packages available to workers. He also began blogging and tweeting about the challenges and difficulty he had to endure as a result of the layoffs.[130]

More and more, former employees who have been downsized or terminated air their views on social media. According to Stacy Parker, managing director of the Blu Ivy Group, "The reality is that most people will use social media, particularly when they are not so happy with the way things have taken place. Especially during a downsizing, it is a very challenging time for the entire employment culture."[131]

Finally, HR can assist in evaluating the downsizing program. Issues include monitoring who left the organization and who remains, job design and redesign, worker adjustment to change, the need for employee counselling, organizational communication, and a comprehensive review of the appropriateness of existing HRM policies and programs (such as training, compensation and benefits, and orientation of employees into the "new" organization).[132] However, research has shown that downsizing employees is professionally demanding and that the "downsizers" may experience social and organizational isolation, a decrease in personal well-being, and poorer family functioning.[133]

Artificial Intelligence and Job Loss

Advancements in artificial intelligence, machine learning, and computerization are being projected to radically change the job market and the nature of work. For instance, a frequently quoted 2013 Oxford University study reached the conclusion that about 47 percent of total U.S. employment is at risk of being replaced by computerization.[134] Similarly, in 2016, the Brookfield Institute for Innovation + Entrepreneurship concluded that about 42 percent of Canadian jobs are at risk of being lost due to automation, while the Organisation for Economic Co-operation and Development's estimate was 38 percent and the C.D. Howe's projection was 35 percent.[135] The Brookfield Institute report identified the occupations most at risk (retail salesperson, administrative assistant, food counter attendant, cashier, and transport truck driver) and jobs with a low risk of becoming obsolete (management, teaching, science, technology, engineering, and math). Of course, not all of the jobs will disappear, but many will change dramatically and new jobs will be created.[136]

A 2017 report, *The Intelligence Revolution: Future-Proofing Canada's Workforce,* observed that the major forces that will change work are (1) robotic process automation, (2) artificial intelligence, and (3) human enhancement technologies, such as devices and wearables aimed at overcoming limitations or improving human capabilities.[137]

Futurist Martin Ford argues that highly routine jobs (such as telemarketing and tax preparation) are almost guaranteed to be automated, while food preparation jobs in the fast food industry have about an 80 percent chance of being replaced by robots (such as Flippy, which is already in place at CaliBurger restaurants).[138]

In late 2017, Walmart brought the self-scanner into 22 Canadian stores, where shoppers carry the scanners with them while they shop and just visit the checkout to pay. In the U.S., shoppers can use a cellphone app to scan products as they shop, and in some stores, they do not even need to go to a checkout—rather, their accounts are charged when they leave the store.[139] Similarly, at Amazon, a warehouse worker whose job was to stack small bins weighing up to 11 kilograms over a 10-hour shift is now employed to monitor several robots in the warehouse and troubleshoot when problems arise. The goal in using robots was to avoid people having to perform monotonous tasks and to reduce the amount of walking around by employees, leaving workers to do jobs that engage them mentally.[140]

Retaining Top Performers

Keeping high-performing employees is often a challenge for both growing and downsized organizations. A study by Right Management indicated that a shortage of talent was the top HR challenge (identified by 34 percent of Canadian executives), followed by low engagement/productivity (24 percent of respondents).[141] Many companies lose half of their employees in three to four years and half of their customers in five years—keeping employees is as critical as retaining customers because without loyal employees, you won't have loyal customers.[142] A survey by Hays indicated that almost 90 percent of Canadian employees would leave their current job for another position (up from 78 percent in 2013), and almost three-quarters would agree to a pay cut for an ideal job. Just over 40 percent of respondents said that company culture (and, in particular, open communication) was their number one reason for seeking a new position.[143]

Of course, some organizations may adopt a strategy in which people are not important and are easily replaceable, and thus they may be willing to accept high levels of employee turnover. One study suggests that the number one reason employees leave their jobs is "shock"—some precipitating event (such as a heated argument with the boss, uncertainty over a corporate merger, or an unexpected and unsolicited job offer) is more likely than job dissatisfaction to cause an employee to leave his or her current job.[144]

BMO's 2014 Labour Day survey looked to the strategies being used by Canadian organizations to retain talented employees. The most common practices included flexible work hours (76 percent); education, training, and development (66 percent); increased health and dental benefits (36 percent); increased paid vacation (29 percent); tuition assistance (27 percent); and telecommuting (25 percent). There were noticeable differences based on firm size: Large businesses were clearly more likely to offer telecommuting (50 percent as compared to 24 percent for small firms) and tuition assistance (49 percent versus 26 percent, respectively).[145]

A study by Professor Tim Gardner indicates that employees who are thinking of quitting often give off behavioural cues and start disengaging at the workplace. The 10 characteristics identified in the research were as follows:

1. Offering fewer constructive contributions in meetings
2. Being reluctant to commit to long-term projects
3. Acting more reserved and quiet

4. Being less interested in advancing in the organization
5. Showing less interest in pleasing the boss than before
6. Avoiding social interactions with the boss and other members of management
7. Suggesting fewer new ideas or innovative approaches
8. Doing the minimum amount of work needed and no longer going beyond the call of duty
9. Participating less in training and development programs
10. Demonstrating a drop in work productivity

Gardner found that if an employee exhibited at least six of these behaviours, his model could predict with 80 percent accuracy that the employee was going to quit.[146]

A Canadian study examining high potential ("HIPO") employee programs revealed that only 10 percent of more than 200 participants believed that senior managers are "highly effective" at spotting talent. About 85 percent of participants indicated that their organization had some type of HIPO program; most of the programs involved identifying high performers (say the top 10 percent) and providing such individuals with leadership development opportunities. More than 80 percent of organizations have not formally evaluated the accuracy of the method used to identify high potential employees. The most common methods used to identify high performers were current job performance (88 percent), supervisor recommendation (70 percent), and upper-level management recommendation (68 percent).[147]

Among the factors in retaining key employees are the following:

- Developing a planned approach to employee retention (which examines the usual company benefits, addresses individual needs, focuses on the long term, is part of the vision of the organization, and is based on investment in employees)
- Becoming an employer of choice with a goal of retaining employees from the day they join the organization
- Communicating the organizational vision and values frequently and in a clear and consistent manner
- Rewarding supervisors and managers for keeping good people
- Using exit interviews to obtain information as to why people are leaving the organization[148]

A number of studies have examined whether there is a relationship between an organization's human resource management practices and employee retention. The findings suggest that employers with high-involvement human resource systems tend to have lower employee turnover.[149]

SUMMARY

The human resource department's role in organizational communication is to create an open, two-way flow of information. Part of the foundation of any organizational communication effort is management's view of employees. If that view is one that sincerely strives to provide an effective downward and upward flow of information, then the human resource department can help develop and maintain appropriate communication systems.

Downward communication approaches include in-house publications, information booklets, employee bulletins, prerecorded messages, email, jobholder reports, and open-book management. Multiple channels are used to help ensure that each message reaches the intended receivers. Perhaps the greatest difficulty in organizational communication is to provide an effective upward flow of information. In-house complaint procedures, manager–employee meetings, suggestion systems, and attitude survey feedback are commonly used tools.

Counselling is the discussion of a problem with an employee to help the worker cope with the situation. It is performed by human resource department professionals as well as supervisors. Counselling programs provide a support service for both job and personal problems, and there is extensive co-operation with community counselling agencies.

Discipline is management action to enforce organizational standards, and it is both preventive and corrective. The hot-stove rule is a useful general guide for corrective discipline. Most disciplinary action is progressive, with stronger penalties for repeated offences. Some disciplinary programs primarily emphasize a counselling approach.

Employee involvement efforts are systematic attempts by organizations to give workers a greater opportunity to take part in decisions that affect the way they do their job and the contribution they make to their organization's overall effectiveness. They are not a substitute for good, sound human resource practices and policies. However, effective EI efforts can supplement other human resource actions and lead to improved employee motivation, satisfaction, and productivity. Whether that involvement is in solving workplace problems or participating in the design of jobs, employees want to know that their contribution makes a difference.

In this era of downsizing and restructuring, it is important to understand the basic principles relating to wrongful dismissal law. Also, there is evidence that many downsizing efforts fail to meet organizational objectives. Human resource professionals have an important role to play in both growing and downsized workplaces.

TERMS FOR REVIEW

constructive dismissal 340
corrective discipline 335
counselling 334
discipline 335
downsizing 351
downward communication 327
due process 336
employee attitude/opinion survey 334
grapevine communication 331
high-involvement work practices 349

hot-stove rule 336
in-house complaint procedures 333
just cause 338
open-door policy 333
preventive discipline 335
progressive discipline 336
self-directed work teams or groups 348
suggestion systems 334
upward communication 331
wrongful dismissal 337

SELF-ASSESSMENT EXERCISE

Procedural and Distributive Justice in the Classroom

Consider a grade you obtained in a course. Research suggests that individuals are concerned with not only the outcome—that is, the grade ("distributive justice")—but also the procedures leading to the decision ("procedural justice"). The following self-test gives you a quick assessment of both procedural and distributive justice. Read each statement and give it a score from 1 to 5 (1 indicating that you strongly disagree with the statement and 5 indicating that you strongly agree with the statement).

1. The grading procedures used to arrive at my grade were applied consistently. _____

2. The grading procedures used to arrive at my grade were free of bias. _____

3. The grading procedures used to arrive at my grade were based on accurate information. _____

4. I was able to express my views and feelings during the grading process. _____

5. The grade I obtained reflected the amount of effort I put into my work. _____

6. The grade I obtained reflected my contribution in the course. _____

7. The grade I obtained is appropriate when I consider the amount of work I did in the course. _____

8. The grade I obtained is fair, given my performance in the course. _____

SCORING

First add up your scores for statements 1 through 4. These statements address the issue of "procedural justice." A higher score is associated with a stronger perception that the procedures used in grading your work were fair. Then add up your scores for statements 5 through 8. These statements measure "distributive justice." A higher score is associated with a belief that the grade you obtained was appropriate, given your contribution.

Source: Adapted from Jason Colquitt, "On the Dimensionality of Organizational Justice: A Construct Validation of a Measure," *Journal of Applied Psychology,* Vol. 86, 2001, pp. 386–400.

REVIEW AND DISCUSSION QUESTIONS

1. Think of a situation in which you learned some new information from the grapevine and took action on the basis of that information. Discuss.

2. List and describe the different types of programs that can be used by the human resource department to improve communication.

3. Discuss differences between preventive and corrective discipline. What examples of either one were applied to you on the last job you had?

4. What is progressive discipline? How does it work? Is its basic approach realistic in work situations? Explain your answer.

CRITICAL THINKING QUESTIONS

1. Employee involvement has become a popular concept. As a manager, what steps would you take to increase EI in your organization?

2. Suppose you are a plant or division manager and you want to improve the quality of work life in your division. What steps would you take?

3. Think of an organization that you have worked in. What high-involvement work practices could be implemented to improve performance?

4. Assume you have been asked to terminate an employee. How would you conduct the termination interview?

ETHICS QUESTION

After completing her Bachelor of Arts and Juris Doctor degrees, Ashley Anderson joined the small but prestigious law firm of Blaney, Delaney and Slaney (BDS Law). Ashley, who finished third in her law school class, is a specialist in patent law and has been working for the firm for seven years. Ashley is single and 33 years of age. By all accounts, she is an excellent lawyer. She has received several awards, has been identified as a top lawyer in patent law by Lexpert, and is one of the top producers at the firm when it comes to billable hours.

A few weeks ago, the law firm became aware that Ashley had posted photos on her Facebook and Instagram accounts. The photos showed Ashley in a number of nude and sexually suggestive poses, and three of the photos showed her wearing a baseball-style hat with the BDS Law logo. In addition, Ashley posted a comment that "BDS Law is a sexist law firm that cares more about profits than it does about its people." BDS Law's ethics policy states that "employees are prohibited from engaging in conduct that may be harmful to the reputation of the firm." Ashley, who is also a part-time model, asserts that the photos are a form of art designed to promote her part-time career as a model, and not harmful to the reputation of BDS Law.

1. Consider the positions of both Ashley and BDS Law. Is Ashley in breach of the BDS Law ethics policy? What discipline, if any, should be imposed on Ashley?

RESEARCH EXERCISE

1. Visit the websites of three employee assistance program (EAP) providers. Compare the programs and approaches of the three providers. What similarities and differences do you observe?

2. Laws relating to dismissal vary among countries. Examine dismissal law websites in Canada, the United States, and one other country. Compare the laws regarding dismissal among the three countries.

INCIDENT 11-1

Character Is Important!

Alex Anderson is an assistant soccer coach and part-time instructor in recreation management at a Canadian university. Alex plays an important role in assessing potential soccer recruits. Alex and the other coaches carefully review information about each athlete (such as watching the athlete play [where feasible], reviewing the résumé, and critically evaluating a recruitment video).

However, Alex has also assumed responsibility for studying the athlete's online profile and has found that such information is very informative. As Alex has stated, "You can learn a lot about the behaviour, motivation, commitment, and interests of each athlete in a few minutes. I like to Google each athlete and check out his or her social media

profile on sites such as Facebook, Twitter, Instagram, and LinkedIn. It doesn't take long and is just due diligence. We don't want problems, and this is just another way of verifying information and screening out those athletes who won't fit in here."

DISCUSSION QUESTIONS

1. Do you support Alex's approach?
2. What are the advantages/disadvantages of reviewing a person's postings on social media as part of the recruitment/selection process?

WE CONNECTIONS: MANAGING EMPLOYEE RELATIONS

The Underperformer

Calvin Brooks rushed toward his desk, frantically looking around him. As he slipped off his jacket and turned on his laptop, he said to the woman in the next cubicle, "Hey, Marcie. Nick hasn't been around here, has he?"

Marcie finished what she was typing and then looked up and said, "Actually, he has already been by looking for you, Cal. He looked pretty mad when he couldn't find you. It wasn't the best day to come in a little late."

Calvin and Marcie Finnegan were junior software engineers working on the same project at WE Connections. Both in their twenties, they had joined the company six months prior, straight out of school.

Cursing under his breath, Cal remarked, "Man. I was hoping he would be tied up with other things, and not thinking about my stuff. I'm still not done the analysis he asked for."

She shrugged. "You've got to know he isn't going to forget. That report was due a week ago. The man is tired of waiting. Why don't you just finish the dang thing?"

"I meant to. Other things keep coming up. I'll definitely finish it today." Calvin nodded determinedly.

One of Marcie's eyebrows went up. "You've said that every day for the last week. I'm starting to doubt that you really mean it."

Calvin laughed. He said, "Oh, I mean it. On some level at least. But this analysis has been dragging on for so long that it has become absolutely painful to do. I must have stared at the data for 20 hours over the last few days. I'm sick of it. I know he'll expect it to be perfect since it has taken so much time, so now I just want to get it over with."

"Everybody wants that, Cal. So do it already."

Cal nodded. "I will. Today. First, just let me check my email. I was waiting to hear from a couple of people."

Serial Procrastination

Marcie shook her head, annoyed. "That's always where you start. Email leads you to Instagram, where you stay until break. When you come back, you make a couple of calls, then it's lunch time. In the afternoon, you walk around looking busy, but really just chatting with people. No wonder you never get your work done, Cal. You are a serial procrastinator."

Offended, Cal said, "Hey! What's with you? Why are you on my back all of a sudden? You're not my boss."

She replied, "That's true. But I'm on this project, too. And whenever someone doesn't do their part, it hurts other people. Paula needs your analysis to write some code. And I need that code for what I'm doing next. Now you're going to be messing me up."

Cal made a face. "C'mon. Who are you trying to kid? You're not sitting here twiddling your thumbs waiting for me. You have lots of work to do."

Domino Effect

Marcie replied angrily, "What do you know about my workload? I have a work plan, and when someone like you doesn't do what they're supposed to, my plan goes out the window. And when you make me late, I'm making someone else late. Sure, it's true that I have lots to do. But the part you're holding up is important, and I sure as heck don't want to spend the next few weekends working nonstop to catch us up just because you can't get your act together."

"Fine! I won't check my email. You happy?" Cal closed the open window on his laptop with a flourish.

Marcie took a breath, and replied, "Not really. Listen, Cal. You're a nice guy. But this is the third report you've handed in late in the last couple of months. Nick is really running out of patience. What if he turfs you? You and I started here together, and I really don't want you to go anywhere, you know?"

Cal laughed, and said, "I'm not going anywhere, Marcie. Nick gets a little mad at me sometimes, but I know

he likes me. I'll be fine. That reminds me. I'm going to *have* to take a quick peek at my email. Someone said they were going to send me a funny golfing video. If it's good, I'll send it to Nick. He loves that kind of thing. That'll get him in a good mood again."

DISCUSSION QUESTIONS

1. What discipline, if any, should Nick impose on Calvin? How should due process be ensured with regards to any discipline that is imposed on Calvin?

2. What impact will there be in both the short term and long term if Nick does not discipline Calvin?

3. If disciplining Calvin does not lead to satisfactory performance, would just cause dismissal be warranted, or should WEC pay "reasonable notice" or compensation in lieu of notice to sever the employment relationship? Explain the rationale behind your decision.

In the next installment of the WE Connections story (at the end of Chapter 12), an overworked employee experiences the health and safety implications of a stressful work situation.

CASE STUDY

Doan v. City of New Halidart

Carl Doan Background

Carl Doan is a 37-year-old employee of the City of New Halidart. He began working for the city as a dispatcher 16 years ago, after completing a community college diploma in business studies. Nine years ago, Doan was promoted to dispatcher-scheduler specialist. The main components of his job involve scheduling transit buses and dispatching buses and access-a-bus vehicles. Note that Doan and the other dispatcher-schedulers are not members of a trade union.

Doan, who currently earns $45,900 a year, is a single father with two children: 14-year-old Horace; and 12-year-old Boris, who is autistic and requires considerable childcare assistance.

Over the past five years, the city has moved to a more automated system of transit dispatching and scheduling. While Doan frequently works on his own, it is important that he communicate with other dispatcher-schedulers concerning transit services. Doan and the other dispatcher-schedulers report to Brian Campbell, who is the supervisor of Transit Services. The city is highly committed to providing quality public services and has invested heavily in both employee training and automating its operations. It

has a good public image, and its slogan—Quality Service Delivery By Quality People—is heavily promoted in the New Halidart area. As part of an information sharing program, Campbell meets with groups of employees on a regular basis. For example, every Tuesday morning is the meeting with the dispatcher-scheduler group. The meetings are fairly informal: Campbell will share relevant business information with employees and address any questions or concerns that employees may have. Typical meetings last about 10 to 15 minutes.

Employee Handbook Provisions

Under Section 11.2 of the City of New Halidart Employee Handbook, the city retains all rights with regard to "the maintenance of discipline at the workplace, including the right to demote or discharge for just cause."

All employees receive a copy of the handbook when they commence employment at the City of New Halidart; every two years, each employee receives an updated version of the handbook. Carl Doan acknowledged receiving the most recent copy last January.

Doan's Previous Record

A review of Doan's file indicates that he has received two citations within the past five years. The disciplinary actions are as follows:

- *28 months ago:* Doan received a written warning for being late for work. He had slept in and was 25 minutes late for his scheduled shift.

- *16 months ago:* Doan was given a five-day suspension (without pay) for inappropriate behaviour at work. He was one of five employees who had made Brian Campbell a special chocolate brownie dessert to celebrate Campbell's birthday. However, as a joke, the group decided to put a laxative in the brownie. Campbell ate the brownie, became ill, and had to miss the following workday. While the employees argued that they were just playing a practical joke, the company viewed the matter as very serious. After reviewing all of the evidence, the employer suspended each of the five employees for five days. In the incident letter placed in each employee's file related to this suspension, the city indicated that the behaviour was clearly unacceptable and that any repeat infractions could result in discharge.

Doan's co-workers generally agree that Doan is a very pleasant guy with a sense of humour. As his close friend Pat Carson said, "Carl is a good person to work with. He does his job well and is very dependable but doesn't take things too seriously."

At the city, the performance appraisal form for the dispatcher-schedulers is very basic. It is determined by averaging the scores of four items (job knowledge, ability to work with others, dependability/accuracy, and handling unexpected vehicle maintenance and operator absences). The appraisal form allows the assessor to give a score anywhere between 1 and 5 (with 1 indicating unsatisfactory performance and 5 indicating outstanding performance) for each of the four items. Each employee has a personal performance appraisal interview with his or her supervisor and signs a form acknowledging that the interview took place (but not that the employee necessarily agrees with the assessment). On his last evaluation, Doan received the following scores:

- Job knowledge: 4.1
- Ability to work with others: 4.2
- Dependability/accuracy: 3.9
- Handling unexpected vehicle maintenance and operator absences: 4.2

In the three years prior, Doan's average performance appraisal scores had ranged from 4.1 to 4.4. The average for Doan's workgroup is around 3.9. As Campbell observes, "All of the dispatcher-schedulers are very good employees. However, that is not surprising—their job is important and we could not tolerate poor performers."

Brian Campbell Background

Brian Campbell is considered by most employees to be a good supervisor. Employees stated that he is fair, conducts performance evaluations in an impartial and timely manner, and gives feedback to employees on a regular basis. However, Campbell has a bad temper and on rare occasions he has "lost it" and been verbally abusive to employees. While these outbursts tend to be quite rare (occurring maybe two or three times a year), employees fear that they will be Campbell's next victim. As one employee stated anonymously, "Brian is a very good supervisor most of the time. However, he takes on a different personality when he is angry, and I just hope that I will not be the one that he verbally attacks. Once you've witnessed one of these outbursts, you can never totally relax around him. This inconsistent behaviour really frightens me."

The Incident

The Friday before last, Carl Doan went to the break room for his afternoon coffee break. During the day shift, employees are entitled to a 15-minute break at 10:30 a.m. and 3:00 p.m. There were about 25 employees in the break room, and Doan went to his usual table. Five other colleagues were also sitting at Doan's table (each table accommodates six people). Don placed his sandwich and water bottle at his spot at the table and then noticed that he had a small cut on his arm. He took a quick sip of his water and then left the break room for about five minutes to wash his arm and put a small bandage on the cut.

Brian Campbell frequently skipped the afternoon break if he had a backlog of work, but when he did take a break, he usually sat at the same table as Carl. Their table was positioned so that Carl and Brian typically took the two seats at the back of the room so that they could sit with their backs to the wall and observe what was going on in the room. Campbell preferred to sit there so that he could see what was happening among the other employees.

When Doan returned from the washroom, he observed that Campbell was sitting at his place as one of the other employees was sitting in the spot Campbell usually occupied. Doan also noticed that his sandwich and water had been pushed to one side.

Doan stated, "Excuse me, Brian, but you are in my spot."

Campbell turned to Doan, gave him a slight smile, and replied, "I don't see your name anywhere on the table. Find a spot somewhere else. And that is an order from your supervisor."

Doan refused to back down. "My drink and sandwich are right in front of you," he declared. "I'm not kidding, Brian. Get out of my spot."

Brian became angry, smashed his fist on Doan's sandwich, and dropped his pen into Doan's water bottle. "Take your sandwich and drink and go somewhere else," he ordered. "I'm not letting you run the garage."

At this point, Doan moved behind Campbell, grabbed the chair Campbell was sitting on, and jerked it backward. Campbell fell on the floor. The water he had in his hand also fell down, and some of it splashed on his body and face. While some of the other employees witnessing the incident laughed, a hush fell over the room when it became evident that Campbell was hurt. He went to the emergency room at the local hospital and was diagnosed with a bruised tailbone. While not serious, the injury required Campbell to miss eight days of work. Doan was sent home and told not to report for work the next day.

On the Monday following the incident, the Human Resources manager, Alex Morrisette, met with a number of the employees (including Pat Carson) who had been present at the table. After reviewing all of the evidence and meeting with Campbell and Doan, the City of New Halidart decided to terminate Doan, who was notified of the termination on Thursday (three days after the investigation).

Eight days after the incident, Carl Doan wrote a formal letter apologizing for his conduct. In the letter, Doan stated that "I didn't mean to hurt Brian, and I am sorry for my actions."

DISCUSSION QUESTIONS

1. Make arguments for both the employer and employee. Does the employer (City of New Halidart) have just cause to terminate Carl Doan?

2. How would you recommend communicating information about the termination with the employees who had observed this incident, and about respectful work practices expected in the future?

CHAPTER 12

Ensuring Health and Safety at the Workplace

Those who suffer (from work-related injuries) include not only the injured worker but his or her family and friends as well. Also, the impact of work injuries on human productivity reaches well beyond the workplace and includes a worker's ability to contribute to family and community.

JULIAN BARLING AND MICHAEL FRONE[1]

LEARNING OBJECTIVES

After studying this chapter, you should be able to:

LO1   Describe the major Canadian laws relating to occupational health and safety.

LO2   Assess the traditional thinking with respect to occupational health and safety issues.

LO3   Explain the new thinking with respect to employee rights relating to occupational health and safety issues.

LO4   Outline the implications for human resource management of safety and health responsibilities.

LO5   Discuss the impact of stress on employees and the workplace.

LO6   Summarize the relationship between health and safety issues and human resource management.

Even today, too many employees are injured at the workplace. Employers, supervisors, and employees must work together to reduce on-the-job injuries and illness:

Vernon Theriault was a miner at the Westray coal mine. On May 9, 1992, he was getting ready to go to work and begin his shift when an explosion at the mine led to the death of 26 miners. As he reflects on what happened at Westray, he believes that politicians have not done enough to make workplaces safer. As Theriault notes, "The bottom line is, the reason I went there is they said it was going to be 20, 25 years of work and you could work all the overtime you want

and (make) $60,000 to $80,000 a year. I was looking after my family and that was No. 1 for me."[2]

At the turn of the twentieth century, the thinking and attitudes of employers and employees toward accident prevention were quite different from today. Comments made during this period by employers illustrate this:

- "I don't have money for frills like safety."
- "Some people are just accident prone, and no matter what you do they'll hurt themselves some way."
- "Ninety percent of all accidents are caused by just plain carelessness."
- "We are not in business for safety."[3]

During this period, the courts used a legal expression, **assumption of risk**, meaning that the worker accepted all the customary risks associated with the occupation he or she worked in. Workers were instructed to protect themselves from special hazards such as extreme heat or molten and sharp metal. Furthermore, the attitudes of employees paralleled those of the employers. Scars and stumps on fingers and hands were often proudly referred to as badges of honour. The thought that safety was a matter of "luck" was frequently reflected in such statements as "I never thought he'd get it; he was always one of the lucky ones," or "When your number's up, there's not much you can do."

Over a four-year period in the early 1900s, records of one steel company show that 1,600 of its 2,200 employees lost time from work because of injury. In other words, 75 percent of this plant's entire workforce lost time from work because of accidents on the job.[4]

The early approach to safety at work used the **careless worker model**. It assumed that most accidents were due to workers' failure to be careful or to protect themselves. Even if training was provided to make workers more aware of the dangers in the workplace, this approach still assumed that it was mainly the worker's fault if an accident happened. A new approach, the **shared responsibility model**, assumes that the best method to reduce accident rates relies on the co-operation of the two main partners: the employer and the employees (who may be represented by a union).[5] Accident rates are reduced when the following occurs:

- Management is committed to safety in the workplace.
- Employees are informed about accident prevention.
- Consultation between the employer and employees takes place on a regular basis (for example, the creation of a health and safety committee).
- There is a trusting relationship between the employer and staff.
- Employees have actual input into the decision-making process.

In Chapter 10, one of the topics was workers' compensation, which has as its aim the compensation of an employee for injuries suffered on the job. These programs have a serious defect: They are after-the-fact efforts. They attempt to compensate employees for accidents and illnesses that have already occurred. Many early supporters of these laws had

> **assumption of risk** Meaning the worker accepts all the customary risks associated with his or her occupation.

> **careless worker model** The early approach to safety in the workplace, which assumed that most accidents were due to workers' failure to be careful or to protect themselves.

> **shared responsibility model** A newer approach to safety in the workplace that assumes the best method to reduce accident rates relies on the co-operation of the employer and the employees (who may be represented by a union).

hoped that costs would force employees to become more safety-conscious. Yet even with greater efforts by employers, accident rates continue to remain high. In addition, toxins and unhealthy work environments continue to create new health hazards.

A home building company and contractor were charged in Alberta after a workplace accident left a father of two paralyzed from the waist down. The employee severed his spinal cord after falling six metres through an open stairwell at a construction site. According to a spokesperson for Occupational Health (Alberta), "The prime employer is always on the hook. If there's another company directing work, they can also be accountable." The contractor who hired the employee (a personal friend for several years) said that the charges were an insult. "It was a tragic accident. If it could have been avoided, it would have been. That is why they're called accidents."[6]

Workplace Injuries and Health Hazards

It is estimated that about three Canadian workers die every working day from an occupational injury or disease. However, the number of work-related injuries has dropped dramatically since the 1980s: from about 50 per 1,000 employed workers in 1986 to about 15 per 1,000 workers today. Every minute worked costs the Canadian economy more than $60,000 in compensation payments to injured workers. Workplace accidents and occupation-related illnesses cost more than $8 billion annually in compensation payments alone. The total cost is more than $19 billion a year when indirect expenses are taken into account, and this does not include the incalculable social toll associated with workplace-related accidents.[7] Employers interested in calculating the direct and indirect costs of workplace accidents and injuries can use an injury cost calculator available from different provincial websites (see, for instance, the one at WorkSafeBC: https://www.worksafebc.com/en/resources/health-safety/interactive-tools/workplace-incident-cost-calculator?lang=en).

Accidents at work are caused by a complex combination of unsafe employee behaviour and unsafe working conditions. Several factors contribute to the complexity of managing safety in the workplace: The effects of some industrial diseases do not show up for years; employers may "clean up" a health or safety problem before an inspector arrives; companies may fail to monitor or disclose health risks; or employees may fail to follow safe practices at the workplace or engage in dangerous behaviour (such as drinking alcohol or taking drugs while on the job).

It is also critical that organizations consider the safety of members of the public who enter onto company property.

In November 2000, two 14-year-old children were killed during the Take Our Kids to Work Day at the

John Deere plant in Welland, Ontario. The fatal accident occurred when they crashed the small vehicle they were driving. An inquest into the accident resulted in several recommendations, including the use of an informed consent form containing health and safety messages and requiring the signature of both the student and a parent or guardian, a requirement that children are under adult supervision at all times, refusing to allow a student to operate a motorized vehicle, and a mandatory orientation program for student participants that addresses health and safety issues.[8]

Workplace Injuries

Data from the Association of Workers' Compensation Boards of Canada provide some perspective on the extent of workplace injury and illness in Canada. While the number of workplace injuries has declined and then levelled off in recent years, the direct cost of injuries (such as lost wages, first aid and medical treatment, rehabilitation, and disability compensation) has not. Moreover, workplace injuries result in several indirect costs (including lost production, recruiting, selecting, and training of new employees, and damage to facilities and equipment) that are incurred by the employer.

Research on the number of time-loss injuries is provided in Figure 12-1, and information on the number of workplace fatalities is contained in Figure 12-2. There are approximately 775,000 occupational injury claims each year, and more than one-third of these claims are accepted time-loss injuries warranting compensation. In Canada in 2016, there were 145,401 lost time claims for men and 95,235 lost claim times for women. 904 workers died as a result of a workplace injury (an average of about three workers each day of the year). April 28 is the National Day of Mourning to commemorate employees killed or injured on the job.

Exposure to asbestos is responsible for about one in three workplace deaths each year since 1996. These deaths represent more fatalities than from highway accidents, fires, and chemical exposures combined. Health professionals believe that the long latency period associated with asbestos (often from 20 to 40 years) will lead to higher death rates. According to Health Canada, "Asbestos poses potential health risks only when fibres are present in the air people breathe. The problem is there's no way of ensuring that all products are always bound or enclosed. Brake pads wear down, renos stir up dust, while pipes and tiles get sawed."[9]

Fishing, construction, manufacturing, and transportation are among the most dangerous industries when considering time-loss injury rates. The most common type of injury involves strains and sprains, followed by cuts, contusions, crushing, or bruises. Evidence from British Columbia reveals that the most common body part involving time lost cases was the back (24 percent of cases). Other common injuries included fingers (11 percent), legs (9 percent), shoulders (8 percent), and ankles (5 percent).[10]

Reynold Hert, now CEO of the BC Forest Safety Council, remembers being a sawmill manager about two decades ago and watching an operator of a lumber-trimming machine stick his hands into the equipment to straighten out a board. Fortunately, the man was not injured but could easily have lost fingers, a hand, or an arm. The man said that taking risks was necessary to avoid costly work disruptions. Hert told him to follow safety procedures and the man had to shut down his machine 90 times during his next shift to straighten out boards, reducing his productivity by about 33 percent. When Hert asked an engineer and maintenance

---

FIGURE 12-1

Number of Accepted Time-Loss Injuries (2000–2016)

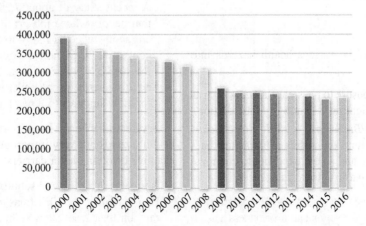

SOURCE: Number of Accepted Time-Loss Injuries: Association of Workers' Compensation Boards of Canada, "National Work Injuries Statistics Program," Association of Workers' Compensation Boards of Canada (AWCBC), National Work Injury/Disease Statistics Program (NWISP).

FIGURE 12-2

Number of Fatalities (2000–2016)

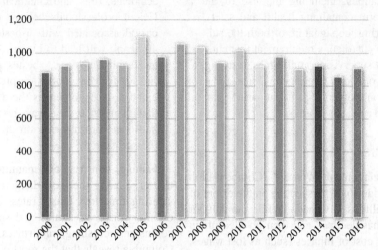

SOURCE: Number of Fatalities: Association of Workers' Compensation Boards of Canada, "National Work Injuries Statistics Program," Association of Workers' Compensation Boards of Canada (AWCBC), National Work Injury/Disease Statistics Program (NWISP).

employee to examine the issue, they found that the machine had a timing flaw, and they were able to fix the problem. The previous year, there were 21 fatalities and approximately 7,000 injuries in the BC forest industry. Hert recognizes that some of the 4,000 employers in the industry may cut corners in order to keep bids as low as possible. According to Hert, investing in safety training may increase short-term costs but the contractors that don't pay attention to safety will find it hard to get work. "When you are staring at the spot where a person died, you realize it is preventable."[11]

The International Labour Organization estimates that more than 2.3 million workers die every year due to workplace accidents or work-related disease. In addition, approximately 313 million accidents at work require employees to take extended absences from the job, and the annual cost to the global economy is about $3 trillion.[12]

Health Hazards

It is possible to combine the various health hazards into three categories:[13]

1. *Physical Agents.* Exposure to physical elements such as noise, temperature, lighting, vibrations, and radiation.
2. *Biological Agents/Biohazards and Chemicals.* Exposure to such natural organisms as parasites, bacteria, insects, viruses, and so on; exposure to chemical compounds or other harmful toxic substances.

   In Fernie, B.C., three men working at a hockey rink died due to an ammonia leak. Ammonia, a colourless gas that is toxic if inhaled, is often used in mechanical refrigeration systems such as those in arenas.

Industry experts reported that more inspections and stricter staffing standards are needed. Other recommendations included training relating to keeping the rink safe and ensuring that maintenance is kept up.[14]

3. *Ergonomically Related Injuries.* Caused by the work environment and including repetitive strain, stress, overexertion/fatigue, and back injuries. In simple terms, *ergonomics* involves the "study of the relationship between people and their jobs." More specifically, ergonomics uses scientific principles to examine the nature of the task that the employee is doing, the equipment or machinery needed to carry out the task, and the environment in which the task is carried out. Some ways in which ergonomics has been applied include preventing back injuries, developing proper work positions, organizing the work space, and managing the light at work.[15]

   A recent study of about 7,300 employees revealed that people whose job primarily involves standing are about twice as likely to have a heart attack or congestive heart failure compared to those whose job largely involves sitting. Moreover, the risk of heart disease (6.6 percent) is actually higher than for daily smokers (5.8 percent).[16]

Awareness of health hazards and preparing for emerging health hazards are very important. Consider the following example involving letter carriers:

Residents of a Montreal suburb were asked by Canada Post to remove the Christmas garlands from the handrails on their front steps. While some residents complained, Canada Post noted that a letter carrier nearly lost a finger when she slipped and caught her hand on a garland wire. In Quebec, letter carriers had almost 600 work accidents during the year, with 80 percent resulting from slips and falls on private property.[17]

In addition, some rather dangerous workplaces may not be subject to the same scrutiny as others. For example, one observer argues that NHL rinks are unsafe workplaces. He asks, "When will authorities responsible for occupational health and safety turn their attention to the professional hockey rink which, after all, is a workplace and subject to regulation?" He argues that British Columbia's health authorities have investigated several cases of workplace violence in recent years but have largely ignored professional sports. He asserts that while hockey involves some inherent risks, injury resulting from fighting, illegal use of the stick, and head shots render the hockey rink an unsafe workplace.[18]

Younger Workers and Workplace Safety

There is growing emphasis on the health and safety of young workers. About one in seven young workers is injured on the job, and approximately one-fourth of all workplace injuries involve employees in the 15 to 29 age group. Among injured workers who are under 25 years of age, more than 50 percent were injured during the first six months of employment, and nearly 20 percent of the injuries and fatalities occurred during the first month on the job. The most common injuries affecting young workers include electrocution and machine injuries. According to the Canadian Centre for Occupational Health and Safety (CCOHS), a number of younger workers are not aware of their health and safety rights and responsibilities at the workplace.

Across the country, governments are trying to make young workers aware of workplace safety. For instance, Alberta has followed the lead of other provinces and introduced the Work Safe Alberta Video Contest in which high school students submit videos addressing issues relating to safe work. The first place prize is $2,000, with $1,500 for second place and $1,000 for third place. The winning videos are available at Work Safe Alberta (https://www.alberta.ca/ohs-high-school-video-contest.aspx).

Many employees fail to appreciate the wide range of health and safety hazards while performing a job. Consider, for example, a student working part-time as a cook at a small restaurant or fast-food outlet. Potential hazards include exposure to biological and chemical elements, ergonomic issues, and a wide variety of safety risks, including electrical shock, cuts, burns, collisions with co-workers, getting a limb or hair caught in a piece of equipment, and so on. For example, a Tim Hortons employee was injured when a car passing through the drive-thru lane hit the worker, who was leaning out the window.[19] The CCOHS documents the risks associated with several jobs often performed by younger workers.

Patrick Desjardins was 17 when he was electrocuted while using a buffer to clean the floor at Walmart in Grand Falls, New Brunswick. The buffer had been purchased at a garage sale. Walmart was fined $120,000 after pleading guilty to health and safety violations, including a failure to ensure that the buffer was suitable, inspected, and well-maintained and failure to take reasonable precautions to ensure the health and safety of its employees. According to Patrick's father, "Walmart can earn $120,000 in 15 seconds. It's not enough but what is enough. As far as I'm concerned, if these workplaces get caught . . . those fines should be increased big time."[20]

LO1 Federal and Provincial Safety Regulations

Each province as well as the federal jurisdiction has detailed legislation addressing health and safety, and most employers and employees are governed by provincial legislation. Although this chapter examines safety legislation at the federal level, students interested in learning about the specific legislation in their province can obtain such information by contacting the relevant provincial government department. Provincial government websites typically contain both the legislative provisions and detailed guides to understanding health and safety law.

At the federal level, the *Canada Labour Code* (Part II) details the elements of an industrial safety program and provides for regulations to deal with various types of occupational safety problems. All provinces and the territories have similar legislation. Part II of the *Code* establishes three fundamental employee rights:

1. The right to know about hazards in the workplace
2. The right to participate in correcting those hazards
3. The right to refuse dangerous work

A key element of health and safety laws is the **workplace health and safety committee**, which is usually required in every workplace with 20 or more employees. These committees have a broad range of responsibilities. Some of the major powers and duties of committees under federal jurisdiction include the following:

> **workplace health and safety committee** A group consisting of representatives of the employer and employees that meets regularly in order to reduce accident rates.

- Meeting at least nine times a year, at regular intervals and during regular working hours
- Considering and expeditiously disposing of health and safety complaints
- Participating in all of the inquiries, investigations, studies, and inspections pertaining to employee health and safety

- Ensuring that adequate records are kept on workplace accidents, injuries, and health hazards

- Participating in the implementation of changes that might affect occupational health and safety

- Inspecting, each month, all or part of the workplace, so that every part of the workplace is inspected at least once a year[21]

Some other relevant federal laws are the *Hazardous Products Act*, the *Transportation of Dangerous Goods Act,* and the *Canadian Centre for Occupational Health and Safety Act.*

Part of the *Hazardous Products Act* and associated regulations concern hazard classification and communication. The primary objectives of Canada's national hazard communication standard, the **Workplace Hazardous Materials Information System (WHMIS)**, include hazard classification, cautionary labelling of containers, the provision of (material) safety data sheets or (M)SDSs, and worker education and training.[22]

> **Workplace Hazardous Materials Information System (WHMIS)**
> Legislation that requires suppliers to label all hazardous products and provide a (material) safety data sheet on each.

Although WHMIS provides information on the use of hazardous materials, other countries have different requirements, and this is problematic with global trade. In an effort to standardize hazardous materials requirements and communications around the globe, the Globally Harmonized System of Classification and Labelling of Chemicals (GHS) was introduced. Consequently, in February 2015, the Hazardous Products Regulations were amended to incorporate the GHS for workplace chemicals (known as WHMIS 2015, see Figure 12-3). This has resulted in new harmonized criteria for hazard classification and safety data sheets.[23]

The *Transportation of Dangerous Goods Act* makes Transport Canada, a federal government agency, responsible for handling and transporting dangerous materials by federally regulated shipping and transportation companies. It requires that such goods be identified, that a carrier be informed of them, and that they be classified according to a coding system.

The *Canadian Centre for Occupational Health and Safety Act* established a public corporation with the following objectives:

(a) to promote health and safety in the workplace in Canada and the physical and mental health of working people in Canada;

(b) to facilitate

(i) consultation and co-operation among federal, provincial, and territorial jurisdictions, and

(ii) participation by labour and management in the establishment and maintenance of high standards of occupational health and safety appropriate to the Canadian situation;

(c) to assist in the development and maintenance of policies and programs aimed at the reduction or elimination of occupational hazards; and

(d) to serve as a national centre for statistics and other information relating to occupational health and safety.[24]

The CCOHS is supervised by a board of governors made up of representatives of the federal government, labour, and employers. Several hundred organizations are now connected electronically with the centre and have access to information relating to health and safety generally and to hazardous materials specifically.

The administration of safety programs comes mainly under provincial jurisdiction. Each province has legislated specific programs for the various industries and occupations within it. Across the country, provinces are following a trend of consolidating health and safety legislation, streamlining the enforcement of the relevant statutes by combining different agencies into one body, and updating safety laws.[25]

For instance, Alberta recently completed a comprehensive review of its health and safety law and introduced new legislation (*Act to Protect the Health and Well-being of Working Albertans*) effective December 15, 2017. Among the major features of the Act are the right to refuse unsafe work, definitions of workplace violence and harassment and an obligation on employers and supervisors to address and prevent such actions at work, a duty on employers to report "near misses" (which enhances learning about what could go wrong and how to fix such issues), and stronger requirements around joint health and safety committees.[26]

Safety Enforcement

In the federal jurisdiction, there have been some significant changes to the *Canada Labour Code* as it relates to health and safety. Among the changes was the removal of references to "health and safety officers," replaced by "the Minister." This change made the minister responsible for exercising the duties historically performed by health and safety inspectors or delegating the duties to another party. Section 141 of the *Canada Labour Code* (Part II) details these powers:

1. The Minister may, in carrying out the Minister's duties and at any reasonable time, enter any work place controlled by an employer and, in respect of any work place, may:

   (a) conduct examinations, tests, inquiries, investigations and inspections or direct the employer to conduct them;

   (b) take or remove for analysis, samples of any material or substance or any biological, chemical or physical agent;

   (c) be accompanied or assisted by any person and bring any equipment that the officer deems necessary to carry out the Minister's duties;

FIGURE 12-3

WHMIS Class and Division Hazard Symbols

| CLASS A – Compressed Gas | |

| CLASS B – Flammable and Combustible Material | |

Division 1: Flammable Gases   *Division 4*: Flammable Solids
Division 2: Flammable Liquids   *Division 5*: Flammable Aerosols
Division 3: Combustible Liquids   *Division 6*: Reactive Flammable Materials

| CLASS C – Oxidizing Material | |

| CLASS D – Poisonous and Infectious Material | |

Division 1: Materials Causing Immediate and Serious Toxic Effects

    Subdivision A : Very Toxic Material
    Subdivision B : Toxic Material

Division 2: Materials Causing Other Toxic Effects

    Subdivision A : Very Toxic Material
    Subdivision B : Toxic Material

Division 3: Biohazardous Infectious Material

| CLASS E – Corrosive Material | |

| CLASS F – Dangerously Reactive Material | |

* The GHS system also defines an Environmental hazards group. This group (and its classes) was not adopted in WHMIS 2018. However, you may see the environmental classes listed on labels and Safety Data Sheets (SDSs). Including information about environmental hazards is allowed by WHMIS 2018

(d) take or remove, for testing, material or equipment if there is no reasonable alternative to doing so;

(e) take photographs and make sketches;

(f) direct the employer to ensure that any place or thing specified by the Minister not be disturbed for a reasonable period of time pending an examination, test, inquiry, investigation or inspection in relation to the place or thing;

(g) direct any person not to disturb any place or thing specified by the Minister for a reasonable period pending an examination, test,

inquiry, investigation, or inspection in relation to the place or thing;

(h) direct the employer to produce documents and information relating to the health and safety of the employer's employees or the safety of the workplace and to permit the Minister to examine and make copies or take extracts from those documents and that information;

(i) direct the employer or an employee to make or provide statements, in the form and manner that the Minister may specify, respecting working conditions and material and equipment that affect the health or safety of employees;

(j) direct the employer or an employee or a person designated by either of them to accompany the Minister while the Minister is in the workplace; and

(k) meet with any person in private or, at the request of the person, in the presence of the person's legal counsel or union representative.[27]

Provincial laws provide similar powers to safety officers under their jurisdiction.

Syncrude Canada was fined $365,000 when a worker in Alberta died. The employee, who was using steam to clear ice on pipes, was struck by a large slab of ice, weighing several hundred kilograms, and was crushed against the metal railings. Most of the money was targeted toward developing a new course at Keyano College in Fort McMurray, and $100,000 was set aside to be used for scholarships in the deceased worker's name.[28]

In Alberta, the introduction of administrative penalties and tickets is leading to the levying of fines on employers and employees. Penalties can include a fine of up to $10,000 a day for each safety violation. On-the-spot tickets to employers, contractors, employees, and suppliers can range from $100 to $500. Mark Hill of the Yukon Workers' Compensation Health and Safety Board reports that, in the Yukon, "Fines have had a dramatic effect on workplace behaviour, with the vast majority of workplaces now ensuring appropriate personal protective equipment is worn (not long ago, this was the exception rather than the rule)." However, safety consultant Alan Quilley disagrees when he asserts that "From my perspective, there is nothing in human history that says we can fine ourselves into excellence."[29]

Nova Scotia recently announced that the province was going to increase fines (from a maximum of $5,000 to $10,000 for a first offence and from $10,000 to $50,000 for a second) and more rigorously enforce safety measures in the construction trades. The changes are aimed at the use of cheaper labourers rather than skilled tradespersons on some construction projects. Duncan Williams, president of the Construction Association of Nova Scotia, stated, "The black market is costing companies that do invest heavily in safety, training, apprenticeship and equipment."[30]

A Nova Scotia employee fell to his death from the sixth floor of an apartment building under construction a few years ago. The Nova Scotia Occupational Health and Safety division laid charges against the employer, Parkland Construction, for failing to provide adequate fall protection, fall protection training, and a safe work plan. A company supervisor was also charged with failing to provide fall protection and failing to take every precaution to protect an employee's health. While initial reports suggested that the company could be fined up to $500,000 and the supervisor could receive a jail term of up to two

years, a provincial court judge ultimately fined the company $70,000 but dismissed charges against the supervisor. Included in the fine was $37,000 to the Nova Scotia Community College to provided bursaries for students entering a program for safety officers and professionals.[31]

As a general principle, an occupational health and safety inspector may enter a business to carry out his or her duties without notice or a warrant. When an OHS (Occupational Health and Safety) inspector arrives at the workplace, the employer should do the following:

1. Be diligent—take notes on everything the inspector says and answer questions directly without a lot of narrative.

2. Be prepared—have the documentation for due diligence in order and follow your safety procedures to the letter (as the inspector may be testing the employer to see if the rules are actually followed).

3. Stay covered—post the safety policy inside the front door and easily visible to the safety inspector, and choose an employee who will be designated to deal with the inspector.[32]

On the other hand, there are examples where safety standards may not be rigorously enforced:

Two explosions at British Columbia sawmills a few months apart resulted in 4 deaths and 40 other workers being badly injured. However, in both cases, the Criminal Justice Branch has been unable to bring charges because WorkSafeBC did not warn the sawmills about the hazards associated with high levels of combustible sawdust and then failed to investigate the incidents properly.[33] In a 2012–2013 review of the health and safety division, Nova Scotia auditor general Jacques Lapointe found that, over a one-year period, more than 1,225 orders (about 32 percent of the total) were not complied with and just 27 of the 100 workplaces with the highest safety risk rating were inspected. According to Lapointe, "You have only a limited number of inspectors with a lot of work to do . . . part of it involves focusing a little better on inspecting targeted workplaces. And make sure inspectors do follow up."[34]

In an examination of 251 cases involving convictions connected to workplace fatalities from 2007 to 2017, a CBC analysis revealed that the median fine was $97,500. However, the median fines differed noticeably among the provinces (the lowest was $26,563 for British Columbia and the highest was $275,00 for Alberta). Although every jurisdiction except Quebec permits a jail sentence, only four provinces have put an employer representative in jail (and almost all jail terms were for 60 days or less). Irene Lanzinger, president of the B.C. Federation of Labour, stated, "The fines need to be greater, they need to be a significant deterrent, but we also need to pursue these cases through the criminal justice system."[35]

Responsibility for Health and Safety

LO2 Historical Views on Responsibility for Health and Safety

So far the focus in this chapter has been on the legal requirements for maintaining a safe and healthy work environment. It should be emphasized, however, that these must be seen as the minimum requirements for employers. A major purpose of occupational health and safety laws is to prevent injuries from happening.

An electrician working on a switchboard in a sewage treatment facility in Dartmouth, Nova Scotia, was badly burned due to electrical arcing resulting from the buildup of silver fines. The electrician successfully sued the Halifax Regional Municipality and was awarded a settlement of $90,000 for extreme pain and loss of his profession, $68,119 for lost income, and $1,713 in special damages. In finding the city liable, Nova Scotia Supreme Court Justice Gerald Moir stated, "The content of the duty of care to the employee included reasonably regular inspection and cleaning of the motor control centres. The failure to inspect or clean for years, if not decades, caused the silver fines to go undetected."[36]

The 2017 list of "Canada's Safest Employers" revealed that leading organizations place considerable attention on safety. At Calgary hospitality firm Horizon North, employees working in food services frequently use knives or a slicer and are required to wear the appropriate cut-resistant gloves. All employees receive basic safety training, and supervisors must complete a three-day Safety Essentials for Supervisors and Managers course. Meetings start with a "safety moment," and proactive reporting of safety incidents is required. According to Bill Anderson, executive vice-president of Quality, Health and Safety, "What can we learn from the incidents last year, so we can continuously work towards zero incidents? If we talk about near misses, for example, possibly we can learn from it."[37]

Historically, it was believed that the responsibility for health and safety rested primarily with the employer. However, this view is changing. A number of jurisdictions have legislation requiring the establishment of joint health and safety committees or health and safety representatives, as mentioned above. The requirement of establishing a joint committee varies among the provinces; for example, a committee may be required if a workplace has a minimum number of employees (typically 10 or 20 workers). The relevant legislation will outline the duties of the committee (such as maintaining records, conducting meetings, inspecting the

workplace, and so on) and the makeup of the committee (number of members, employee representation on the committee, and so on).

No law, by itself, can make a workplace safe. It is far more effective—and less costly in the long run—if the responsibility for safety becomes a concern for everyone: top management, supervisors, and employees.

A bus driver was attacked from behind and punched in the face and shoulder by an intoxicated female passenger while driving down a Winnipeg street. The union representing transit drivers has argued for the provision of face shields to drivers and training in self-defence. Winnipeg Transit has installed on-bus video- and audio-recording devices and is revising employee training to include basic self-defence skills. While the use of face shields is being studied, there are concerns that they may impact the ability of the drivers to operate buses and provide quality customer service.[38]

Many organizations neglect safety issues when designing orientation programs. A comprehensive safety orientation program will address several issues, such as fire safety, smoking at the workplace, accident procedures, personal clothing, protective equipment, material and chemical hazards, waste disposal, safety representatives and the safety committee, occupational health, and the safety policy or policies in existence. It is important that employees understand the various issues and know how to respond in a crisis situation.[39]

Similarly, employers often fail to consider the safety issues related to shift work. According to the Institute for Work and Health, about 30 percent of Canadians work shift work or are on call. Shift workers may experience higher stress and may be prone to an increase in accidents and mistakes due to such factors as sleepiness and fatigue. One study indicated that individuals working outside of regular daytime hours are 1.5 times more likely to be injured at work, and this rate increases around 2.5 times if a person alternates working between day and night shifts. In addition, shift workers may not eat properly, and those on longer shifts may be at a greater risk of exposure to health hazards. Of particular note is that shift workers are most at risk when they are driving home from work.[40]

Research from the University of Pennsylvania study revealed that chronic disruptions in a person's sleep cycle, which is often experienced by shift workers, could lead to damaged neurons in the brain and permanent brain damage. There is also evidence that shift workers are more likely to have a higher risk of injury at work, and preliminary studies suggest a link with heart disease, mental health issues, and certain types of cancer.[41] A Global Corporate Challenge Insights study reported that about one in five employees is sleep deprived. Also, 93 percent of poor sleepers were more likely to show signs of workplace fatigue, which is a common symptom of "excessive daytime sleepiness" (EDS).

EDS, in turn, is associated with higher rates of absenteeism and greater accident and injury rates at work.[42]

LO3 Recent Views on Responsibility for Health and Safety

In today's workplaces, health and safety are joint responsibilities by top management, supervisors, and employees, and often have dedicated people or groups responsible for health and safety of all employees.

Top Management

Top management must set policies and make concern for health and safety part of the organization's culture and strategy. This ensures that health and safety aspects will be considered whenever business decisions are made and training programs developed. A failure on the part of managers to pay attention to health and safety issues is being considered seriously by the courts in Canada. Consider the following cases:

> Petro-Canada was fined $150,000 after a worker at a refinery was severely burned when steam and scalding water poured out of a tank. Shaw Cable Systems was fined $75,000 when an employee was severely burned after making contact with an unguarded and uninsulated power line. The company failed to appoint a safety watcher and failed to provide safety equipment where there was a high-voltage hazard. TDL Spring and Suspension Specialists was fined $120,000 for violating safety regulations after an employee died when a sidebin on a recycling truck he was working on fell and crushed the worker. The sidebin had blocking pins to prevent the bin from falling, but they were not used and the employer failed to provide proper tools to prevent the bin from falling.[43]

Some organizations, recognizing that they lack the internal expertise to address safety issues, are now outsourcing some health and safety needs. Options for such firms include hiring a health and safety expert on a part-time or contract basis or seeking the assistance of a firm that specializes in health and safety. While the cost of a health and safety consultant generally ranges from about $50 to $150 or more per hour, companies often save three to five times the cost of the consulting bill by reducing the number of safety incidents at the workplace. Here's what one safety consultant had to say:

> "We get invited to a workplace that has just bought all new work stations and ergonomic chairs. And they would have ended up saving all that money, and prevented musculoskeletal injuries, if they had just asked for advice beforehand. The earlier an ergonomist is brought in, the cheaper it is. For every dollar you

Safety gear, such as that worn by construction workers, is essential to reducing work injuries. Should penalties be imposed for not wearing it?

spend at the design stage, it will cost you a hundred times more to fix it at the implementation stage."[44]

The Bill C-45 amendments to the *Criminal Code* imposed a new duty on individuals and organizations. Section 217.1 of the *Criminal Code* states this:

> "Everyone who undertakes, or has the authority, to direct how another person does or performs work or performs a task is under a legal duty to take reasonable steps to prevent bodily harm to that person, or any other person, arising from that work or task."

The first Bill C-45 conviction involved the death of an employee in Quebec:

> Transpavé, a Quebec stone-paving manufacturer, was fined $110,000 for criminal negligence causing death after a 23-year-old employee was crushed by a machine being used with an unplugged safety device. The employee's mother was disappointed with the amount of the fine, saying that she expected the fine to be millions of dollars.[45]

There has been a lot of criticism about Bill C-45, which celebrated its tenth anniversary in 2014, and relatively few cases have resulted from the legislation. In the *R. v. Metron Construction* case, six employees got on a swing stage to go down 14 stories. The swing, which had only two lifelines, collapsed and four of the workers died in the fall. Subsequent investigation revealed that the swing stage was defective and failed to meet Ontario safety standards. In addition, three employees, including the site supervisor, had marijuana in their system. Metron pleaded guilty to criminal negligence charges and the judge imposed a $200,000 fine. However, the Court of Appeal felt that the fine did not reflect the moral blameworthiness and gravity of Metron's conduct and substituted a fine of $750,000. In addition, Metron construction project manager Vadim Kazenelson was sentenced to three-and-a-half years in prison in early 2016 but appealed his conviction. However, in early 2018, the Ontario Court of Appeal upheld the decision of the trial judge.[46]

Other countries are also developing legislation making safety violations a criminal offence:

A British firm was the first company to be charged with corporate manslaughter under the United Kingdom's 2007 *Corporate Manslaughter Act.* A 27-year-old geologist was killed when the pit he was working near collapsed. Cotswold Geotechnical Holdings director Peter Eaton was charged and convicted of gross negligence manslaughter and fined £385,000. An organization is guilty of corporate manslaughter if "the way senior management organizes or manages the business activities causes a person's death and amounts to a gross breach of the firm's duty of care owed to the person who died."

Since the legislation was passed, there have been more than 20 convictions. However, the greatest value of the act may lie in the symbolism of a statutory offense called "corporate manslaughter."[47]

One CEO, Robert Watson of SaskPower, tendered his resignation after a report indicated that workplace safety was not enough of a priority. SaskPower was ordered to remove more than 100,000 smart meters that had been installed in homes after it was found that at least eight of the meters had caught fire. The province's Economy Minister stated that "Watson took responsibility for the problems experienced with this project. He felt it was time that there was new leadership." A review revealed that the meter project was rushed, no one was responsible for the overall program, and there was insufficient attention to customer safety.[48]

Supervisors

As part of their management training, supervisors must become proficient in managing safety, which means knowing about health and safety laws, safety regulations, training in observing safety violations, and learning communication skills to convey the necessary information to their employees.

On her second day on the job at a British Columbia quarry, Kelsey Anne Kristian died after a 30-ton truck she had parked began rolling and crushed her. In 2015, about eight years after the incident, charges of criminal negligence causing death were filed against two supervisors and the company Slave Lake Quarries. Kristian had never driven such a large truck and her training only involved an oral review by her supervisor on using air brakes. Charges against the two supervisors were stayed while the company pleaded guilty and was fined $115,000. Kristian's mother felt that the fine was a slap on the wrist: "I would have loved to see someone go to jail, even if it was just for a year, house arrest. I would have loved to see someone pay."[49]

The ingredients of an effective safety training program include the following:

- Accident investigation and analysis
- Communication skills and report writing
- Overview of legislative requirements
- Meeting with management and objective setting
- Organization and responsibility of joint health and safety committee
- Team problem-solving/problem-solving techniques
- Audits and inspections
- Principles of occupational health and safety
- Ergonomics

An issue that supervisors may have to deal with, but feel uncomfortable about, involves an employee's right to refuse unsafe work. It is important that the supervisor knows the provincial legislation relating to work refusals and recognizes the importance of taking every work refusal seriously (even if the supervisor believes that the work is safe).

David Law, a lawyer specializing in health and safety, believes that "whenever employees feel so concerned about their health risks that they would resort to such a drastic measure as refusing to work, the first thing you do is shut up and listen. To dismiss out of hand would be disrespectful about an issue that, in the employee's perception, could have serious, harmful consequences. People are often very poor judges of risk, but if we don't listen to them, what can they conclude except that we don't care?"[50]

Almost 90 percent of safety professionals report seeing workers not wearing personal protective equipment (PPE) when they should have, with 29 percent reporting that this has happened on numerous occasions. The most common compliance challenges involving PPE relate to eye protection, hearing guards, and respiratory protection or masks. The two most pressing workplace issues relating to safety involve worker compliance and managing safety with fewer workers.[51]

There are also examples where supervisors do not assume proper responsibility for safety. A British Columbia mine run by Imperial Metals Corp. spilled millions of cubic metres of waste into nearby waterways. According to a local United Steelworkers executive, workers had warned company officials of safety issues months before the spill. In his words, "Not everybody's saying it, but you get guys coming in who are saying that it's looking dangerous." It was not known whether the warnings stayed with supervisors or went higher up the organization.[52]

Employees

While employers are responsible for providing a safe work environment, and supervisors are responsible for the safety of their people in the workplace, employees are responsible for working safely. Employees must be trained to understand safety rules and how to operate equipment safely.

> Teenager Sarah Wheelan began working part-time at a deli counter of a supermarket. Standard practice was to clean the machines between each use. Rather than taking the machine apart and washing the blade, the practice was to hold one's hand to a spinning blade and clean the blade. While Wheelan did not lose any fingers or suffer any injuries, it took her about two months to get up the courage to confront her supervisor, concerned that she would look stupid or unable to handle the pressure and responsibility of the job. Her supervisor, a butcher, told her that new butchers would frequently nick themselves or lose a finger—that was just the nature of the job. One week later, Wheelan quit.[53]

It is also important that a system of enforcement is in place, understood, and followed. If necessary, progressive discipline has to be applied for violation of safety rules in the same way as for other rule violations.

There is a growing, but fairly recent, recognition that employers need to consider the needs of female employees when it comes to health and safety. For example, safety protection gear and equipment such as tools and harnesses may not be suitable for female employees. In addition, training programs need to be examined—how to carry equipment, for instance, may differ depending on a person's height, weight, and strength.[54]

Good safety performance should be recognized and rewarded by managers. On the other side, unsatisfactory practices should be documented and corrected. Rewarding good performance is preferable. The objective of safety incentives should be to promote safety awareness and should therefore benefit as many workers as possible. Group awards may help to reinforce safety-consciousness through peer pressure. In addition, the importance of safety training cannot be overemphasized:

> Thirty-two miners in Esterhazy, Saskatchewan, were trapped one kilometre below ground while a fire burned at the Mosaic potash mine. The miners stayed in "refuge stations" (chambers that can be sealed off and are equipped with food, water, and beds) and waited to be rescued. The situation ended with the rescue of the miners, and it was acknowledged that their safety training had been invaluable. As one miner said, "Follow every rule you were taught, even if they don't make sense, and it all works out in the end."[55]

A typical Occupational Health and Safety (OHS) training session may involve a day or more of in-class training and more than 500 slides that are communicated to the participants. Recognizing that traditional programs were not meeting their objectives in terms of keeping employees safe at work, the Canadian Manufacturers and Exporters set up a two-year project to examine OHS training. The result was a new training program offered both face-to-face and over the Internet with homework assignments completed at the workplace. Among the features of the training were videos showing employees how to conduct a task-and-hazard analysis and role-play simulations, and training set up for workers with low levels of literacy or understanding of English.[56]

The failure to train can have serious consequences:

> A 17-year-old boy suffered an asthmatic attack at a Tim Hortons in London, Ontario. The teenager was able to say "help" and "phone" but the staff told him that the phone was not for public use and directed him to a pay phone across the street. A customer witnessing the incident called 911 and stayed with the boy until medical help arrived. Norm Keith, a Toronto lawyer, noted that "employers have a general duty to ensure that everyone, not just workers, are safe in the workplace. Assuming the worst—a pandemic, health concerns, someone fainting at work because of a health incident—you have to have a plan that deals with that." As a result of the incident, Tim Hortons employees will be given a refresher course and training on what to do in an emergency situation.[57]

Organizations operating in foreign countries may need to provide specialized training to workers going to such locations. To meet this requirement, progressive employers are recognizing the importance of employee training in global hot spots (areas of political, social, or civil unrest that are potentially dangerous).[58]

LO4 Implications for Human Resource Management

Human resource professionals should ensure consistent enforcement of all safety and health rules. If one worker is allowed to violate safety rules, other workers may follow—and if an accident results, the employer may be subject to penalties.

In the United States, Walmart was fined $2 million after a temporary maintenance employee was trampled to death by bargain-hungry shoppers. Although the company was not charged criminally, it implemented a new crowd-management plan.[59]

Transocean Ltd. rewarded top executives with bonuses for achieving "the best year in safety performance in our company's history." Most senior managers received two-thirds of their maximum safety bonus despite the fact that an explosion of a company oil rig killed 11 people and spilled more than 750 million litres of oil into the Gulf of Mexico. The company said that it still had an exemplary safety record because it met or exceeded a number of internal safety targets.[60]

Health and safety law permits an employee to refuse to work when working conditions are perceived to be unsafe. In such instances, the employee should report the circumstances of the matter to his or her supervisor or to the supervisor's manager and to the safety committee in the firm. In most jurisdictions, an employee with reasonable cause to believe that the work is unsafe will not receive any loss in pay for refusing to work.

Changes in Ontario law now make safety training mandatory. All supervisors and employees covered by the OHSA are required to complete a one-hour training program that is designed to inform the parties of their rights and responsibilities in creating a culture of safety. As noted by Rob Ellis of MySafeWork, "Most Canadians still don't understand that they have the right to say no to unsafe work, and I find it shocking that most Canadians still fear putting up their hand and reporting unsafe work."[61]

When charged with a health and safety offence, a company's best defence is "due diligence," which means that the company took all reasonable steps to avoid the particular event. In examining the organization's behaviour, the court considers several factors, including the magnitude of the risks involved and the nature of the potential harm, with a focus on the part of the safety program designed to prevent the accident in question. An effective safety program only helps establish due diligence—preparing a defence based on due diligence begins well before an accident ever happens.[62]

Health and Safety Audit

With increased attention on health and safety, more and more organizations are having a health and safety audit conducted. Some of these audits are voluntary and others are as a result of being targeted by government health and safety officials. While health and safety audits vary, they may include a review of the employer's occupational health and safety documentation (such as training records, manuals, etc.), a tour of the workplace, and interviews (and/or surveys) of front-line employees, supervisors, and senior management. Of course, some employers may decide to take the risk and not comply with health and safety standards.

However, failing to comply may be a risky proposition:

The Transportation Safety Board of Canada (TSB) found that 254 incidents involving Canadian National, Canadian Pacific, and Montreal, Maine and Atlantic (MMA—the railway involved in the Lac-Mégantic, Quebec, derailment that killed 47 people) were not reported over a seven-year period. The TSB has made it clear that the railroads are expected to comply with the regulations, and a spokesperson for Canadian National stated that "CN will continue to focus on every safety incident as a leading indicator of potentially more serious accidents."

Following up on the case, in January 2018, three rank-and-file MMA employees were acquitted of charges of criminal negligence causing death. However, six former employees pleaded guilty to failing to test the train's handbrakes. One employee was sentenced to six months of community service and the others were fined $50,000 (the maximum fine permitted).[63]

Consequently, a growing number of employers are being more proactive; and, rather than waiting for a provincial audit, they are either conducting internal audits or hiring consultants to assess the health and safety system. A number of provinces, such as Nova Scotia, provide detailed information on how to establish and evaluate a health and safety system.[64]

Safety Climate

According to an HR manager for a Calgary road-building company, "Safety is all about the way you run your business. Wherever you see poor safety there is always a poor-run company. The unfortunate aspect is that the ownership isn't even aware that it is poorly run. If a company has a poor attitude toward safety, it makes us wonder if that attitude is indicative of other aspects of their business."[65]

Why should employers and human resource professionals be concerned with safety climate? There is growing evidence that safety climate is an important factor affecting safety knowledge and motivation. Neal and Griffin, two leading scholars specializing in workplace safety, have developed a framework for conceptualizing safety climate (perceptions about the value of safety in an organization) and safety behaviour.[66] They assert that safety climate is an important factor affecting safety knowledge and motivation, which in turn impacts safety behaviour (see Figure 12-4).

About a decade ago, and faced with one of the worst injury rates in the country, Saskatchewan introduced a new educational campaign called "Mission Zero" in an effort to reduce workplace deaths and injuries. The chair of the Saskatchewan Workers' Compensation Board (WCB) noted that safety requires that employers and employees work together with the same goal

FIGURE 12-4

A Framework for Conceptualizing Safety Climate and Safety Behaviour

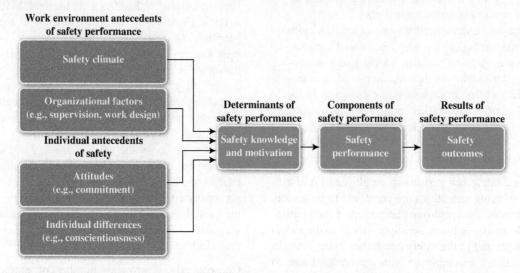

SOURCE: Andrew Neal and Mark Griffin (2004), "Safety climate and safety at work," in Julian Barling and Michael Frone (Eds.), *The Psychology of Workplace Safety,* Washington, DC: American Psychological Association, p. 17.

of a safe work environment and asserted that safety is "an attitude thing" with a culture where safety is out front. The program is still going strong—according to Donna Kane, VP of HR and Team Support at WCB, "We believe every injury is preventable and that's why Mission Zero is core to everything we do." According to WCB CEO Peter Federko, "We've seen the biggest reductions in the time-loss injury rate since we introduced Mission-Zero. Employers and employees alike have embraced the notion that injuries are predictable and preventable."[67]

Neal and Griffin outline eight dimensions of a safety climate. Organizational level dimensions include the following:

- *Management commitment to safety* (Does management place a high priority on safety and communicate and act on safety issues effectively?)

- *Human resource management practices* (To what extent are the HRM practices of the organization perceived to enhance safety?)

- *Safety systems* (To what extent are hazard management systems, incident investigation, and safety policies and procedures perceived to be effective and of high quality?)

Local work group dimensions include the following:

- *Supervisor support for safety* (including placing a high priority on safety and responding to safety issues)

- *Internal group processes* (communication and support for safety issues within the group)

- *Boundary management* (quality of communication between the group and other stakeholders)

- *Risk* (Are the work tasks perceived to be hazardous, dangerous, or unsafe?)

- *Work pressure* (Is workload perceived to exceed the employee's capacity to perform the work safely?)

The importance of top management commitment is critical:

A report to the House of Commons described the "culture of fear" at Canadian National Railways. CN received a score of 1 out of 5 when evaluated on its efforts to implement the safety management standards introduced as an update to the *Railway Safety Act.* Railway workers described how difficult it was to develop a safety culture when they were working in a culture of fear in which they feared reprisals and disciplinary action if they voiced concerns relating to safety. There was evidence that safety management systems were getting little more than lip service, thus increasing the risk of train derailments and other accidents. According to one former employee, "We had it drummed into our heads if trains aren't running on time, somebody would want to know why and it could mean our jobs."[68]

Downsizing and Safety

Another issue that is beginning to attract attention is the relationship between downsizing and employee safety. This is particularly relevant in light of the number of downsizings announced in recent years. The research evidence suggests that downsizing creates job insecurity, which is strongly

Spotlight *on* ETHICS

A Question of Safety

Consider the following situation and make a note of your answer on a separate sheet of paper.

You are a supervisor at a local dairy. Your job involves supervising employees who work in the dairy while another individual is responsible for supervising the employees who deliver milk to various stores. In the past six months, the labour market has been fairly tight and your company has been having problems attracting and retaining good delivery people.

Two weeks ago, the human resource management department hired a new milk delivery employee named Lucy Lynn. Lucy's job involves driving a milk van and making deliveries to grocery stores. By all accounts, Lucy is a very competent and reliable employee, and the human resource professional who hired her did so without any hesitation. Lucy is also the mother of one of your best friends. Lucy, who is 54 years of age, was recently downsized from her job as a delivery person at a large courier company.

Two days ago, you were invited to dinner at Lucy's house. Lucy commented on how much she was enjoying her new job and how grateful she was to obtain employment so quickly. Lucy had recently gone through a messy divorce, and you were aware that she was having some financial problems.

Just after dinner, you went out to the kitchen and found Lucy sitting on a chair with her head resting on the kitchen table. When you asked whether she was okay, she replied that "Everything is fine. It's just that over the last few months, I have been getting really bad headaches and have had three or four dizzy spells. When my head starts whirling, I just need to sit down and put my head between my knees. It's no big deal—the dizziness passes in a few minutes. I'm telling you this in confidence. Please don't tell anyone at work. I can't afford to lose my job."

What are you going to do? Complicating the decision is that you know the company asks individuals who will be driving company vehicles to provide a detailed medical history. The questions include whether the individual has experienced dizzy spells and severe headaches. After completing the form, individuals are required to sign that they have answered the questions honestly and to the best of their ability.

associated with low levels of job satisfaction. Low job satisfaction, in turn, is related to *safety motivation* (the motivation to perform a job in a safe manner) and *safety knowledge* (an understanding of safe operating procedures). When safety motivation is low, employees are less likely to comply with safety procedures and carry out their work in a safe manner (what is known as *safety compliance*). Finally, lower levels of safety compliance are associated with more workplace accidents. It is suggested that during a downsizing, employees concerned with keeping their jobs view productivity as more important than safety. However, in downsizings in which employees perceived that the safety climate was positive and the organization viewed safety as very important, the negative outcomes associated with job insecurity were not seen.[69]

LO5 Workplace Stress

The term *stress management* is now part of the regular vocabulary of managers and employees, but what is "workplace stress"? *Workplace stress* is "the harmful physical and emotional responses that can happen when there is

a conflict between job demands of the employee and the amount of control the employee has over meeting those demands."[70] Although high levels of stress are usually associated with poorer job performance, not all stress is harmful. Moderate levels of stress may actually increase workplace performance.

A ComPsych survey indicated that 59 percent of employees have high levels of stress, with extreme fatigue/feeling out of control; 35 percent report having constant but manageable stress; and 6 percent indicate having low stress levels. In terms of the impact of stress, 35 percent of employees report losing one hour or more a day in productivity due to stress, 55 percent miss one to two days due to stress, 31 percent miss three to six days, and 14 percent miss more than six days a year.[71]

Similarly, a study of more than 7,300 employees by Globe Careers/Howatt HR Consulting revealed that about 6 out of 10 people felt stressed and on edge. Respondents were placed in one of five categories (Calm to Losing It) based on their scores on a Quality of Life scale. In the Calm group, 26 percent were senior managers or executives,

96 percent said they put 80 percent or more effort into their job each day, 2 percent indicated suffering from a mental health issue, and 16 percent reported calling in sick more than four days a year. For the Losing It group, only 9 percent were senior managers or executives, 52 percent said they put 80 percent or more effort into their job every day, 4 percent responded that they suffered from a mental health issue, and 48 percent stated that they called in sick more than four days a year. The Losing It group were more likely to report not being a good fit for their job, that the work culture was not positive, that they had trouble sleeping, that they suffered from headaches, that they did not receive adequate performance feedback, and that they would leave the organization if they could.[72]

It is estimated that stress-related absences cost the Canadian economy more than \$4.5 billion a year, have increased more than threefold since 1995, and average about 20 days in length. Health Canada suggests that each dollar invested in the prevention of stress is worth about \$3.40 in future savings.[73]

Is stress associated with quitting a job? A recent Monster Canada report reveals that about 25 percent of Canadians have quit a job while a further 17 percent also considered it because of stress. Women were more likely than men to quit for stress-related reasons (28 percent compared to 22 percent). Employees earning less than \$40,000 a year were most likely to leave a job due to stress (38 percent), while 27 percent of workers earning between \$40,000 to \$59,000 reported quitting due to stress. The two most important stress factors were workload and office politics.[74]

The actual experience or the perceived threat of a corporate takeover, merger, downsizing, or plant closing, all of which could put large numbers of employees out of jobs, can lead to a variety of symptoms of stress that can harm employees' job performance. These symptoms involve both mental health and physical health. Persons who are stressed may become nervous, easily provoked to anger, and chronically worried about things.

There is a growing body of research indicating that stress may be associated with cardiovascular disease (in particular, among employees in psychologically demanding jobs that allow workers little control over the work process), musculoskeletal disorders (such as back injuries), psychological disorders (for example, depression and burnout), workplace injuries, suicide, cancer, ulcers, and impaired immune functions.[75] In addition, employer immunity from lawsuits as a result of contributing to the workers' compensation system is being eroded as more courts allow employees to sue their employers for stress resulting from a poisoned work environment.

Although there has been a lot of effort aimed at protecting employees from physical harm at work, experts are now calling for greater attention to psychological safety at work. According to Lorne Zon, former CEO of the Canadian Mental Health Association (Ontario Division), "We expect psychological safety in our schools and communities, and we should be able to count on it in the workplace. If employees don't feel safe speaking to their managers or co-workers, because they are afraid of recrimination, the workplace is not psychologically safe and productivity will be affected."[76]

In early 2013, the National Standard on Psychological Health and Safety in the Workplace was published. The purposes of the National Standard are to identify and eliminate hazards in the workplace that pose a risk of psychological harm to a worker and assess and control the risks associated with hazards that cannot be eliminated, implement structures and practices that support and promote psychological health and safety in the workplace, and foster a culture that promotes psychological health and safety in the workplace.[77]

Causes of Stress at Work

A model of job stress has been developed by the National Institute for Occupational Safety and Health in the United States.[78] According to the model, exposure to stressful working conditions (called "job stressors") can directly influence the health and safety of employees. However, the model also recognizes that individual and situational factors can intervene to strengthen or weaken the relationship between stressful job conditions and the risk of injury or illness. Examples of individual and situational factors include one's outlook or attitude, the presence of a support network of co-workers or friends, and the balance between work and family life.

Although major distress can occur from only one stressor, usually **stressors** combine to affect an employee in a variety of ways until distress develops.

> **stressors** Stressful working conditions that can directly influence the health and safety of employees.

While almost any job condition may cause stress (depending upon an employee's reaction to it), there are, however, a number of job conditions that frequently cause stress for employees. Some of the major causes of workplace stress are outlined in Figure 12-5.

It is also possible to distinguish between *acute stressors,* which occur infrequently but are extremely stressful events (such as a major organizational change), and *chronic stressors,* which are the ongoing, daily problems and hassles that occur at work. While many wellness programs are aimed at chronic stress, organizations regularly ignore the impacts on employees associated with major organizational changes.

With many employers cutting back on staff, employees are being told to work smarter, but there is evidence that many are not able to face the added pressure. One study found that as people work longer hours, their risk of injury and illness goes up. This includes workplace accidents, depression, hypertension, stress, cardiovascular disease, and chronic infections.[79]

Recent evidence from Statistics Canada revealed that more than one in four workers (about 3.7 million working

FIGURE 12-5

Causes of Workplace Stress

Factors Unique to the Job

- Relationships at work
- Workload
- Work pace/variety/meaningfulness of work
- Autonomy
- Hours of work/shift work
- Physical environment (noise, air quality, etc.)
- Isolation (physical or emotional)

Role in the Organization

- Role conflict/role ambiguity
- Level of responsibility

Relationships at Work

- Supervisors/co-workers/subordinates
- Threat of violence, harassment, and so on

Organizational Climate

- Participation (or nonparticipation) in decision making
- Management style
- Communication patterns

Career Development

- Under- or overpromotion
- Job security
- Career-development opportunities
- Overall job satisfaction

SOURCE: Based on "Major Causes of Workplace Stress." Adapted from L.R. Murphy (1995), "Occupational stress management: Current status and future direction," *Trends in Organizational Behavior,* pp. 1–14.

adults) reported life as being "highly stressed." For highly stressed individuals, the main source of stress was, in fact, work (63 percent), followed by finances (12 percent), time (12 percent), and family issues (8 percent). Respondents with poorer physical and mental health were more likely to be highly stressed. Workers who were mainly stressed about work tended to be well-educated and have white-collar jobs, workers anxious about finances had lower incomes and less skilled jobs, and women were more likely to be stressed about family matters.[80]

What are the most stressful jobs? A 2017 CareerCast study revealed that the most stressful jobs are enlisted military personnel, firefighter, airline pilot, police officer, and event coordinator. The least stressful jobs included diagnostic medical sonographer, hair stylist, audiologist, university professor, and medical records technician.[81]

Poor supervision can cause stress. For example, the following stressful conditions are mostly created by poor supervision: an insecure workplace climate, lack of performance feedback, and inadequate authority to match one's responsibilities. Workers frequently complain in private about "bad bosses."

A study of workers in Finland revealed that a bad boss may be hazardous to employee health. Employees who perceived that they were being treated fairly at work by their supervisors had a 30 percent lower risk of coronary heart disease compared with co-workers who did not believe that their supervisors treated them fairly.[82]

A general and widely recognized cause of stress is *change of any type* because it requires adaptation by employees. Change tends to be especially stressful when it is major, unusual, or frequent. One particular type of change that dominated the 1990s and is becoming more common since the global financial crisis is organizational downsizing. In many organizations, the "survivors" of workplace change are being asked to work longer hours and do more with limited resources. Working in such an environment may increase both employee stress and the probability of having an accident. As well, downsizing may have an impact on an employee's family. Research suggests that the job loss of a parent affects that parent's children. Perceptions of the job insecurity of a parent were associated with negative attitudes toward work and lower grades on exams.[83]

Evidence from the Global Business and Economic Roundtable on Addiction and Mental Health indicates that about 18 to 25 percent of American and Canadian workers suffer from depression, and employers are losing billions of dollars due to lost productivity and a lower capacity to compete. In order to build a healthy workplace, CEOs must value a psychologically healthy and safe workplace and be willing to walk the talk.[84] Consider the impact of stress on Canadian call centre workers:

A study of call centre employees revealed that employees in the industry suffer higher rates of stress and emotional difficulty than workers in other industries. The call centre industry currently employs about half a million Canadians. It is estimated that among 100 recent hires at a call centre, 14 percent may experience high levels of stress and 10 percent may experience high levels of depression. Each day about 10 percent of employees call in sick, turnover may run as high as 50 percent or more a year, and the cost of training a replacement employee is more than $6,000. As observed by Karen Seward, senior vice-president at Shepell, "It doesn't take long to do the math to figure out the impact of this on a company's profits."[85]

Burnout

Burnout is a condition of mental, emotional, and sometimes physical exhaustion that results from substantial and prolonged stress. It can occur for any type of employee, whether one is a professional employee, secretary, or labourer. There is growing concern over what has become known as *presenteeism,* which describes an employee who is able to

> **burnout** A condition of mental, emotional, and sometimes physical exhaustion that results from substantial and prolonged stress.

© Tom Grill/Getty Images.

Too much stress on the job can lead to employee burnout. What measures can an employer take to reduce stress? Can stress be avoided?

come to work but is inhibited from achieving optimal levels of productivity due to ongoing health issues.[86] One employee described a burned-out associate in the following way: "His body is here today, but his mind stayed home."

With respect to burnout, the human resource department's role is a proactive one to help employees prevent burnout before it occurs. For example, the human resource department can train supervisors to recognize stress and rearrange work assignments to reduce it. Jobs may be redesigned, staff conflicts resolved, counselling provided, and temporary leaves arranged. Weeks or months of rest, reassignment, or treatment may be required before recovery occurs. Some emotional or health damage can be permanent. International evidence suggests that health issues are a global concern:

> The Global Wellness Institute notes that many of the world's 3.2 billion workers are unwell with 45 percent employed in low-skill or manual jobs and 77 percent in part-time, temporary, vulnerable, or unpaid jobs. Moreover, 38 percent suffer from excessive pressure on the job, and 24 percent are actively disengaged from work. It is estimated that the economic burden of unwell workers is in the range of 10 to 15 percent of global economic output. For the United States alone, the costs of unwellness are estimated at $2.2 trillion a year (about 12 percent of GDP), with the cost breakdown arising from chronic disease ($1,100 billion), work-related injuries and illnesses ($250 billion), work-related stress ($300 billion), and disengagement at work ($550 billion).[87]

Stress and Job Performance

Stress can be either helpful or harmful to job performance. When there is no stress, job challenges are absent and performance tends to be low. As stress increases, performance tends to increase because stress helps a person call up resources to meet job requirements. It is a healthy stimulus to encourage employees to respond to challenges. Eventually it reaches a plateau that represents approximately a person's top day-to-day performance capability. At this point, additional stress tends to produce no more improvement. Finally, if stress becomes too great, performance begins to decline because stress interferes with it. An employee loses the ability to cope, becomes unable to make decisions, and is erratic in behaviour.

Major causes of stress at the workplace include workload (39 percent), people issues (31 percent), and juggling work and personal life (19 percent). In terms of impact on productivity, 23 percent of respondents indicate productivity is unaffected by stress, 41 percent lose 15 to 30 minutes a day in productivity due to stress, and 36 percent lose one hour or more as a result of stress.[88]

There are several solutions to the problem of workplace stress. Curative solutions try to correct the outcome of stress, while preventive solutions attempt to change the cause of stress. In terms of *curative measures,* some employers give employees the opportunity to relax through such activities as aerobic exercises, yoga, and meditation. Some companies have counselling professionals on staff, employ an external consulting service that provides assistance in diagnosing the causes of stress and developing ways to cope with it, and are looking at or using video counselling as a means of helping employees. While video counselling is at times the only option for employees in remote locations, it also gives employees more flexibility in scheduling counselling sessions. However, it is important that the counselling platform meets privacy requirements (such as PIPEDA), has appropriate technology support, and allows for multiple participants.[89]

With regard to *preventive measures,* there are different approaches to dealing with stress at the workplace. First, organizations can establish stress management training sessions and EAP assistance to help workers deal with stress. Second, some organizations are looking at improving working conditions in order to reduce stress at work—the employer needs to identify stressful situations and design strategies to reduce or eliminate the stressors. In managing stress, it may be necessary to bring in outside experts.[90]

Management should look at the structure of the organization and the design of jobs. Several Canadian organizations have developed programs that provide workers with more diversified tasks, greater control over decisions that affect their work, and a chance for wider participation in the overall production process. Figure 12-6 shows some of the specific actions that the human resource department should take to reduce employee stress and burnout.

The Stress Audit

Human resource managers must be sensitive to the many possible sources and causes of stress at the workplace. It is possible to evaluate the extent of dysfunctional stress by performing a stress audit, which assists in identifying the causes of stress.[91] The stress audit asks the following questions:

- Do any individuals demonstrate physiological symptoms?
- Is job satisfaction low, or are job tension, turnover, absenteeism, strikes, or accident proneness high?
- Does the organization's design contribute to the symptoms described?
- Do interpersonal relations contribute to the symptoms described?
- Do career-development variables contribute to the symptoms described?
- What effects do personality, socio-cultural influences, and the nonwork environment have on the relationship between the stressors—individual careers, interpersonal relations, and organizational design—and stress?

Mental Health

It is estimated that mental health problems and illnesses cost the Canadian economy more than $50 billion a year directly and $6 billion annually for lost productivity resulting from related absenteeism. Approximately 6.7 million Canadians have a mental health problem or illness, about half a million Canadians are absent in any given week as a result of mental health issues, and around 30 percent of disability claims and 70 percent of disability costs are attributable to mental illness.[92] A Conference Board of Canada report indicated that about 44 percent of Canadians experienced a mental health issue and only 26 percent perceived that their supervisor "effectively managed mental health issues." The report also revealed that employees on disability

FIGURE 12-6

Actions to Reduce Stress

- Ensure that an employee's workload is compatible with the individual's capabilities and resources.
- Design jobs to provide meaningful opportunities for employees to use their skills.
- Clearly define employee roles and responsibilities.
- Provide workers with the opportunity to participate in decision making.
- Improve the communications process.
- Increase opportunities for social interaction among employees.
- Develop appropriate work schedules.
- Train managers and employees to be sensitive to the symptoms of stress.
- Establish a stress management policy.

SOURCE: National Institute for Occupational Health and Safety, *Stress at Work.*

Spotlight *on* HRM

Parents' Job Anxiety Wreaks Havoc on Children

A Queen's University researcher has documented a relationship that HR specialists have long recognized—children absorb the job anxieties of their parents. Business professor Dr. Julian Barling surveyed 154 commerce undergraduates and their parents and found that children's perceptions of their parents' job insecurities affect their attitudes about work and jobs and, indirectly, their grades.

Barling, an expert in work and family relationships at the Kingston, Ontario, university, said that he undertook the study because "we need to be aware of how the next generation is being affected by current insecurity in the workplace." In his study, he found a close correlation between students' perceptions and their midterm grades. Barling considers school performance to be a matter of great concern because "how children perform at school affects their self-esteem and how they are perceived by peers, teachers, and families. And, in the long term, grades obtained will influence the educational and occupational opportunities open to them."

In a companion study . . . in the *Journal of Applied Psychology,* Barling writes that children's perceptions of their parents' job insecurity also affect their beliefs and attitudes toward work. He notes that the waves of layoffs in both the public and private sectors in the last decade may produce "a generation of young people with pre-existing negative work beliefs and attitudes which may not be amenable to change."

Parents Anxious Over More Than Security

Barling is not alone in his observations. "Professor Barling has quantified something I have been observing for well over a decade—children are sponges and readily absorb their parents' anxiety and ambivalence about work," said Barbara Moses, president of BBM Human Resource Consultants, Inc., and author of *Career Intelligence.* She added that parental anxieties

extend beyond job insecurity to include dissatisfaction with promotions, wages, workload, and perquisites.

"Is it any wonder that children are ambivalent? They see their parents tired and complaining, or more likely, they rarely see their parents. They grow to feel their parents are abused by work, and work denies them access to their parents. They see their parents as victims of their jobs and careers. And, despite these sacrifices, their employers treat them badly and let them go."

HR's Role Goes beyond EAPs

Moses said HR professionals have a role to play in reducing employee anxiety and the communication of this anxiety to sons and daughters. "At a minimum, HR should ensure that corporate communications do not unnecessarily incite job anxiety among employees," she said. "In addition, HR can promote career management among employees. Career support services reassure employees that they will be okay even if they lose their jobs. Encourage them to talk the language of employability rather than job security."

The assistance can be provided through support groups and Employee Assistance Programs, although Moses and others say EAPs are insufficient because they are reactive rather than proactive, and fail to address the needs of employees who do not identify themselves as anxious.

Sam Klarreich, president of the Berkeley Centre for Wellness, described the success of a support group he was involved with a few years ago at Imperial Oil. "We set up a group to help employees deal with on-the-job stress. We brought guest speakers, reprinted and shared articles on stress, held group discussions, published a newsletter. By working together the group members learned better ways to cope with stress. The program was such a success the group grew from an initial membership of 20 to over 200."

SOURCE: © Canadian HR Reporter, December 29, 1997, pp. 16, 20. Reprinted by permission of Canadian HR Reporter. © Copyright Thomson Reuters Canada Ltd. (2015), Toronto, Ontario, 1-800-387-5164. https://www.hrreporter.com

who leave for more than 12 weeks have about a 1 in 2 chance of returning to work.[93] However, some employers are making major strides in helping employees.

Willow Bean Café in Vancouver has six employees, all of whom are also clients of the Canadian Mental Health Association. According to Elisha Brodeur, employment support coordinator for the café, the program "trains clients of CMHA in an actual café setting. They're people who have maybe faced more barriers to finding employment due to mental health problems or struggles with mental illness."[94]

The 2016 Sun Life Canadian Health Index report indicated that about 29 percent of Canadians were impacted by a mental health issue and 66 percent indicated that deteriorating health is a top concern as people age. The same report from 2014 revealed that more than three-quarters of participants indicated that they are stressed out, with the most important factors being personal or household finances (41 percent), trying to maintain a budget (31 percent), unexpected expenses (30 percent), personal relationships (29 percent), and work life (25 percent). About 29 percent of respondents reported never or rarely participating in at least 30 minutes of physical activity a day.[95]

A 2017 study by Ipsos found that 40 percent of Canadians indicated that mental health disrupted their lives in the past year. Based on a "mental health index," 41 percent of Canadians are at a high risk for mental illness. Moreover, 23 percent of respondents reported taking medication to help with their mental health and about 500,000 Canadians miss work every week because of mental health concerns.[96]

In order to get a more complete picture of mental health in the workplace, it is important to also consider the influence of life at home. A study of almost 2,000 employees from 63 organizations reveals that mental health in an organization does not exist in a vacuum. Fewer mental health problems were associated with living with a partner, living in households with young children, living with higher household incomes, living with fewer work–family conflicts, and living with greater access to social network support away from work. In addition, work-related factors (including support for employees, higher use of skills, job security, and meeting expectations of job recognition) were also related with fewer mental health issues.[97]

HR professionals may need to develop a greater understanding of mental illness issues and diagnoses. The *Diagnostic and Statistical Manual of Mental Disorders (DSM)*, which is considered to be the authoritative source for the diagnosis of mental illness, had its first major revision in nearly 20 years. Major changes included new diagnostic criteria, greater attention to culture and gender, and a developmental focus. The DSM is used by several parties, including arbitrators, employers and HR professionals, workers' compensation decision-makers, and mental health professionals.[98] Consider the following arbitration case:

A 38-year-old labourer at a Toronto dairy manufacturing plant was diagnosed with severe mental health conditions. The employee's behaviour became quite erratic and the employer ultimately terminated the worker because of the safety risk. An arbitrator ruled that the employer had examined accommodation to the point of undue hardship and concluded that the employee should not be reinstated to active duty. However, the company was ordered to reinstate the employee for three months without compensation solely for the purpose of allowing the employee to apply for long-term disability benefits.[99]

Saskatchewan recently amended its *Workers' Compensation Act* and stated that all forms of psychological injuries will be presumed to be work-related. The change was in response to data indicating that about half of the claims for psychological injury were being declined because the employee was unable to establish a link to employment or establish the nature of the injury. Employers expressed concern with the legislation because psychological injury is not defined, because an organization having a large number of claims could have a higher premium for workers' compensation, and because bogus or frivolous claims could drain employer resources.[100]

Fitness and Employee Wellness Programs

Fitness, wellness, and lifestyle programs have become quite popular in organizations and have been shown to have a positive impact on reducing stress and absenteeism and increasing productivity. A UK study of more than 1,000 employees revealed that 39 percent of employees reported that losing weight was their top health issue, followed by managing stress (26 percent), and getting more exercise (17 percent).[101]

Many employees want access to health promotion programs in the workplace, and the National Wellness Survey Report for 2013 indicates that more than 90 percent of Canadian organizations with 50 or more employees and almost 60 percent of smaller employers offer at least one type of wellness initiative. The most common wellness initiatives were flexible work programs (49 percent), first aid/CPR courses (36 percent), staff appreciation events (28 percent), time off in lieu of overtime (27 percent), involvement of employees in work scheduling (27 percent), and flu shot programs (24 percent). However, 87 percent of employers do not measure the health status of employees and 75 percent are not confident that they have the knowledge or support to effectively address employee mental health needs. About 47 percent of employers are using incentive programs to encourage participation in wellness initiatives. The biggest barriers to adopting wellness initiatives were lack of budget (28 percent), lack of staffing (21 percent), lack of ability to quantify benefits (19 percent), little knowledge of wellness (19 percent), and lack of conviction of cost savings (18 percent).[102]

According to the Conference Board of Canada, only 32 percent of employers had a formal wellness strategy, while just under one-half (48 percent) were relying on informal strategies, and 20 percent had no wellness strategy.[103]

Starting in 2011, the safest employers in Canada have been recognized at the Canada's Safest Employer Awards ceremony. In addition to awards in 10 industries, there is also a wellness and psychological safety award and, beginning in 2015, a young worker safety and best health and safety culture award. In 2017, Niagara Casinos won awards for wellness and psychological safety. Five years ago, the company (which has about 4,000 employees with an average age of 49) overhauled its wellness program. Among the initiatives were healthy alternatives in the cafeterias, wellness centres at each location, and resilience training for casino dealers.[104]

A recent Aon Hewitt survey of Canadian employers indicated that about 92 percent of employers believe that an integrated approach to managing health is essential but only 20 percent see their programs as in the top ranges of integration. Among the most common wellness initiatives were employee assistance programs (93 percent), lunch and learns (59 percent), health spending accounts (55 percent), newsletters (45 percent), and fitness memberships (42 percent). About 39 percent had online fitness classes and 23 percent had a smoking cessation program.[105]

Is an employer allowed to restrict job applicants to nonsmokers? According to Krista McMullin of Smoke-Free Nova Scotia, "Having smokers can mean more lost time, indirect health care costs, longer breaks, and less productivity." However, providing support for smokers indicates that an employer cares about its employees. While the law is currently unsettled, it can be argued that an addiction to smoking is a disability, thus raising the possibility of a human rights complaint.[106]

The average annual cost to an employer for each smoker is estimated by the Conference Board of Canada to be $4,256. Part of the cost is related to absenteeism with smokers, on average, taking more than two extra sick days a year than nonsmokers. In addition, unsanctioned smoke breaks result in a loss of $3,842 per employee. Further, smokers and those who recently quit smoking are 2.3 times more likely to be off work for three months or more a year due to chronic health issues.[107]

How effective are wellness programs? While most evaluations have come from large American corporations with comprehensive programs, the evidence indicates that such programs do the following:

- Improve employee health
- Decrease health care costs
- Improve employee satisfaction
- Decrease absenteeism and turnover
- Improve corporate image
- Reduce disability claims

A review of 73 published studies revealed an average savings-to-cost ratio of $3.50 to $1.00 due to reduced absenteeism and health care costs. A meta-analysis of 43 studies indicated an average reduction of 28 percent in sick leave absenteeism and a 30 percent reduction in workers' compensation and disability management claims associated

© Dougal Waters/Getty Images

More and more companies are promoting health by providing health programs. Would the money be better spent by paying bonuses that serve to motivate employees?

with health promotion.[108] Specific programs also show significant benefits:

A British Columbia initiative called UPnGO is a workplace wellness program being tried out at five major companies. It is estimated that only 20 percent of Canadians get the recommended two-and-a-half hours per week of moderate to vigorous physical activity. Employees in the UPnGo program complete an initial assessment and are then given an individual step goal. The goals of the program include trying to improve on traditional participation rates in fitness programs and to specifically target employees who are less physically active and sedentary.[109]

In evaluating the success of wellness programs, employers are focusing on positive feedback from participants, good participation, improved employee morale, and reduced absenteeism. Only 19 percent of organizations were using a positive return on investment as a measure of success. When asked to identify health risk concerns, the three biggest issues included poor stress management skills, lack of exercise by employees, and an inability to balance work and family issues.[110] Some employers are being creative in trying to help workers get healthier:

One approach involves imitating digital games and having employees track health performance online. In many instances, employees form teams and monitor their results. There is some concern that employees may feel manipulated or pressured by co-workers to help the team win. In one organization, employees posted messages criticizing co-workers who were dragging the team down.[111]

There is some recent evidence that positive results from employee wellness programs are associated with the involvement of organizational leadership and the provision of stress management initiatives. The most effective wellness programs include wellness competitions (83 percent), counselling on nutrition (63 percent), fitness programs (60 percent), wellness seminars and health fairs (53 percent), and health screening (52 percent).[112]

Although labour unions have been strong supporters of health and safety initiatives, organized labour has not always been an advocate of wellness programs: Unions are often skeptical about employer motivations behind wellness programs and there is a concern that employee information may be collected and tracked to be used in attendance management.

Other Contemporary Safety Issues

Workplace Security

The events of September 11, 2001, increased employer and employee awareness of workplace security issues. This has led to a reassessment of security policies used to make workplaces safe. In addition to terror concerns, other issues include preparations for a disaster (such as an earthquake or flood) and access to workplace property by an intruder:

> While schools are generally well prepared for a lockdown, many employers are not. However, the attack at the National War Memorial and subsequent firing of shots on Parliament Hill in October 2014 have made employers more aware of the importance of having a lockdown procedure. According to Ann Wyganowski, director of the Toronto Disaster Recovery Information Exchange, "Employers should conduct a proper internal and external assessment ahead of time. Training is also important. You need to do the drills."[113]

A number of organizations have developed emergency plans (such as evacuation of buildings), implemented training programs associated with security issues, assessed the work site for hazards and security shortcomings, and established safety competencies for managers and supervisors.[114] However, not all employees feel secure at work:

> Letter carriers in Montreal have been subject to more than a dozen attacks by assailants seeking keys to mailboxes to steal credit cards, passports, and other documents. The keys provide access to grey boxes, community mailboxes, and apartments. While there are allegations of thousands of thefts from community mailboxes, Canada Post says it doesn't have data on such thefts. According to Canadian Union of Postal Workers president Mike Palacek, "We've been asking for this information for years and Canada Post refuses to release it. We all realize community mailboxes are a problem and far less secure than door-to-door delivery."[115]

Some firms have taken proactive measures to increase security for employees:

> During the global financial crisis, TD Bank became concerned about robberies. Consequently, it trained 33,000 employees in robbery prevention. A training needs assessment was completed and the company also partnered with the RCMP and an armed robbery prevention association with the goal of making the training as realistic as possible. The training included elearning, instructor-led discussions, role-plays, informal discussions, and ongoing coaching. The bank has seen several benefits from the training, including a reduction in robberies, increased safety to employees and customers, and a positive return on investment.[116]

Sick Building Syndrome (SBS)

Sick building syndrome is used to describe situations in which employees experience acute health and comfort effects that appear to be linked to the length of time spent in a building but no specific illness or cause can be identified. However, the term *building-related illness* is used when symptoms of diagnosable illness are identified and are attributable directly to airborne contaminants in a building.[117]

People spend up to 90 percent of their lives indoors, and a growing number report becoming sick while working in a particular building. Symptoms range from headaches to dizziness to nausea, to eye, ear, or throat irritation, to allergic reactions. Sick building syndrome may be caused by major combustion pollutants (caused, for instance, by malfunctioning heating systems), biological air pollutants (such as mites, mould, and dander), volatile organic compounds (including pesticides, solvents, and cleaners), and heavy metals (such as lead). Human resource professionals should take proactive steps to prevent sick building syndrome.[118] However, sick building syndrome is not always easy to detect:

> The Alberta Court of Appeal building has been abandoned since 2001. Following renovations to the building, there were numerous complaints from lawyers, judges, and other workers of watery eyes, fatigue, and irritated lungs. It took a considerable time to figure out the problem, but eventually it was determined that air quality was the problem—the new, airtight building trapped moisture inside the walls, leading to the growth of toxic mould. It is estimated that about 4 percent of the population react to mould spores and that between 30 to 50 percent of new or refurbished buildings cause sick building syndrome.[119]

Workplace Violence

One area of safety management that has been neglected to some extent concerns workplace violence. However, a scan of newspapers and television reports indicates that workplace violence is not a rare event. In this era of restructuring and productivity improvement, there have been a number of accounts of terminated employees returning to the workplace and injuring or killing other employees. For example, Chuang "Ray" Li, a computer programmer at Ceridian Canada in Toronto, allegedly stabbed four of his former co-workers after being fired and is facing several charges, including attempted murder. As a result, jurisdictions across the country have developed legislation to address the issue.[120] Consider the experiences of health care workers:

> A recent study of nurses revealed that 68 percent report experiencing at least one incident of violence during the past year and 20 percent experienced nine or more violent incidents. Three-quarters have witnessed at least one incident of violence against a co-worker, and 26 percent lost time at work due to violence on the job.[121]

Evidence from the United States indicates that about 9 percent of workplace deaths were homicides, with four-fifths of the deaths resulting from gunshots. Workplace violence is the second-highest cause of workplace death for women (behind traffic accidents), with 22 percent of the fatal workplace injuries to women resulting from homicide. In terms of deaths per 100,000 workers, U.S. evidence indicates that the highest-risk jobs (in order of risk of death) include taxi drivers, law enforcement officers, hotel clerks, gas station attendants and security guards, liquor store workers, detective or protective service workers, and jewellery store workers. The jobs with the greatest risk of workplace violence are police officers, security guards, taxi drivers, prison guards, bartenders, mental health professionals, gas station attendants, and convenience or liquor store clerks.[122] Measures aimed at preventing or reducing the incidence of workplace violence include an anti-violence/zero-tolerance policy, self-defence training, and safety and security measures.

A 2012 study from the United States indicates that 36 percent of organizations had at least one incident of workplace violence during the previous five years. In the event of a threat of violence from an employee, the HR department (90 percent) and management staff (45 percent) were most commonly identified as being responsible to handle the issue. Verbal threats were most common, followed by pushing or shoving, robbery, fist-fighting, and stalking.[123]

Additional U.S. research on workplace violence revealed that about two million workers become victims of workplace violence every year. Health care professionals experienced more injuries from workplace violence than all other industries combined, and 44 percent of teachers reported being physically attacked while at school over a one-year period. Workplace violence is the second leading cause of death on the job for women. Since 2010, there

have been more than 150 employee-on-employee killings; two-thirds of workplace homicides are committed by a person not close to the employee, and robberies make up about 85 percent of workplace violence deaths. It is estimated that $3 or more is saved for every dollar invested in workplace safety.[124]

A study entitled *Violence and Aggression in the Workplace* involved a survey of Canadian CEOs. The results indicated that the three most common incidents of workplace violence were loud screaming or yelling; destruction of employer property during a fit of anger; and throwing a telephone, pen, or some other office object in anger. Based on CEO perceptions, the top three contributors to workplace violence were consumption of drugs and alcohol, lack of management authority, and poor morale.[125]

With the growth of the Internet and social media, one of the most recent threats at the workplace involves "cyberstalking," which is the use of electronic communications to harass or threaten another individual. Based on 2013 data, the most common ways in which cyberstalking escalated included Facebook (29 percent), phone (25 percent), text messaging (24 percent), and Twitter (17 percent).[126] Although one might expect that careful selection of new hires may be an important step in reducing workplace violence, a recent study places more attention on situational factors and poor management:

> According to Julian Barling, co-author of a study entitled *Supervisor-Targeted Aggression*, "In trying to understand why people behave aggressively in the workplace, we should give primary responsibility to situational rather than personal considerations." Barling believes that in creating a healthy work environment where workers are treated fairly, quality supervision is important in reducing workplace violence. Moreover, when an act of workplace violence does occur, he suggests looking inside the workplace for a potential cause rather than assuming that the worker has a psychological problem.[127]

In workplace violence lawsuits, courts in the United States are placing a much heavier onus on employers to take reasonable care in making sure that the workplace is safe. Factors considered by the courts include the crime rate in the neighbourhood, the security measures in place at the business, the lighting of the buildings and grounds, the architectural design of the buildings, and recommendations from security consultants.

It is estimated that workplace violence costs well over $8 billion a year, with costs including medical care, disability and workers' compensation, higher insurance rates, negative public relations and company image, consulting fees, greater security measures, and lower morale and productivity. Experts point out that under Bill C-45, employers and executives may be criminally liable for failing to take reasonable steps to prevent workplace violence and accidents. Proactive suggestions include careful employee selection, development of a comprehensive policy on workplace violence, employee training, assessment of the likelihood of workplace violence, and rigorous security standards.[128]

Jamie Pasieka, who worked at a Loblaw warehouse in Edmonton, stopped at a military surplus store on his way to work, purchased two large knives, and allegedly attacked several co-workers, leaving two dead and four injured. According to Glenn French of the Canadian Initiative on Workplace Violence, an incident of workplace violence is very complex because "there is an environmental impact, there's witness and bystander impact, and, of course, there's the impact on the individual (victim) and the individual's family."[129]

Workplace bullying can cause mental health problems yet many employers are not aware of national standards aimed at protecting the psychological health of employees. Consultant Valerie Cade notes that there is no well-established definition of bullying, but her definition is this: "Workplace bullying is deliberate, disrespectful, and repeated behaviour toward someone or many people, for the bully's gain." According to Cade, envy is at the root of all bullying, and nice, effective people are frequently targeted. The bully's goal is to take something away from the victim (such as praise from somebody or relationships at work).[130]

Another issue that is gaining more attention is the link between domestic violence and other facets of an employee's life, including his or her life at work. A study by Western University and the Canadian Labour Congress revealed that about one in three respondents said that they had experienced a domestic violence incident during their lives (17 percent of men, 38 percent of women, and 65 percent of participants in the transgender/other category). Prevalence of domestic violence was particularly high for respondents with disabilities, Indigenous respondents, and individuals indicating that their sexual orientation was not heterosexual. Almost 54 percent of participants who reported experiencing domestic violence said that at least one abusive act occurred at or close to their workplace, 38 percent reported that domestic violence affected their ability to get to work, and just under 9 percent reported losing a job because of domestic violence. The most common abuse acts at or near the workplace included abusive phone calls or text messages (41 percent), stalking or harassment near the workplace (21 percent), and the abuser coming to the workplace (18 percent).[131]

Ergonomics

An area of health and safety that is attracting more attention is ergonomics (also known as *human factors*

engineering). As discussed in Chapter 2, ergonomics focuses on the interaction between employees and their total working environment.[132] An ergonomics program seeks to ensure that the physical and behavioural characteristics of the employee are compatible with the work system (including methods of work, machines and equipment, the work environment, and the workplace or work station layout).[133]

While a number of organizations wait until employees complain about the work system or sustain an injury, proactive employers aim to ensure that the work system is compatible with employees; recent research indicates that it is important to incorporate wellness initiatives into ergonomic and safety programs.[134] Consultants specializing in ergonomics can assist organizations in the design and implementation of the work system.

Two common types of injuries that may be reduced by the application of ergonomic principles are (1) overexertion and lower back injury and (2) repetitive-strain injuries (RSI), which may include cumulative trauma disorder (CTD), overuse syndrome (OS), and musculoskeletal injury (MSI). Repetitive-strain injuries are caused by repeated actions resulting in muscle or skeletal strain.

According to Statistics Canada, about 15 percent of Canadians (4.5 million individuals) are affected by repetitive strain injuries (RSIs). RSIs are the most frequent type of lost-time injuries and the largest source of lost-time injury costs in the country.[135]

The treatment of repetitive-strain injuries is complex and varied. Some of the approaches used include physical treatments (such as physiotherapy or chiropractic treatments), postural treatments (often aimed at correcting bad habits relating to posture), relaxation (such as meditation), exercise and stretching, acupuncture, and cognitive behavioural therapy (with a focus on coping with pain).[136] A properly designed work station can play a major role in reducing workplace injuries. The key factors in designing an ergonomically sound work station relate to the layout of the work station, the characteristics of control and display panels, seating arrangements at the work station, and lighting quality and quantity.[137] While a number of organizations have moved to an open-office concept, workers complain about such things as reduced privacy and noise spillover:

One woman at a public relations firm could not concentrate while a co-worker in an adjoining cubicle completed the ritual of clipping his nails. Another employee complained about the lack of privacy when she spoke on the phone to a former boyfriend, while a different employee lamented hearing a co-worker blurt out a crude phrase to tell a client he had to use the washroom.[138]

AIDS

A chapter on occupational health and safety would be incomplete if no reference was made to acquired immune deficiency syndrome (AIDS) or the human immunodeficiency virus (HIV) that causes AIDS. There are an estimated 75,500 individuals in Canada living with AIDS.[139] Both HIV and AIDS have a potentially immense impact on the human resource function.[140]

AIDS and Human Resource Management

Consider the following case that occurred more than 30 years ago:

Ron Lentz was hired January 4, 1988, by the Toronto Western Hospital as a nurse and fired on January 23. He complained to the Ontario Human Rights Commission that he was discriminated against because he was HIV-positive. The commission agreed and negotiated with the hospital a settlement that included reinstatement, about $14,000 in back pay, $1,400 in benefits, $5,000 in legal fees, restoration of seniority, and a clean employment record.[141]

This case points to challenges that human resource managers have to face if one of their employees is HIV-positive or develops AIDS, or if a job applicant happens to mention that he or she has an HIV-related infection. It is a breach of human rights laws to discriminate against that person. But what if colleagues refuse to work with that person? What if a supervisor expresses concern about the employee's contact with customers? To be prepared for such questions, each employer should establish a policy and have an action plan in place before a case arises among employees or their dependants. Some recommendations on how to set up a successful AIDS program are outlined below.

1. A *policy* regarding HIV-infected employees should
    - protect an employee's right to privacy;
    - guarantee the employee will not be isolated from other workers; and
    - keep those diagnosed with AIDS productive as long as they are able.

2. *Mandatory training* for managers, supervisors, and union leaders should
    - present facts on HIV;
    - address personal concerns about AIDS in the workplace;
    - reiterate the company's policy;
    - help with job restructuring; and
    - discuss how to manage co-worker concerns.

3. *Education programs* for all employees should
    - explain policy;
    - present facts on transmission and prevention;
    - encourage empathy for those with AIDS; and
    - provide workshops or forums for frank, open discussion.

4. *Counselling and support* should be provided to
    - help employees with AIDS cope with their disease;
    - assist others in coming to terms with an HIV-infected co-worker; and
    - explore with supervisors the issues involved in managing AIDS.[142]

Despite the considerable amount of information on HIV and AIDS, many individuals are still not well informed about the disease. One of the problems human resource managers must deal with is the lack of knowledge on the part of employees. There are still questions asked such as "Can I get AIDS from germs in the air? From touching an infected worker? From a toilet seat? From infected water in a swimming pool? From insect bites?" It has been found that a comprehensive education program for co-workers can halt the hysteria that often results when a colleague is diagnosed with HIV or AIDS.[143]

LO6 Occupational Health and Safety Strategy

It must be continually stressed that top management's involvement in setting health and safety policies is essential. If top management does not assume a leadership role, it sets an example by its inaction, and middle managers, first-line supervisors, and employees will behave accordingly. Part of an effective occupational health and safety strategy is to clearly assign responsibilities for plant safety and health programs to ensure that the company's policies are carried out. An occupational health and safety committee with enforcement authority is a very helpful tool to implement health and safety policies. Such a committee should be made up of representatives of management and employees, ideally with balanced representation. This increases the probability that the committee's decisions are accepted as fair by the employees.

It is important to have a control process in place. Causes of accidents should be identified and either eliminated or controlled to prevent recurrence. The human resource department should use its information system to monitor for patterns of accidents or health problems that may be otherwise overlooked. An effective training program is another critical part of a good occupational health and safety program. Moreover, a number of organizations are hiring occupational health and safety specialists to design and administer comprehensive workplace health and safety programs. Finally, management should continually encourage safety awareness on the part of supervisors and employees.

SUMMARY

Occupational health and safety has become an important aspect of organizations and will have an even higher priority for human resource managers in the future. The federal and provincial governments have created a variety of laws that require the attention of human resource professionals. Most occupational health and safety acts now require the establishment of safety committees in companies with 20 or more employees.

The Workplace Hazardous Materials Information System (WHMIS) is a comprehensive plan that requires suppliers to provide detailed information about any danger their material may pose, but it also asks the user to make sure that the information is available and that employees are trained to understand it.

Accident prevention is a major concern, but human resource managers should not forget to look at the psychological aspect of the work environment. Stress-related losses—absenteeism, turnover, low productivity, accidents, and so on—cost Canada billions of dollars each year. Preventive programs such as employee assistance programs, professional counselling, time management, and fitness programs can go a long way to reduce stress-related costs.

AIDS and the workplace is an important issue facing human resource managers. Some organizations will experience individual cases of AIDS or HIV that can lead to severe friction among work groups and irrational actions from some frightened employees. Human resource managers should be prepared for this by providing appropriate training and communication programs.

TERMS FOR REVIEW

assumption of risk 362
burnout 378
careless worker model 362
shared responsibility model 362

stressors 376
Workplace Hazardous Materials Information System (WHMIS) 366
workplace health and safety committee 365

SELF-ASSESSMENT EXERCISE

Work–Life Balance Quiz

Do you find it difficult to balance the different roles in your life? If so, you're not alone—58 percent of Canadians report "overload" as a result of the pressures associated with work, home and family, friends, physical health, and volunteer and community service.

Take this quiz to see if you're in balance.

ARE YOU IN BALANCE?
More than ever before, Canadians play many different roles in their lives. They are workers, parents, spouses, friends, caregivers of elderly relatives, and volunteers in their communities. They must also make room in their lives for taking care of their own physical and mental well-being. Not surprisingly, achieving balance among all these competing priorities can be difficult. This overload can be heightened by new technologies that were actually intended to make our work lives easier—through email, cellphones, and other electronic devices, many workers are expected to be available 24/7, making the achievement of a balance between work and the rest of our lives even more difficult.

Achieving work–life balance means having equilibrium among all the priorities in your life—this state of balance is different for every person. But, as difficult as work–life balance is to define, most of us know when we're out of balance. To find out more about your own personal balance, take the Work–Life Balance Quiz.

Disclaimer

This is not a scientific test. Information provided is not a substitute for professional advice. If you feel that you may need advice, please consult a qualified health care professional.

WORK–LIFE BALANCE QUIZ

	Agree	Disagree
1. I feel like I have little or no control over my work life.	○	○
2. I regularly enjoy hobbies or interests outside of work.	○	○
3. I often feel guilty because I can't make time for everything I want to.	○	○
4. I frequently feel anxious or upset because of what is happening at work.	○	○
5. I usually have enough time to spend with my loved ones.	○	○
6. When I'm at home, I feel relaxed and comfortable.	○	○
7. I have time to do something just for me every week.	○	○
8. On most days, I feel overwhelmed and overcommitted.	○	○
9. I rarely lose my temper at work.	○	○
10. I never use all my allotted vacation days.	○	○
11. I often feel exhausted—even early in the week.	○	○
12. Usually, I work through my lunch break.	○	○
13. I rarely miss out on important family events because of work.	○	○
14. I frequently think about work when I'm not working.	○	○
15. My family is frequently upset with me about how much time I spend working.	○	○

WHAT YOUR SCORE MEANS

Give yourself one point for agreeing with statements 2, 5, 6, 7, 9, and 13. Give yourself one point for disagreeing with statements 1, 3, 4, 8, 10, 11, 12, 14, and 15.

0–5: Your life is out of balance—you need to make significant changes to find your equilibrium. But you can take control!

6–10: You're keeping things under control—but only barely. Now is the time to take action before you're knocked off balance.

11–15: You're on the right track! You've been able to achieve work–life balance—now, make sure you protect it.

Source: Canadian Mental Health Association: http://www.cmha.ca/

REVIEW AND DISCUSSION QUESTIONS

1. Explain the legal term *assumption of risk*.
2. What factors affect occupational accidents?
3. What responsibilities do joint occupational health and safety committees have?
4. Explain the requirements of the Workplace Hazardous Materials Information System (WHMIS).

CRITICAL THINKING QUESTIONS

1. Develop a strategy and identify the implementation steps you would follow to lower the incidence of workplace accidents in your organization.
2. Think about a time when you felt under considerable stress. What were the causes of that stress? What efforts (by you and/or others) were or could have been taken to reduce the stress?
3. What can be done to prepare an organization for an AIDS case?
4. Consider an organization that you have worked in. Critically review its safety procedures and training. Evaluate the organization in terms of the presence of physical, biological, and chemical hazards. Also be sure to address issues relating to ergonomics.

ETHICS QUESTION

What Gets Measured Gets Acted On

As part of its wellness program, your employer has decided to provide every employee with a wearable wrist band to track fitness and health data. Although wearing such a monitor is not mandatory, there is considerable pressure on employees to participate in the wellness initiative. According to the manager of Wellness Programs, "More than 60 percent of our workforce is overweight, and several employees have serious health issues. We all know that what gets measured gets acted on. If we improve the health of our employees, everyone wins. Employees feel better, are less likely to get sick and be absent, and both engagement and productivity improve."

1. Outline the ethical issues relating to tracking employee fitness and health data.

2. Are there any practices/policies that could enhance the likelihood of the wellness initiative being successful?

RESEARCH EXERCISE

1. Visit the Justice Laws Website (https://laws-lois.justice.gc.ca/) and examine the relevant sections of the *Canada Labour Code* that deal with occupational health and safety. Also, explore other websites that address health and safety law within your province.

2. Go to the website of the American Institute of Stress (https://www.stress.org/). Check out three other websites that also have information on workplace stress. Compare the information from the various sites.

INCIDENT 12-1

Safety at Canada Chemicals Ltd.

Canada Chemicals Ltd. is a large wholesaler of industrial chemicals in Ontario. It handles swimming pool supplies, industrial solvents, fertilizers, and special lubricants. The sales and clerical operations caused few safety worries, but the warehouse facilities caused Sam Peterson sleepless nights. Sam's title was manager of safety and security. He had worked in the human resource department since his job was created in 1992.

His biggest problem was the warehouse manager, Garfield McKenney. Gar simply did not appreciate safety. Nearly every action Sam took to improve safety resulted in objections from Gar, especially if it meant warehouse workers were to be slowed or delayed in their jobs. Most of the workers liked Sam, but they paid more attention to Gar. The only time employees wore their safety goggles, shoes, and acid-resistant gloves was when Sam was around. They knew

Gar did not care and would not discipline good workers for safety violations unless company property was damaged.

One day a case of sulphuric acid was dropped, badly burning a new employee. The employee recovered after four weeks and two plastic surgery operations. Immediately after the accident, Sam requested a meeting with Gar, the human resource manager, and the general manager.

DISCUSSION QUESTIONS

1. If you were the general manager, what would you do to gain greater co-operation on safety from (a) Gar and (b) the workers under him?

2. Should Sam be given authority to discipline those who violate safety rules?

WE CONNECTIONS: ENSURING HEALTH AND SAFETY

Stress in the Workplace

When Rebecca, WE Connections' new HR specialist, saw Julie Moore, the project manager, in the lunchroom, hunched over some papers and furiously scribbling some notes, her face broke into a grin. She hadn't seen Julie in weeks and was delighted for the chance to catch up with her. She quickly walked over and touched her on the arm.

When Julie looked up, Rebecca almost gasped. The woman looked like she hadn't slept in weeks.

The last time they had spoken, Julie had been full of life. Her face had been animated as she had excitedly talked about a new project that she was taking on. Due to an internal staffing shortage, Alex had asked her to juggle two major projects at the same time. One client was in a city two hours north of WE Connections. The other was located an hour-and-a-half south. Both required a lot of face time with the clients, so Julie had been driving for hours almost every day. If she wasn't with one client, she was with the other, or she was on a conference call with a member of her staff.

Sitting down at the table, and trying to hide her shock, Rebecca said, "Julie, I haven't seen you in a few weeks. How are things going?"

Julie managed a feeble smile. "Things are good, I guess. I'm surviving."

Rebecca's first instinct was to tell Julie that she looked tired, but she bit her tongue. That kind of comment never helped anyone. It just let the person know they were not looking their best. Instead, she said, "How are the two projects going? I heard there were some hiccups, but you managed to keep everything going."

Living on the Edge of Disaster

Shrugging, Julie said, "Just barely. It feels like I'm always one moment away from disaster. Every moment I'm awake I'm either working or driving. My husband says he doesn't even recognize me anymore." With one hand, she attempted to rub some of the tension from her neck.

"Well, it's great to see you here. I'm glad you finally got back to home base. I hope that means things are slowing down for you." Rebecca smiled encouragingly.

"I wish! If anything, things are ramping up. I just came into town today because I had a doctor's appointment this morning that I had already rescheduled several times. I thought I'd use the chance to talk to my people here before I head out

again. We just worked through lunch, and I was just making notes on what I have to do next. It seems that every time there is a task that isn't getting done, it gets added to my list. I guess it's good to be needed. I just wish people would stop calling in sick all of a sudden. I've had three people call in this week. That's not really being a team player, is it?"

Julie straightened the pile of papers that was in front of her, and stuffed them into her bag. She added, "Well, I guess I better keep going. Nice to see you, Rebecca."

Before she stood up, Rebecca put a hand on her arm, and said, "Hold up a second. Are you sure you're okay? I'm worried that you're doing too much. All of this pressure can't be good for you."

Physical Effects of Stress

Julie laughed, and said, "You sound like my doctor. She wanted me to take a week off—starting today. I guess my blood pressure is up, and she didn't like hearing about my headaches and insomnia. Obviously, she doesn't realize that this is all part of the job. Stepping away, even for a couple of days, just isn't possible."

She stood up to go, but added, "Ha! Can you imagine what Alex would say if I bailed in the middle of these two projects? He calls me seven times a day to get updates on everything, watching every single thing I do to make sure I'm not messing up, freaking out when I miss anything. If I stepped away, even for a day, he would be the one with the real medical emergency!" She chuckled at the thought and waved as she walked away.

Rebecca watched her go, troubled by the conversation.

DISCUSSION QUESTIONS

1. What are the causes of Julie's stress?

2. What are the potential outcomes if this workload continues for Julie?

3. What could Rebecca (or the company) do to reduce the stress that Julie is experiencing?

4. What do you think it is like for the employees on Julie's team?

In the final installment of the WE Connections story (at the end of Chapter 13), an HR staff member worries that there may be a union-organizing drive going on at the company.

CASE STUDY

Perth Metro Transit

Bonita Cousins is a 38-year-old bus driver with Perth Metro Transit (PMT). She has been with PMT for 15 years, is a good performer (her performance ratings have been between 4.0 and 4.2 on a five-point scale over the past five years), and is well liked by both co-workers and her supervisor. She has only one previous disciplinary offence—a written warning two years ago for being 18 minutes late.

Last Friday, Bonita was driving her bus on her route on the outskirts of Perth. There were 24 passengers on the bus, and as she drove along Kings Park Road, she observed a woman in her early twenties being attacked by a man in his late twenties. She immediately pulled the bus over to the side of the road, jumped out, and ran to assist the woman. The incident occurred about 150 feet from where the bus was parked. The assailant, upon seeing Cousins approaching, ran away into the park. Cousins accompanied the woman back to the bus, called the police for assistance, and contacted her supervisor.

In discussing the incident with her supervisor, Cousins admitted that the bus was idling and that the passenger doors were left open while she was in the park.

According to three passengers, an eight-year-old boy sitting three rows from the front of the bus got up and sat in the bus driver's seat while Cousins was away from the bus. The boy's mother was sending a text message when the boy went to the driver's seat. The mother was quickly informed of the situation by other passengers, and she got up and brought her son back to their seat. The evidence is clear that the boy did not touch the gear shift or gas/brake pedals but merely sat in the bus driver's seat for a short period of time.

Bus drivers receive yearly training on safety issues (including proper procedures to follow in the event a driver has to leave the bus). The employee handbook states that "a bus driver should never leave his or her bus unattended. If you need to leave the bus, make sure that the engine is turned off, you remove the key, you have passengers get off the bus, and you lock the bus. Failure to follow such procedures constitutes a serious breach of the employment contract, and dismissal is an appropriate remedy."

DISCUSSION QUESTIONS

1. Is there just cause to dismiss Bonita? Explain your answer.

2. Would your response to question 1 be different if Bonita had left the bus unattended to rescue a cat stuck in a tree? An elderly person crossing the road? Justify your response.

3. What can PMT do to improve its safety practices and policies?

CHAPTER 13

The Union–Management Framework

HRM focuses on the shared interests of workers and managers in the success of their enterprise. Conflict is de-emphasized in favour of "win–win" scenarios where problems are solved or put aside to fulfill organizational objectives. By contrast, industrial relations assumes conflict is inherent in the employment relationship.

DAPHNE GOTTLIEB TARAS, ALLEN PONAK, AND MORLEY GUNDERSON[1]

LEARNING OBJECTIVES

After studying this chapter, you should be able to:

LO1 Discuss the major reasons why workers join unions.

LO2 Describe the structure of Canadian unions.

LO3 Summarize the core legal principles relating to collective bargaining.

LO4 Explain how a union organizing campaign is carried out.

LO5 Outline the key steps in negotiating a union contract.

LO6 List common techniques to resolve disputes.

LO7 Describe how unions affect the human resource management environment.

LO8 Suggest ways to build union–management co-operation.

Workers may join together and form a union. A **union** is an organization with the legal authority to represent workers, negotiate the terms and conditions of employment with the employer, and administer the collective agreement.

> **union** An organization with the legal authority to represent workers, negotiate the terms and conditions of employment with the employer, and administer the collective agreement.

Many successful companies have one or more unions among their employees. While unionized organizations are often lumped together, there is growing evidence that the quality of the relationship between an employer and union is a major factor in predicting firm performance. Still, the presence of a union places limits on the role of human resource management, and many managers find these new limitations hard to accept:

CUPE Local 118 in Saint John, New Brunswick, had a clause in its contract with the city that guaranteed a minimum of 293 full-time outside employees. The clause, which was introduced in the early 1980s,

FIGURE 13-1

Industrial Relations and Human Resource Perspectives on Workplace Conflict

Industrial Relations Perspective

1. Conflict stems from an employer–employee power imbalance.
2. Conflict between labour and management is enduring.
3. Correcting the power imbalance between labour and management often requires institutional intervention in the forms of union representation and legislation.
4. Conflict can be constructive even when the conflict is addressed in an adversarial, non-problem-solving fashion.

Human Resource Perspective

1. Conflict stems from poor management.
2. Conflict can be partially reduced by organizational and workplace innovations that build an employer–employee unity of interests.
3. Conflict can further be reduced by co-operative, mutual gains-oriented problem-solving techniques.
4. As a result of improved management, conflict will fade from the employment relationship.

SOURCE: Adapted from D. Lewin (2001), "IR and HR perspectives on workplace conflict: What can each learn from the other?" *Human Resource Management Review, 11,* p. 453–85.

has been renewed several times to avoid damaging union–management relations and labour unrest. Terry Totten, former city manager for more than 15 years, believed that the clause was fundamentally wrong and impaired the ability of the city to save money by contracting out services. Totten asserted that the clause would only be removed when the economic climate was right and council had the political will to remove the clause. Union officials reported that the clause was introduced to stop corruption, poor-quality work, and kickback schemes with outside contractors, and they believe that the clause has benefited both employees and taxpayers.[2]

As shown in Figure 13-1, the industrial relations and human resource perspectives on workplace conflict are somewhat different.

LO1 Why Employees Seek Union Representation

Unions do not just happen. They are frequently caused by some management action or inaction that workers perceive as unfair. For example, in a 6:1 decision, the Supreme Court of Canada held that the RCMP's internal system for negotiating workplace issues was grossly unfair and gave Mounties the right to join a union.[3] Once a union is organized, it becomes the employees' bargaining agent and the employer is legally obligated to meet with the union and bargain a labour contract called a **collective agreement**. The collective agreement, which is known as the "rule book" by some managers and union officials, addresses a variety of issues, such as wages and benefits, hours of work, and working conditions, as well as related issues, including grievance procedures, safety standards, probationary periods, and work assignments. The collective agreement is usually negotiated between the local union's bargaining committee and the human resource or industrial relations department.

The collective agreement places restrictions on management's rights in managing the workplace. When a new collective agreement is negotiated, it is important that supervisors and managers dealing with unionized employees are made aware of the terms of the agreement and provided with training regarding the interpretation and application of the new agreement. All too often, a union grievance arises because the supervisor did not understand the terms of the collective agreement.

collective agreement
A labour contract that addresses a variety of issues, such as wages and benefits, hours of work, working conditions, grievance procedures, safety standards, probationary periods, and work assignments; usually negotiated between the local union's bargaining committee and the human resource or industrial relations department.

Causes of Unionization

Why do employees join unions? The reasons for joining a union vary from person to person, and there is no single force that motivates people to join unions. Instead, perceptions are shaped by a variety of reasons. The *union push explanation* asserts that some employees are pushed or forced into joining a union because of employer treatment of the workforce, peer pressure by co-workers to join a union, or collective agreement provisions requiring an employee to join if he or she wants the job in question. The *union pull explanation* states that employees are pulled into the union because of the benefits of union representation (such as higher wages, greater benefits, job security, and grievance representation).

Consider the following organizing drive at a Halifax coffee shop:

In 2013, Just Us! Coffee Roasters Co-op was presented with unfair labour practice charges relating to the dismissal of two employees who were alleging that they were terminated for trying to start a union. Just Us! was started by two social workers and sold itself as a fair-trade workers' co-op. While there was a health care plan, an employee had to work 30 hours a week to meet the full-time requirement. In addition, the store manager was responsible for scheduling, and employees who weren't close to the manager got fewer shifts, more night or weekend shifts, and "clopens" or split shifts requiring employees to open and close the store.

The Service Employees International Union commenced an organizing drive at Just Us! and 90 percent of the employees voted for the union. The parties got down to serious but "amicable" bargaining and struck a three-year deal that addressed such issues as work scheduling, wages, worker control of tips, and an improved grievance procedure. One employee stated, "Unionizing was a transformative process. We realized we don't have to sit back and take whatever management gives us." Debra Moore, one of the company's founders, noted that "with the union things are so much clearer and better. We can go to the union if we are not happy. The down side is that we can't be flexible. We have to stick to the contract."[4]

Fast forward a few years and the coffee shop is still going strong. One of the original union organizers observed that "without a union an employer can fire you whenever they feel like it. If you're visibly queer or trans, that unemployment period is likely to be much longer." The general manager similarly responded, "In a café situation, a lot of the staff don't have a lot of work or life experience and it's hard to stand up to an owner or a business and negotiate. Having a union gave both sides a voice, created a platform for the staff to discuss their concerns in a productive way, and have led to a formulated method to deal with their issues."[5]

When considering union joining, it is important to distinguish between the desire for union representation and the opportunity to join a union.[6] Three factors—job dissatisfaction, individual attitudes toward unions in general, and perceived union instrumentality (beliefs about what unions can do for an employee)—appear to be most important in an individual's decision to join a union.[7]

Reasons for not joining a union are equally diverse. Workers who want to become managers may believe union membership damages their chances for promotion. Other employees view unions as "just another boss" that leads to extra costs, such as union dues or lost wages from strikes. Likewise, past experiences or isolated stories of union wrongdoing may cause some people to form a negative opinion of collective action. Also, employer policies and supervisory treatment may be fair, and, consequently, employees are not motivated to join a union.

As the following example shows, people within a community may have vastly differing views concerning unionization:

In the small town of Brooks, Alberta, a strike shut down the Lakeside Packers slaughterhouse. Management was determined to open the plant (which employed about one-quarter of the town's population) during the dispute, which divided the town. While some citizens strongly supported the employees and their union, others were concerned that the strike would hurt other businesses in the community and leave lasting divisions among the town's residents. Striking workers were very upset—despite an Alberta Labour Relations Board order that banned strikers from doing more than delaying vehicles seeking to enter the plant, workers were committed to restricting access to the facility. As one worker stated, "If they kill us, they can go in. This is modern slavery for me."[8]

Canadians' Views toward Unions

A survey by Leger of 1,400 Canadian adults examined their attitudes toward unions. While the survey provides important information, the results are aggregated and important differences may exist among workers based on demographic characteristics. For a few of the questions, responses from a Nanos survey are presented. Some of the major findings with regard to attitudes toward work and employers are reported below:

- Among Canadians who are not unionized, 19 percent reported that they were very or somewhat interested in being unionized, 2 percent didn't know or refused to respond, and 79 percent did not want to be unionized.

© The Canadian Press/Fred Lum

Having a union means strikes and walkouts. Are unions necessary in today's organizational environment, with labour and pay equity laws safeguarding workers?

- Among current union members, 71 percent would prefer to be unionized. Among formerly unionized workers 46 percent would prefer to be unionized.

- Among respondents, 71 percent of current union members believed that unions are as relevant today as they have ever been. Support for this statement dropped to 46 percent for former union members and 42 percent for respondents who had never been in a union.

- When forming a union in or removing a union from the workplace, 86 percent of current union employees and 83 percent of nonunion employees believe that a secret ballot vote should be required.[9]

A CAUT Harris-Decima poll conducted at about the same time revealed that about 70 percent of participants agreed that unions are still needed, about 42 percent indicated that they would never join a union, 40 percent supported the position that governments should have the right to impose contracts on public sector unions, and about 44 percent felt that public sector unions should not have the right to strike.[10]

Incidents reported in the media may impact the views of individuals. Consider, for instance, the decision by Caterpillar to shut down an Ontario plant:

In February of 2012, Caterpillar announced that it would close its Electro-Motive plant in London, Ontario. The announcement came about a month after the company had locked out 450 workers when they refused a 50 percent pay cut. Caterpillar argued that the closure was necessary because the plant was unsustainable. Shortly before the closure, Caterpillar announced that its quarterly earnings were up 58 percent and it had a record profit of almost $5 billion. According to Ken Lewenza, Sr., president of the Canadian Auto Workers (CAW) at the time, "The closure was a callous move. From Day 1, we believed that Caterpillar was trying to provoke a crisis by forcing deep cuts that were not possible." Ontario Federation of Labour president Sid Ryan observed that "job loss like this is going to decimate towns across the country."[11]

Employer Views toward Unions

A *Canadian HR Reporter* survey of human resource professionals examined their views toward unions. The study revealed several important trends:

- Of participants, 27 percent thought the union had the upper hand in bargaining, while 52 percent did not.

- 52 percent believed that economic conditions had pitted unionized workers against management.

- 42 percent reported that the number of grievances had increased over the previous three years, 44 percent indicated no change, and 13 percent believed there had been a decrease.

- 62 percent perceived that there was a growing trend for employers and unions to work together to find solutions to problems.

- 19 percent of respondents believed that unions had had a large financial impact on the employer, while 57 percent indicated that the financial impact of unions had been small.

- 36 percent of participants thought that the employer's relationship with the union would get worse over the next five years, 39 percent believed that it would stay about the same, and 24 percent thought that it would improve.[12]

The bitter labour disputes of the past few years have attracted considerable media and public attention. Some commentators argue that unions are fighting to survive. Ken Georgetti, former president of the Canadian Labour Congress, stated, "There used to be a time when we had great respect from the public. But we've lost that. There's this notion that unions are just out for themselves and not for society. You get that label hung on you, and you have to work to get rid of it."[13] It is argued that unions must engage the new workforce if they are to survive. While strikes and threats of strikes have been common in the past, Jim Stanford, an economist with Unifor, observes that "the confrontations are overwhelmingly driven by the employers' side. Almost all of the strikes and conflicts have been defensive from the perspective of the union. They're trying to hang on to what they have."[14]

LO2 Labour Unions: Goals and Structure

Labour unions alter the work environment. Their presence changes the relationship between employees and the organization, and the human resource department's involvement in union-related issues is not always well received by lower levels of management, who believe that their ability to make workplace decisions has been eroded.

Unions have a major effect on the work environment, but in many other ways the environment remains unchanged. Supervisors and managers retain their primary responsibility for employee performance. Profit objectives and budgetary goals are often not shared with the union (although this is changing in some organizations). As well, unions do not reduce the need for effective human resource policies and procedures. In short, management must still manage, and the union does not assume the responsibilities of the human resource department. To understand how and why unions influence human resource management, it is necessary to examine their goals and structure.

Union Goals and Philosophy

A union's objectives are influenced internally by the wishes of its members, the aspirations of its leaders, and the financial and membership strength of the union. Like other organizations, unions are open social systems that are also affected by their external environment: The financial condition of the employer, the gains of other unions, inflation and unemployment rates, and government policies all influence the union's objectives.

Yet among all these internal and external considerations, there exists a common core of widely agreed-upon objectives. Writing almost 100 years ago, one prominent labour leader stated that the mission for the labour movement was to protect workers, increase their pay, improve their working conditions, and help workers in general.[15] This approach has become known as **business unionism**, primarily because it recognizes that a union can survive only if it delivers a needed service to its members in a businesslike manner. But some unions have chosen to address broader social issues of politics and economics when such concerns are in the best interests of their members. This second kind of union, engaged in what is called **social (or reform) unionism**, tries to influence the economic and social policies of government at all levels—municipal, provincial, and federal.[16] In practice, union leaders pursue the objectives of social unionism by

> **business unionism** A type of unionism whose mission is to protect workers, increase their pay, improve their working conditions, and help workers in general; it recognizes that a union can survive only if it delivers a needed service to its members in a businesslike manner.

speaking out for or against government programs. For example, many union leaders oppose substantial government intervention into collective bargaining because it takes away or limits the right of the union to engage in free collective bargaining with management.

> **social (or reform) unionism** A type of unionism that tries to influence the economic and social policies of government at all levels. In practice, union leaders pursue such objectives by speaking out for or against government programs.

A number of unions have developed programs to help members deal with issues at the workplace. Consider, for example, the Women's Advocate program:

> The program, which was developed by the Canadian Auto Workers (now part of Unifor), is aimed at providing trained workplace advocates/representatives to help women (and men) deal with such issues as partner abuse and workplace harassment by making workers aware of community resources and workplace supports. The importance of employer support is noted. According to Julie White, former director of Unifor's Women's Department, "It's really important we have that management support person to go through because, ultimately, if a woman needs time off work, it's not the union that can authorize that, it's the management support system."[17]

Human resource management is influenced by both business and social unionism goals. The growth of benefits discussed in Chapter 10 has resulted partly from union pressure. Even nonunionized employers have added many benefits in order to remain competitive in the labour market or to forestall unionization among their employees.

Union Structure and Functions

It has been argued that employees lost direct contact with business owners as organizations grew larger, so unions emerged to help workers influence workplace decisions.[18] Through unions, workers were able to exert control over their jobs and their work environment.[19] Then, when attempts were made by employers to cut wages or employment, the employees relied on unions to resist these actions.[20] The most important levels of union structure are local unions, national and international unions, and labour congresses.

Local Unions

For most union members and industrial relations practitioners, the **local unions**, or locals, are the most important part of the union structure. They provide the members, the revenue, and the power of the entire union movement. Historically, the two major types of unions were

> **local unions** Branches of a union that are locally based and form part of a larger (often national or international) union.

craft and industrial unions. **Craft unions** are composed of workers who possess the same skills or trades; these include, for example, all the carpenters who work in the same geographical area. **Industrial unions** include the unskilled and semiskilled workers at a particular location. When an employer has several locations that are unionized, employees at each location are usually represented by a different local union. An example would be the United Food and Commercial Workers.

> **craft union** A type of union composed of workers who possess the same skills or trades.
>
> **industrial union** A type of union that includes the unskilled and semiskilled workers at a particular location.

Figure 13-2 shows the structure of a typical local. The union steward is usually elected by the workers and helps them present their problems to management. If the steward of an industrial union cannot help the employee, the problem is given to the grievance committee, which takes the issue to higher levels of management or to the human resource department. In craft unions, the steward, who is also called the representative, usually takes the issue directly to the business agent, who is often a full-time employee of the union.

National and International Unions

Many local unions are part of a larger union, which may be a *national union,* such as Unifor or the Canadian Union

of Public Employees, or an *international union,* such as the United Steelworkers or the International Brotherhood of Teamsters. National unions are based in Canada, while international unions have their headquarters outside of the country (typically in the United States).

National and international unions exist to organize and help local unions. They also pursue social objectives of interest to their members and frequently maintain a staff that assists the local unions with negotiations, grievance handling, and expert advice. Some national and international unions leave many key decisions (including bargaining a collective agreement) with their local unions. In other relationships, the national or international union plays a very active role in local union affairs. Figure 13-3 shows the membership of the largest unions in Canada. Note that the two largest unions represent public sector employees.

Canadian Labour Congress

The **Canadian Labour Congress (CLC)** represents many unions in Canada and has about 3.3 million members. The president, Hassan Yussuff, was elected in 2014. The CLC has five main functions: (1) representing Canada at the International Labour Organization, (2) influencing public policy at the federal level, (3) enforcing the code of ethics set out in its constitution, (4) providing services (such as research and education) for its member unions, and (5) resolving jurisdictional disputes among its member unions.

> **Canadian Labour Congress (CLC)** An organization, with a membership of about 3.3 million, that represents many unions in Canada.

While the Canadian Labour Congress is the largest labour federation, it is not the only one. In addition to other federations at the national level, there are also federations operating at the provincial and municipal or regional level (for instance, the Quebec Federation of Labour and the Ottawa and District Labour Council).

Secession

In 1960, about two-thirds of union members belonged to an international union. Over the past half-century, that percentage has declined noticeably so that now only about 25 percent of union members belong to international unions.[21] This trend, referred to as *secession,* has been motivated, in part, by a desire for more autonomy on the part of Canadian locals and the development of policies aimed at specifically addressing the needs of Canadian workers. The most dramatic breakaway occurred in 1985 when the Canadian Auto Workers union (now part of Unifor), led by former president Bob White, severed ties with the United Auto Workers and held its founding convention in Toronto. Canadian members of international unions have often complained that they receive a disproportionately small share of union benefits.

FIGURE 13-2

Structure of a Typical Local Union

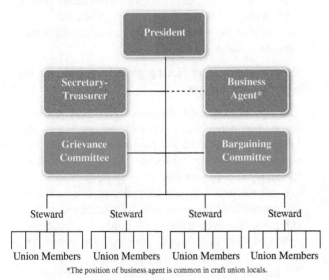

*The position of business agent is common in craft union locals.

Based on Human Resources and Social Development Canada (2003), "Structure of a Typical Union," Public Works and Government Services Canada.

FIGURE 13-3

Membership in Canada's Largest Unions (2015)

Union	Membership (000s)
Canadian Union of Public Employees	635
National Union of Public and General Employees	360
Unifor	300
United Food and Commercial Workers Canada	248
United Steelworkers of America	190
Public Service Alliance of Canada	181
Social Affairs Federation	135
Service Employees International Union	126
Labourers' International Union	97
Teamsters Canada	93

Based on *Labour Organizations in Canada 2015,* Employment and Social Development Canada.

Trends in Union Membership

Union Growth and Decline

In 2017, about 4.5 million workers were covered by collective agreements (union coverage rate of 30.4 percent). In terms of industry sector, education was the most highly unionized, at 73 percent, followed closely by public administration (72 percent), utilities (64 percent), and health care and social assistance (55 percent). The lowest rates of unionization were in the agricultural (4.4 percent), scientific, professional and technical services (4.6 percent), and accommodation/food services sectors (6.9 percent).[22]

A number of employers in small business and the service sector (such as retail) have been determined to remain union free:

More than a decade ago, the United Food and Commercial Workers (UFCW) began an organizing drive at Walmart in Weyburn, Saskatchewan. The union and employer were unable to reach an agreement during bargaining and a decertification vote was commenced. The UFCW objected to the vote but the Supreme Court of Canada refused to hear the case, and by a vote of 51 to 5, the union was decertified. According to the local union president, "The process has been really, totally frustrating. Nine years battling this out in the courts, that's not very consistent of how you would see labour relations go between a union and an employer."[23]

However, unions are placing greater emphasis on organizing service employers:

The United Food and Commercial Workers (UFCW) union, which represents most of the employees at Loblaws (Canada's largest food retailer), turned its efforts to organizing the second-largest food retailer (Sobeys). Sobeys sent a letter to employees indicating that the union merely wanted their dues money and emphasized the good and open relationship the company has with employees. Loblaws executives indicated that they would welcome the move to remove the competitive disadvantage of paying 35 percent higher wage payments to employees. By 2014, the UFCW represented employees at more than 350 Sobeys, Safeway, IGA, and Freshco stores and at a number of distribution warehouses across Canada.[24]

In recent years, the number of women members in Canadian unions has been increasing rapidly. In 1967, women made up only 20 percent of total union membership; now, more than 50 percent of union members are female—the unionization rate for women surpassed that for men for the first time in 2004. While about one in six female employees belonged to a union in 1967, that ratio has doubled over 35 years and now about one in three women are union members. Thirty years ago, four out of ten male employees were union members; today that proportion has fallen to under three in ten. In terms of age, the density rate is 16 percent for workers ages 15 to 24, 29 percent for those between 25 and 34, 31 percent for workers from ages 35 to 44, 35 percent for workers from 45 to 54, and 34 percent for those ages 55 and older.

Unions today are acknowledging that traditional approaches to organizing and collective bargaining are becoming less relevant today. Many Canadians view union workers as being in a blue-collar or government occupation so there is a growing recognition of the need to appeal to other employees. For example, Unifor has decided to try to attract young workers to the union movement. According to Anna Goldfinch, formerly with the Canadian Federation of Students, "There is more and more underemployment, precarious employment for youth. Unions need to start communicating that they're applicable in any workforce—and that unions will reflect young people more and more as young people start to participate in them."[25]

Moreover, low wage employees may look to unions to protect their rights and improve conditions of work:

On January 1, 2018, the Ontario government raised the minimum wage to $14. This was met with resistance by a number of employers, including some Tim Hortons franchises, which decided to change paid breaks to unpaid and to cut some employee benefits. It became clear that there was a major power imbalance between employers and low wage employees without the resources to fight back. As noted by Martin Regg Cohn, "If employers trample on their rights, minimum wage workers have to stand up for themselves—by joining a union that can push back against companies. Unions can keep a watchful eye on abuses, enable members to file grievances, and tap into the collective resources of the larger labour movement."[26]

In comparing unionization across provinces, Newfoundland had the highest rate (39 percent), followed closely by Quebec (38 percent), while the lowest union density was in Alberta (25 percent). Also of note is the lower probability that a part-time worker will be unionized (the union density rate for full-time workers is 31 percent compared with 23 percent for their part-time counterparts). In addition, larger workplaces are more likely to be unionized—about 13 percent of employees in firms with fewer than 20 employees were unionized, 30 percent in firms with 20 to 99 employees, 41 percent in firms with 100 to 500 employees, and 54 percent in firms with more than 500 employees.[27]

On the global scene, a number of countries have experienced a decline in union density (that is, union members as a percentage of the paid nonagricultural workforce) (although Spain, Ireland, and Luxembourg have seen an increase). Explanations for the decline in union representation include (1) the decline in the manufacturing sector, (2) the constraints that the globalization of financial markets have put on macroeconomic policies, and (3) competition from developing countries with low labour costs, resulting in the loss of low-skilled, labour-intensive jobs in high-wage countries.[28]

Back in the mid-1980s, about 30 percent of workers in OECD countries were unionized. About 30 years later, that number has declined to about 17 percent. Similarly, the percentage of employees covered by a collective agreement has declined from 45 to 33 percent over the same time period. When considering selected OECD countries, union density varies across countries, as shown in Figure 13.4.[29]

FIGURE 13-4

Union Density in Select OECD Countries

Country	Union Density
Iceland	91.8%
Sweden	67.0%
Italy	37.3%
Canada	26.5%
United Kingdom	24.7%
Germany	17.7%
Japan	17.4%
Australia	17.0%
France	11.2%
United States	10.6%
South Korea	9.0%

SOURCE: Neil McCarthy (2017, June 20), "Which countries have the highest levels of union membership?" *Forbes.*

The Impact of Union Representation

Strikes

Members of the public frequently associate unions with strikes. However, the reality is that most collective agreements are settled without the union's resorting to strike action or the employer's locking out the workers. Still, there are exceptions:

> In 2009, approximately 1,800 City of Windsor (Ontario) inside and outside workers went on strike. By the six-week mark of the strike, frustration was setting in. A bar owner reported that her employees were harassed by city workers for removing the bar's garbage during the strike, and a newspaper columnist said his car was vandalized after he wrote an article about taking garbage to a private firm. There were allegations of individuals putting clothes hangers in tall grass to prevent it from being mowed and spreading nails on the road leading to a private waste disposal site. The local CUPE president insisted that there were no reports of union picketers doing any of that. Rather, one CUPE member stated that he suffered a broken ankle and cuts to his face after a confrontation with a private contractor cutting grass, and other picketers revealed that they had been nudged by people seeking to drive past the picket line. One picketer was the victim of a hit-and-run and another was put in a headlock by an irate driver.[30]

In studying why strikes occur, it is possible to classify strikes into one of two categories:

1. *Strikes as Mistakes/Misjudgment.* At least some strikes occur because the parties have uncertain and imperfect information when trying to negotiate an agreement or because one or both negotiation teams are inexperienced negotiators. For example, some negotiators easily become frustrated when bargaining and make their "final offer" too early or without carefully considering the implications of shutting down bargaining.
2. *Strikes as Collective Voice.* In a number of instances, the decision to go out on strike is not because of a mistake or misjudgment but because of a perception on the part of workers that they are not being treated fairly. A strike is considered a mechanism by which to voice discontent to management:[31]

> A prolonged strike between the City of Ottawa and OC Transpo showed how adversarial a dispute can become and its impact on labour–management relations. The city wanted more control over route assignments and scheduling in an effort to improve the quality of the transit service, but the union was strongly opposed. As one union member stated, "This offer is going to destroy my family life. I won't be home for my family." The scheduling issue had the most impact on drivers with more seniority, and some of the other employees were anxious to return to work. According to one attendant, "In this economy, I don't think anybody wants to be out of work for a long period of time."[32]

In a strike environment, there are several issues to consider. An extended strike puts considerable financial pressure on employees. As well, the family is at risk for more than just financial reasons: Normal family patterns and routines are seriously disrupted. Physical and emotional harm may also be an issue. Once the dispute is settled, employees have to return to a workplace and to work teams that just a few days before were divided by a fundamental conflict. While companies need to get on with business, the human issues do not go away by themselves. It can take four to six weeks to return to normal working conditions, and some workplaces are never really the same.[33]

What factors distinguish firms with lower strike activity? Strikes were less common in smaller firms and in organizations where

- workers had more autonomy in the workplace;
- the employer introduced progressive human resource management practices;
- the union was in a strategically weak position; and
- employers had a large share of the market.[34]

How common are strikes and lockouts? Data on the number of strikes and lockouts, the number of workers involved, and the person-days not worked are provided in Figure 13-5. Over the 2013–2017 period, the greatest number of strikes and lockouts (and the largest number of person-days not worked) was in 2015. Obviously, a small number of large strikes in a given year can markedly affect the number of workers involved and the person-days not worked.

Quebec and British Columbia prohibit the use of replacement workers if there is a strike or lockout. However, some employer groups are arguing that the ban on replacement workers does not reduce the number of strikes or lockouts or days lost due to work stoppages. In addition, employers argue that the legislation discourages investment by employers in Quebec.[35]

> Some strikes can take well over a year to resolve. Employees at the Voisey's Bay (Newfoundland) nickel mine finally settled with Brazilian mining firm Vale, ending a bitter 18-month strike. According to United Steelworkers spokesperson Boyd Bussey, the use of replacement workers by Vale made the dispute particularly nasty. In Bussey's words, "It's been a cold couple of years on the picket line. At the end of the day, these workers resolved to take on the company and they came through with flying colours."[36]

FIGURE 13-5

Strikes and Lockouts in Canada

Year	Number of Strikes and Lockouts	Workers Involved (000)	Person-Days Not Worked (000)
2003	266	79	1,730
2004	297	259	3,185
2005	260	199	4,148
2006	151	42	793
2007	206	66	1,771
2008	188	41	875
2009	157	67	2,162
2010	174	58	1,202
2011	149	91	1,351
2012	281	137	904
2013	165	205	205
2014	153	80	1,711
2015	237	429	1,846
2016	189	44	632
2017	192	207	1,201

SOURCE: Based on Work Stoppages by Jurisdiction and Year, ESDC, 2018.

Sometimes workers do not go out on strike but come up with other approaches to put pressure on an employer. After about 200 Air Berlin pilots called in sick one day, approximately 100 flights had to be cancelled. The pilots' union indicated that it was surprised by the absences and stated that it had not encouraged pilots to call in sick.[37]

Recent Supreme Court of Canada decisions addressed important issues relating to strikes. First, the court struck down Saskatchewan legislation that prevented public sector workers from going on strike. According to Lori Johb of the Saskatchewan Federation of Labour, "Workers aren't generally keen to strike. Without that right, we really had no power, we had no ability to achieve fair, collective bargaining for all the members."[38] The court also ruled that a part of Alberta's privacy legislation violated the right of a union to free speech by prohibiting the union from videotaping employees crossing a picket line. The court recognized the importance of freedom of expression in labour disputes with picketing representing a particularly critical form of expression.[39]

In commenting on the recent Supreme Court of Canada decisions, union labour lawyer Chris Paliare stated the following:

"The very notion of collective bargaining implies that there is an imbalance between workers and employers. So unless you have an inherently anti-union bent, you have to accept that workers need the fundamental right to bargain collectively, to be protected from unfair labour practices, and to take strike action in order to address that imbalance."[40]

One issue that frequently comes up after a strike is settled concerns rebuilding the labour–management relationship. A strike changes the relationship, often leads to workplace conflict, and typically destroys the trust between the parties:

> When a seven-week strike at CBC ended, management announced plans to hire consultants to "reintegrate" the workers with their managers. The reaction from most employees was "They've got to be [expletive] kidding." According to one consultant, "There is always a dramatic erosion in trust of management after a strike, which creates lingering resentment, and lack of productivity unless it is addressed properly." While each strike is different, some companies ask outside consultants with expertise in psychology and social work to conduct confidential debriefing sessions for employees. As well, some organizations have "return to work" training programs (again run by consultants) for managers; the programs focus on role plays, dealing with employees, and getting the team back and running. In addition, employees should be made aware of the EAP program and other assistance available to them.[41]

Wages and Benefits

What are the effects of unions on wages and benefits? The average hourly wage for full-time unionized employees at the beginning of 2018 was $30.32 an hour (compared with $25.47 for nonunion workers).[42] Moreover, as indicated in Figure 13-6, unionized employees tend to have more comprehensive benefit plan coverage.

Unions and Productivity

One major issue of interest for human resource management and industrial relations practitioners is the relationship between unionization and productivity. On one hand, it can be argued that unions have a "monopoly" face that creates economic inefficiency by introducing restrictive and inflexible work rules, withdrawing labour in the form of a strike if an employer fails to meet union demands, and increasing compensation costs. On the other hand, it can also be asserted that unions have a "voice" face that increases productivity by reducing turnover, enhancing employee morale, improving communications with workers, and "shocking" management into using more efficient workplace practices.[43] Studies have shown that unions

- reduce employee turnover (fewer quits);
- increase tenure with the firm; and
- raise productivity or output per worker.[44]

FIGURE 13-6

Union Status and Work Conditions

Work Condition	Union Employees	Nonunion Employees
% of employees with pension coverage	82.8	32.9
% of employees with supplemental health plan coverage	83.7	44.4
% of employees with dental plan coverage	77.0	41.9
% of employees with paid sick leave	77.2	44.7
% of employees with paid vacation leave	84.1	65.3
% of employees with flextime option	16.7	27.1
% of employees in job sharing arrangement	12.1	6.8
Average annual paid vacation leave (days)	20.9	15.1

SOURCE: "Strikes and Lockouts in Canada," adapted from the Statistics Canada publication "Perspectives on Labour and Income," Catalogue No. 75-001, Autumn, 2000.

Spotlight *on* **HRM**

Making Peace at Work

Communication is vital to rebuilding a workplace after a labour dispute, the experts say. Here are tips from Steve Kennedy, Ottawa-based mental-health practitioner for employee assistance provider FGIworld:

- Before employees return, managers should discuss how the new agreement changes the workplace and how they will welcome back the staff.

- Employees and managers may need counselling to help them recover if they experienced conflicts at the picket line. "It's important from the get-go to acknowledge that both sides have a legal right to do what they did," Mr. Kennedy says.

- As soon as possible after employees return, managers should acknowledge that the strike caused stresses and that efforts will be made to relieve them. A full-scale staff meeting is best.

- Attendance at the meeting should be mandatory. "The message is not 'Come if you want to,'" Mr. Kennedy says. Employees usually are anxious to participate.

- To help employees refocus, managers should state goals clearly and express optimism. They should also commit to supporting employees and trying to better resolve issues in the future.

- Allow ample time for employee questions and discussions.

- Managers should set up processes to discuss and resolve any outstanding issues among teams or individuals.

- Employees should be encouraged to take stock of their role and consider what they can do to create a better work environment. They should also remember that managers are human, too.

Based on Wallace Immen (2005, October 5), "How to heal ab Bruised workplace," *The Globe and Mail*, pp. C1, C2.

However, the relationship between unionization and productivity is open to considerable debate and has not been universally agreed upon. In fact, management perceptions are opposite to some of the empirical work: While managers from both the union and nonunion sectors tend to believe that unions lower productivity, some studies indicate that in a number of industries, productivity is actually higher in unionized firms. There is also evidence that unions recognize the importance of increasing productivity:

The International Boilermakers Union believed that union members who were shutting down work sites illegally, sleeping on the job, and being disrespectful were giving the union a bad name. As a result, the union got tough and decided to adopt a zero-tolerance policy for poor worker behaviour. As one senior union official stated, "A majority of our members are honest, hard-working, skilled tradespeople. Unfortunately, a small group are destroying other members' careers with their personal agenda of bad attitudes, late starts, early quits, poor productivity, absenteeism, and job disruptions." The union

implemented a new policy with strict guidelines addressing union member behaviour.[45]

In most jurisdictions, employers have the right to operate during a strike but some choose not to:

According to one labour relations expert, "The employer has to calculate very carefully if bringing in replacement workers is going to exacerbate the bitterness of the dispute. After a strike it takes a while to put the relationship back together. There's a lot of bitterness left over. The employer takes some chance of exacerbating that when they bring in replacement workers—at a substantial cost to the labour–management relationship over the long term."[46]

LO3   The Legal Environment

Government shapes the union management framework through both the enactment of laws and in their role as employer. Unlike the United States, where employers and unions across the country are regulated by the *National*

Labour Relations Act, in Canada the federal government and each province has its own labour legislation. This division of responsibilities for trade union law is a result of the *British North America Act* (now the *Constitution Act, 1867*), which specifies the powers of the federal government and the provinces.

The issue of jurisdiction over labour relations is significant for human resource practitioners. The Canadian Parliament is restricted in its jurisdiction over labour relations matters to organizations involved in interprovincial trade and commerce (e.g., banks, airlines, railways, and federal government agencies). All other organizations fall under the jurisdiction of the provinces. It has been estimated that less than 10 percent of the Canadian labour force comes under federal jurisdiction. Consequently, it is important that human resource practitioners are aware of the appropriate legislation.

Although the traditional view is that the employer and union should be free to sit down and negotiate a collective agreement, we are seeing increasing government intervention in the bargaining process at both the provincial and national level. For instance, in Nova Scotia, the government is overhauling and radically altering the education system with minimal consultation. One of the changes, which has been strongly opposed by the Nova Scotia Teachers' Union, involves the removal of principals and vice-principals from the bargaining unit. Such individuals will be given one year to decide whether they want to return to the classroom or leave the bargaining unit.[47] Buzz Hargrove, former president of the Canadian Autoworkers Union, stated, "There's no respect left for the collective bargaining process. It's about government coming in on behalf of employers and defending employers, almost guaranteeing they're going to win the dispute . . . it's so anti-democratic, it's so un-Canadian."[48]

The Common Core of Canadian Labour Legislation

The fact that each province and the federal jurisdiction have their own labour relations statutes makes dealing with unions somewhat more difficult, particularly for employers

operating in more than one province. Some of the key aspects of Canadian labour law (which will be discussed in more detail later) include the following:

- *Right to Join a Union.* Employees have the right to join a trade union of their choice and participate in the union's activities.
- *Good Faith Bargaining.* In attempting to negotiate a collective agreement, both labour and management have a duty to "bargain in good faith."
- *No Strikes or Lockouts during the Life of the Collective Agreement.* It is illegal for a union to strike or an employer to lock out employees during the life of the contract.
- *Prohibition on Unfair Labour Practices.* All jurisdictions have legislation prohibiting unfair labour practices by employers and unions.
- *Conciliation.* The right of a union to strike or an employer to lock out employees is (in most provinces) delayed until the conciliation process has been exhausted.

While each province and the federal jurisdiction have some unique features in their labour laws, there is a "common core" of provisions contained in the various labour relations acts (refer to Figure 13-7).[49]

Labour Relations Boards

To enforce labour legislation, the federal and all provincial governments have created **labour relations boards (LRBs)**. These agencies investigate violations of the law and have the power to determine (1) whether a person is an employee for the purposes of the law; (2) whether an employee is a member of a trade union; (3) whether an organization is an appropriate bargaining agent for bargaining purposes; (4) whether a collective agreement is in force; and (5) whether any given party is bound by it. The enforcement procedures of an

> **labour relations boards (LRBs)** Boards set up in the federal and provincial jurisdictions to administer labour relations legislation.

FIGURE 13-7

Common Characteristics of Federal and Provincial Labour Legislation

1. All jurisdictions create labour relations boards to decide who has the right to participate in collective bargaining and what bargaining unit should be permitted to represent those who are organized.
2. Most jurisdictions prohibit strikes during the life of an agreement.
3. Most jurisdictions contain regulations that delay strike action until a conciliation effort has been made and has failed.
4. All jurisdictions require that a collective agreement be in force for at least one year.
5. All jurisdictions specify and prohibit certain "unfair labour practices" by management and unions.

LRB Procedures for Redressing Unfair Labour Practices

1. The aggrieved individual or organization contacts the appropriate LRB office (federal or provincial) and explains the alleged violation.

2. If the case appears to have merit, the LRB informs the other party of the complaint and asks for a response.

3. The LRB gives the parties involved the opportunity to present evidence and to make representations. If the complaint cannot be solved informally, the LRB conducts an official hearing with the interested parties present and usually represented by legal counsel.

4. On the basis of the evidence, the board will either dismiss the case or, if one party is found guilty of a violation, issue a cease-and-desist order. In the event of noncompliance, this order is enforceable in a court of law.

5. It is up to the courts to decide whether a verdict can be appealed or not. In any case, an appeal can be made in matters of jurisdiction, failure to pursue legitimate complaints, and procedural irregularities.

LRB relating to unfair labour practice allegations are summarized in Figure 13-8.

In comparison to traditional courts of law, LRBs are more flexible in their procedures for resolving a conflict. They may rely on expert evidence instead of adhering to precedents, suggest a compromise, or even impose a solution upon the parties. In all jurisdictions, the boards' decisions are final and binding and cannot be appealed except on procedural matters.

When charges have been filed against an employer, the human resource department usually assists the organization's lawyer in preparing the case. For example, the HR department may be involved in compiling job descriptions, performance appraisals, attendance records, and other documents that help the company prove its case. Consider the following:

> Patrick Veinot was an employee of Vale Canada, a nickel mining and metals company, and vice-president of his local union. During a long and bitter strike, Veinot was charged with criminal harassment after an employee, who crossed the picket line, was assaulted. Vale investigated the incident, concluded that Veinot had verbally harassed the employee and encouraged another striking worker to assault the employee, and terminated Veinot's employment (but Veinot was subsequently acquitted of the charges). Veinot was also prohibited from going onto the employer's property. After the strike ended, Veinot was appointed a vice-president of the local union— the company would contact him by phone to discuss grievances but refused to let Veinot on the company property. The union grieved the employer's action and the labour board held that banning Veinot from company property was interference with union activities. The company was ordered to stop such interference and allow Veinot on the property for the purpose of union meetings.[50]

LO4 The Collective Bargaining Process

Union Organizing

It is worth remembering that a union exists only when workers create it. While unions may use professional organizers, the outcome of the organizing drive depends primarily upon the employees. George Meany, the first president of the American Federation of Labor and Congress of Industrial Organizations (AFL-CIO) in the United States, once said this:

> "Despite the well-worn trade union phrase, an organizer does not organize a plant. Now, as in the beginning, the workers must organize themselves. The organizer can serve only as an educator; what he or she organizes is the thinking of the workers."[51]

In addition to professional organizers, employees interested in unionization often play an important role in convincing co-workers to join the union. During regular working hours, employees are not allowed to discuss unionization with co-workers. However, several other techniques are used to encourage workers to sign **authorization cards**, including handbills, speeches, conversations, and even home visits. Depending on the jurisdiction, a union is typically certified either on the basis of card signatures or as a result of an election. Some unions are particularly creative in the organizing process:

authorization cards
Cards signed by workers to join a union; depending on the jurisdiction, a union may be certified either on the basis of card signatures or as a result of an election.

> The United Food and Commercial Workers (UFCW) have developed a Youth Internship Program that

involves youth activists who are given the opportunity to work with union representatives to learn negotiating skills and experience hands-on union organizing campaigns. Travel and accommodation expenses as well as lost wages are covered by the union. The UFCW also has a program—Talking Union—where union representatives and members visit high schools, colleges, and universities and provide students who are new to the workforce with information on labour history and workplace rights.[52]

Union organizers educate the workers by explaining how the union can help employees and reduce mistreatment of workers. However, professionals only assist workers; they do not cause workers to join a union. Even experienced organizers find it difficult to organize a well-managed and growing company with proactive human resource practices.[53] Still, some unions are using new technology to help organize workers:

> Some union activists are advocating using the Internet to build support through virtual organizing and virtual picketing. Derek Blackadder, a CUPE organizer, tried to organize a group of workers using Facebook but was banned from the network for having too many friends. However, an email campaign by a colleague was used to have Facebook administrators restore his privileges. Some experts believe social networks are particularly appropriate for union organizing as unions are very committed to increasing membership of young people (who are primary users of social networks).[54]

Prior to many union organizing campaigns, there are signs of employee interest in union representation. Of particular importance is the work environment. For example,

are the turnover and absenteeism rates higher than the norms for the industry and community? Is morale poor? Are pay and benefits below average for the industry? Does the employer have a procedure for resolving employee complaints or issues, and, if so, is the process used by workers? Changes in employee behaviour may also suggest that a union drive is under way (see Figure 13-9). However, these are only indications of a *possible* union drive.

> An organizing drive at a Denny's restaurant signalled the use of class-action litigation as a new organizing strategy for unions. The Denny's case involved the charging of agency fees by companies recruiting temporary foreign workers for the restaurant. The BC Supreme Court supported the filing of a class-action lawsuit, a strategy that has been used in the United States with difficult-to-organize and exploited workers who may be unable or unwilling to bring a case on their own against their employer.[55]

Once a union drive begins, management's choice of responses becomes limited in several important ways. A labour relations board (LRB) will protect workers from management reprisals. For example, the discipline of union supporters is illegal, unless the employer can prove that the basis for punishment was not involvement in a union but improper behaviour.

Employer lawyer Jamie Knight identified three stages to an employer's defence in the event that an employer is committed to remaining union free. Stage 1 involves removing the incentive to unionize through effective human resource management (such as competitive wages and benefits, fair and reasonable policies, excellent communication with employees, and a complaint and suggestion system that allows employees to voice their concerns without the threat of reprisal). Stage 2, which occurs when card signing

---

FIGURE 13-9

Employee Behaviour That Suggests Union Activity

- Obvious signs—such as finding a union flyer
- Change in employee turnover
- Exit interview language—comments on a negative work environment
- Employee language—such as common labour management terms like *arbitration* and *unfair labour practice*
- Employee communication behaviour change—less co-operative behaviour by workers
- New employee alliances—among those interested in unionization
- Social media language—involving unionization
- Employee phone time—discussing union activities
- Emotions running high—negative portrayal of working conditions
- Employee routines change—such as lunch breaks

Based on "Are You Missing These 10 Signs of Union Organizing Activity?" *UnionProof*, http://www.unionproof.com

Spotlight *on* ETHICS

Hiring a Union Supporter

Consider the following situation and make a note of your answer on a separate sheet of paper.

You are a recent university graduate and three months ago started working for a small manufacturing firm. The company currently has 17 employees, including 10 labourers who are responsible for product assembly. Although wage levels in the firm are slightly above average when compared to the competition in the immediate area, the business owner is known as a tough manager who isn't exactly a "people person."

While your official title is assistant manager of operations, your job involves some aspects of production as well as marketing. Although the hours are long, you have found the job to be quite rewarding and have enjoyed the exposure to the "real world of business." Four days ago, the owner of the business came to you and asked you to also assume responsibility for human resources, saying, "I'm not into all that people management stuff but we are expanding and I know we've got to have somebody do it. You can pretty much do what you want when it comes to hiring—the only thing that's important to me is that we don't ever get a union around here."

Yesterday, the owner dropped by your office to tell you that the company was going to need to hire two labourers. He said, "Here's a chance for you to use some of that stuff you learned in university. I've been doing most of the hiring around here but I'm just getting too busy. As I mentioned the other day, the only thing I want is to be sure that we don't get a union around here. Oh, also, the people you hire better be good! I'll let you in on a little secret—when you bring someone in for an interview, ask them the usual stuff about qualifications and so on. Then, carefully bring the conversation around to unions. But you've got to be careful—I don't want the labour board down here bothering us. I usually bring up some labour dispute— the NHL collective bargaining situation, a strike by the post office or nurses, or some other union issue. If you are careful, you can find out what the person really thinks about unions. And, obviously, if you think that they are sympathetic to unions, don't hire them. It's worked for me for more than 25 years. Whatever you do, don't mess this up!"

On one hand, you know the views of the business owner concerning unions. On the other hand, you are fully aware that under Canadian labour law, employees have the right to join a union and participate in its activities and that it is illegal to discriminate against employees or job candidates because they are interested in union representation. What are you going to do in this situation?

begins, involves discussing the impacts of unionization (such as the union becoming the exclusive bargaining agent, the requirement for employees to pay dues, and the need to carefully assess union promises) and the need to avoid unfair labour practice charges. In Stage 3, when an election is about to be held, the employer is advised to encourage employees to get out and vote because the chance of a union victory may decline as voter turnout increases.[56]

When unions are organizing, labour relations boards pay particularly close attention to the actions of employers. Unlike the United States, Canadian labour law provides employers with relatively little freedom to counter a union organizing drive.[57] Both the context and content of statements about unionization are carefully examined by LRBs. Consequently, employers are well advised to obtain prudent legal advice in the wake of a union organizing campaign.

Canadian LRBs are quite vigilant in enforcing unfair labour relations practices. Human resource administrators should stress to every member of management, from supervisor to chief executive officer, the following two cautions:

1. Can management actions be judged as unfair labour practices by the LRB?
2. Will management actions provide fuel for the organizing drive?

In Prince Edward Island, two fish processing plants were closed down upon the arrival of union organizers. The PEI Labour Relations Board ordered the employer, Polar Foods, to compensate 150 workers for lost wages (a total settlement of almost $500,000) following evidence at an unfair labour practices hearing that Polar Foods closed the plants to avoid unionization.[58]

FIGURE 13-10

Unfair Labour Practices by Management

Every jurisdiction in Canada has specific provisions dealing with unfair labour practices by management. Some of the most common provisions addressing unfair labour practices are provided below. Activities that management may not engage in include the following:

1. Interfering in the formation of a union or contributing to it financially (although there have been allowances for the providing of an office for the union to conduct business and for paid leave for union officials conducting union business)
2. Discriminating against an employee because the individual is or is not a member of a trade union
3. Discriminating against an employee because that individual chooses to exercise rights granted by labour relations statutes
4. Intimidating or coercing an employee to become or not become a member of a union

When an unfair labour practice is committed by any member of management, it can lead to expensive, time-consuming lawsuits and (in some instances) automatic certification of the union. Moreover, union supporters can point to management violations as further justification for a union.

Unfair Labour Practices

To prevent employers from interfering with employee rights, the law prohibits specific **unfair labour practices** by management. These legal prohibitions are summarized in Figure 13-10. They require that management neither interfere with nor discriminate against employees who undertake collective action.

Unfair labour practices by unions are also prohibited. A summary of such practices is provided in Figure 13-11.

> **unfair labour practices**
> Practices by management such as interfering with or discriminating against employees who undertake collective action. Unions may also commit unfair labour practices.

Obtaining Bargaining Rights

Legal recognition or bargaining rights may be obtained in three ways: (1) through voluntary recognition, (2) through certification by a labour relations board, and (3) through a prehearing vote or automatic certification resulting from unfair labour practice.

1. *Voluntary recognition* occurs if a union has organized a majority of employees and the employer is satisfied that the union did not apply undue pressure in the organization process. The employer then accepts the union as the legal bargaining agent without any involvement of a third party.
2. *Regular certification* may take different forms (depending on the jurisdiction):
   - In some provinces, if a substantial number of employees (usually between 50 and 65 percent, depending on jurisdiction) sign union cards, the labour relations board may certify the unit without an election. If the union is unable to get enough

FIGURE 13-11

Unfair Labour Practices by Unions

While every jurisdiction has laws regulating trade union conduct, some of the most important unfair labour practice provisions are presented below. Activities that a union is not permitted to engage in include the following:

1. Seeking to compel an employer to bargain collectively with the union if the union is not the certified bargaining agent
2. Attempting, at the workplace and during working hours, to persuade an employee to become or not become a union member
3. Intimidating, coercing, or penalizing an individual because he or she has filed a complaint or testified in any proceedings pursuant to the relevant labour relations statute
4. Engaging in, encouraging, or threatening illegal strikes
5. Failing to represent employees fairly

employees to sign cards to qualify for automatic certification but still gets a significant number of card signatures (typically between 35 and 45 percent of bargaining-unit members, again depending on the jurisdiction), an election is mandatory. A secret ballot is taken under the supervision of the labour relations board at the employer's place of business. If the union loses, another election among the same employees cannot be held for one year. If the union wins (that is, the majority of eligible employees who vote cast ballots in favour of the union), then the employer must prepare to negotiate with the union and attempt to reach a collective agreement.

- Other provinces do not automatically certify unions based on card signatures. Rather, an election is held if there is sufficient support for the union in the form of signed cards. Again, the union is certified if the majority of the ballots cast are in favour of the union. While employers generally favour a mandatory secret ballot vote for certification, the legislative change away from certification on the basis of card signatures was strongly opposed by unions. Amendments to the certification process are not uncommon:

> Ontario's *Fair Workplaces, Better Jobs Act, 2017,* has some interesting features that will impact union organizing in the province. For instance, a union able to show at least 20 percent membership support can obtain employee contact information (such as name, phone number, and email) from the employer. Also, the Act provides for off-site or electronic voting.[59]

3. *Prehearing votes* are taken in cases when there are significant indications that an employer has committed unfair labour practices to prevent unionization. In such a case a union can ask an LRB to conduct a prehearing vote. In addition, most jurisdictions provide for automatic certification if employer actions (in the form of unfair labour practices) are such that the true wishes of employees may not be known.[60]

In Jonquière, Quebec, a Walmart suddenly closed down a few months after the employees became the first Walmart store to unionize in 2004. The closure was on the day an arbitrator was selected to resolve the dispute. A legal battle that took about a decade was ultimately decided when the Supreme Court of Canada ruled that the employees were entitled to compensation.[61]

LO5 Negotiating a Collective Agreement

Once a union is certified, the various labour relations statutes require both the union and management to bargain in good faith. This means that both sides are required to make

a reasonable effort to negotiate a collective agreement. The failure of either party to do so can lead to unfair labour practice charges.

The collective bargaining process has three overlapping phases. Preparation for negotiations is the first and often the most critical stage. The success of the second stage, face-to-face negotiations, largely depends on how well each side has prepared, the skill of the management and union negotiators, and the bargaining power of each side. The third phase involves the follow-up activities of contract administration. An organization may establish an industrial relations department or create a labour relations specialist position within the human resources department to administer the collective agreement and coordinate contract negotiations. In recent years, we have seen a trend toward longer collective agreements:

> Over the past 30 years, the average length of collective agreements has doubled (from 20 to 40 months). Unions have generally preferred shorter agreements while employers often sought longer deals. According to labour lawyer Will Cascadden, "Because bargaining involves multiple meetings, bargaining is usually a time-consuming expensive process. Employers have to allocate significant resources figuring out what the bargaining positions are and what positions you are going to take on those issues."[62]

© CP/Sean Kilpatrick

Postal strikes tend to have a serious impact on customers, especially small businesses. Should postal strikes be prohibited? Could such prohibitions be done legally?

Preparing for Negotiations

The purpose of negotiations is to achieve a *collective agreement*. The agreement specifies the rights and responsibilities of management and the union. Detailed preparations are required if each party is to achieve its objectives.[63]

Labour relations specialists need to monitor the environment to obtain information about likely union demands. A number of strategies can be employed. The labour relations department must be sensitive to the rate of inflation and the settlements made by other unions.

One set of bargaining issues revolves around **management rights**. These rights provide management with the freedom to operate the business subject to any terms in the collective agreement.[64] They often include the right to reassign employees to different jobs, to make hiring decisions, and to decide other matters important to management.

> **management rights**
> Rights that provide management with the freedom to operate the business subject to any terms in the collective agreement.

Under what is known as the *residual rights theory* of management, employers argue that they have the authority over all issues not contained in the collective agreement. On the other hand, union leaders assert that residual rights do not exist and that they are free to bargain over any issue affecting workers. Most collective agreements have a *management rights clause*. A typical clause might be as follows:

> Nothing in this agreement shall be deemed to restrict management in any way in the performance of all functions of management except those specifically abridged or modified by this agreement.[65]

In negotiating a collective agreement, management may want to include contract language that increases its flexibility at the workplace. For example, supervisors may want all job descriptions to include the phrase "and other duties assigned by management." This clause prevents workers from refusing work because it is not in their job description. The clause also gives supervisors greater freedom in assigning employees. Labour relations specialists in the human resource department may use a variety of sources (such as surveys, discussions, focus groups, provisions in other collective agreements, and information from grievance claims) to discover which rights are important.

Negotiating with the Union

After preparing for bargaining, the second phase of negotiations is face-to-face bargaining with the union. Discussions often start as much as 60 to 90 days before the end of the present contract. If the negotiations are for a first contract, they begin after the union is recognized by the employer or wins a certification election.

Negotiations cover a variety of issues relating to terms and conditions of employment, including wages, hours of work, and working conditions. These areas are interpreted broadly. *Wages* refer to all forms of compensation, such as pay, insurance plans, retirement programs, and other benefits and services. *Hours of work* include the length of the workday, breaks, holidays, vacations, and any other component of the work schedule. *Working conditions* involve such issues as safety, supervisory treatment, and other elements of the work environment. The contents of a collective agreement are only limited by the ingenuity of the parties. For instance:

> Canadian Blood Services (Edmonton) permits employees to take up to three days off to attend their wedding. In PEI, the Labourers International Union negotiated a clause that prohibits the use of cellphones and smart phones during work hours, and in Quebec, CBC and Groupe TVA agreed to a clause guaranteeing an employee salary and benefits if the individual is incarcerated for refusing to divulge a confidential source.[66]

Successful bargaining usually begins with easy issues in order to build a pattern of give-and-take. Negotiations almost always take place in private, permitting more open discussion of the issues. When deadlocks occur, several tactics can keep negotiations moving toward a peaceful settlement. By settling easy issues first, bargainers often point to this progress and say, "We've come too far to give up on this impasse. Surely, we can find a solution." This sense of past progress may increase the resolve of both sides to find a compromise.

> Richard Dixon, former vice-president and human resources officer at NAV Canada, stated, "In any unionized environment, if you're sitting at the collective bargaining table, you're sitting across from

Union leaders, like politicians, are elected. Are there other similarities?

individuals who know the business very well. When trying to introduce a new business process or negotiate a more streamlined way of doing things, the HR professionals who don't know the business as well as the people on the other side of the table could have their pockets picked."[67]

Compromises may be achieved by offering counterproposals that take into account the needs of the other party. For example, Air Canada and its pilots reached an agreement without resorting to strike action or arbitration for the first time since 1996. In addition to reopener clauses, the 10-year contract also provided for profit sharing for union members using a formula similar to that applied for executive bonuses.[68]

Many management teams will exclude top executives. They are kept out of negotiations because top managers are often not experienced in collective bargaining. Also, their exclusion gives management bargainers a reason to ask for a temporary adjournment when the union introduces demands that require a careful review. Rather than refusing the union's suggestion, management bargainers may ask for a recess to confer with top management (using the adage "My hands are tied").

Experienced bargainers realize that the other side must achieve some of its objectives. If the employer is powerful enough to force an unacceptable contract on the union negotiating team, the union membership may refuse to ratify the contract, or union officials and members may refuse to co-operate with management once the collective agreement goes into effect. In addition, if management does not bargain in good faith, the union may file unfair labour practice charges.

Using Mutual Gains Bargaining

Rather than use the traditional adversarial approach to negotiating a collective agreement, some unions and employers are employing *mutual gains bargaining*. This approach moves away from the us-versus-them or win–lose attitude in favour of a win–win approach, in which both parties work together to solve common problems. However, labour unions are often skeptical about win–win bargaining, as one senior union official asserts:

It has been our experience that most employers only become "less adversarial" and talk about co-operation when they want something that will benefit them. Many employers have approached unions wanting to extract concessions, normally accompanied by promises of future employer co-operation. It is also usually followed by an acute case of amnesia on the part of the company. Any level of co-operation between the union and company must be accompanied by a commitment that front-line supervisors are prepared to treat our members with dignity and respect on the shop floor. Without that commitment, co-operation between the union and company is meaningless.[69]

Note that mutual gains bargaining does not mean "soft" bargaining or one side giving in. Rather, both parties sit down at the bargaining table as equals and engage in joint problem-solving activities. The process is usually preceded by training in conflict resolution for both employer and union representatives. In addition, mutual gains bargaining requires substantial commitment, trust, and respect, and a long-term focus on the part of both labour and management.

What does a mutual gains enterprise need to succeed? At the workplace level, it is important to have high standards of employee selection, broad design of tasks and a focus on teamwork, employee involvement in problem solving, and a climate based on co-operation and trust. At the human resource policy level, key elements include a commitment to employment stabilization, investment in training and development, and a contingent compensation strategy that emphasizes participation, co-operation, and contribution. Finally, at the strategic level, there must be a strong commitment from top management to the mutual gains concept, business strategies that support and are aligned with the mutual gains model, and an effective voice for human resource management in strategy making.[70]

Research by the Conference Board of Canada revealed that 36 percent of employers and 42 percent of unions have attempted interest-based or mutual gains bargaining techniques.[71]

Still, many labour relations experts are somewhat skeptical about interest-based bargaining, as one labour lawyer points out:

"If you ask seasoned negotiators (about interest-based bargaining), they'll give you the look of death and say, 'Are you crazy?' Mutual gains bargaining requires both sides to invest so much time and energy in being trained in things like 'What do you need?' 'What are our needs?' 'How do we negotiate in a collaborative fashion?' But to go from traditional bargaining into mutual interest takes a diametric mind-shift. You need to invest the resources and the relationship has to be mature enough."[72]

Approving the Proposed Agreement

The bargaining stage of negotiations is completed when the agreement has been approved. Often final approval for the employer rests with top management. Negotiations are not complete until the union also approves the proposed agreement. Typically, the union bargaining team submits the proposal to the membership for ratification. If a majority of the members vote for the proposal, it replaces the previous collective agreement. If members reject it, union and management bargainers reopen negotiations. Administration of the collective agreement begins when both sides sign it.

LO6 Conciliation and Mediation

What happens in the event that negotiations between labour and management break down? In their legislation, all jurisdictions provide for **conciliation** and mediation services. Actually, in most provinces, no strike action is permitted before a conciliation effort has been made and has failed.[73] A 10-year review of conciliation cases in Nova Scotia revealed that conciliation officers settled more than 90 percent of the cases.[74] However, the results vary among provinces, and some jurisdictions have not come close to matching the 90 percent figure.

conciliation Use of a government-appointed third party to explore solutions to a labour–management dispute.

Conciliators are appointed by the federal or provincial minister of labour, at the request of either one or both of the parties involved or at the discretion of the ministers. A conciliator is requested to submit a report to the minister within a specified time period. If conciliation fails, strikes or lockouts can legally commence, usually two weeks after the submission of the conciliator's report. Although labour relations legislation may include an option to have a conciliation board meet with the parties, this is used infrequently.

With reference to **mediation**, often a mediator will meet separately with each bargaining team, especially when the negotiations take place in a hostile atmosphere. Effective mediation requires a high degree of sensitivity, patience, and expertise in the psychology of negotiation.

mediation Use of a neutral third party to help settle a labour–management dispute.

Administering the Collective Agreement

Upon ratification by union members and approval by management, the parties begin living with the collective agreement. What happens if the parties have a disagreement regarding the interpretation of a term of the agreement? As discussed below, alleged violations of the agreement typically go through the **grievance procedure**. A *grievance* is defined as a complaint by an employee or employer that alleges that some aspect of a collective agreement has been violated. Almost every collective agreement in Canada contains some type of formalized procedure for resolving disputes. Furthermore, labour legislation typically requires that a grievance that cannot be resolved between the parties be

grievance procedure A formalized procedure for resolving disputes if the parties have a disagreement regarding the interpretation of a term of the collective agreement.

submitted to an arbitrator or arbitration board whose decision is final and binding. To give an example, consider the following case:

> A 46-year-old Ottawa city worker was found to have altered the water meter at both his current and former residence. The employer met with the worker, who admitted to tampering with the meter and agreed to reimburse the city for almost $7,000 to cover unrecorded water usage. The employee admitted turning off the meter on several occasions (such as on heavy laundry days or when filling his pool). Although the employee had 23 years of service without performance or disciplinary issues and the misconduct was off-duty and not directly related to his employment, an arbitrator upheld the termination of the employee.[75]

Grievance Procedures

While either management or the union may file a grievance when the collective agreement is violated, most workplace decisions are made by management. Consequently, most grievances are filed by the union. The grievance procedure consists of an ordered series of steps. Figure 13-12 describes the steps that an employee's grievance typically passes through. An example further demonstrates how grievances may occur:

> Preboarding screeners at the Edmonton International Airport, who are members of Teamster Local 362, have filed more than 900 grievances resulting from delayed or missed breaks. Although all workers are entitled to two or three half-hour breaks based on shift length, employer GardaWorld changed its interpretation of the clause so that all required security lines could be open. Union officials reported that at least four workers soiled themselves after being denied bathroom breaks. Union vice-president and business agent Jordan Madarash stated, "Morale is low, absenteeism is higher. It's not a fun place to work right now, wondering if you are going to get a break to get your food if you are a diabetic."[76]

The number of steps in the grievance procedure and the staff involved at each step will vary from organization to organization, but most grievance procedures have between three and five steps. The purpose of a multistep grievance procedure is to allow higher level managers and union representatives to look at the issue from different perspectives and to assess the consequences of pursing the matter further. This approach increases the chance that the dispute gets resolved without going to arbitration

Although an employee may prefer to bring his or her case to court rather than arbitration, this may not be permissible. For instance, former Canadian Football League receiver Arland Bruce's lawsuit against the CFL and former league commissioner Mark Cohon will not be going

FIGURE 13-12

Typical Steps in a Union–Management Grievance Procedure

- *Preliminary discussion.* The aggrieved employee discusses the complaint with the immediate supervisor with or without a union representative. At this stage, or at any other step in the process, management may resolve the grievance to the satisfaction of the union, or the union may decide to drop the grievance. Otherwise, the grievance proceeds to the next step in the process.
- *Step 1.* The complaint is put in writing and formally presented by the shop steward to the first-level supervisor. Normally, the supervisor must respond in writing within a contractually specified time period, usually two to five days.
- *Step 2.* The chief steward takes the complaint to the department superintendent. A written response is required, usually within a week.
- *Step 3.* The complaint is submitted to the plant manager/chief administrative officer by the union plant or grievance committee. Again, a written response is typically required.
- *Step 4.* If Step 3 does not solve the dispute, arrangements are made for an arbitrator or an arbitration board to settle the matter.

to court. Bruce was alleging in his lawsuit that he had sustained permanent and disabling head trauma while playing football and has post-concussive symptoms, including depression and paranoia. The Supreme Court of Canada refused to hear Bruce's appeal, following its earlier decision that unionized employees must use labour arbitration for disputes arising from their collective agreements.[77]

Handling Grievances

Once a grievance has been filed, management should seek to resolve it fairly and quickly. Failure to do so can be seen as a disregard for employee needs and is not conducive to building and maintaining effective labour relations. However, in resolving grievances, management should consider several issues. Most important, grievances should be settled on their merits. Complaints need to be carefully investigated and decided on the facts. Second, the cause of each grievance should be recorded. A large number of grievances coming from one or two departments may indicate poor supervision or a lack of understanding of the contract. Third, the final solution to the grievance needs to be explained to those affected:

Shahab Makholi, an immigrant from Iran, was hired as a welder by a Mississauga company that manufactures fire doors. Makholi injured his hand at work and had to have a splint put on it. He continued working and was ultimately assigned alternate duties. Eventually, his lead hand assigned Makholi to do work that he couldn't perform and he went to the production manager's office to complain. After some discussion, the employer concluded that Makholi wanted to be laid off and documentation was prepared. Makholi was dismissed, which he ultimately grieved. The arbitrator, in reinstating Makholi, noted that Makholi could not read or write English, the company did not make a substantial effort to explain the importance of the dismissal

documentation, no union representative was present at the termination meeting although the agreement required that the union be notified of any layoffs, and Makholi was instructed not to tell the union what had happened.[78]

Arbitration

All jurisdictions require that collective agreements include a provision for final settlement by **arbitration**, without stoppage of work, of all differences concerning the interpretation or administration of a contract. This means that as long as a collective agreement is in force, any strike or lockout is illegal. An arbitrator may be selected from a list provided by the appropriate ministry of labour, or the parties may agree to the selection of an arbitrator. The arbitrator's decision is final and cannot be changed or revised, except in rare instances (such as corruption, fraud, or a breach of natural justice).[79] There is growing concern that the arbitration process is becoming too costly, too slow (some cases take two years or more to be resolved), and too legalistic.[80]

arbitration The settling of a dispute between labour and management by a third party.

Arbitration holds two potential problems for labour relations practitioners: costs and unacceptable solutions. An arbitration case can cost both the union and employer several thousand dollars. There are also time commitment costs in terms of preparing for arbitration, attending the actual hearings, and following up on the case. From the perspective of management, a potential problem occurs when an arbitrator renders a decision that is against management's best interests. Since the ruling is binding, it may drastically alter management's rights and set a precedent for future cases. For example, if an arbitrator accepts the union's argument of extenuating circumstances in a disciplinary case, those extenuating circumstances may be cited in future cases. Consider the following case and decide if the employee should be terminated:

> Mark Davis was a Toronto Transit Commission fare collector who had been employed for 25 years. After gesturing at a customer with his middle finger, Davis was suspended for two days and required to take sensitivity training on dealing with difficult customers, workplace violence, and professional conduct. One day after completing the training, Davis commented to a co-worker, "If anything ever happened, like losing my job, I'd have no problem coming in and shooting them. I'd die for that cause." Davis indicated that he would only shoot managers (three of whom he named). The co-worker subsequently told her shop steward and a manager about the comments and Davis was terminated from employment. Although Davis stated that he was only joking and had no animosity for anyone, an arbitrator upheld the dismissal.[81]

This decision shows that once an employer goes to arbitration, the decision is turned over to a third party. In dismissal cases, the union will typically argue that discharge is an inappropriate penalty and the possibility exists that an arbitrator may agree with the union position. Consequently, it is important that an employee grievance is treated seriously by management representatives and that the organization attempts to resolve grievances with the union in a fair and timely manner. However, there may be some instances where arbitration is unavoidable.

Contract Provisions

Every collective agreement contains specific terms and provisions. A number of the most common ones are listed in Figure 13-13. These clauses are important because they define the rights and obligations of the employer and the union. For instance, union security is a very important issue from the union's perspective. In addition, some of the most frequent disputes concern seniority and discipline.

FIGURE 13-13

Common Provisions in Union–Management Agreements

- *Union recognition.* Normally near the beginning of a contract, this clause states management's acceptance of the union as the sole representative of designated employees.

- *Union security.* To ensure that the union maintains members as new employees are hired and present employees quit, a union security clause is commonly demanded by the union. Union security provisions are discussed later in the chapter.

- *Wage rates.* The amount of wages to be paid to workers (or classes of workers) is specified in the wage clause.

- *Cost of living.* Unions may negotiate automatic wage increases for workers when price levels go up. For example, one approach is for wages to go up in response to an increase in the consumer price index above some specified amount.

- *Insurance benefits.* This section specifies which insurance benefits the employer provides and how much the employer contributes toward these benefits. Frequently included benefits are life and supplemental hospitalization insurance and dental plans.

- *Pension benefits.* The amount of retirement income, years of service required, penalties for early retirement, employer and employee contributions, and vesting provisions are described in this section if a pension plan exists.

- *Income maintenance.* To provide workers with economic security, some contracts give guarantees of minimum income or minimum work. Other income maintenance provisions include severance pay and supplements to employment insurance.

- *Time-off benefits.* Vacations, holidays, rest breaks, washup periods, and leave-of-absence provisions typically are specified in this clause.

- *Seniority clause.* Unions seek contract terms that require human resource decisions to be made on the basis of seniority. Often, senior workers are given preferential treatment in job assignments, promotions, layoffs, vacation scheduling, overtime, and shift preferences.

- *Management rights.* Management must retain certain rights to do an effective job. These may include the ability to require overtime work, decide on promotions, design jobs, and select employees. This clause reserves to management the right to make decisions that management thinks are necessary for the organization's success.

- *Discipline.* Prohibited employee actions, penalties, and disciplinary procedures are either stated in the contract or included in the agreement by reference to those documents that contain the information.

- *Dispute resolution.* Disagreements between the union and management are resolved through procedures specified in the contract.

- *Duration of agreement.* Union and management agree on a time period during which the collective agreement is in force.

Union Security

Can an employee be required to join a union as a condition of employment? An employer and union can negotiate clauses dealing with union security and, in some jurisdictions, compulsory dues checkoff is required.

The highest form of union security is the *closed shop* (found in about 8 percent of agreements), which requires that an employee be a union member prior to obtaining employment and pay dues to the union. The closed shop, which is frequently operated through a hiring hall, is common in construction and longshore industries.

Under a **union shop** security arrangement, the employer is free to hire an individual, but, as a condition of employment, the new hire must join the union within a specified period of time after being hired and must pay union dues. If the individual refuses to join the union, the employer is required to terminate the worker's employment. About 40 percent of agreements have a union shop provision.[82]

> **union shop** A union security provision in which employers may hire anyone they want, but all new employees must join the union within a specified period and pay dues.

The *Rand Formula* requires an employer to deduct union dues at source from the wages of an employee and remit the funds to the union. However, the employee is not required to join the union. In some jurisdictions, dues checkoff clauses must be negotiated; in other jurisdictions, compulsory dues checkoff is enshrined in law.

While the amount of dues varies, it is typically in the range of about 1 to 1.5 percent of an employee's earnings. Most workers covered by a collective agreement are subject to a dues checkoff requirement.[83] Some jurisdictions allow workers who object to joining a union on the basis of religious grounds to pay the equivalent amount to a registered charity.

In an *open shop,* an individual does not have to join the union and is not required to pay dues.

Seniority

Unions typically prefer to have employee-related decisions determined by the length of the worker's employment, called **seniority**. Seniority assures that promotions, overtime, layoffs, and other employee concerns are handled without favouritism. As well, the influence of seniority is not restricted to the union environment; several nonunion organizations also place considerable weight on seniority in making human resource decisions.

> **seniority** Length of the worker's employment, which may be used for determining order of promotion, layoffs, vacation, etc.

Seniority is often very important in deciding layoff rights. For example, when a company plans a layoff, the most recently hired workers are typically the first to go.

The remaining employees probably receive higher wages if there is a premium for service with the organization. Thus, the higher paid employees are retained, even though the layoff may have been implemented as a cost-reduction measure. Moreover, layoffs may undermine a company's employment equity plan, since employees hired through the employment equity program may have low seniority.

Discipline

Unions often challenge the discipline of a union member. Due to the difficulty of trying to list employee behaviours that may warrant discipline, many collective agreements provide the employer with the right to discipline or discharge if "just cause" exists. In any disciplinary action, management must abide by the terms of the collective agreement. Arbitration cases are frequently lost because management failed to establish grounds for disciplinary action, neglected to document past disciplinary procedures, and failed to adhere to the provisions of the collective agreement.

In deciding discipline and discharge cases, the starting point is the collective agreement. However, many collective agreements have a provision indicating that the employer must have "just cause" to discipline or discharge an employee. In determining just cause, a number of factors may be important:

- Nature and seriousness of the offence
- Due process and procedure
- Past record of the grievor
- Seniority and age of the grievor
- Knowledge of rules
- Previous warnings from management
- Lax enforcement/condonation by management in the past
- Unequal treatment of employees
- Provocation by management
- Isolated incident
- Sincere apology/remorse on the part of the grievor[84]

Although an employer may believe that clear grounds for discipline or dismissal exist, arbitrators consider a number of issues in making their decisions:

A Beer Store employee in Ontario took a Toronto Maple Leafs shirt from a case of beer being returned by a customer. Cases of beer containing Maple Leafs shirts were part of a special promotion, and the employee's daughter was a big Leafs fan. The employee put the shirt in his coat pocket (with part of it hanging out) and went to serve a customer. The employer terminated the employee as part of its zero-tolerance theft policy while the employee argued that he had intended to ask his supervisor whether he could keep the shirt. An arbitrator ruled that the employee, who had 23 years of service with the employer, had not intended to steal the shirt and replaced the termination with a three-day suspension.[85]

Past Practice

The actions of managers and union officials sometimes change the meaning of the agreement. A **precedent** is a new standard that arises from the past practices of either

> **precedent** A new standard that arises from the past practices of either the company or the union.

party. Once a precedent results from unequal enforcement of disciplinary rules, the new standard may affect similar cases in the future.

The fear of past practices usually causes two changes in human resource policies and procedures. First, employee-related decisions are often centralized in the human resource department. Supervisors are stripped of their authority to make decisions on layoffs, discipline, and other employee matters. Instead, supervisors are required to make recommendations to the human resource department to ensure uniformity and consistency of application and to prevent precedents.

The second change is to increase the training of supervisors in the administration of the contract. Training is needed to ensure that supervisors administer the collective agreement in a consistent manner. For example, if each supervisor applies a different standard to tardiness, some employees may be disciplined while others with more lenient supervisors may not receive any penalty. In time, the union might argue that unequal treatment makes it unfair to discipline those who are late. Through centralization and training, human resource departments create a more uniform enforcement of the contract.

Public Sector Bargaining

When Parliament passed the **Public Service Staff Relations Act (PSSRA)** in 1967, it essentially gave federal civil servants bargaining rights similar to those granted workers in the private sector—usually the right to bargain for wages,

> **Public Service Staff Relations Act (PSSRA)** Provides federal public servants with the right to unionize and either opt for compulsory arbitration or strike if a deadlock in bargaining occurs.

hours, and certain working conditions. More important, it also gave them the right to strike. This is in contrast to civil servants in the United States, who since 1962 have had the right to bargain collectively but not to withhold their services. Under the PSSRA, the methods of conflict resolution

are different from those in the private sector. Before a bargaining agent can give notice that it wishes to bargain, a decision must be made as to whether a conciliation-strike procedure or a binding-arbitration procedure will be used should a deadlock occur. The union has the right to choose different procedures for each subsequent collective agreement. If the strike route has been chosen, conciliation procedures must be followed before a strike can begin.

Another difference from the private sector is that the law allows the employer to designate certain employees as performing essential services, thus divesting them of the right to strike. The union, however, may challenge the list of "designated employees," in which case the Public Service Staff Relations Board makes the final decision.

A comparison of the federal and provincial legislation for government employees reveals little uniformity across Canada. While municipal government employees generally fall under the same legislation as private sector workers, the legislation applicable to provincial civil servants varies markedly. For instance, Saskatchewan government employees come under the same legislation as private sector employees; in some provinces there is specific legislation applicable only to provincial government employees; and in other jurisdictions, there may be two or more statutes applicable to government employees. In addition, some provinces markedly restrict or prohibit strikes by public sector workers.[86]

Public sector labour disputes can present major challenges:

On October 16, 2017, about 12,000 college teachers represented by the Ontario Public Service Employees Union went on strike, affecting around 500,000 college students. The major issues concerned the ratio between full and contract employees, job security, academic freedom, and compensation. The strike ultimately came to an end when the Ontario Liberal government passed back-to-work legislation on November 19 and an arbitrator set a new four-year contract one month later. However, the union initiated a court charter challenge in early 2018, alleging that the back-to-work legislation violated workers' rights.

Even though students and faculty are back to class, repercussions from the dispute are still being felt. A condensed schedule meant cutting and skimming over course material. Some faculty lost external research funding, stress and anxiety increased, and students missed employment opportunities. For example, one student had secured full-time employment with the federal government upon her anticipated graduation in December, but one of her courses was delayed by the strike and, consequently, her employment contract was changed to temporary status.[87]

LO7 Human Resource Practices in the Union Environment

A study by the Industrial Relations Centre at Queen's University provides insights on the labour relations profession in Canada. Among the major findings are the following:

- The four activities that labour relations professionals are most involved in are conflict resolution management, coaching with regard to labour relations best practices, administration of the collective agreement, and grievance settlement.

- From a knowledge perspective, the most important areas are understanding the union–management perspective, conflict resolution, labour statutes, and negotiation.

- In terms of skills required to perform day-to-day work, the top four skills include communication, active listening, relationship building, and collective agreement interpretation.

- When considering the labour relations profession, 59 percent are optimistic about the future of the profession, 15 percent are pessimistic, and 26 percent are unsure.

- The top three perceived opportunities for the profession are talent management, union–management collaboration and partnership, and strategic labour relations.[88]

While there is a significant and growing body of information about human resource management from the perspective of the employer, less attention has been paid to examining which human resource management practices are found within unionized workgroups.

A key issue for human resource management practitioners involves obtaining union involvement in managing change. Bob White, former president of the Canadian Labour Congress, had this to say about unions and change:

"For workers, change will be judged to be positive if higher productivity is shared in the form of better wages and benefits; if change results in more rather than less security of employment; if change gives workers access to new skills and opportunities; and if change improves the overall quality of working life in terms of the ability of workers to make a productive contribution."[89]

A survey of Canadian union officials examined a number of human resource issues in the unionized environment. Concerning human resource management policies, union officials were asked to indicate whether a number of specific HRM programs or practices applied to bargaining-unit

employees. As revealed in Figure 13-14, more than 95 percent of units had a policy addressing sexual harassment, 86 percent had an orientation program for new hires, 86 percent had an employee assistance plan (EAP), and 66 percent had some type of formal performance appraisal system. About 51 percent of respondents reported that the employer shared business information with union members.

Union officials were also asked to indicate whether bargaining-unit employees were involved in a number of specific team-based and incentive programs (Figure 13-14). As the figure reveals, 28 percent of the union locals reported having work teams, 22 percent had quality circles, and 40 percent had problem-solving groups. Unions have generally stayed away from contingency compensation plans such as profit sharing, productivity sharing, and employee stock ownership plans; overall, less than 20 percent of respondents reported having such plans.

Implications of Union Avoidance Approaches

In nonunion facilities, an implicit objective of many employers is to remain nonunion. Employers frequently adopt either a *union suppression* or a *union substitution* approach in order to avoid unionization. The union suppression approach involves fighting union representation. An employer may try to intimidate workers, threaten to close or move the plant or facility, or discriminate against union supporters.

An employer in the food services industry heard that four of the workers were discussing unionization as a means of improving wages and working conditions. Senior management learned about the issue and decided to terminate six employees—the four union activists and two other employees who were considered poor performers. The termination notices were issued under the guise of incompetent work performance.

The union substitution approach examines what unions bring to the employment relationship and then tries to introduce such features into the nonunion workplace. This approach requires that human resource specialists do the following:

- Design jobs that are personally satisfying to workers.
- Develop plans that maximize individual opportunities while minimizing the possibility of layoffs.
- Select workers who are well qualified.
- Establish fair, meaningful, and objective standards of individual performance.
- Train workers and managers to enable them to achieve expected levels of performance.

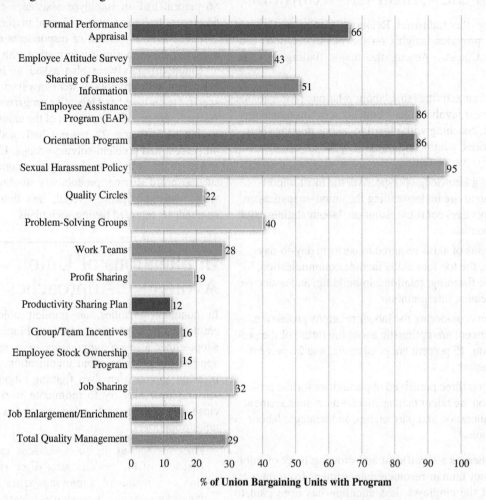

FIGURE 13-14

HRM Practices/Programs among Canadian Unions

SOURCE: Terry H. Wagar (2009), *Human Resource Management and Workplace Safety: A Study of Canadian Union Officials,* unpublished report, Saint Mary's University.

- Evaluate and reward behaviour on the basis of actual performance.
- Provide employees with a "voice" in the workplace.
- Implement a compensation plan in which wages/salary and benefits parallel those available in the union sector.

The union substitution approach is advocated by many HR practitioners, consultants, and labour lawyers. Employer lawyer Jamie Knight has this to say:

"Nonunion companies that want to remain non-union should steal some of their best features from their competitors' collective agreements. Often a collective agreement will contain provisions that do not contradict an efficient and effective operation.

Employers should have a nonunion dispute resolution process. Dealing with complaints is the biggest challenge in a nonunion workplace."[90]

On the other hand, Canadian labour relations legislation requires that workers need to take the initiative in establishing collective bargaining relationships, knowing that many employers are opposed to unions. Consequently, the beginning of the new union–management relationship is already characterized by conflict and adversarialism.[91] Roy Adams, professor emeritus of industrial relations at McMaster University, argues that the practice of union avoidance sabotages the right to bargain collectively and contravenes the International Labour Organization's Declaration of Fundamental Principles and Rights at Work, which includes the effective recognition of the right to bargain collectively. In North America, this right is generally not available until workers go through an arduous certification procedure, which results in an adversarial relationship.[92]

LO8 Managing in a Union Environment

When unions are present, the human resource function is changed. In many organizations, the human resource department is expanded by the addition of specialists in labour relations, who deal with such critical areas as negotiations and contract administration, while human resource professionals attend to their more traditional roles. Although some organizations establish separate industrial relations departments to deal with labour relations issues, industrial relations is often considered a subset of human resource management.

Unionization may be associated with greater centralization of employee record-keeping and discipline to ensure uniformity of application. This change can mean that line managers lose some of their authority to the human resource department. They may also find their jobs more difficult because of the new rules imposed by the contract—while management has the right to act, the union may have the right, under the contract, to react to management's actions.

Line managers may become dissatisfied because their authority diminishes while their responsibility increases. These added responsibilities are likely to result from requests of human resource professionals, who may need to monitor the work environment more closely and need more information from the line managers. For example, the line manager may have to compile new reports on such issues as absenteeism, lateness, productivity, and employee grievances. (A growing number of organizations are using computer technology to collect such information.) Such demands on supervisors may create friction between line managers and human resource staff members.

The presence of a union means that management has less freedom to make unilateral changes. No longer can an employer simply decide which changes to implement. Instead, collective agreement provisions and labour laws must also be considered.

Labour–Management Cooperation

Some unions and employers are moving toward greater co-operation, and there is increasing acceptance that labour and management must work together if they are to survive and prosper in the highly competitive global economy.[93]

Some employers and unions are using or considering "evidence-based labour relations." According to Cooper, Jackson, and Irish, "Both unions and employers are expressing an interest in partnering on initiatives to tackle challenges related to health and safety, precarious work, and marginalized groups." The parties also may be interested in grievance metrics, such as grievances as a percentage of unionized headcount, arbitrated grievances as a percentage of grievances open, and percentage of grievances closed. A 2015 Conference Board Report revealed that both employers and unions viewed arbitration as a "cumbersome, unpredictable process."[94]

There is growing evidence that organizational performance is enhanced when labour and management co-operate. For example, research using data from both employers and unions indicated that a more positive labour climate was associated with perceptions of higher productivity, enhanced product or service quality, and greater customer or client satisfaction.[95] However, co-operation is a very challenging process:

A recent survey of the City of Edmonton's communication branch revealed low morale and allegations of workplace harassment, disrespect, and bullying. The City's engagement survey showed that only 27 percent of respondents reported having "trust and confidence in my branch's leadership team's ability to achieve the city's goals" while just 30 percent indicated that "the City inspires me to do my best work." One employee stated that she would be criticized at large meetings, get yelled at, and have people go behind her back to her supervisor. Another finally quit after seeing man after man get promoted and stated, "It was awful. My mental health deteriorated over the years I was there." The branch is now under new leadership that is committed to improving the work environment.[96]

Obstacles to Cooperation

Industrial relations specialists often seek union co-operation to improve the organization's effectiveness. However, co-operation may not be politically attractive to union leaders, who see little gain in co-operating with management. In fact, if leaders do co-operate, they may be accused by workers of forgetting the union's interests. These accusations can mean defeat by political opponents within the union. Thus, co-operation may not be in the union leader's best interests.

In addition to political obstacles, union leaders may mistrust management. For example, bitter remarks during an organizing drive or arbitration case may convince union officials that human resource specialists are anti-union. Within this climate, co-operative gestures are often seen as tricks or gimmicks aimed at hurting the union. If co-operative proposals threaten the members or leaders, mistrust increases and co-operation usually fails.

While employers often have good reasons for seeking more cooperation with their unionized workforce, a

---

FIGURE 13-15

Methods of Building Labour–Management Cooperation

Managers and human resource specialists can build cooperation between the employer and the union through the following:

- *Prior consultation* with union leaders to defuse problems before they become formal grievances
- *Sincere concern* for employee problems and welfare even when management is not obligated to do so by the collective agreement
- *Training programs* that objectively communicate the intent of union and management bargainers and reduce biases and misunderstandings
- *Joint study committees* that allow management and union officials to find solutions to common problems
- *Third parties* who can provide guidance and programs that bring union leaders and managers closer together to pursue common objectives

---

number of co-operative programs have the underlying goal of increasing managerial domination in the workplace. As well, some employers use cooperation to "stress the system" by reducing employees or resources, giving workers more tasks, or speeding up the assembly line; such practices may dramatically increase the stress level of workers and dehumanize the workplace.[97]

Building Labour–Management Cooperation

An employer and union interested in greater labour–management co-operation have several options to consider. Some of the most common co-operative efforts are summarized in Figure 13-15. One of the most basic actions is prior consultation with the union. While not every management decision must be approved by the union, actions that affect unionized employees may result in grievance filing unless explained in advance to the union.

A growing number of unionized organizations are among the "Best Workplaces in Canada" winners. Some observers believe that cooperation between unions and employers is key as the parties move away from the "us-versus-them" mentality. For example, at Toronto East General Hospital, employees and union stewards are involved in all joint committees with managers, including the staff satisfaction committee. General Mills believes that all employees need to have a sense of ownership of the company's success. The company shares minutes from weekly executive team meetings with all employees and encourages employee input into decisions.[98]

Human resource specialists can also build cooperation through a sincere concern for employees. This concern may be shown through the prompt settlement of grievances. As well, employers can establish programs (such as employee assistance programs and job counselling) that assist employees who are experiencing personal difficulties.

Training programs are another way to build cooperation. After a new contract is signed, the human resource department often trains only managers. The union does the same for its leaders. The result is that both sides continue their biases and misunderstandings. If human resource management sponsors training for both the union and management, a common understanding of the contract is more likely to be brought about. The training can be as simple as taking turns paraphrasing the contract, or outside neutral parties can be hired to do the training. Either way, supervisors and union officials end the training with a common understanding of the contract and a new basis for co-operation.

When a complex problem confronts the union and employer, *joint study committees* are sometimes formed. For example, one organization recently set up a joint committee with its union to establish a policy on sexual harassment. Other employers use joint study committees to address such issues as workplace rules, quality of work life, technological change, budget reduction strategies, and safety. However, union participation and support is absolutely essential:

At Toronto Hydro, the company implemented a recognition program in which employees who demonstrated certain behaviours that reduced costs, improved productivity, or surpassed performance standards would receive a nonmonetary reward of up to $300. The union strongly opposed the program on the grounds that it pitted workers against each other and violated the union's right to be the exclusive bargaining agent for the employees, refused management's offer to develop the program, and filed a grievance. The arbitrator found in favour of the union. HR consultant Eric Cousineau commented, "What Toronto Hydro should have done right from the start is to do it with the union, not to the union."[99]

A final method of building cooperation is through the use of third parties, such as consultants or government agencies, who may act as change agents or catalysts to cooperation. For example, in Nova Scotia, the provincial government has established and delivers a variety of joint union–management programs (including grievance mediation, joint supervisor–steward training, and labour–management committees) with the goal of increasing cooperation in the workplace.

There is no single best approach to building cooperation. Since each relationship is unique, the methods used will depend upon the situation. Improving union management relations is an important function that can be addressed by human resource professionals in unionized organizations.

SUMMARY

The labour–management framework consists of unions, government, and management. Although each union is unique, unions share the common objectives of protecting and improving their members' wages, hours, and working conditions. To further these objectives, the union movement has created local, national, and international structures, plus federations at the provincial and federal levels.

In Canada, the federal government has jurisdiction in labour relations matters over Crown corporations, airlines, most railways, communication companies, and federal government agencies—or approximately 10 percent of the labour force. All other organizations fall under the jurisdiction of the provinces, which have enacted separate but similar legislation.

Unionization often occurs when workers perceive the need for a union as a response to unsatisfactory treatment by management. During the organizing process, management's response is limited by laws and employee reactions. The employer's primary defence is sound policies implemented by competent supervisors before unionization begins.

If workers form a union, federal or provincial law requires management and the union to bargain in good faith. The success of the employer at the bargaining table is affected by its actions before negotiations begin. Negotiations with the union usually result in a "collective agreement" that must be approved by union members and top management. Once negotiated, the collective agreement is administered by the union and management.

In administering the agreement, human resource specialists face several challenges. For example, contract clauses place limits on management, day-to-day administration of the contract can lead to precedents, and limitations often result from the resolution of disputes through the grievance procedure or arbitration.

Although unions may represent the employees, management remains ultimately responsible for organizational performance and effectively utilizing the human resources. Through prior consultation, sincere concern for employees, training programs, joint study committees, or third parties, human resource specialists can lay the foundations of a co-operative union–management relationship.

TERMS FOR REVIEW

arbitration 413
authorization cards 405
business unionism 396
Canadian Labour Congress (CLC) 397
collective agreement 393
conciliation 412
craft union 397
grievance procedure 412
industrial union 397
labour relations boards (LRBs) 404

local unions 396
management rights 410
mediation 412
precedent 416
Public Service Staff Relations Act (PSSRA) 416
seniority 415
social (or reform) unionism 396
unfair labour practices 408
union 392
union shop 415

SELF-ASSESSMENT EXERCISE

What Are Your Views toward Unions?

The following self-test gives you a quick assessment of your attitudes toward unions. Read each statement and give it a score from 1 to 5 (with 1 indicating that you strongly disagree with the statement and 5 indicating that you strongly agree with the statement).

1. Unions give members their money's worth.   _____

2. Unions improve job security for their members.   _____

3. Unions protect workers against unfair actions by the employer.   _____

4. Unions represent the wishes of their members.   _____

5. Unions are a positive force in our society.   _____

6. Unions are still needed today.   _____

7. Unions need more power.   _____

8. Laws should be changed to make it easier to get a union at the workplace.   _____

9. I would prefer to work in a unionized job.   _____

10. If a union was organizing my workplace, I would vote for the union.   _____

SCORE

Add up your score for each of the statements. A higher score is associated with a more positive view of unions.

REVIEW AND DISCUSSION QUESTIONS

1. In your own words, summarize the primary objectives of unions.

2. What distinguishes craft and industrial unions from each other?

3. What roles do labour relations boards serve in labour–management relations?

4. In preparing to negotiate an agreement with a union, what types of information would you gather before arriving at the bargaining table?

5. If you were asked to explain why various types of people are on the employer's bargaining team, what reasons would you give for (a) the company lawyer, (b) the director of industrial relations, (c) a wage and salary specialist, (d) a benefit specialist, and (e) the assistant plant manager?

6. Since grievance procedures are found in most contracts, both managers and unions must want them. Explain why both managers and unions want grievance procedures.

CRITICAL THINKING QUESTIONS

1. "Unions do not happen, they are caused by management." Do you agree or disagree with this statement? Why?

2. If you had to advise the manager of a small chain of bakeries how to prepare for a possible strike, what would you suggest?

3. Suppose an employee in your department is an active member of the union, but is performing improperly. After several sessions with the employee, performance is still unacceptable. What type of support would you want to gather before you terminated that employee? What legal complications might result from your action?

4. If you worked in the human resource department of a small company that is suddenly unionized, what changes would you expect to occur in the human resource department?

5. What role do you think federal and provincial governments will play in future labour–management relations? What actions can unions and management take to reduce the probability of future government involvement?

6. Obtain a copy of two different collective agreements. Compare and contrast the contract items and the grievance procedure.

ETHICS QUESTION

You are a community college instructor and have completed one full year of teaching. All college instructors are unionized and represented by the College Teachers Union (CTU). It is now early November of your second year at the college and the previous collective agreement expired on September 1. Bargaining between the parties has not been going well and the employer and union are far apart on two issues: academic freedom and the hiring of full-time instructors. More than 60 percent of the instructors are part-time, and the union believes that those part-time instructors should be hired into any new full-time positions (based on seniority and experience) unless they do not meet the basic qualifications for the position. The employer is arguing that it wants to keep the current practice of conducting an outside search for any full-time position because it wants to be able to hire the best candidate (who may or may not be currently working for the college).

Negotiations have reached an impasse, the parties have completed conciliation, and the union has called for a strike in 48 hours. You are mixed on whether to cross the picket line or not. On one hand, you know that 84 percent of instructors voted for strike action, you have some appreciation for the issues under dispute, and you have heard that unions do not take kindly to members who cross the picket line. On the other hand, the issues are not overly important to you personally. There is a strong feeling that the academic issue can be resolved without too much difficulty, and the issue relating to the hiring of part-time instructors doesn't affect you directly as you are a full-time instructor. In addition, you feel a loyalty to your students, and, with a student loan of $22,000, you don't want to be off work for any length of time.

Are you going to support the union or cross the picket line? Be sure to address any ethical issues involved in your decision.

RESEARCH EXERCISE

1. Visit the website of the International Labour Organization (https://www.ilo.org/global/lang--en/index.htm). What are the major objectives of the ILO? What are some of the major issues affecting workers around the world?

2. Go to the website for the Canadian Labour Congress (http://canadianlabour.ca/). Also visit the website for a provincial federation of labour (for instance, the Nova Scotia Federation of Labour: http://nslabour .ca/). Compare and contrast the functions of the two federations. What similarities and differences exist? What assistance do the federations provide to organized labour?

INCIDENT 13-1

My Work Was Done!

Francis Foster is a 42-year-old unionized employee at a sports and recreation facility operated by the municipality. Foster has been with the municipality for 14 years, and his work performance has been "acceptable." Foster's main responsibilities include operating the Zamboni at the arena, keeping the arena clean, maintaining the fields at the baseball and soccer fields, and helping customers who have rented the facilities.

Depending on operational and scheduling requirements, Foster may work a day or night shift. Some evenings, the arena or sports fields may not be fully booked, or bad weather may mean that the sports fields are not available for customers. Ten months ago, a new supervisor was appointed; in four meetings with employees and in monthly emails, she made it clear that employees were not allowed to leave work early even if the arena or sports fields was not booked or in use. Four months after this meeting, a customer who had booked the arena from 10:00 to 11:00 p.m. showed up with his team at about 9:20 p.m. and found the arena doors locked. Calls to the arena number went unanswered. Foster was on duty that evening but said that the booking had slipped his mind, he was away from the arena doing other maintenance work, and had forgotten to bring his cell phone with him that day. After conducting an investigation and discussing the grievance with the union, the employer and union agreed that Foster receive a three-day suspension.

After a few complaints in recent months (e.g., occasionally, the ice at the rink was not flooded before a rental; one customer had difficulty finding Foster when there

was an issue with the booking), the municipality decided to secretly monitor Foster's behaviour over a 10-day period. During the 10 days, Foster was found to have taken extended breaks (ranging from 7 to 34 minutes) on seven occasions and to have left early on six of the ten shifts (6, 34, 48, 11, 23, and 54 minutes early, respectively). After being presented with the evidence, Foster insisted that there must be mistakes with the data. Although he admitted leaving a bit early once in a while, he insisted that he never left when there was a booking. Foster also stated that his former supervisor had said it was fine to leave early if there were no bookings and all of the required maintenance work had been completed. After conducting an investigation and meeting with the parties, the municipality decided to terminate Foster. The union is grieving Foster's dismissal.

DISCUSSION QUESTIONS

1. Make arguments for the union and for the employer.
2. What penalty (if any) should Foster receive?

WE CONNECTIONS: UNION–MANAGEMENT FRAMEWORK

Shhh . . .

As she walked down the hallway, Charlotte noticed a number of people clustered around the desk of Scott Browski. From the way they were leaning in, it looked as though they were talking about something juicy. Although she had things to do, she pivoted to see what was going on. As the HR specialist, she was expected to stay tuned in to what people were talking about. Plus, it was 2:00 p.m., and she wouldn't mind a mini-break for a little chitchat. Maybe there was some good gossip going around. As she neared the group, someone looked up, noticed her coming, and gestured to the rest.

Immediately, the conversation stopped.

This was puzzling to Charlotte. Usually, she was readily included in whatever conversation was underway. She said, "Hey. What's going on?"

Several people muttered, "Nothing." They quickly scattered, except for Scott, who smiled at her and said, "What's new with you, Charlotte? Staying out of trouble?"

She shrugged and replied, "Oh, you know. Same old. What's going on here? That was kind of weird just now. Why did everyone take off when I came along?"

Scott paused for a moment as he looked at her straight on, then he smiled again and said, "Just chatting about

things. Guess everyone wants to get back to work so they don't get in trouble."

Feeling exasperated, Charlotte said, "Oh, Scott. Get real. People won't get in trouble for chatting, and you know it."

He turned back to his laptop and opened a program, obviously about to begin working. Over his shoulder, he said, "I don't know if that's true, Charlotte. I've gotten in trouble for less than that."

Taking a breath, Charlotte refused to take the bait. She murmured a goodbye and began to walk toward her office. Scott had been written up a few times in the previous six months, and he complained about it to Charlotte every chance he got. She was tired of trying to convince him that he had been treated fairly.

Difficult Conversations

When Rebecca, the HR manager, had joined WEC, she had helped the company develop a performance management system to help deal with some of the poor performance that was happening. That had led to more difficult conversations with employees. Most employees saw that as a good thing, but Scott wasn't one of them. His old boss, Oliver Caine, had let him get away with murder. Fairly recently, he had been assigned to a new project manager, Travis

Dobson, and this boss didn't let much slide. Scott had been written up three times, but he still wasn't very keen on getting in line. He spent a lot of time venting to people about how unfairly he had been treated. Charlotte wasn't sure, but she had the impression that Scott's days at WEC were numbered.

Potential Union Drive

As she walked down the hallway toward her desk, Charlotte had a scary thought. The week before, she had noticed that someone had tacked a union flyer on the lunchroom bulletin board. She had quickly taken it down and had been relieved to see that it was generic. In other words, it had not been a flyer specifically targeting WEC employees. That would have been a clear sign that there was an active organizing drive. At the time, she had thought it was just a fluke. People were always putting random things on that bulletin board.

After seeing the secretiveness of the people who had been talking to Scott, she began to piece together a number of little things. She realized that there could be a union organizing drive going on. She wondered if Scott and his friends had connected with a union. It was unusual for white-collar workers to get unionized, but it did happen.

When she got back to her desk, she pulled Scott's personnel file. Her heart sank when she saw his past employment history. Right before WEC, he had worked at a heavily unionized firm. There was no doubt that WEC employees worked long, hard hours. Someone like Scott might not have too much trouble convincing people that a union was a good idea.

She got up to go find Rebecca. Maybe now was the time for Scott to go.

DISCUSSION QUESTIONS

1. What are the indicators that there may be a union organizing drive happening at WEC?

2. What would be the costs and benefits of unionization for WEC and their employees?

3. What should the HR team do if the company would prefer to remain union-free?

CASE STUDY

Traveller Inn Hotels

Labour Management Relations

Traveller Inn hotels are well recognized throughout Canada and offer rooms and suites that attract families and business travellers. Room rates are competitive with similar chains across the country. There are 392 unionized employees across the four Vancouver hotels, and they are represented by the Hotel Employees Union (HEU). The members of HEU generally work the front desk or are involved in maintenance, housekeeping, or food services at the hotels.

All four of the Traveller Inn hotels in the Vancouver area have been unionized for eight years. Contract negotiations between the two parties have been difficult, but five years ago, the employer reached a three-year agreement with the union (HEU). Two years ago, the Traveller Inn negotiation team and HEU signed another three-year contract—negotiations again were very challenging, but a conciliator was able to help the parties reach an agreement.

Ledonna Johnson, vice-president of human resources, has asked you to carefully review the situation at the Vancouver hotels and prepare a report. Some information relating to labour relations issues at the four Vancouver hotels is summarized in Table 1.

Since signing the new contract, employee grievances have increased by about 9 percent a year. The company is concerned about the amount of time being spent by company officials, union representatives, and employees in contract negotiations and administering the collective agreement.

According to one of the Vancouver hotel managers who participated in the latest round of bargaining, "During contract negotiations, we met with the union bargaining team on a weekly basis. Each meeting was a good six or seven hours, and it took us almost four months to ultimately hammer out a contract. Things were further complicated by spending four days in conciliation. Furthermore, we seem to be spending way too much time dealing with grievances. Our wages are competitive with similar hotels in the Vancouver area, but morale is low and turnover is clearly a problem at all four hotels."

A review of company records revealed the following grievance pattern, as shown in Table 1.

While some of the grievances involved more than one issue, most of them were single-issue matters. The breakdown of grievances based on the type of issue was also available, as shown in Table 2.

A survey of managers and employees at the four hotels was recently completed. All of the managers and 331 of the 392 unionized employees completed the survey. The survey was conducted by a Vancouver consultant with expertise in

TABLE 1

Grievance Pattern at Traveller Inn Hotels

Total grievances filed	502
Number of grievances settled at:	
Step 1—First-level supervisor stage	75
Step 2—Second-level supervisor stage	288
Step 3—Senior HR manager stage	129
Arbitration	10

TABLE 2

Grievance Issues at Traveller Inn Hotels

Types of Grievance Issues	
Lateness or absenteeism	194
Overtime allocation	98
Other discipline or discharge	36
Job scheduling	97
Job posting	35
Multiple-issue disputes	42

TABLE 3

Initial Results from the Labour–Management Survey

PART A		
Workplace Performance Measures	**Average Management Response**	**Average Union Response**
Workplace productivity	3.76	3.56
Service quality	3.88	3.43
Union member morale	3.66	2.33
Union member job satisfaction	3.71	2.28
Quality of union member/supervisor relations	4.01	2.95

Note: Each of these questions uses a 5-point scale (1 = Very low; 5 = Very high).

PART B		
Labour Climate Measures	**Average Management Response**	**Average Union Response**
Grievances are settled promptly	4.04	2.82
The working conditions are fair	4.28	3.18
The parties co-operate to solve problems	3.78	2.55
The parties share information	3.65	2.37
The relationship is adversarial	2.91	4.10

Note: Each of these questions uses a 5-point scale (1 = Very low; 5 = Very high).

labour relations and was supported by both the company and union (with the understanding that the completed survey forms would go directly to the consultant and that the survey results would be provided in summary form to both the company and union).

As Johnson noted, "We didn't think the union would co-operate, and we needed it on board in order to survey the unionized workers. I'm getting a sense that both management and the union are getting concerned about the impact of the negative labour relations climate on our ability to compete in a very competitive Vancouver market." Some of the initial findings from the survey are provided in Table 3.

Survey Comments

Survey participants were also permitted to make comments on the survey. A total of 104 union respondents made comments. Most of the comments concerned a few major issues (a few are presented below):

Workload: "It is crazy here at times. I work in food services and we are frequently understaffed when it is busy."

"The weekends are terrible, especially when we have sports teams in. The rooms take twice as long to clean, some of the rooms are disgusting, and people are always coming in late or calling in sick."

Scheduling and Supervision: "I'm generally OK with working overtime, but after being on the front desk from midnight to 8:00 a.m., I'm just too tired."

"I'm in housekeeping and when it is super busy, you can only do so many rooms. If I take too long, I hear about it from my supervisor. And if the rooms aren't cleaned properly, I hear about that, too. You can't have it both ways, especially when people don't show up or guests are late checking out of their rooms."

DISCUSSION QUESTIONS

1. Assume that you assigned to examine labour relations at the Travellers Inn. Review the material for Ledonna Johnson, and briefly summarize your major findings.

2. What specific recommendations would you give Ledonna? Are there any programs or initiatives that you would suggest?

References

CHAPTER 1

1. Leif Edvinsson, accessed September 22, 2018, from https://www.12manage.com/quotes_hr.html
2. Canadian Business, Canada's 15 top companies by market cap: Investor 500 2016, 2016, accessed September 18, 2018, from http://www.canadianbusiness.com/lists-and-rankings/best-stocks/2016-biggest-companies-by-market-cap/
3. How stuff works, downloaded September 18, 2018, from http://www.howstuffworks.com/innovation/inventions/top-5-nasa-inventions.htm#page=1
4. National Aeronautical and Space Administration, downloaded September 18, 2018, from http://mars.jpl.nasa.gov/mars2020/
5. Ulrich, D., Yonger, J., Brockbank, W., and Ulrich, M. (2012), HR talent and the new HR competencies, *Strategic Human Resource Review,* downloaded September 18, 2018, from http://www.researchgate.net/publication/235295245
6. Bloomberg BMA (2015), HR department benchmarks and analysis 2015–2016, ISBN 978-1-63359-087-8, accessed September 18, 2018, from https://www.bna.com/uploadedFiles/BNA_V2/HR/Products/Surveys_and_Reports/HR%20Department%20Benchmark%20and%20Analysis%202015-16_Executive%20Summary.pdf
7. Harder, J. (2015, March), Engage your long-time employees to improve performance, *Harvard Business Review,* accessed September 18, 2018, from https://hbr.org/2015/03/engage-your-long-time-employees-to-improve-performance
8. Ulrich, D., Yonger, J., Brockbank, W., and Ulrich, M. (2012), HR talent and the new HR competencies, *Strategic Human Resource Review,* doi:10.1108/14754391211234940, accessed January 6, 2018, from http://www.researchgate.net/publication/235295245
9. Daft, R. L. (1995), *Organizational theory and design,* St. Paul, West Publishing; Zheng, W., Yang, B., and McLean, G. N. (2010), Linking organizational culture, structure, strategy, and organizational effectiveness: Mediating role of knowledge management, *Journal of Business Research, 63*(7), 763–771.
10. Walmart (2014), *Annual Report,* accessed September 18, 2018, from http://cdn.corporate.walmart.com/66/e5/9f-f9a87445949173fde56316ac5f/2014-annual-report.pdf
11. Purpose and Values, Target, downloaded September 22, 2018, from https://corporate.target.com/about/purpose-values
12. Verma, S. (2012), The relentless pursuit of perfection: The Lexus brand strategy, *Business 2 Community,* accessed January 6, 2018, from https://www.business2community.com/branding/the-relentless-pursuit-of-perfection-the-lexus-brand-strategy-0307457
13. van der Hoop, J. (2016), *10 examples of innovative HR practices and policies that amplify success,* accessed September 18, 2018, from https://www.talentsorter.com/10-examples-innovative-hr-practices-policies/
14. SHRM (2016), *2016 human capital benchmarking report,* accessed September 18, 2018, from https://www.shrm.org/hr-today/trends-and-forecasting/research-and-surveys/Documents/2016-Human-Capital-Report.pdf
15. *State of the American workplace: Employee engagement insights for US business leaders* (2013), accessed September 18, 2018, from http://www.gallup.com/file/services/176708/State_of_the_American_Workplace
16. Brown, D. (2003, May 5), HR issues top of mind for execs worldwide: Study, *Canadian HR Reporter,* p. 1.
17. *State of the American workplace: Employee engagement insights for US business leaders* (2013), accessed September 18, 2018, from http://www.gallup.com/file/services/176708/State_of_the_American_Workplace_
18. Porter, M. E. (1980), *Competitive Strategy: Techniques for Analyzing Industries and Competition,* New York, p. 300; Porter, M. E. (2008), *Competitive Strategy: Techniques for Analyzing Industries and Competitors,* Simon and Schuster.
19. *Canada's best managed companies* (n.d.), accessed September 22, 2018, from https://www2.deloitte.com/ca/en/pages/canadas-best-managed-companies/topics/best-managed.html
20. Ministry of Finance, Government of Canada (2017), *Fall economic statement,* accessed September 22, 2018, from https://www.budget.gc.ca/fes-eea/2017/docs/statement-enonce/fes-eea-2017-eng.pdf
21. Conference Board of Canada (2017), *Canadian outlook executive summary: Autumn 2017,* Ottawa: The Conference Board of Canada.
22. Conference Board of Canada (2017), *Canadian outlook executive summary: Autumn 2017,* Ottawa: The Conference Board of Canada.
23. Conference Board of Canada (2017), *Canadian outlook long-term economic forecast: Mid-year update—2017,* Ottawa: The Conference Board of Canada.
24. The World Bank (2016), *Exports of goods and services (% of GDP) 2016,* accessed September 22, 2018, from https://data.worldbank.org/indicator/NE.EXP.GNFS.ZS
25. Schwab, K. (2017), World Economic Forum, *The global competitiveness report: 2017–2018.*
26. Immigration, Refugees and Citizenship Canada (2017), *2017 annual report to Parliament on immigration,* accessed September 22, 2018, from https://www.canada.ca/en/immigration-refugees-citizenship/corporate/publications-manuals/annual-report-parliament-immigration-2017.html
27. Gerszak, R. (2017), Canada aims for immigration boost to buttress economy as population ages, *Global and Mail,* accessed September 22, 2018, from https://www.theglobeandmail.com/news/politics/canada-to-admit-40000-more-immigrants-a-year-by-2020-under-liberals-new-three-year-plan/article36800775/
28. Lee, C. C., Strohl, K., Fortenberry, M., and Cho, C. Y. S. (2017), Impacts of human resources management innovations on productivity and effectiveness in a medium-size non-profit organization, *Global Journal of Management and Marketing, 1*(1), 51.
29. Schwab, K. (2017), World Economic Forum, *The global competitiveness report: 2017–2018.*
30. Conference Board of Canada (2015), *How Canada performs: Innovation,* accessed September 22, 2018, from http://www.conferenceboard.ca/hcp/provincial/innovation.aspx
31. Conference Board of Canada (2011), *How Canada performs: Patents,* accessed September 22, 2018, from http://www.conferenceboard.ca/hcp/provincial/innovation/patents.aspx
32. McCarty, D., and Jinks, B. (2012, January 19), Kodak files for bankruptcy as digital era spells end to film, Bloomberg.com, accessed September 22, 2018, from https://www.bloomberg.com/news/articles/2012-01-19/kodak-photography-pioneer-files-for-bankruptcy-protection-1-
33. Kupfer, M. (2016, December 21), CRTC declares broadband internet access a basic service, *CBC News,* accessed September 22, 2018, from

http://www.cbc.ca/news/politics/
crtc-internet-essential-service-1.3906664

34. Internet World Statistics (2017), Global competitiveness index, *World Economic Forum report 2016,* accessed September 22, 2018, from https://www.internetworldstats .com/list3.htm

35. Akkirman, A. D., and Harris, D. L. (2005), Organizational communication satisfaction in the virtual workplace, *Journal of Management Development, 24*(5), 397–409; Fuhr, J. P., and Pociask, S. (2011), Broadband and telecommuting: Helping the U.S. environment and the economy, *Low Carbon Economy, 2*(01), 41.

36. Stats Canada Census Profile, 2016 Census, accessed September 22, 2018, from http://www12.statcan.gc.ca/census-recensement/2016/dp-pd/prof/details/page .cfm?Lang=E&Geo1=PR&Code1=01&-Geo2=&Code2=&Data=-Count&SearchText=Canada&-SearchType=Begins&Search-PR=01&B1=All&TABID=1

37. Smart Commute, accessed September 22, 2018, from https://smartcommute.ca/ more-options/telus/

38. Gallant, M. (2015), Getting the most out of a remote workforce, *Canadian HR Reporter,* accessed September 22, 2018, from http://www.hrreporter.com/ article/25690-getting-the-most-out-of-a-remote-workforce/

39. Mota, D. (2015), Keeping data safe takes several solutions, accessed September 22, 2018, from http://insurancenewsnet.com/ oarticle/2015/03/02/keeping-data-safe-takes-several-solutions-a-602265.html# .VRX1bPnF-OM

40. Dobbs, R., Ramaswamy, S., Stephenson, E., and Viguerie, S. P. (2014), Management institution for the next 50 years, *McKinsey Quarterly,* accessed September 22, 2018, from http://www.mckinsey.com/insights/ strategy/management_intuition_for_the_ next_50_years?cid=other-eml-ttn-mip-mck-oth-1410

41. Bersin, J. (2013), Big data in human resources: A world of haves and have-nots, *Forbes,* accessed September 22, 2018, from http://www.forbes.com/sites/ joshbersin/2013/10/07/big-data-in-human-resources-a-world-of-haves-and-have-nots/

42. Bosco, F. A., Uggerslev, K. L., and Steel, P. (2017), metaBUS as a vehicle for facilitating meta-analysis. *Human Resource Management Review, 27,* 237–254, accessed September 22, 2018, from http:// dx.doi.org/10.1016/j.hrmr.2016.09.013; Baker, C. A., Bosco, F. A., Uggerslev, K. L., and Steel, P. (2016), metaBUS: An open search engine of I-O research findings, *The Industrial-Organizational Psychologist,* accessed September 22, 2018, from http://www.siop.org/tip/july16/ metabus.aspx; Bosco, F. A., Steel, P., Oswald, F. L., Uggerslev, K. L., and Field,

J. G. (2015), Cloud-based meta-analysis to bridge science and practice: Welcome to metaBUS, *Personnel Assessment Decisions, 1,* 3–17.

43. Hernandez, J. (2017, May 8), Forest sector losing jobs—but desperately needs more skilled workers, *CBC News,* accessed November 22, 2018, from https://www.cbc .ca/news/canada/british-columbia/forest-sector-losing-jobs-but-desperately-needs-more-skilled-workers-1.4103694.

44. Daniels, J. (2018). From strawberries to apples, a wave of agriculture robotics may ease the farm labor crunch, *CNBC,* accessed September 22, 2018, from https:// www.cnbc.com/2018/03/08/wave-of-agriculture-robotics-holds-potential-to-ease-farm-labor-crunch.html

45. Dobson, S. (2017), Job fair focuses on transgender community, *Canadian HR Reporter,* accessed September 22, 2018, from http://www.hrreporter.com/ recruitment-and-retention/35394-job-fair-focuses-on-transgender-community/

46. Adapted from Statistics Canada, Table 14-10-0018-01, accessed September 23, 2018, from https://www150.statcan.gc.ca/ t1/tbl1/en/tv.action?pid=1410001801

47. Ibid.

48. Government of Canada (2017), *Maximizing Canada's engagement in the global knowledge-based economy: 2017 and beyond,* accessed March 17, 2018, from http://www.horizons.gc.ca/en/content/ maximizing-canada%E2%80%99s-engagement-global-knowledge-based-economy-2017-and-beyond%C2%A0

49. Alberta Government (n.d.), *Alberta's Occupational Demand and Supply Outlook 2015–2025,* accessed September 23, 2018, from http://work.alberta.ca/documents/ occupational-demand-and-supply-out-look-2015-2025.pdf

50. World Bank (2012), *China 2030—Building a modern, harmonious, and creative high-income society,* Washington: The World Bank, accessed September 23, 2018, from http://www.worldbank.org/content/ dam/Worldbank/document/China-2030-complete.pdf

51. Morgan, J. (2016, June 7), Say goodbye to knowledge workers and welcome to learning workers, *Forbes,* accessed September 23, 2018, from https://www .forbes.com/sites/jacobmorgan/2016/06/07/ say-goodbye-to-knowledge-workers-and-welcome-to-learning-workers/ #1720dbf02f93

52. Connelly, C. Zweig, D., Webster, J., and Trougakos, J. P. (2012, January), Knowledge hiding in organizations, *Journal of Organizational Behavior, 33*(1), pp. 64–88.

53. Statistics Canada, "Education in Canada: Key results from the 2016 census." downloaded September 23, 2018, from https://

www150.statcan.gc.ca/n1/daily-quotidien/ 171129/dq171129a-eng.pdf

54. Human Resources Development Canada, *Quarterly Labour Market and Income Review,* Vol. 3, No. 1, Summer 2002, p. 13.

55. Canadian School Boards Association, "Pisa results: Canadian students score high in performance, Canadian education system scores high in equity," downloaded September 23, 2018, from http://cdnsba .org/all/education-in-canada/pisa-results-canadian-students-score-high-in-performance-canadian-education-system-scores-high-in-equity

56. Conference Board of Canada, Adults with inadequate literacy skills, accessed September 23, 2018, from http://www.con-ferenceboard.ca/hcp/provincial/education/ adlt-lowlit.aspx

57. Statistics Canada 2016 Census, accessed September 23, 2018, from http://www12 .statcan.gc.ca/census-recensement/2016/ dp-pd/prof/details/page.cfm?Lang=E&-Geo1=PR&Code1=01&Geo

58. Ibid.

59. Workplace Education–PEI, "Creating Partnerships with Business and Industry," Charlottetown: April 2000.

60. Corporate Council on Education, "Employability Skills Profile," a program of the National Business and Education Centre, Ottawa: The Conference Board of Canada, undated.

61. "Our Coming Old Age Crisis," *Maclean's,* January 17, 1983, p. 24.

62. Adapted from Statistics Canada, "Projected population, by projection scenario, age and sex, as of July 1" Table 17-10-0057-01, accessed September 23, 2018, from https://www150.statcan.gc.ca/t1/tbl1/en/ tv.action?pid=1710005701

63. Adapted from Statistics Canada, "Projected population, by projection scenario, age and sex, as of July 1," Table 17-10-0057-01, accessed September 23, 2018, from https://www150.statcan.gc.ca/t1/tbl1/en/ tv.action?pid=1710005701

64. Dobson, S. (2017). Older tech workers face ageism in hiring. *Canadian HR Reporter,* accessed September 23, 2018, from http:// www.hrreporter.com/recruitment-and-retention/34985-older-tech-workers-face-ageism-in-hiring/

65. Statistics Canada, "Retirement age by class of worker, annual," Table 14-10-0060-01, accessed September 23, 2018, from https://www150.statcan.gc.ca/t1/tbl1/en/ tv.action?pid=1410006001

66. Stinchcombe, J. (2013). Attracting older workers while helping others retire, *Canadian HR Reporter,* accessed September 23, 2018, from http://www .hrreporter.com/article/18012-attracting-older-workers-while-helping-others-retire/

67. Nyhof, P. (2000, May 22), Managing Generation X: The Millennial challenge, *Canadian HR Reporter, 13*(10), pp. 7–8.

68. Vander Wier, M. (2017), 4 generations, 4 approaches to work, *Canadian HR Reporter*, accessed September 23, 2018, from http://www.hrreporter.com/article/32294-4-generations-4-approaches-to-work/

69. Ibid.

70. CBC, True Canadians: Multiculturalism in Canada debated, accessed September 23, 2018, from https://www.cbc.ca/archives/entry/true-canadians-multiculturalism-in-canada-debated

71. Statistics Canada (2016), Immigration and ethnocultural diversity highlight tables, accessed September 23, 2018, from http://www12.statcan.gc.ca/census-recensement/2016/dp-pd/hlt-fst/imm/Table.cfm?Lang=E&T=31&Geo=01

72. Porter, J. (1965), *The Vertical Mosaic: An Analysis of Social Class and Power in Canada,* Toronto: University of Toronto Press; see also Murray, V. V. (1974), Canadian cultural values and personnel administration, in H. Jain, ed., *Contemporary Issues in Canadian Personnel Administration,* Scarborough, ON: Prentice-Hall; Kalman, B. (2010), *Canada: The Culture,* Crabtree Publications.

73. Statistics Canada, 2011 Census.

74. Ethics & Compliance initiative (2016), 2016 Global Business Ethics Survey, accessed September 23, 2018, from https://higherlogicdownload.s3.amazonaws.com/THEECOA/11f760b1-56e0-43c6-85da-03df2ce2b5ac/UploadedImages/research/GBESFinal.pdf

75. Shen, L. (2017), The 10 biggest business scandals of 2017, *Fortune Magazine,* accessed September 23, 2018, from http://fortune.com/2017/12/31/biggest-corporate-scandals-misconduct-2017-pr/

76. Ibid.

77. L. Kohlberg (1976), Moral stages and moralization: The cognitive-development approach, in T. Lickona, ed., *Moral Developmental and Behavior: Theory, Research, and Social Issues,* New York: Holt, Rinehart and Winston, pp. 31–35.

78. Harper, C. (2015), *Organizations: Structures, processes and outcomes,* Routledge.

79. Vu, U. (2008, July 14), "Strategic" over-used in HR, *Canadian HR Reporter,* p. 8.

80. Bamberger, P. A., Meshoulam, I., and Biron, M. (2014), *Human Resource Strategy: Formulation, Implementation, and Impact,* Routledge.

81. Bamberger, P., and Meshoulam, I. (2000), *Human Resource Strategy,* Thousand Oaks, CA: Sage Publications, p. 57.

82. Statistics Canada, Work stoppages in Canada, by jurisdiction and industry based on the North American Industry Classification System (NAICS), Employment and Social Development Canada–Labour Program, adapted from CANSIM Table 278-0015, accessed March 30, 2018.

83. Manyika, J. (2017), Technology, jobs, and the future of work, McKinsey Global Institute, accessed September 23, 2018, from https://www.mckinsey.com/~/media/McKinsey/Global%20Themes/Employment%20and%20Growth/Technology%20jobs%20and%20the%20future%20of%20work/MGI-Future-of-Work-Briefing-note-May-2017.ashx

84. Brown, D. (2003, April 7), Innovative HR ineffective in manufacturing firms, *Canadian HR Reporter,* p. 1.

85. Gibbons, J., and Woock, C. (2009, March 23), Evidence-based HR in action, *Canadian HR Reporter,* pp. 16, 20.

86. SHRM Customized Human Capital Benchmarking Report (2017), accessed September 23, 2018, from https://www.shrm.org/ResourcesAndTools/business-solutions/Documents/Human-Capital-Report-All-Industries-All-FTEs.pdf

87. Aon (2018), Efficiency, effectiveness, and employee experience, accessed September 23, 2018, from http://www.aon.com/human-capital-consulting/consulting/HR_Effectiveness.jsp

88. BC Human Resource Management Association, accessed March 3, 2012, from http://www.hrmetricsservice.org/

89. Deloitte & Touche Human Resource Consulting Services (1994), *The State of the Human Resources Management Function in Canada,* p. ii.

90. Number adapted from reported registrants in both CPHR/CRHA Canada, accessed March 30, 2018, and the Human Resource Professional Association (HRPA), accessed March 30, 2018.

91. Human Resource Professional Association, accessed October 17, 2018, from https://www.hrpa.ca/Documents/Public/Thought-Leadership/CEO-Perspective-Research-Highlight.pdf

92. Peoplefluent (2014), *The evolving role of HR,* White paper.

93. Conference Board of Canada (2013), International Ranking—Labour Productivity Growth, accessed September 23, 2018, from https://www.conferenceboard.ca/hcp/Details/Economy/measuring-productivity-canada.aspx

94. Muzyka, D., and Hodgson, G. (2017), To boost productivity, Canada needs to focus on innovation, *The Globe and Mail,* accessed September 23, 2018, from https://www.theglobeandmail.com/report-on-business/rob-commentary/to-boost-productivity-canada-needs-to-focus-on-innovation/article26283449/

95. Ibid.

CHAPTER 2

1. Philip C. Grant (1988, February), What use is a job description? *Personnel Journal, 67*(2), p. 50.

2. Vu, U. (2006, March), How Purolator dealt with skyrocketing costs, *Canadian Human Rights Reporter, 19,* pp. 9–10.

3. SHRM, Survey findings: Job analysis activities, accessed September 24, 2018, from http://www.shrm.org/research/survey-findings/articles/pages/2014-Job-Analysis-Activities.aspx

4. Economic Research Institute (2012), Conducting job analysis, *StudyLib,* accessed September 24, 2018, from https://studylib.net/doc/8845126/conducting-job-analysis---eri-economic-research-institute

5. Cleary, J., and Cochie, M. (2011), Core skill set remains same in newspaper job ads, *Newspaper Research Journal, 32*(4), 68–82, accessed September 24, 2018, from https://doi.org/10.1177/073953291103200406

6. *Canadian Human Rights Reporter,* Vol. 6, 1985, p. 6.

7. IC&RC, IC&RC announces updated alcohol and drug counselor (ADC) job analysis, accessed September 24, 2018, from http://internationalcredentialing.org/Resources/Documents/ADC_JA_Finished_Announcement.pdf

8. Purdue Research Foundation (1989), *Position Analysis Questionnaire,* West Lafayette, IN; see also: Position Analysis Questionnaire, accessed September 24, 2018, from http://www.paq.com/?FuseAction=bulletins.job-analysis-questionnaire

9. Dierdorff, E. C., and Wilson, M. A. (2003), A meta-analysis of job analysis reliability, *Journal of Applied Psychology, 88,* pp. 635–646.

10. CBC News (2011, December), CP freight train derails near Golden, B.C., accessed September 24, 2018, from http://www.cbc.ca/news/canada/british-columbia/story/2011/12/27/bc-cp-train-derailment.html

11. O*Net OnLine, Summary report for loco-motive engineers, accessed September 24, 2018, from http://www.onetonline.org/link/summary/53-4011.00

12. Wickström, G., and Bendix, T. (2000), The "Hawthorne effect"—what did the original Hawthorne studies actually show? *Scandinavian Journal of Work, Environment & Health, 26*(4), 363–367. Accessed September 24, 2018, from http://www.jstor.org/stable/40967074

13. SHRM Survey findings: Job analysis activities, accessed September 24, 2018, from http://www.shrm.org/research/surveyfindings/articles/pages/2014-Job-Analysis-Activities.aspx

14. Human Resources and Skills Development Canada (2011), National Occupational Classification, accessed September 24, 2018, from http://www5.hrsdc.gc.ca/NOC/

15. Entrepreneur Media (2010, October), How to write a job analysis and description, *Start Your Own Business: The Only*

Start-Up Book You'll Ever Need (5th ed.), October 2010, accessed September 24, 2018, from http://www.entrepreneur.com/article/56490

16. Dobson, S. (2017, April 17), Salespeople in spotlight after complaints, *Canadian HR Reporter,* accessed September 25, 2018, from http://www.hrreporter.com/culture-and-engagement/33165-salespeople-in-spotlight-after-complaints/

17. Bates, S. (2013), Majority of new hires say job is not what they expected, *SHRM Blog,* accessed September 25, 2018, from https://blog.shrm.org/workplace/majority-of-new-hires-say-job-is-not-what-they-expected

18. Gilbert, F., and Gerstner, G. (2011), Chapter 7: Benchmarking, in J. Geller and A. H. Mazur (Eds.), *Global Business Driven HR Transformation: The Journey Continues,* Deloitte Development LLC.

19. Cooper, K. C. (2000), *Effective Competency Modeling & Reporting,* New York: AMACOM, AMA Publications; Hill, J. (2012, January), Competency model helps HR build value, *Canadian Human Rights Reporter, 25*(2), pp. 20–21.

20. Woods, S. A., and Hinton, D. P. (2017), What do people really do at work? Job analysis and design, in *An Introduction to Work and Organizational Psychology: An International Perspective (*3rd ed.), edited by Nik Chmiel, Franco Fraccaroli, and Magnus Sverke, John Wiley & Sons, Ltd.

21. Hill, J. (2012, January), Competency model helps HR build value, *Canadian Human Rights Reporter, 25*(2), pp. 20–21.

22. Campion, M. A., Fink, A. A., Ruggeberg, B. J., Carr, L., Phillips, G. M., and Odman, R. B. (2011), Doing competencies well: Best practices in competency modeling, *Personnel Psychology, 64*(1), 225–262.

23. Stetz, T. A., and Chmielewski, T. L. (2015), Competency modeling documentation, *SHRM-SIOP Science of HR White Paper Series,* accessed September 25, 2018, from http://www.siop.org/SIOP-SHRM/SHRM-SIOP_Competency_Modeling_Documentation.pdf

24. Woods, S. A., and Hinton, D. P. (2017), What do people really do at work? Job analysis and design, in *An Introduction to Work and Organizational Psychology: An International Perspective* (3rd ed.), edited by N. Chmiel, F. Fraccaroli, and M. Sverke, John Wiley & Sons, Ltd.

25. Passariello, C. (2006, October 9), Louis Vuitton tries modern methods on factory line, *The Wall Street Journal,* pp. A1, A15.

26. Inman, R. (1996, July), Workflow, *Transactions, 28*(7), pp. 555–556.

27. Salvendy, G. (2012), *Handbook of Human Factors and Ergonomics,* John Wiley & Sons.

28. Chahardoli, S., Motamedzade, M., Hamidi, Y., Golmohammadi, R., and Soltanian, A. R. (2014), Relationship between job design, performance and job satisfaction among Bank employees, *Journal of Health and Safety at Work,* 4(3), pp. 75–84.

29. AWCBC Online Community—Annual KSM Standard Report 2013, accessed September 25, 2018, from https://aoc.awcbc.org/KsmReporting/KsmSubmissionReport/2

30. Statistics Canada (2014, September 26), Canada's population estimates: Age and sex, 2014, *The Daily,* accessed September 25, 2018, from http://www.statcan.gc.ca/daily-quotidien/140926/dq140926b-eng.htm

31. Salvendy, G. (2012), *Handbook of Human Factors and Ergonomics,* John Wiley & Sons.

32. Chisholm, P. (2001, March 5), Redesigning work, *Maclean's,* p. 36.

33. Hackman, J. R., and Oldham, G. (1980), *Work Redesign,* Reading, MA: Addison-Wesley; Sparrow, P. (2000), New employee behaviours, work designs and forms of work organization: What is in store for future of work? *Journal of Managerial Psychology, 15*(3), pp. 202–218.

34. Prevention of Musculoskeletal Injuries in Poultry Processing (2013), *Occupational Safety and Health Administration, U.S. Department of Labor,* OSHA 3213-12R 2013, accessed September 25, 2018, from https://www.shrm.org/resourcesandtools/hr-topics/risk-management/documents/osha3213.pdf

35. Mohr, R. D., and Zoghi, C. (2006, January), *Is Job Enrichment Really Enriching?* Working paper, University of Chicago, accessed September 25, 2018, from http://www.bls.gov/ore/pdf/ec060010.pdf

36. Booth, P. (1994), *Challenge and Change: Embracing the Team Concept,* Ottawa: Conference Board of Canada; Sagie A., and Aycan, Z. (2003, April), A cross-cultural analysis of participative decision-making in organizations, *Human Relations,* pp. 453–473.

37. Engardio, P. (2007, August 20), Managing a global workforce, *Business Week,* pp. 48–51; Marquez, J. (2008, September 22), Connecting a virtual workforce, *Workforce Management,* pp. 18–28.

38. Balkema, A., and Molleman, E. (1999), Barriers to the development of self-organizing teams, *Journal of Managerial Psychology, 14*(2), pp. 134–150.

39. Stetz, T. A., and Chmielewski, T. L. (2015), Competency modeling documentation, *SHRM-SIOP Science of HR White Paper Series.*

CHAPTER 3

1. A. Rahman bin Idris and D. Eldridge (1998), Reconceptualising human resource planning in response to institutional change, *International Journal of Manpower, 19*(5), p. 346.

2. IBM Corporate website, accessed April 17, 2018, from https://www.ibm.com/annualreport/2013/bin/assets/2013_ibm_strategy.pdf

3. Korn Ferry Institute (2016, May 31), The Right Workforce, Today and Tomorrow, accessed September 23, 2018, from https://www.kornferry.com/institute/the-right-workforce-today-and-tomorrow

4. Baron, A., Clake, R., Turner, P., and Pass, S. (2010), Workforce planning: Right people, right time, right skills, Chartered Institution of Personnel and Development.

5. Kreissl, B. (2018), Five more HR trends for 2018, accessed September 25, 2018, from http://www.hrreporter.com/columnist/hr-policies-practices/archive/2018/01/16/five-more-hr-trends-for-2018/

6. Stauss, M. (2014, January 15), Nordstrom to plant Canadian flagship in Toronto, *The Globe and Mail.*

7. Laura Hamill, Ph.D., appointed chief people officer at Limeade (2015, March 24), *Market Wired,* accessed September 25, 2018, from http://www.marketwired.com/press-release/laura-hamill-phd-appointed-chief-people-officer-at-limeade-2003269.htm; Nielsen, S. (2018), The evolution of CHROs, *Canadian HR Reporter,* accessed September 25, 2018, from http://www.hrreporter.com/columnist/the-c-suite/archive/2018/02/27/the-evolution-of-chros/

8. Mills, D. Q. (2001), Planning with people in mind, *Harvard Business Review,* pp. 97–105.

9. How to predict employee turnover using SAP InfiniteInsight (2014, December 1), accessed September 23, 2018, from https://blogs.sap.com/2014/12/01/how-to-predict-employee-turnover-using-sap-infiniteinsight/

10. Boudreau, J. (2014, September 5), Predict what employees will do without freaking them out, *Harvard Business Review.*

11. HR Analytics Factsheets (2018, June 13), accessed September 23, 2018, from https://www.cipd.co.uk/knowledge/strategy/analytics/factsheet

12. Cappelli, P. (2017, June 2), There's no such thing as big data in HR, *Harvard Business Review,* accessed September 23, 2018, from https://hbr.org/2017/06/theres-no-such-thing-as-big-data-in-hr

13. Phillips, J., & Phillips, P. (2009), Measuring return on investment in HR, *Strategic HR Review, 8,* pp. 12–19. doi:10.1108/14754390910990946

14. Bailey, S. (2018), Its population shrinking, Newfoundland and Labrador aims to lure back diaspora, *CTV News,* accessed September 23, 2018, from https://www.ctvnews.ca/canada/its-population-shrinking-newfoundland-and-labrador-aims-to-lure-back-diaspora-1.3826026

15. Mutikani, L. (2018), Americans voluntarily quitting jobs as labour market

tightens, *Canadian HR Reporter,* accessed September 23, 2018, from http://www.hrreporter.com/recruitment-and-retention/35911-americans-voluntarily-quitting-jobs-as-labour-market-tightens/

16. MacLeod, A. (2018), BC minimum wage to top $15 by 2021, *The Tyee,* accessed September 25, 2018, from https://thetyee.ca/News/2018/02/08/BC-Minimum-Wage-Top-15-By-2021/

17. Biro, M. M. (2017), The impact of technology on HR and what's ahead, *Huffpost,* accessed September 25, 2018, from https://www.huffingtonpost.com/meghan-m-biro-/the-impact-of-technology-_1_b_9294208.html; E. Brynjolfsson and A. McAfee (2011, October 17), *Race against the Machine: How the Digital Revolution Is Accelerating Innovation, Driving Productivity, and Irreversibly Transforming Employment and the Economy,* Digital Frontier Press.

18. DeNisco Rayome, A. (2018), Demand for AI talent exploding: Here are the 10 most in-demand jobs, *TechRepublic,* accessed September 25, 2018, from https://www.techrepublic.com/article/demand-for-ai-talent-exploding-here-are-the-10-most-in-demand-jobs/

19. McKinsey Global Institute (2017), How automation and technology are affecting work, accessed September 25, 2018, from https://www.mckinsey.com/global-themes/employment-and-growth/technology-jobs-and-the-future-of-work#section 2

20. The Canadian Press (2018, February 19), Bombardier may lay off hundreds at Quebec railway plant if no orders come in, *Global News,* accessed September 23, 2018, from https://globalnews.ca/news/4033984/bombardier-may-lay-off-hundreds-at-its-quebec-railway-plant-if-no-orders-come-in/

21. Baertlein, L., and McLeod, H. (2017), For Whole Foods workers, fears of robots, drones and culture clash, *Canadian HR Reporter,* accessed September 25, 2018, from http://www.hrreporter.com/recruitment-and-retention/33758-for-whole-foods-workers-fears-of-robots-drones-and-culture-clash/

22. Wang, D. (2016), 4 examples of companies that nailed organizational change, *TinyPulse,* accessed September 25, 2018, from https://www.tinypulse.com/blog/sk-examples-of-companies-that-nailed-organizational-change

23. Delbecq, A. L., and Van de Ven, A. H. (1971), A group process model for problem identification and program planning, *The Journal of Applied Behavioral Science, 7*(4), 466–492.

24. Delbecq, A. L., Van de Ven, A. H., and Gustafson, D. H. (1975), *Group Techniques for Progress Planning: A Guide to Nominal and Delphi Process,* Glenview, IL: Scott, Foresman; Bartwrek,

J. M., and Muringhan, J. K. (1984), The nominal group technique: Expanding the basic procedure and underlying assumptions, *Group and Organizational Studies, 9,* pp. 417–432.

25. Dalkey, N., & Helmer, O. (1963), An experimental application of the Delphi method to the use of experts, *Management science, 9*(3), 458–467.

26. SHRM (2016), Strategic planning: How can a skills inventory be used for strategic HR planning? Accessed September 25, 2018, from https://www.shrm.org/resourcesandtools/tools-and-samples/hr-qa/pages/howcanaskillsinventorybeusedforstrategichrplanning.aspx

27. Cognology, accessed September 25, 2018, from http://www.cognology.com.au

28. SHRM (2012), Succession planning: What is a 9-box grid? Accessed September 25, 2018, from https://www.shrm.org/resourcesandtools/tools-and-samples/hr-qa/pages/whatsa9boxgridandhowcananhrdepartmentuseit.aspx

29. Posner, B. Z., and Kouzes, J. M. (1987), Leadership Practices Inventory (LPI): A self-assessment and analysis, accessed September 25, 2018, from https://www.lpionline.com/lpi_individual.html

30. Walker, J. (1976, June), Human resource planning: Managerial concerns and practices, *Business Horizons,* pp. 56–57; see also Odiorne, G. (1986, December), The crystal ball of HR strategy, *Personnel Administrator,* pp. 103–106; Byrne, J., and Cowan, A. (1986, September), Should companies groom new leaders or buy them? *BusinessWeek,* pp. 94–96.

31. Government of Alberta, *Alberta's Short-Term Employment Forecast: 2017–2019,* accessed September 25, 2018, from https://work.alberta.ca/documents/short-term-employment-forecast.pdf

32. Government of Alberta, *Alberta's Occupational Demand and Supply Outlook 2015–2025,* accessed September 25, 2018, from https://work.alberta.ca/documents/occupational-demand-and-supply-outlook-2015-2025.pdf

33. Government of Alberta, 2012 Alberta Labour Mobility Survey Report.

34. Statistics Canada (n.d.), The migration of infrastructure tradespersons, accessed September 25, 2018, from http://www.statcan.gc.ca/pub/75-006-x/2014001/article/14011-eng.htm

35. *Canadian HR Reporter* (2016), Agriculture sector reliance on temporary foreign workers growing: Report, accessed September 23, 2018, from https://www.hrreporter.com/article/31882-agriculture-sectors-reliance-on-temporary-foreign-workers-growing-report/

36. Barrett, A., and Kelly, E. (2012), The impact of Ireland's recession on the labour market outcomes of its immigrants, *European Journal of Population, 28*(1),

accessed November 30, 2018, from https://doi.org/10.1007/s10680-011-9249-7

37. CBC News (2014), Temporary Foreign Worker Program linked to joblessness: Report, accessed September 25, 2018, from http://www.cbc.ca/news/business/temporary-foreign-worker-program-linked-to-joblessness-report-1.2620551

38. Employment and Social Development Canada, Temporary Foreign Worker Program, accessed September 25, 2018, from http://www.esdc.gc.ca/eng/jobs/foreign_workers/index.shtml

39. Employment and Social Development Canada (n.d.), Overhauling the Temporary Foreign Worker Program, accessed September 23, 2018, from https://www.canada.ca/en/employment-social-development/services/foreign-workers/reports/overhaul.html

40. Smith, S. (2018) Temporary foreign workings gaining permanent residence in Canada on the rise, *Canadian Immigration News,* accessed September 25, 2018, from https://www.cicnews.com/2018/02/temporary-foreign-workers-gaining-permanent-residence-in-canada-on-the-rise-0210221.html#gs.8DesqJo

41. Hrvatin, V. (2018), Farmers dismayed as government to begin unannounced temporary foreign worker checks, *National Post,* accessed September 25, 2018, from http://nationalpost.com/news/canada/farmers-dismayed-as-government-begins-unannounced-temporary-foreign-worker-audits

42. Koven, P. (2014), Agrium Inc. targeted by another activist investor, *Financial Post,* accessed September 25, 2018, from http://business.financialpost.com/news/mining/agrium-inc-in-crosshairs-of-another-activist-investor/

43. CBC News (2017), Agrium, PotashCorp merger will "impact the entire industry," including thousands of farmers: Prof, accessed September 25, 2018, from http://www.cbc.ca/news/canada/saskatchewan/agrium-potashcorp-merger-nutrien-1.4465479

44. Berkow, L. (2011, March 29), Tech labour crunch looming in Canada, *Financial Post,* accessed September 25, 2018, from http://business.financialpost.com/2011/03/29/tech-labour-crunch-looming-in-canada/

45. Raphelson, S. (2018), Trucking industry struggles with growing driver shortage, *Here and Now Compass,* accessed September 25, 2018, from https://www.npr.org/2018/01/09/576752327/trucking-industry-struggles-with-growing-driver-shortage

46. HRSDC, accessed September 25, 2018, from http://www23.hrsdc.gc.ca/w.2lc.4m.2@-eng.jsp

47. Ontario Ministry of Labour, Employment Standards, accessed September 25,

2018, from http://www.labour.gov.on.ca/english/es/

48. Marzucco, L., and Hansez, I. (2016), Outplacement adequacy and benefits: The mediating role of overall justice, *Journal of Employment Counseling, 53*(3), 130–143.

49. Stacho, Z., and Stachová, K. (2015), Outplacement as part of human resource management, *Procedia Economics and Finance, 34,* pp. 19–26.

50. Howell, D. (2015), Heavy oil industry needs "lifestyle change," conference told, *Edmonton Journal,* accessed September 25, 2018, from https://edmontonjournal.com/news/local-news/heavy-oil-industry-needs-lifestyle-change-conference-told

51. Investopedia, Phased retirement, accessed September 25, 2018, from http://www.investopedia.com/terms/p/phased-retirement.asp#axzz1uJouTga0

52. University of Toronto, Retirement, from *Academic Administrative Procedures Manual,* accessed September 25, 2018, from http://www.aapm.utoronto.ca/retirement

53. Higgins, C. (2018), I'm a designer and I job share with an AI, *Insight,* accessed September 25, 2018, from http://workplaceinsight.net/im-a-designer-and-i-job-share-with-an-ai/

54. *EI Monitoring and Assessment Report 2012V: EI Work-Sharing Benefits,* ESDC, accessed September 25, 2018, from http://www.esdc.gc.ca/eng/jobs/ei/reports/mar2012/chapter2_5.shtml

55. Heathfield, S. M. (2016), Job share advantages and disadvantages, *The Balance,* accessed September 25, 2018, from https://www.thebalance.com/job-share-good-and-bad-1918169

56. CBC News (2012, April 2), 300 people vie for 30 part-time bar jobs, accessed September 25, 2018, from http://www.cbc.ca/news/canada/windsor/story/2012/04/02/wdr-service-industry-windsor.html

57. Statistics Canada (2015), Full time employment, 1976–2014, accessed September 25, 2018, from http://www.statcan.gc.ca/pub/11-626-x/11-626-x2015049-eng.htm

58. Fantini, J., and de Piante, L. (2009, March 23), Temporary lay-offs risk dismissal claims, *Canadian HR Reporter,* p. 5.

59. Government of Alberta, Termination and termination pay, accessed September 25, 2018, from https://www.aberta.ca/termination-pay.aspx

60. UPS, accessed September 25, 2018, from https://ups.managehr.com/screening/hourly/apply.aspx?l=WABOE&p=1&src=&ref=136212272

61. Milley, P. A. S. (2015), Well, what did you expect? Setting expectations for probationary employees, Atlantic Employers' Council, accessed September 25, 2018, from http://www.smss.com/abcnewsletter/AEC/2015_Spring/A2.html?utm_source=-Mondaq&utm_medium=syndication&utm_campaign=View-Original

62. Dujay, J. (2017), Outsourcing in spotlight with CIBC replacing staff, *Canadian HR Reporter,* accessed September 25, 2018, from http://www.hrreporter.com/recruitment-and-retention/33422-outsourcing-in-spotlight-with-cibc-replacing-staff/

63. Kearns, K. (2015), 9 great examples of crowd-sourcing in the age of empowered customers, *Tweak Your Biz,* accessed September 25, 2018, from http://tweakyourbiz.com/marketing/2015/07/10/9-great-examples-crowdsourcing-age-empowered-consumers/

64. Ligaya, A. (2014, November 2), Canadian interactive studio to produce Marvel's e-magazine for blockbuster movies, *Financial Post,* accessed September 25, 2018, from http://business.financialpost.com/entrepreneur/canadian-interactive-studio-to-produce-marvels-e-magazine-for-blockbuster-movies/

65. Lawson, T. (2015), Accomodating an aging workforce, *Canadian HR Reporter,* accessed September 25, 2018, from http://www.hrreporter.com/article/24481-accommodating-an-aging-workforce/

66. Dobson, S. (2016, May 30), Despite benefits, many employers not offering job rotations: Survey, *Canadian HR Reporter,* accessed September 25, 2018, from http://www.hrreporter.com/article/27741-despite-benefits-many-employers-not-offering-job-rotations-survey/

67. Wallace, T. (2015), Measuring workforce planning success—Dealing with skill and luck, *LinkedIn,* accessed September 25, 2018, from https://www.linkedin.com/pulse/measuring-workforce-planning-success-dealing-skill-luck-wallace

68. CB Staff & Steve Brearton (2015, January 23), The biggest layoffs in Canadian history, *Canadian Business,* accessed September 25, 2018, from http://www.canadianbusiness.com/lists-and-rankings/the-biggest-layoffs-in-canadian-history/

69. Groysberg, B., and Connolly, K. (2015), The three things CEOs worry about the most, *Harvard Business Review, 16.*

70. Kavanagh, M. J., and Johnson, R. D. (Eds.) (2017), *Human resource information systems: Basics, applications, and future directions,* Sage Publications.

71. Dobson, S. (2017, November 27), Building effective HR analytics, *Canadian HR Reporter,* accessed September 23, 2018, from https://www.hrreporter.com/article/35255-building-effective-hr-analytics/

72. Gale, S. F. (2014), Special report: HRMS vendors say, "Hey, you, get onto my cloud," *Workforce,* accessed September 23, 2018, from https://www.workforce.com/2014/08/07/special-report-hrms-vendors-say-hey-you-get-onto-my-cloud/

73. Sage Software Systems, accessed September 25, 2018, from http://www.sagehrms.com/

74. Min, C., Y. (2018, March 3), Big data boss, *The Business Times,* accessed September 25, 2018, from https://www.businesstimes.com.sg/brunch/big-data-boss

75. *HR Technologist* (2018, February 20), Moorepay launches new People Analytics solution, accessed September 25, 2018, from https://www.hrtechnologist.com/news/payroll-administration/moorepay-launches-new-people-analytics-solution/

76. Predictive Analysis World, Predictive Analysis Guide, accessed September 25, 2018, from http://www.predictiveanalyticsworld.com/predictive_analytics.php

77. Young, L. (2017, November 13), Analytics give Andrea Scheelar HR edge (National HR Awards), *Canadian HR Reporter,* accessed September 25, 2018, from http://www.hrreporter.com/article/35119-analytics-give-andrea-scheelar-hr-edge-national-hr-awards/

78. Flamholtz, E. G. (2012), *Human resource accounting: Advances in concepts, methods and applications,* Springer Science & Business Media.

79. N. Chaudhry and M. Roomi (2010), Accounting for the development of human capital in manufacturing organizations: A study of the Pakistani textile sector, *Journal of HRCA: Human Resource Costing & Accounting, 14*(3), pp. 178–195. Retrieved from ProQuest.

CHAPTER 4

1. Canadian Charter of Rights and Freedoms, as part of the *Constitution Act* of 1982.

2. Ibid.

3. Dobson, S. (2011, September 26), 24-hour shift for medical residents quashed, *Canadian HR Reporter,* pp. 1, 11.

4. Canadian Human Rights Commission (2010), Your guide to understanding the Canadian Human Rights Act, accessed October 30, 2018, from https://www.chrc-ccdp.gc.ca/eng/content/your-guide-understanding-canadian-human-rights-act.

5. *Canadian Human Rights Act,* Paragraph 2, Subsection (a).

6. See Canadian Human Rights Commission (2016), *2016 Annual Report to Parliament,* accessed November 20, 2018, from https://2016.chrcreport.ca/index.php; New Brunswick Human Rights Commission (2018, March), *Annual Report 2016–2017,* accessed November 20, 2018, from https://www.gnb.ca/

7. Bernier, L. (2014, February 10), No easy answer for competing rights cases, *Canadian HR Reporter,* pp. 1, 8.

8. See Time, F. (n.d.), Height qualifications to become a flight attendant, *Chron,* accessed November 20, 2018, from https://

work.chron.com/height-qualifications-become-flight-attendant-27467.html

9. See Equity Challenge Unit (2014), Unconscious bias, accessed November 20, 2018, from https://www.ecu.ac.uk/guidance-resources/employment-and-careers/staff-recruitment/unconscious-bias/; see also: Billan, R. (2017, April 3), Surfacing unconscious bias, *Canadian HR Reporter,* p. 16.

10. Dobson, S. (2017, May 15), Feds try to blank out bias, *Canadian HR Reporter,* pp. 1, 9.

11. Starbucks to shut 8,000 U.S. outlets for bias training after protests (2018, April 17), *CBC News.*

12. Bundale, B. (2018, March 23), Black janitors allege racial discrimination, plan to file human rights complaint, *The Star.*

13. Vander Weir, M. (2017, March 20), Rise of racial incidents challenging employers, *Canadian HR Reporter,* pp. 1, 12.

14. Pulse Survey (2011, October 24), *Canadian HR Reporter,* p. 14.

15. Canadian Press (2014, September 9), Tribunal orders penalty against firm that said it only hired white men, *Chronicle Herald,* p. A13.

16. Silliker, A. (2012, November 21), Matthew, you're hired. Good luck next time, Samir, *Canadian HR Reporter,* pp. 1. 20. A report of the full study *Why Do Some Employers Prefer to Interview Matthew but Not Samir?* is available at http://mbc.metropolis.net/assets/uploads/files/wp/2011/WP11-13.pdf

17. Bernier, L. (2016, April 18), Resume whitening common among job applicants, *Canadian HR Reporter,* pp. 1, 12.

18. Stam, L. (2017, December 20), Religious accommodation in the workplace, *Employment and Human Rights Law in Canada,* accessed November 20, 2018, from https://www.canadaemploymenthumanrightslaw.com/2017/12/religious-accommodation-in-the-workplace/. See also: Kreissl, B. (2011, May 3), Religion in the workplace, *HR Reporter,* accessed November 20, 2018, from https://www.hrreporter.com/columnist/hr-policies-practices/archive/2011/05/03/religion-in-the-workplace/.

19. Silliker, A. (2013, January 14), 7 in 10 firms not hiring older workers, *Canadian HR Reporter,* pp. 1, 10.

20. Rubin, J. (2014, June 2), Ageism not easy to circumnavigate, *Canadian HR Reporter,* p. 12; Sun Life Canada (2015), *2015 Canadian Unretirement Index Report,* accessed November 20, 2018, from https://cdn.sunlife.com/static/ca/Learn%20and%20Plan/Market%20insights/Canadian%20Unretirement%20index/2015_Sun_Life_Canadian_Unretirement_Index_Report_en.pdf

21. The aging workforce (2013, November 18), *Canadian HR Reporter,* p. 11.

22. Ryan, D. (2018, January 14), From choice or necessity, more people are working post-65, *Vancouver Sun.*

23. Bernier, L. (2013, December 16), Retirement incentives: Proceed with caution, *Canadian HR Reporter,* pp. 3, 8.

24. Smith, J. (2014, November 3), Pregnant server not on tap for bar owner, *Canadian HR Reporter,* p. 5.

25. Bernier, L. (2014, December 1), Discrimination alive and well around pregnancy, breastfeeding, *Canadian HR Reporter,* pp. 3, 6.

26. Bernier, L. (2014, June 16), Pregnant workers more vulnerable to health risks, *Canadian HR Reporter,* p. 3.

27. Zaman, N. (2017, May 15), Dressing down discriminatory dress codes, *Canadian HR Reporter,* pp. 5, 15.

28. Dobson, S. (2014, May 5), Male-wanted job ads, *Canadian HR Reporter,* pp. 1, 10.

29. Booking.com research reveals gender bias in the tech industry is not limited to IT and engineering (2017, November 8), *Booking.com,* accessed November 20, 2018, from https://news.booking.com/bookingcom-research-reveals-gender-bias-in-the-tech-industry-is-not-just-limited-to-it-and-engineering/

30. CHRC, *Annual Report 1999,* pp. 7, accessed November 20, 2018, from http://publications.gc.ca/collections/collection_2017/ccdp-chrc/HR1-1999-eng.pdf.

31. Brodsky, G., Day, S., and Peters, Y. (2012, March), *Accommodation in the 21st Century,* Canadian Human Rights Commission, p. 42, accessed November 20, 2018, from https://www.chrc-ccdp.gc.ca/eng/file/1379/download?token=uNCLYhk_

32. Dobson, S. (2013, September 20), Employer on the hook for lost wages, damages in vile case, *Canadian HR Reporter,* pp. 1, 2.

33. CBC Stories (n.d.), *CBC News,* accessed November 20, 2018, from https://www.cbc.ca/news2/background/samesexrights/newsarchive.html

34. Ghoussoub, M. (2017, December 15), Supreme court rules employees can allege workplace harassment against people from other companies, *CBC News.*

35. See Bernier, L. (2016, September 19), Gay-friendly policies attract LGBTQ—and straight—workers: Survey, *Canadian HR Reporter,* pp. 1, 7.

36. Ibbitson, J. (2017, June 15), Canada shows leadership in advancing human rights, *Globe and Mail.*

37. Kreissl, B. (2013, February 25), Coping with gender reassignment surgery, *Canadian HR Reporter,* p. 27.

38. Dobson, S. (2017, December 11) Job fair focuses on transgender community, *Canadian HR Reporter,* pp. 1, 7.

39. Lowrie, M. (2018, March 22), Duclos defends gender-neutral language amid criticism from opposition, *Canadian HR Reporter.*

40. McClelland, C. (2016, May 30), An employer's last-minute childcare obligations may trigger the duty to accommodate, *Blaney McMurtry,* accessed November 3, 2018, from https://www.blaney.com/articles/an-employees-last-minute-childcare-obligations-may-trigger-the-duty-to-accommodate

41. Beaumont, M. (2014, August 26), When childcare interferes with work: When is an employer's duty to accommodate triggered? *Thompson, Doreman, and Sweatman,* accessed November 20, 2018, from https://www.tdslaw.com/resource/when-childcare-interferes-with-work-when-is-an-employers-duty-to-accommodate-triggered/

42. Dobson, S. (2017, August 7), Supreme Court confirms that employers can terminate workers with disabilities, *Canadian HR Reporter,* pp. 1, 8.

43. Starbucks settles with dwarf fired from barista job (2011, August 18), *Reuters.*

44. Grant, T. (2014, February 28), The (dis)ability edge, *The Globe and Mail,* pp. B6, B7.

45. Ibid.

46. Filsinger, K. (2010), *Employment Law for Business and Human Resources Professionals* (2nd ed.), Toronto: Emond Montgomery, pp. 128–130.

47. Ibid.

48. Ibid.

49. McQuigge, M. (2017, December 30), What will Canada's new accessibility law in 2018 look like? *Toronto Star.*

50. Silliker, A. (2012, February 13), People with episodic disabilities valuable talent, *Canadian HR Reporter,* pp. 1, 19.

51. Wafer, M. (2016, February 4), Employees with disabilities can have a positive impact on profitability, *Globe and Mail.*

52. Silliker, A. (2013, May 6), 70 percent of employers hire workers with disabilities, *Canadian HR Reporter,* pp. 1, 9.

53. Branigan, M., and Aitken, J. (2017, October 2), Enabling change: From disability to inclusion, *Canadian HR Reporter,* p. 16.

54. Canadian Human Rights Commission (n.d.), Correctional service agrees to hire ex-convict, News Release, Ottawa: Government of Canada.

55. For a nice summary of the historic Janzen and Govereau sexual harassment case, see: Hammond, S. (2011, August 15), The historic fight against sexual harassment, *Canadian HR Reporter,* p. 31.

56. Theodore, T. (2012, March 28), RCMP faces suit by female officers, *Chronicle Herald,* B1, B3.

57. Hill, B. (2018, February 22), Lead plaintiff in sexual harassment suit says RCMP has done nothing to make female employees safer, *Global News.*

58. See Ebosswatch.

59. Canadian Human Rights Commission (n.d.), Your guide to understanding the Canadian Human Rights Act, accessed November 3, 2018, from https://www.chrc-ccdp.gc.ca/eng/content/your-guide-understanding-canadian-human-rights-act-page1

60. Smith, J. (2010, November 29), When banter crosses the harassment line, *Canadian HR Reporter,* pp. 5, 27.

61. Bernier, L. (2014, July 14), Ostracism an often-overlooked form of workplace bullying, finds study, *Canadian HR Reporter,* p. 3.

62. AVG Technologies (2013, January 31), Social media stokes workplace privacy fears, *AVG Now,* accessed November 20, 2018, from http://now.avg.com/social-media-stokes-workplace-privacy-fears

63. Barrow, L. (2014, March 10), Unmasking the face of workplace cyber-bullying, *Canadian HR Reporter,* p. 10.

64. MeToo: Moment or movement? (2018, February 9), *AngusReid.*

65. Employment and Social Development Canada (2017), *Harassment and Sexual Violence in the Workplace Public Consultations: What We Heard,* ESDC.

66. NRG Research Group (2017, December 18), *Sexual Harassment and Sexual Violence Survey Backgrounder.*

67. *Canadian Human Rights Act,* Paragraph 60, Section 2.

68. Heathfield, S. M. (2018, November 1), How to handle an employee sexual harassment complaint, *The Balance Careers,* accessed November 20, 2018, from https://www.thebalancecareers.com/how-to-address-an-employee-sexual-harassment-complaint-1916862.

69. See Nova Scotia Human Rights Commission (n.d.), Resolving disputes: About the process, accessed November 22, 2018, from https://humanrights.novascotia.ca/resolving-disputes/about-process.

70. Ontario Human Rights Commission, *Taking the Pulse: Peoples' Opinions on Human Rights in Ontario,* 2017.

71. Schwarz, J. (2017, October 16), Best practices for gender equity, *Canadian HR Reporter,* p. 14.

72. See Dalhousie University (n.d.), Indigenous Blacks & Mi'kmaq Initiative, *Schulich School of Law,* accessed November 20, 2018, from https://www.dal.ca/faculty/law/indigenous-blacks-mi-kmaq-initiative.html.

73. Statistics Canada (2017, March 8), *Women in Canada: A Gender-based Statistical Report.*

74. Government of Canada (2009), Public Sector Equitable Compensation Act, *Justice Laws Website,* accessed October 31, 2018, from https://laws-lois.justice.gc.ca/eng/acts/P-31.65/. See also Government of Canada (n.d.), FAQ: Pay equity reform, accessed October 31, 2018, from https://www.canada.ca/en/treasury-board-secretariat/services/innovation/equitable-compensation/frequently-asked-questons-pay-equity-reform.html.

75. CBC News (2011, November 17), Postal workers win 28-Year pay equity fight.

76. Dobson, S. (2014, March 24), Ugly, racist altercation caught on video at Sears, *Canadian HR Reporter,* pp. 1, 12.

77. Valentine, J. (2017, September 9), Opinion: Sport has power to bring diverse people together, *Edmonton Journal.*

78. Statistics Canada (2017, August 2), *Same Sex Couples in Canada in 2016.*

79. Statistics Canada, *Projections of the Diversity of the Canadian Population: 2006–2031,* Catalogue No. 91-551-x; see also Statistics Canada, *Immigration and Ethnocultural Diversity in Canada,* Catalogue No. 99-010-X2011001; and Employment and Social Development Canada, *Canadians in Context—People with Disabilities,* 2015.

80. Keung, N. (2017, October 20), Sunshine approach to diversity in federal public service working, study says, *Toronto Star.*

81. DePalma, A. (1991, November 12), Women can be hindered by lack of "Boys' Network," *Boulder Daily Camera,* p. B9.

82. Li, A. (2012, April 12), Justice of the Peace suspended for sexually harassing female court staff, *Toronto Star.*

83. Wyman, O. (2016), *Women in Financial Services.* See also McFarland, J. (2014, December 5), Canada's bank sector lauded for gender diversity in world ranking, *The Globe and Mail,* p. B4.

84. Canadian Board Diversity Council, 2016 Annual Report Card, accessed from https://www.boarddiversity.ca

85. Friesen, J. (2015, February 26), Program aims for diversity on boards, *The Globe and Mail,* p. A4.

86. Canadian Board Diversity Council, *Annual Report Card,* 2016.

87. May, C. (2016, March 11), Canada 26/150 Michael Bach, Canadian Race Relations Foundation; see also Dobson, S. (2011, November 7), Catalyst honours champions of women in business, *Canadian HR Reporter,* pp. 1, 17.

88. Klie, S. (2006, February 27), Muslims face discrimination in workplace, *Canadian HR Reporter,* pp. 1, 16.

89. Kandola, R. (1995), Managing diversity: New broom or old hat? *International Review of Industrial and Organizational Psychology, 10,* pp. 131–167.

90. Immen, W. (2012, February 11), Immigrants looking for a better welcome in Canadian workplaces, *The Globe and Mail,* p. B17.

91. Gallagher-Louisy, C. (2014), What gets measured gets done: Measuring the return on investment of diversity and inclusion, Canadian Institute of Diversity and Inclusion.

92. McMahon, A. (2010), Does workplace diversity matter? A survey of empirical studies on diversity and firm performance, 2000–09, *Journal of Diversity Management, 5*(3), pp. 37–48.

93. Herring, C. (2009), Does diversity pay? Race, gender and the business case for diversity, *American Sociological Review, 74*(2), pp. 208–224.

94. RBC addressing unconscious bias to root out blind spots (2015, March 31), *The Globe and Mail;* and Mediacorp (2015), *2015 Canada's Best Diversity Employers,* p. 18.

95. Hire Immigrants Ottawa (2018), Shopify: A creative experiment to access immigrant talent.

96. Siu, B. (2011, August 15), *HR Manager's Guide to Managing Diversity and Employment Equity,* Carswell; see also Silliker, A. (2011, August 15), Making managers accountable for diversity, *Canadian HR Reporter,* pp. 12, 14.

97. Arsenault, D. (2011, February 1), Firefighting hiring plan under fire, *The Chronicle Herald,* pp. A1, A2; see also Lightstone, M. (2011, March 9), HRM to change fire service recruiting process, *The Chronicle Herald,* p. A6.

98. Silliker, A. (2013, January 28), Majority of employers lack IEP integration policies, *Canadian HR Reporter,* pp. 1, 10.

99. Canada Post (2016), *2016 Social Responsibility Report,* accessed November 20, 2018, from https://www.canadapost.ca/assets/pdf/aboutus/2016_csrreport_en.pdf

100. Royal Bank of Canada (2017), *All of Us: What We Mean When We Talk About Inclusion,* 6 Degrees Reports.

101. Blakes builds a diverse pipeline to corporate law (2015, March 31), *The Globe and Mail;* Mediacorp (2015), *2015 Canada's Best Diversity Employers,* p. 11.

CHAPTER 5

1. *Canadian HR Reporter* (2018, January 4), Talent shortages see employers changing hiring tactics.

2. Johne, M. (2011, October 7), The hunt for talent at an emerging giant, *The Globe and Mail.*

3. Uggerslev, K. L., Fassina, N. E., and Kraichy, D. (2012), Recruiting through the stages: A meta-analytic test of predictors of applicant attraction at different stages of the recruiting process, *Personnel Psychology, 65,* pp. 597–660; Saks, A., and Uggerslev, K. (2010), Sequential and combined effects of recruitment information on applicant attraction, *Journal of Business and Psychology, 25,* pp. 351–365.

4. Liedtke, M. (2010, June 14), 5 PR nightmares that were handled better than the BP oil spill, *The Huffington Post,* accessed November 27, 2018, from http://www.huffingtonpost.com/2010/06/14/5-pr-

disasters-handled-be_n_611010
.html#s99783&title=Exxon_Valdez_Spill

5. Chapman, D., Uggerslev, K., Carroll, S., Piasentin, K., and Jones, D. (2005), Applicant attraction to organizations and job choice: A meta-analytic review of the correlates of recruiting outcomes, *Journal of Applied Psychology, 90,* pp. 928–944.

6. Carey, D. (2008, September 10), Using the virtual world of Second Life to snag young IT talent, *Itbusiness.ca,* accessed November 27, 2018, from http://www.itbusiness.ca/it/client/en/home/News.asp?id=49854

7. Employment and Social Development Canada, Publications Centre (2016, January), *Canadian Occupational Projection System 2015 Projections: Imbalances Between Labour Demand and Supply 2015–2024,* accessed November 27, 2018, from http://occupations.esdc.gc.ca/sppc-cops/maint/file/download/SSPB-EPD-COPS2015IndustrialSummaries-Report-20151210-EN-FINAL.pdf

8. Tom Long, Toronto-based partner of executive recruiter Egon Zehnder International Inc. quoted by Wallace Immen (2006, February 22), Going abroad to get ahead, *The Globe and Mail,* p. C1.

9. Results of surveys by Global Recruitment Consultancy Robert Walters, Korn/Ferry International, 2005 Survey of Executives Worldwide, reported in Wallace Immen (2006, February 22), Going abroad to get ahead, *The Globe and Mail,* p. C1.

10. Turcotte, M. (2015, November 27), Persons with disabilities and employment, accessed November 27, 2018, from http://www.statcan.gc.ca/pub/75-006-x/2014001/article/14115-eng.htm

11. NCR Graduate Gateway, accessed November 27, 2018, from https://www.ncr.com/careers/work-at-ncr/early-careers

12. Uggerslev, K. L., Fassina, N. E., and Kraichy, D. (2012), Recruiting through the stages: A meta-analytic test of predictors of applicant attraction at different stages of the recruiting process, *Personnel Psychology, 65,* pp. 597–660.

13. Heneman, H., Judge, T., Smith, V., and Summers, R. (2010), *Staffing Organizations* (2nd ed.), Canada: McGraw-Hill Ryerson.

14. Vander Wier, M. (2017, August 7), Training up leaders the Facebook way, *Canadian HR Reporter.*

15. Vander Wier, M. (2018, January 17), No easy answers for employers facing major minimum wage hikes., *Canadian HR Reporter,* accessed November 28, 2018, from http://www.hrreporter.com/compensation-and-benefits/35683-no-easy-answers-for-employers-facing-major-minimum-wage-hikes/

16. Vander Wier, M. (2017, August 7), Training up leaders the Facebook way, *Canadian HR Reporter.*

17. Boosting accessibility could life economic activity by $16.8 billion: Report (2018, February 23), *Canadian HR Reporter.*

18. Vancouver International Airport: Recruiting people with disabilities (n.d.), *go2hr,* accessed November 28, 2018, from https://www.go2hr.ca/recruitment/vancouver-international-airport-recruiting-people-with-disabilities

19. Green, L. T. (2017, April 17), Organically produced diversity and inclusion, *Canadian HR Reporter.*

20. Galt, V. (2006, February 24), Better shifts, better training, better pay, *The Globe and Mail,* p. C1.

21. Employment and Social Development Canada's Canadian Occupational Projection System (COPS) is found at http://occupations.esdc.gc.ca/sppc-cops/w.2lc.4m.2@-eng.jsp;jsessionid=kzua-46TfLTk8Wx5RvIXYH7qDg-FvpRRH7spY_Tr2fkgDe2iFV3gs!-1348758053 (accessed November 28, 2018)

22. *Construction and Maintenance: Looking forward, national summary* (2018, January), Buildforce Canada, accessed November 28, 2018, from http://www.buildforce.ca/en/system/files/products/2018_National_Summary_Constr_Maint_Looking_Forward.pdf

23. Bernier, L. (2016, March 7), Lessons to be learned in mass recruitment, *Canadian HR Reporter.*

24. Nursing careers (n.d.), Government of Canada, accessed November 28, 2018, from http://www.hc-sc.gc.ca/fniah-spnia/services/nurs-infirm/empl/profil-eng.php

25. Leadem, R. (2017, November 6), The 15 tech companies with the highest signing bonuses, *Entrepreneur,* accessed November 28, 2018, from https://www.entrepreneur.com/slideshow/304043

26. McDonald's FAQs (n.d.), *McDonald's Careers* website, accessed November 28, 2018, from https://corporate.mcdonalds.com/mcd/corporate_careers2/benefits/highlights_of_what_we_offer/balance_work_and_life.html

27. Cain, A. (2017, November 17), 8 unbelievable perks that come with working for Google, *Business Insider,* accessed November 28, 2018, from https://www.businessinsider.com/google-employee-best-perks-benefits-2017-11

28. Kang, S. K., DeCelles, K. A., Tilcsik, A., and Jun, S. (2016), Whitened resumés: Race and self-presentation in the labor market, *Administrative Science Quarterly, 61,* 469–502.

29. Giang, V., and Lockhart, J. (2012, May 7), BUSTED: This is what happened to 10 executives who lied about their resumes, *Business Insider,* accessed November 28, 2018, from https://www.businessinsider.com/9-people-who-were-publicly-shamed-for-lying-on-their-resumes-2012-5#the-ceo-of-a-major-software-firm-lied-about-getting-an-mba-from-stanford-the-companys-stock-dove-when-the-truth-surfaced-9.

30. E-mail is now the preferred way to receive resumes (2000, July), *HR Focus, 77*(7), p. 8.

31. Canada's top 100 employers (2012), *Canada Visa,* accessed November 28, 2018, from https://www.canadavisa.com/canada-immigration-discussion-board/threads/canadas-top-100-employers-2012.85113//

32. Lindzon, J. (2014, September 8), Why is our great tech talent leaving the country? *The Globe and Mail.*

33. Kreissl, B. (2015, March 10), How effective are employee referral programs? *Canadian HR Reporter.*

34. Dineen, B., Ling, J., Ash, S., and DelVecchio, D. (2007), Aesthetic properties and message customization: Navigating the dark side of web recruitment, *Journal of Applied Psychology, 92*(2), pp. 356–372.

35. Breaugh, J. (2012), Recruiting and attracting talent: A guide to understanding and managing the recruitment process, *SHRM Foundation's Effective Practice Guidelines Series,* pp. 1–43.

36. Saks, A. M., and Uggerslev, K. L. (2010), Sequential and combined effects of recruitment information on applicant attraction, *Journal of Business and Psychology, 25,* pp. 351–365.

37. Breaugh, J. (2009), Employee recruitment: Current knowledge and important areas for future research, *Human Resource Management Review, 18,* pp. 103–118; Saks, A. M. (2005), The impracticality of recruitment research, in A. Evers, O. Smit-Voskuyl, and N. Anderson (Eds.), *Handbook of Personnel Selection,* Oxford, UK: Basil Blackwell, pp. 47–72.

38. Santora, M. (2008, March 3), To recruit caseworkers, a dose of reality, *New York Times,* p. B3; Mooney, J. (2008, April 20), The faces of those who knock on difficult doors, *New York Times,* p. B1.

39. Kanar, A. M., Collins, C. J., and Bell, B. S. (2015), Changing an unfavorable employer reputation: The roles of recruitment message-type and familiarity with employer, *Journal of Applied Social Psychology, 45*(9), pp. 509–521, accessed November 28, 2018, from https://scholar.google.ca/scholar?oi=bibs&cluster=17355287522975962504&btnI=1&hl=en

40. Kang, S. K., DeCelles, K. A., Tilcsik, A., and Jun, S. (2016), Whitened résumés: Race and self-presentation in the labor market, *Administrative Science Quarterly, 61*(3), pp. 469–502; Gaucher, D., Friesen, J., and Kay, A. C. (2011), Evidence that gendered wording in job advertisements exists and sustains gender inequality, *Journal of Personality and Social Psychology, 101*(1), pp. 109–128.

41. Breaugh, J. (2012), Recruiting and attracting talent: A guide to understanding and managing the recruitment process, *SHRM Foundation's Effective Practice Guidelines Series,* pp. 1–43.

42. Snell, A. (2001, February 26), Best practices for Web site recruiting, *Canadian HR Reporter,* p. G7.

43. Smedley, K. (2016, August 8), Does Pokemon GO game reveal future of graduate recruitment? *Canadian HR Reporter.*

44. Young, L. (2017, November 13), City of Edmonton uses podcasts in recruitment (National HR Awards), *Canadian HR Reporter.*

45. Dobson, S. (2010, April 5), Recruitment technology evolving, *Canadian HR Reporter,* p. 14.

46. Klie, S. (2005, December 19), Lights, camera and recruitment, *Canadian HR Reporter,* p. 1.

47. Swartz, M. (1997, June 2), Jobs are online: What about job seekers? *Canadian HR Reporter,* p. 21.

48. Freedman, A. (2002, March 6), The Web worldwide, *Human Resource Executive,* pp. 44–48.

49. Kraichy, D., and Chapman, D. (2014), Tailoring web-based recruiting messages: Individual differences in the persuasiveness of affective and cognitive messages, *Journal of Business and Psychology, 29,* pp. 253–268.

50. Allen, D. G., Biggane, J. E., Otondo, R., and Van Scotter, J. (2013), Reactions to recruitment web sites: Visual and verbal attention, attraction, and intentions to pursue employment, *Journal of Business and Psychology, 28*(3), pp. 263–285.

51. Jones, D., Willness, C., and Madey, S. (2014), Why are job seekers attracted by corporate social performance? Experimental and field tests of three signal-based mechanisms, *Academy of Management Journal, 57,* pp. 383–404.

52. Walker, H. J., Feild, H. S., Bernerth, J. B., and Becton, J. B. (2012), Diversity cues on recruitment websites: Investigating the effects on job seekers' information processing, *Journal of Applied Psychology, 97*(1), pp. 214–224, accessed from http://dx.doi.org/10.1037/a0025847

53. Crisp, D. (2008, July 14), Highlights from the HRPS global conference, *Canadian HR Reporter,* p. 11.

54. Grensing-Pophal, L. (2013, September 9), Which is best For HR consultants—LinkedIn or Google+? *SHRM,* accessed November 28, 2018, from https://blog.shrm.org/trends/which-is-best-for-hr-consultants-linkedin-or-google

55. Maurer, R. (2018, April 23), Screening candidates' social media may lead to TMI, discrimination claims, *SHRM,* accessed November 28, 2018, from https://www.shrm.org/resourcesandtools/hr-topics/talent-acquisition/pages/screening-social-media-discrimination-claims.aspx.

56. Employment and Social Development Canada website, accessed November 28, 2018, from https://www.canada.ca/en/employment-social-development.html

57. *Government of Canada Services for You,* Catalogue No. PF4-2/2000, Minister of Public Works and Government Services, 2000.

58. Kusch, L. (2014, August 22), Headhunter hired to fill physician vacancies: Eastern health authority counting on results, *Winnipeg Free Press,* accessed November 28, 2018, from http://www.winnipegfreepress.com/local/headhunter-hired-to-fill-physician-vacancies-272262331.html

59. Kreissl, B. (2010, October 4), Problems with employee referrals, *Canadian HR Reporter,* p. 34.

60. Curtis, A. (2011, May 23), Filling those niche roles, *Canadian HR Reporter,* p. 17; Benefits to using specialty recruitment firms (2011, May 23), *Canadian HR Reporter,* p. 17.

61. Pachner, J. (2014, July 29), Canada's elite headhunters face a daunting—and key—question: As the sector booms, is it better to be big or nimble? *Perry-Martel International,* accessed November 28, 2018, from https://perrymartel.com/articles/inside-tumultous-world-executive-recruiting/.

62. Liegel, O. (2016), How do executive search firms get paid? *Quora,* accessed November 28, 2018, from https://www.quora.com/How-do-executive-search-firms-get-paid

63. Dobson, S. (2015, September 21), Video interviews advance Loblaw's on-campus recruitment (National HR Awards), *Canadian HR Reporter.*

64. Turban, D. (2001), Organizational attractiveness as an employer on college campuses: An examination of the applicant population, *Journal of Vocational Behavior, 58,* pp. 293–312; Cable, D., and Yu, T. (Eds.) (2013), *The Oxford Handbook of Recruitment;* Top 5 best practices for information sessions (n.d.), *Haskayne Career Connections,* University of Calgary, accessed November 28, 2018, from http://haskaynecareerconnections.wordpress.com/category/campus-recruitment-best-practices/

65. Best practices for campus recruitment centres, *NACE,* accessed November 3, 2018, from http://www.naceweb.org/KnowledgeCenter.aspx?fid=786&menuID=88&ispub=False&nodetype=3&navurl=

66. Laurie, N., and Laurie, M. (2000, January 17), No holds barred in fight for students to fill internship programs, *Canadian HR Reporter,* p. 15.

67. Dobson, S. (2010, September 20), Staying in touch with alumni networks, *Canadian HR Reporter,* pp. 19–22.

68. Leonard, B. (2013, December 20), Hiring vets the right way, *SHRM Articles,* accessed November 28, 2018, from http://www.shrm.org/hrdisciplines/staffingmanagement/articles/pages/hiring-vets-the-right-way.aspx

69. Hemmadi, M. (2015, March 16), The freelance economy prompts the rise of a new kind of temp agency, *Canadian Business, 88,* pp.14–16, accessed November 28, 2018, from http://www.canadianbusiness.com/innovation/the-new-temp-agency/

70. About us (n.d.), *Adecco,* accessed November 28, 2018, from https://www.adecco.ca/en-ca/about-adecco-staffing/

71. Kerr, A. (2004, June 30), Accounting firm makes sure to stay in touch with past staff, *The Globe and Mail,* p. C1.

72. McCord, P. (2018, January–February), How to hire, *Harvard Business Review,* accessed November 28, 2018, from https://hbr.org/2018/01/how-to-hire

73. P4E Career Fair 2018, accessed February 18, 2018, from https://www.partners4employment.ca/home.htm

74. Giving job fairs a fair shot (2008, November 17), *Canadian HR Reporter,* p. 21.

75. Silliker, A. (2012, May 7), More firms hiring contract workers, *Canadian HR Reporter,* accessed November 28, 2018, from http://www.hrreporter.com/articleview/13016-more-firms-hiring-contract-workers

76. Moffat, A. (2009, May 4), The line between employees and temps, *Canadian HR Reporter,* pp. 18–19.

77. Heneman, H., Judge, T., Smith, V., and Summers, R. (2010), *Staffing Organizations* (2nd ed.), Canada: McGraw-Hill Ryerson.

78. Dobson, S. (2015, August 10), Interview process getting longer, *Canadian HR Reporter.*

CHAPTER 6

1. Wright, D. (2014, November 10), *Tell Stories, Get Hired: Innovative Strategies to Land Your Next Job and Advance Your Career,* WCS Publishers.

2. Gee, K. (2017, June 26), In Unilever's radical hiring experiment, resumes are out, algorithms are in, *Fox Business,* accessed November 28, 2018, from http://www.foxbusiness.com/features/in-unilevers-radical-hiring-experiment-resumes-are-out-algorithms-are-in

3. Collins, C. (2007, March), *Research report on phase 5 of Cornell University/Gevity Institute Study: Human resource management practices and firm performance in small businesses: A look at differences across industries* (CAHRS Working Paper #07-10), Ithaca, NY: Cornell University, School of Industrial and Labor Relations, Center for Advanced Human Resource Studies, accessed November 28, 2018,

from http://digitalcommons.ilr.cornell.edu/cahrswp/465

4. Valpy, M. (2006, February 27), Human-rights victory brings little relief, *The Globe and Mail*, p. A6.

5. Petroleum Labour Market Information (n.d.), *PSAC*, accessed November 28, 2018, from https://www.psac.ca/leadership/petroleum-hr-council-projects/

6. Schmidt, J. A., Chapman, D. S., and Jones, D. A. (2015), Does emphasizing different types of person-environment fit in online job ads influence application behavior and applicant quality? Evidence from a field experiment, *Journal of Business and Psychology, 30,* 267–282, 10.1007/s10869-014-9353-x

7. Dobson, S. (2015, August 10), Rewording the job ad, *Canadian HR Reporter.*

8. Brienza, L. (2018, January 2), 5 reasons why an applicant tracking system makes sense, *Canadian HR Reporter.*

9. Kreissl, B. (2017, October 2), So many job applicants, so little time, *Canadian HR Reporter.*

10. Mann, S. L., and Chowhan, J. (2011, December), Selection practices in Canadian firms: An empirical investigation, *International Journal of Selection and Assessment, 19,* pp. 435–437.

11. Society for Human Resource Management Research (2016, April 18), *Talent acquisition: Selection,* accessed November 28, 2018, from https://www.shrm.org/hr-today/trends-and-forecasting/research-and-surveys/Documents/Talent-Acquisition-Selection.pdf

12. Gulati, A. (2015, February 26), The hidden benefits of employer branding, *SHRM Articles,* accessed November 28, 2018, from http://www.shrm.org/hrdisciplines/staffingmanagement/articles/pages/benefits-employer-branding.aspx

13. Allen, D. G. (2008), Retaining talent: A guide to analyzing and managing employee turnover, *SHRM Foundation's Effective Practice Guidelines Series;* Hom, P. W., and Griffeth, R. W. (1995), *Employee Turnover,* Cincinnati, OH: South-Western College Publishing.

14. Allen, D. G. (2008), Retaining talent: A guide to analyzing and managing employee turnover, *SHRM Foundation's Effective Practice Guidelines Series.*

15. Hansell, S. (2007, January 3), Google answer to filling jobs is an algorithm, *NY Times,* downloaded November 28, 2018, from http://www.nytimes.com/2007/01/03/technology/03google.html

16. Catano, V. M., Wieser, W. H., Hackett, R. D., and Methot, L. L. (2010), *Recruitment and Selection in Canada* (4th ed.), Canada: Nelson Education Ltd; Heneman III, H., Judge, T., Smith, V., and Summers, R. (2010), *Staffing Organizations* (2nd Canadian ed.), McGraw-Hill Ryerson.

17. Hunter, J. E., and Hunter, R. F. (1984), Validity and utility of alternative predictors of job performance, *Psychological Bulletin, 96,* pp. 72–98; Allen, D. G. (2008), Retaining talent: A guide to analyzing and managing employee turnover, *SHRM Foundation's Effective Practice Guidelines Series.*

18. Brown, D. (2004, October 11), Waterloo forced to fire top bureaucrat weeks after hiring, *Canadian HR Reporter*, p. 3.

19. U.S. Equal Employment Opportunity Commission (2006, November 20), *Appeals court upholds EEOC sex discrimination claim against Dial.*

20. Canadian Human Rights Commission (2007, March), *Guide to screening and selection in employment,* accessed November 28, 2018, from http://www.chrc-ccdp.ca/eng/content/guide-screening-and-selection-employment

21. Krajewski, H., and Goffin, R. (2009, August), Choosing the right personality test for the job, *Canadian HR Reporter, 22,* p. 14.

22. Judge, T. A., and Zapata, C. P. (2015), The person-situation debate revisited: Effect of situation strength and trait activation on the validity of the big five personality traits in predicting job performance, *Academy of Management Journal, 58,* pp. 1149–1179.

23. Judge, T. A., and Zapata, C. P. (2015), The person-situation debate revisited: Effect of situation strength and trait activation on the validity of the big five personality traits in predicting job performance, *Academy of Management Journal, 58,* pp. 1149–1179; Blickle, G., Wendel, S., and Ferris, G. R. (2010), Political skill as moderator of personality–Job performance relationships in socioanalytic theory: Test of the getting ahead motive in automobile sales, *Journal of Vocational Behavior, 76,* pp. 326–335; Methot, J. R., Lepine, J. A., Podsakoff, N. P., and Christian, J. S. (2015), Are workplace friendships a mixed blessing? Exploring tradeoffs of multiplex relationships and their associations with job performance, *Personnel Psychology,* pp. 1–45.

24. Griffin, B., and Hesketh, B. (2004), Why openness to experience is not a good predictor of job performance, *International Journal of Selection and Assessment, 12,* pp. 243–251; Timmerman, T. A. (2004), Relationships between NEO-PI-R personality measures and job performance ratings of inbound call center employees, *Applied Human Resource Management Research, 9,* pp. 35–38.

25. Rogelberg, S. J. (2007), Personality assessment, *Encyclopedia of Industrial and Organizational Psychology,* Thousand Oaks, CA: Sage Publications, pp. 612–615.

26. Salgado, J. F., Anderson, N., Moscoso, S., Bertua, C., de Fruyt, F., and Rolland, J. P. (2003), A meta-analytic study of general mental ability validity for different occupations in the European Community, *Journal of Applied Psychology, 88,* pp. 1068–1081; Ohme, M., and Zacher, H. (2015), Job performance ratings: The relative importance of mental ability, conscientiousness, and career adaptability, *Journal of Vocational Behavior,* doi: 10.1016/j.jvb.2015.01.00

27. NFL combine 2012: 10 of the most pathetic Wonderlic scores ever (2012, February 14), *Bleacher Report,* accessed November 28, 2018, from http://bleacherreport.com/articles/1065284-nfl-combine-2012-10-most-patheticwonderlic-scores-ever

28. Murphy, K. R., Cronin, B. E., and Tam, A. P. (2003), Controversy and consensus regarding the use of cognitive ability testing in organizations, *Journal of Applied Psychology, 88,* pp. 660–671; Berry, C. M., and Zhao, P. (2015), Addressing criticisms of existing predictive bias research: Cognitive ability test scores still overpredict African Americans' job performance, *Journal of Applied Psychology, 100,* pp. 162–179.

29. McDaniel, M. A., and Nguyen, N. T. (2001), Situational judgment tests: A review of practice and constructs assessed, *International Journal of Selection and Assessment, 9,* pp. 103–113; Rockstuhl, T., Ang, S., Ng, K.-Y., Lievens, F., and Van Dyne, L. (2015), Putting judging situations into situational judgment tests: Evidence from intercultural multimedia SJTs, *Journal of Applied Psychology, 100*(2), pp. 464–480, accessed November 28, 2018, from http://dx.doi.org/10.1037/a0038098

30. Doerner, W. G., and Nowell, T. (1999), The reliability of the behavioural-personnel assessment device (B-PAD) in selecting police recruits, *Policing: An International Journal of Police Strategies and Management, 22*(3), pp. 343–352.

31. Real Assessment Centre Examples (n.d.), *AssessmentDay Practice Text Experts,* accessed November 28, 2018, from https://www.assessmentday.co.uk/assessmentcentre/real-examples.html

32. Arthur, W., Day, E. A., McNelly, T. L., and Edens, P. S. (2003), A meta-analysis of the criterion-related validity of assessment center dimensions, *Personnel Psychology, 56,* pp. 125–154; Collins, J. M., Schmidt, F. L., Sanchez, K. M., McDaniel, M. A., and Le, H. (2003), Can basic individual differences shed light on the construct meaning of assessment center evaluations? *International Journal of Selection and Assessment, 11,* pp. 17–29.

33. Cook, I. (2012), The gamification of human resources, *Canadian HR Reporter, 25*(2), pp. 31–32; Jackson, S. (2000), Hire top performing managers with performance-based micro assessments, *Canadian HR Reporter, 13*(7), pp. 11–12; Sillup, S.

(1992), Applicant screening cuts turnover costs, *Personnel Journal*, pp. 115–116.

34. Insurance Bureau of Canada (n.d.), Cargo theft, accessed November 28, 2018, from http://www.ibc.ca/on/business/business-crime/cargo-theft

35. Burke, D. (2017, February 16), A company's most costly thieves already have keys to the building, *CBC News*, accessed November 28, 2018, from http://www.cbc.ca/news/canada/nova-scotia/employee-theft-business-loss-money-1.3983773

36. Government of Ontario (2000), *Ontario Employment Standards Act*, accessed November 28, 2018, from http://www.e-laws.gov.on.ca/html/statutes/english/elaws_statutes_00e41_e.htm

37. Sturman, M. C., & Sherwyn, D. (2007). The truth about integrity tests: The validity and utility of integrity testing for the hospitality industry [Electronic article]. Cornell Hospitality Report, 7(15), 6-13. More information about the Stanton Survey can be found at https://www.plotkingroup.com/search/?SearchTerm=Stanton+Survey (accessed November 28, 2018).

38. Van Iddekinge, C., Roth, P., Raymark, P., and Odle-Dusseau, H. (2012, May), The criterion-related validity of integrity tests: An updated meta-analysis, *Journal of Applied Psychology, 97*(3), pp. 499–530.

39. Furnham, A. (2015, August 11), Can you really test someone for integrity? *Fortune*, accessed November 28, 2018, from http://fortune.com/2015/08/11/hiring-integrity-test/

40. Popovich, P., and Wanous, J. P. (1982, October), The realistic job preview as a persuasive communication, *Academy of Management Review*, p. 571.

41. Breaugh, J. A. (2009), Recruiting and attracting talent: A guide to understanding and managing the recruitment process, *SHRM Foundation's Effective Practice Guidelines Series;* Earnest, D. R., Allen, D. G., and Landis, R. S. (2011), Mechanism linking realistic job previews with turnover: A meta-analytic path analysis, *Personnel Psychology, 64,* pp. 865–897.

42. Kotlyar, I., and Abelman, R. (2003, December), Simulation turns recruitment into a two-way street: Applicants can get a better sense of the job while the company gets a sampling of how the candidate will perform, *Canadian HR Reporter, 16*(21), p. G6.

43. Dinesen,D. (2018, April 5), Notable trends from BackCheck, accessed November 28, 2018, from http://www.backcheck.net/notable-trends-from-backcheck.htm

44. Leggatt, H. (2010, September), Germany bans Facebook as employee screening tool, *BizReport*.

45. Silliker, A. (2012, March 31), Tread carefully with social media checks, Human Resources Institute of Alberta.

46. Shiffman, L. (2007, November 12), Employers use Facebook information when hiring, *North by Northwestern,* accessed November 28, 2018, from http://www.northbynorthwestern.com/story/employers-use-facebook-information-when-hiring/

47. Moffatt, A. (2008, August 11), The danger of digging too deep, *Canadian HR Reporter*, p. 5.

48. Silliker, A. (2017, April 1), Are you hiring your next injury? *Canadian Occupational Safety,* accessed November 28, 2018, from http://www.cos-mag.com/occupational-hygiene/33142-are-you-hiring-your-next-injury/

49. Silliker, A. (2017, April 1), Are you hiring your next injury? *Canadian Occupational Safety,* accessed November 28, 2018, from http://www.cos-mag.com/occupational-hygiene/33142-are-you-hiring-your-next-injury/

50. Substance abuse top health and safety risk in sawmills: Both workers, managers worry about dangers of alcohol and drug use (2017, December 22), *Canadian Occupational Safety Magazine,* accessed November 28, 2018, from https://www.cos-mag.com/article/35493-substance-abuse-top-health-and-safety-risk-in-sawmills/.

51. Health Canada (2012), *Canadian Alcohol and Drug Use Monitoring Survey: Summary of Results for 2012,* accessed November 28, 2018, from https://www.canada.ca/en/health-canada/services/health-concerns/drug-prevention-treatment/drug-alcohol-use-statistics/canadian-alcohol-drug-use-monitoring-survey-summary-results-2012.html.

52. Government of Canada (n.d.), Substance use in the workplace, *Canadian Centre for Occupational Health and Safety,* accessed November 28, 2018, from http://www.ccohs.ca/oshanswers/psychosocial/substance.html

53. *Milazzo v Autocar Connaisseur* (2003) 47 C.H.R.R. D/468. More recently, the Tribunal followed this finding in *Dennis v Eskasoni Band Council* (September 2008); *Alberta (Human Rights and Citizenship Commission) v Kellogg Brown & Root* (2007) ABCA 426. Leave to appeal denied by SCC May 29, 2008.

54. Canadian Human Rights Commission Policy on Alcohol and Drug Testing (2009, October), *Canadian Human Rights Commission.*

55. Warkentin, J. (2008, April 17), Kellogg Brown & Root: Discrimination and pre-employment drug testing, *The Court,* Osgoode Hall Law School, York University, accessed November 28, 2018, from http://www.thecourt.ca/kellogg-brown-root-discrimination-and-pre-employment-drug-testing/

56. Rubin, J., and Sultan, S. (2005, March 9), Drug and alcohol testing: Where are we now? *Canadian HR Reporter*, p. 15.

57. Fleming, J. (2017, September 4), Managing marijuana, *Canadian HR Reporter.*

58. Adapted from Das, H. (2006), *Recruitment, Selection and Deployment,* Toronto: Pearson Education, p. 320.

59. Whitten, D. (2005, June 20), Steering clear of contract landmines, *Canadian HR Reporter*, p. 5.

60. Judge, T., Higgins, C., and Cable, D. (2000), The employment interview: A review of recent research and recommendations for future research, *Human Resource Management Review, 10,* pp. 383–406; Conway, J. M., Jako, R. A., and Goodman, D. F. (1995), A meta-analysis of interrater and internal consistency reliability of selection interviews, *Journal of Applied Psychology, 80,* pp. 565–579.

61. Dobson, S. (2017, May 15), Feds try to blank out bias, *Canadian HR Reporter.*

62. Klie, S. (2008, April), Biases creep into interviews, *Canadian HR Reporter*, p. 2.

63. Gardiner, H., and Hackett, R. (1997), Employment interviewing: A review and analysis of Canadian human rights cases, Jacques Barrette (ed.), *ASAC 1997 (Human Resource Division) Proceedings, 18*(9), pp. 46–55.

64. Canadian Human Rights Commission (2007), *Guide to Screening and Selection in Employment,* accessed November 28, 2018, from https://www.chrc-ccdp.gc.ca/eng/content/guide-screening-and-selection-employment

65. Survey by Professors David Zweig and Derek Chapman, quoted by Shannon Klie (2005, December 19), Armchair psychology doesn't make for good hiring choices, *Canadian HR Reporter*, p. 3.

66. Maurer., R. (2017, May 16), Digital video upgrades the hiring experience, *Society for Human Resource Management,* accessed November 28, 2018, from https://www.shrm.org/resourcesandtools/hr-topics/talent-acquisition/pages/digital-video-upgrades-the-hiring-experience.aspx.

67. Chapman, D. S., Uggerslev, K. L., and Webster, J. (2003, December), Applicant reactions to technology-mediated interviews: A field investigation, *Journal of Applied Psychology, 88,* pp. 944–953.

68. Klie, S. (2008, April), Biases creep into interviews, *Canadian HR Reporter, 21,* p. 8.

69. Canadian Human Rights Commission (2007, March), *Guide to Screening and Selection in Employment,* accessed November 28, 2018, from https://www.chrc-ccdp.gc.ca/eng/content/guide-screening-and-selection-employment

70. Employers know within 5 minutes if candidate good fit (2015, March 6), *Canadian HR Reporter,* accessed November 28,

2018, from http://www.hrreporter.com/articleview/23713-employers-know-within-5-minutes-if-candidate-good-fit#sthash.SOgMlUrq.dpuf

71. Hunter, J. E., and Hunter, R. F. (1984), Validity and utility of alternative predictors of job performance, *Psychological Bulletin, 96,* pp. 72–98; see also Schwind, H. F. (1987), How well do interviews predict future performance? *The Human Resource,* June–July, pp. 19–20.

72. Cascio, W. (2006), *Managing Human Resources* (7th ed.), New York: McGraw-Hill Irwin, p. 199.

73. Hunter, J. E., and Schmidt, F. L. (1983), Quantifying the effects of psychological interventions on employee job performance and work force productivity, *American Psychologist, 38,* pp. 473–478; see also Hunter, J. E., and Schmidt, F. L. (1982), Fitting people to jobs: The impact of personnel selection on national productivity, in Marvin D. Dunnette and E.A. Fleishman (Eds.), *Human Capability Assessment,* Hillsdale, NJ: Lawrence Erlbaum Associates.

74. Dunnette, M. D. (1966), *Personnel Selection and Placement,* Belmont, CA: Wadsworth.

75. Hunter, J. E., and Schmidt, F. L. (1982), Fitting people to jobs: The impact of personnel selection on national productivity, in Marvin D. Dunnette and E.A. Fleishman, (Eds.), *Human Capability Assessment,* Hillsdale, NJ: Lawrence Erlbaum Associates; Schmidt, F. L., Hunter, J. E., McKenzie, R. C., and Muldrow, T. W. (1979), Impact of valid selection procedures on work force productivity, *Journal of Applied Psychology, 64,* pp. 609–626; Alexander, R. B., and Barrick, M. R. (1987), Estimating the standard error of projected dollar gains in utility analysis, *Journal of Applied Psychology, 72,* pp. 463–474; Hunter, J. E. (1981, January 15), *The Economic Benefits of Personnel Selection Using Ability Tests: A State of the Art Review Including a Detailed Analysis of the Dollar Benefit of U.S. Employment Service Placement and a Critique of the Low Cutoff Method of Test Use,* Washington, DC: U.S. Employment Service, U.S. Department of Labor; Schmidt, F. L., Hunter, J. E., and Pearlman, K. (1982), Assessing the economic impact of personnel programs on work force productivity, *Personnel Psychology, 35*(3), pp. 333–343; Cascio, W. F. (1982), *Costing Human Resources: The Financial Impact of Behaviour in Organizations,* Boston, MA: Kent Publishing; Cascio, W. F., and Silbey, V. (1979), Utility of the assessment centre as a selection device, *Journal of Applied Psychology, 64,* pp. 107–118; Cascio, W. F., and Philips, N. F. (1979), Performance testing: A rose among thorns? *Personnel Psychology, 32,* pp. 751–766.

76. Adapted from Cascio, W. (2006), *Managing Human Resources* (7th ed.), New York: McGraw-Hill Irwin, p. 199.

77. Hunter, J. E., and Schmidt, F. L. (1983), Quantifying the effects of psychological interventions on employee job performance and work force productivity, *American Psychologist, 38,* pp. 474–477.

78. See, for example, Hunter, J. E., and Schmidt, F. L. (1982), Fitting people to jobs: The impact of personnel selection on national productivity, in Marvin D. Dunnette and E.A. Fleishman (Eds.), *Human Capability Assessment,* Hillsdale, NJ: Lawrence Erlbaum Associates; Schmidt, F. L., Hunter, J. E., McKenzie, R. C., and Muldrow, T. W. (1979), Impact of valid selection procedures on work force productivity, *Journal of Applied Psychology, 64,* pp. 609–626; Cascio, W. (2006), *Managing Human Resources* (7th ed.), New York: McGraw-Hill Irwin; Schmidt, F. L., Hunter, J. E., and Pearlman, K. (1982), Assessing the economic impact of personnel programs on work force productivity, *Personnel Psychology, 35*(3), pp. 333–343. See also Cranshaw, S. F. (1986), The utility of employment testing for clerical/administrative trades in the Canadian military, *Canadian Journal of Administrative Sciences, 3*(2), pp. 376–385; Cranshaw, S. F., Alexander, R. A., Weisner, W. H., and Barrick, M. R. (1987), Incorporating risk into selection utility: Two models of sensitivity analysis and risk simulation, *Organizational Behaviour and Decision Processes, 40,* pp. 270–286.

79. Dunnette, M. D. (1966), *Personnel Selection and Placement,* Belmont, CA: Wadsworth, p. 174.

80. Taylor, H. C., and Russell, J. T. (1939), The relationship of validity coefficients to the practical effectiveness of tests in selection: Discussion and tables, *Journal of Applied Psychology, 23,* pp. 565–578.

CHAPTER 7

1. Bauer (2010), Onboarding new employees: Maximizing success, SHRM Foundation's Effective Practice Guidelines Series.

2. Hom, P., Lee, T. W., Shaw, J. D. and Hausknecht, J. P. (2017), 100 years of turnover research, *Journal of Applied Psychology, 102,* pp. 530–545; Saks, A., and Gruman, J. A. (2012), Getting newcomers on board: A review of socialization practices and introduction to socialization resources theory, in Wanberg (Ed.), *The Oxford Handbook of Organizational Socialization,* pp. 27–55, Oxford: Oxford University Press.

3. Koenig, M. E. D. (2018, January 15), What is KM? Knowledge management explained, *KMWorld,* accessed November 28, 2018, from http://www.kmworld.com/Articles/Editorial/What-Is/What-is-KM-Knowledge-Management-Explained-122649.aspx

4. Yerema, R., and Leung, K. (2011, October 6), *Employer Review: EllisDon Corporation,* accessed from http://www.eluta.ca/top-employer-ellisdon

5. Cotsman, S., and Hall, C. (2018, January), *Learning Cultures Lead the Way: Learning and Development Outlook* (14th ed.), The Conference Board of Canada.

6. Association for Talent Development (2014), *2014: State of the Industry,* accessed November 28, 2018, from https://www.td.org/publications/research-Reports/2014/2014-State-of-the-Industry

7. Cotsman, S., and Hall, C. (2018, January), *Learning Cultures Lead the Way: Learning and Development Outlook,* (14th ed.), The Conference Board of Canada.

8. Hall, C. (2018, March 7), Learning and development outlook: Stay ahead of the curve—Focus on strengthening your learning culture, *The Conference Board of Canada,* accessed November 28, 2018, from http://www.conferenceboard.ca/e-library/abstract.aspx?did=9350

9. Vander Wier, M. (2018, March 1), Building a learning nation, *Canadian HR Reporter.*

10. Aguinis, H., and Kraiger, K. (2009), Benefits of training and development for individuals and teams, organizations, and society, *Annual Review of Psychology, 60,* pp. 451–474; Aguinis, H., and O'Boyle, E. (2014), Star performers in twenty-first century organizations, *Personnel Psychology, 67*(2), pp. 313–350; Arthur Jr., W., Bennett Jr., W., Edens, P. S., and Bell, S. T. (2003), Effectiveness of training in organizations: A meta-analysis of design and evaluation features, *Journal of Applied Psychology, 88,* pp. 234–245.

11. Vloeberghs, D., Pepermans, R., and Thielemans, K. (2005), High-potential development policies: An empirical study among Belgian companies, *Journal of Management Development, 24,* pp. 546–558; Maurer, T. J. (2002, March), Employee learning and development orientation: Toward an integrative model of involvement in continuous learning, *Human Resource Development Review, 1*(1), pp. 9–44.

12. Bauer, T. (2010), Onboarding new employees: Maximizing success, SHRM Foundation's Effective Practice Guidelines Series.

13. Canada ranks 4th globally for highest employee turnover (2018, March 15), *Canadian HR Reporter.*

14. Klein, H. J., Polin, B., and Sutton, K. L. (2015), Specific onboarding practices for the socialization of new employees, *International Journal of Selection and Assessment, 23,* pp. 263–283, accessed from https://doi.org/10.1111/ijsa.12113

15. Klein, H. J., and Polin, B. (2012), Are organizations on board with best practices onboarding? in Wanberg (Ed.), *The Oxford Handbook of Organizational Socialization:* 267–287, Oxford: Oxford University Press.

16. Conference Board of Canada (2011, August), Bringing new hires up to speed: How structured onboarding can help: Briefing.

17. Merhar, C. (2016, February 4), Employee retention—The real cost of losing an employee, *PeopleKeep,* accessed March 22, 2018, from https://www.peoplekeep.com/blog/bid/312123/employee-retention-the-real-cost-of-losing-an-employee

18. Canada ranks 4th globally for highest employee turnover (2018, March 16), *Canadian HR Reporter,* accessed November 28, 2018, from https://www.hrreporter.com/culture-and-engagement/36271-canada-ranks-4th-globally-for-highest-employee-turnover/

19. Royal Bank of Canada (2018), *RBC at a glance: Q1/2018,* accessed March 18, 2018, from http://www.rbc.com

20. Gutierrez, K. (2016, May 6), The true cost of not providing employee training, *Shift Disruptive Elearning,* accessed November 28, 2018, from https://www.shiftelearning.com/blog/the-true-cost-of-not-providing-employee-training

21. Heneman III, H., Judge, T., Smith, V., and Summers, R. (2010), *Staffing Organizations* (2nd Canadian ed.), Toronto: McGraw-Hill Ryerson, 2010.

22. Desuyo, T. (n.d.), How to shorten new hire time to productivity with 90+day onboarding, *Atrivity,* accessed November 28, 2018, from https://blog.atrivity.com/how-to-shorten-new-hire-time-to-productivity-with-90day-onboarding

23. Dujay, J. (2017, November 13), Strong employee engagement good for Vision Critical's bottom line (National HR Awards, Winner: Best Employee Engagement Program), *Canadian HR Reporter.*

24. Dobson, S. (2011, March 28), Mix of online, face-to-face programs ensure success in orientation, *Canadian HR Reporter, 24*(6), pp. 13, 17.

25. Korte, R. (2010, February), First, get to know them: A relational view of organizational socialization, *Human Resource Development International, 13*(1), pp. 27–43.

26. Vander Wier, M. (2018, April 6), $15 minimum wage challenges retailers, *Canadian HR Reporter.*

27. Citizenship and Immigration Canada (2015), *Immigration Overview: Permanent residents by category and source area,* accessed November 28, 2018, from https://open.canada.ca/data/en/dataset/2fbb56bd-eae7-4582-af7d-a197d185fc93?_ga=2.96482975.1678281054.1518800815-781687463.1495736649

28. Aguinis, H., and Kraiger, K. (2009), Benefits of training and development for individuals and teams, organizations, and society, *Annual Review of Psychology, 60,* 451–474.

29. Gutierrez, K. (2016, July 28), Training Millenials: 7 things you should do right now, *Shift Disruptive eLearning,* accessed November 28, 2018, from https://www.shiftelearning.com/blog/training-millennials-elearning

30. Dobson, S. (2011), Mix of online, face-to-face programs ensure success in orientation, *Canadian HR Reporter, 24*(6), pp. 13–17.

31. DiGirolamo, J. (2015), Coaching for professional development, *SHRM-SIOP Science of HR White Paper Series.*

32. Cotsman, S., and Hall, C. (2018, January), *Learning Cultures Lead the Way: Learning and Development Outlook* (14th ed.), The Conference Board of Canada.

33. Mest, E. (2016, May 3), Best Western invests in virtual reality training, *Hotel Management,* accessed November 28, 2018, from https://www.hotelmanagement.net/operate/best-western-invests-virtual-reality-training

34. RCMP (2018), RCMP Academy looking for contract scenario actors, accessed November 28, 2018, from http://www.rcmp-grc.gc.ca/depot/ctp-pfc/actors-needed-acteurs-recherches-eng.htm

35. Harris, P. (2011, October), Learning you can bank on, *T+D, 65*(10), pp. 40–42.

36. Howard, D. (2016, November/December), Innovation in educational technology, *Trends: Training Industry Magazine,* accessed November 28, 2018, from http://www.nxtbook.com/nxtbooks/trainingindustry/tiq_20161112/index.php#/24

37. Fink, C. (2017, October 30), VR training next generation of workers, *Forbes,* accessed November 28, 2018, from https://www.forbes.com/sites/charliefink/2017/10/30/vr-training-next-generation-of-workers/#6df4f77164f5

38. Fink, C. (2017, October 30), VR training next generation of workers, *Forbes,* accessed November 28, 2018, from https://www.forbes.com/sites/charliefink/2017/10/30/vr-training-next-generation-of-workers/#6df4f77164f5

39. Gronstedt, A. (2008), All aboard! The web 3D train is leaving the station, *T+D,* pp. 22–24.

40. Global Knowledge and Deloitte win gold for training excellence in internal learning (2010, November 23), *Business Wire.*

41. Kosoff, M. (2015, April 9), LinkedIn just bought online learning company Lynda for $1.5 billion, accessed November 28, 2018, from http://www.businessinsider.com/linkedin-buys-lyndacom-for-15-billion-2015-4

42. About us (n.d.), *Udacity,* accessed November 28, 2018, from https://www.udacity.com/us.

43. Moldoveanu, M. (2018, March 1), Education 2.0: The destructive reconstruction of higher learning, *Canadian HR Reporter.*

44. Hewitt, A. (2016, March), *Developing Canada's future workforce: A survey of large private-sector employers,* Ottawa: Business Council of Canada.

45. Costen, W., Johanson, M., and Poisson, D. (2010), The development of quality managers in the hospitality industry: Do employee development programs make cents?" *Journal of Human Resources in Hospitality & Tourism, 9,* pp. 131–141.

46. Dugan, B., and O'Shea, P. G. (2014, February), Leadership development: Growing talent strategically, *SHRM-SIOP Science of HR While Paper Series.*

47. Tarique, I., and Schuler, R. (2012, September 15), Global talent management literature review, *SHRM Foundation.*

48. Tarique, I., and Schuler, R. S. (2010), Global talent management: Literature review, integrative framework, and suggestions for further research, *Journal of World Business, 45*(2), pp. 122–133; Vaiman, V., Scullion, H., and Collings, D. (2012), Talent management decision making, *Management Decision, 50,* pp. 925–941; Silzer, R., and Church, A. (2009), Identifying and assessing high-potential talent: Current organizational practices, in R. Silzer and B. E. Dowell (Eds), *Strategy Driven Talent Management: A Leadership Imperative,* San Francisco, CA: Jossey-Bass, pp. 213–280.

49. Aguinis, H., and Kraiger, K. (2009), Benefits of training and development for individuals and teams, organizations, and society, *Annual Review of Psychology, 60,* 451–474.

50. Aguinis, H., and O'Boyle, E. (2014), Star performers in twenty-first century organizations, *Personnel Psychology, 67*(2), pp. 313–350; Becker, B. E., Huselid, M. A., and Beatty, R. W. (2009),*The Differentiated Workforce: Transforming Talent into Strategic Impact,* Harvard Business Press.

51. Thunnissen, M., Boselie, P., and Fruytier, B. (2013), Talent management and the relevance of context: Towards a pluralistic approach, *Human Resource Management Review, 23*(4), pp. 326–336; Thornton, III, G. C., Hollenbeck, G. P., and Johnson, S. K. (2010), Selecting leaders: Executives and high potentials, in J. L. Farr and N. T. Tippins (Ed.), *Handbook of Employee Selection,* New York, NY: Routledge/Taylor & Francis Group, pp. 823–840; Tansley, C., and Tietze, S. (2013), Rites of passage through talent management progression stages: An identity work perspective, *The International Journal of Human*

Resource Management, 24, pp. 1799–1815.

52. Brown, P. T. (2010), Having their backs: Improving managers' skills in developing others, *T+D,* pp. 61–64.

53. Wexley, K. N., and Latham, G. P. (2001), *Developing and Training Human Resources in Organizations* (3rd ed.), New York: Prentice Hall.

54. Feloni, R. (2016, February 11), Here's the presentation Google gives employees on how to spot unconscious bias at work, *Business Insider,* accessed November 28, 2018, from http://www.businessinsider.com/google-unconscious-bias-training-presentation-2015-12

55. Thanos, K., and Kourtesopoulou, A. (2008), Human resource training and development: The outdoor management method, *Choregia, 4,* 32–44. doi:10.4127/ch.2008.4.1.32-44

56. Search B.C.'s Top Employers (2012, July), The Great Little Box Company, accessed from http://www.eluta.ca/top-employer-great-little-box-company

57. Dobson, S. (2016, May 30), Despite benefits, many employers are not offering job rotations: Survey, *Canadian HR Reporter.*

58. Finney, R. (2006), Winning Project Teams, white paper.

59. Kirkpatrick, D. L. (1959), Techniques for evaluating training programs, *Journal of the American Society of Training Directors, 13,* pp. 3–9, 21–26.

60. 2017 Training Industry Report (2017), *Training Magazine,* accessed November 28, 2018, from https://trainingmag.com/trgmag-article/2017-training-industry-report/.

61. Wiscombe, J. (2010, December 1), IBM Corp. 2010 WINNER: *Global Outlook,* Resource Library.

62. Akkermans, J., Kubasch, S. (2017), #Trending topics in careers: A review and future research agenda, *Career Development International, 22*(6), pp. 586–627, accessed November 28, 2018, from https://doi.org/10.1108/CDI-08-2017-0143

63. Adekola, B. (2011, May), Career planning and career management as correlates for career development and job satisfaction—A case study of Nigerian bank employees, *Australian Journal of Business and Management Research, 1*(2), pp. 100–112.

64. Petrieglieri, G., Ashford, S., and Wrzesniewski, A. (2018, March–April), Thriving in the gig economy, *Harvard Business Review,* accessed November 18, 2018, from https://hbr.org/2018/03/thriving-in-the-gig-economy

65. Chew, J., and Girardi, A. (2008), Is career management the panacea to retaining vital staff? *International Journal of Management and Marketing Research, 1*(1), pp. 83–98.

66. Swisher, K. (2013, February 22), "Physically Together" : Here's the Internal Yahoo No-Work-From-Home Memo for Remote Workers and Maybe More, accessed November 18, 2018, from http://allthingsd.com/?p=297562&ak_action=printable

67. Albison, C., and Correll, S. (2013, March 13), Benefit of office face time a myth, *CNN,* accessed November 28, 2018, from http://www.cnn.com/2013/03/13/opinion/albison-correll-women-face-time/; Fell, S. S. (2004, April 7), How "Face Time" hurts productivity and why remote work can help, *LinkedIn,* accessed November 28, 2018, from https://www.linkedin.com/pulse/20140407183936-60144-how-face-time-hurts-productivity-and-remote-work-helps; Is job hopping losing its stigma? (2014, December 18), *Cision: PR NewsWire* [Ottawa], accessed November 28, 2018, from https://www.prnewswire.com/news-releases/is-job-hopping-losing-its-stigma-300011719.html.

68. Is job hopping losing its stigma? (2014, December 18), *Cision: PR NewsWire* [Ottawa], accessed November 28, 2018, from https://www.prnewswire.com/news-releases/is-job-hopping-losing-its-stigma-300011719.html.

69. Lee, C. I. S. G., Bosco, F. A., Steel, P., and Uggerslev, K. L. (2017), A metaBUS enabled meta-analysis of career satisfaction, *Career Development International, 22*(5), pp. 565–582, accessed November 18, 2018, from https://doi.org/10.1108/CDI-08-2017-0137

70. Baruch, Y. (2014), The development and validation of a measure for protean career orientation, *The International Journal of Human Resource Management,* doi:10.1080/09585192.2014.896389

71. Proctor & Gamble, P&G Business School (2011), P&G Live Events–Testimonials.

72. Schein, E., and Van Maanen, J. (2013), *Career Anchors: The Changing Nature of Work and Careers Self Assessment* (4th ed.), Wiley.

73. Glass, A. (2007), Understanding generational differences for competitive success, *Industrial and Commercial Training, 39*(2), pp. 98–103.

74. Patagonia (2011), *Environmentalism: What We Do– Environmental Internships,* accessed November 28, 2018, from http://www.patagonia.com/us/patagonia.go?assetid=1963

75. Employee testimonials (n.d.), Concord National, accessed November 28, 2018, from http://concordnational.com/careers/employee-testimonials/.

76. Holland, John. 1973. *Making Vocational Choices: a theory of careers.* (Prentice-Hall). Nota, L., and Soresi, S. (2018), *Counseling and Coaching in Times of Crisis and Transition,* Taylor & Francis.

77. Sampson, J. (2009), Modern and postmodern career theories: The unnecessary divorce, *The Career Development Quarterly,* 51(1), pp. 91–96; Baruch, Y. (2009), *Managing Careers—Theory and Practice,* Essex: Pearson Education Limited; Barnett, B., and Bradley, L. (2007), The impact of organisational support for career development on career satisfaction, *Career Development International,* 12(7), pp. 617–636.

78. Personal communication by the first author with a Ford HR executive at the Cologne plant in Germany.

79. BMO Harris Bank (n.d.), Find your perfect fit, accessed November 28, 2018, from https://bmoharriscareers.com/find-your-perfect-fit/

CHAPTER 8

1. Meyers, J. (2013, March 13), Bill Gates lambasts D.C. dysfunction, *Politico,* accessed on November 28, 2018, from https://www.politico.com/story/2013/03/bill-gates-on-dc-you-dont-run-a-business-like-this-088830

2. Aguinis, H. (2013), *Performance management* (3rd ed.), Upper Saddle River, NJ: Pearson/Prentice Hall.

3. Chancellor, E. (2018, March 19), The pitfalls of managing by measurement, *Canadian HR Reporter.*

4. The pitfalls of managing by measurement (2018, March 19), *Canadian HR Reporter,* accessed October 30, 2018, from http://www.hrreporter.com/columnist/human-resources-guest-blogger/archive/2018/03/19/the-pitfalls-of-managing-by-measurement/

5. DeNisi, A., and Smith, C. E. (2014), Performance appraisal, performance management, and firm-level performance: A review, a proposed model, and new directions for future research, *The Academy of Management Annals, 8*(1), pp. 127–179. doi:10.1080/19416520.2014.873178

6. Miller, S. (2012, May 25), Integrating performance management and rewards at Microsoft, *SHRM,* accessed October 30, 2018, from https://www.shrm.org/resourcesandtools/hr-topics/compensation/pages/rewardsatmicrosoft.aspx

7. Chiodo, S. (2010, December), Objective performance development, *Canadian HR Reporter,* pp. 28, 34.

8. Pulakos, E. P. (2004), *Performance Management: A Roadmap for Developing, Implementing and Evaluating Performance Management Systems,* Alexandria, VA: SHRM Foundation.

9. Mueller Hanson, R. A., and Pulakos, E. (n.d.), Putting the "performance" back in performance management, SHRM-SIOP Science of HR White Paper Series, accessed October 30, 2018, from https://www.shrm.org/hr-today/trends-and-forecasting/special-reports-and-expert-views/

Documents/SHRM-SIOP%20
Performance%20Management.pdf

10. Cooper, D. J., Ezzamel, M., and Qu, S. Q. (2017), Popularizing a management accountant idea: The case of the Balanced Scorecard, *Contemporary Accounting Research, 34*(2), pp. 991–1025. https://doi .org/10.1111/1911-3846.12299

11. Lucco, J. (2017, September 12), A full balanced scorecard example (including 6 templates), *ClearPoint Strategy.com,* accessed November 28, 2018, from https://www .clearpointstrategy.com/full-exhaustive-balanced-scorecard-example/.

12. Dobson, S. (2011, December), Performance reviews valued by employees: Poll, *Canadian HR Reporter, 24,* p. 22.

13. Online Staff (2012, October 16), Compensation practices becoming more formal, rigorous, *SHRM,* accessed November 28, 2018, from https://www .shrm.org/resourcesandtools/hr-topics/ compensation/pages/compensation-salary-incentives.aspx

14. Aguinis, H. (2013), *Performance Management* (3rd ed.), Pearson; Kreissl, B. (2017, May 2), Should performance management be based on objective standards? *Canadian HR Reporter.*

15. Lamothe, C. (2016, November 14), Off target: Are performance reviews missing the mark? *Canadian HR Reporter;* Oppedisano, T. (2017, February 21), Changing gears to get results, *Canadian HR Reporter.*

16. Bhui, K., Dinos, S., Standfeld, S., and White, P. (2012), A synthesis of the evidence for managing stress at work: A review of the reviews reporting on anxiety, depression, and absenteeism, *Journal of Environmental and Public Health,* accessed November 28, 2018, from http:// dx.doi.org/10.1155/2012/515874; Steel, P., Schmidt, J., Uggerslev, K., and Bosco, F. (2018), The effects of personality on job satisfaction and life satisfaction: A meta-analytic investigation accounting for bandwidth-fidelity and commensurability, *Human Relations.*

17. Aguinia, H. (2012), *Performance Management* (3rd ed.), Pearson.

18. Uggerslev, K., and Sulsky, L. (2002), Presentation modality and indirect performance information: Effects on ratings, reactions, and memory, *Journal of Applied Psychology, 87,* pp. 940–950.

19. Richardson, H. A., and Taylor, S. G. (2012), Understanding input events: A model of employees' responses to requests for their input, *Academy of Management Review, 37*(3), pp. 471–491.

20. Vander Wier, M. (2017, March 6), Are your employees disengaged? Coaching can help, say experts, *Canadian HR Reporter.*

21. Vigoda-Gadot, E., and Angert, L. (2007), Goal setting theory, job feedback, and OCB: Lessons from a longitudinal study, *Basic and Applied Social Psychology, 29*(2), pp. 119–128, doi:10.1080/01973530701331536; McEwan, D., Ruissen, G. R., Eys, M., Zumbo, B., and Beauchamp, M. (2017), The effectiveness of teamwork training on teamwork behaviors and team performance: A systematic review and meta-analysis of controlled interventions, *PLOS one,* accessed November 28, 2018, from https://doi.org/10.1371/journal .pone.0169604

22. Welch, J. (2001), *Straight from the Gut,* New York: Warner Business Books.

23. Chakkirala, A. (2013, January 22), HR professionals' love-hate equation with the bell curve, *Recruitment India,* accessed November 28, 2018, from http:// recruitmentindiaonline.blogspot.com/ 2013/02/the-hr-professionals-love-hate-equation.html

24. Pulakos, E., Mueller-Hanson, R., O'Leary, R., and Meyrowitz, M. (2012), *Building a high-performance culture: A fresh look at performance management,* SHRM Foundation's Effective Practice Guidelines Series, accessed November 28, 2018, from https://www.shrm.org/foundation/ourwork/ initiatives/resources-from-past-initiatives/ Documents/Building%20a%20High%20 Performance%20Culture.pdf

25. Vinogradova, M. L., Kulyamina, O. S., Larionova, A. A., Maloletko, A. N., and Kaurova, O. V. (2016), The use of MBO (Management of Objectives), method of attraction and evaluation of effectiveness of investments to the tourism and hospitality, *International Review of Management and Marketing, 6*(S2), pp. 241–246.

26. Grote, R. C. (2000, January 1), Performance appraisal reappraised, *Harvard Business Review.*

27. Pulakos, E. D. (2004), *Performance Management: A Roadmap for Developing, Implementing and Evaluating Performance Management Systems,* SHRM Foundation, Alexandria, VA.

28. Zenger, J. (2016, March 10), How effective are your 360-degree feedback assessments? *Forbes,* accessed November 28, 2018, from https://www.forbes.com/sites/jackzenger/ 2016/03/10/how-effective-are-your-360-degree-feedback-assessments/2/ #219c11cd2614

29. Heathfield, S. (2018, January 4), 360 degree feedback: See the good, the bad and the ugly, *The Balance,* accessed November 28, 2018, from https://www.thebalance.com/ 360-degree-feedback-information-1917537

30. Dineen, K. (2015, May), Pros vs cons of employee self-evaluations, *Helios,* accessed November 28, 2018, from https://www.helioshr.com/2015/05/pros-vs-cons-of-employee-self-evaluations/

31. Caruso, K. (2014, January 7), 4 benefits of using peer appraisal in employee performance reviews, *Via People,* accessed November 28, 2018, from http://web .viapeople.com/viaPeople-blog/bid/99056/ 4-Benefits-of-Using-Peer-Appraisal-in-Employee-Performance-Reviews

32. Silliker, A. (2011), Management behaviours closely linked to engagement: Study, *Canadian HR Reporter, 24*(8), pp. 3, 6.

33. Klie, S. (2011, January), Shift in strategy requires new leadership skills, *Canadian HR Reporter,* p. 14; Toronto Pearson Passenger Data (2015), accessed November 28, 2018, from http://www .torontopearson.com/uploadedFiles/GTAA/ Content/About_GTAA/Statistics/04-Apr15-passenger.pdf

34. Aguinis, H. (2012), *Performance Management* (3rd ed.), Pearson.

35. Heathfield, S. (2018, January 4), 360 degree feedback: See the good, the bad and the ugly, *The Balance,* accessed November 28, 2018, from https://www.thebalance.com/ 360-degree-feedback-information-1917537

36. Uggerslev, K. L., and Sulsky, L. M. (2008), Using frame-of-feference training to understand the implications of rater idiosyncrasy for rating accuracy, *Journal of Applied Psychology, 93,* pp. 711–719; Loignon, A., Woehr, D., Thomas, J., Loughry, M., Ohland, M., and Ferguson, D. (2018), Facilitating peer evaluation in team contexts: The impact of frame-of-reference rater training, *Academy of Management Learning & Education, 16*(4).

37. Managing employee performance (2018, September), *Society for Human Resource Management,* accessed November 28, 2018, from https://www.shrm.org/resource-sandtools/tools-and-samples/toolkits/ pages/managingemployeeperformance .aspx.

38. Pulakos, E., Mueller-Hanson, R., O'Leary, R., and Meyrowitz, M. (2012), *Building a high-performance culture: A fresh look at performance management,* SHRM Foundation's Effective Practice Guidelines Series, accessed November 28, 2018, from https://www.shrm.org/foundation/ourwork/ initiatives/resources-from-past-initiatives/ Documents/Building%20a%20High%20 Performance%20Culture.pdf

39. Gaumond, J. (2008, January), 5 tips to perfecting performance reviews, *Canadian HR Reporter, 21,* p. 2; Chiodo, S. (2010, December), Objective performance development, *Canadian HR Reporter, 23,* p. 22.

40. Silliker, A., (2013, June 17), Employee engagement levels sliding, *Canadian HR Reporter.*

41. Pulakos, E., Mueller-Hanson, R., O'Leary, R., and Meyrowitz, M. (2012), *Building a high-performance culture: A fresh look at performance management,* SHRM Foundation's Effective Practice Guidelines Series, accessed November 28, 2018, from https://www.shrm.org/foundation/ourwork/ initiatives/resources-from-past-initiatives/

Documents/Building%20a%20High%20 Performance%20Culture.pdf

42. Western Canada HR trends report (2016, Fall), *Torch,* accessed November 28, 2018, from http://cphr.ca/wp-content/ uploads/2017/02/Western-Canada-HR-Trends-Report-2016.pdf

43. Silzer, R., and Dowell, B. E. (Ed.) (2010), *Strategy-Driven Talent Management: A Leadership Imperative,* San Francisco: Jossey-Bass.

44. Ruddy, T., and Anand, P. (2010), Managing talent in blobal organizations, in R. Silzer and B. E. Dowell (Eds.), *Strategy-Driven Talent Management: A Leadership Imperative,* San Francisco: Jossey-Bass.

45. Gorsline, K. (2010), Talent management comes of age, *Canadian HR Reporter, 23*(14), p. 9; Silzer, R., and Dowell, B. E. (Ed.), *Strategy-Driven Talent Management: A Leadership Imperative,* San Francisco: Jossey-Bass.

46. Hendry, I. (2011), Hail talent management, *Canadian HR Reporter, 24*(13), pp. 13–14.

47. Brown, W. (2017, November 13), Approaching comp differently to remain competitive, *Canadian HR Reporter;* Introduction to the human resources discipline of compensation (2017, May 5), accessed April 5, 2018, from https://www .shrm.org/resourcesandtools/tools-and-samples/toolkits/pages/introcompensation .aspx

48. Adapted from How To Guides: How to Establish a Performance Improvement Plan (2018, March 2), Society for Human Resource Management How To Guides, accessed on October 30, 2018, from https://www.shrm.org/resourcesandtools/ tools-and-samples/how-to-guides/pages/ performanceimprovementplan.aspx

49. Workopolis (2017, December 27), How to give a negative performance review, accessed November 28, 2018, from https:// hiring.workopolis.com/article/how-to-give-a-negative-performance-review/.

50. Secord, H. (2008, March), Performance improvement plan guidelines, *Canadian Labour Relations and Employment Law Topics,* accessed November 28, 2018, from http://www.cch.ca/newsletters/Business/ March2008/Article2.htm

51. Olson, R. (2011, November), Terminating a worker for poor performance, *Canadian HR Reporter, 24,* p. 19.

52. Clark, M. (2017, August 7), Finally, performance management is about managing performance, *Canadian HR Reporter.*

CHAPTER 9

1. Former U.S. Representative for Utah, accessed November 28, 2018, from https://www.brainyquote.com/quotes/ jason_chaffetz_720147

2. Introduction to the human resources discipline of compensation (2017, May 5), *Society for Human Resource Management.*

3. Building a market-based pay structure from scratch, (2018, January 12), *SHRM,* accessed November 28, 2018, from https:// www.shrm.org/resourcesandtools/tools-and-samples/toolkits/pages/buildingamarket-basedpaystructurefromscratch.aspx

4. Planning & Design: Compensation Philosophy: What are the advantages or disadvantages of a lead, match or lag compensation strategy? (2015, December 2), *Society for Human Resource Management,* accessed November 28, 2018, from https:// www.shrm.org/resourcesandtools/tools-and-samples/hr-qa/pages/cms_024253.aspx

5. Felonie, R. (2015, April 11), Inside Google's policy to "pay unfairly"—why 2 people in the same role can earn dramatically different amounts, *Business Insider,* accessed November 28, 2018, from http://www.businessinsider.com/ google-policy-to-pay-unfairly-2015-4

6. Performing job evaluations (2016, October 27), Society for Human Resource Management.

7. EL-Hajji, M. A. (2015), The Hay System of job evaluation: A critical analysis, *Journal of Human Resource Management and Labor Studies, 3,* pp. 1–22. doi:10.15640/jhrmls.v3n1a1

8. Korn Ferry Hay Guide Chart. Accessed December 12, 2018 from: https://www .kornferry.com/solutions/products/ hr-training-korn-ferry-hay-guide-chart

9. Building a market-based pay structure from scratch (2018, January 12), *Society for Human Resource Management,* accessed November 28, 2018, from https:// www.shrm.org/resourcesandtools/tools-and-samples/toolkits/pages/buildingamarket-basedpaystructurefromscratch.aspx

10. Building a market-based pay structure from scratch (2018, January 12), *Society for Human Resource Management,* accessed November 28, 2018, from https:// www.shrm.org/resourcesandtools/tools-and-samples/toolkits/pages/buildingamarket-basedpaystructurefromscratch.aspx

11. Building a market-based pay structure from scratch (2018, January 12), *Society for Human Resource Management,* accessed November 28, 2018, from https:// www.shrm.org/resourcesandtools/tools-and-samples/toolkits/pages/buildingamarket-basedpaystructurefromscratch.aspx

12. Compensation practices becoming more formal, rigorous (2012, October 16), *Society for Human Resource Management,* accessed November 28, 2018, from https:// www.shrm.org/ResourcesAndTools/hr-topics/compensation/Pages/Compensation-Salary-Incentives.aspx

13. Ledford, Jr., G., and Heneman III, H. (2011, June), Skill-Based Pay, *SHRM-SIOP White Paper Series,* accessed November 28, 2018, from http://www.siop .org/SIOP-SHRM/SIOP_SHRM_Skill_ Based_Pay.pdf

14. Ledford, Jr., G., and Heneman III, H. (2011, June), Skill-Based Pay, *SHRM-SIOP White Paper Series,* accessed November 28, 2018, from http://www.siop .org/SIOP-SHRM/SIOP_SHRM_Skill_ Based_Pay.pdf

15. Ledford, Jr., G., and Heneman III, H. (2011, June), Skill-Based Pay, *SHRM-SIOP White Paper Series,* accessed November 28, 2018, from http://www.siop .org/SIOP-SHRM/SIOP_SHRM_Skill_ Based_Pay.pdf

16. Ledlow, A. (2007, August 1), Shell upgrades Brockville lubricants plant, *Truck News,* accessed November 28, 2018, from https://www.trucknews.com/features/ shell-upgrades-brockville-lubricants-plant/

17. Lawler, E. E. (2008, February), *Rewarding Excellence: Pay Strategies for the New Economy,* San Francisco: Jossey-Bass.

18. Lawler, E. E. (2008, February), *Rewarding Excellence: Pay Strategies for the New Economy,* San Francisco: Jossey-Bass.

19. Lawler, E. E. (2008, February), *Rewarding Excellence: Pay Strategies for the New Economy,* San Francisco: Jossey-Bass.

20. Columbus, L. (2017, May 13), IBM predicts demand for data scientists will soar 28% by 2020, *Forbes,* accessed November 28, 2018, from https://www .forbes.com/sites/louiscolumbus/2017/ 05/13/ibm-predicts-demand-for-data-scientists-will-soar-28-by-2020/ #184ada9e7e3b

21. See Morgan, G. (2014, April 6), Rising to the challenge of Canada's skills shortage, *The Globe and Mail,* for an overview of current skill shortages.

22. Building a market-based pay structure from scratch (2018, January 12), *Society for Human Resource Management,* accessed from www.shrm.org/resourcesandtools/ tools-and-samples/toolkits/pages/ buildingmarket-basedpaystructurefrom-scratch.aspx

23. Building a market-based pay structure from scratch (2018, January 12), *Society for Human Resource Management.*

24. Vander Wier, M. (2018, January 17), No easy answers for employers facing major minimum wage hikes, *Canadian HR Reporter,* accessed November 28, 2018, from http://www.hrreporter.com/ compensation-and-benefits/35683-no-easy-answers-for-employers-facing-major-minimum-wage-hikes/

25. Macewan, A. (2014, July/August), The minimum wage and inflation, *Dollars and Sense,* accessed November 28, 2018, from http://dollarsandsense.org/archives/2014/ 0714macewan.html

26. Employment and Social Development Canada (n.d.), Federally regulated businesses and industries, *Government of Canada,* accessed April 13, 2018, from https://www.canada.ca/en/employment-social-development/programs/

employment-equity/regulated-industries
.html

27. Brown, W. (2017, November 13),
Approaching comp differently to remain
competitive, *Canadian HR Reporter.*

28. Compensation Programs and Practices
Survey (2016, August), *WorldatWork,*
accessed November 28, 2018, from https://
www.worldatwork.org/docs/research-
and-surveys/survey-brief-survey-on-
compensation-programs-and-practices-
2016.pdf

29. Designing and managing incentive compensation programs (2018, January 12),
Society for Human Resource Management,
accessed November 28, 2018, from https://
www.shrm.org/ResourcesAndTools/
tools-and-samples/toolkits/Pages/
designingincentivecompensation.aspx

30. Designing and managing incentive compensation programs (2018, January 12),
Society for Human Resource Management,
accessed November 28, 2018, from https://
www.shrm.org/ResourcesAndTools/tools-
and-samples/toolkits/Pages/designingin-
centivecompensation.aspx

31. Lazear, E. (2000), Performance pay and
productivity, *American Economic Review,*
90(5), pp. 1346–1361.

32. Connick, W. (2017, July 16), Tying sales
compensation to sales quotas, *The Balance,*
accessed November 28, 2018, from https://
www.thebalance.com/tying-sales-
compensation-to-sales-quotas-2917118

33. Cronin, Z. (2018, April 4), 5 inside
sales compensation plan examples that
will motivate your reps to win revenue,
ringDNA, accessed November 28, 2018,
from https://www.ringdna.com/blog/
these-inside-sales-compensation-plan-
templates-will-motivate-your-reps-to-win-
revenue

34. Compensation programs and practices
survey (2016, August), *WorldatWork,*
accessed November 28, 2018, from https://
www.worldatwork.org/docs/research-
and-surveys/survey-brief-survey-on-
compensation-programs-and-practices-
2016.pdf

35. Leadem, R. (2017, November 6), The 15
tech companies with the highest signing
bonuses, *Entrepreneur.com,* accessed
November 28, 2018, from https://www
.entrepreneur.com/slideshow/304043

36. Dobson, S. (2013, May 6), Retention
bonuses help during time of crisis:
Experts, *Canadian HR Reporter.*

37. Dobson, S. (2013, May 6), Retention
bonuses help during time of crisis:
Experts, *Canadian HR Reporter.*

38. Designing and managing incentive
compensation plans (2018, January 12),
Society for Human Resource Management,
accessed November 28, 2018, from https://
www.shrm.org/ResourcesAndTools/
tools-and-samples/toolkits/Pages/
designingincentivecompensation.aspx

39. Moultry, L. (2018, October 23), The
advantages of using money to motivate
employees, *Chron.com,* accessed
November 28, 2018, from http://
smallbusiness.chron.com/advantages-
using-money-motivate-employees-22056
.html

40. Cherniak, B. (2013, October 15), How
to share profits with your staff without
running into problems, *Financial Post,*
accessed November 28, 2018, from http://
business.financialpost.com/entrepreneur/
how-to-share-profits-with-your-staff-
wihout-running-into-problems

41. Reynolds, J. N. (2014), *Sharing Profits:
The Ethics of Remuneration, Taxes and
Shareholder Return,* New York: Palgrave
Macmillan.

42. O'Boyle, E., Patel, P., and Gonzalez-Mule,
E. (2016), Employee ownership and firm
performance: A meta-analysis, *Human
Resource Management Journal, 26,*
pp. 425–448.

43. Serebrin, J. (Updated 2017, March 24),
Beau's brewery to remain independent by
selling ownership to employee, *The Globe
and Mail,* accessed November 28, 2018,
from https://www.theglobeandmail.com/
report-on-business/small-business/sb-
growth/beaus-brewery-to-remain-
independent-by-selling-ownership-to-
employees/article30046219/

44. Shore, R. (2016, June 1), Succession
planning increasingly includes employee
ownership, *Vancouver Sun,* accessed
November 28, 2018, from http://van-
couversun.com/business/local-business/
succession-planning-increasingly-
includes-employee-ownership

45. Robertson, K. (2010, November 23, updated
2017, March 26), Leave your company in
good hands, *The Globe and Mail,* accessed
November 28, 2018, from www
.theglobeandmail.com/report-on-business/
small-business/sb-managing/succession-
planning/leave-your-company-in-good-
hands/article1316184/

46. Webster, S. (2018, January 30), The
difference between base salary and total
compensation, *The Chron.com,* accessed
November 28, 2018, from http://
smallbusiness.chron.com/difference-
between-base-salary-total-compensation-
21449.html

47. Managing total rewards across the EMEA
region—can one size fit all? (2012,
November), *Towers Watson,* accessed
November 28, 2018, from http://www
.towerswatson.com/en-za/insights/ic-types/
survey-research-results/2012/11/managing-
total-rewards-across-the-emea-region-can-
one-size-fit-all

48. O'Grady, R. (2018, April 1), Being too
conservative a dangerous game, *Canadian
HR Reporter.*

49. Gidwaney, V. (2014, September 1), 5 tips
for creating tailored benefit packages for

your employees, *The Inc.com,* accessed
November 28, 2018, from https://www.inc
.com/veer-gidwaney/5-tips-for-creating-
tailored-benefit-packages-for-your-
employees.html

50. Moyser, M. (2017, March 8), Women and
paid work, *Statistics Canada,* accessed
November 28, 2018, from http://www
.statcan.gc.ca/pub/89-503-x/2015001/
article/14694-eng.htm

51. Ryan, C. (2012, February 12), Tesco pay
showdown contains a wider warning,
Canadian HR Reporter.

52. Equal pay for equal work? A look at the
wage gap between men and women in
the U.S. and Canada (2013, February
15), *CBC: George Stroumboulopoulos
Tonight,* accessed November 28, 2018,
from http://www.cbc.ca/strombo/news/
equal-pay-for-equal-work-a-look-at-the-
wage-gap-between-men-and-women-in-va;
see also Adshade, M. (2013, January
22), Do women choose lower pay? (The
gender wage gap explained), *Canadian
Business,* accessed November 28, 2018,
from http://www.canadianbusiness.com/
blogs-and-comment/gender-wage-gap/

53. Dujay, J. (2017, April 3), LCBO casual
workers in Ontario achieve equal pay for
equal work, *Canadian HR Reporter.*

54. Humber, T. (2018, April 1), Cross money
off taboo topic list, *Canadian HR Reporter.*

55. Equal Pay for Male and Female Employees
Who Are Performing Work of Equal Value,
interpretation guide for Section 11 of the
Canadian Human Rights Act, Ottawa:
Canadian Human Rights Commission,
undated.

56. Gurchiek, K. (2018, March 20), Wages
are unequal between white and black men
even when other factors are comparable,
Society for Human Resource Management,
accessed November 28, 2018, from
https://www.shrm.org/resourcesandtools/
hr-topics/behavioral-competencies/
global-and-cultural-effectiveness/pages/
wages-are-unequal-between-white-and-
black-men-even-when-other-factors-are-
comparable.aspx

57. Hayninck, E. (2017, June 12), Pay equity
still a challenge after 30 years, *Canadian
HR Reporter.*

58. Hayninck, E. (2017, June 12), Pay equity
still a challenge after 30 years, *Canadian
HR Reporter.*

59. Bamberge, P., and Belogolovsky, E.
(2010), The impact of pay secrecy on
individual task performance, *Personnel
Psychology, 63*(4), 965–996. doi:10.1111/
j.1744-6570.2010.01194.x

60. Lawler, E. E. (2008, February), *Rewarding
Excellence: Pay Strategies for the New
Economy,* San Francisco: Jossey-Bass.

61. Baylor, R., and Sharer, C. (2017, June
27), Delaware becomes latest state and
local entity to ban salary history questions
in interviews, *WorldatWork,* accessed

November 28, 2018, from https://www
.worldatwork.org/docs/public-policy/
government-affairs-news-bytes/2017/6-
june/delaware-becomes-latest-state-and-
local-entity-to-ban-salary-history-
questions-in-interviews.html

62. Adler, A., Gundersen, A. (2007, June 29),
*International Dimensions of Organizational
Behavior,* Cengage Learning.

63. Compensation practices becoming more
formal, rigorous (2012, October 16),
Society for Human Resource Management,
accessed November 28, 2018, from https://
www.shrm.org/resourcesandtools/hr-
topics/compensation/pages/compensation-
salary-incentives.aspx

CHAPTER 10

1. Sir Richard Branson, founder, Virgin
Group, *VirginPulse,* accessed November 30,
2018, from https://www.virginpulse.com/
about-us/

2. Hadzima, J. (n.d.), How much does an
employee cost? *Boston Business Journal,*
accessed November 3, 2018, from http://
web.mit.edu/e-club/hadzima/pdf/how-
much-does-an-employee-cost.pdf

3. About Husky (n.d.), *Husky.com,* accessed
November 30, 2018, from http://www
.husky.co/EN-US/About-us.aspx.

4. LaRochelle-Cote, S., and Uppal, S.
(2011), The financial well-being of the
self-employed, *Statistics Canada,* accessed
November 30, 2018, from https://www
.statcan.gc.ca/pub/75-001-x/2011004/
article/11535-eng.htm

5. Paterson, J. (2016, February 9), What
are the top 5 employee benefits? *Benefits
Canada,* accessed November 30, 2018,
from https://www.benefitscanada.com/
uncategorized/what-are-the-top-5-
employee-benefits-76725

6. Barnett, J. C., and Berchick, E. R. (2017,
September 12), Health insurance coverage
in the United States: 2016, *United States
Census Bureau,* accessed November 30,
2018, from https://www.census.gov/
library/publications/2017/demo/p60-260
.html

7. Stewart, N. (2015), *Benefits Benchmarking
2015,* The Conference Board of Canada.

8. Statistics Canada (2017, July 21), Pension
plans in Canada, as of January 1, 2016,
The Daily, accessed November 30, 2018,
from http://www.statcan.gc.ca/daily-
quotidien/170721/dq170721d-eng.htm

9. Statistics Canada (2017, July 21), Pension
plans in Canada, as of January 1, 2016,
The Daily, accessed November 30, 2018,
from https://www150.statcan.gc.ca/n1/
daily-quotidien/170721/dq170721d-
eng.htm

10. Statistics Canada (2017, July 21), Pension
plans in Canada, as of January 1, 2016,
The Daily, accessed November 30, 2018,
from http://www.statcan.gc.ca/daily-
quotidien/170721/dq170721d-eng.htm

11. Statistics Canada (2017, July 21), Pension
plans in Canada, as of January 1, 2016,
The Daily, accessed November 30, 2018,
from http://www.statcan.gc.ca/daily-
quotidien/170721/dq170721d-eng.htm

12. Think your defined benefit pension is
money in the bank? Think again (2017,
September 14), *Financial Post,* accessed
November 30, 2018, from http://business
.financialpost.com/personal-finance/
retirement/sears-defined-pension-plan-
slap-a-reminder-that-savings-should-be-
diversified

13. Stewart, N. (2015), *Benefits Benchmarking
2015,* The Conference Board of Canada.

14. Finch, C. (2012, September 27), Corporate
cell phones: Perk or penalty? *CIO From
IDG,* accessed November 30, 2018, from
https://www.cio.com/article/2371046/
consumer-technology/corporate-cell-
phones--perk-or-penalty-.html

15. Attridge, M. (2017, June 16), Future
Trends in Organizational Risk
Management, Keynote Presentation, 16th
Annual Conference, *Employee Assistance
European Forum,* accessed November 30,
2018, from https://archive.hshsl.umaryland
.edu/handle/10713/6721

16. LifeWorks (2017, November 1),
Employee Assistance Program, accessed
November 30, 2018, from https://
www.lifeworks.com/ca/solution/
employee-assistance-program-eap/

17. Providing employee benefits continues to
be a significant cost for employers (2015,
November 9), *The Conference Board of
Canada,* accessed November 4, 2018,
from http://www.conferenceboard.ca/
press/newsrelease/15-11-09/Providing_
Employee_Benefits_Continues_To_Be_A_
Significant_Cost_For_Employers.aspx

18. Stewart, N. (2015), *Benefits Benchmarking
2015,* The Conference Board of Canada.

19. The Associated Press (2013, June 10),
Some employers letting workers buy,
sell vacation time, *CBC News,* accessed
November 4, 2018, from http://www.cbc
.ca/news/business/some-employers-
letting-workers-buy-sell-vacation-time-
1.1400197

20. Stewart, N. (2015), *Benefits Benchmarking
2015,* The Conference Board of Canada.

21. Henry, J. (2018, February 15), Applied
artificial intelligence is no longer an
advantage: It's a necessity, *Mobile
Business Insights,* accessed November 4,
2018, from https://mobilebusinessinsights
.com/2018/02/applied-artificial-
intelligence-is-no-longer-an-advantage-its-
a-necessity/; see also https://www.johnpaul
.com/

22. Stewart, N. (2015), *Benefits Benchmarking
2015,* The Conference Board of Canada.

23. See Blue Cross Canada, http://www
.bluecross.ca/en/index.html.

24. Watson Wyatt Consulting, 34th Annual
Canadian Salary Survey.

25. Beyer, L. (2011, October 12), Heightened
awareness of benefits plays pivotal role in
employee experience, *Workforce,* accessed
November 30, 2018, from http://www
.workforce.com/2011/10/26/heightened-
awareness-of-benefits-plays-pivotal-role-
in-employee-experience/

26. Demangos, P. (2017, March 17), Sounding
board: Five ways to cut benefit costs
while preserving value for staff, *Benefits
Canada,* accessed November 30, 2018,
from http://www.benefitscanada.com/
benefits/health-benefits/sounding-board-
five-ways-to-cut-benefit-costs-while-
preserving-value-for-staff-95143.

27. Demangos, P. (2017, March 17), Sounding
board: Five ways to cut benefit costs
while preserving value for staff, *Benefits
Canada,* accessed November 30, 2018,
from http://www.benefitscanada.com/
benefits/health-benefits/sounding-board-
five-ways-to-cut-benefit-costs-while-
preserving-value-for-staff-95143

28. Wilson, C. (2014, September 26), Benefits
column: How to retain employees, *Benefits
Canada,* accessed November 30, 2018,
from http://www.benefitscanada.com/
benefits/other/benefits-column-how-to-
retain-employees-56197; see also Bruce, S.
(2015, February 25), Voluntary benefits:
Low cost, high reward! *HR Daily Advisor,*
accessed November 30, 2018, from http://
hrdailyadvisor.blr.com/2015/02/25/
voluntary-benefits-low-cost-high-reward/
#more-10002

29. Miller, S. (2016, November 30),
Employers alter benefits to attract, retain
employees, SHRM finds, *SHRM,* accessed
November 30, 2018, from https://www
.shrm.org/resourcesandtools/hr-topics/
benefits/pages/alter-benefits-attract-retain
.aspx

30. Cameron, D. (2012, February 28), Design
your benefits to drive behavior, *Benefits
Canada,* accessed November 30, 2018,
from http://www.benefitscanada.com/
benefits/health-benefits/design-your-
benefits-to-drive-behaviour-25492

CHAPTER 11

1. Sinek, S. (2010), How great leaders inspire
action, TED Talk.

2. Fairlie, P. (2009, June 15), Five must-
haves of meaningful work, *Canadian HR
Reporter.*

3. Balthazard, C. (2011, January 17), Problem
managers: It doesn't take many to spoil the
bunch, *Canadian HR Professional,* p. 11.

4. Internet use boosts productivity, study
finds (2009, April 10), *Times-Colonist*
(Victoria), p. C12.

5. Smith, J. (2014, January 24), Why your top
talent is leaving in 2014, and what it'll take
to retain them, *Forbes.com,* accessed
November 30, 2018, from https://www
.forbes.com/sites/jacquelynsmith/2014/01/
24/why-your-top-talent-is-leaving-in-

2014-and-what-itll-take-to-retain-them/#2b230c3a6ea1

6. Penn Schoen Berland (2016), *Dell and Intel Future Workforce Study Global Report,* accessed November 30, 2018, from https://www.emc.com/collateral/analyst-reports/dell-future-workfoce-study-global.pdf

7. Hackbarth, N. (2016, February 2), HR trends, tactics and strategies for improving the employee experience, *Quantum Workplace.*

8. Should you "friend" your co-workers? (2017, September 12), *OfficeTeam.*

9. The high flyers of Air Canada impress the world: Canada's Top Employers 2015 Winners (2014), *The Globe and Mail* and Mediacorp, p. 13.

10. Tibbetts, J. (2009, January 5), Fired on Facebook, spa worker cries foul as controversy rages, *Edmonton Journal,* p. A5.

11. 8 Uses of the intranet for HR (2012, September 4), *Noodle,* accessed November 30, 2018, from https://vialect.com/intranet-solutions/intranet-uses-for-hr

12. Finney, M. I. (1997, January), Harness the power within, *HR Magazine,* pp. 66–74.

13. Greengard, S. (1997, March), 12 ways to use an intranet, *Workforce,* p. 94.

14. Leveraging the value of employee self-service portals (2015, August 25), *Society for Human Resource Management,* accessed November 30, 2018, from https://www.shrm.org/resourcesandtools/tools-and-samples/toolkits/pages/leveraging-value-of-employee-self-service-portals.aspx

15. Zielinski, D. (2016, December 20), New assistive technologies aid employees with disabilities, *Society for Human Resource Management.*

16. How to protect your company from misuse of electronic communications (2000, April), *HRFocus,* p.7.

17. Zimmerman, K. (2017, March 26), Is your cell phone killing your productivity at work? *Forbes;* Stothart, C., Mitchum, A., & Yehnert, C. (2015), The attentional cost of receiving a cell phone notification, *Journal of Experimental Psychology: Human Perception and Performance, 41*(4), pp. 893–897, doi:http://dx.doi.org/10.1037/xhp0000100

18. Immen, W. (2009, June 3), Tweet at work, your boss may thank you, *The Globe and Mail,* p. B14.

19. Evans, P. (2017, November 14), Canadians more connected, but at possible cost to work-life balance, StatsCan says, *CBC News.*

20. Massey, A. (2005, September 26), Blogging phobia hits employers, *Canadian HR Reporter,* pp. 15, 17.

21. Akitunde, A. (2013, August 15), Employees gone wild: 8 reasons you need a social media policy today, accessed November 30, 2018, from https://www.americanexpress.com/us/small-business/openforum/articles/employee-social-media-policy/?linknav=us-openforum-search-article-link1

22. Working hard or hardly working? (2017, July 19), *OfficeTeam.*

23. Kinni, T. (2016, July 7), Does social media enhance employee productivity? *MIT Sloan Management Review.*

24. Dangers lurking in mobile devices (2011, November 7), *Canadian HR Reporter,* pp. 19, 25.

25. Facebook for pleasure, not business (2013, September 9), *Canadian HR Reporter,* p. 2.

26. *Nearly Half of Canadian Small Business Owners Now Use Social Media for Their Businesses: BMO Report* (2015), Bank of Montreal.

27. Bernier, L. (2014, December 15), Held hostage, *Canadian HR Reporter,* pp. 1, 8.

28. Gesenhues, A. (2013, September 27), Survey: 71% of companies concerned over social media risks, but only 36% provide employee training, *Marketing Land,* accessed November 30, 2018, from https://marketingland.com/survey-71-of-companies-concerned-about-social-media-risks-only-36-do-social-media-training-60212

29. Schachter, H. (2015, January 5), Why you need a chief reputation officer, *The Globe and Mail,* p. B6.

30. Buccongello, C. (2013, September 23), Technology presents challenges, opportunities, *Canadian HR Reporter,* pp. 14, 18.

31. How is HR using social media? (2011, November 21), *Canadian HR Reporter,* p. 15.

32. Silliker, A. (2012, January 30), Tread carefully with social media checks, *Canadian HR Reporter,* pp. 1, 11.

33. Statistics Canada (2005), *Workplace and Employee Survey Compendium,* Ottawa: Statistics Canada.

34. See Kapel, C., and Thompson, M. (2005, January 17), Effective communications link employees to business and customers, *Canadian HR Reporter,* p. 12.

35. Bernier, L. (2014, June 2), Before you hit Send, *Canadian HR Reporter,* pp. 1, 8.

36. Lobo, V. (2009, June 6), Dealing with the social media monster, *Canadian HR Reporter.*

37. For more information on privacy issues see Keenan, T. (2014), *Technocreep,* Greystone.

38. See WorkSmart Productivity Tool.

39. Erskine, B. (2012, February 7), CIBC emails will be used as evidence at trial, *Chronicle Herald,* p. C6.

40. Brookbank, W., and Ulrich, D. (2003), *Competencies for the New HR,* Ann Arbor, MI: University of Michigan Business School.

41. A detailed examination of the use of HR technology is found in "Guide to HR Technology," supplement to *Canadian HR Reporter* (2001, October 22).

42. McIninch, D. (2013, September 9), Managing HR in the cloud, *Canadian HR Reporter,* pp. 21, 22.

43. Bernier, L. (2014, January 24), 5 areas where social media shines, *Canadian HR Reporter,* pp. 12, 14.

44. Sloss, J. (2014, November 3), New tools, new rules, *Canadian HR Reporter,* p. 15.

45. Kelly, H. (2018, February 2), Amazon's idea for employee-tracking wearables raises concerns, *CNNTech.*

46. Caudron, S. (1997, May), Blow the whistle on employment disputes, *Workforce,* pp. 50–57; see also Roche, W., Teague, P., and Colvin, A. (2015), *The Oxford Handbook of Conflict Management in Organizations,* Oxford University Press.

47. Colvin, A. (2011), An empirical study of employment arbitration: Case outcomes and processes, *Journal of Legal Empirical Studies, 8,* pp. 1–23.

48. Wagar, T. H. (2001), Grievance procedures in the non-union environment, *Labour Arbitration Yearbook,* pp. 127–136; see also Colvin, A. (2004), The relationship between employee involvement and workplace dispute resolution, *Relations Industrielles, 59,* pp. 681–702.

49. These are just some of the issues discussed in Feuille, P., and Chachere, D. R. (1995), Looking fair or being fair: Remedial voice procedures in nonunion workplaces, *Journal of Management, 21,* pp. 27–42.

50. Mitchell, T. (2014, September 8), Is this thing on? *Canadian HR Reporter,* p. 27.

51. Marksberry, P., Church, J., and Schmidt, M. (2014), The employee suggestion system: A new approach using latent semantic analysis, *Human Factors and Ergonomics in Manufacturing and Service Industries, 24,* pp. 29–39.

52. Veder, B. (2013, August 12), If you build it, they will come, *Canadian HR Reporter,* p. 16.

53. Levitt, H. A. (2009), *The Law of Dismissal in Canada* (3rd ed.), Aurora, ON: Canada Law Book.

54. Falcone, P. (1997, February), The fundamentals of progressive discipline, *HR Magazine,* pp. 90–94.

55. Silliker, A. (2013, June 17), HR, lawyers working hand-in-hand, *Canadian HR Reporter,* pp. 1, 8.

56. This material is based largely on the video *Discipline without Punishment (Revised),* which was released in 1996 by Owen Stewart Performance Resources. Also see Watson, T. (2014, April 15), Discipline without punishment: A best practices approach to disciplining employees, *Watson Training & Development,* accessed November 30, 2018, from https://www.watson-training.com/blog2/46-discipline-with-punishment-a-best-practices-approach-to-disciplining-employees.html

57. CEOs talk (2004, December 6), *Canadian HR Reporter,* p. 10.

58. Levitt, H. A. (2009), *The Law of Dismissal in Canada* (3rd ed.), Aurora, ON: Canada Law Book.

59. *Wallace v. United Grain Growers Ltd.,* Supreme Court of Canada, October 30, 1997; see also *Potter v. New Brunswick Legal Aid Services Commission,* March 6, 2015.

60. Wagar, T. H. (1996, June), Wrongful dismissal: Perception vs. reality, *Human Resources Professional,* pp. 8, 10.

61. See Rudner, S. (2008, September 22), Just cause—back from the dead, *Canadian HR Reporter;* MacDonald, N. (2008, September 22), Progressing toward just cause, *Canadian HR Reporter;* Filsinger, K. (2010), *Employment Law for Business and Human Resources Professionals,* Toronto: Emond Montgomery.

62. Jackson, D. (2006, March 15), 6 months' severance for 8 months work, *Chronicle Herald* (Halifax), pp. 1, 2.

63. Zinejda, R. (2016, September 14), *Wilson v. Atomic Energy:* More than unjust dismissals, *thecourt.ca.*

64. Levitt, H. (2009, March 18), Promise of job for life proves costly for employer, *Times-Colonist* (Victoria), p. B7.

65. Dobson, S. (2012, January 16), Employees behaving badly, *Canadian HR Reporter,* pp. 1, 8.

66. Possibility of internal sabotage alarming (2011, August 15), *Canadian HR Reporter,* p. 4.

67. For more information on just cause see Scott, R., and Certosimo, M. L. O. (2002), *Just Cause: The Law of Summary Dismissal in Canada,* Aurora, ON: Canada Law Book; and Levitt, H. A. (2009), *The Law of Dismissal in Canada* (3rd ed.), Aurora, ON: Canada Law Book.

68. ClearView Strategic Partners (2013, July 3), Theft, abuse and cooking the books: 42% of Canadians admit witnessing misconduct at work, *MarketWired,* accessed November 30, 2018, from http://www.marketwired.com/press-release/theft-abuse-cooking-the-books-42-of-canadians-admit-witnessing-misconduct-at-work-1808042.htm

69. Levitt, H. A. (2009), *The Law of Dismissal in Canada* (3rd ed.), Aurora, ON: Canada Law Book.

70. Smith, J. (2012, January 30), Opportunity knocks but employee does not answer, *Canadian HR Reporter,* pp. 5, 8.

71. Sultan, S. (2015, March 23), Keeping the good faith: The Supreme Court clarifies constructive dismissal and emphasizes honesty, candidness and communication, *Ontario Bar Association,* accessed November 30, 2018, from https://www.oba.org/Sections/Labour-Employment-Law/Articles?page=7

72. Straszynski, P. (2011, June 20), Proving just cause just not enough, *Canadian HR Reporter,* p. 10.

73. An excellent source of information on reasonable notice awards is Sproat, J. (2012), *Wrongful Dismissal Handbook* (6th ed.), Toronto: Carswell; see also Levitt, H. (2009, March 7), Four factors drive severance packages, *Telegraph-Journal* (Saint John), p. E7; and MacLeod Law Firm (2013, January 8), Wrongful dismissal update: What is reasonable notice of termination, accessed November 30, 2018, from https://www.macleodlawfirm.ca/employers/2013/01/wrongful-dismissal-update-what-is-reasonable-notice-of-termination/

74. Johnson, B. (2017, April 17), A look at notices of resignation, *Canadian HR Reporter,* p. 31.

75. Smith, J. (2014, May 19), 6-month notice of resignation upheld for BlackBerry executive keen to join Apple, *Canadian HR Reporter,* p. 5.

76. Dobson, S. (2015, February 9), Target bows out, *Canadian HR Reporter,* pp. 1, 2.

77. Minken, R. (2012, March 26), $20 million award upheld by appeal court, *Canadian HR Reporter,* p. 5.

78. Rudner, S. (2008, September 22), Just cause—back from the dead, *Canadian HR Reporter.*

79. More detail on these points is provided in Connor, J. (2000, January), Disarming terminated employees, *HR Magazine,* pp. 113–116; see also Bell, D. (2009, June 15), No easy way to say you're fired, *Canadian HR Reporter;* Nebenzahl, D. (2009, May 31), Ethics of dismissal: Boss must do it in person and with privacy, *The Province* (Vancouver), p. A39.

80. Dobson, S. (2018, March), No discounts for Walmart, *Canadian HR Reporter,* pp. 1, 9.

81. Mitchell, T. (2014, October 6), A look at the various pitfalls of specifying notice periods in contract, *Canadian HR Reporter,* p. 15.

82. Jaekel, M., and Bilotta, L. (2014, February 24), Tempering high risk terminations, *Canadian HR Reporter,* pp. 17, 20.

83. Gray, J. (2014, November 4), Court sides with Globe in dispute over settlement, *The Globe and Mail,* p. B2.

84. Astor, M. (2017, July 25), Microchip implants for employees? One company says yes, *New York Times.*

85. Klie, S. (2010, November 19), Employees more litigious: Survey (2010, November 19), *Canadian HR Reporter,* pp. 10–11.

86. St. Denis, J. (2015, March 30), Saanich monitoring software was violation of employees' privacy rights: Privacy watchdog, *Business Vancouver,* accessed November 30, 2018, from https://biv.com/article/2015/03/saanich-computer-monitoring-software-violated-empl

87. Eichler, L. (2014, November 1), What you do after hours matters, too, *The Globe and Mail,* p. B17.

88. Privacy Commissioner: Health Canada violated privacy laws by disclosing personal health information of over 40,000 Canadians (2015, March 16), Canadian Privacy Law Blog, accessed November 30, 2018, from https://blog.privacylawyer.ca/2015/03/privacy-commissioner-health-canada.html

89. Vander Wier, M. (2017, October 2), Saliva testing helps with disability management, *Canadian HR Reporter,* pp. 1, 9.

90. Therrien, D. (2015, January 29), In business, privacy is money, *Chronicle Herald,* p. A11.

91. Humber, T. (2011, March 14), Here's the memo on Facebook—again, *Canadian HR Reporter,* p. 18; see also: Some US employers asking for applicants' Facebook login info (2012, March 21), *Chronicle Herald,* p. C6; Doorey, D. (n.d.), Ontario Human Rights Commission issues statement on employer requests for Facebook passwords, *The Law of Work,* accessed November 30, 2018, from http://lawofwork.ca/?p=5026

92. *R. v. Cole,* Supreme Court of Canada, October 19, 2012; *R v. Telus Communications,* Supreme Court of Canada, March 27, 2013; *R v. Vu,* Supreme Court of Canada, November 7, 2013.

93. Rudner, S., and MacDonald, N. (2014, Monday, June 9), The law, surveillance and employee privacy, *The Globe and Mail.*

94. Levitt, H. (2009, January 24), Spy without cause—and pay price, *Vancouver Sun,* p. H5.

95. See Canada's Anti-Spam Legislation, Government of Canada, for more information; see also Bouw, B. (2014, March 24), New anti-spam law "a big deal" for small business, *The Globe and Mail.*

96. Dobson, S. (2013, February 25), Hamilton workers caught in the act, *Canadian HR Reporter,* pp. 1, 12.

97. Shields, R. (2014, May 5), Training around privacy, *Canadian HR Reporter,* pp. 12, 104; Gray, J. (2013, June 14), Ruling could make random alcohol testing tougher, *The Globe and Mail.*

98. Gray, J. (2013, June 14), Ruling could make random alcohol testing tougher, *The Globe and Mail.*

99. Dujay, J. (2017, September 4), Concerns raised over tracking of migrant workers in British Columbia, *Canadian HR Reporter,* pp. 10, 16.

100. *Canadian Cannabis Survey,* Health Canada, December 2017.

101. Vander Wier, M. (2018, January), Are employers ready? *Canadian HR Reporter,* pp. 1, 11.

102. Stam, L. (2017, October 2), Employers aren't hamstrung when it comes to marijuana at work, *Canadian HR Reporter,* p. 19.

103. Employers boost morale (2009, February 24), *Canadian HR Reporter.*

104. Sirota, D., and Klein, D. (2013), The enthusiastic employee: How companies profit by giving workers what they want (2nd ed.).

105. Becker, B. E., Huselid, M. A., Pickus, P. S., and Spratt, M. F. (1997, Spring), HR as a source of shareholder value: Research and recommendations, *Human Resource Management,* pp. 39–47.

106. Foster, L. (2016, May 2), Best practices in HR linked to better business performance, *Canadian HR Reporter,* pp. 1, 6.

107. Tomlinson, A. (2001, November 5), Loyalty isn't dead but it does need some critical care, *Canadian HR Reporter,* p. 3; for more information on Fred Reichheld's work on loyalty, see http://www .loyaltyeffect.com/loyaltyrules/index.html.

108. A good review of this perspective is presented in Parker M., and Slaughter, J. (1988, October), Management by stress, *Technology Review,* pp. 37–44; see also Mehri, D. (2006), The darker side of lean: An insider's perspective on the realities of the Toyota production system, *Academy of Management Perspectives, 20,* pp. 21–42.

109. Dobson, D. (2011, October 10), Virtual teams expected to grow: Survey, *Canadian HR Reporter,* p. 3.

110. Huselid, M. (1995, June), The impact of human resource management practices on turnover, productivity, and corporate financial performance, *Academy of Management Journal,* pp. 635– 672; see also Pfeffer, J. (2005), Producing sustainable competitive advantage through the effective management of people, *Academy of Management Executive, 19,* pp. 95–108; Michie, J., and Sheehan-Quinn, M. (2001), Labour market flexibility, human resource management and corporate performance, *British Journal of Management, 12,* pp. 2187–2306; Becker, B., and Huselid, M. (2006), Strategic human resources management: Where do we go from here? *Journal of Management, 32,* pp. 898–925; Messersmith, J., Patel, P., and Lepak, D. (2011), Unlocking the black box: Exploring the link between high-performance work systems and performance, *Journal of Applied Psychology, 96,* pp. 1105–1118; Shin, D., and Konrad, A. (forthcoming), Causality between high-performance work systems and organizational performance, *Journal of Management.*

111. AON Hewitt (2018), *Trends in Global Employee Engagement.*

112. Becker, B. E., Huselid, M. A., Pickus, P. S., and Spratt, M. F. (1997, Spring), HR as a source of shareholder value: Research and recommendations, *Human Resource Management,* pp. 39–47.

113. Pfeffer, J., and Veiga, J. (1999, May), Putting people first for organizational success, *Academy of Management Executive,* p. 43.

114. Link, D. (2003, August 11), HR self service applications grow in number and depth, *Canadian HR Reporter,* pp. 9, 11.

115. Rousseau, D. (1996), Changing the deal while keeping the people, *Academy of Management Executive, 10,* pp. 50–59.

116. O'Reilly, B. (1994, June 13), The new deal: What companies and employees owe one another, *Fortune,* p. 44.

117. Ligaya, A. (2017, October 13), Sears closing after 65 years in Canada: Court grants complete liquidation, *Global News;* Jackson, E. (2017, November 27), The alarm bells should go off: Postmedia, Telstar deal will see 36 community papers closed, *Financial Post;* Marowits, R. (2018, January 16), Yellow Pages cuts roughly 500 jobs across Canada to reduce spending, *Toronto Star.*

118. Kozlowski, S. W. J., Chao, G. T., Smith, E. M., and Hedlund, J. (1993), Organizational downsizing: Strategies, interventions, and research implications, in C. L. Cooper and I. T. Robertson (Eds.), *International Review of Industrial and Organizational Psychology, 8,* pp. 263–332.

119. Cameron, K. (1994, Summer), Strategies for successful organizational downsizing, *Human Resource Management,* p. 192.

120. Ibid.

121. Cascio, W. (2002), *Responsible Restructuring: Creative and Responsible Alternatives to Layoffs,* San Francisco: Berrett-Koehler.

122. X Factor firing goes viral as employee hijacks Twitter account (2013, January 31), *National Post.*

123. See, for instance, Nixon, R. D., Hitt, M. A., Lee, H.-U., and Jeong, E. (2004), Market reactions to announcements of corporate downsizing actions and implementation strategies, *Strategic Management Journal, 25,* pp. 1121–1129; Love, E. G., and Nohria, N. (2005), Reducing slack: The performance consequences of downsizing by large industrial firms, *Strategic Management Journal, 26,* pp. 1087–1108. A very good review of the literature is in Datta, D., Guthrie, J., Basuil, D., and Pandey, A. (2010), Causes and effects of employee downsizing: A review and synthesis, *Journal of Management, 36,* pp. 281–348.

124. Arenburg, P. B. (2015, January 13), Shock of a sudden job loss, *Chronicle Herald,* pp. B1, B4.

125. Duffy, A. (2009, March 14), Forest workers lose hope as downturn deepens; log loader no longer gives a damn, *Times-Colonist* (Victoria), p. B1.

126. Cameron, K. (1994, Summer), Strategies for successful organizational downsizing, *Human Resource Management,* p. 192.

127. Cameron, K., Freeman, S., and Mishra, A. (1991), Best practices in white collar downsizing: Managing contradictions, *Academy of Management Executive, 5,* pp. 57–73.

128. Campeau, M. (2017, February 20), Organizational change leads to increase in sick leave: Study, *Canadian HR Reporter,* pp. 1, 8.

129. See, for instance, Wagar, T. H. (1996, June), What do we know about downsizing? *Benefits and Pensions Monitor,* pp. 19–20, 69.

130. Mishra, A. (2009, January 17), Zappos uses social networks for announcing downsizing, accessed November 30, 2018, from http://www.trustiseverything.com/blog/zappos-uses-social-networks-for-announcing-downsizing/

131. Bernier, L. (2014, September 8), Your employer brand in 140 characters, *Canadian HR Reporter,* p. 11.

132. These issues are discussed in more detail in Mone, M. (1994, Summer), Relationships between self-concepts, aspirations, emotional responses, and intent to leave a downsizing organization, *Human Resource Management,* pp. 281–298.

133. Wright B., and Barling, J. (1998, December), The executioners' song: Listening to downsizers reflect on their experiences, *Canadian Journal of Administrative Sciences,* pp. 339–355; see also Clair, J., and Dufresne, R. (2004), Playing the Grim Reaper: How employees experience carrying out a downsizing, *Human Relations, 57,* pp. 1597–1625.

134. Frey, C., and Osborne, M. (2013), *The Future of Employment,* Oxford Martin Programme on Technology and Employment.

135. See Lamb, C. (2016, June), *The Talented Mr. Robot—The Impact of Automation on Canada's Workforce,* The Brookfield Institute for Innovation; Arntz, M., Gregory, T., and Zierahn, U. (2016), *The Risk of Automation for Jobs in OECD Countries: A Comparative Analysis,* OECD Social Employment and Migration Working Papers, No. 189, OECD; Oschinski, M., and Wyonch, R. (2017), *Future Shock? The Impact of Automation on Canada's Labour Market,* C.D. Howe Institute.

136. 42% of Canadian jobs at high risk of being affected by automation, new study suggests (2016, June 15), *CBC News,* accessed November 30, 2018, from https://www.cbc.ca/news/business/automation-job-brookfield-1.3636253

137. See Deloitte and Human Resources Professional Association of Canada

(2017), *The Intelligence Revolution: Future-proofing Canada's Workforce.*

138. Mahdawi, A. (2017, June 26), What jobs will still be around in 20 years? Read this to prepare your future, *The Guardian.*

139. Sagan, A. (2017, October 25), Retail jobs being put at risk, experts say, *Chronicle Herald.*

140. Wingfield, N. (2017, September 18), As Amazon pivots toward automation, workers assume more "engaging" roles, *Globe and Mail.*

141. What's the top HR challenge? (2012, March 12), *Canadian HR Reporter,* p. 4.

142. This is discussed in more detail in Reichheld, F. F. (1996), *The Loyalty Effect,* Boston: Harvard Business School Press.

143. Hays (2017), *What People Want,* accessed November 30, 2018, from http://www .hays.com/resources/what-people-want-2017/index.htm

144. Galt, V. (2005, September 10), Shock: The number 1 reason people leave their jobs, *The Globe and Mail,* p. B10.

145. Bank of Montreal (2014, August 28), Annual BMO Labour Day Survey: How Are Canadian Businesses Retaining Talented Employees? accessed November 30, 2018, from https:// newsroom.bmo.com/2014-08-28-Annual-BMO-Labour-Day-Survey-How-Are-Canadian-Businesses-Retaining-Talented-Employees

146. Brooks, C. (2014, February 21), 10 signs your employee is ready to quit, *Business News Daily.*

147. Karakowsky, L., and Kotlyar, I. (2011, December 5), Think you know your high performers? *Canadian HR Reporter,* p. 23.

148. Solomon, C. M. (1997, August), Keep them! Don't let your best people get away, *Workforce,* pp. 46–51.

149. See, for example, Batt, R. (2002), Managing customer services: Human resource practices, quit rates, and sales growth, *Academy of Management Journal, 45,* pp. 587–597; Hughes, L. (2006, January), The effects of human resource management and union member status on employees' intentions to quit, Queen's University Industrial Relations Centre Research Program.

CHAPTER 12

1. Barling J., and Frone, M. (Eds.) (2004), *The Psychology of Workplace Safety,* Washington: APA, p. 4.

2. Gorman, M. (2011, May 9), Westray miner: Workplace safety still lags, *Chronicle Herald,* p. A3; see also Gorman, M. (2012, May 9), Westray legacy: Better safety, in theory, *Chronicle Herald,* p. A3.

3. Bird, Jr., F. E. (1974), *Management Guide to Loss Control,* Atlanta, GA: Institute Press.

4. Ibid.

5. Kelloway, E. K., Francis, L., and Montgomery, J. (2006), *Management of Occupational Health and Safety* (3rd ed.), Toronto: Nelson.

6. Charges laid in workplace accident (2008, November 13), *Calgary Herald,* p. B5.

7. Schwartz, D. (2014, April 28), Workplace safety by the numbers, *CBC News,* accessed November 30, 2018, from https:// www.cbc.ca/news/canada/workplace-safety-by-the-numbers-1.2622466; see also Human Resources and Social Development Canada (2010), *Occupational Injuries and Diseases in Canada: 1996–2008,* Ottawa, ON: Government of Canada.

8. Grant, T. (2001, June 18), Inquest reports on kids at Work tragedy, *Canadian HR Reporter,* pp. 13.

9. Grant, T. (2014, December 5), Asbestos top source of workplace deaths in Canada, *The Globe and Mail,* pp. A1, A6.

10. See Association of Workers' Compensation Boards of Canada; It hurts where? (2013, September 9), *Canadian HR Reporter,* p. 4.

11. Luke, P. (2009, March 15), Safety yields bigger returns, *The Province* (Vancouver), p. A28.

12. Buehler, M., Werna, E., and Brown, M. (2017, March 23), More than 2 million people die at work each year: Here's how to prevent it, *World Economic Forum.*

13. Kelloway, K., and Francis, L. (2010), *Management of Occupational Health and Safety* (5th ed.), Toronto: Nelson.

14. Krugel, L. (2017, October 19), Bodies removed from B.C. arena following ammonia leak, evacuation order persists, *National Post;* Karstens-Smith, G. (2018, March 18), After B.C. ammonia deaths, experts say inspections, training needed at Canadian ice rinks, *National Post.*

15. See also Kelloway, E. K., Francis, L., and Montgomery, J. (2006), *Management of Occupational Health and Safety* (3rd ed.), Toronto: Nelson.

16. Dobson, S. (2017, September 18), Prolonged standing carries health risks, *Canadian HR Reporter,* pp. 1, 10.

17. Perreaux, P. (2010, December 24), For letter carriers, 'tis the season to be cautious, *The Globe and Mail,* p. A7.

18. Hume, S. (2012, April 5), NHL rinks are an unsafe workplace, *Vancouver Sun.*

19. Tim's worker hurt (2014, November 4), *Chronicle Herald,* p. A7.

20. Marcoux, J., and Annable, K. (2017, November 30), Penalties when workers die on the job don't go far enough, say labour groups, families, *CBC News.*

21. For more information, see Justice Laws Website, Canada Labour Code, Part II.

22. Health Canada, Workplace Hazardous Materials Information System.

23. Callaghan, J. (2013, October 21), GHS set to replace WHMIS—sort of—in 2015, *Canadian HR Reporter,* p. 12.

24. More information on the Canadian Centre for Occupational Health and Safety is available from the Centre's website, and from its annual reports.

25. The websites for the various provincial governments are very informative.

26. Dobson, S. (2018, February), Alberta revamps its safety rules, *Canadian HR Reporter,* pp. 1, 8.

27. See a full copy of the *Canada Labour Code.*

28. Syncrude fined for worker's death (2011, February 22), *Chronicle Herald,* p. E2.

29. Dobson, S. (2013, October 21), Alberta OHL levying cash fines against employers, workers, *Canadian HR Reporter,* p. 6, accessed November 30, 2018, from https:// www.hrreporter.com/article/19179-alberta-ohs-levying-cash-fines-against-employers-workers/

30. Nova Scotia to increase fines, step up enforcement around skilled trades (2018, February 28), *The Chronicle Herald.*

31. Parkland Construction charged after worker Alan Fraser's death (2015, February 18), *CBC News,* accessed November 30, 2018, from https://www.cbc .ca/news/canada/nova-scotia/parkland-construction-charged-after-worker-alan-fraser-s-death-1.2961502; also see: Parkland Construction given $70,000 penalty for 2013 workplace death (2016, May 19), *Chronicle Herald.*

32. Aceto-Guerin, A. (2013, March 11), What to do when an OHS inspector shows up, *Canadian HR Reporter,* p. 13.

33. Hunter, J. (2014, April 15), Safety board blamed for lack of prosecution in deadly blast, *The Globe and Mail,* pp. A1, A12.

34. Jackson, D. (2013, November 21), AG: Safety process lax, *Chronicle Herald,* pp. B1, B2.

35. Marcoux, J., and Annable, K. (2017, November 30), Penalties when workers die on the job don't go far enough, say labour groups, families, *CBC News.*

36. Borden Colley, S. (2005, June 21), HRM must pay badly burned worker, *Chronicle Herald* (Halifax), p. B1.

37. Horizon North managers constantly reinforcing safety (2017, October 24), *Canadian Occupational Safety.*

38. Giroday, G. (2009, May 6), Face shields for bus drivers sought, *Winnipeg Free Press,* p. B1.

39. Pomfret, B. (1999, January 25), Sound employee orientation program boosts productivity and safety, *Canadian HR Reporter,* pp. 17, 19.

40. See Institute for Work and Health; see also Brooks Arenburg, P. (2015, January 30), Tough haul of shiftwork, *Chronicle Herald,* pp. B1, B2.

41. Bernier, L. (2014, April 21), Losing sleep over losing sleep, *Canadian HR Reporter,* pp. 1, 7.

42. Smith, S. (2014, December 22), Stress, fatigue and reduced productivity: The true cost of sleepless workers, *EHS Today,* accessed November 30, 2018, from https://www.ehstoday.com/health/stress-fatigue-and-reduced-productivity-true-cost-sleepless-workers

43. See: Petro-Canada fined after worker burned (2008, December 11), *Times-Colonist* (Victoria), p. A7; Slade, D. (2009, March 21), Shaw fined $75K after employee burned, *Calgary Herald,* p. B2; Truck repair firm fined $120K after worker killed on job (2009, May 13), *Ottawa Citizen,* p. D4.

44. Young, L. (1999, May 17), Are you sure you've got health and safety covered? *Canadian HR Reporter,* pp. 18–19.

45. First Bill C-45 conviction and fine (2008, April 30), *Daily Commercial News; see also* Perreault, M. C., with Lemelin, V., and Levac, P. (2008, May), The Transpavé Inc. case: A Quebec company pays for its negligence, *In Fact and in Law,* accessed November 30, 2018, from https://www.lavery.ca/DATA/PUBLICATION/965_en~v~the-transpave-inc-case-a-quebec-company-pays-for-its-negligence.pdf

46. McCann, M. (2013, September 25), ONCA: $750,000 fine under Bill C-45, *Lexology,* accessed November 30, 2018, from https://www.lexology.com/library/detail.aspx?g=9ad07d74-7955-43a6-b5a7-3d445d936c65. Also see: Perkel, C. (2018, January 30), Supervisor's conviction, prison term upheld in deadly Toronto scaffolding collapse, *Canadian Press.*

47. Lim, E. (2017, November 8), Piercing the corporate veil: Assessing the effectiveness of the Corporate Manslaughter and Corporate Homicide Act 2007 ten years on, *Cambridge University Law Society,* accessed November 30, 2018, from https://culs.org.uk/per-incuriam/legal-updates/piercing-corporate-veil-assessing-effectiveness-corporate-manslaughter-corporate-homicide-act-2007-ten-years/

48. Grant, C. (2014, October 28), SaskPower head quits after study of safety, *Chronicle Herald,* p. B6.

49. Annable, K., Marcoux, J., and Marcoux, V. L. (2017, November 30), The price of death, *CBC News.*

50. Vu, U. (2004, August 9), Right to refuse dangerous work expands, *Canadian HR Reporter,* pp. 1, 2.

51. High rate of non-compliance with safety protocols (2011, August 15), *Canadian HR Reporter,* p. 4.

52. Dhillon, S. (2014, August 9), Mine workers said to have reported safety worries in months before spill, *The Globe and Mail,* p. A7.

53. Humber, T. (2008, October 20), Target: Zero fatalities, *Canadian HR Reporter.*

54. Dobson, S. (2011, October 10), Making sure the shoe—and hard hat—fits, *Canadian HR Reporter,* pp. 20, 26.

55. Cook, T. (2006, January 31), Miners' safety training paid off, *Chronicle Herald* (Halifax), p. A3.

56. Faulk, J. (2012, March 12), Conveying safety messages—in any language, *Canadian HR Reporter,* pp. 11, 18.

57. Silliker, A. (2013, April 8), Will your staff help if a customer falls ill? *Canadian HR Reporter,* pp. 1, 12.

58. Kenning, S. (2013, May 20), Employee safety in global hot spots, *Canadian HR Reporter,* p. 16.

59. Walmart to pay $2 million after employee trampled to death (2009, May 14), *Canadian HR Reporter.*

60. Robertson, J. (2011, April 3), Firm gives kudos despite spill, *Chronicle Herald,* p. A8.

61. Bernier, L. (2013, December 16), Safety training to be mandatory in Ontario, *Canadian HR Reporter,* pp. 1, 6.

62. Black, D. (1999, May 31), Due diligence: Your company's best defence against an occupational health and safety offence, *Canadian HR Reporter,* pp. 17, 19.

63. Blatchford, A. (2014, October 28), Safety board seeks rail accident data, *Chronicle Herald,* p. B4. Also see: Brunette, A., and Nakonechny, S. (2018, February 5), Former MMA bosses plead guilty to federal charges in Lac-Mégantic tragedy, *CBC News.*

64. Occupational Health and Safety (n.d.), *A How-to Guide for an Occupational Health and Safety Policy and Program,* accessed November 30, 2018, from https://novascotia.ca/lae/healthandsafety/docs/GuideOHSPolicy.pdf

65. Stewart, R. (2005, March 28), The challenge of creating a culture of safety, *Canadian HR Reporter,* p. 11.

66. Neal, A., and Griffin, M. (2004), Safety climate and safety at work, in J. Barling and M. Frone (Eds.), *The Psychology of Workplace Safety,* Washington: APA, pp. 15–34.

67. Chabun, W. (2009, May 11), Safety a state of mind, *Leader Post* (Regina), p. D1. See also: Saskatchewan's top employers 2015 (2015), *Star Phoenix and Leader Post,* p. 11. Also see: Johnstone, B. (2016, April 26), WCB CEO credits Mission: Zero with improved injury rate in Saskatchewan, *Regina Leader-Post.*

68. Simpson, S. (2008, May 31), Report attacks CN's approach to safety, *Vancouver Sun,* p. A3; see also: Nicol, J., and Seglins, D. (2013, October 24), CN hiding derailment, falsifying stats, employees allege, *CBC News.*

69. For an interesting review of the safety–job insecurity issue, see Probst, T. (2004), Job insecurity: Exploring a new threat to employee safety, in J. Barling and M. Frone (Eds.), *The Psychology of Workplace Safety,* Washington: APA, pp. 63–80; see also: McKelvey, J., and Colwick, J. (2009, October 1), Leading through downsizing, *Occupational Health and Safety,* accessed November 30, 2018, from https://ohsonline.com/articles/2009/10/01/leading-through-downsizing.aspx

70. Canadian Centre for Occupational Health and Safety (2000, April 28), Workplace stress, accessed November 30, 2018, from https://www.ccohs.ca/oshanswers/psychosocial/stress.html

71. ComPsych (2017, October 30), Three out of five employees are highly stressed, according to ComPsych Survey, *2017 Stress Pulse Survey,* accessed November 30, 2018, from https://www.compsych.com/press-room/press-article?nodeId=37b20f13-6b88-400e-9852-0f1028bd1ec1

72. Livingston, G. (2018, July 9), Survey says: We're stressed (and not loving it), *The Globe and Mail,* p. B17; see also Grant, T. (2015, February 2), Working it out, *The Globe and Mail,* p. L1, L6.

73. See: Managing stress at work: A how-to for employers (n.d.), Canadian Federation of Independent Business, accessed November 30, 2018, from https://www.cfib-fcei.ca/en/tools-resources/managing-stress-work-how-employers

74. Dube, D. E. (2017, August 16), Stress is the reason 1 in 4 Canadians quit their job, *Global News.*

75. International Labour Organization (2012, Feburary 20), *Encyclopaedia of Occupational Health and Safety* (4th ed.), Waldorf, MA: ILO, accessed November 30, 2018, from https://www.ilo.org/safework/info/publications/WCMS_113329/lang--en/index.htm

76. Mental health association calling for psychological safety in workplaces (2010, December 7), *The Globe and Mail,* p. E7.

77. For more information and to download the National Standard, see https://www.mentalhealthcommission.ca.

78. National Institute for Occupational Safety and Health (1999), *Stress at Work,* Washington, DC: U.S. Department of Health and Human Services, accessed November 30, 2018, from https://www.cdc.gov/niosh/docs/99-101/

79. Boesveld, S. (2009, March 2), Exhaustion, longer hours, heavier workload, greater responsibility, unbearable stress juggling, *The Globe and Mail,* p. L1.

80. Crompton, S. (2011, October 13), What's stressing the stressed? Main sources of stress among workers, *Canadian Social Trends,* Statistics Canada, accessed November 30, 2018, from https://www150.statcan.gc.ca/n1/pub/11-008-x/2011002/article/11562-eng.htm

81. CareerCast (2017), The most stressful jobs of 2017, accessed November 30,

2018, from https://www.careercast.com/jobs-rated/most-stressful-jobs-2017

82. Bad bosses may affect health of workers (2005, October 28), *The Globe and Mail,* p. C2.

83. Burn, D. (1997, December 29), Parents' job anxiety wreaks havoc on children, *Canadian HR Reporter,* pp. 16, 20.

84. Silliker, A. (2012, January 30), Employers in best position to fight depression, *Canadian HR Reporter,* pp. 3, 8.

85. Morris, H. (2008, September 2), Study finds high levels of stress at call centres, *Ottawa Citizen,* p. D8.

86. Higginbottom, K. (2018, April 20), The price of presenteeism, *Forbes,* accessed November 30, 2018, from https://www.forbes.com/sites/karenhigginbottom/2018/04/20/the-price-of-presenteeism-2/#72a599d67f9c

87. Young, O., and Johnson, K. (2016, January), *The Future of Wellness at Work,* Global Wellness Institute.

88. ComPsych (2017, October 30), Three out of five employees are highly stressed, according to ComPsych Survey, *2017 Stress Pulse Survey,* accessed November 30, 2018, from https://www.compsych.com/press-room/press-article?nodeId=37b20f13-6b88-400e-9852-0f1028bd1ec1

89. Veder B., and Beaudoin, K. (2014, March 24), Face-to-face—But not in person, *Canadian HR Reporter,* p. 20.

90. National Institute for Occupational Safety and Health (1999), *Stress at Work,* Washington, DC: U.S. Department of Health and Human Service, accessed November 30, 2018, from https://www.cdc.gov/niosh/docs/99-101/

91. Ibid.

92. Mental Health Commission of Canada, *Making the Case for Investing in Mental Health in Canada,* accessed November 30, 2018, from https://www.mentalhealthcommission.ca/sites/default/files/2016-06/Investing_in_Mental_Health_FINAL_Version_ENG.pdf

93. Boyer, C., and Chenier, L. (2014, November 17), Does workplace wellness really matter? *Canadian HR Reporter,* p. 19.

94. Bernier, L. (2013, November 4), Breaking down barriers—1 cup at a time, *Canadian HR Reporter,* pp. 18, 20.

95. Sun Life Canadian Health Index (2014); see also 2016 Sun Life Canadian Health Index, accessed November 30, 2018, from https://cdn.sunlife.com/static/ca/Learn%20and%20Plan/Market%20insights/Canadian%20Health%20index/Canadian_Health_Index_2016_en.pdf

96. Chai, C. (2017, May 5), 500,000 Canadians miss work each week due to mental health concerns, *Global News.*

97. Marchand, A., Durand, P., Haines, V., and Harvey, S. (2014), The multilevel determinants of worker mental health: Results from the SALVEO Study, *Social Psychiatry and Psychiatric Epidemiology.*

98. Dobson, S. (2013, September 23), Mental health Bible overhauled, *Canadian HR Reporter,* pp. 1, 11.

99. Smith, J. (2013, February 11), Safety trumps accommodation for worker with mental illness, *Canadian HR Reporter,* p. 5.

100. Vander Wier, M. (2016, November 28), Saskatchewan workers' psychological injuries presumed work-related, *Canadian HR Reporter,* pp. 1, 7.

101. ComPsych (2013, January 14), Weight loss is employees' top new year's resolution, according to ComPsych Survey, accessed November 30, 2018, from https://www.prnewswire.com/news-releases/weight-loss-is-employees-top-new-years-resolution-according-to-compsych-survey-186797221.html

102. *Sun Life Buffet National Wellness Survey, 2013.*

103. Conference Board of Canada (2017), *Wellness Initiatives: Trends in Organizational Health Initiatives.*

104. Vander Wier, M. (2017, October 30), Niagara casinos awarded for wellness, psychological safety, *Canadian HR Reporter,* pp. 6, 16.

105. Aon Hewitt (2013, March), Rapid Response Survey on Wellness, accessed November 30, 2018, from http://www.aon.com/canada/attachments/thought-leadership/rapidresponse/report_rr_march2013.pdf

106. Dobson, S. (2013, May 6), Smokers need not apply, *Canadian HR Reporter.*

107. Shields, R. (2014, May 5), Training around privacy, *Canadian HR Reporter,* p. 12.

108. Gray, J. (2013, June 14), Ruling could make random alcohol testing tougher, *The Globe and Mail.*

109. Bernier, L. (2016, May 2), Fitness program helps to end sedentary behaviour, *Canadian HR Reporter,* pp. 1, 10.

110. See *Canadian HR Reporter,* April 11, 2005, p. 20. See also https://www.worksmartlivesmart.com.

111. Becker, B. E., Huselid, M. A., Pickus, P. S., and Spratt, M. F. (1997, Spring), HR as a source of shareholder value: Research and recommendations, *Human Resource Management,* pp. 39–47.

112. Successful wellness programs involve leadership, stress management (2018, March 1), *Benefits Canada.*

113. Dobson, S. (2014, November 17), Are you prepared for a lockdown? *Canadian HR Reporter,* pp. 1, 8.

114. Safety strategies for a post-Sept. 11 world (2002, October), *HRFocus,* pp. 3–5.

115. Rakobowchuk, P. (2015, March 6), Several attacks leave letter carriers worried, *Chronicle Herald,* p. A12; Larsen, K. (2017, June 5), Union asks Canada Post to come clean on scope of mail theft from community boxes, *CBC News.*

116. Dobson, S. (2010, November 29), Learning to avoid the bad guys, *Canadian HR Reporter,* pp. 24, 26.

117. This material is taken from the U.S. Environmental Protection Agency, see https://www.epa.gov/iaq/pubs/sbs.html

118. This information is based on an article by Morgan, K. (1998, February– March), Sick building syndrome, *Human Resources Professional,* pp. 39–40.

119. Zolfagharifard, E. (2014, February 18), Are energy efficient homes making us ill? *Daily Mail Online,* accessed November 30, 2018, from https://www.dailymail.co.uk/sciencetech/article-2562146/Are-energy-efficient-homes-making-ILL-Toxic-mould-caused-poor-air-circulation-trigger-sick-building-syndrome.html

120. See The Canadian Initiative on Workplace Violence, accessed November 30, 2018, from workplaceviolence.ca; see also Bernier, L. (2014, May 5), Termination nightmare: Stabbing rampage raises unsettling questions, *Canadian HR Reporter,* pp. 1, 8.

121. Mojtehedzadel, S. (2017, November 5), Violence against health-care workers "out of control," survey finds, *Toronto Star.*

122. Botelho, G. (2014, September 28), Workplace violence: Know the numbers, risk factors and possible warning signs, *CNN,* accessed November 30, 2018, from https://www.cnn.com/2014/09/27/us/workplace-violence-questions-answers/index.html

123. See https://www.shrm.org; see also Society for Human Resource Management (1999), *1999 Workplace Violence Survey,* Alexandria, VI: SHRM.

124. Lebron, A. (2017, October 30), The latest on workplace violence statistics, *RaveMobileSafety.*

125. COMPAS (2007, February 26), *Violence and Aggression in the Workplace,* accessed November 30, 2018, from http://www.compas.ca/data/070226-ViolenceInTheWorkplace-PB.pdf

126. Most common ways in which cyber stalking cases escalated in 2013 (n.d.), *statista,* accessed November 30, 2018, from https://www.statista.com/statistics/291257/cyber-stalking-victims-how-case-escalated/

127. Klie, S. (2005, November 21), Screening new hires won't end workplace violence, study says, *Canadian HR Reporter,* pp. 1, 3.

128. Viollis P., and Mathers, C. (2005, March 14), Companies need to re-engineer their cultural thinking about workplace violence, *Canadian HR Reporter,* p. 19.

129. Bernier, L. (2014, April 7), Picking up the pieces, *Canadian HR Reporter,* pp. 1, 8.

130. Mellor, C. (2014, May 31), Battling bullies, *Chronicle Herald,* pp. B1, B2.

131. Western University and Canadian Labour Congress (2014), *Can Work Be Safe, When Home Isn't?* accessed November 30, 2018, from http://makeitourbusiness.ca/sites/makeitourbusiness.ca/files/DVWork_Survey_Report_2014_EN_0.pdf

132. Kelloway, K., and Francis, L. (2010), *Management of Occupational Health and Safety* (5th ed.), Toronto: Nelson.

133. Hagan, P., Montgomery, J., and O'Reilly, J. (2009), *Accident Prevention Manual for Business and Industry* (13th ed.), Washington, DC: National Safety Council.

134. Don't forget to tie workplace wellness programs into ergonomics and safety programs (n.d.), *KED,* accessed November 30, 2018, from https://www.kedproductivity.com/articles/don%E2%80%99t-forget-tie-workplace-wellness-programs-ergonomics-and-safety-programs

135. See: Painful disorders focus on International Repetitive Strain Injury Day (2017, February 28), *Canadian Occupational Safety.*

136. For further information, see http://www.tifaq.org/information/rsi.html.

137. Ergonomic issues are discussed in much more detail in Kelloway, E. K., Francis, L., and Montgomery, J. (2006), *Management of Occupational Health and Safety* (3rd ed.), Toronto: Nelson.

138. Stuart, N. (2000, October 6), Open offices drive workers up the wall, *The Globe and Mail,* p. B11.

139. See *Canada's 2016 Global AIDS Response Progress Report,* accessed November 30, 2018, from http://www.unaids.org/sites/default/files/country/documents/CAN_narrative_report_2016.pdf

140. Information on AIDS can be obtained from the Canadian AIDS Society; see also UNAIDS 2011 World Aids Day Report.

141. Breckenridge, J. J. (1988, June 29), Nurse with AIDS gets job back, but row over dismissal goes on, *The Globe and Mail,* p. A10.

142. *Business Week* (1993, February 1), p. 53; see also the HIV/AIDS Toolkit developed by the Society for Human Resource Management, accessed November 30, 2018, from https://vcurrtc.org/resources/printview.cfm/335

143. The Canadian Human Rights Commission has considerable information about AIDS on its website. Similarly, information is readily available from provincial human rights commissions. For example, see the Ontario Human Rights Commission's Policy on HIV/Aids-Related Discrimination.

CHAPTER 13

1. Gunderson, M., Ponak, A., and Gottlieb Taras, D. (2005), *Union–Management Relations in Canada* (4th ed.), Toronto: Pearson, p. 10.

2. Chilibeck, J. (2008, December 23), Clause that clogs the wheel, *Telegraph Journal,* p. C1.

3. Fine, S. (2015, January 17), Mounties win the right to unionize, *The Globe and Mail,* p. A10.

4. Kimber, S. (2015, January–February), Brewhaha, *Atlantic Business,* pp. 26–34.

5. Cameron, M. (2015, August 27), Unionized coffee shops grind out a future, *The Coast.*

6. Murray, M. (1995), Unions: Membership, structure and actions, in M. Gunderson and A. Ponak (Eds.), *Union–Management Relations in Canada* (3rd ed.), Don Mills, ON: Addison-Wesley.

7. Barling, J., Fullagar, C., and Kelloway, K. (1992), *The Union and Its Members: A Psychological Approach,* New York: Oxford University Press.

8. Brethour, P. (2005, October 17), Bitter strike divides Alberta town, *The Globe and Mail,* pp. 1, 7.

9. Leger (2013, October), *LabourWatch State of the Unions 2013,* accessed November 30, 2018, from https://www.labourwatch.com/docs/research/Leger_State_of_the_Unions_October_2013_Report.pdf

10. CAUT Harris-Decima (2013, November 29), *CAUT Harris-Decima Public Opinion Poll.*

11. Leslie, K. (2012, February 4), Caterpillar closes plant after lockout, *Chronicle Herald,* p. B2. For a review of the Caterpillar closure and its implications, see Grant, T. (2012, February 22), The Caterpillar shutdown's stark warning for the industrial heartland, *The Globe and Mail,* pp. A8–A9.

12. Silliker, A. (2011, December 5), Canada's labour relations at the crossroads, *Canadian HR Reporter,* pp. 1, 9.

13. Allemang, J. (2012, March 24), Organized labour is fighting to survive, *The Globe and Mail.*

14. Taber, J. (2012, March 7), Union tensions on the rise, *The Globe and Mail,* pp. A1, A4.

15. Gompers, S. (1919), *Labor and the Common Welfare,* Freeport, NY: Books for Libraries Press, p. 20.

16. An editorial in *Canadian Labour,* June 1968, p. 5.

17. Dobson, S. (2013, April 8), CAW's women's advocate program presented at UN session, *Canadian HR Reporter,* p. 3.

18. Tannenbaum, F. (1921), *The Labour Movement, Its Conservative Functions and Consequences,* New York: Alfred A. Knopf.

19. Perlman, S. (1928), *A Theory of the Labour Movement,* New York: Macmillan.

20. Lipton, C. (1967), *The Trade Union Movement in Canada, 1827–1959,* Montreal, QC: Canadian Social Publications, p. 4.

21. Union coverage in Canada—2013 (2014, June), Workplace Information and Research Division, Labour Program, Employment and Social Development Canada.

22. Statistics Canada (2017), *Labour Force Survey.* See Tables 282-0220 and 282-0223.

23. Nanji, S. (2013, September 9), Walmart workers reject union, *Canadian HR Reporter,* pp. 1, 11.

24. Sova, G. (2009, January 15), Union targeting second-largest food retailer, *Canadian HR Reporter;* see also: UFCW (2014, June 30), Canada's leading union committed to representing members impacted by Sobeys announcement, accessed November 30, 2018, from http://www.ufcw.ca/index.php?option=com_content&view=article&id=4088:canada-s-leading-union-committed-to-representing-members-impacted-by-sobeys-announcement&catid=546&Itemid=6&lang=en

25. Nanji, S. (2014, January 27), Labour pains, *Canadian HR Reporter,* pp. 16–17.

26. Cohn, M. R. (2018, January 24), Why Tim Hortons' foul play gives unions a big assist, *Toronto Star.*

27. Uppal, S. (2011, October), *Unionization 2011,* accessed November 30, 2018, from https://www150.statcan.gc.ca/n1/en/pub/75-001-x/2011004/article/11579-eng.pdf?st=ykOnu1Nn

28. Why trade unions are declining (2015, September 29), *The Economist,* accessed November 30, 2018, from https://www.economist.com/the-economist-explains/2015/09/29/why-trade-unions-are-declining.

29. McCarthy, N. (2017, June 20), Which countries have the highest levels of union membership? *Forbes.*

30. Wilhelm, T. (2009, May 22), Tension rising on the line: City strike turns ugly, *Windsor Star,* p. A1.

31. Godard, J. (1992, October), Strikes as collective voice: A behavioral analysis of strike activity, *Industrial and Labor Relations Review,* pp. 161–175.

32. Adam, M., and Deachman, B. (2009, January 6), Transit workers vow to strike as long as it takes, *Ottawa Citizen,* p. A1.

33. Herald, D. (2002, September 9), Back to work doesn't mean back to normal, *Canadian HR Reporter,* pp. 8, 11.

34. Godard, J. (1992, October), Strikes as collective voice: A behavioral analysis of strike activity, *Industrial and Labor Relations Review,* pp. 161–175.

35. Klie, S. (2011, February 28), Labour debate rages in Quebec, *Canadian HR Reporter,* pp. 1, 2.

36. Voisey's Bay mine strike over (2011, February 1), *Chronicle Herald,* p. C3.

37. See: Massive pilot sick-out makes Air Berlin cancel 100 flights (2017, September 12), *Fortune.*

38. Blanchfield, M. (2015, January 31), Top court OKs right to strike, *Chronicle Herald,* p. A5.

39. Gray, J., and Fletcher, J. (2013, November 16), Top court's ruling on union rights hailed as victory for freedom of expression, *The Globe and Mail,* p. A19.

40. Melnitzer, J. (2016, February), The right to strike: Supreme Court's labour trilogy has wide ranging impacts, *Lexpert Magazine.*

41. Immen, W. (2005, October 5), How to heal a bruised workplace, *The Globe and Mail,* pp. C1, C2.

42. Statistics Canada (2018), Labour Force Survey, CANSIM 282-0073.

43. Freeman, R. B., and Medoff, J. L. (1984), *What Do Unions Do?* New York: Basic Books.

44. Gunderson, M., and Hyatt, D. (2009), Union impact on compensation, productivity, and management of the organization, in M. Gunderson and D. Gottlieb Taras (Eds.), *Canadian Labour and Employment Relations* (6th ed.), Toronto: Pearson.

45. Tomlinson, A. (2002, August 12), Union cracks down on workers with bad habits, *Canadian HR Reporter,* pp. 1, 11.

46. Klie, S. (2005, October 24), Replacement workers put pressure on the union but at what cost? *Canadian HR Professional,* pp. 11, 12.

47. Campbell, F. (2018, February 15), Principals given one year to decide: Leave union or go back to classroom, *The Chronicle Herald.*

48. Dobson, S. (2011, November 7), Collective bargaining under fire: Hargrove, *Canadian HR Reporter,* pp. 3, 18.

49. Adams, G. W. (2012), *Canadian Labour Law* (2nd ed.), Aurora, ON: Canada Law Book.

50. Smith, J. (2012, February 13), Vale must open its gates to fired worker: Board, *Canadian HR Reporter,* pp. 5, 8.

51. Meany, G. (1976, July), Organizing a continuing effort, *The American Federationist,* p. 1.

52. See http://www.ufcw1006a.ca/ for more information about these initiatives.

53. For an interesting view of union organizing in the United States, see Fulmer, E. (1991), Step by step through an organizing campaign, *Harvard Business Review, 59,* pp. 94–102.

54. Harris, L. (2008, June 25), Technology providing organizing options, *Canadian HR Reporter.*

55. Roper, T. (2013, February 25), Class-action litigation—new tool for unions, *Canadian HR Reporter,* pp. 23, 24.

56. Knight, J. (2013, October 21), What you can do if a union comes knocking, *Canadian HR Reporter,* p. 5.

57. Adams, G. W. (2012), *Canadian Labour Law* (2nd ed.), Aurora, ON: Canada Law Book.

58. Fish processor pays for union-busting closures (2005, December 5), *Canadian HR Reporter,* p. 2.

59. Dujay, J. (2018, January), New tools for unions in Ontario, *Canadian HR Reporter,* pp. 1, 17.

60. Adams, G. W. (2012), *Canadian Labour Law* (2nd ed.), Aurora, ON: Canada Law Book.

61. Marin, S. (2014, June 28), Wal-Mart staff win case, *Chronicle Herald,* p. A14.

62. Dujay, J. (2017, September 4), Are longer-term agreements the new normal? *Canadian HR Reporter,* pp. 26–27.

63. Walton, R. E., Cutcher-Gershenfeld, J. E., and McKersie, R. B. (1994), *Strategic Negotiations: A Theory of Change in Labor–Management Relations,* Boston: Harvard Business School Press.

64. McQuarrie, F. (2011), *Industrial Relations in Canada* (3rd ed.), Mississauga: Wiley.

65. Peirce, J. (2003), *Canadian Industrial Relations* (2nd ed.), Scarborough, Prentice Hall.

66. Nanji, S., and Foster, L. (2014, February 24), With this contract, I thee wed, *Canadian HR Reporter,* p. 15.

67. Developing HR's business skills (2004, September 13), *Canadian HR Reporter,* p. 9.

68. Keenan, G. (2014, October 7), Air Canada, pilots reach tentative 10-year agreement, *The Globe and Mail,* p. B4.

69. Fraser, M. J. (2001, September 10), Labour skeptical about win-win, *Canadian HR Reporter,* pp. 11, 12.

70. Kochan, T. A., and Osterman, P. (1994), *The Mutual Gains Enterprise,* Boston, MA: Harvard Business School Press.

71. Lendvay-Zwickl, J. (2005), *The Canadian Industrial Relations System: Current Challenges and Future Options,* Ottawa: Conference Board of Canada.

72. Vu, U. (2005, February 28), Interest wanes on interest-based? *Canadian HR Reporter,* pp. 6, 9.

73. Each jurisdiction has defined procedures relating to conciliation and mediation. As well, the distinction between these terms has been blurred. Consequently, human resource professionals need to consult the relevant legislation for their jurisdiction.

74. See the Nova Scotia Department of Labour Annual Reports for the 1992 to 2001 period.

75. Smith, J. (2014, May 5), City worker's water use doesn't wash, *Canadian HR Reporter,* p. 5.

76. Kent, G. (2017, October 25), Airport security screeners soiled themselves after they weren't allowed breaks, union says, *Edmonton Journal.*

77. Ralph, D. (2018, March 15), Supreme Court drops Arland Bruce's concussion case against CFL, *CBC Sports.*

78. Smith, J. (2013, October 7), Employee's complaint wasn't layoff request, *Canadian HR Reporter,* pp. 5, 6.

79. The judicial review of labour board and arbitration decisions is a very technical area of labour law. For an in-depth treatment, see: Charney, R. L., and Brady, T. E. F. (2008), *Judicial Review in Labour Law,* Aurora, ON: Canada Law Book.

80. These issues are discussed in more detail in: Wagar, T. H. (1997), The arbitration process: Employer and union views, in W. Kaplan, J. Sack, and M. Gunderson (Eds.), *Labour Arbitration Yearbook 1996–1997,* Toronto: Lancaster House, pp. 3–11; see also: McQuarrie, F. (2011), *Industrial Relations in Canada* (3rd ed.), Mississauga: Wiley.

81. Smith, J. (2017, May 15), Worker fired for shooting threats, *Canadian HR Reporter,* p. 10.

82. Giles, A., and Starkman, A. (2005), The collective agreement, in M. Gunderson, A. Ponak, and D. Gottlieb Taras, *Union–Management Relations in Canada* (5th ed.), Toronto: Pearson Addison Wesley, p. 306.

83. Ibid.

84. For a comprehensive review of the arbitration process, see: Brown, D. J. M., and Beatty, D. M. (2011), *Canadian Labour Arbitration* (4th. ed.), Aurora, ON: Canada Law Book.

85. Harris, L. (2004, November 8), Promotional T-shirt runs afoul of zero tolerance, *Canadian HR Reporter,* p. 5.

86. An excellent summary of the legislative requirements applicable to public sector workers is found in Adams, G. W. (2012), *Canadian Labour Law* (2nd ed.), Aurora, ON: Canada Law Books.

87. See Battersby, S. J. (2017, October 1), Everything you need to know about the Ontario colleges strike, *Halifax Metro;* Campean, T. (2018, January 24), Faculty union launches charter challenge over Ontario college strike, *Globe and Mail;* Dunne, N. (2018, January 28), Ontario college strike aftermath continues to impact students, faculty, *Ottawa Citizen.*

88. Juniper, P., Hill, A., and Raza, T. (2012), *An Inquiry into the State of Labour Relations in Canada,* Kingston, ON: Queen's University IRC.

89. This quote is taken from Human Resources Development Canada and the Organisation for Economic Co-operation and Development (1997), *Changing Workplace Strategies: Achieving Better Outcomes for Enterprises, Workers and Society,* Hull: HRDC.

90. Galt, V. (2002, February 18), Benefits seen in union-like workplace, *The Globe and Mail,* p. C1.

91. Adams, R. (2000), Canadian industrial relations at the dawn of the 21st century—prospects for reform, *Workplace Gazette, 3,* pp. 109–115.

92. Adams, R. (2006), *Labour Left Out: Canada's Failure to Protect and Promote Collective Bargaining as a Human Right,* Ottawa: Canadian Centre for Policy Alternatives.

93. See, for instance: Cooke, W. N. (1990), *Labor–Management Cooperation,* Kalamazoo, MI: W. E. Upjohn Institute; Kochan, T. A., and Osterman, P. (1994), *The Mutual Gains Enterprise,* Boston, MA: Harvard Business School Press.

94. Cooper, J., Jackson, S., and Irish, L. (2017, October 30), Evidence-based labour relations, *Canadian HR Reporter,* p. 14.

95. See, for instance: Wagar, T. H. (1997, Winter), Is labor–management climate important? Some Canadian evidence, *Journal of Labor Research,* pp. 101–112; and Dastmalchian, A. (2008), Industrial relations climate, in P. Blyton, N. Bacon, J. Fiorito, and E. Heery (Eds.), *The Sage Handbook of Industrial Relations,* London, UK: Sage, pp. 548–568.

96. Stolte, E. (2017, November 15), A punch in the face: Morale takes deep dive in city's communication branch, *Edmonton Journal.*

97. Grenier, G., and Hogler, R. (1991, August), Labor law and managerial iIdeology: Employee participation as a social control system, *Work and Occupations,* pp. 313–333. For an excellent discussion of management by stress, see: Parker, M., and Slaughter, J. (1999, October), Management by stress, *Technology Review,* pp. 37–44.

98. Unionized organizations make their mark (2010, April 13), *The Globe and Mail,* pp. GPTW1, GPTW9, accessed November 30, 2018, from http://v1 .theglobeandmail.com/partners/free/sr/ greatplacestowork/great-places-to-work-2010.pdf

99. Brown, D. (2002, March 11), Union says recognition divides workers, *Canadian HR Reporter,* pp. 1, 13.

Glossary

360-degree performance appraisal:
Combination of self, peer, supervisor, and subordinate performance evaluation.

ability tests: Tests that assess an applicant's capacity or aptitude to function in a certain way.

ads: Advertisements in a newspaper, magazine, and so on, that solicit job applicants for a position.

alternate work arrangements: Nontraditional work arrangements (e.g., flextime, telecommuting) that provide more flexibility to employees while meeting organizational goals.

alumni associations: Associations of alumni of schools, colleges, or other training facilities.

applicant tracking system (ATS): A database of potential candidates that enables a good match between job requirements and applicant characteristics and also enlarges the recruitment pool.

apprenticeships: A form of on-the-job training in which junior employees learn a trade from an experienced person.

arbitration: The settling of a dispute between labour and management by a third party.

assumption of risk: Meaning the worker accepts all the customary risks associated with his or her occupation.

attrition: Loss of employees due to their voluntary departures from the firm through resignation, retirement, or death.

authorization cards: Cards signed by workers to join a union; depending on the jurisdiction, a union may be certified either on the basis of card signatures or as a result of an election.

automation: The shift toward converting work that was traditionally done by hand to being completed by mechanical or electronic devices.

autonomy: In a job context, independence—having control over one's work and one's response to the work environment.

awareness training: Training employees to develop their understanding of the need to manage and value diversity.

balanced scorecard: An integrated organizational performance measuring approach that looks at organizational learning and innovation, financial management, internal operations, and customer management.

behavioural description interviews: Interviews that attempt to find out how job applicants responded to specific work situations in the past.

behaviourally anchored rating scales (BARS): Evaluation tools that rate employees along a rating scale by means of specific behaviour examples on the scale.

benefit audit: A system to control the efficiency of a benefit program.

biographical information blank (BIB): A type of application blank that uses a multiple-choice format to measure a job candidate's education, experiences, opinions, attitudes, and interests.

blind ads: Job ads that do not identify the employer.

blogs: Web logs—online journals, diaries, or serials published by a person or group of people.

bona fide occupational requirement (BFOR): A justified business reason for discriminating against a member of a protected class; also known as bona fide occupational qualification (BFOQ).

burnout: A condition of mental, emotional, and sometimes physical exhaustion that results from substantial and prolonged stress.

business unionism: A type of unionism whose mission is to protect workers, increase their pay, improve their working conditions, and help workers in general; it recognizes that a union can survive only if it delivers a needed service to its members in a businesslike manner.

buy-back: A method of convincing an employee who is about to resign to stay in the employ of the organization, typically by offering an increased wage or salary.

Canada Pension Plan (CPP): A mandatory, contributory, and portable pension plan applicable to all employees and self-employed persons in Canada. Public service employees have their own pension plan, the Public Service Pension Plan (PSPP), but it is coordinated with the Canada Pension Plan.

Canadian Charter of Rights and Freedoms: Federal law enacted in 1982, guaranteeing individuals equal rights before the law.

Canadian Human Rights Act: A federal law prohibiting discrimination.

Canadian Human Rights Commission (CHRC): Supervises the implementation and adjudication of the *Canadian Human Rights Act*.

Canadian Labour Congress (CLC): An organization, with a membership of about 3.3 million, that represents many unions in Canada.

Canadian Occupational Projection System (COPS): Provides up to 10-year projection of Canadian economy and human resource needs.

career management: A series of formal and less formal activities designed and managed by the organization to influence the career development of one or more employees.

career planning and development: The process through which someone becomes aware of his or her interests and needs, motivations, etc.,

in terms of a career, and engages in a lifelong series of activities in pursuit of that career.

careless worker model: The early approach to safety in the workplace, which assumed that most accidents were due to workers' failure to be careful or to protect themselves.

Chartered Professional in Human Resources (CPHR): Human resource practitioner, formally accredited to practice, who reflects a threshold professional level of practice.

collective agreement: A labour contract that addresses a variety of issues, such as wages and benefits, hours of work, working conditions, grievance procedures, safety standards, probationary periods, and work assignments; usually negotiated between the local union's bargaining committee and the human resource or industrial relations department.

communication standards: Formal protocols for internal communications within an organization to eliminate sex/gender, racial, age, or other biases in communications.

compa-ratio: An index that indicates how an individual's or a group's salary relates to the midpoint of their relevant pay grades.

comparative evaluation methods: A collection of different methods that compare one person's performance with that of co-workers.

compensatory approach: An approach where a higher score on a predictor may compensate a low score on another.

competency: A knowledge, skill, ability, or behaviour associated with successful job performance.

competency matrix: A list of the level of each competency required for each of a number of jobs.

competency model (competency framework): A list of competencies required in a particular job.

competitive advantage: An advantage that exists when the firm is able to deliver the same value and benefits as competitors but at a lower cost (cost advantage), or when the firm is able to deliver unique value or benefits that exceed those of competing products (differentiation advantage).

computer-interactive performance tests: Performance tests using computer simulations that can measure skills, comprehension, spatial visualization, judgment, etc.

concentration: A condition that exists when a department or employer has a greater proportion of members of a protected class than are found in the employer's labour market.

conciliation: Use of a government-appointed third party to explore solutions to a labour–management dispute.

constructive dismissal: A major change in the terms of the employment contract that results in an employee's resigning.

consultants: Professionals who provide expert advice and counsel in a particular area.

contract (or contingent)worker: A freelancer (self-employed, temporary, or leased employee) who is not part of the regular workforce who provides goods or services to another entity under the terms of a specific contract.

contributory plans: Benefits that require the employer to contribute to the cost of the benefit.

core dimensions of diversity: Age, ethnicity and culture, sex/gender, race, religion, sexual orientation, and capabilities.

corrective discipline: Discipline that follows a rule infraction.

cost leadership strategy: Strategy to gain competitive advantage through lower costs of operations and lower prices for products.

cost–benefit analysis: Analysis undertaken to assess the cost-effectiveness of a project or program.

costs: Expenses related to attracting recruits.

counselling: The discussion of a problem with an employee, with the general objective of helping that employee resolve the issue or cope with the situation so that he or she can become more effective.

craft unions: A type of union composed of workers who possess the same skills or trades.

cross-training: Training employees to perform operations in areas other than their assigned jobs.

crowdsourcing: The act of a company or institution taking a function once performed by employees and outsourcing it to an undefined (and generally large) network of people in the form of an open call.

cultural forces: Challenges facing a firm's decision makers because of cultural differences among employees or changes in core cultural or social values occurring at the larger societal level.

cultural mosaic: The Canadian ideal of encouraging each ethnic, racial, and social group to maintain its own cultural heritage, forming a national mosaic of different cultures.

cultural norms: Values and norms that determine behaviours of individuals and groups in different cultures.

defined benefits (DB) plan: A benefits plan whose benefits are defined by a formula based on age and length of service, with the employer assuming responsibility for funding.

defined contribution (DC) plan: A benefits plan based on amounts contributed by the employer and the employee, with the final pension depending on amounts contributed, investment income, and economic conditions at retirement.

Delphi technique: The soliciting of predictions about specified future events from a panel of experts, using repeated surveys until convergence in opinions occurs.

demographic changes: Changes in the demographics of the labour force (e.g., education levels, age levels, participation rates) that occur slowly and are usually known in advance.

development: Planned activities aimed at providing employees with enhanced skills and competencies for the future.

differential validity: Test validation process aimed at discovering the validity of a test for various subgroups, e.g., females and members of visible minorities.

differentiation strategy: Strategy to gain competitive advantage by creating a distinct product or offering a unique service.

discipline: Management action to encourage compliance with organization standards.

diversity and inclusion audits: Audits to uncover underlying dimensions, causes, interdependencies, and progress-to-date on diversity and inclusion matters.

diversity and inclusion training programs: Training programs aimed at importing new skills to motivate and manage a diverse and inclusive workforce.

diversity committee: A committee entrusted to oversee diversity efforts, implement processes, and serve as a communication link.

diversity management: Recognizing differences among employees belonging to heterogeneous groups and creating a work environment in which members of diverse groups feel comfortable.

downsizing: Reducing employment to improve efficiency, productivity, and competitiveness.

downward communication: Information that begins at some point in the organization and feeds down the organization hierarchy to inform or influence others.

drug tests: Tests that determine whether a job applicant uses marijuana, cocaine, or other drugs.

due process: In a disciplinary situation, following proper, established rules and procedures and giving employees the opportunity to respond to allegations.

duty to accommodate: Requirement that an employer must accommodate the employee to the point of "undue hardship."

economic forces: Economic factors facing Canadian business today, including global trade forces and the force to increase one's own competitiveness and productivity levels.

educational attainment: The highest educational level attained by an individual worker, employee group, or population.

educational institutions: High schools, technical schools, community colleges, and universities where applicants for job positions are sought.

efficiency: Achieving maximal output with minimal input.

employee assistance programs (EAPs): Comprehensive company programs that seek to help employees and their family members overcome personal and work-related problems.

employee attitude/opinion survey: A systematic method of determining what employees think of their organization.

employee log: An approach to collecting job- and performance-related information by asking the jobholder to summarize tasks, activities, and challenges in a diary format.

employee referrals: Recommendations by present employees to the recruiter about possible job applicants for a position.

employee self-service (ESS): A feature of an HRIS that allows employees to access and view their own records and make changes where applicable.

Employment and Social Development Canada (ESDC): Federal department that provides programs and services for employers and present and potential employees.

Employment Equity Act: Federal law to remove employment barriers and to promote equality.

employment equity programs: Developed by employers to undo past employment discrimination or to ensure equal employment opportunity in the future. Called affirmative action programs in the United States.

Employment Insurance (EI): A program to help alleviate the financial problems of workers in Canada during the transition from one job to another.

employment interview: A formal, in-depth, face-to-face, or, more recently, a phone or video conference between an employer and a job applicant to assess the appropriateness of the applicant for the job under consideration.

employment references: Evaluations of an employee's past work performance and job-relevant behaviours provided by past employers.

employment tests: Devices that assess the probable match between applicants and job requirements.

enterprise-wide systems: Systems that link an organization's entire software application environment into a single enterprise solution.

environmental considerations: The influence of the external environment on job design; includes employee ability, availability, and social expectations.

equal pay for equal work: The principle or policy of equal rates of pay for all employees in an establishment performing the same kind and amount of work, regardless of sex, race, or other characteristics of individual workers not related to ability or performance.

equal pay for work of equal value: The principle of equal pay for men and women in jobs with comparable content; based on criteria of skill, effort, responsibility, and working conditions; part of the *Canadian Human Rights Act*.

ergonomics: The study of relationships between physical attributes of workers and their work environment to reduce physical and mental strain and increase productivity and quality of work life.

evaluation interviews: Performance review sessions that give employees feedback about their past performance or future potential.

external equity: Perceived fairness in pay relative to what other employers are paying for the same type of work.

extrapolation: Extending past rates of change into the future.

feedback: Information that helps evaluate the success or failure of an action or system.

flexible benefits programs: Programs that allow employees to select the mix of benefits and services that will answer their individual needs. Also known as cafeteria benefit programs.

flexible retirement: Programs that provide retirees with the opportunity to work after they have retired and provide them with significant flexibility in terms of how they work, what they work on, when they work, and where.

focus group: A face-to-face meeting with five to seven knowledgeable experts on a job and a facilitator to collect job- and performance-related information.

focus strategy: Strategy to gain a competitive advantage by focusing on the needs of a specific segment of the total market.

forced distributions: A method of evaluating employees that requires raters to categorize employees.

forecasts: Estimates of future resource needs and changes.

full-time employees: Employees who work 37.5 to 40 hours in a workweek.

functional authority: Authority that allows staff experts to make decisions and take actions normally reserved for line managers.

gamification: The use of rules, competition, and teamwork to encourage engagement by mimicking games.

glass ceiling: Invisible but real obstructions to career advancement of women and people of visible minorities, resulting in frustration, career dissatisfaction, and increased turnover.

grapevine communication: Informal communication within an organization that arises from normal social interaction.

grievance procedure: A formalized procedure for resolving disputes if the parties have a disagreement regarding the interpretation of a term of the collective agreement.

guaranteed annual wage (GAW): A benefits plan by which an employer assures employees that they will receive a minimum annual income regardless of layoffs or a lack of work.

harassment: Occurs when a member of an organization treats an employee in a disparate manner because of that person's sex, race, religion, age, or other protective classification.

health insurance: Health and medical insurance provided by provincial governments with assistance from the federal government.

high-involvement work practices: A set of human resource practices aimed at increasing employee performance.

hot-stove rule: The principle that disciplinary action should be like what happens when you touch a hot stove: It is with warning, immediate, consistent, and impersonal.

human resource accounting (HRA): A process to measure the present cost and value of human resources as well as their future worth to the organization.

human resource audit: An examination of the human resource policies, practices, and systems of a firm (or division) to eliminate deficiencies and improve ways to achieve goals.

human resource development (HRD): A function of human resource management that integrates the use of onboarding, training, and employee and career development efforts to improve individual, group, and organizational effectiveness.

human resource information system (HRIS): A system that gathers, analyzes, summarizes, and reports important data for formulating and implementing strategies by HR specialists and line managers.

human resource management: The leadership and management of people within an organization using systems, methods, processes, and procedures that enable employees to optimize their performance and in turn their contribution to the organization and its goals.

human resource plan: A firm's overall plan to fill existing and future vacancies, including decisions on whether to fill internally or to recruit from outside.

human resource planning: A process used to determine future human resource requirements and the business processes that will be needed to support and enable those resources by anticipating future business demands, analyzing the impacts of these demands on the organization, determining the current availability of human resources and the applicable business processes, and making decisions on how to effectively adapt and utilize firms' human resources.

in-house complaint procedures: Formal methods through which an employee can register a complaint.

incentive pay: Compensation that is directly tied to an employee's performance, productivity, or both.

indexation: A method of estimating future employment needs by matching employment growth with a selected index, such as the ratio of production employees to sales.

inducements: Monetary, nonmonetary, or even intangible incentives used by a firm to attract recruits.

industrial unions: A type of union that includes the unskilled and semiskilled workers at a particular location.

integrity tests: Employment tests that measure an applicant's honesty and trustworthiness.

internal equity: Perceived equity of a pay system across different jobs within an organization.

interview: An approach to collecting job- and performance-related information by a face-to-face meeting with a jobholder, typically using a standardized checklist of questions.

interviewee errors: Interviewee mistakes, such as boasting, not listening, or not being prepared, that reduce the validity and usefulness of an interview.

interviewer errors: Mistakes like biases and domination that reduce the validity and usefulness of the job interview.

intranet: An organization-specific internal computer network.

job: A group of related activities and duties.

job analysis: Systematic study of a job to discover its specifications, skill requirements, and so on, for wage-setting, recruitment, training, or job-design purposes.

job analysis questionnaires: Checklists used to collect information about jobs, working conditions, and other performance-related information in a uniform manner.

job application form: A company's form that is completed by a job applicant, indicating the applicant 's contact information, education, prior employment, references, special skills, and other details pertaining to the position.

job code: A code that uses numbers, letters, or both to provide a quick summary of the job and its content.

job description: A recognized list of functions, tasks, accountabilities, working conditions, and competencies for a particular occupation or job.

job design: Identification of job duties, characteristics, competencies, and sequences, taking into consideration technology, workforce, organization character, and environment.

job enlargement: Adding more tasks to a job to increase the job cycle and draw on a wider range of employee skills.

job enrichment: Adding more responsibilities and autonomy to a job, giving the worker greater powers to plan, do, and evaluate job performance.

job evaluations: Systematic processes of assessing job content and ranking jobs according to a consistent set of job characteristics and worker traits.

job fairs: Trade-show-style fairs with many employers showcasing their companies and jobs to potential recruits.

job families: Groups of different jobs that are closely related by similar duties, responsibilities, skills, or job elements.

job grading: A form of job evaluation that assigns jobs to predetermined job classifications according to their relative worth to the organization.

job identity: The key part of a job description, including job title, location, and status.

job performance standards: The work performance expected from an employee on a particular job.

job ranking: A form of job evaluation in which jobs are ranked subjectively according to their overall worth to the organization.

job rotation: Moving employees from one job to another to allow them more variety and to learn new skills.

job sharing: A plan whereby available work is spread among all workers in a group to reduce the extent of layoffs when production requirements cause a substantial decline in available work.

job specification: A written statement that explains what a job demands of jobholders and the human skills and factors required.

just cause: Legal grounds for termination, such as employee misconduct or incompetence.

key job: A job that is common in the organization and in a labour market (e.g., janitors, drivers, secretaries) and that is used to determine pay scales.

knowledge management: The process of capturing, distributing, and effectively using knowledge.

knowledge tests: Tests that measure a person's information or knowledge.

knowledge workers: Members of occupations generating, processing, analyzing, or synthesizing ideas and information (such as scientists and management consultants).

labour market analysis: The study of a firm's labour market to evaluate the present or future availability of different types of workers.

labour relations boards (LRBs): Boards set up in the federal and provincial jurisdictions to administer labour relations legislation.

labour shortage: Insufficient supply of qualified talent to fill the demand for labour.

learning curve: A visual representation of the rate at which one learns given material.

learning principles: Guidelines to the ways people learn most effectively.

line authority: Authority to make decisions about production, performance, and people.

local unions: Branches of a union that are locally based and form part of a larger (often national or international) union.

long-term disability insurance: A benefit plan providing the employee with an income in the case of long-term illness or injury.

management or leadership inventory: Comprehensive reports of available management capabilities in the organization.

management rights: Rights that provide management with the freedom to operate the

business subject to any terms in the collective agreement.

management-by-objectives (MBO) approach: Requires an employee and superior to jointly establish performance goals for the future; employees are subsequently evaluated on how well they have obtained these objectives.

manager self-service (MSS): A feature of an HRIS that allows managers to view and access their employees' records and add relevant information.

managing diversity: Ability to manage individual employees with different cultural values and lead teams made up of diverse employees.

Markov analysis: Forecast of a firm's future human resource supplies, using transitional probability matrices reflecting historical or expected movements of employees across jobs.

mediation: Use of a neutral third party to help settle a labour–management dispute.

medical evaluation: Assessment of physical and/or mental health of an applicant through self-reports and/or medical examination by a preferred physician.

mentor: Someone who offers informed career guidance and support on a regular basis.

mentoring programs: Programs encouraging members of disadvantaged groups (e.g., women) to work with a senior manager who acts like a friend and guide in achieving career success.

merit raise: A pay increase given to individual workers according to an evaluation of their performance.

mission statement: A statement outlining the purpose and long-term objectives of the organization.

multiple cut-off approach: An approach where scores are set for each predictor and each applicant is evaluated on a pass–fail basis.

National Occupational Classification (NOC): An occupational classification created by the federal government, using skill level and skill types of jobs.

natural justice: Minimum standards of fair decision making imposed on persons or bodies acting in a judicial capacity.

needs assessment: A diagnosis that presents problems and future challenges that can be met through training or development.

nominal group technique: A focused group discussion where members meet face-to-face or digitally, write down their ideas, and share them. All new thoughts on a topic are recorded and ranked for importance.

noncomparative evaluation methods: Appraisal methods that evaluate an employee's performance according to preset data, and not by comparing one person's performance with that of co-workers.

observation: An approach to collecting job- and performance-related information by direct observation of jobholders by a specialist.

old boys' network: Set of informal relationships among male managers providing increased career advancement opportunities for men and reinforcing a male culture.

onboarding: The process of integrating and acculturating new employees into the organization and providing them with the tools, resources, and knowledge to become successful and productive.

open-door policy: A company policy that encourages employees to address their problems to higher levels of management.

organization structure: The product of all of an organization's features and how they are arranged—people, objectives, technology, size, age, and policies.

organizational culture: The core beliefs and assumptions that are widely shared by all organizational members.

organizational goals: An organization's short- and long-term outcomes that human resource management aims to support and enable.

organizational policies: Internal policies that affect recruitment, such as "promote-from-within" policies.

orientation programs: Programs that familiarize new employees with their roles, the organization, its policies, and other employees.

outplacement: Assisting employees to find jobs with other employers.

outsourcing: Contracting tasks to outside agencies or persons.

panel interview: An interview using several interviewers with one applicant.

part-time employees: Persons working fewer than the required hours for categorization as full-time workers and who are ineligible for many supplementary benefits offered by employers.

pay equity: A policy to eliminate the gap between the income of men and women, ensuring that salary ranges correspond to value of work performed.

pay secrecy: A management policy not to discuss or publish individual salaries.

Pension Benefits Standards Act: A federal act regulating pension plans in industries under the jurisdiction of the Government of Canada.

performance appraisal: The process by which organizations evaluate employee job performance over a period of time.

performance management: The continuing process of identifying, measuring, and developing the performance of individuals and teams and aligning performance with the strategic goals of the organization.

performance measures: The ratings used to evaluate employee performance.

performance standards: The benchmarks against which performance is measured.

performance tests: Tests that measure the ability of job applicants to perform specific components of the job for which they are to be hired.

personality tests: Questionnaires designed to reveal aspects of an individual's character or temperament.

phased retirement: Gradual phase in to retirement with loss or reduction of pension benefits.

piecework: A type of incentive system that compensates workers for each unit of output.

point system: A form of job evaluation that assesses the relative importance of the job's key factors in order to arrive at the relative worth of jobs.

portability clauses: Clauses that allow accumulated pension rights to be transferred to another employer when an employee changes employers.

position: A collection of tasks and responsibilities performed by an individual.

precedent: A new standard that arises from the past practices of either the company or the union.

predictive analysis: The process of selecting, exploring, analyzing, and modelling data to create better business outcomes.

preventive discipline: Action taken prior to an infraction to encourage employees to follow standards and rules.

proactive human resource management: A human resource management approach wherein decision makers anticipate problems or challenges both inside and outside the organization and take action before they impact the organization.

production bonuses: A type of incentive system that provides employees with additional compensation when they surpass stated production goals.

productivity: The ratio of a firm's outputs (goods and services) divided by its inputs (people, capital, materials, energy).

professional search firms: Agencies that, for a fee, recruit specialized personnel for a company.

profit-sharing plan: A system whereby an employer pays compensation or benefits to employees, usually on an annual basis, in addition to their regular wage, on the basis of the profits of the company.

progressive discipline: The use of stronger and stronger penalties for repeated offences.

provincial human rights laws: All provinces have their own human rights laws with discrimination criteria, regulations, and procedures.

Public Service Staff Relations Act (PSSRA): Provides federal public servants with the right to unionize and either opt for compulsory arbitration or strike if a deadlock in bargaining occurs.

ranking method: A method of evaluating employees that ranks them from best to worst on some trait.

rate range: A pay range for each job class.

rating scale: A scale that requires the rater to provide a subjective evaluation of an individual's performance.

reactive human resource management: A human resource management approach wherein decision makers respond to problems or challenges as they arise rather than anticipate them.

realistic job preview (RJP): Involves showing the candidate the type of work, equipment, and working conditions involved in the job before the hiring decision is final.

reasonable accommodation: Voluntary adjustments to work or workplace that allow employees with special needs to perform their job effectively.

recruiter habits: The propensity of a recruiter to rely on methods, systems, or behaviours that led to past recruitment success.

recruitment: The process of finding and attracting capable applicants to apply for employment and accept job offers that are extended to them.

red-circled rate: A rate of pay higher than the contractual, or formerly established, rate for the job.

reference letters: Written evaluations of a person's job-relevant skills, past experience, and work-relevant attitudes.

regulations: Legally enforceable rules developed by governmental agencies to ensure compliance with laws that the agency administers.

reliability: A selection device's ability to yield consistent results over repeated measures; also, internal consistency of a device or measure.

relocation programs: Company-sponsored benefits that assist employees who must move in connection with their job.

replacement charts: Visual representations of who will replace whom when a job opening occurs.

replacement summaries: Lists of likely replacements for each job and their relative strengths and weaknesses.

résumé: A brief voluntary listing of an applicant's work experience, education, personal data, and other information relevant to the job.

retention: A company's ability to keep employees.

role-playing: A training technique that requires trainees to assume different identities in order to learn how others feel under different circumstances.

secondary dimensions of diversity: Education, status, language, and income levels.

selection: The identification of candidates from a pool of recruits who best meet job requirements, using tools such as application blanks, tests, and interviews.

selection process: A series of specific steps used by an employer to decide which recruits should be hired.

selection ratio: The ratio of the number of applicants hired to the total number of applicants available.

self-directed work teams or groups: Teams of workers without a formal, employer-appointed supervisor who decide among themselves most matters traditionally handled by a supervisor.

seniority: Length of the worker's employment, which may be used for determining order of promotion, layoffs, vacation, etc.

severance pay: Payment to a worker upon permanent separation from a company.

sexual harassment: Unsolicited or unwelcome sex- or gender-based conduct that has adverse employment consequences for the complainant.

shared responsibility model: A newer approach to safety in the workplace that assumes the best method to reduce accident rates relies on the co-operation of the employer and the employees (who may be represented by a union).

short-term disability plan: A benefit plan crediting a number of days to be used as sick leave.

situational interviews: Interviews that attempt to assess a job applicant's likely future response to specific situations, which may or may not have been faced by the applicant in the past.

situational judgment test: A test that places applicants in hypothetical scenarios and asks them to indicate how they would respond from a list of alternatives.

skill- or knowledge-based pay: A pay system based on the employee's mastery of skills or knowledge (in contrast to the more common job-based pay).

skill-building training: Training employees in interpersonal skills to correctly respond to cultural differences at the workplace.

skills inventories: Summaries of each worker's knowledge, skills, abilities, experiences, and other attributes.

social (or reform) unionism: A type of unionism that tries to influence the economic and social policies of government at all levels. In practice, union leaders pursue such objectives by speaking out for or against government programs.

social expectations: The larger society's expectations about job challenge, working conditions, and quality of work life.

socialization: The process by which people adapt to an organization through learning and accepting the values, norms, and beliefs held by others in the organization.

sponsor: A person in an organization who can create career development opportunities for others.

staff authority: Authority to advise, but not to direct, others.

staffing table: A list of anticipated employment openings for each type of job.

stages of an interview: Key phases in an employment interview: interview preparation, creation of rapport, information exchange, termination, and evaluation.

startup costs: The additional costs associated with a new employee because the new employee is typically less efficient than an experienced worker; the new worker also requires additional supervisory time.

stereotyping: The process of using a few observable characteristics to assign someone to a preconceived social category.

strategic human resource development: The identification of needed skills and active management of employees' learning in relation to corporate strategies.

strategic human resource management: Integrating the strategic needs of an organization into the organization's choice of human resource management systems and practices to support the organization's overall mission, strategies, and performance.

stressors: Stressful working conditions that can directly influence the health and safety of employees.

structured interviews: Interviews wherein a predetermined checklist of questions usually asked of all applicants is used.

subjective approach: An approach where the decision maker looks at the scores received by the various applicants on predictors, subjectively evaluates all of the information, and comes to an overall judgment.

succession planning: The process of making long-range management development plans to fill human resource needs.

suggestion systems: Formal methods of generating, evaluating, and implementing employee ideas.

supplemental unemployment benefits (SUB): Private plans providing compensation for wage loss to laid-off workers.

support groups: Groups of employees who provide emotional support to a new employee who shares a common attribute with the group (e.g., racial or ethnic membership).

systemic discrimination: Any company policy, practice, or action that is not openly or intentionally discriminatory but has an indirect discriminatory impact or effect.

talent management: "A systemic attraction, identification, development, engagement/retention, and deployment of those individuals with high potential who are of particular value to the organization."

task identity: The feeling of responsibility or pride that results from doing an entire piece of work, not just a small part of it.

task significance: Knowing that the work one does is important to others in the organization or to outsiders.

temporary-help agencies: Agencies that provide supplemental workers for temporary vacancies caused by employee leave, sickness, etc.

total reward model: Inclusion of everything employees value in an employment relationship.

training: Planned activities aimed to provide employees with enhanced skills to perform their current jobs.

transference: Applicability of training to job situations; evaluated by how readily the trainee can transfer the learning to his or her job.

transition matrices: Describe the probabilities of how quickly a job position turns over and what an incumbent employee may do over a forecast period of time, such as stay in the current position, move to another position within the firm, or accept a job in another organization.

underutilization: A condition that exists when a department or employer has a lesser proportion of members of a protected class than are found in the employer's labour market.

unfair labour practices: Practices by management such as interfering with or discriminating against employees who undertake collective action. Unions may also commit unfair labour practices.

union: An organization with the legal authority to represent workers, negotiate the terms and conditions of employment with the employer, and administer the collective agreement.

union shop: A union security provision in which employers may hire anyone they want, but all new employees must join the union within a specified period and pay dues.

unstructured interviews: Interviews using few if any planned questions to enable the interviewer to pursue, in depth, the applicant's responses.

upward communication: Communication that begins in the organization and proceeds up the hierarchy to inform or influence others.

validity: A key attribute of a selection device that indicates its accuracy and relationship to job-relevant criteria.

validity generalization: Using validity evidence accumulated for other jobs or applicant populations to guide employment test choices until local validation study results can be acquired.

variety: An attribute of jobs wherein the worker has the opportunity to use different skills and abilities, or perform different activities.

vesting: A provision in employer-provided retirement plans that gives workers the right to a pension after a specified number of years of service.

virtual reality/augmented reality: Use of modern computer technology to create a 3D environment.

wage and salary surveys: Studies of the wages and salaries paid by other organizations within the employer's labour market.

walk-ins/write-ins: Job seekers who arrive at or write to the organization in search of a job without prior referrals and not in response to a specific ad.

weighted application blank (WAB): A job application form in which various items are given differential weights to reflect their relationship to criterion measures.

wiki: A type of server program that allows multiple users to contribute to a website.

work arrangement: A firm's use of work hours, schedules, and location to ensure that the goals of the organization and the needs of employees are optimally met.

work flow: The sequence of and balance between jobs in an organization needed to produce the firm's goods or services.

work practices: The set ways of performing work in an organization.

workers' compensation: Compensation payable by employers collectively for injuries sustained by workers in the course of their employment.

working conditions: Facts about the situation in which the worker acts; includes physical environment, hours, hazards, travel requirements, and so on, associated with a job.

workplace diversity: Includes important human characteristics that influence employee values, their perceptions of self and others, behaviours, and interpretations of events.

Workplace Hazardous Materials Information System (WHMIS): Legislation that requires suppliers to label all hazardous products and provide a (material) safety data sheet on each.

workplace health and safety committee: A group consisting of representatives of the employer and employees that meets regularly in order to reduce accident rates.

wrongful dismissal: The termination of an employee without just cause or without giving the employee reasonable notice or compensation in lieu of notice.

Index